MARKETING
STRATEGY

MARKETING STRATEGY

O.C. Ferrell

Colorado State University

Michael D. Hartline

Louisiana State University

George H. Lucas Jr.

U.S. Learning, Inc.

David Luck

Southern Illinois University

THE DRYDEN PRESS

HARCOURT BRACE COLLEGE PUBLISHERS

FORT WORTH PHILADELPHIA SAN DIEGO NEW YORK ORLANDO AUSTIN SAN ANTONIO
TORONTO MONTREAL LONDON SYDNEY TOKYO

Publisher	George Provol
Acquisitions Editor	Bill Schoof
Product Manager	Lisé Johnson
Developmental Editor	Rebecca Linnenburger
Project Editor	John Haakenson
Art Director	Burl Sloan
Production Manager	Eddie Dawson
Electronic Publishing Coordinator	Kathi Embry

ISBN: 0-03-024801-9
Library of Congress Catalog Card Number: 98-070999

Address for orders:
The Dryden Press
6277 Sea Harbor Drive
Orlando, FL 32877-6777

Address for editorial correspondence:
The Dryden Press
301 Commerce Street, Suite 3700
Fort Worth, Texas 76102

Website address:
http://www.hbcollege.com

Dedication

To my wife, Linda
— O.C. Ferrell

To my wife, Marsha, and my daughters, Meghan and Madison
— Michael Hartline

To my wife, Linda, and my sons, Taylor and Austin
— George Lucas

To my wife, Adele
— David J. Luck

The Dryden Press Series in Marketing

PREFACE

Marketing Strategy provides a practical, straightforward approach to analyzing, planning, and implementing marketing strategies. Our focus is the creative process involved in applying the knowledge and concepts of marketing to the development of marketing strategy. Integration of marketing's many decisions and coordination with functional areas of business are important to the success of both companies and nonprofit organizations. Twenty-two cases are available in this book to prepare students in critical thinking, decision making and the development of an entrepreneurial spirit.

Marketing Strategy provides a comprehensive framework for the development of competitive marketing strategies that achieve organizational goals and objectives and build competitive advantage. The core of our strategic market planning framework is the organization's analysis of internal strengths and weaknesses and external opportunities and threats (SWOT analysis). Our framework describes all the activities and processes necessary to develop a marketing plan, including the implementation, evaluation, and control of a firm's marketing activities. We stress that effective marketing strategies and plans are developed in concert with the organization's mission and goals as well as plans from other functional areas. The end result of the strategic market planning process is an overall strategic market plan that outlines the activities and resources required to fulfill the organization's mission and achieve its goals and objectives. We offer many examples of successful planning and implementation to illustrate how to capitalize on an organization's strengths and gain competitive advantage.

Purpose

This book was written to address the challenges of strategic market planning in a rapidly changing environment. We view strategic market planning not only as a process for achieving organizational goals, but also to build long-term relationships with customers. Creating a customer orientation takes an imaginative, visionary, and courageous leader, one who is capable of relinquishing control over the organization. We have therefore integrated the importance of customer orientation throughout the entire text. Topics such as creating a competitive advantage based on customer value, the implementation process, and the internal marketing process are thoroughly covered. We have also included social, ethical, electronic commerce, and global considerations throughout the text as well as covered specifically in Chapter 10. Addressing these issues in strategic market planning can help organizations gain competitive advantage in our dynamic marketing environment.

While our framework provides for the use of sophisticated research and decision-making processes, we have employed a practical perspective that will permit marketing managers in any size organization to develop and plan a marketing strategy. We have avoided esoteric, abstract, and highly theoretical material that does not relate to typical marketing strategy decision making in most organizations. The marketing plan template that we include in Appendix B has been used by a number of organizations in successfully planning their marketing strategies. Many companies report great success in using our planning approach partially due to the ease of communicating the plan to all functional areas of the business.

Target Audience

This text is relevant for a number of educational environments, including undergraduate, graduate, and corporate university courses. At the undergraduate level, it is appropriate for the capstone course or any second-level integrating course, often labeled "marketing management," "marketing strategy," or "marketing policies." At this level, it provides an excellent framework to use with cases and/or a computer simulation approach to teaching. At the graduate level, the book is appropriate for courses dealing with strategic market planning, competitive marketing strategies, or as a supplement for any course that takes a case or computer simulation focus. A growing segment of the market, corporate training can utilize this text when educating business professionals who are developing marketing plans of their own or interpreting and implementing the plans of others.

Cases

Most of the cases in the text were written specifically for this book and describe the strategic situations of real-world, indentifiable organizations. All of the cases were updated to Spring 1998. Because these cases feature real companies, students have an opportunity to update them, using the library or company Web sites, to find the latest information. In addition to cases prepared specifically for this book, instructors can customize a casebook from the cases listed on the Dryden case library at http://www.dryden.com/mktng/marketingcase/. Many additional resources for students can be found at the text's web site at http://www.dryden.com/mktng/ferrell/. These resources include a guide for analyzing and preparing case studies as well as links to company Web sites for all cases.

Key Features of *Marketing Strategy*

- Twenty-two cases providing up-to-date opportunities to apply the text material to real world situations. A final integrating case can be used for an independent case study or as the background for developing a marketing plan.

- An emphasis on the development of the marketing plan, including the "how" and "why" of each of its component parts. The SWOT (strengths, weaknesses, opportunities, and threats) analysis approach to marketing planning used in the text is both powerful and easy to use.

- A detailed and comprehensive set of Marketing Plan Worksheets provided in Appendix A helps to ensure that students and/or managers do not omit important factors in developing strategic marketing plans. It is also useful for organizing the vast amounts of data and information collected during the marketing planning process.

- An example marketing plan, provided in Appendix B, illustrates the format and writing style used in creating an actual marketing plan document.

- Integration of the global aspects of marketing planning throughout the text, with more detailed coverage provided in Chapter 10. Many of the cases focus on global marketing issues and decisions.

- Coverage of ethics and social responsibility issues in Chapter 10 that will help satisfy AACSB requirements in this important area. A specific case, Columbia HCA provides an opportunity to explore the relationship of marketing ethics and marketing strategy.

- Coverage of the role of electronic commerce and the Internet is discussed in Chapter 10. The collection of relevant data and information through electronic sources is thoroughly discussed in Chapter 3.

- Examples of the challenges that real organizations face as they engage in strategic marketing planning and management. Well-known companies such as Apple Computer, Home Depot, Wal-Mart, Kodak, and Microsoft illustrate many of the issues faced in developing marketing strategy.

- A completely user-friendly text that is both easy to read and understand, with numerous exhibits, a complete subject index, and familiar marketing terminology.

- A state-of-the-art Web site to support the text material and cases.

- Additional reading material not found in the text, including a tutorial on how to perform case analysis.

- Online exercises for each chapter in the text.

- Links to useful Web sites, including important sources of research data and information.

- Online exams to help prepare students for actual course exams.

- A downloadable, electronic version of the marketing plan Worksheets found in Appendix A.

- Helpful information on choosing a marketing career, developing an individualized marketing plan, and finding a good marketing job.

For instructors, the Web site provides the following:

- Password-protected site

- Additional reading material not found in the text

- Downloadable, electronic versions of the lecture outlines and case notes from the Instructor's Resource Manual. These additional materials can be downloaded for editing before using them in the classroom.

Instructor's Resource Materials

The Instructor's Resource Manual with text bank and case notes for *Marketing Strategy* is available to assist the instructor using our text. We provide the following teaching aids:

- Detailed lecture outlines to guide class discussion. The outlines can be used to review chapter content quickly before class or to gain an overview of the entire book. These outlines can also be downloaded from our text's Web site. Instructors can download the outlines and add their own personal notes and examples before class.

- A test bank consisting of multiple choice and discussion questions.

- Case teaching notes that provide a uniform format to help the instructor evaluate cases before use, or to assist instructors in leading case analysis and class discussion. These case notes are also available on our text's Web site. While there are many approaches to using cases in class, our notes are designed to help the instructor identify key issues and alternatives as they relate to the content of the case and corresponding text chapters.

- Transparency masters from the exhibits and tables in the text. Through the use of the text's web site, instructors can also download additional presentation materials that are not found in the text.

- In addition to these materials, additional instructional aids can be found on our text's web site, http://www.dryden.com/mktng/ferrell/. Professors may choose from any of these teaching materials, tailoring them to their specific goals and course schedules. In addition, the text and cases may be supplemented with articles, business simulations, and/or videos.

ACKNOWLEDGMENTS

Throughout the development of this text, several extraordinary individuals provided their talent and expertise to make important contributions to the book. A number of individuals have made many useful comments and recommendations as reviewers of this text. We appreciate the generous help of these reviewers:

Brett Boyle, *DePaul University*

Bill Carner, *University of Texas-Austin*

Ken Clow, *Pittsburg State University*

Jim Fair, *Campbellsville College*

Jim Grimm, *Illinois State University*

Oliver Heil, *University of California, Los Angeles*

Ronald E. Michaels, *Central Florida*

Mary Mobley, *Augusta College*

Don Sciglinpaglia, *San Deigo State University*

Anil Sharma, *Frostburg State University*

Michael J. Swenson, *Brigham Young University*

We deeply appreciate the assistance of Gwyneth M. Vaughn who played a major role in editing, organizing and refining chapter content.

Barbara Gilmer assisted with many aspects of the project, including the cases and instructor's manual. Thanks also are due to Denise Kleiner, Barbara-Jean Ross, James G. "Trey" Maxham, Thomas S. Corcoran, Melissa Johnson, Debbie Thorne LeClair, Brent Wren, Neil Herndon, Don Roy, and Salvadore Trevino. Also, thanks goes to Jeffery A. Krug for his work on the final integrating case.

A special thanks to Jim Grimm at Illinois State University for class testing the manuscript in the Spring of 1998.

The editorial and production staff at Dryden cannot be thanked enough. These people include Bill Schoof, Acquisitions Editor; Rebecca Linnenburger, Developmental Editor; Eddie Dawson, Production Manager; John Haakenson, Project Editor; Burl Sloan, Art Director; Adele Krause, Picture & Rights Editor; and Kathi Embry, Electronic Publishing Coordinator.

Finally, we express appreciation for the support and encouragement of our families, and our colleges at the University of Memphis, Louisiana State University, Colorado State University, and U.S.Learning, Inc.

ABOUT THE AUTHORS

O.C. Ferrell, Ph.D.
Colorado State University

O.C. Ferrell (Ph.D., Louisiana State University) is a Professor of Marketing and Business Ethics at Colorado State University. He is a past president of the Academic Council of the American Marketing Association. He chaired the American Marketing Association Ethics Committee that developed the AMA Code of Ethics and more recently co-chaired an AMA Marketing Exchange Colloquium in Vienna, Austria. He is co-chair of the 1999 Academy of Marketing Science Annual Conference. He is also a Southern Marketing Association Fellow and a Southwestern Marketing Association Fellow.

Dr. Ferrell teaches marketing strategy courses at the graduate and undergraduate levels including the capstone marketing course. He taught a course on competitive marketing strategies at Thammasat University in Bangkok, Thailand using an early draft of this text. In addition, he is the author or co-author of 15 books and approximately 60 academic articles.

Dr. Ferrell has extensive experience speaking and assisting businesses and professional associations. He has been a major event speaker for organizations such as General Motors, Society of American Florists, Water Quality Association, and National Bank of Commerce of Mississippi. He served as a marketing and business ethics expert witness for a number of leading law firms throughout the United States.

Dr. Ferrell and his wife Linda live in Ft. Collins and enjoy skiing, golf, fishing, and international travel.

Michael D. Hartline, Ph.D.
Louisiana State University

Michael D. Hartline received his Ph.D. from the University of Memphis and his MBA and BS from Jacksonville State University (Alabama). He taught at the University of Arkansas at Little Rock before joining the marketing faculty of the E. J. Ourso College of Business Administration at Louisiana State University in 1994.

Dr. Hartline has won awards for teaching and research excellence and has made many presentations to industry and academic groups. He has served as a consultant to several for-profit and non-profit organizations in the areas of marketing plan development, market feasibility analysis, customer satisfaction measurement, employee training, and pricing policy.

Dr. Hartline and his wife Marsha live in Baton Rouge with their two daughters, Meghan and Madison, and a psychotic Chihuahua named Nugget. His hobbies include church activities, golf, personal computing, college football, and reading.

George H. Lucas Jr., Ph.D.
President, U.S.Learning, Inc.

George Lucas has spent his entire career in the customer relationship develop-ment business. After receiving his bachelors degree from the University of Missouri, Columbia, Lucas served in field sales positions with American Hospital Supply Cor-poration and Pitney Bowes. He then returned to Missouri University to complete his MBA, and later his Ph.D. Following graduate school he accepted a position on the Graduate Faculty of Texas A&M University's Marketing Department, where he served as one of the founding Faculty Committee members for the now interna-tionally recognized Center for Retailing Studies. While there he was also a research fellow for the Institute for Ventures in New Technology (INVENT). In 1987, he joined the faculty of the University of Memphis, where he served as a full professor on the Graduate Faculty of the Fogelman College of Business and Economics until January 1998. He now serves as president of U.S.Learning, Inc., a corporate training firm. He is highly regarded as a marketing strategy, international marketing, retail-ing, personal selling, and negotiation speaker, trainer, and researcher, and has pub-lished numerous articles in leading marketing and business journals. Dr. Lucas is frequently quoted in the business sections of magazines, newspapers, and trade pub-lications, and is a featured presenter in one of the most frequently aired cable tele-vision programs on personal selling.

He lives in Memphis with his wife Linda and sons, Taylor and Austin. His hob-bies include golf, fishing, and coaching youth soccer.

David J. Luck, Ph.D.
Southern Illinois University

David Luck received his Ph.D. from the University of Texas after receiving a bache-lors degree from Dartmouth College, 1934, and a masters from University of Penn-sylvania, 1940.

Dr. Luck has taught in marketing faculties at several universities—most notably Michigan State University, University of Illinois, and Southern Illinois University. He has published several books in marketing strategy and marketing research. His chief focus has been strategies for product development. He has also conducted marketing research in Ford Motor Company and has had consulting roles at many business firms.

Dr. Luck is a highly respected scholar who has played an important role in the development of marketing thought.

His contributions have helped shape marketing theory and practice over the past 50 years.

Brief Table of Contents

Table of Contents

Strategic Market Planning

Introduction

To be successful, every organization requires effective planning and a marketing strategy that achieves its goals and objectives *and* satisfies customers. Without effective strategic market planning, it is unlikely that Intel will be able to develop a new processor that boosts your PC's performance, that Microsoft will be able to upgrade its Windows operating system to enhance your work and entertainment tasks, or that your university will be able to offer the courses you need and want to complete your education. These organizations engage in the process of strategic market planning to capitalize on their strengths in order to provide goods and services that satisfy your needs and wants. Every organization—from your favorite local restaurant to giant global food corporations, from city, state, and federal governments to charities such as Habitat for Humanity and the American Red Cross—is involved in developing and/or implementing marketing strategies.

This book is about strategic marketing management, including the process of planning, organizing, implementing, and controlling marketing activities. In this book, we provide an orderly process for developing customer-oriented strategic market plans and strategies that match an organization with its internal and external environments. Our approach uses practical methods that reflect how this process actually occurs. We focus on real-world applications of market planning and the development of the marketing plan. We assume that the reader has at least some basic knowledge of marketing principles.

In this first chapter, we introduce the strategic market planning process. We begin by examining the overall market planning process and defining the terms and concepts used throughout the book. Then, we discuss each step in the process by considering the hierarchy of decisions that must be made in strategic market planning. Next, we introduce the marketing plan and discuss its role and importance. Finally, we explore how customer-oriented organizations use strategic market planning for success.

An Overview of Strategic Market Planning

The process of strategic market planning includes identifying or establishing an organizational mission and goals, corporate strategy, marketing goals and objectives, marketing strategy, and finally, a marketing plan. The process begins with an in-depth analysis of the organization's internal and external environments. This analysis aids the planner in determining the organization's internal strengths and weaknesses and identifying external opportunities and threats. Based on an exhaustive examination of these relevant environmental issues, the firm next establishes its organizational mission, goals, and objectives; the corporate or business-unit strategy; functional goals and objectives; functional strategies; implementation; and evaluation and control. This process is depicted in Exhibit 1.1.

Although our emphasis in this book is on the processes and concerns necessary to develop a customer-oriented marketing strategy and marketing plan, we should stress that effective marketing strategies and plans are developed in concert with the organization's mission and goals, as well as the plans from other functional areas. Developing a marketing strategy is impossible without organizational goals and objectives and marketing goals and objectives that establish specific, intended outcomes to be attained when the strategy is executed through the marketing plan.

To fulfill its mission and achieve its goals and objectives, an organization needs a strategy, a term derived from an ancient Greek word that means "art of the general." Although the term is based on the art of directing military campaigns, marketing strategies involve the selection and analysis of target markets (the group of people the organization wants to reach) and the creation and maintenance of an appropriate marketing mix (product, distribution, promotion, and price) that satisfies the needs of customers in those target markets. General Motors' Saturn division, for example, represents one of the first really innovative efforts by a U.S. automaker to define and service a target market by offering reliability, service, quality, and value, as well as production capability. Saturn's strategy includes innovation in all marketing mix elements, particularly pricing, advertising, and the personal-selling process. The company further enhances relationships with customers through homecoming weekends at Spring Hill, Tennessee, which bring in thousands of Saturn owners.[1] These efforts help create a community of Saturn owners who identify with the image of buying and owning a Saturn, which in turn helps Saturn fulfill its goals and objectives as part of General Motors' overall strategy. Thus, the marketing strategy may be viewed as the fundamental means or idea for reaching marketing objectives, but all marketing strategies should be grounded in the overall strategic market planning process described in Exhibit 1.1.

As indicated in Exhibit 1.1, planning efforts within each functional area will result in the creation of a useful plan for each area. Because this text is concerned with marketing, we are interested in a particular type of functional plan—the marketing plan. A marketing plan is a written document or blueprint governing all the firm's marketing activities, including the implementation, evaluation, and control of marketing activities. The marketing plan serves a number of purposes, including its role as a "road map" for implementing the marketing strategy and achieving its objectives. It informs the plan's participants of their role and function. It specifies how resources are to be allocated and includes the specific marketing tasks, the responsibilities of individuals, and the timing of all marketing activities.

The end result of the strategic market planning process is an overall strategic market plan, an outline of the activities and resources required to fulfill the organization's mission and achieve its goals and objectives. The strategic market plan takes into account not only marketing, but *all* functional aspects of a business that must be

EXHIBIT 1.1   The Strategic Market Planning Process

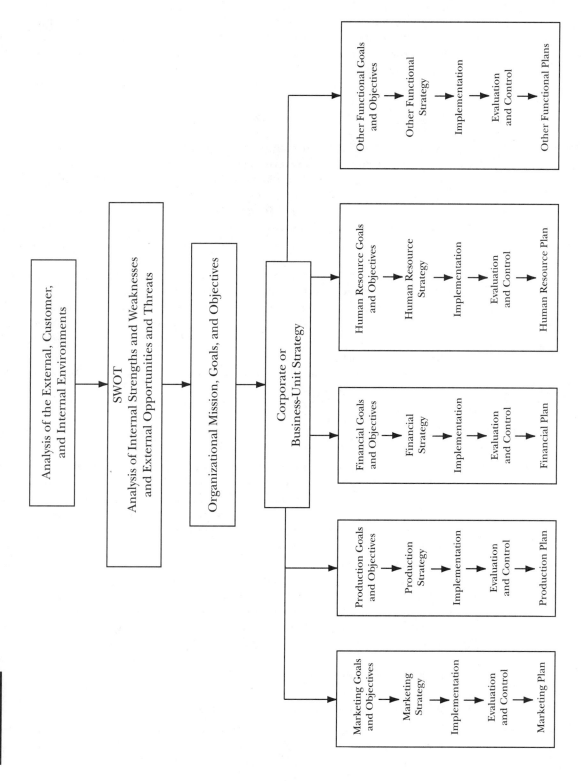

coordinated by senior management, including production/operations, finance, human resources management, accounting, and research and development. Thus, the strategic market plan encompasses the planning process for the entire organization. Because change is constant within the marketing environment, strategic market planning is a continuous process.

The Strategic Market Planning Process

As shown in Exhibit 1.1, the strategic market planning process begins with an analysis of the organization's external, customer, and internal (organizational) environments. This analysis plays a key role in strategic marketing management. As we shall see in Chapter 3, planning requires analyzing data and considering the views of those involved in decisions. The evaluation of internal strengths and weaknesses and external opportunities and threats (SWOT analysis) is an excellent comprehensive framework to use to structure the output from the environmental analysis. We explore SWOT analysis in detail in Chapter 4.

All strategic decision making depends on a comprehensive and accurate analysis of the organization's internal and external environments. Examples of variables to consider related to internal strengths and weaknesses include financial resources, human resources, physical assets, product quality, corporate culture, value systems, marketing ethics, and social responsibility. Honda's reputation for quality, for instance, represents a strength that gives the firm an extra edge in the market for automobile sales. Examples of variables to consider related to external opportunities and threats include competition, customers, technology, legal and regulatory activities, social issues, and economic conditions. GTE, for example, exploited an opportunity in the form of a loophole in the Telecommunications Act of 1996 that permitted the local phone service company to compete in long-distance markets while its "Baby Bell" rivals could not.[2]

A company should develop strategies that match strengths and opportunities, convert weaknesses to strengths, minimize liabilities where weaknesses coincide with threats, and minimize the impact of limitations where weaknesses coincide with opportunities. In the case of GTE, the opportunity granted by the legal loophole allowed the firm to package local and long-distance telephone services together, giving GTE a cost advantage. Moreover, the company's local telephone service gives it access to detailed customer information that long-distance carriers do not traditionally have. Although GTE's advantage may be tested in court, in the meantime it is making the best of the opportunity to build a substantial long-distance customer base.[3]

An orderly approach for sequencing decision stages is helpful to make decisions effective and efficient. Although our focus is on marketing strategy and marketing plans, the following decisions must be addressed in strategic market planning whether the functional area of interest is marketing, production, finance, human resources, accounting, or some other area.

Organizational Mission, Goals, and Objectives

Three words are often used, sometimes interchangeably, to describe an organization's aspirations: mission, goals, and objectives. This is due to widespread confusion regarding the nature and role of each of these components.

A mission statement defines an organization and describes its reason for being, what and whom it represents, and the values or beliefs for which it stands. Intel, for example, says that its mission is to "Do a great job for our customers, employees, and stockholders by being the preeminent building block supplier to the computing industry worldwide."[4] The mission tends to be a much broader concept than a goal or objective. It is means-focused (for example, what a firm stands for and does), as opposed to the ends-focus of goals and objectives (what it hopes to achieve).

Goals are general statements of desired accomplishments expressed in qualitative terms. They are important because they provide direction for the firm and create a set of priorities it will use in evaluating alternatives and making resource allocation decisions. Consider a goal to "develop the highest quality products in the industry." This statement correctly does not contain information about where the firm stands now, or even what evaluation tool will be used to determine the quality ranking of competitive products. It does, however, provide a target for achievement, thus playing a major role in directing resource allocation decisions. Because of their nature, goals are sometimes referred to as qualitative objectives. For example, one of General Motors' goals is that the customer be satisfied with the "total ownership experience."

Goals without objectives are largely meaningless because progress is impossible to track without a measurable yardstick. Objectives are specific and quantitative benchmarks that can be used to gauge progress toward the achievement of a previously established goal. For example, an objective "to increase market share from 17 percent to 20 percent during the fiscal year," includes the present level of achievement, the desired level of achievement, and the time period for the objective to be reached. All of these components must be present in a well-devised objective, along with the specific employees or groups who are responsible for the accomplishment of the desired outcome.

In Exhibit 1.1, we refer to both organizational goals/objectives and marketing goals/objectives. Setting objectives at both levels is a necessary step in planning because everything that is decided should be measured and controlled to achieve optimal performance levels. In addition, marketing goals and objectives must be consistent with organizational goals and objectives. Without objectives, the degree of success achieved by the implemented marketing plan is very difficult to determine.

Corporate or Business-Unit Strategy

All organizations need a corporate strategy, the central scheme or means for utilizing and integrating resources in the areas of production, finance, research and development, human resources, and marketing to carry out the organization's mission and achieve the desired goals and objectives. For example, Enron, a large electric utility, has led the drive for deregulation in the electric power industry in the hope that it can generate more competition that allows electric consumers to shop around to find the best value. If Enron's strategy is effective and legislators and regulators permit greater competition in the electric power business, the company will have positioned itself to be able to sell electricity over wide geographic areas.[5] Corporate strategy also focuses on the businesses in which the firm will participate and how to divide resources among them. When Barnes & Noble decided to open its own online bookstore, for example, it was a major corporate strategic shift in resource allocation. B&N had to make a commitment to build Web sites and acquire and learn competencies it did not have for its physical stores. By providing greater discounts for online purchases, Barnes & Noble had to evaluate the possibility of cannibalizing its traditional businesses and annoying its customers through dual distribution.[6]

Larger firms often find it beneficial to devise separate strategies for each strategic business unit (SBU), or subsidiary, division, product line, or other profit center within the parent firm. Business-unit strategy determines the nature and future direction of each business unit, including its competitive advantages, the allocation of its resources, and the coordination of the functional business areas (marketing, production, finance, human resources, etc.). Sony, for example, has a number of SBUs, including Sony Music (music CDs and videos), Sony Electronics (consumer electronics, business and professional products, and computer products), Sony Movies (films and videos from Sony subsidiaries such as TriStar, Columbia, and Sony Pictures Classic Films), Sony Television (Sony-produced television shows, including "Seinfeld," "Jeopardy," and "Days of Our Lives"), Sony Games (video games and game players), Sony Theatres (movie theaters), Sony Gear (entertainment-related collectibles and apparel), and Sony Worldwide (music and talk-radio-based radio programming). Each of these units has its own goals, objectives, and strategies. In small businesses, corporate strategy blurs with business-unit strategy. Although we use both terms, corporate and business-unit strategy apply to all organizations, from large corporations to small businesses and nonprofit organizations.

In the strategic market planning process, issues such as competition, differentiation, diversification, coordination of business units, and environmental issues all tend to emerge as corporate strategy concerns. Corporations must try to match their resources and strengths with the opportunities and threats in the environment. It should be obvious that a component of corporate and business-unit strategy is to take into account customer-orientation and marketing mix decisions. Corporate and business-unit strategy also rests on the firm's organizational culture and value structure.

An important consideration in selecting a corporate or business-unit strategy is the firm's capabilities. In marketing, this includes the firm's abilities in target market selection, product development, promotion, distribution, and pricing—the marketing strategy. Capabilities also relate to the firm's ability to match its strengths to opportunities in the marketplace. The firm's strengths relative to competitors are also pertinent, as are its abilities to identify and consider all competitive threats.

When a firm possesses capabilities that allow it to serve customers' needs better than the competition, it is said to have a competitive, or differential, advantage. Although a number of advantages are based on functions other than marketing— such as human resources, research and development or production—these functions often create important competitive advantages that can be exploited through marketing activities. For example, Barr Laboratories, a pharmaceutical firm, markets a generic version of a blood thinner that was the eleventh most prescribed drug in the United States. Although Barr faces opposition from brand name pharmaceuticals, its lower price gives it a distinct competitive advantage—for now.[7]

In planning, it is important to identify differential advantages in relation to competitors, especially those of particular value to targeted markets. The key issue is the firm's ability to have customers believe the various aspects of its business are superior to those of its competitors. When it comes to differential advantages, customer perceptions are everything. When Barr Laboratories introduced its generic blood thinner, its profit rocketed to a 57 percent gain.[8] Barr's differential advantage or perceived position of relative superiority was price with product quality being perceived as equal to the competition.

However, a differential competitive advantage based on price is difficult to sustain. Only when a firm can sustain its advantage can it ensure long-term success. A sustainable competitive advantage is one that competitors cannot copy, or can copy only slowly over the long term with significant investments. If another pharmaceutical company introduces a comparably priced generic blood thinning product, Barr Laboratories will lose its differential advantage.

In order to achieve desired goals and objectives, corporate and business-unit strategies provide general approaches to making the business successful. For example, a firm within a specific industry could establish a differential advantage through price leadership, service quality/customer partnering, research and development, innovative distribution, or as a low-cost supplier. IBM has a corporate strategy that attempts to provide this type of differential advantage. By cutting costs, improving quality, and continuing to be the leader in mainframe computers, IBM has been able to maintain its leadership position in the computer industry.

Marketing Goals and Objectives

Marketing and all other business functions must support the organization's mission and goals, translating these into objectives with specific quantitative measurements. For example, a firm's goal to increase return on investment might translate into a marketing objective of a 15 percent increase in sales in the next fiscal year. Therefore, marketing objectives must be consistent with organizational goals. Marketing objectives should be expressed in clear, simple terms so that all marketing personnel understand what type and level of performance is desired. In other words, a marketing objective should be written so that its accomplishment can be measured accurately. In addition, marketing objectives should be expressed in terms of a unit of measurement, such as sales volume (in dollars or units), profitability per unit, percentage gain in market share, sales per square foot, average customer purchase, percentage of customers in the firm's target market who prefer its products, or some other measurable achievement.

Marketing objectives should be reconsidered for each planning period. Perhaps no strategy was found in the previous planning period to meet the stated objectives. Or perhaps some brilliant inspiration was found that propelled the firm beyond those objectives. In either case, realism demands that marketing objectives be revised to remain consistent with the next edition of the marketing plan. In Chapter 5, we fully discuss the importance and establishment of marketing goals and objectives.

Marketing Strategy

An organization's marketing strategy is designed to provide a total integration of efforts that focus on achieving the marketing objectives. The marketing strategy involves selecting one or more target markets and then developing a marketing mix (product, price, promotion, distribution) that satisfies the needs and wants of members of that target market. AutoZone, for example, targets do-it-yourself "shadetree mechanics" by offering an extensive selection of automotive replacement parts, maintenance items, and accessories at low prices.

Although the marketing strategy involves selection of a target market and development of a marketing mix, these decisions are not made in a vacuum. The marketing strategy must (1) fit the needs and purposes of the selected target market, (2) be realistic given the organization's available resources and environment, and (3) be consistent with the organization's mission, goals, and objectives. Within the context of the total strategic market planning process, the marketing strategy must be evaluated to determine its effect on the organization's sales, costs, image, and profitability. In Chapter 6 we will explore specific marketing strategy decisions, including market segmentation and target marketing, marketing mix issues, and differentiation and positioning. Chapter 7 will take a broader look at marketing strategy decisions, including criteria for selecting the marketing strategy, creating a competitive advantage based on customer value, and marketing strategies for services and business-to-business markets.

Marketing Implementation

Marketing implementation involves activities that actually execute the marketing strategy. One of the more interesting aspects of marketing strategy is that all organizations have at least two target markets: an external market (customers) and an internal market (employees). The more traditional definition of a target market refers to the external customer market. However, in order for any marketing strategy to be implemented successfully, the organization must rely on the commitment and knowledge of its employees—its internal target market. For this reason, organizations often execute internal marketing activities that are designed to ensure the implementation of external marketing activities. We discuss marketing implementation and internal marketing in depth in Chapter 8.

Maintaining a customer focus is extremely important throughout the market planning process and particularly during implementation. The marketing concept is a widely accepted business philosophy that states that an organization should try to provide products that satisfy customers' needs through a coordinated set of activities that allow the organization to achieve its goals. One of the key aspects of the marketing concept is the coordination of activities. As a result, it is important for the marketing manager to maintain contact and to interact with other functional managers who are involved in executing the overall strategic market plan. For example, accurate and timely distribution almost always depends on accurate and timely production. By maintaining contact with the production manager, the marketing manager helps to ensure effective marketing strategy implementation (by ensuring timely production) and, in the long run, customer satisfaction. One reason that marketing implementation is often difficult to achieve is that executing a marketing strategy depends on the coordinated execution of other functional strategies (i.e., production, research, human resources, etc.).

Evaluation and Control

In some ways, the evaluation and control phase of the planning process is an end *and* a beginning. On one hand, evaluation and control occur after the marketing strategy has been implemented. In fact, the implementation of any marketing strategy would be incomplete without an assessment of its success and the creation of control mechanisms to provide and revise the strategy, its implementation, or both if necessary. On the other hand, evaluation and control serve as the beginning point for the planning process in the next planning cycle.

Because strategic market planning is a never-ending process, managers should have a system for monitoring and evaluating implementation outcomes on an ongoing basis. Managers use a variety of financial and planning tools to aid in the evaluation of implementation success. Likewise, managers set performance standards based on marketing objectives to control marketing activities. We discuss the evaluation and control process further in Chapter 9.

The Marketing Plan

The result of the strategic market planning process described in the first portion of this chapter is a series of plans for each functional area of the organization. For the marketing department, the marketing plan provides a detailed formulation of the actions necessary to carry out the marketing program. A great deal of effort and organizational commitment are required to create and implement a marketing plan. To assist your efforts, we devote all of Chapter 2 to a discussion of the structure of the marketing plan, and we provide an example of a marketing plan in Appendix B.

The marketing plan is a report or document that addresses the information that was discovered in the planning process. The results of the environmental analysis, marketing goals and objectives, and the key elements of the marketing strategy should have been clearly specified in writing during the strategic market planning process. Here, the marketing strategy is described in rather broad terms. Such a general statement is not suitable for directing implementation, nor is it intended to be. The marketing plan is the action document. It is the handbook for marketing implementation, evaluation, and control.

A critical aspect of the marketing plan is its ability to communicate to other colleagues, particularly top management. Top managers look to the marketing plan for an explanation of the elements of the marketing strategy and for a justification of needed resources, like the marketing budget.[9] The marketing plan also communicates to line managers and other employees by giving them points of reference to chart the progress of marketing implementation.

A survey of marketing executives on the importance of the marketing plan revealed:

> ... the *process* of preparing the plan is more important than the document itself.... A marketing plan does compel attention, though. It makes the marketing team concentrate on the market, on the company's objectives, and on the strategies and tactics appropriate to those objectives. It's a mechanism for synchronizing action.[10]

Purposes and Significance of the Marketing Plan

The purposes of a marketing plan must be understood to appreciate its significance. A good marketing plan will fulfill these five purposes in detail:

1. It explains both the present and future situation of the organization. This includes the environmental and SWOT analyses and the firm's past performance.

2. It specifies the outcomes that are expected (goals and objectives) so that the organization can anticipate its situation at the end of the planning period.

3. It describes the specific actions that are to take place so that the responsibility for each action can be assigned. This helps to ensure that the marketing strategies are implemented.

4. It identifies the resources that will be needed to carry out the planned actions.

5. It permits the monitoring of each action and its results so that controls may be implemented. Feedback from monitoring and control provides information to start the planning cycle again in the next time frame.

These five purposes are very important to various persons in the firm. Line managers are particularly interested in the third purpose because they are responsible for ensuring that marketing actions are implemented. Middle-level managers have a special interest in the fifth purpose, as they want to ensure that tactical changes can be made if needed. These managers must also be able to evaluate why the marketing strategy does or does not succeed.

The most pressing concern for success may lie in the fourth purpose. The marketing plan is the means of communicating the strategy to top executives who make the critical decisions regarding the productive and efficient allocation of resources. Very sound marketing plans can prove unsuccessful if implementation of the plan is not adequately funded. Resource allocation is an especially important aspect of marketing planning given the recent trend of corporate downsizing in U.S. businesses. It is important to remember that marketing is not the only business function to compete for scarce resources. Other functions such as finance, research and development, and human resources have strategic plans of their own. It is in this vein that the marketing plan must "sell itself" to top management.

Organizational Aspects of the Marketing Plan

The marketing plan is based on strategic market planning. In large firms with several business units, the product manager (or brand/market manager) may play a major role in developing the plan. Many firms, however, place this responsibility in the hands of a top marketing executive. A Conference Board survey found that among manufacturing firms, nearly twice as many gave this responsibility to a marketing vice president or director than to a brand/market manager, unit-level manager, or planning committee.[11]

The fact that many marketing plans are developed by top managers does not necessarily refute the logic of having the unit manager prepare the plan. However, the unit manager should want and expect a higher-level marketing executive to provide direction in the preparation of the plan to increase the odds of the plan being approved. In the Conference Board survey, approximately 60 percent of all industrial, consumer, and service firms assigned the final approval of the marketing plan to the president, chairman, or CEO.[12] In some firms with multiple business units, the plan goes up only to the head executive of that unit for approval. Many companies also have executive committees that evaluate and screen marketing plans before they are submitted to the approving executive. Therefore, when a unit manager writes a marketing plan, it must be clear and persuasive to win the approval of the series of decision makers through which it is routed.

Strategic Market Planning in the Customer Oriented Organization

The main pillar of marketing thought and practice over the last 50 years has been the marketing concept, which focuses on customer satisfaction and the achievement of the firm's objectives. Although some firms are quite good at following the marketing concept, others pay only lip service to it. Unfortunately, the marketing plan cannot realize its full potential unless the entire firm is focused on meeting customer needs. Because our emphasis in this book is on the processes and concerns necessary to develop a customer-oriented marketing strategy and marketing plan, it is important to understand this concept and how it fits into the strategic planning process.

A customer-oriented organization concentrates on discovering what buyers want and providing it in such a way that the firm achieves its own objectives as well. Such a company has an organizational culture that effectively and efficiently produces a sustainable competitive advantage. It focuses on customer analysis, competitor analysis, and the integration of the firm's resources to provide customer value and satisfaction, as well as long-term profits.[13] Top management of the Chili's restaurant chain, for example, believes that well-trained, competent, and friendly staff will provide customers with the best service in the restaurant industry. Chili's takes a middle-of-the-road strategy by offering a more upscale menu than that offered by regular fast-food chains, but at prices that are more affordable than establishments offering fine cuisine. To enhance its customers' satisfaction, Chili's created a concept called "sizzle service," an approach in which servers are trained to acknowledge customers quickly. Chili's also recognizes that managers provide leadership in promoting a customer-oriented culture. Managers' attitudes toward service, employee training, and creating a service culture in each restaurant are important to Chili's success.[14]

Customer-oriented organizations such as Chili's strive to build meaningful long-term buyer-seller relationships. The term relationship marketing refers to "long-term, mutually beneficial arrangements in which both the buyer and seller focus on value enhancement through the creation of more satisfying exchanges."[15] FedEx, for example, has built a reputation for quality service by building strong relationships with customers. To enhance these relationships, the company developed a World Wide Web site that enables customers to manage their FedEx accounts and even track their packages.

In order to be a customer-oriented organization, a firm must also adopt a market orientation, which requires generating and responding to market intelligence throughout the entire organization.[16] Many companies that are leaders in their fields have mastered market orientation. Home Depot, for example, has more than twice the industry average return on equity. Sony continues to outperform its competition by nearly every financial measure. Southwest Airlines has redefined the concept of market orientation in the airline business by providing low fares, on-time departures, and dedicated employees who are eager to serve customers.

It is almost impossible to talk about the marketing concept and market orientation without addressing customer value. Value refers to customers' perceptions about the benefits received from using a product relative to the costs and risks associated with acquiring it. Benefits consist of quality, service, and need-fulfillment, while costs include time, effort, opportunity costs, and an overall subjective evaluation of risk, in addition to the monetary price of the product. It is also significant to note that diverse customers desire different kinds of value. No one goes into Wal-Mart or Target expecting highly personalized service. On the other hand, the customer expects Wal-Mart to provide "always the low price." Likewise, most customers do not expect Southwest Airlines to provide meals, reserved seats, or nonstop flights, but they do expect on-time departures, quality standardized operations, and low fares, along with upbeat, caring employees and a fun environment. At some point in time, customers make decisions about value based on an emotional response that "it just feels right." By focusing on value, the marketing concept can be a way to achieve marketing objectives. A value orientation is developed through strategic market planning that attempts to forge long-term relationships with customers.

To be a truly customer-oriented organization, a firm should focus on creating satisfying exchanges that provide value for both buyers and sellers. This requires ongoing ethical and socially responsible behavior and constant communication efforts. Avon, for example, recognizes that breast cancer is a major concern of its target market—women—and that addressing this concern helps build stronger relationships with customers while contributing to society. So, when Avon sales representatives market cosmetic products door-to-door, they also bring information about breast cancer and sell $2 Breast Cancer Awareness pins and $3 writing pens. These efforts have helped Avon's Breast Cancer Awareness Crusade raise $16.5 million to fund breast cancer education and early detection services at the community level, while bringing the firm positive media attention and increasing sales.[17] Because we believe ethics and social responsibility should be considered during the strategic market planning process, we will take a closer look at issues such as these in Chapter 10.

Building a Customer-Oriented Organization

For an organization to be truly customer-oriented, it must take a completely different perspective on the organization and structure of the marketing function. A traditional marketing firm is often very authoritative, with decision-making authority emanating from the top. Front-line employees must "answer" to front-line managers, who answer to mid-level managers, who answer to top managers, etc. The customer-oriented approach, however, decentralizes decision-making to facilitate feedback from customers. In this type of organization, every level of the firm is focused on serving customer needs.

Like the traditional design, the levels in a customer-oriented organization must "answer" to the levels above them. However, answering to the next level under this design does not mean yielding to authority. Rather, employees in a customer-oriented firm answer to the next level by taking any actions necessary to ensure that each level performs its job well. The role of the CEO in a customer-oriented organization is to ensure that his or her employees have everything they need to perform their jobs well. This "helping mentality" includes removing obstacles, providing resources, and becoming a cheerleader, teacher, and coach.[18] This same mentality is carried upward through all levels of the organization, including customers. Thus, the job of a front-line manager is to ensure that front-line employees are capable and efficient. The end result of the customer-oriented design is a complete focus on customer needs.

The decision as to which design to adopt will determine the relative importance of marketing within the firm. As you might suspect, the marketing function occupies a critical position in a truly customer-oriented firm. Marketing is important to traditionally designed firms as well, but its role is mainly one of selling the firm's products, not satisfying customer needs. The prominence of marketing in a customer-oriented firm can create one problem: Other functional areas may come to resent marketing's increased importance. This issue must be dealt with because the development of a good marketing plan depends on coordination with other functional areas.

Obviously, creating a customer-oriented organization takes time. The CEO cannot simply redraw the organizational chart and pronounce the firm to be customer-oriented. One of the major stumbling blocks to creating a customer-oriented firm is the top manager's own predisposition to be a boss rather than a leader. As one author puts it:

> Most managers have risen to the top by their ability to achieve results. They have succeeded in overcoming the bureaucratic inertia of their environments by the force of their personalities and their autocratic attitudes. They do not know that there is a better way—not to just release their own energies but the creative and enthusiastic energies of all their employees.[19]

Creating a customer-oriented organization takes an imaginative, visionary, and courageous leader, one who is capable of relinquishing control over the organization. A customer-oriented firm gives its employees the resources they need to perform their jobs, trains them well, and then trusts them to serve customers effectively. Although some managers will see the risks as being too great, the rewards can be enormous.

Using Strategic Planning to Build Relationships and Create Value

Strategic market planning should be viewed as a process to build long-term relationships with customers and achieve organizational objectives. It should become obvious that without the establishment of an organizational mission and corporate strategy, it would be impossible to gauge success. Without an effective marketing strategy and a marketing plan, it will not be possible to capitalize on the strengths and gain competitive advantage. It is necessary to implement the marketing concept and determine the appropriate marketing strategy to provide the right level of value to the customer.

To make strategic market planning work requires a purposeful focus in the planning processes and implementation of the marketing plan. According to authors Michael Treacy and Fred Wiersema, the goal is to "choose your customer, narrow your focus, and dominate your market."[20] According to these authors, market leaders choose a single best total cost, product, or total solution and then build their strategic plan and organization to succeed.[21] No company can be successful at being all things to all customers. Following the strategic planning process we outline in this book will help you determine what your firm does best so that you can choose a strategy that matches your firm's strengths to opportunities in the marketplace. This process helps successful customer-oriented organizations excel in planning strategies that satisfy their customers and achieve their own goals and objectives. We begin this process in the next chapter with a detailed look at the marketing plan itself.

14   *Chapter 1*   Strategic Market Planning

Key Insights from Chapter 1

Strategic market planning:

- involves identifying or establishing an organizational mission and goals, corporate strategy, marketing goals and objectives, marketing strategy, and ultimately, a marketing plan.
- must be coordinated with all functional business areas to ensure that the organization's goals and objectives will be considered in the development of each functional plan, one of which is the marketing plan.
- develops a marketing strategy, which includes selecting and analyzing target markets and creating and maintaining an appropriate marketing mix to satisfy the needs of customers in those target markets.
- creates a marketing plan, the written document or blueprint governing all the firm's marketing activities, including the implementation, evaluation, and control of marketing activities.
- ultimately results in a strategic market plan that outlines the activities and resources required to fulfill the organization's mission and achieve its goals and objectives.

The strategic market planning process:

- begins with an exhaustive examination of the organization's internal and external environments, which is then used to determine its internal strengths and weaknesses and external opportunities and threats (SWOT analysis).
- establishes the firm's mission, goals, and objectives.
- establishes corporate strategy and, if appropriate to the size and complexity of the firm, business-unit strategy.
- establishes marketing-level goals and objectives that support the organization's mission, goals, and objectives.
- develops a marketing strategy that integrates organizational efforts and achieves marketing objectives.
- provides for the implementation, evaluation, and control of the marketing strategy to ensure its success.

The marketing plan:

- provides a detailed formulation of the actions necessary to execute the marketing program and thus requires a great deal of effort and organizational commitment to create and implement.
- serves as an important communication vehicle to top management and to line managers and employees.
- is an important document, but not nearly as important as the knowledge gained from going through the market planning process.
- fulfills five purposes:
  1. explains both the present and future situation of the organization.
  2. specifies the expected outcomes.
  3. describes the specific actions that are to take place and assigns responsibility for each action.

4. identifies the resources needed to carry out the planned actions.

5. permits the monitoring of each action and its results so that controls may be implemented.

- is most often prepared by the marketing manager/director but is ultimately approved by the organization's president, chairman, or CEO.

A customer-oriented organization:

- concentrates on discovering what buyers want and providing it in such a way that the firm achieves its own objectives as well.

- uses relationship marketing to build long-term, mutually beneficial arrangements in which both the buyer and seller focus on value enhancement through the creation of more satisfying exchanges.

- develops a market orientation through the generation of and response to market intelligence throughout the entire organization.

- decentralizes decision-making authority to facilitate customer feedback.

- considers marketing to be a critically important function within the firm.

- uses the strategic planning process to build relationships and create value.

CHAPTER 2

Developing the Marketing Plan

Introduction

A good marketing plan requires a great deal of information from many different sources. Your job in developing the marketing plan is to pull all of this information together in an efficient and timely manner. As you do so, it is important that you constantly keep in mind "the big picture" to avoid getting caught up in the details. This requires looking at the marketing plan holistically rather than as a collection of related elements.

Unfortunately, adopting a holistic perspective is rather difficult in practice. It is easy to get deeply involved in developing marketing strategy only to discover later that the strategy is inappropriate for the organization's marketing environment. Consider what happened when America Online implemented a strategy to offer services at a flat rate of $19.95 per month. Although the strategy seemed like a good idea, the resultant surge in demand for AOL's services revealed that the new pricing strategy was inappropriate because the firm wasn't set up to handle the volume of new customers. AOL's customers quickly became aggravated when they got busy signals instead of Internet access, resulting in a class-action lawsuit against the company. To resolve the problem, the company was forced to spend millions of dollars to increase capacity.[1] Although America Online anticipated an increase in customer demand for its services, the company certainly did not expect the massive difficulties that it encountered. If the firm's managers had taken a more holistic approach in developing its marketing plan, the company could have initiated a new pricing strategy that was more consistent with its marketing environment and organizational resources. The hallmark of a well-developed marketing plan is its ability to achieve its stated goals and objectives.

In this chapter, we will explore the marketing plan in detail. We begin by examining the structure of a typical marketing plan, which should include analyses of the firm's internal, external, and customer environments; analyses of the firm's strengths, weaknesses, opportunities, and threats; a statement of the firm's marketing goals and objectives; an outline of the marketing strategy for achieving those ends; a blueprint of how the plan will be implemented; and an explanation of how the plan will be evaluated and controlled. We conclude by considering some common problems encountered in creating marketing plans and how marketing plans can be used to achieve organizational objectives.

The Structure of the Marketing Plan

All marketing plans should be well organized to ensure that all relevant information is considered and included. The outline of a typical marketing plan is illustrated in Exhibit 2.1. We say this outline is "typical" because there are many other ways to organize a marketing plan. In fact, marketers use many different planning approaches, with plans written for strategic business units (SBUs), product lines, individual products/brands, or specific markets. Although the actual outline used is not that important, most plans will share common elements described here.

EXHIBIT 2.1   **The Structure of a Typical Marketing Plan**

I. Executive Summary
  A. Synopsis
  B. Major aspects of the marketing plan

II. Environmental Analysis
  A. Analysis of the external environment
  B. Analysis of the customer environment
  C. Analysis of the internal (organizational) environment

III. SWOT Analysis (Strengths, Weaknesses, Opportunities, & Threats)
  A. Strengths
  B. Weaknesses
  C. Opportunities
  D. Threats
  E. Matching, converting, minimizing, and avoiding strategies

IV. Marketing Goals and Objectives
  A. Marketing Goals
  B. Marketing Objectives

V. Marketing Strategies
  A. Target market(s)
  B. Marketing mix for each target market
  C. Key customer and competitor reactions

VI. Marketing Implementation
  A. Structural issues
    1. Approach to implementation
    2. Internal marketing
    3. Communication
    4. Decision-making authority
    5. Employee motivation
  B. Activities, responsibilities, and budgets
  C. Implementation timetable

VII. Evaluation and Control
  A. Financial assessment
  B. Marketing control

Regardless of the specific outline you select for a marketing plan, you should keep three points in mind. First, the marketing plan outline should be comprehensive. This point is the most critical because having a complete outline ensures that no important information is omitted. Second, the outline should flow in a logical manner. It is important to remember that the marketing plan must ultimately sell itself to top managers. An illogical outline could force top managers to reject or underfund the marketing plan. Finally, the marketing plan outline should be flexible enough to be modified to fit the unique planning needs of the specific firm. Because every firm is different, using an outline that does not fit the company would be detrimental to the planning process.

In the following sections, we examine each element of the typical marketing plan structure shown in Exhibit 2.1. You will find that these elements are common to all marketing plans.

Executive Summary

The executive summary is a synopsis of the overall marketing plan with an outline that conveys the main thrust of the marketing strategy and its execution. The purpose of the executive summary is to provide an overview of the plan so the reader can quickly identify key issues or concerns related to his or her role in the planning process. Therefore, the executive summary does not provide detailed information found in the environmental or SWOT analyses, or any other detailed information that supports the final plan. Instead, this synopsis introduces the major aspects of the marketing plan, including sales projections, costs, and performance evaluation measures.

Managers may need to know what information is contained in the plan for other planning or implementation issues. Ultimately, many users of a marketing plan may ignore some of the details because of their respective roles in the organization. The CEO, for example, may be more concerned with the overall cost and expected return of the plan, and less interested in how the plan is to be implemented. On the other hand, significant detail should be contained in the body of the marketing plan so that effective decisions can be made with full understanding of the logic in the plan.

Others outside the immediate organization may be given a copy of the marketing plan. For example, a financial institution or an investment banker may want to read the marketing plan before approving any needed financing. Suppliers, investors, or others who have a stake in the success of the organization are sometimes given access to the marketing plan. In these cases, the executive summary becomes critical as a means of conveying a concise overview of the plan and its objectives, costs, and returns.

Although the executive summary is the first part of a marketing plan, it should always be the last element to be prepared because it is easier (and more meaningful) to write after the entire marketing plan has been developed. There is another good reason to write the executive summary last: It may be the only element of the marketing plan that is read by a large number of people. As a result, the executive summary must accurately condense the entire marketing plan.

Environmental Analysis

The next major section of the marketing plan is the environmental analysis, which summarizes all the pertinent information obtained about three key business conditions:

the external environment, the customer environment (i.e., target markets), and the firm's internal (organizational) environment. Analysis of the external environment should include all relevant external factors—economic, competitive, social, political/legal, and technological—that can exert considerable direct and indirect pressures on the firm's marketing activities. The analysis of the customer environment should examine the current situation with respect to the needs of the target market (consumer or business-to-business), anticipated changes in these needs, and how well the firm's products are presently meeting these needs. The analysis of the firm's internal environment should consider such issues as the availability and deployment of human resources, the age and capacity of equipment or technology, the availability of financial resources, and the power and political struggles within the firm's structure. In addition, the planner should scrutinize the firm's current marketing objectives and performance. The information for an environmental analysis may be obtained internally through the firm's information system, or it may have to be obtained externally through primary or secondary marketing research. We will take a closer look at the process of environmental analysis in Chapter 3.

A clear and comprehensive environmental analysis is one of the most difficult parts of developing a marketing plan. This difficulty arises in part because the environmental analysis must be simultaneously comprehensive in scope and focused on key issues in order to prevent information overload, a task actually made more complicated by technological advances.[2] High-speed modems, the Internet, overnight delivery services, and fax machines have made data more accessible and data collection and transmission faster than ever. However, easier access and faster speed also lead to a glut of information for the planner to synthesize. Unless the precise uses of data are identified beforehand, gathering relevant internal and external environmental data can quickly become overwhelming.

To help prevent information overload, the collection and organization of environmental data should be an ongoing effort. Once collected and organized, this data can be stored and analyzed within the firm's marketing information system (MIS) so that up-to-date information about the firm's environment is available when needed. Such a system can provide relevant input to the SWOT analysis by synthesizing findings into a series of conclusions.

Analysis of SWOT (Strengths, Weaknesses, Opportunities, and Threats)

The SWOT analysis focuses on the internal factors (strengths and weaknesses) and external factors (opportunities and threats)—derived from the environmental analysis in the preceding section—that give the firm certain advantages and disadvantages in satisfying the needs of its target market(s). These strengths, weaknesses, opportunities, and threats should be analyzed relative to market needs and competition. This analysis helps the company determine what it does well and where it needs to make improvements.

STRENGTHS AND WEAKNESSES   Strengths and weaknesses are internal issues that are unique to the firm conducting the analysis. Strengths refer to factors that give the firm an edge in meeting the needs of its target markets, i.e., a competitive advantage. Such factors may include strong resources (e.g., financial, human), a patented technology, sharp manufacturing or marketing skills, even a well-known brand name. For example, as the most popular car ever made, the name and cachet of the Volkswagen "Beetle" represents a strength for the German car maker. Volkswagen recently decided to capitalize on that strength by introducing a "new Beetle" that looks like Herbie the Love Bug but has updated safety devices, such as antilock brakes, air bags, and a front-mounted engine. Volkswagen hopes that baby boomer nostalgia for the car, which was sold in the United States from 1949 to 1979, will fuel sales of 50,000 units in 1999.[3] Any analysis of company strengths must be customer-focused because strengths are meaningful only when they assist the firm in serving customer needs.

Weaknesses refer to any deficiencies that a company might have in marketing strategy development or implementation. Weaknesses should also be examined from a customer perspective because customers often perceive weaknesses that the company cannot see. For example, many companies take their logos for granted, even to the point of ignoring the design of their logos for decades. A case in point is Sailor Jack, the mascot of the Cracker Jack snack-food brand, which was last redesigned in the late 1960s. When research ascertained that Sailor Jack was not contributing to consumers' identification of the brand, a major weakness in the crowded snack-food market, managers recognized that it was time for a new look. The new Jack is bright eyed and blond with an unmistakable all-American image. The new logo is also larger to help make the Cracker Jack package stand out on the shelf.[4]

Taking a customer-oriented approach to the SWOT analysis allowed Cracker Jack to spot a weakness that it had ignored for years. A true customer-oriented approach to SWOT allows a company to develop marketing strategies that align its strengths with customer requirements and preferences and minimize the exposure of its weaknesses. Only those strengths that relate to satisfying customers should be considered true competitive advantages. Likewise, weaknesses that directly affect customer satisfaction should be considered competitive disadvantages.

OPPORTUNITIES AND THREATS Opportunities and threats are external issues that may affect all organizations, even those that do not compete with the planning firm. Thus, both opportunities and threats exist independently of the firm creating the marketing plan. Both can greatly affect the operations of the firm and the outcomes of the marketing plan, however. Like strengths and weaknesses, opportunities and threats should be analyzed relative to market needs and the abilities of competitors.

Opportunities refer to favorable conditions in the environment that could produce rewards for the organization if acted upon properly. That is, opportunities are situations that exist but that must be acted upon in order to yield benefits for the firm. Consider, for example, the decade-long trend of increases in restaurant takeout orders, which was prompted by baby boomers who preferred takeout meals to sitting in restaurants with their young children. As these baby boomers age and their children move out of the house, however, the demand for full-service sit-down meals is expected to soar, creating a tremendous opportunity for restaurant firms to expand sales and market share. By 2010, full-service restaurants are expected to sell up to 189 million more meals per year to aging baby boomers.[5]

Threats, on the other hand, refer to conditions or barriers that may prevent the firm from reaching its objectives. Like opportunities, threats must be acted upon to prevent them from limiting the firm's performance. The July 1, 1997, turnover of Hong Kong to China by Great Britain was seen as a tremendous threat to most firms doing business in Hong Kong. Although the Chinese government promised to preserve Hong Kong's business climate, many feared that corruption and bureaucracy could jeopardize their business interests.[6]

MATCHING STRENGTHS AND WEAKNESSES TO THE ENVIRONMENT   One of the most important outcomes of a good SWOT analysis is matching internal strengths to external opportunities. When companies match their strengths to opportunities, they create capabilities that can be used to generate competitive advantages in meeting the needs of customers. In fact, these matched strengths and opportunities often become the focus of the firm's marketing strategy. Viacom, for example, entered the world of retailing after matching its knowledge of entertainment marketing to opportunities available in retailing. Viacom's stores are divided into boutiques that are associated with its six well-known entertainment brands: MTV, VH1, Nickelodeon, Nick at Nite, Paramount Pictures, and *Star Trek*. By entering the entertainment retailing segment, Viacom hopes to make its name as well known to consumers as its major competitors, Disney and Warner Brothers.[7]

Another important outcome of a good SWOT analysis is finding ways to convert weaknesses into strengths and reposition threats into opportunities. In some cases, companies can successfully transform weaknesses or threats into competitive advantages. When the state of California passed clean-air legislation that mandated zero-emission vehicles by 1997, for example, car makers immediately began plans to develop vehicles that complied with the legislation. But when California postponed the deadline to 2003, most car makers slowed their development efforts. General Motors and Honda, however, continued to move full-speed ahead and in 1997 both introduced the first line of all-electric vehicles to the U.S. market. By launching their new vehicles ahead of the mandated schedule, GM and Honda not only converted a potential threat, they also gained a competitive advantage over other carmakers.[8]

SWOT analysis has gained widespread acceptance because it is a simple framework for organizing and evaluating a company's strategic position when developing a marketing plan. It provides the best framework for planning that we have been able to identify. Like any straightforward framework, SWOT analysis can be misused unless the appropriate research is conducted to identify key variables that will affect the performance of the firm. We will take a closer look at the SWOT analysis in Chapter 4.

Marketing Goals and Objectives

Marketing goals and objectives are formal statements of the desired and expected outcomes resulting from the marketing plan. This section of the marketing plan is based on a careful study of the SWOT analysis and should contain objectives related to matching strengths to opportunities and/or the conversion of weaknesses or threats. It is important to remember that neither goals nor objectives can be developed without a clearly defined mission statement. All marketing goals should be based on the firm's mission, and all marketing objectives should flow from marketing goals.

Goals are broad, simple statements of what is to be accomplished through the marketing strategy. The major function of goals is to guide the development of objectives and to provide direction for resource allocation decisions. Marketing objectives are more specific and are essential to planning. Marketing objectives should be stated in quantitative terms to permit reasonably precise measurement. To return to Viacom, the goal of the company was to make the Viacom name as well known to consumers as Disney or Warner Brothers. This is a simple, nonspecific goal of what is to be accomplished via the marketing strategy.[9] A possible objective stemming from this goal might be to increase consumer recognition of the Viacom name by 20 percent by 1999. The quantitative nature of marketing objectives makes them easier to implement after the strategy has been developed.

Regardless of the types of goals or objectives, all marketing personnel must understand exactly what the company is trying to achieve. Each goal and objective should be communicated to employees in such a way that the expected outcomes are understood. Having quantitative marketing objectives facilitates this communication to employees. Because goals and objectives are so important to the success of marketing strategy, we devote Chapter 5 to them.

Marketing Strategies

The strategy section of the marketing plan outlines how the firm will achieve its marketing objectives. In Chapter 1, we said that marketing strategies involve selecting and analyzing target markets and creating and maintaining an appropriate marketing mix (product, distribution, promotion, and price) to satisfy the needs of those target markets. Thus, in the broadest sense, marketing strategy refers to how the firm will manage its relationships with customers in a manner that gives it an advantage over the competition.

Target market selection is the first stage of this process. The marketing plan should clearly define target markets in terms of one or more important segmentation variables: demographic, geographic, psychographic, product usage, and so on. This step is extremely important because marketers must understand the needs of their customers before they can develop a marketing mix to satisfy those needs. In developing a marketing mix, the firm should determine how the elements of the mix—product, price, distribution, and promotion—will work together to satisfy the needs of specific target market segments.

It is at the marketing mix level of the marketing plan where the firm will detail how it will gain a competitive advantage. To gain an advantage, the firm must obviously do something better than the competition: Its products must be of higher quality than competitive offerings, its prices must be consistent with the level of quality (value), its distribution methods must be as efficient as possible, and its promotions must be more effective in communicating with target customers. It is also important that the firm attempt to make these advantages sustainable. Many retailers, for example, maintain sustainable advantages over their competition through location. Most McDonald's stores are strategically located to take advantage of traffic patterns. Many new Wal-Mart stores have a McDonald's restaurant rather than a snack bar. Such locations provide a sustainable advantage because they are almost impossible for competitors to match directly or copy.[10]

The final portion of the strategy section of the marketing plan outlines the expected reactions to implementing the chosen marketing strategy. It is important that planners put themselves in the customer's position to try to understand how customers will react to the marketing strategy. In other words, what are the key benefits that customers perceive they will receive as a result of the marketing strategy? This section of the marketing plan must also detail the potential competitive reactions to the marketing strategy. What will competitors do in response to changes in the firm's marketing strategy? A good understanding of the potential customer and competitor reactions may suggest areas where the marketing strategy needs to be changed. Recognizing the need for a change of strategy at this stage is far better than recognizing the need *after* the strategy has been implemented.

Marketing Implementation

The implementation section of the marketing plan describes how the marketing strategies delineated in the previous section will be performed. Marketing implementation is the process of executing the marketing strategy by creating specific actions that will ensure that the marketing objectives are achieved. This section of the marketing plan answers several questions with respect to the strategies outlined in the preceding section:

1. What specific actions will be taken?
2. How will these activities be performed?
3. When will these activities be performed?
4. Who is responsible for the completion of these activities?
5. How will the completion of plan activities be monitored?
6. How much will these activities cost?

Without a good plan for implementation, the success of the marketing strategy is seriously jeopardized. For this reason, the implementation phase of the marketing plan is just as important as the marketing strategy phase.

A well-developed plan for implementation involves several considerations. First, the marketing manager should ensure that structural elements are in place to facilitate the implementation of the marketing plan. These elements include selecting an overall approach to implementation, communicating the requirements and benefits of the marketing plan to all employees, granting decision-making authority to frontline employees who are responsible for implementing the plan, and motivating employees to give their full efforts to the marketing plan. Second, specific activities for each element of the marketing mix must be clearly outlined, including assigning a budget and a responsible employee to each activity. Finally, the overall timetable of implementation must be developed to ensure that all activities are executed at the appropriate times.

It is important to recognize that employees at all levels of the firm are critically important to marketing implementation. In fact, we feel so strongly about the importance of employees that we subscribe to the "implementation axiom": *Organizations do not implement strategies, people do!* As a result, there are many issues that are critical to implementation success: leadership, employee motivation, communication, training, etc. The significance of employees in marketing implementation has led many experts to label people as the "Fifth P" of the marketing mix (with the other four "Ps" being, of course, product, price, promotion, and place). We will explore these and many other key implementation issues in Chapter 8.

Evaluation and Control

The final section of the marketing plan details how the results of the plan will be evaluated and controlled. The first part of evaluation and control is a financial assessment of the marketing plan. Financial projections are based on estimates of costs, sales, and revenues. In reality, budgetary considerations play a key role in the identification of alternative strategies. The financial realities of the firm must be monitored at all times. For example, proposing to expand into new geographic areas or alter products without financial resources is a waste of time, energy, and opportunity. Even if funds are available, the strategy must be a "good value" and provide an acceptable return on investment to be a part of the final plan.

The second part of the control process is marketing control, which involves establishing performance standards, assessing actual performance by comparing it with these standards, and, if necessary, taking corrective action to reduce discrepancies between desired and actual performance. Performance standards can be based on sales volume increases, market share increases, profitability, or even advertising standards such as brand name recognition or recall. Regardless of the standard selected, all measures of performance must be agreed upon before the results of the plan can be assessed. Internal performance data and external environmental relationships must be identified and monitored to ensure an appropriate evaluation and diagnosis before corrective actions can be taken.

Finally, should it be determined that the marketing plan is not living up to expectations, the firm can use a number of tools to pinpoint potential causes for the discrepancies. One such tool is the marketing audit, a systematic examination of the firm's marketing objectives, strategy, and performance.[11] The marketing audit can help isolate weaknesses in the marketing plan and recommend actions to help improve performance. The control phase of the planning process also outlines the actions that can be taken to reduce the differences between planned and actual performance. We will take a close look at evaluation and control in Chapter 9.

Problems in Creating Marketing Plans[12]

In the past decade, many firms have changed the focus and content of their marketing plans. Of these changes, the one most frequently mentioned by marketing planners is an increased emphasis on the customer. For most firms, this change has required shifting their focus from the company's products to the unique requirements of specific target market segments. Other important changes in marketing plans include better analysis of the competition, more specific objectives and measurement, and more reasoned and realistic planning.

Although most marketing plans have become more customer-oriented, specific, and realistic, many marketing planners and executives remain dissatisfied with the results of their efforts. The problems most commonly cited in the development of marketing plans are (1) getting companywide consensus and cooperation and (2) finding enough time to prepare a good plan. Other common problems are listed in Exhibit 2.2. Despite efforts to create more practical marketing plans, lack of realism remains a major limitation of most marketing plans. This issue and other major shortcomings are presented in Exhibit 2.3. Note that 33 percent of service firms believe their marketing plans are not specific enough and 26 percent feel their

EXHIBIT 2.2	Common Problems in Preparing Marketing Plans

Problem	Percentage of Firms Listing the Problem		
	Industrial Product Firms	Consumer Product Firms	Service Firms
Hard to get consensus/cooperation	18%	5%	21%
Not enough time to prepare properly	16	18	7
Hard to make forecasts	10	8	0
Plans not taken seriously enough	5	0	10
Company isn't market-oriented	2	3	14
Too much focus on short term	2	7	0
Not enough useful information	8	8	3
Unrealistic top management goals	5	5	3
Not enough top management commitment	3	3	3
Not enough strategic thinking	4	3	7
Market changes too fast	4	3	3
Have to plan too far ahead	3	2	0
Inertia/resistance to change	1	5	3

Source: Howard Sutton, *The Marketing Plan in the 1990s* (New York: The Conference Board, 1990), 61.

marketing plans place too much emphasis on short-term results. Despite these problems and shortcomings, most executives expect market planning and the creation of the marketing plan to become even more important in the future.

Using the Marketing Plan

The creation and implementation of a complete marketing plan will allow the organization to achieve not only its marketing objectives, but its business-unit and corporate objectives as well. However, it is important to understand that the marketing plan is only as good as the information it contains and the effort and creativity that went into its creation. As a result, the importance of having an ongoing system of collecting relevant marketing information cannot be overstressed. Equally important is the role of managerial judgment throughout the strategic market planning process. Managers must always weigh any information against its accuracy—and their own intuition—when making marketing decisions.

We should also note that the marketing plan outline that we described in this chapter should serve as a structure for the written document rather than a series of sequential planning steps. In practice, many of the elements in the marketing plan are decided upon simultaneously. For example, the actual development of marketing strategies must take into account how those strategies will be implemented.

EXHIBIT 2.3	Major Shortcomings of Marketing Plans		
Shortcoming	*Percentage of Firms Listing the Shortcoming*		
	Industrial Product Firms	Consumer Product Firms	Service Firms
Not realistic enough	19%	14%	11%
Too much emphasis on short term	10	14	26
Not specific enough	16	12	33
Not enough market information	16	16	11
Not taken seriously enough	13	9	15
Inadequate performance measures	8	12	15
Not sufficiently up-to-date	9	18	7
Not enough strategic emphasis	12	14	7
Not enough competitive analysis	17	5	7
Objectives not well defined	3	11	15
Inadequate contingency plans	9	9	4
Not enough focus on customers	3	11	4
Not executed well	7	4	7
Not enough input from other groups	5	5	4
Not integrated with other plans	7	2	4
Not adequately communicated	4	0	4
Takes too much time and effort	3	4	0

Source: Howard Sutton, *The Marketing Plan in the 1990s* (New York: The Conference Board, 1990), 62.

Except in small organizations where one person both creates and approves the marketing plan, the authority to approve the marketing plan is vested in executives above the marketing level. Therefore, the final marketing plan is submitted to that executive, group, or committee that has the authority to give final approval for budgets and other resources. The completion of the formal, written document is not the most critical goal. It is more important that top management approves the marketing plan, provides the necessary resources to implement the plan, and convinces nonmarketing areas to fulfill their role in implementing the marketing plan. Before the marketing plan gains final approval, top managers usually ask these two important questions:

1. Will the proposed marketing plan achieve the desired marketing, business unit, and corporate goals and objectives?
2. Are there alternative uses of resources that would better meet corporate or unit objectives than the marketing plan that has been submitted?

It is crucial that managers at the approval stage make efficient and timely decisions with respect to the marketing plan. To give the plan every chance for success, very little time should elapse between the completion of the plan and its implementation.

Finally, although the creation of a marketing plan is an important milestone in strategic market planning, it is by no means the final step. Some of the information used to create the plan may, and often does, turn out to be inaccurate. Many of the managerial assumptions or projections used in the analysis often turn out differently when the plan is actually put into practice, as America Online learned when it offered its $19.95 flat rate fee to customers. Likewise, there is usually a meaningful difference between the intended marketing strategy and the strategy that actually takes place. These realities point out that the marketing plan must be flexible enough to be adjusted on an ongoing basis.

Developing Your Own Marketing Plan

Writing a comprehensive marketing plan is a very time-consuming endeavor. This is especially true if the marketing plan is being developed for the first time. Initially, most of your time will be spent on the environmental analysis. Although this analysis is a very demanding part of the marketing plan, without a thorough understanding of the total marketing environment, the marketing plan has little chance for success.

After conducting the environmental analysis, you will spend most of your time revising the remaining elements of the marketing plan to ensure that they mesh with each other. Some plan writers find it productive, once the first draft has been written, to put the plan away for a day or so. Then, they review the plan with a fresher perspective and fine tune sections that need changing in order to arrive at the final marketing plan document. Because the revision process often takes more time than expected, it is wise to begin the planning process far in advance of when the plan is due.

Ideally, once the first marketing plan has been developed, it should be regularly updated as new data and information are collected. Many companies update their marketing plans on a quarterly basis to ensure that the marketing strategy remains consistent with changes in the external, customer, and internal environments. Using this approach, the company will always have a working plan that covers 12 months into the future. At the end of the first year when the annual marketing plan must again be formally developed, the marketing manager will face a much less difficult task than the first time around.

The remaining chapters of this book discuss each section of the marketing plan in detail. Additionally, in Appendix A, we have provided worksheets to assist you in developing each section of your own marketing plan. As you complete these worksheets, you will be organizing all of the information you will need to write your final marketing plan. To help you get started, we have provided an example of a marketing plan in Appendix B.

We should stress again that most organizations have their own unique format and terminology to describe the elements of their marketing plans. Consequently, you should not regard the outline presented in Exhibit2.1 and the marketing plan worksheets in Appendix A as the only format available for creating your marketing plan. Every marketing plan is and should be unique to the organization for which it was created. So, as you complete the worksheets, you should make any changes, additions, or deletions that you feel are necessary to adapt our outline to the specific circumstances of your organization.

Key Insights from Chapter 2

Developing a marketing plan:

- requires a great deal of information from many different sources that must be pulled together in an efficient and timely manner.
- involves taking a holistic approach toward the elements of the marketing plan.

The structure of the marketing plan:

- should be well organized and comprehensive to ensure that no important information is omitted.
- should flow in a logical manner to ensure that the marketing plan can sell itself to top managers.
- should be flexible enough to be modified to fit the unique planning needs of the specific firm.

Includes seven major elements:

- *Executive Summary*: a synopsis of the overall marketing plan that conveys the main thrust of the marketing strategy and its execution.
- *Environmental Analysis*: a summary of the pertinent information obtained about the external environment, the customer environment, and the firm's internal environment.
- *SWOT Analysis*: an analysis of the internal factors (strengths and weaknesses) and external factors (opportunities and threats) that give the firm certain advantages and disadvantages in satisfying the needs of its target market.
- *Marketing Goals and Objectives*: formal statements of the desired and expected outcomes resulting from the marketing plan.
- *Marketing Strategies*: a blueprint for how the firm will achieve its marketing objectives through selection of one or more target markets and the development of a marketing mix appropriate for those target markets.
- *Marketing Implementation*: the process of executing the marketing strategy by creating specific actions that will ensure that the marketing objectives are achieved.
- *Evaluation and Control*: an explanation of how the results of the plan will be measured and assessed.

The practice of creating the marketing plan:

- has changed over the past decade to include an increased emphasis on the customer, better analysis of the competition, more specific objectives and measurement, and more reasoned and realistic planning.
- faces a number of challenges, including getting companywide consensus and cooperation and finding enough time to prepare a good plan.
- is still plagued by insufficient realism.
- is gaining increased emphasis today and in the future.

Using the marketing plan requires:

- an ongoing system of collecting relevant marketing information.
- good managerial judgment.

- getting top management to approve the marketing plan, provide the necessary resources to implement the plan, and convince nonmarketing areas to fulfill their role in implementing the marketing plan.
- being flexible enough to adjust the plan as necessary.

CHAPTER 3

Environmental Analysis

Introduction

In this chapter, we begin the process of developing the marketing plan by examining the major elements of environmental analysis and illustrating how environmental data can be structured to assist in the formulation of marketing strategies. Managers in all organizations, large and small, devote a major portion of their time and energy to developing plans and making decisions. Good planning and decision making require access to and analysis of data to generate usable information in a timely manner. Although environmental analysis is but one of several tasks performed by marketing managers, it is perhaps the most important task, as practically all decision making and planning depends on how well the analysis is conducted.

There are many issues to be considered in environmental analysis. An outline of these issues is shown in Exhibit 3.1. It is important that any effort at environmental analysis be well-organized, systematic, and supported by sufficient resources (e.g., people, equipment, information). However, the most important aspect of environmental analysis is that it should be *an ongoing effort*. Rather than taking place only in the days and weeks immediately preceding the formation of strategies and plans, the collection, distribution, and analysis of pertinent environmental data must be ingrained in the culture of the organization. This ongoing effort ensures that the organization is always able to assess its strengths and weaknesses accurately, while simultaneously monitoring the environment to uncover any opportunities and threats. This effort drives the development of the SWOT analysis addressed in the next chapter.

In this chapter, we will examine several issues related to environmental analysis, the components of environmental analysis, and the collection of environmental data and information to facilitate strategic marketing planning. Although environmental analysis has traditionally been one of the most difficult aspects of market planning, recent advances in technology, particularly with respect to computers and the Internet, have made the collection of environmental data and information much easier and more efficient. A wealth of environmental data is free for the asking. This chapter examines the different types of environmental data that are needed for market planning, as well as many sources where such data may be obtained.

EXHIBIT 3.1	Issues in Environmental Analysis

The external environment
  Competitive forces
  Economic growth and stability
  Political trends
  Legal and regulatory factors
  Changes in technology
  Cultural trends

The customer environment
  Who are our current and potential customers?
  What do our customers do with our products?
  Where do our customers purchase our products?
  When do our customers purchase our products?
  Why (and how) do our customers select our products?
  Why do potential customers not purchase our products?

The internal environment
  Current objectives and performance
  Level of available resources
  Organizational culture and structure

Important Caveats of Environmental Analysis

Before we move forward in our discussion, you should be aware of three important caveats regarding environmental analysis. Understanding these caveats can help overcome potential problems throughout the environmental analysis.

Environmental Analysis Is Not a Panacea

Although it is true that a comprehensive environmental analysis can lead to better planning and decision making, analysis itself is not enough. Put another way, environmental analysis is a necessary, but insufficient, prerequisite for effective strategic planning. The analysis must be combined with the manager's intuition and judgment to make the results of the analysis useful for planning purposes. Environmental analysis is not intended to replace the manager in the decision-making process. Its purpose is to *empower* the manager with information for decision making.

Environmental analysis empowers the marketing manager because it encourages both *analysis and synthesis* of information. From the view of the marketing manager, environmental analysis involves taking things apart: be it a customer segment, to study the heavy users; a product, to understand the relationship between its features and customers' needs; or competitors, to weigh their strengths and weaknesses. The purpose of taking things apart is to understand why people, products, or organizations perform the way they do. After this dissection is complete, the manager can then synthesize the information to gain an overall "big picture" understanding of the complex decisions to be made. The result of this synthesis of information is a marketing strategy that integrates complex decisions regarding target markets and the marketing mix.

Data Is Not the Same as Information

Throughout the planning process, managers regularly face the question: "How much data and information do I need?" The answer sounds simple, but in practice it is not. Today, there is no shortage of data for analysis purposes. The cost of collecting and storing vast amounts of data has dropped dramatically over the past decade. Computer-based marketing information systems are becoming commonplace. Online systems, such as intranets and databases, allow managers to retrieve data in a matter of minutes. The truth is that managers are more likely to be overwhelmed with data rather than face a shortage.

Although data is easy to find, good information is not. In simple terms, data is a collection of numbers that have the potential to provide information. Data, however, does not become informative until a person, or computer program, transforms it in a manner that makes it *useful* to decision makers. Generating useful information requires that data be of high quality. As the saying goes, "Garbage in, garbage out." It is a good idea for the manager to be curious, perhaps even suspicious, of the quality of data being used for planning and decision making. We discuss issues related to data collection later in this chapter.

The Benefits of Data Analysis Must Outweigh the Costs

Environmental analysis is valuable only to the extent that it improves the quality of the resulting plans and decisions. For example, data that costs $4,000 to acquire, but improves the quality of the decision by only $3,999, should not be part of the analysis process. Although the costs of acquiring data are easy to determine, the benefits of improved decisions are quite difficult to estimate. Managers must constantly ask: "Where do I have knowledge gaps?" "How can these gaps be filled?" "What are the costs of filling these gaps?" and "How much improvement in decision making will be gained as a result of acquiring this information?" By asking these questions, managers can find a happy medium between jumping to conclusions and "paralysis by analysis," or constantly postponing a decision due to a lack of information. Perpetually analyzing data without making any decisions is usually not worth the added expense.

Components of Environmental Analysis

Environmental analysis is one of the most difficult parts of developing the marketing plan. Although an organization should maintain an ongoing effort to collect and organize data about the marketing environment, managers are often faced with something less than a well-ordered flow of information. As mentioned earlier, managers have the responsibility of assessing the quality, adequacy, and timeliness of the data and information used for analysis and synthesis. Unfortunately, dynamic internal and external environments often create breakdowns in the effort to develop effective information flows. This dynamism can be especially troubling when the firm attempts to collect and analyze data in international environments.

The environmental analysis should provide the manager with as complete a picture as possible about the organization's current and future situation with respect to three key environments: the external environment, the customer environment, and the organization's internal environment. To examine these three environments properly, the manager should look at both internal and external sources of data and information. As we discuss later in the chapter, a great deal of this information is available through secondary sources. However, if the required data or information is not available, it may have to be collected through primary marketing research. Whatever the source, having data and information readily available makes for an easier and more comprehensive environmental analysis.

The External Environment

The first and broadest issue in environmental analysis is an assessment of the external environment, which includes all the external factors—competitive, economic, political, legal/regulatory, technological, and sociocultural—that can exert considerable direct and indirect pressures on both domestic and international marketing activities. Exhibit 3.2 provides a framework for analyzing factors in the external environment. As this framework suggests, the issues involved in examining the external environment can be divided neatly into separate categories (i.e., competitive, economic, legal, etc.). However, some environmental issues fall into multiple categories.

For example, a strike by UPS employees created a situation that led to changes in several environmental sectors. From a competitive perspective, the strike handed other package delivery firms (FedEx, Airborne Express, U.S. Postal Service) a golden opportunity to increase sales and market share. However, companies that depend on UPS to deliver shipments to their customers faced a tremendous threat to their livelihood. On the economic front, the strike not only put UPS employees out of work, it also led to an economic slowdown in UPS hub cities. It also brought to a head the debate over part-time vs. full-time employment and benefits. The strike became a political issue as President Bill Clinton was continually pressured to invoke the Taft-Hartley Act to force striking UPS employees back to work. Finally, on a cultural level, many people began to debate the wisdom of being so dependent on overnight delivery services such as UPS. Although situations like the UPS strike are rare, they do illustrate how seemingly isolated events can affect many different aspects of the external marketing environment.

COMPETITIVE FORCES   In most industries, customers have choices and preferences in terms of the goods and services they can choose. Thus, when the marketing manager defines the target markets the firm will serve, he or she simultaneously selects a set of competing firms. The current and future actions of these competitors must be constantly monitored, and hopefully even be anticipated. The major problem in analyzing competing firms is one of identification. That is, how does the manager answer the question "Who are our current and future competitors?" To arrive at an answer, the manager must look beyond the obvious examples of competition. Most firms face four basic types of competition:

1. Brand competitors, which market products that are similar in features and benefits to the same customers at similar prices.
2. Product competitors, which compete in the same product class, but with products that are different in features, benefits, and price.
3. Generic competitors, which market very different products that solve the same problem or satisfy the same basic customer need.
4. Total budget competitors, which compete for the limited financial resources of the same customers.

EXHIBIT 3.2   **A Framework for Analyzing the External Environment**

1. Competitive forces
   a. Who are our major brand, product, generic, and total budget competitors? What are their characteristics in terms of size, growth, profitability, strategies, and target markets?
   b. What are our competitors' key strengths and weaknesses?
   c. What are our competitors' key marketing capabilities in terms of products, distribution, promotion, and pricing?
   d. What response can we expect from our competitors if environmental conditions change or if we change our marketing strategy?
   e. Is this competitive set likely to change in the future? If so, how? Who are our new competitors likely to be?

2. Economic forces
   a. What are the general economic conditions of the country, region, state, and local area in which our firm operates?
   b. Overall, are our customers optimistic or pessimistic about the economy?
   c. What is the buying power of customers in our target market(s)?
   d. What are the current spending patterns of customers in our target market(s)? Are customers buying less or more of our product and why?

3. Political forces
   a. Have recent elections changed the political landscape within our domestic or foreign markets? What type of industry regulations do newly elected officials favor?
   b. What are we currently doing to maintain good relations with elected political officials? Have these activities been effective? Why or why not?

4. Legal and regulatory forces
   a. What changes in international, federal, state, or local laws and regulations are being proposed that would affect our marketing activities?
   b. Do recent court decisions suggest that we should modify our marketing activities?
   c. Do the recent rulings of federal, state, local and self-regulatory agencies suggest that we should modify our marketing activities?
   d. What effect will changes in global trade agreements (e.g. NAFTA and GATT) have on our international marketing opportunities?

5. Technological forces
   a. What impact has changing technology had on our customers?
   b. What technological changes will affect the way we operate or manufacture our products?
   c. What technological changes will affect the way we conduct marketing activities, such as distribution or promotion?
   d. Are there any current technologies that we are not using to their fullest potential in making our marketing activities more effective and efficient?
   e. Do any technological advances threaten to make our product(s) obsolete? Does new technology have the potential to satisfy previously unmet or unknown customer needs?

6. Sociocultural forces
   a. How are society's demographics and values changing? What effect will these changes have on our product(s)? pricing? distribution? promotion? people?
   b. What problems or opportunities are being created by changes in the diversity of our customers and employees?
   c. What is the general attitude of society about our industry, company, and product(s)? Could we take actions to improve this attitude?
   d. What consumer or environmental groups could intervene in the operations of our industry or company?
   e. What ethical issues should we address?

Examples of each type of competition for selected product markets are presented in Exhibit 3.3. In the fast-growing sport-utility vehicle (SUV) segment of the automobile industry, for example, Ford Explorer, Chevrolet Blazer, Toyota 4Runner, and Honda Passport are all brand competitors. However, each faces competition from other types of automobile products, such as minivans, passenger cars, and trucks. Some of this product competition even comes from within each company's own product line (e.g., Ford's Explorer, Taurus, Windstar, and F-150 pickup). SUVs also face generic competition from Honda motorcycles, Schwinn bicycles, Hertz car rental, and public transportation—all of which offer products that satisfy the same basic customer need for transportation. Finally, customers have many alternative uses for their available dollars rather than purchasing an SUV: They can take a long and exotic vacation, install a pool in the backyard, buy a boat, start an investment fund, or pay off their debt.

Although all types of competition are important, brand competitors rightfully receive the greatest attention because consumers typically see the different products

---

EXHIBIT 3.3   **Major Types of Competition**

Sport/Utility Vehicles (Need: Transportation)

Brand Competition	Product Competition	Generic Competition	Total Budget Competition
Ford Explorer	Minivans	Rental cars	Home remodeling
Toyota 4Runner	Cars	Motorcycles	Family vacation
Honda Passport	Trucks	Bicycles	Debt reduction

Soft Drinks (Need: Thirst)

Brand Competition	Product Competition	Generic Competition	Total Budget Competition
Coke	Tea	Water	Candy bars
Pepsi	Juice		Potato chips
Dr Pepper	Beer		Gum

Movies (Need: Entertainment)

Brand Competition	Product Competition	Generic Competition	Total Budget Competition
Titanic	HBO	Football game	Shopping
Jurassic Park	Showtime	Video arcade	Pizza delivery
Star Wars	Video rental	Rock concert	Magazines

College (Need: Education)

Brand Competition	Product Competition	Generic Competition	Total Budget Competition
Harvard	Trade school	Correspondence	New car
LSU	Community	school	Vacation
Florida State	college	CD-ROM	Savings

of these firms as direct substitutes for each other. For this reason, strategies aimed at getting consumers to switch brands are a major issue in market planning directed toward beating brand competitors. McDonald's and Burger King have engaged in massive promotional campaigns designed to get customers to switch to their respective products. Recently, Burger King has made serious inroads into McDonald's once-dominant market share. In response, McDonald's began test marketing a new weapon: the 99¢ Quarter Pounder Big and Tasty, which includes lettuce, tomato, and mayonnaise. The sole purpose of the new sandwich is to get Burger King customers to switch from the similarly priced Whopper sandwich.[1]

Competitive analysis has received greater attention recently for several reasons: more intense competition from sophisticated competitors, increased competition from foreign firms, shorter product life cycles, and dynamic environments, particularly in the area of technological innovation. Growing numbers of companies are adopting formalized methods of identifying competitors, tracking their activities, and assessing their strengths and weaknesses. The core of competitive analysis involves observing, tracking, and analyzing the total range of competitive activity, including competitors' sources of supply, technological capabilities, financial strength, manufacturing capacities and qualities, marketing abilities, and target markets. Competitive analysis should progress through the following stages:

1. Identify all current and potential brand, product, generic, and total budget competitors.

2. Assess each key competitor by ascertaining its size, growth, profitability, objectives, strategies, and target markets.

3. Assess each competitor's strengths and weaknesses, including the major competencies that each possesses within its functional areas (marketing, research and development, production, human resources, etc.).

4. Focus the analysis on each competitor's marketing capabilities in terms of its products, distribution, promotion, and pricing.

5. Estimate each competitor's most likely strategies and responses under different environmental situations, as well as its reactions to the firm's own marketing efforts.

There are many sources that can be used to gather information on current or potential competitors. Company annual reports are useful for determining a firm's current performance and future direction. An examination of a competitor's mission statement can also provide information, particularly with respect to how the company defines itself. A thorough scan of a competitor's World Wide Web site can also uncover information—such as the mission statement, product specifications, and prices—that can greatly improve the competitive analysis. Other valuable information sources include business periodicals and trade publications that provide newsworthy tidbits about companies. There are also numerous commercial databases that provide a wealth of information on companies and their marketing activities. Examples of these databases are shown in Exhibit 3.4. The information contained in these databases can be purchased in print form, on CD-ROM, or through a direct online connection with the data provider. We discuss data collection in more detail later in this chapter.

| EXHIBIT 3.4 | Major Sources of Competitive Information |

COMPUSERVE

Business Demographics: "Business to Business Report" details number of employees and states percentages for all SIC codes. "Advertisers Service Reports" provides employee counts and number of establishments by employee size for retail trade businesses. Both are available for various geographic units.

IQuest: A gateway to more than 850 databases, including magazines, newspapers, indexes, conference proceedings, newsletters, government documents, and patent records.

Magazine Database Plus: Full-text magazine articles from more than 90 magazines.

Marketing/Management Research Center: Indexes and full text of major business magazines, indices to market and industry research reports, and company news releases.

DIALOG

ABI/INFORM®: Information on business management and administration for approximately 800 publications.

ARTHUR D. LITTLE/ONLINE: Industry forecasts, technology assessments, product and market overviews, and public opinion surveys.

D&B-DUN'S ELECTRONIC BUSINESS DIRECTORY: Information for over 8.7 million businesses and professionals in the U.S. Includes address, telephone number, SIC code and description, and number of employees.

EMPLOYEE BENEFITS INFOSOURCE™: Comprehensive information on all aspects of employee benefit plans.

INVESTEXT®: More than 320,000 full-text reports written by analysts at investment banks and research firms worldwide.

MOODY'S® CORPORATE FILES: Descriptive and financial information on all companies traded on the New York and American Stock Exchanges, as well as 1,300 other companies traded over the counter.

PTS NEWSLETTER DATABASE™: Full text from over 500 business and trade newsletters covering 50 industries.

NEXIS

Analyst Research: Brokerage house reports on companies and industries, structured by data type or category.

Company: Over 170 files of business and financial information, including thousands of in-depth company and industry research reports from worldwide investment banks, research firms, SEC filings, Standard & Poor's, and more.

Consumer Goods: Information from over 40 trade publications and brokers' reports on the cosmetics, drugs, electronics, food beverages, retail, and apparel industries.

LEXPAT®: Full text of U.S. patents issued since 1975 by the U.S. Patent and Trademark Office.

Marketing: Information from trade publications and other sources on advertising, marketing, market research, public relations, sales and selling, promotions, consumer attitudes and behavior, demographics, product announcements, and reviews.

PROMT/PLUS: Overview of markets and technology. Tracks competitors, identifies and monitors trends, analyzes specific companies and industries, and assesses various advertising and promotion techniques.

DOW JONES NEWS RETRIEVAL

Comprehensive Company Reports: Detailed financial and business information on public companies.

Dow Jones Business Newswires: Continuously updated news from seven different news wires.

Dow Jones Text Library: Full-text articles from nearly 500 local, regional, and national publications and over 600 newsletters and two news wires.

Dun & Bradstreet Financial Profiles & Company Reports: In-depth financial, historical, and operational reports for public and private companies.

Japanese Business News: Same-day coverage of major Japanese business, financial, and political news.

Statistical Comparisons of Companies & Industries: Comparative stock price, volume, and fundamental data on companies and industries.

Standard & Poor's Profiles and Earnings Estimates: Company reports with descriptive and statistical data.

Top Business, Financial & Economic News: Summaries of the day's business and financial stories.

Source: Reprinted from *Sales and Marketing Management,* January 1993, 40. Copyright © 1993 Sales and Marketing Management. Used with permission.

ECONOMIC GROWTH AND STABILITY   If there is one truism about any economy, it is that it will inevitably change. Therefore, current and expected conditions and changes in the economy can have a profound impact on marketing strategy. A thorough examination of economic factors requires marketing managers to gauge and anticipate the general economic conditions of the nation, region, state, and local area in which they operate. These general economic conditions include inflation, employment and income levels, interest rates, taxes, trade restrictions, tariffs, and the current and future stages of the business cycle (prosperity, stagnation, recession, depression, and recovery).

Equally important economic factors include consumers' overall impressions of the economy and their ability and willingness to spend. Consumer confidence (or lack thereof) can greatly affect what the firm can or cannot do in the marketplace. In times of low confidence, consumers may not be willing to pay higher prices for premium products, even if they are able to do so. In other cases, consumers may not have the ability to spend, regardless of the state of the economy. Another important factor is the current and anticipated spending patterns of consumers in the firm's target market. If consumers are buying less (or more) of the firm's products, there could be important economic reasons for the change.

In the past 20 years, most American families have experienced little growth in income. Those that have seen their incomes increase were already in the top 20 percent of incomes in the United States.[2] This trend has led to a major increase in the number of discount retailers in the United States. The Gap, for example, opened its chain of Old Navy stores to compete directly with major discounters like Wal-Mart and Kmart. The clothing at Old Navy, however, is more distinctive and of higher quality than traditional discount clothing.[3] By remaining attuned to the state of the economy, The Gap was able to adapt its traditional marketing strategy to compensate for economic changes within the nation.

POLITICAL TRENDS   Although the importance will vary from firm to firm, most organizations should attempt to maintain good relations with elected political officials. Organizations that do business with government entities, such as defense contractors, must be especially attuned to political trends. Elected officials who are negatively disposed toward a firm or its industry are more likely to create or enforce regulations that are unfavorable for the firm. For example, the anti-tobacco trend in the U.S. made its way into politics in 1997 when the White House and Congress began to debate a proposed settlement between the tobacco companies and the attorneys general of several states. These political discussions could have serious consequences for the tobacco industry, ranging from a complete ban on all cigarette advertising to the regulation of nicotine levels by the Food and Drug Administration. If tobacco companies are forced to overhaul their U.S. marketing activities, they will likely turn to other markets, including Japan. In Japan, 50 percent of men and 35 percent of women smoke, and Japanese law does not restrict the promotion or distribution of cigarettes.[4]

Many managers view political factors as being beyond their control and do little more than adjust the firm's strategies to accommodate changes in those factors. Other firms, however, take a more proactive stance by seeking to influence elected officials. For example, some organizations publicly protest legislative actions, while others seek influence more discreetly by routing funds to political parties or lobbying groups. Whatever the approach, managers should always stay in touch with the political landscape.

LEGAL AND REGULATORY FACTORS   Numerous laws and regulations have the potential to influence marketing decisions and activities. The simple existence of these laws and regulations causes many firms to accept this influence as a predetermined aspect of market planning. For example, most organizations comply with procompetitive legislation rather than face the penalties of noncompliance. In reality, most laws and regulations are fairly vague (for instance, the Americans with Disabilities Act), often forcing firms to test the limits of certain laws by operating in a legally questionable manner. Vagueness of the law is particularly troubling for Internet-based marketers, who face a number of ambiguous legal issues such as copyrights, liability, taxation, and legal jurisdiction.[5] For reasons such as these, the marketing manager should carefully examine recent court decisions to better understand the law or regulation in question. New court interpretations can point to future changes in existing laws and regulations. The marketing manager should also examine the recent rulings of federal, state, local and self-regulatory trade agencies to determine their effects on marketing activities.

Companies that engage in international marketing activities should also consider changes in the trade agreements between nations. The implementation of the North American Free Trade Agreement (NAFTA), for example, essentially created an open market of roughly 374 million consumers. Since NAFTA went into effect, many U.S. firms have begun, or expanded, operations in Canada and Mexico. Likewise, the most recent Uruguay Round of negotiations on the General Agreement on Tariffs and Trade (GATT) greatly affected the international marketing strategies of companies in the United States and 116 other nations. As a result of these negotiations, U.S. apparel manufacturers will experience a 25 percent reduction in tariffs on their products. Other industries will see similar changes to their international legal environments.

CHANGES IN TECHNOLOGY   When most people think about technology, they tend to think about new "things" such as cellular telephones, high-speed computers, medical breakthroughs, or interactive television. However, technology actually refers to the way we accomplish specific tasks or the processes we use to create the "things" we consider to be new. Of all the new technologies created in the past 20 years, none has had a greater impact on marketing than advances in computer technology and digital electronics. These technologies have changed the way consumers and employees live their daily lives and the way that marketers operate in fulfilling their needs. In some cases, changes in technology can be so profound that they make a firm's products obsolete. Vinyl long-playing (LP) records and typewriters are good examples.

Many changes in technology assume a frontstage presence in creating new marketing opportunities. By frontstage technology, we mean those advances that are most noticeable to customers. Such technology can have a profound impact on the ways that customers live their lives and on the marketing activities that firms must engage in to fulfill their needs. For example, advances from cellular telephones to CD-ROM software to microwave and convection ovens have spawned entirely new industries aimed at fulfilling previously unrecognized customer needs. Many frontstage technologies are aimed at increasing customer convenience. One of the most profound changes in frontstage technology as we move toward the year 2000 is likely to be interactive marketing.[6] Through interactive television or computer systems, consumers are increasingly able to shop for practically anything from the comfort and convenience of their own home. Marketers must be ready to make the necessary changes in their activities to accommodate the expected high demand for interactive marketing and other frontstage technologies.

These and other technological changes can also assume a backstage presence when their advantages are not necessarily apparent to consumers. Advances in backstage technology can affect marketing activities by making them more efficient and effective. For example, advances in computer technology have made warehouse storage and inventory control more efficient and less expensive. Similar changes in communication technology, such as cellular telephones, laptop computers, and software programs such as Lotus Notes, have made field sales representatives more efficient and effective in their dealings with managers and customers.

CULTURAL TRENDS   Sociocultural factors are those social and cultural influences that cause changes in attitudes, beliefs, norms, customs, and lifestyles. These forces profoundly affect the way people live and help determine what, where, how, and when customers buy a firm's products. The list of potentially important sociocultural trends is far too long to examine each one here. Examples of some of these trends are shown in Exhibit 3.5. Two of the more important trends, changes in demographics and customer values, are briefly discussed below.

There are many changes taking place in the demographic makeup of the U.S. population. For example, most of us know that the population as a whole is growing older as a result of advances in medicine and healthier lifestyles. By 2030, a full 65 percent of the population is expected to be over the age of 65.[7] Marketers of health care, recreation, tourism, and retirement housing can expect large increases in demand over the next several decades. Other important changes include a decline in the teenage population, an increasing number of singles, and still greater participation of women in the work force. The increase in the number of two-income and single-parent families has, for example, led to a massive increase in demand and retail shelf space for convenient frozen entrees and meals. Our growing focus on health and low-fat nutrition has led many of the marketers of these meals to modify their products and advertising messages to get more consumers to try them.

One of the most important demographic changes taking place is the increasing diversity of the U.S. population. The number of legal immigrants coming to the United States has steadily risen during the past 30 years. By the turn of the century, the U.S. population will have shifted to a three-group ethnic majority: whites, African-Americans, and Hispanics. These changes create both threats and opportunities for most firms. A diverse population means a diverse customer base. Firms must alter their marketing practices, including the way they recruit and select employees, to match these changing customer segments. For example, African-American, Asian, and Hispanic women were ignored by cosmetics companies for a long time. These women had a very difficult time finding makeup in shades appropriate for their skin tones. Now, virtually all cosmetics companies offer product lines designed specifically for these previously untapped markets.

Changes in our cultural values can also create problems and opportunities for marketers. Cultural values have shifted away from the materialism and conspicuous consumption of the 1980s to become more focused on quality and value in the

---

EXHIBIT 3.5   **Trends in the Sociocultural Environment**

Lifestyles Trends

Clothing has become more casual

Americans have less time for leisure activities

Spending time at home is more common

Less shopping in malls, more shopping from home

Growing focus on health and nutrition

Cleanliness has become less important

Time spent watching television has declined

Time spent using computers has increased

Minivans and sport-utility vehicles have become very popular

Demographic Trends

Baby-boomers are growing older

Appearance of a new baby boom (21 and under)

Increasing number of single-member/individual households

Increasing participation of women in the work force

Increasing number of single-parent families

Increasing population diversity, especially growth in the number of Asian-Americans

Increasing legal immigration

Polarization of income levels (decline of middle class)

Changes in Cultural Values

Less conspicuous consumption

Value-oriented consumption (good quality, good price)

Increasing importance of family and children

Increasing concerns about the natural environment

Giving back to the community

Less tolerance of smoking in public places

More tolerance of varying individual lifestyles

---

things we buy. The increasing importance placed on family and children has caused many firms to respond with safer toys and more family-oriented entertainment. Increased concerns about the natural environment have also led marketers to take actions. Many firms, such as Wal-Mart and Procter & Gamble, are active in recycling programs and use recycled materials in packaging.

As you can see, the external environment encompasses a wide array of important factors that must be carefully analyzed before developing the marketing plan. Although the external environment is the largest of the three environments we will consider, it is not necessarily the most important. As we look next at the customer environment, you will note that parts of the external environment, particularly sociocultural factors, overlap with the customer environment. The difference is that the analysis of the customer environment is more specific, focusing solely on the specific target markets of the firm.

The Customer Environment

In the second part of environmental analysis, the marketing manager must examine the customer environment to assess the current and future situation with respect to customers in the firm's target markets. During this analysis, information should be collected that identifies (1) the firm's current and potential customers, (2) the prevailing needs of current and potential customers, (3) the basic features of the firm's and competitors' products that are perceived as meeting customers' needs, and (4) anticipated changes in customers' needs.

In assessing the firm's target markets, the marketing manager must attempt to understand all relevant buyer behavior and product usage statistics. One method that the manager can use to collect this information is the 5–W model: Who, What, Where, When, and Why. We have adapted and applied this model to target market analysis, as shown in Exhibit 3.6. Organizations that are truly customer-oriented should know their customers well enough that they have easy access to the types of information that answer these questions. If not, the firm may have to conduct marketing research to understand fully the current situation of its target markets.

WHO ARE OUR CURRENT AND POTENTIAL CUSTOMERS?   Answering the "who" question requires an examination of the relevant characteristics that define target markets. The marketing manager should look at demographic characteristics (gender, age, income, occupation, education, ethnic background, family life cycle, etc.), geographic characteristics (where customers live, density of the target market, etc.), and psychographic characteristics (attitudes, opinions, interests, motives, lifestyles, etc.) in defining the firm's target markets. Depending on the type of products sold by the firm, purchase influencers, such as children or spouses, may be important as well. For business-to-business marketers, the analysis must focus on the decision-making unit (DMU). Is the buying decision made by a single individual or by a committee? What positions in the organization are the major purchase influencers?

WHAT DO OUR CUSTOMERS DO WITH OUR PRODUCTS?   The "what" question entails an assessment of how customers consume and dispose of the firm's products. Here the marketing manager might be interested in identifying how often products are consumed (sometimes called the usage rate), differences between heavy and light users of products, whether complementary products are used during consumption, and what customers do with the firm's products after consumption. Before customers and marketers became more concerned about the natural environment, many firms looked only at how their customers used products. Today, marketers are increasingly interested in how customers dispose of products, such as whether customers recycle the product or its packaging.

WHERE DO OUR CUSTOMERS PURCHASE OUR PRODUCTS?   The "where" question is mainly one of distribution. Until recently, most firms looked solely at traditional channels of distribution, such as brokers, wholesalers, and retailers. Thus, the marketing manager would have been concerned with the types of retailers that the firm's customers patronized. Today, however, many other forms of distribution are available. The fastest growing form of distribution today is nonstore retailing, which includes vending machines, door-to-door selling, direct marketing through catalogs or infomercials, and electronic merchandising through computers, interactive television,

EXHIBIT 3.6	The Expanded 5-W Model for Customer Analysis

1. **Who are our current and potential customers?**
   a. What are the demographic, geographic, and psychographic characteristics of our customers?
   b. Who actually purchases our products?
   c. Do these purchasers differ from the users of our products?
   d. Who are the major influencers of the purchase decision?
   e. Who is financially responsible for making the purchase?

2. **What do our customers do with our products?**
   a. In what quantities and in what combinations are our products purchased?
   b. How do the heavy users of our products differ from the light users?
   c. Are complementary products used during the consumption of our products?
   d. What do our customers do with our products after consumption?
   e. Are our customers recycling our products or our packaging?

3. **Where do our customers purchase our products?**
   a. From what types of intermediaries are our products purchased?
   b. Does electronic commerce have an effect on the purchase of our products?
   c. Are our customers increasing their purchasing from nonstore outlets such as catalogs, home shopping networks, or the Internet?

4. **When do our customers purchase our products?**
   a. Are the purchase and consumption of our products seasonal?
   b. To what extent do promotional events affect the purchase and consumption of our products?
   c. Do the purchase and consumption of our products vary based on changes in physical/social surroundings, time perceptions, or the purchase task?

5. **Why (and how) do our customers select our products?**
   a. What are the basic features provided by our products and competitors' products?
   b. What are the customer needs that are fulfilled by the benefits delivered by our products and competitors' products?
   c. How well do our products and competitors' products meet the comprehensive set of needs of our customers?
   d. How are the needs of our customers expected to change in the future?
   e. What methods of payment do our customers use when making a purchase?
   f. Are our customers prone to developing close long-term relationships with us and our competitors, or do they buy in a transactional fashion (primarily based on price)?

6. **Why do potential customers not purchase our products?**
   a. What are the basic needs of noncustomers that are not being met by our products?
   b. What are the features, benefits, or advantages of competing products that cause noncustomers to choose them over our products?
   c. Are there issues related to distribution, promotion, and pricing that cause customers to not purchase our products?
   d. What is the potential for converting these noncustomers to our products?

Source: Adapted from Donald R. Lehmann and Russell S. Winer, *Analysis for Market Planning* (Plano, TX: Business Publications, Inc., 1988), 89-96.

and video kiosks.[8] Likewise, many manufacturers are bypassing traditional distribution channels in favor of selling through their own outlet stores or Internet Web pages. Major computer manufacturers such as Dell, Gateway 2000, and Micron sell their products directly to customers via the telephone and the Internet. In the future, most computer software will be sold over the Internet rather than through retail outlets.

WHEN DO OUR CUSTOMERS PURCHASE OUR PRODUCTS?   The "when" question refers to any situational influences that may cause customer purchasing activity to vary over time. This includes broad issues, such as the seasonality of the firm's products and the variability in purchasing activity caused by promotional events. The "when" question also includes more subtle influences that can affect purchasing behavior, such as physical and social surroundings, time perceptions, and the purchase task. For example, a customer may purchase Bud Light beer for regular home consumption, but purchase an import or microbrew when visiting a bar (physical surroundings), going out with friends (social surroundings), or throwing a party. Customers can also vary their purchasing behavior based on the time of day or how much time they have to search for alternatives. Variation by purchase task depends on what the purchase is intended to accomplish. For example, a customer may purchase brand A for her own use, brand B for her children, and brand C when the purchase is intended as a gift.

WHY (AND HOW) DO OUR CUSTOMERS SELECT OUR PRODUCTS?   The "why" question involves identifying the basic need-satisfying benefits provided by the firm's products. The potential benefits provided by the features of competing products should also be analyzed. This question is important because customers may purchase the firm's products to fulfill needs that the firm never considered. The answer to the "why" question can also aid in identifying unsatisfied or undersatisfied customer needs. During the analysis, it is also important to identify potential changes in customers' current needs and the needs that customers may have in the future. Finally, the "how" part of this question refers to the means of payment that customers use when making a purchase. The availability of credit makes it much easier for customers to take possession of a product.

WHY DO POTENTIAL CUSTOMERS NOT PURCHASE OUR PRODUCTS?   Part of understanding why customers choose a firm's products is the realization that many potential customers choose not to purchase them. Although there are many potential reasons why customers might not purchase a firm's products, some reasons might include:

- Customers have a basic need that the product does not fulfill.
- The product does not match noncustomers' lifestyle or image.
- Competing products have better features or benefits.
- The product is too expensive for some customers.
- Noncustomers may have high switching costs.
- Noncustomers are simply unaware of the product's existence.
- Noncustomers have misconceptions about the product (poor image).
- Poor distribution makes the product hard to find.

Once the reasons for nonpurchase have been identified, the manager should make a realistic assessment of the potential for converting noncustomers into customers. For example, after research indicated that many consumers and small business owners had not yet purchased a computer due to the high cost of buying the latest technology, computer manufacturers developed stripped-down computers that sell for less than $1,000. These bare-bones computers use older technology that is adequate for most home and small business applications, including Internet access.[9]

Once the marketing manager has analyzed the firm's current and potential customer groups, the information can be used to identify and select specific target markets for the revised marketing strategy. The firm should target those customer segments where it can create and maintain a sustainable advantage over its competition. We will discuss these aspects of marketing strategy in Chapters 6 and 7.

The Internal Environment

The final aspect of environmental analysis is a critical evaluation of the firm's current and anticipated internal environment with respect to its objectives and performance, allocation of resources, structural characteristics, and political and power struggles. A framework for analyzing the internal environment is shown in Exhibit 3.7.

EXHIBIT 3.7   A Framework for Analyzing the Internal Environment

1. **Review of marketing goals, objectives, and performance**
   a. What are our current marketing goals and objectives?
   b. Are our marketing goals and objectives consistent with the mission, goals, and objectives of the firm? Are they consistent with recent changes in the marketing or customer environments? Why or why not?
   c. How are our current marketing strategies performing in terms of sales volume, market share, profitability, and communication (e.g. awareness and preference) objectives?
   d. How does our current performance compare to other firms in the industry? Is the performance of the industry as a whole improving or declining? Why?
   e. If our performance is declining, what is the most likely cause? Are our marketing objectives inconsistent? Is the strategy flawed? Was the strategy poorly implemented?
   f. If our performance is improving, what actions can we take to ensure that our performance continues to improve? Is the improvement in performance due to a better-than-anticipated environment or superior planning and implementation?

2. **Review of current and anticipated organizational resources**
   a. What is the state of our current organizational resources (e.g., financial, human, experience, relationships with key suppliers or customers)?
   b. Are these resources likely to change for the better or worse in the near future?
   c. If the changes are for the better, how can we utilize these added resources to our advantage in meeting customer needs better than competitors?
   d. If the changes are for the worse, what can be done to compensate for these new constraints on our resources?

3. **Review of current and anticipated structural issues**
   a. What are the positive and negative aspects of the current and anticipated culture of the firm?
   b. What issues related to internal politics and power struggles might affect our marketing activities?
   c. What is the overall position and importance of the marketing function as seen by other functional areas? Are key executive positions expected to change in the future?
   d. How will the overall customer-orientation of the firm (or lack thereof) affect our marketing activities?
   e. Does the firm emphasize a long- or short-term planning horizon? How will this emphasis affect our marketing activities?
   f. Currently, are there positive or negative issues with respect to motivating our employees, especially those in customer-contact positions (i.e., sales, customer service)?

CURRENT OBJECTIVES AND PERFORMANCE　First, the marketing manager must assess the firm's current marketing goals, objectives, and performance. A periodic assessment of the firm's marketing goals and objectives is necessary to ensure that they remain consistent with the organization's mission and the changing marketing environment. This analysis serves as an important input to later stages of the marketing plan.

The marketing manager should also evaluate the performance of the current marketing strategy with respect to sales volume, market share, profitability, or other relevant measures. Additionally, performance should be analyzed relative to overall industry performance. Poor or declining performance may be the result of (1) retaining marketing goals and objectives that are inconsistent with the current realities of the external or customer environments, (2) a flawed marketing strategy, (3) poor implementation, or (4) changes in the external or customer environments that are beyond the control of the firm. The causes for poor or declining performance must be pinpointed before marketing strategies can be developed to correct the situation.

LEVEL OF AVAILABLE RESOURCES　Second, the marketing manager must review the current and anticipated levels of organizational resources that can be used for marketing purposes. This review includes the analysis of the firm's financial, human, and experience resources, as well as any resources the firm might hold in key relationships with supply chain partners, strategic alliance partners, or customer groups. An important element of this analysis is to gauge whether the level of these resources is likely to change in the near future. Additional resources might be used to create competitive advantages in meeting customer needs. If resource levels are expected to decline, the marketing manager must find ways to compensate for this as he or she establishes marketing goals, objectives, and strategy.

ORGANIZATIONAL CULTURE AND STRUCTURE　Finally, the marketing manager should review current and anticipated structural issues that could affect marketing activities. One of the most important issues in this review is the internal culture of the firm. In some organizations, marketing does not hold a prominent position in the political hierarchy. This situation can create challenges for the marketing manager in acquiring resources and gaining approval of the marketing plan. The internal culture also includes any anticipated changes in key executive positions within the firm. The marketing manager could have difficulty in dealing with a new production manager who fails to see the benefits of marketing. Other structural issues to be considered include the overall customer orientation of the firm, the relative emphasis on long- versus short-term planning, and issues in the motivation of the firm's employees. A careful consideration of each of these issues is necessary if the marketing manager is to create a realistic marketing plan that is capable of being successfully implemented.

Other key structural issues must also be evaluated. For example, the marketing manager must remain keenly aware of any internal political and power struggles that can affect marketing activities. These types of issues typically surface immediately after a key executive leaves the company. After the murder of fashion mogul Gianni Versace, for example, his company faced a creative leadership crisis just when it was trying to become a global brand name in the highly competitive fashion industry.[10]

The marketing manager must also be aware of the overall position and importance of the marketing function as seen by other functional areas. In some companies, marketing does not have enough influence to ensure that its plans are fully funded and supported by top management. The overall customer-orientation of the firm (or lack thereof) can also affect marketing activities, as can the company's emphasis on short- or long-term results. Top managers who are concerned only with short-term profits are unlikely to see the importance of a marketing plan that attempts to create long-term customer relationships.

Collecting Environmental Data and Information

To perform a complete environmental analysis, the marketing manager must invest time and money to perform research to uncover data that is pertinent to the development of the marketing plan. This effort will always involve the collection of secondary data, which is compiled inside or outside the organization for some purpose other than the current analysis. However, if the required data or information is not available, primary data may have to be collected through marketing research. Accessing secondary data sources is usually preferable as a first option because they can be obtained more quickly and at less cost than collecting primary data. In this section, we will examine the different sources of environmental data and challenges in collecting this data.

Sources of Environmental Data

In general, there are four basic sources of secondary data: internal, government, periodicals/books, and commercial data sources. Examples of each type of data source are illustrated in Exhibit 3.8. Note that many of these data sources are available in both print and electronic forms. Let's look at the major strengths and weaknesses of these sources.

INTERNAL DATA SOURCES   The organization's own records are the best source of data on current objectives, performance, and available resources. Internal sources may also be a good source of data on customer needs, attitudes, and behavior. Internal data also has the advantage of being relevant and believable because the organization itself is responsible for its collection and organization.

One of the biggest problems with internal data is that it is often not in a form that is readily accessible to the marketing manager. Box after box of printed company records that sit in a warehouse are hardly useful for marketing planning. To overcome this problem, many organizations maintain extensive marketing information systems (MISs) that make data easily accessible and interactive. Many of these systems are computerized, and some take the form of "intranets" because their interactive capability uses the same technology and browser software associated with the World Wide Web. Intranets enable employees to access internal data such as customer profiles and product inventory and to develop their own internal Web pages and share details of their activities and projects with other company employees across the hall or the world. FedEx, for example, has more than 60 intranets and plans to equip its 30,000 office employees around the world with Web browsers so that they can navigate both the ever-expanding company intranet as well as the

EXHIBIT 3.8	Sources of Secondary Data

This is only a partial list of the many different sources that are available. It is not meant to be exhaustive. Because the Internet is dynamic, some of the Web addresses (URLs) shown here may have changed. Visit our Web site at http://www.dryden.com/mktg/ferrell/ for up-to-date links to these and other sites.

1. **Internal Sources**

   Company annual reports, balance sheets, income statements, invoices, inventory records, databases on the intranet or MIS, previous research studies. Some of this information is available on company Web sites. Some good examples include:
   - *FedEx* (http://www.fedex.com/us/about/)
   - *IBM* (http://www.ibm.com/IBM/)
   - *Saturn* (http://www.saturn.com/communication/index6.html)
   - *AutoZone* (http://www.autozone.com/about/index.html)
   - *Nissan* (http://www.nissan.co.jp/GCC/Japan/Annual/index.html)
   - *Revlon* (http://www.revlon.com/corp/)

2. **Government Sources**

   U.S. government data sources are too numerous to provide a complete listing. Some of the best sources include:

   Bureau of the Census (http://www.census.gov) provides raw data on practically every imaginable demographic, economic, or social aspect of U.S. business and society in general. Some of the best Census Bureau sources include:
   - *Statistical Abstract of the United States* (http://www.census.gov/stat_abstract)
   - *Economic Census* (http://www.census.gov/econ/www/econ_cen.html), including the Census of Retail Trade, and the Census of Wholesale Trade
   - *Statistics of U.S. Businesses* (http://www.census.gov/epcd/www/sb001.html)

   U.S. Industrial Outlook (http://www.jobtrak.com/jobsearch_docs/indoutlk.html) provides projections on production, sales, employment, shipments, etc., all by industry.

   Federal Trade Commission (http://www.ftc.gov) provides reports, speeches, and other facts about competitive, antitrust, and consumer protection issues.

   FedWorld (http://www.fedworld.gov) offers links to various federal government sources of industry and market statistics.

   Edgar Database (http://www.sec.gov/edgarhp.htm) provides comprehensive financial data (10K reports) on public corporations in the U.S.

   Small Business Administration (http://www.sba.gov) offers numerous resources for small businesses, including industry reports, maps, market analyses (national, regional, or local), library resources, and checklists.

   Chambers of Commerce (http://chamber-of-commerce.com) supplies demographic information on consumers and businesses within selected geographical areas.

3. **Periodicals and Books**

   The examples listed below are excellent sources of business and marketing information. Many sources are available in both print and electronic formats. Although some sources are free and available on the Internet, most require paid subscriptions. Many local libraries, particularly university libraries, subscribe to these information services.

   Business Periodicals Index maintains a listing of business-related articles that appear in a vast array of publications. Online versions found in libraries often contain short abstracts of each article. The index is updated monthly.

   Moody's Manuals (http://www.moodys.com) and *Hoover's Manuals* (http://www.hoovers.com) both provide basic information about major corporations, including industry and company overviews and analyses.

   Standard and Poor's Industry Surveys (http://www.compustat.com) offers in-depth analyses and current statistics about major industries and corporations.

   Trade Associations, Trade Magazines, and Trade Journals offer information on their membership and readers, as well as articles on competing products and companies. Some of the better examples include:
   - *American Marketing Association* (http://www.ama.org)
   - *Sales and Marketing Executives* (http://www.smei.org)

EXHIBIT 3.8　　**Sources of Secondary Data**　*(continued)*

- *Advertising Age* (http://www.adage.com)
- *Adweek* (http://www.adweek.com)
- *Chain Store Age* (http://www.chainstoreage.com)
- *Progressive Grocer* (http://www.progressivegrocer.com)
- *Sales and Marketing Management* (http://www.salesandmarketing.com)

Encyclopedia of Associations, available on CD-ROM, provides information on 140,000 major professional and trade organizations around the world.

American Demographics (http://www.demographics.com) provides articles, links to other databases, and tips for finding marketing information.

Fast Company (http://www.fastcompany.com) provides information on state-of-the-art business concepts, business trends, executive profiles, and cases studies.

Academic Journals, such as the *Journal of Marketing* (http://www.ama.org/pubs) or the *Harvard Business Review* (http://www.hbsp.harvard.edu/groups/hbr/index.html).

General Business Magazines offer a wealth of information on a wide variety of industries and companies. The information tends to focus on newsworthy items about specific industries and companies. Some widely read examples include:

- *The Wall Street Journal* (http://www.wsj.com)
- *Fortune* (http://www.fortune.com)
- *Inc. Magazine* (http://www.inc.com)
- *Business Week* (http://www.businessweek.com)
- *Forbes* (http://www.forbes.com)

Business News Sources provide the latest information related to business and financial news. Some examples include:

- *Bloomberg* (http://www.bloomberg.com) provides business trends, financial news, regional business reports, business briefs in many different languages.
- *AudioNet* (http://www.audionet.com/business) provides written summaries and commentary on business topics. Also offers real-time events such as radio programs and stockholders meetings.
- *AmCity* (http://www.amcity.com) offers business newspaper coverage for many U.S. cities and specialized publications on selected industries.
- *Ecola* (http://www.ecola.com/news) is a good source of local and regional coverage of business trends.
- *NewsPage* (http://www.newspage.com) offers headline news from a variety of sources, company press releases, and industry publications.

4. **Commercial Sources**

Commercial sources generally charge a fee for their services. However, much of their data and information are invaluable to many companies, particularly packaged goods firms. Some commercial sources provide limited information on their Internet sites.

A. C. Nielsen Company (http://www.acnielsen.com) supplies data and reports on retail sales of products and brands through the use of scanner technology. The company also provides data on television and magazine audiences.

Information Resources, Inc. (http://www.infores.com) is second only to Nielsen as a marketing research firm. IRI specializes in supermarket scanner data and the impact of promotions on sales of brands and products in supermarkets.

Mediamark Research, Inc. (http://www.mediamark.com/) provides a wealth of data on television markets and selected industries through annual reports that focus on customer demographics and brand preferences.

Other Subscription-Based Services sell a variety of data to interested companies. Common examples include:

- *Arbitron* (http://www.arbitron.com)
- *Dun and Bradstreet* (http://www.dnb.com)
- *Audit Bureau of Circulation* (http://www.accessabc.com)
- *Audits and Surveys* (http://www.surveys.com)

external World Wide Web.[11] Intranets provide an opportunity for companywide marketing intelligence that permits coordination and integration of efforts to achieve a true market orientation.

GOVERNMENT SOURCES   If it exists, the government has probably collected data about it. The sheer volume of available information on the economy, our population, and business activities is the major strength of most government data sources. Government sources also have the added advantages of being easily accessed and low in cost. The major drawback to government data is timeliness. Although many government sources are updated annually, some are updated much less frequently (e.g., the census). As a result, some government sources may be out of date and not particularly useful for market planning purposes.

PERIODICALS/BOOK SOURCES   The articles and research reports that are available in periodicals and books provide a gamut of information about many organizations, industries, and nations. Timeliness is a major strength of these sources, as most are written about current environmental trends and business practices. Some sources, such as academic journals, provide detailed results of research studies that may be pertinent to the manager's planning efforts. Others, such as trade publications, focus on specific industries and the issues that characterize them. The biggest drawback to periodical and book sources is relevance to the specific problem at hand. That is, despite the wealth of information that is available, finding data or information that pertains to the manager's unique situation is often like looking for that proverbial needle in a haystack.

COMMERCIAL SOURCES   Commercial sources are almost always relevant to a specific issue because they deal with the actual behaviors of customers in the marketplace. Firms such as A. C. Nielsen and Simmons monitor a variety of behaviors from food purchases in grocery stores to media usage characteristics. Data can also be analyzed by specific customer segments, product category, or geography. The most obvious drawback to commercial sources is cost. Although this is not a problem for large organizations, small companies often cannot afford the expense. However, some commercial sources provide limited access to some data and information for free. Additionally, companies often find "off-the-shelf" studies less costly than conducting primary research.

A BLEND OF SOURCES   The environmental analysis should always begin with an examination of secondary data sources due to their availability and low cost. Each type of secondary data has its advantages and disadvantages. For that reason, the best approach to secondary data collection is one that blends data and information from a variety of sources. However, if the needed secondary data is not available, out of date, inaccurate or unreliable, or irrelevant to the specific problem at hand, the manager may have little choice but to collect primary data through marketing research. Primary marketing research has the major advantages of being relevant to the specific problem, as well as trustworthy due to the control the manager has over data collection. However, primary research is extremely expensive and time consuming. There are a number of approaches to primary data collection as outlined in Exhibit 3.9.

EXHIBIT 3.9	Approaches to Collecting Primary Data

Approach	Pros and Cons
Observation Researcher records overt behavior of customers in natural settings	Avoids direct contact with respondents. Accurately describes customer behavior. Too descriptive; does not test causality. Subject to the biases of the observer.
Focus Groups A gathering of six to ten people who openly discuss a specific subject with a skilled moderator	In-depth exploration of an issue. Very useful before a large-scale survey. Very small sample size. Can be biased by moderator.
Surveys Interviews conducted via mail, telephone, e-mail, or personal contact	Very useful in describing and analyzing. Useful in describing entire populations. Response rates are declining due to long surveys, respondent skepticism, and unethical practices.
Experiments Selecting matched subjects and exposing them to different treatments while controlling for extraneous variables	Best suited to examine cause and effect relationships. Can test changes in levels of marketing mix variables. Difficult to control extraneous variables. Expensive.

Overcoming Problems in Data Collection

Despite the best intentions, problems usually arise in collecting environmental data. One of the most common problems is an incomplete or inaccurate assessment of the situation for which data is being gathered to address. After expending a great degree of effort in collecting environmental data, the manager may be unsure of the usefulness or relevance of what has been collected. In some cases, the manager might even suffer from severe information overload. To prevent these problems from occurring, the marketing problem must be accurately and specifically defined before any data is collected. The problem is often caused by top managers who do not adequately explain their needs and expectations to the marketing researcher.

Another common difficulty is the expense of collecting environmental data. Although data collection does have associated costs (even if the data is free), it need not be prohibitively expensive. The key is to find alternative data collection methods or sources. For example, an excellent way for some businesses to collect data is to engage the cooperation of a local college or university. Many professors seek out marketing projects for their students as a part of course requirements. Likewise, to help overcome the costs of conducting surveys, many researchers are distributing surveys via e-mail to respondents who agree to be contacted. Although this method has some unresolved problems (such as reliability), the potential time and cost savings are attractive to most researchers.[12]

A third issue is the time it takes to collect environmental data. Although this is certainly true with respect to primary data collection, the collection of secondary data can be quite easy and fast. Online data sources, such as those listed in Exhibit 3.8, are quite accessible. Even if the manager has no idea where to begin the search, the powerful search engines and indexes available on the World Wide Web make it easy to find data. Exhibit 3.10 summarizes the strengths and weaknesses of some of the major WWW search tools. Online data sources have become so good at data retrieval that the real problem involves the time needed to sort through all of the available information to find something that is truly relevant.

A final challenge is finding a way to organize the vast amount of data and information that are collected during the environmental analysis. Clearly defining the marketing problem and blending different data sources are the first steps toward finding all of the pieces to the puzzle. The next step is to convert the data and information into a form that will facilitate strategy development. One method of organizing this information into a catalyst for strategy formulation is the development of a SWOT analysis, which involves classifying data and information into categories labeled strengths, weaknesses, opportunities and threats (SWOT). This SWOT framework is the focus of our next chapter.

Key Insights from Chapter 3

Environmental analysis:

- is perhaps the most important task of the marketing manager because practically all decision making and planning depends on how well the analysis is conducted.
- should be an ongoing effort that is well organized, systematic, and supported by sufficient resources.
- involves analysis and synthesis to understand why people, products, and organizations perform the way they do.
- is not intended to replace the marketing manager in the decision-making process, but to empower him or her with information for decision making.
- forces managers to ask continually, "How much data and information do I need?"
- is valuable only to the extent that it improves the quality of the resulting decisions. Marketing managers must avoid "paralysis by analysis."
- should provide as complete a picture as possible about the organization's current and future situation with respect to the external environment, the customer environment, and the organization's internal environment.

EXHIBIT 3.10   **Pros and Cons of Major Internet Search Tools**

HotBot
www.hotbot.com

Pros: Highly rated search engine with customizable output

Outstanding user interface; extremely fast

Cons: Overwhelming number of options

Infoseek
www.infoseek.com

Pros: Staged searching from broad to specific topics

Good at searching for specific types of data (images, news, companies, live Web events)

Best at processing plain English questions

Cons: Overwhelming number of results

Altavista
www.altavista.digital.com

Pros: Great for finding "hard-to-find" information

Good at finding everything on a given subject

Cons: Fewer features than HotBot or Infoseek

Information overload

Excite
www.excite.com

Pros: Concept searching: Excite finds related words and ideas

Useful when a search can be described in different ways

Indexed, rated, and reviewed sites

Cons: Information overload

Deja News
www.dejanews.com

Pros: Only searches in newsgroups

Good at finding specific threads of information or people

Useful for understanding what people think and what people are talking about

Cons: Only searches in newsgroups

Inference Find
www.inference.com/ifind

Pros: Parallel searching: Ifind submits a query to several search engines simultaneously, then merges the results

Good for fast, simple searching of unique words

Cons: Lowest common denominator: complex searches are limited to what each individual search engine can process

Lycos
www.lycos.com

Pros: Can confine search to top 5 percent of Web sites

Multimedia searching: Lycos allows the user to display or play files directly from the search results page

Cons: Results are less comprehensive than other search engines

Cluttered with shopping sites, stock quotes, maps, etc.

Sources: Reva Basch, "Find Anything Online," *ComputerLife*, August 1997, 59-74; Ed Bott, "Search-Engine Secrets," *PC Computing*, March 1997, 298-301.

Analysis of the external environment:

- is the broadest issue in environmental analysis.
- surveys the competitive, economic, political, legal and regulatory, technological, and sociocultural factors in the firm's external environment.

Analysis of the customer environment:

- examines the firm's customers or target markets.
- can be investigated by using the expanded 5–W model:
    - *Who* are our current and potential customers?
    - *What* do our customers do with our products?
    - *Where* do our customers purchase our products?
    - *When* do our customers purchase our products?
    - *Why* (and how) do our customers select our products?
    - *Why* do potential customers not purchase our products?

Analysis of the internal environment:

- assesses the firm's current marketing goals, objectives, and performance, and evaluates how well the current marketing strategy is working.
- includes a review of the current and anticipated levels of organizational resources.
- must include a review of current and anticipated structural issues that could affect marketing activities.

Environmental data and information:

- can be collected from a wide array of internal, government, periodical, book, and commercial sources, as well as primary marketing research.
- can be collected and organized through the firm's own marketing information system (MIS).

Problems that can occur during data collection include:

- an incomplete or inaccurate definition of the marketing problem.
- ambiguity about the usefulness or relevance of the data that is collected.
- severe information overload.
- the expense and time associated with data collection.
- finding ways to organize the vast amount of data and information that is collected.

CHAPTER 4

SWOT: The Analysis of Strengths, Weaknesses, Opportunities, and Threats

Introduction

The environmental analysis, as discussed in Chapter 3, can generate a great deal of data and information for marketing planning. But information, in and of itself, provides little direction to managers preparing to enter the strategic planning process. If information is not structured in a meaningful way that clarifies both present and anticipated situations and provides some direction for action, analysis can become a sterile, "academic" process. This absence of structure and direction is frequently the cause of the widely known malady, "information overload." People afflicted with this planning malady have massive numbers of bits and pieces of information about how things are, but they lack direction.

A widely used framework for organizing and utilizing the bits and pieces of information gained from the environmental analysis is a SWOT (strengths and weaknesses, opportunities and threats) analysis, the focus of this chapter. A SWOT analysis encompasses both the internal and external environments of the firm. Internally, the framework addresses a firm's strengths and weaknesses on key dimensions such as financial performance and resources; human resources; production facilities and capacity; market share; customer perceptions of product quality, price, and product availability; and organizational communication. The assessment of the external environment organizes information on the market (customers and competition), economic conditions, social trends, technology, and government regulation. When performed correctly, a SWOT analysis can drive the process of creating a sound marketing plan. SWOT analysis can be especially useful in discovering strategic advantages that can be exploited in the firm's marketing strategy. But before we look at the SWOT analysis, we first need to consider some important issues.

Important Issues in SWOT Analysis

SWOT analysis is a simple, straightforward model that provides direction and serves as a catalyst for the development of viable marketing plans. It fulfills this role by structuring the assessment of the fit between what an organization can (strengths) and cannot (weaknesses) presently do, and the environmental conditions working for (opportunities) and against (threats) the firm. In fact, SWOT analysis is so simple and makes so much sense that its value in planning is often underestimated. However, this simplicity often leads to SWOT analyses that are unfocused and performed rather poorly.[1] In this section, we will explore the benefits of a SWOT analysis and discuss directives for conducting a productive one.

The discussion that follows has been strongly influenced by the writings of Nigel Piercy, a British author who has worked extensively to make SWOT and other strategic planning tools more meaningful and productive for managers.[2] As a planning tool, SWOT is not inherently productive or unproductive. Rather, the way that SWOT is used will determine whether it yields benefits for the market planning process or wastes management time.

Benefits of SWOT Analysis

The effective use of SWOT analysis delivers several key benefits to a manager as he or she creates the marketing plan, and these are outlined in Exhibit 4.1. The first benefit is *simplicity*. SWOT analysis requires no extensive training or technical skills to be used successfully, only an understanding of the nature of the company and the industry in which it operates. Because specialized training and skills are not necessary, the use of SWOT analysis can actually reduce the costs associated with strategic planning. Since the late 1980s, many companies have elected to eliminate their costly strategic planning departments when they realized that specialized training was not required. Many of these departments were filled with highly trained employees who had great analytical skills, but very little understanding of the business or industry for which they were planning.

Closely related to its simplicity is the *flexibility* of SWOT. It can enhance the quality of an organization's strategic planning even without extensive marketing information systems. However, when comprehensive systems are present, they can be structured to feed information directly into a SWOT framework. In addition, the presence of a comprehensive MIS, though not needed, can make repeated SWOT analyses run more smoothly and efficiently.

SWOT analysis allows the planner to *integrate* and *synthesize* diverse information, both of a quantitative and qualitative nature. It organizes information that is widely known, as well as information that has only recently been acquired or discovered. SWOT analysis can also deal with a wide diversity of information sources. SWOT can help push the planning team toward agreement as it uncovers and flushes out potentially harmful disagreements. All of these different forms of information are inherent to, and sometimes problematic for, the strategic planning process. SWOT helps transform this information diversity from a weakness of the planning process into one of its major strengths.

A final major benefit of SWOT is its ability to *foster collaboration* between managers of different functional areas. By learning what their counterparts do, what they know, what they think, and how they feel, the marketing manager can solve problems and fill voids in the analysis *before* the marketing plan is finalized. The SWOT framework provides a process that generates open information exchange in advance of the actual marketing strategy development process.

| EXHIBIT 4.1 | Major Benefits of SWOT Analysis |

Simplicity

Specialized training and technical skills are not required. The analyst needs only a comprehensive understanding of the firm and the industry within which it operates.

Lower Costs

Expensive training and, in some cases, whole planning departments can be eliminated or reduced due to SWOT's simplicity

Flexibility

An extensive marketing information system is not required to be used successfully. However, SWOT is capable of incorporating the output of any information system into its planning structure.

Integration

SWOT has the ability to integrate and synthesize diverse sources of information.

Collaboration

SWOT analysis fosters collaboration and open information exchange between the managers of different functional areas. This collaboration helps to uncover and eliminate potentially harmful disagreements and fills voids in the analysis before reaching the actual planning stage.

Directives for a Productive SWOT Analysis

The degree to which a firm receives the full benefits of a SWOT analysis will depend on the way the framework is used. If done correctly, SWOT can be a strong catalyst for the planning process. If done haphazardly or incorrectly, it can be a great waste of time and other valuable resources. Following the simple directives listed below will help ensure that the former and not the latter takes place. These directives are outlined in Exhibit 4.2.

STAY FOCUSED   A major mistake planners often make in conducting a SWOT analysis is to complete one generic analysis for the entire organization or unit. Such an approach tends to produce stale, meaningless generalizations that come from the tops of managers' heads or from press release files. Although this type of effort may make managers feel good and provide a quick sense of accomplishment, it does little to add to the creativity and vision of the planning process.

When we say SWOT analysis, we really mean SWOT analys*es*. In most firms, there should be a series of analyses, each focusing on a specific product/market combination. For example, a single SWOT analysis for the Chevrolet division of General Motors would not be focused enough to be meaningful. Instead, separate analyses for each brand in the division would be more appropriate (Geo, Corvette, Lumina, Caprice, Suburban, etc.). Such a focus enables the marketing manager to look at the specific mix of product, price, promotion, and distribution presently being used in a given market. This focus also allows the manager to

---

EXHIBIT 4.2	**Directives for a Productive SWOT Analysis**

Stay Focused

A single, broad analysis leads to meaningless generalizations. Separate analyses for each product/market combination are recommended.

Search Extensively for Competitors

While major brand competitors are the most important, product, generic, and total budget competitors should not be overlooked.

Collaborate with Other Functional Areas

SWOT analysis promotes the sharing of information and perspective across departments. This cross-pollination of ideas allows for more creative and innovative solutions to marketing problems.

Examine Issues from the Customers' Perspective

Customers' beliefs about the firm, its products, and marketing activities are critically important in SWOT analysis. The term "customers" is broadly defined to include customers, employees, stockholders, and other relevant stakeholders.

Separate Internal Issues from External Issues

If an issue would exist even if the firm did not exist, the issue should be classified as external. Marketing strategies and tactics are not the same as market opportunities.

---

analyze the specific environmental issues that are relevant to the particular product/market. Chevrolet's Suburban, for example, competes in the sport/utility market where competitors are releasing new models at a staggering pace.[3] Consequently, market planning for the Suburban should differ substantially from market planning for Chevrolet's Corvette and Geo brands. If needed, separate product/market analyses can be combined to examine the issues that are relevant for the entire strategic business unit, and business unit analyses can be combined to create a complete SWOT for the entire organization. The only time a single SWOT would be appropriate is when an organization has only one product/market combination.

Besides increased relevance, another major benefit of a focused SWOT is its ability to identify knowledge gaps. The identification of such gaps depends on the firm's ability to gather market intelligence. Virgin Atlantic Airlines, for example, is quite effective at gathering information on its competitors. Virgin's employees fly on competing flights, use competing reservation systems, and linger in airport terminals to observe competing flight operations. This information helped Virgin upgrade its services, tailor products to customers' needs, and enhance its promotional efforts, and thereby take away a large portion of British Airway's transatlantic business.[4]

SEARCH EXTENSIVELY FOR COMPETITORS   Information on competitors and their activities is an important aspect of a well-focused SWOT analysis. The key is not to overlook any competitor, whether a current rival or one on the horizon. As we discussed in Chapter 3, the firm will focus most of it efforts on brand competition. As the SWOT analysis is conducted, the firm must watch for any current or potential direct substitutes for its products. Product, generic, and total budget competitors are important as well. Looking for all four types of competition is important because many planners never look past brand competitors. Thus, although the SWOT analysis should be focused, it must not be myopic.

Even industry giants can lose sight of their potential competitors by focusing exclusively on brand competition. Kodak, for example, had always taken steps to maintain its market dominance over rivals such as Fuji, Konica, and Polaroid in the film industry. However, entering the market for digital cameras completely changed Kodak's set of competing firms. Kodak was forced to turn its attention to giants like Sony and Canon in the fast-growing market for digital cameras. But, while Kodak was distracted, Fuji announced a major price cut on film that took Kodak by surprise.[5] Likewise, major beer-makers Anheuser-Busch and Miller were caught napping when microbrews—such as Samuel Adams and Pete's Wicked—began to steal their market share.

COLLABORATE WITH OTHER FUNCTIONAL AREAS   A major benefit of SWOT analysis is that it generates information and perspective that can be shared across a variety of functional areas in the organization. The SWOT process should be a powerful stimulus for communication outside normal channels. The final outcome of a properly conducted SWOT analysis should be an amalgam of information from many areas. Managers in sales, advertising, production, research and development, finance, customer service, inventory control, quality control, and others areas should learn what other managers see as the firm's strengths, weaknesses, opportunities, and threats. This allows the marketing planner to come to terms with multiple perspectives before actually creating the marketing plan.

As the SWOT analyses from individual areas are combined, the marketing manager can identify opportunities for joint projects and cross-selling of the firm's products. In a large organization, the first time a SWOT is undertaken may be the initial point at which managers from some areas have ever formally communicated with each other. Such "cross-pollination" can generate a very conducive environment for creativity and innovation. Moreover, research has shown that the success of introducing a new product, especially a radically new product, is extremely dependent on the ability of different functional areas to collaborate and integrate their differing perspectives. This collaboration must occur horizontally across divisions and vertically between different levels of management.[6]

EXAMINE ISSUES FROM THE CUSTOMERS' PERSPECTIVE   Beyond internal performance and the resources of the firm that are addressed in the early phases of the strength/weakness assessment, every issue in a SWOT analysis must be examined from the customers' perspective. To do this, the analyst must constantly ask questions such as:

- What do our customers (and noncustomers) believe about us as a company?
- What do our customers (and noncustomers) think of our product quality, customer service, price and overall value, convenience, and promotional messages in comparison to our competitors?

- What is the relative importance of these issues, not as we see them, but as our customers see them?

Marketing planners must also gauge the perceptions of each customer segment that the firm is attempting to target. For example, older banking customers, due to their reluctance to use automatic teller machines and online banking services, may have vastly different perceptions of a bank's convenience than younger customers. Each customer segment's perceptions of external issues, such as the economy or the environment, are also important. It matters little, for example, that managers think the economy is improving if customers have slowed their spending because they think the economy is weak.

Examining every issue from the customers' perspective also includes the firm's internal customers: its employees. The fact that management perceives the firm as offering competitive compensation and benefits is unimportant. The real issue is what the employees think. Employees are also a valuable source of information on strengths, weaknesses, opportunities, and threats that management may have never considered. Some employees, especially front-line employees, are closer to the customer and can offer a different perspective on what customers think and believe. For example, research indicates that employees are a valuable source of information regarding the effectiveness of a firm's advertising.[7] Other types of customers, such as brokers and investors who are involved in providing capital for the firm, should also be considered. The key is to examine every issue from the most relevant perspective. Exhibit 4.3 shows how taking the customers' perspective can help managers interpret the clichés they might develop and breaks them down into meaningful customer-oriented strengths and weaknesses.

EXHIBIT 4.3	**Breaking Down Common Managerial Clichés into Potential Strengths and Weaknesses**	
Cliché	*Potential Strengths*	*Potential Weaknesses*
"We are an old, established firm."	Stable after-sales service Experienced Trustworthy	Old-fashioned Inflexible No innovation
"We are a large supplier."	Comprehensive product line Technical expertise Stable supplier High status	Bureaucratic Deals only with large accounts Impersonal
"We have a comprehensive product line."	Wide variety Single-source supplier Convenient	Shallow assortment Limited expertise in specific products
"We are the industry standard."	Wide product adoption High status and image Good marketing leverage	Vulnerable to changes in technology Limited view of potential competition

Source: Adapted from Nigel Piercy, *Market-Led Strategic Change* (Oxford, United Kingdom: Butterworth-Heineman, Ltd., 1992), 261.

Taking the customers' perspective is the centerpiece of a well-done SWOT analysis. Prior to SWOT, managers tend to see issues the way *they* think they are (e.g., "We offer a high quality product"). The SWOT analysis process forces managers to change their perceptions to the way customers and other important groups see things (e.g., "The product is really overpriced given the features and benefits it offers in comparison to the strongest brand competitor"). The contrast between these two perspectives often leads to the identification of a gap between management's version of reality and customers' perceptions. Managers must determine if it is realistic for the firm to be seen as they see it.

SEPARATE INTERNAL ISSUES FROM EXTERNAL ISSUES   As you conduct a SWOT analysis, it is important to keep the internal issues separate from the external ones. Internal issues are the firm's strengths and weaknesses, while external issues refer to opportunities and threats in the firm's external environments. The key test to differentiate a strength or weakness from an opportunity or threat is to ask, "Would this issue exist if the firm did not exist?" If the answer is yes, the issue should be classified as external.

At first glance, the distinction between internal and external issues seems simplistic and immaterial. However, failure to understand the difference between internal and external issues is one of the major reasons for a poorly conducted SWOT analysis. This happens because managers tend to get ahead of themselves by listing their marketing strategies and tactics as opportunities.[8] Opportunities and threats exist independently of the firm. Strategies and tactics are what the firm intends to do about its opportunities and threats *relative to* its own strengths and weaknesses.

In summary, the SWOT analysis should be directed by Socrates' advice: "Know thyself." This knowledge should be realistic, and it must be as customers (external and internal) and other key groups see the company. If managers find it difficult to make an honest and realistic assessment of these issues, they should recognize the need to bring in outside experts/consultants to oversee the process. As you have seen from this discussion, we would expand Socrates' advice to include "Know thy customer," "Know thy competitors," and in general, "Know thy environment." We will look further at these issues in the next section as we explore the elements of the SWOT framework.

The Elements of SWOT Analysis

The environmental analysis discussed in Chapter 3 serves the important role of identifying the key factors that should be tracked by the firm and organizing them within a system that will monitor and distribute information on these factors on an ongoing basis. This process feeds into and helps define the boundaries of the SWOT analysis that will be used as a catalyst for the development of the firm's marketing plan. The role of SWOT analysis is to take the information from the environmental analysis and separate it into internal issues (strengths and weaknesses) and external issues (opportunities and threats). Once this is done, SWOT analysis next determines if the information indicates something that will assist the firm in accomplishing its objectives (a strength or opportunity), or if it is indicative of an obstacle that must be overcome or minimized to achieve desired outcomes (weakness or threat).

The issues that can be considered in a SWOT analysis are numerous and will vary depending on the particular firm and industry being analyzed. To aid your search for relevant issues, we have provided a list of potential strengths, weaknesses, opportunities, and threats in Exhibit 4.4. The items in this list are meant to illustrate some potential issues to be considered in a SWOT analysis. Our role here is not to reiterate issues from the environmental analysis, but instead to cast them in a new light. In the next few sections, we'll look at how the information from an environmental analysis can be structured in the SWOT framework.

Strengths and Weaknesses

Relative to market needs and competitors' characteristics, the manager must begin to think in terms of what the firm can do well and where it may have deficiencies.

EXHIBIT 4.4   **Potential Issues to Consider in a SWOT Analysis**

Potential Internal Strengths
- abundant financial resources
- any distinctive competence
- well-known as the market leader
- economies of scale
- proprietary technology
- patented processes
- lower costs
- good market image
- superior management talent
- better marketing skills
- outstanding product quality
- partnerships with other firms
- good distribution skills
- committed employees

Potential External Opportunities
- rapid market growth
- rival firms are complacent
- changing customer needs/tastes
- opening of foreign markets
- mishap of a rival firm
- new uses for product discovered
- economic boom
- deregulation
- new technology
- demographic shifts
- other firms seek alliances
- high brand switching
- sales decline for a substitute
- new distribution methods

Potential Internal Weaknesses
- lack of a strategic direction
- weak spending on R&D
- very narrow product line
- limited distribution
- higher costs
- out-of-date products
- internal operating problems
- weak market image
- poor marketing skills
- limited management skills
- undertrained employees

Potential External Threats
- entry of foreign competitors
- introduction of new substitutes
- product life cycle in decline
- changing customer needs/tastes
- rival firms adopt new strategies
- increased regulation
- recession
- new technology
- demographic shifts
- foreign trade barriers
- poor performance of ally firm

Strengths and weaknesses exist inside the firm, or in key relationships between the firm and its customers or other organizations (channel members, suppliers, alliances, etc.). Given that SWOT analysis must be customer focused to gain maximum benefit, a strength is really meaningful only when it is useful in satisfying a customer need. When this is the case, that strength becomes a capability.[9]

Wal-Mart, for example, did not surge ahead of Kmart and Sears in the early 1990s because its products were much different. It did so through the use of its major strengths in information processing/communications, transportation, and distribution systems to build supplier relationships that were more effective (getting the right merchandise on the sales floor in a timely fashion and keeping the proper level of inventory in stock) and efficient (reducing waste and shifting marketing activities to the partner most efficient in carrying them out).[10] Wal-Mart's strengths are meaningful only because they enable the retailer to satisfy customers' needs for lower prices, good selection, and product availability. When strengths like these are matched to specific customer needs, they become the firm's capabilities. Wal-Mart was able to translate these capabilities into unique competitive advantages because it was better able to meet customers' needs than Kmart or Sears.

A customer-focused SWOT analysis can also uncover a firm's potential weaknesses. Although some weaknesses may be harmless, those that relate to specific customer needs should be minimized if possible. In the crowded minivan market, for example, no one product possesses all three important features that customers look for in a minivan—performance, reliability, and safety. The top-selling Dodge Caravan is rated highest in performance; however, it rates much lower in reliability and safety. Customers looking for the most reliable minivan are likely to choose the Honda Odyssey, while those looking for the safest opt for the Ford Windstar. To help downplay its weaknesses in reliability and safety, Dodge aggressively promotes the Caravan as the best-selling minivan because of its top-notch performance.[11]

The role of the internal portion of SWOT is to determine where resources are available or lacking so that strengths and weaknesses can be spotted. The marketing manager can then develop marketing strategies that match these strengths with opportunities and thereby create new capabilities, which will then be part of subsequent SWOT analyses. At the same time, the manager can develop strategies to overcome the firm's weaknesses, or find ways to minimize the negative effects of these weaknesses.

Opportunities and Threats

Managers who are caught up in developing strengths and capabilities may ignore the external environment. Such a mistake can lead to an efficient organization that is no longer effective when changes in the external environment impede the firm's ability to deliver value to its targeted customer segments. These changes can occur in the rate of overall market growth and in the competitive, economic, political/legal, technological, or sociocultural environments. This section will look at examples of how changes in the external environment can create opportunities or threats for a firm.

CHANGES IN THE COMPETITIVE ENVIRONMENT   One of the most prevalent trends in the U.S. economy in recent years has been the rapid decline in the number of small, independently owned retail businesses. Small mom-and-pop supermarkets and locally owned bookstores are already extinct or severely endangered. Likewise, many locally owned restaurants around the country are struggling due to the growth of large, national restaurant chains. The latest businesses to face extinction are neighborhood hardware stores, which have watched their customers move to hardware giants such as Home Depot and Lowes. Retail cooperatives Ace Hardware and True Value have taken bold steps to shield themselves from this competitive threat: Ace ended its relationship with several other cooperatives, while True Value merged with ServiStar to form the TruServ Corp. Both Ace Hardware and TruServ are actively adding new retailers to their systems in order to maintain a national image and increase their buying power. Although they are still not price-competitive with Home Depot or Lowes, both cooperatives expect to survive by offering outstanding service and convenient locations.[12]

CHANGES IN THE SOCIOCULTURAL ENVIRONMENT   In Chapter 3, we discussed a few of the social and cultural influences that cause changes in attitudes, beliefs, norms, customs, and lifestyles. One of the these changes has been consumers' increasing desire for Tex-Mex and other southwestern food products. In recent years, sales of Mexican-food products have grown at an annual rate of about 12 percent. This trend went unnoticed by major food producers for a long time. The Heinz Company, for example, was very comfortable with the largest share of the ketchup market. Although its market share remained strong, the change in consumer tastes toward Tex-Mex food produced a surprising result: Mexican sauces and salsa surpassed ketchup to become consumers' most preferred condiment.[13] Heinz immediately recognized the existence of a viable opportunity and responded by introducing two versions of salsa-style ketchup.[14] Though Heinz's strategy was sound, its salsa ketchup eventually failed due to poor distribution during the implementation phase: The product was placed in the salsa aisle of the supermarket rather than with other ketchup brands.[15]

Product modifications are often used to take advantage of market opportunities. However, these changes can also create potential new competitive threats. When Heinz introduced salsa-flavored ketchup, it added Old El Paso and Pace to its set of brand competitors that previously included Hunt's and Del Monte. The actions of other companies can also change the competitive set. For example, Heinz, Old El Paso, and Pace face stiff competition from retailers such as Taco Bell and Chi-Chi's that have recently entered the grocery market for Mexican food.

CHANGES IN THE POLITICAL/LEGAL ENVIRONMENT   Regulatory actions by government agencies often restrict the activities of firms in affected industries. The Americans With Disabilities Act of 1990 placed restrictions on the way firms construct their places of business and design jobs. Companies with significant investments in facilities that did not comply with the law saw its implementation as a major threat. Conversely, companies that market products designed to assist disabled shoppers and employees saw the act as a key opportunity.

In a similar fashion, lawsuits against the tobacco industry may lead to dramatic changes in the way cigarette companies market their products. A proposed settlement agreement between the industry and the attorneys general of several states represents a threat that could result in a ban on some types of cigarette advertising and the regulation of nicotine by the FDA.[16] Likewise, health care reforms at the state level in recent years have been an opportunity for benefits consulting firms (such as Sedgwich Noble Lourdes) that help employers refine their health insurance programs.

CHANGES IN THE INTERNAL ORGANIZATIONAL ENVIRONMENT   Elements within an organization's internal environment can also have an impact on marketing activities. Changes in the structuring of departments, lines of authority, top management, or the internal political climate can all create internal weaknesses that must be considered during the SWOT analysis and in the development of the marketing plan. McDonald's, for example, has recently been feeling increased competitive pressure from Burger King and Wendy's. In an effort to boost market share, McDonald's opened new stores, introduced new sandwiches, and developed new promotional campaigns. In its responses to these threats, however, McDonald's failed to gain the complete cooperation of its network of franchisees (which account for 85 percent of the firm's North American sales). When their stores' sales began to fall, individual franchisees started banding together to gain power and protect their interests. The increasing power of the franchisees has forced McDonald's to pull several advertising campaigns due to a lack of franchisee support.[17] Before, McDonald's was accustomed to getting its way with franchisees. Now, the shift in power from McDonald's to its franchisees has created an internal weakness that the company must address as it develops and implements new marketing strategies.

SWOT-Driven Strategic Planning

The preceding examples illustrate how issues gleaned from an analysis of external environments can be coordinated in a SWOT analysis. In the final section of the chapter, we will consider how a firm can use its set of strengths, weaknesses, opportunities, and threats to drive the development of strategic plans that will allow the firm to achieve its goals and objectives. Remember that SWOT analysis should not be an academic exercise to classify information correctly. Rather, it should serve as a catalyst to facilitate and guide the creation of marketing strategies that will produce desired results.[18] The process of organizing information within the SWOT analysis can help the firm see the difference between where it thinks it is, where others see it as being, and where it hopes to be. To utilize SWOT analysis successfully as a catalyst for strategic planning, the manager must recognize four issues:

1. The assessment of the firm's strengths and weaknesses involves looking beyond the firm's current products. The manager should also assess the firm's business processes that are key to meeting customers' needs. This entails offering "solutions" to customers' problems rather than specific products.

2. The key to the successful achievement of the firm's goals and objectives depends on the ability of the firm to transform key strengths into capabilities by matching them with opportunities in the marketing environment. Capabilities can become competitive advantages if they provide better value to customers than competitors' offerings.

3.   Firms can convert weaknesses into strengths, and even capabilities, by investing strategically in key areas (namely, customer support, R&D, promotion, employee training) and by linking key areas more effectively (such as linking human resources to marketing). Likewise, threats can often be converted into opportunities if the right resources are available. One of the key benefits of strategic market planning is a better foundation for resource allocation decisions.

4.   Key weaknesses that are not converted into strengths become limitations. These limitations will become obvious and meaningful to customers and other groups as they interact with the firm. Limitations must be minimized.[19]

To address these issues properly, the marketing manager should appraise every strength, weakness, opportunity, and threat to determine its total impact on the firm's marketing efforts. This assessment will also give the manager an idea of the basic strategic options that might be available to emphasize the firm's capabilities or convert/minimize its weaknesses and threats. One method of conducting this SWOT assessment is to create and analyze a SWOT matrix. Let's look at how a marketing manager might conduct this assessment.

Analysis of the SWOT Matrix

Exhibit 4.5 shows a SWOT matrix, a four-cell array that planners can use to categorize information at the conclusion of the SWOT analysis. At this point, the manager must evaluate each cell of the matrix in order to match strengths to opportunities, convert weaknesses to strengths, and convert threats to opportunities. Weaknesses and threats that cannot be converted should be minimized or avoided. To begin this evaluation, the manager should assess the magnitude and importance of each

EXHIBIT 4.5   **The SWOT Matrix**

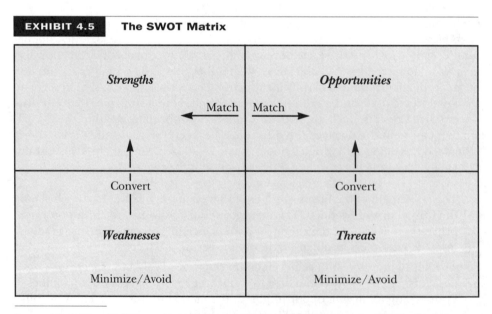

Source: Adapted from Nigel Piercy, *Market-Led Strategic Change* (Oxford, UK: Butterworth-Heineman, Ltd., 1992): 260.

element in the SWOT matrix. These ratings should ideally be based on customers' perceptions rather than those of the marketer. Customers' perceptions can be collected through focus group research. If customers' perceptions cannot be gathered, the manager's rating should be based on intuition and expertise.

It is not mandatory that the cells of the SWOT matrix be assessed quantitatively, but it can be quite informative to do so. Exhibit 4.6 illustrates how this assessment would be conducted (using information from the sample marketing plan in Appendix B). To quantify the magnitude of each element within the matrix, one might use a scheme of 3 (high), 2 (medium), 1 (low) for each positive element (strength or opportunity) and -1 (low), -2 (medium), and -3 (high) for each negative element (weakness or threat). The importance of each element should also be rated. For example, one could use a scheme of 3 (very important), 2 (average importance), and 1 (weak importance) for both positive and negative elements. If an element is given an importance rating of 0, it should be dropped from the matrix. To rank the items within each cell, the manager multiplies the magnitude

---

EXHIBIT 4.6	**Quantitative Assessment of Elements within the SWOT Matrix**

This analysis was conducted for a local retailer of Johnston & Murphy (J&M) shoes. See Appendix B for the complete marketing plan. The ratings in each cell are based on customer perceptions.

Strengths	M	• I	= R		*Opportunities*	M	• I	= R
Reputation for quality	3	3	9		Demand for good service	3	3	9
Excellent service	3	3	9		Demand for high quality			
High car traffic location	3	2	6		and value	3	3	9
Affluent location	2	2	4		Time-poor consumers	2	3	6
Excellent J&M catalog	3	1	3		No high-end competitors			
Good repeat business	2	1	2		in the area	2	3	6
					Women are major purchasers	2	2	4
					Growing population in area	2	2	4

Weaknesses	M	• I	= R		*Threats*	M	• I	= R
Poor awareness of location	-3	3	-9		Consumers are price			
Poor foot traffic location	-3	3	-9		sensitive	-3	3	-9
J&M shoes are expensive	-3	2	-6		No complementary retailers			
J&M's promotion stresses					in the shopping center	-3	3	-9
features rather than					Decreased spending on			
benefits of ownership	-2	2	-4		clothing and accessories	-2	2	-4
					Popularity of resoling			
					shoes	-2	1	-2

M = magnitude of element
I = importance of element
R = final rating of the element

Magnitude scale: ranges from +3 for most favorable to -3 for most unfavorable

Importance Scale: ranges from 3 (highest importance) to 1 (lowest importance)

rating by the importance rating. Remember that the magnitude and importance ratings should be heavily influenced by information on customer perceptions, not just the perceptions of the manager.

Those elements with the highest numerical rankings (positive or negative) should receive the greatest attention in guiding the development of marketing strategy. A sizable strength in an important area must certainly be emphasized in order to convert it into a key capability. On the other hand, a fairly small and insignificant opportunity would not play a central role in the planning process. The magnitude and importance of opportunities and threats will depend on the particular product market. For example, a dramatic increase in new housing starts would be very important for the lumber industry, but inconsequential for an industry such as semiconductors. Although the magnitude of the opportunity is the same, the importance ratings are different.

After the magnitude and importance of each element in the SWOT matrix have been assessed, the manager then turns his or her attention toward finding competitive advantages by matching strengths to opportunities. The manager should also attempt to develop strategies that convert weaknesses and threats, and to minimize/avoid those weaknesses or threats that cannot be converted. We examine this stage of SWOT-driven strategic planning in the next few sections.

Matching Strengths to Opportunities to Create Competitive Advantages

The most important, natural, and often most effective strategic option is to match the firm's strengths with the opportunities that the SWOT analysis identified/uncovered in the environment. Key strengths that are compatible with important and sizable opportunities are most likely to be converted into capabilities. Remember that capabilities that allow a firm to serve customers' needs better than the competition give it a competitive advantage. Although competitive advantages can arise from many internal or external sources, some common sources of competitive advantage are listed in Exhibit 4.7.

REAL VS. PERCEIVED CAPABILITIES AND ADVANTAGES When we refer to capabilities or competitive advantages, we usually speak in terms of real differences between competing firms. After all, capabilities and competitive advantages stem from real strengths possessed by the firm. However, the capabilities and competitive advantages that any firm possesses are often based more on perception than reality. Most customers make purchase decisions based on their own perceptions of the firm's capabilities and advantages. How customers see a company is how that firm is. Regardless of the facts about a company, if customers perceive the company as slow to react, impersonal, or having excessively high priced or out-of-date products, that is quite simply the way that firm is. Customer perceptions, not market realities, drive customers' attitudes, intentions, purchase, and repurchase behaviors.

Effectively managing customer's perceptions has been a challenge for marketers for generations. The problem lies in developing and maintaining capabilities and competitive advantages that customers can easily understand, and that solve specific customers needs. Capabilities or competitive advantages that do not translate into specific benefits for customers are of little use to a firm. In recent years, many successful firms have developed capabilities and competitive advantages based on one of three strategies: operational excellence, product leadership, and customer intimacy. To be successful, firms should be able to execute all three strategies. However, the most

EXHIBIT 4.7	Sources of Competitive Advantage

External Sources of Competitive Advantage	*Internal Sources of Competitive Advantage*

• Customer Relations
  Brand loyal customers
  Long-term relationships
  Barriers to brand switching
• Legal
  Patents and trademarks
  Tax advantages
  Zoning laws
  Global trade restrictions
• Supplier Relations
  Strategic alliance agreements
  Good working relationships
  High volume of supplier's sales
	• Product-related advantages
	  Brand equity
	  Exclusive products
	  Superior quality
	  Superior features
	  Outstanding service
	  Research and development
	  Product guarantees and warranties
	• Price-related advantages
	  Lower production costs
	  Economies of scale
	  Large volume buying
	  Low cost distribution
	• Promotion-related advantages
	  Company image
	  Large promotion budget
	  Superior sales force
	  Creativity
	• Distribution-related advantages
	  Efficient distribution system
	  Just-in-time inventory control
	  Superior information systems
	  Exclusive distribution outlets
	  Convenient locations
	• Other internal advantages
	  Superior management talent
	  Excellent research department
	  Strong organizational culture

successful firms choose one area at which to excel, then actively manage customer perceptions so that customers believe that the firm does indeed excel in that area.[20]

Firms employing a strategy of operational excellence tend to focus on efficiency of operations and processes. These firms typically operate at lower costs than their competitors, allowing them to deliver goods and services to their customers at lower prices or a better value. Southwest Airlines, for example, offers a no-frills service—no meals or advanced seating—and uses nearly identical 737 aircraft in order to keep costs down and maintain some of the lowest fares in the industry. Firms that focus on product leadership typically excel at technology and product development. As a result, these firms usually offer customers the most advanced, highest quality goods and services in the industry. For example, Microsoft, which dominates the market for personal computer operating systems with its Windows program, continues to upgrade and stretch the technology underlying its operating systems while creating complementary software that solves customers' needs, like the Microsoft Office suite of products. Organizations that practice customer intimacy work very hard to know their customers and understand their needs better than the competition. These firms attempt to get very close to their customers by seeking their input on how to make the firm's goods and services better or how to solve specific customer problems. These firms also attempt to create long-term relationships between themselves and their customers. Airborne Express, for example, provides ultra-early delivery, same-day courier service, special handling of difficult products, and solutions for customers that competitors cannot match.[21]

To implement a strategy of operational excellence, product leadership, or customer-intimacy successfully, a firm must possess certain core competencies, as outlined in Exhibit 4.8. Organizations that boast such competencies are more likely to create a competitive advantage than those that do not. However, before a competitive advantage can be translated into specific customer benefits, the firm's target market(s) must recognize that its competencies give it an advantage over the competition. Exhibit 4.8 includes a list of attributes that customers might use to describe a company that possesses each particular competitive advantage. The core competencies are internal (strength) issues, while specific attributes refer to activities that customers will notice as they interact with the firm.

Once a firm achieves success in using one of the three competitive advantage strategies, it must then continually invest to maintain its core competencies. Blockbuster Video is an example of a firm that has declined in performance because it lost its edge in operational excellence. Blockbuster decided to insource its distribution system to help make it number one in the industry. Unfortunately, Blockbuster's distribution efficiency was much lower than that of its former outside distribution partner. Distribution slowed and became more expensive when all products had to be hand-packed for delivery to the stores. This resulted in stolen products, slower arrival of new titles to the store shelves, and lower profit margins. Because it did not possess a core competency in distribution, Blockbuster was unable to maintain its operational excellence strategy.[22]

MATCHING STRENGTHS TO OPPORTUNITIES: AN EXAMPLE   How does a marketing manager go about the process of matching company strengths to opportunities in the environment? To illustrate this process, refer back to Exhibit 4.6 and the SWOT analysis of the Johnston & Murphy retail store. The analysis indicates that J&M possesses two major strengths—its reputation for quality and excellent personal service—that match two sizable opportunities—demand for good service and demand for high quality/value. The store can emphasize these two capabilities in the marketing strategy to create a competitive advantage based on superior product quality (a product leadership strategy) and/or customer service (a customer intimacy strategy). The resulting marketing plan could then be designed around a promotional campaign that informs potential customers of the superior quality and service available at Johnston & Murphy's. In addition, J&M's strengths of a high-traffic location and excellent catalog match consumers' lack of shopping time. To take advantage of these capabilities, the marketing strategy might also include an emphasis on customer shopping convenience. A direct mail campaign to qualified customers might also be part of the marketing strategy.

EXHIBIT 4.8	Core Competencies and Company Attributes for Competitive Advantage Strategies

A. **Operational Excellence**

Core competencies

- √ Totally dependable product supply
- √ Expedient customer service
- √ Effective demand management
- √ Low-cost operations

Attributes of operationally excellent firms

1. Deliver a combination of acceptable price, consistent quality, and convenient exchange processes.
2. Target a broad, heterogeneous market of price-sensitive buyers.
3. Focus their marketing plans on price leadership.
4. Provide several standardized product options that sufficiently meet a variety of customer needs.
5. Make frequent, minor product modifications, but keep products in the acceptable range of cost and quality.
6. Pass scale economies on to customers in the form of lower prices.
7. Plan operations centrally to find the most efficient means for carrying out all business processes.
8. Invest to achieve efficiency-driven production systems.
9. Develop information systems geared toward capturing and distributing information on inventories, shipments, customer transactions, and costs.
10. Let customers reap the benefits of lower prices by adapting customers' needs to standardized product offerings.
11. Assess most managerial decisions on a profit-margin basis.
12. Maintain a system where waste = death, and efficiency improvement is highly rewarded.

B. **Product Leadership**

Core competencies

- √ Basic research/rapid research interpretation
- √ Applied research geared toward product development
- √ Rapid exploitation of market opportunities
- √ Excellent marketing skills

Attributes of product-leading firms

1. Frequently introduce products that push the envelope of new technology.
2. Target narrow, homogeneous market segment(s).
3. Expect some product failures and try to learn from them.
4. Focus their marketing plans on the rapid introduction of high quality, technologically sophisticated products in order to create customer loyalty.
5. Move ideas rapidly from concept to commercialization.
6. Make products and solutions obsolete with their own innovations.
7. Scan the environment constantly in search of new opportunities.
8. Focus on an attitude of "How can we make this work?" rather than on "Why can't we make it work?"
9. Support flexibility and adaptability in all aspects of business.
10. View success and failure differently than other organizations (both are fairly fleeting and part of the game).
11. Protect their decentralized entrepreneurial environment above all else.
12. Maintain a system where complacency = death, and creativity is highly rewarded.

C. **Customer Intimacy**

Core competencies

- √ Exceptional skills in discovering customer needs

(continued)

EXHIBIT 4.8	Core Competencies and Company Attributes for Competitive Advantage Strategies *(continued)*

√ Problem solving proficiency
√ Flexible product/solution customization
√ A customer relationship management mind-set
√ A wide presence of collaborative (win-win) negotiation skills

Attributes of customer-intimate firms

1. Emphasize providing customized products (both goods and services) that meet a variety of unique customer needs.
2. Carefully select customer prospects with whom to pursue a relationship.
3. Focus their marketing plans on developing and maintaining an intimate knowledge of customer requirements.
4. Deliver comprehensive solutions that are a good value, without fear or apology for charging a higher price.
5. Consistently "reinvent" solutions as their customers' problems and needs change.
6. See customer loyalty as the firm's greatest asset.
7. Decentralize most decision-making authority to the customer-contact level.
8. Assess relationships on a long-term, even lifetime basis.
9. Avoid one-time sales transactions in order to pursue long-term customer relationships.
10. Exceed customer expectations consistently.
11. Seek to solve customers' problems *proactively,* rather than take a reactionary approach.
12. Regularly form strategic alliances with other companies to address customers' need set in a comprehensive fashion.
13. Have advanced levels of problem/opportunity identification and solution development.
14. Have a system where customer loss = death, and accomplishments that generate customer loyalty are highly and visibly rewarded.

Source: Michael Treacy and Fred Wiersema, *The Discipline of Market Leaders* (Addison-Wesley, 1995).

Converting Weaknesses and Threats

What should a firm do about highly ranked weaknesses and threats? The answer is to design marketing strategies that attempt to convert important weaknesses into strengths and important threats into opportunities. Such strategies are often based on the development of new products and/or new markets. Remember that Heinz transformed a competitive threat into an opportunity when it developed its line of new salsa-flavored products. Heinz's expertise with tomato-based products made this product introduction more feasible, but until it acknowledged the threat and took action to make its product offering consistent with customers' tastes, Heinz was vulnerable to competitive activities.

Finding new markets for a firm's products is also a viable conversion strategy. For example, to suppress the ever-constant threat posed by Pepsi, Coca-Cola often takes a market development approach that converts its threats into opportunities. When apartheid ended, Coca-Cola immediately reopened its offices in South Africa to maintain its brand presence. Pepsi was somewhat slower in responding. By developing the South African market faster than Pepsi, Coca-Cola became the dominant brand. As a result, Pepsi was eventually forced to liquidate its South African bottling business.[23] Now, the South African market represents a strength for Coca-Cola that the company can leverage as it increases its brand presence throughout the African continent.

In some cases, conversion strategies depend on the investment of additional resources, typically financial resources. To return to our Johnston & Murphy example (see Exhibit 4.6), J&M's weaknesses of poor awareness and poor foot traffic might be converted by devoting more money to the store's promotion. The addition of signs along the street or in the shopping center can make customers more aware of the store's location. Sometimes, the conversion of a weakness or threat requires additional spending in research and development. For example, Outboard Marine, a dominant player in the $11 billion U.S. boating industry, faced a serious market threat when bass fishermen wanted a more powerful marine engine. Outboard Marine's most powerful 150–horsepower engine was not selling well. After investing in extensive research and development, the company introduced a new 175–horsepower engine billed as the biggest advance in recreational boating since 1909. Sporting the latest in technology, Outboard Marine's two-stroke engine was smoother, quieter, 30 percent more fuel efficient, and 80 percent cleaner in exhaust emissions.[24] Because of its investment in state-of-the-art technology, Outboard Marine now possesses a superior competitive advantage in the recreational boating industry.

One issue that sometimes arises in the analysis of weaknesses and threats is the identification of major liabilities. A liability occurs when a weakness remains paired with a threat. In Exhibit 4.6, note that one of Johnston & Murphy's weaknesses (J&M shoes are expensive) coincides with one of its major threats (consumers are price sensitive). What should J&M do to convert this liability? The company could develop a line of lower-priced shoes for price-conscious customers. However, such a strategy would be inconsistent with the high quality/high price image of J&M's shoes. A more consistent approach might be to stress product quality, good value, and image in J&M's advertising. This strategy would also help to convert J&M's fourth weakness of not stressing the benefits of owning J&M shoes. Increased personal selling and customer service might also be viable ways of justifying higher prices to customers.

Strategies for Minimizing/Avoiding Weaknesses and Threats

In some cases, weaknesses and threats cannot be successfully converted in the short or long run. When this occurs, the firm must adopt strategies that avoid these issues or minimize their repercussions. One such strategy is to become a niche marketer. A firm lacking funds, facilities, or expertise for extensive research and development, for example, should not attempt to position itself as a cutting-edge producer. Instead, it may want to focus on a specific niche, such as low price or extensive distribution, for customers in the price-conscious or convenience segments.

Changes in customer demographics often create threats that are difficult to minimize or avoid. Shopping malls are a good example. As the demographic characteristics of their customers change, some malls have adopted niche strategies aimed at focusing on specific customer segments.[25] Consider Somerset Square, a cluster of small, specialty stores in Glastonbury, Connecticut, that focuses exclusively on working women. Its 27 stores include two restaurants, three children's clothing stores, and a variety of women's clothing stores. In Atlanta, Greenbriar Mall decided to cater exclusively to African-American customers when it discovered that 94 percent of its shoppers were African-American. Stores in Greenbriar Mall offer a broad assortment of Afrocentric apparel and merchandise.

Another strategy for minimizing or avoiding weaknesses and threats is to reposition the product. Changes in demographics, declining sales, or competitive actions are common reasons for product repositioning. The classic example of repositioning is Miller beer. In the 1970s, Miller was touted as "The Champagne of Beers" and marketed to affluent customers. However, the company managed to capture just 3.4 percent of the market with this strategy. After the "Miller Time" campaign and a new focus on blue-collar customers, Miller's market share skyrocketed to 22 percent. A more recent repositioning involved Kentucky Fried Chicken. When customers became more health conscious, the company gradually changed its name to KFC and added grilled, broiled, and baked items to the menu. Other notable repositioning campaigns include those for orange juice ("It's not just for breakfast anymore") and 7–Up ("The Uncola").

Despite a company's best efforts, some weaknesses and threats simply cannot be minimized or avoided. When this situation occurs, the firm is said to have a limitation. Limitations occur most often when the firm possesses a weakness or faces a threat that coincides with one of its opportunities. Limitations can be particularly troublesome if they are obvious to consumers. Note that in Exhibit 4.6, one of Johnston & Murphy's threats (no complementary retailers in the shopping center) coincides with one of its opportunities (time-poor consumers). Because most time-poor consumers demand the convenience of one-stop shopping, they are less likely to patronize isolated retailers. Hence, the J&M retailer faces the limitation of not being located among a group of retailers that could offer the convenience of having clothing, shoes, and accessories all in one shopping area.

How does a company deal with its limitations? One way is to diversify, thus reducing the risk of operating solely within a single business unit or market. In our example above, Johnston & Murphy can diversify by opening a second retail outlet in an area where complementary retailers exist, such as a mall. Likewise, tobacco giants R. J. Reynolds and Philip Morris diversified into industries such as beer, liquor, frozen foods, and soft drinks in the face of serious threats to their tobacco interests.

Moving Beyond SWOT Analysis

At the conclusion of the SWOT analysis, the marketing manager should have a rough outline of potential marketing activities that can be used to take advantage of capabilities and convert weaknesses and threats. At this stage, however, there are likely to be many potential directions for the manager to pursue. Because most firms have limited resources, it is difficult to accomplish everything at once. Now, the manager must prioritize all potential marketing activities and develop specific goals and objectives for the marketing plan. We turn our attention to setting goals and objectives in Chapter 5.

Key Insights from Chapter 4

SWOT analysis:

- links a company's ongoing environmental analysis and the development of the marketing plan.
- structures the information from the environmental analysis into four categories: strengths, weaknesses, opportunities, and threats.
- uses the structured information to drive the selection of the firm's strategy.

Major benefits of SWOT analysis are:

- *simplicity*—SWOT analysis can be conducted without extensive training or technical skills.
- *lower costs*—SWOT's simplicity eliminates the need for and the expense of formal training.
- *flexibility*—SWOT analysis can be performed with or without extensive marketing information systems.
- *integration*—SWOT analysis has the ability to integrate and synthesize diverse types of information, both quantitative and qualitative, from various areas of the firm.
- *collaboration*—SWOT analysis has the ability to foster collaboration between functional areas of the firm that are interdependent, but may have little additional contact with each other.

Five key directives for a productive SWOT analysis are:

- stay focused by using a series of SWOT analyses, each focusing on a specific product/market combination.
- search extensively for competitors, whether they be a present competitor or a future one.
- collaborate with other functional areas by sharing information and perspectives.
- examine issues from the customers' perspective by constantly asking the question, "What do our customers think/believe and what does this issue mean for them?" This includes examining the issues from the perspective of the firm's internal customers, its employees.
- separate internal issues from external issues. The key test to differentiate an internal issue from an external issue is to ask this question: "Would this issue exist if the firm did not exist?" If the answer is yes, the issue should be classified as external.

Strengths and weaknesses:

- exist inside the firm or in key relationships between the firm and its other channel members, suppliers, or customers.
- are meaningful only when they assist or hinder the organization in satisfying a customer need.
- should focus on the business processes or "solutions" that are key to meeting consumer needs.

Opportunities and threats:

- involve issues that occur in the firm's external environments.
- should not be ignored as the firm gets caught up in developing strengths and capabilities for fear of creating an efficient, but ineffective, organization.
- may stem from changes in the competitive, sociocultural, political/legal, or internal organizational environments.

SWOT-driven strategic planning:

- should serve as a catalyst to structure the generation of marketing strategies that will produce desired results.

- is facilitated by using the four-cell SWOT matrix to categorize information at the conclusion of the analysis. As a part of this process, the magnitude and importance of each strength, weakness, opportunity, and threat is evaluated, quantitatively if desired.

- should always be based on customer perceptions, not the perceptions of the manager.

- strives to create capabilities by matching the firm's strengths with its opportunities.

- focuses on creating competitive advantages by matching company strengths to market opportunities. Many successful firms use one of three strategies to create competitive advantages: operational excellence, product leadership, or customer intimacy.

- provides guidance on how the firm might structure its marketing strategy to convert weaknesses and threats, and minimize/avoid those weaknesses and threats that cannot be converted.

CHAPTER 5

Missions, Goals, and Objectives

Introduction

To this point, we have carefully analyzed the marketing, customer, and internal environments and determined the strengths, weaknesses, opportunities, and threats that face the organization. Now, in the next five chapters, we turn our attention to laying out the organization's marketing plan. In this chapter, we will look at three important issues: the organization's mission and the formulation of its marketing goals and objectives. These critical issues are sometimes overlooked as managers move quickly to develop the firm's marketing strategy and marketing plan. This is a grievous error. Deciding on strategies without carefully determining what the organization stands for and what it is trying to accomplish is like deciding whether you will fly, take the train, or drive before you decide whether to travel and where to go.

As we work our way through these issues, it is important to keep in mind that a firm's strategy should not be developed secretly by top management and handed down to employees—a top-down planning approach. Successful strategic planning requires top-down, bottom-up, and horizontal planning and communication. Managers should carefully listen to lower-level employees to ensure the plans are realistic for the day-to-day operation of the business. At the same time, top managers should communicate their vision for the future of the organization to lower-level employees. This top-down/bottom-up process helps to gain the commitment of all employees to the final plan, a critical element for its success. Likewise, although each functional unit will develop its own strategies and plans, developing marketing goals, objectives, and strategies requires input from all functional areas of the firm. This input represents the horizontal communication aspect of strategic planning.

We begin this chapter with an exploration of organizational mission statements, including their components, focus on customers, and width and stability. Next we look at the goals and objectives derived from the mission statement, including their characteristics and specific issues in their development. Finally, we look at how goals and objectives guide the next stages of the strategic-planning process.

The Mission Statement

Before turning our attention to marketing goals and objectives, we must first examine the importance of the organization's mission statement. Understanding the organization's mission helps to ensure compatible marketing goals and objectives. A mission statement is a clear and concise statement (a paragraph or two at most) that explains the organization's reason for being. If you ask many businesspeople "What is your reason for being?" their response is likely to be, "to make money." Although that is what they are trying to accomplish, it is not their *raison d'être*. Profit has a role in this process, of course, but it is a goal or objective of the firm, not its mission. The mission statement identifies what the firm stands for and its basic philosophy for operating. Profit and other performance outcomes are "ends," and thus are out of place and tend to confuse the mission statement. All firms, no matter how large or small, need public mission statements. Sigma Marketing Concepts has only ten employees but it has developed a mission statement to communicate its purpose to its customers and employees. On its Web site, for example, the firm has the following statement:

> Sigma Marketing Concepts is a provider of custom printing and related services focused on meeting customer needs through creativity, flexibility and on-time performance. Sigma values its partnership with customers, suppliers and employees, emphasizing long-term relationships and mutual trust.

Mission statements can be accompanied by shorter statements that elaborate on what the firm stands for. These brief descriptions are sometimes referred to as vision or value statements. For example, FedEx's vision puts people first, then service, then profit. Although the terms are often used interchangeably, the mission statement should be the most critical and *comprehensive* statement of an organization's *raison d'être*. Organizations may use a variety of terms to express what the mission statement accomplishes. What this statement is called is not nearly as important as what it contains. We will look at that issue next.

Elements of the Mission Statement

A well-devised mission statement for any organization, unit within an organization, or single-owner business should answer the same five basic questions. These questions should clarify for the firm's employees and anyone else who reads the statement:

1. Who are we?
2. Who are our customers and what do they value?
3. What does our organization stand for?
4. What makes our organization unique?
5. What impressions does this organization want key publics (i.e., customers, employees, citizens, regulatory agencies) to have of us?[1]

A mission statement that delivers a clear answer to each of these questions installs the cornerstone for the rest of the marketing plan. If the cornerstone is weak, or not in line with the foundation laid in the preliminary steps, the entire plan will have no real chance of long-term success.

The mission statement is the one portion of the strategic plan that should not be held confidential. It should tell everyone—customers, employees, investors, competitors, regulators, and society in general—what the firm stands for and why it exists. Mission statements facilitate public relations activities and communicate to customers and others important information that can be used to build trust and long-term relationships. The mission statement should be included in annual reports and major press releases, framed on the wall in the personnel office, and possessed by every employee of the organization. Goals, objectives, strategies, budgets, tactics, and implementation plans are not for public viewing. A mission statement kept secret, however, is of little value to the firm.

Customer-Focused Mission Statements

In recent years strategic planners have come to realize that, in line with the marketing concept, mission statements should be customer-oriented. Peoples' lives and businesses should be enriched because they have had dealings with the firm. A focus on profit in the mission statement displaces this customer orientation. A profit orientation means that something positive happens for the owners and managers, not necessarily the customers.

The need for a customer-oriented mission statement was illustrated by the Tylenol cyanide tragedy that occurred in 1982. After several deaths resulted from outside tampering with Tylenol capsules, the public expressed concern about the safety of the popular pain reliever. McNeilab, the subsidiary of Johnson & Johnson that markets Tylenol, made the decision to remove all packages of capsules from all store shelves, at a direct cost of $100 million. When asked about the difficulty of this decision, managers declared that the choice was obvious given Johnson & Johnson's mission statement. That statement, developed decades earlier by the firm's founders, establishes that Johnson & Johnson's primary responsibility is to the doctors, nurses, patients, parents, and children who prescribe or use the company's products. Given this responsibility, the choice for management was an easy one: Destroy any products that might harm people. If J&J's mission had been focused on profit maximization, the managers might have chosen to base their decision on probabilities and prior damage settlements. Because the mission dictated the firm's response to the crisis, Tylenol became an even more dominant player in the pain-reliever market after the tragedy. In a time of crisis, the public got a clear picture of where the firm's priorities stood. The firm received a clear reminder in the form of its mission statement, a very useful tool in such difficult times.[2]

Other highly successful firms also name customers as the top priority in their mission statements. Home Depot, the largest retailer in the home improvement segment, clearly asserts in its mission statement that concern for customers comes before consideration for merchandise: "Customer service is the bottom line at The Home Depot." The firm's track record suggests that this statement is more than just "lip service." During major disasters, Home Depot keeps stores open, even when stores are damaged or without electricity, sometimes even using flashlights to ensure customers can obtain needed supplies. Dillard's Department Stores, another highly successful retailer, states that its mission is to provide reasonably priced, brand name merchandise to middle- and upper-income shoppers in attractive, well-stocked stores staffed with polite, not pushy, salespeople.[3]

Note that the Dillard's mission identifies the customer segment it is targeting, in this instance using income as the segmentation criterion. This is a recommended aspect of a customer focused mission statement. The mission for JCPenney targets an identical group as Dillard's, but is more specific in terms of the merchandise it will market to this segment: " . . . (target middle- and upper-middle income consumers) who shop the centers where JCPenney is located for ego-sensitive apparel, accessories, and home furnishings."[4] Authors of a book on mission statements have identified the statements in Exhibit 5.1 as the best they found. As you read each one, consider how well it answers the five questions presented at the beginning of this section, as well as the factors for consideration that precede and follow the exhibit.

Mission Width and Stability

In devising a mission statement, management should be extremely concerned about the statement's width. If the statement is too broad, it will be meaningless to those who read and build on it. A mission of "making all people happy around the world by providing them with entertaining products" sounds splendid but provides almost no information. This can lead companies to establish plans and strategies in areas where their strengths are limited. Such endeavors almost always result in failure. Exxon's foray into office products—a move that cost the firm millions—is an example of the end result of a mission statement that provided little direction. Sears had a similar experience when it expanded into real estate and financial services. In the end, Sears was forced to sell off everything but its core retailing business. Silicon Graphics learned this lesson after success with three-dimensional graphics computers. Its realistic 3D graphics became the choice of Hollywood film makers, engineers, and scientists. But it lost track of its mission and jumped into new markets it knew very little about, such as interactive cable TV and digital film studios, while neglecting marketing, inventory management, and quality control. The company lost its direction and its performance declined rapidly.[5] In short, a well-designed mission should not strangle the organization, but it must help keep the firm from moving too far afield.

Overly narrow mission statements that constrain the vision of the firm can prove just as costly. Early in this century, the railroads defined their organizations as being in the business of owning and operating trains. Consequently, the railroad industry wasn't concerned about the invention of the airplane. After all, they thought, the ability to fly had nothing to do with trains or the railroad business. Today, we know that the passenger and time-sensitive freight business is dominated by firms such as American, Southwest, and Northwest Airlines, rather than Burlington, Union Pacific, and Santa Fe. The railroads missed this major opportunity because their missions were too narrowly tied to railroads, as opposed to a more appropriate definition encompassing the transportation business.

Blockbuster Entertainment, Inc.'s purchase of Sound Warehouse, Inc. is an example of seizing a new opportunity. Blockbuster, the largest chain of video rental stores in the U.S., bought the seventh-largest record retail chain because of its desire to move its retail expertise into the audio arena. Such a move from a largely rental business to one focusing on sales, and from video to audio, may have been a modification of the firm's mission and strategic plan. However, Blockbuster's more recent move into sales of CDs, videos, T-shirts, toys, books, and magazines proved disastrous because these products have lower margins than video rentals. New

EXHIBIT 5.1	Mission Statements

The following mission statements have been identified as being among the best to come from corporate strategic planning efforts. Remember that these mission statements were customized to fit the needs and goals of specific organizations, not to match the criteria we established in this chapter.

Ben & Jerry's

Ben & Jerry's is dedicated to the creation and demonstration of a new corporate concept of linked prosperity. Our mission consists of three interrelated parts:

Product Mission: To make, distribute, and sell the finest quality, all-natural ice cream and related products in a wide variety of innovative flavors made from Vermont dairy products.

Social Mission: To operate the company in a way that actively recognizes the central role that business plays in the structure of society by initiating innovative ways to improve the quality of life of a broad community—local, national and international.

Economic Mission: To operate the company on a sound financial basis of profitable growth, increasing value for our shareholders, and creating career opportunities and financial rewards for our employees.

Boeing

To be the number one aerospace company in the world and among the premier industrial concerns in terms of quality, profitability, and growth.

Boston Beer Company

We are the Boston Beer Company.

We make the Best Beer in America.

We treat others as we would like to be treated ourselves.

We sell our beer with enthusiasm, energy for our jobs and respect for our customers. As a company, we seek to add value to our customers, by providing them with a superior product at a favorable price; to our employees, by providing them with employment which encourages personal growth and pride at favorable compensations; to our investors, by providing a superior return on their investment; and to our communities, by providing taxes, charitable contributions, and community support.

Because we represent the Company at all times, we act in a manner which increases the respect of others for the Boston Beer Company and its people.

We constantly seek ways to improve our own skills and how we do our jobs.

We are committed to making Samuel Adams the largest and most respected craft or imported beer in the United States before 2006.

Leo Burnett

The mission of the Leo Burnett Company is to create superior advertising.

In Leo's words: "Our primary function in life is to produce the best advertising in the world, bar none. This is to be advertising so interrupting, so daring, so fresh, so engaging, so human, so believable and so well-focused as to themes and ideas that, at one and the same time, it builds a quality reputation for the long haul as it produces sales for the immediate present."

Celestial Seasonings

Our mission is to grow and dominate the U.S. specialty tea market by exceeding consumer expectations with:

The best tasting, 100 percent natural hot and iced teas, packaged with Celestial art and philosophy, creating the most valued tea experience.

Through leadership, innovation, focus, and teamwork we are dedicated to continuously improving value to our consumers, customers, employees, and stakeholders with a quality-first organization.

Dayton Hudson

We are in business to please our customers...to provide greater value than our competitors.

- By giving customers what they seek in terms of quality merchandise that is both fashion-right and competitively priced.
- By having the most wanted merchandise in stock and in depth in our stores.
- By giving customers a total shopping experience that meets or exceeds their expectations for service, convenience, environment, and ethical standards.

Everything we do—throughout our organization—should support and advance the accomplishment of this mission.

Gerber

The people and resources of the Gerber Products Company are dedicated to assuring that the company is the world leader in, and advocate for, infant nutrition, care, and development.

(continued)

EXHIBIT 5.1   **Mission Statements**   *(continued)*

Intel Corporation

Do a great job for our customers, employees and stockholders by being the preeminent building block supplier to the computing industry.

Johnson & Johnson

We believe our first responsibility is to the doctors, nurses and patients, to mothers and fathers and all others who use our products and services. In meeting their needs, everything we do must be of high quality. We must constantly strive to reduce our costs in order to maintain reasonable prices. Customers' orders must be serviced promptly and accurately. Our suppliers and distributors must have an opportunity to make a fair profit.

We are responsible to our employees, the men and women who work with us throughout the world. Everyone must be considered as an individual. We must respect their dignity and recognize their merit. They must have a sense of security in their jobs. Compensation must be fair and adequate, and working conditions clean, orderly and safe. We must be mindful of ways to help our employees fulfill their family responsibilities. Employees must feel free to make suggestions and complaints. There must be equal opportunity for employment, development and advancement for those qualified. We must provide competent management, and their actions must be just and ethical.

We are responsible to the communities in which we live and work and to the work community as well. We must be good citizens—support good works and charities and bear our fair share of taxes. We much encourage civic improvements and better health and education. We must maintain in good order the property we are privileged to use, protecting the environment and natural resources.

Our final responsibility is to our stockholders. Business must make a sound profit. We must experiment with new ideas. Research must be carried on, innovative programs developed and mistakes paid for. New equipment must be purchased, new facilities provided and new products launched. Reserves must be created to provide for adverse times. When we operate according to these principles, the stockholders should realize a fair return.

Merck & Co., Inc.

The mission of Merck & Co., Inc. is to provide society with superior products and services—innovations and solutions that satisfy customer needs and improve the quality of life—to provide employees with meaningful work and advancement opportunities and investors with a superior rate of return.

The Park Lane Group

The Park Lane Group is a leader in building, developing, and managing radio stations in small and medium-size markets. Park Lane and our member stations provide extraordinary service to the communities in which we operate, outstanding growth and development opportunities for our people, and significant returns to our investors. Stations of The Park Lane Group are role models which set a standard for quality small-medium market radio, and the Park Lane Group is the model of outstanding radio group development and management.

Reader's Digest

The Reader's Digest Association, Inc. is built on a heritage of service. Today our company is a global publisher and world leader in direct mail marketing. Our magazines, books and home entertainment products provide customers with hours of reading, listening and viewing pleasure. The legacy of service and quality live on—timeless ideals guiding us in our mission: to profitably develop, produce and market high quality products that enrich, inform and entertain people all over the world.

The Ritz-Carlton

The Ritz-Carlton Hotel company will be regarded as the quality and market leader of the hotel industry worldwide.

We are responsible for creating exceptional, profitable results with investments entrusted to us by efficiently satisfying customers.

The Ritz-Carlton Hotels will be the clear choice of discriminating business and leisure travelers, meeting planners, travel industry partners, owners, partners and the travel agent community.

Founded on the principles of providing a high level of genuine, caring, personal service; cleanliness; beauty, and comfort, we will consistently provide all customers with their ultimate expectations, a memorable experience and exceptional value. Every employee will be empowered to provide immediate corrective action should customer problems occur.

Meeting planners will favor the Ritz-Carlton Hotels. Empowered sales staff will know their own product and will always be familiar with each customer's business. The transition of customer requirements from Sales to Conference Services will be seamless. Conference Services will be a partner to the meeting planner, with General Managers showing interest through their presence and participation. Any potential problem will be solved instantly and with ease for the planner. All billings will be clear, accurate and timely. All of this will create a memorable, positive experience for the meeting planner and the meeting participants.

Key account customers will receive individualized attention, product and services in support of their organization's objectives.

All guests and customers will know we fully appreciate their loyalty.

EXHIBIT 5.1   **Mission Statements** *(continued)*

The Ritz-Carlton Hotels will be the first choice for important social business events and will be the social centers in each community. Through creativity, detailed planning, and communications, banquets and conferences will be memorable.

Our restaurants and lounges will be the first choice of the local community and will be patronized on a regular basis.

The Ritz-Carlton Hotels will be known as positive, supportive members of their community and will be sensitive to the environment.

The relationship we have with our suppliers will be one of mutual confidence and teamwork.

We will always select employees who share values. We will strive to meet individual needs because our success depends on the satisfaction, effort and commitment of each employee. Our leaders will constantly support and energize all employees to continuously improve productivity and customer satisfaction. This will be accomplished by creating an environment of genuine care, trust, respect, fairness and teamwork through training, education, empowerment, participation, recognition, rewards and career opportunities.

Saturn

Market vehicles developed and manufactured in the United States that are world leaders in quality, cost and customer satisfaction through the interaction of people, technology and business systems and to transfer knowledge, technology and experience through General Motors.

Steelcase

Old: Our mission is to provide the world's best office environment products, services, systems, and intelligence...designed to help people in offices work more effectively.

New: Helping people work more effectively.

Tom's of Maine

To serve our customers by providing safe, effective, innovative, natural products of high quality.

To build a relationship with our customers that extends beyond product usage to include full and honest dialogue, responsiveness to feedback, and the exchange of information about products and issues.

To respect, value and serve not only our customers, but also our co-workers, owners, agents, suppliers, and our community; to be concerned about and contribute to their well-being, and to operate with integrity so as to be deserving of their trust.

To provide meaningful work, fair compensation, and a safe, healthy work environment that encourages openness, creativity, self-discipline, and growth.

To contribute to and affirm a high level of commitment, skill and effectiveness in the work community.

To recognize, encourage, and seek a diversity of gifts and perspectives in our worklife.

To acknowledge the value of each person's contribution to our goals, and to foster teamwork in our tasks.

To be distinctive in products and policies which honor and sustain our natural world.

To address community concerns, in Maine and around the globe, by devoting a portion of our time, talents, and resources to the environment, human needs, the arts, and education.

To work together to contribute to the long-term value and sustainability of our company.

To be a profitable and successful company, while acting in a socially and environmentally responsible manner.

UPS

- Customers—Serve the ongoing package distribution needs of our customers worldwide and provide other services that enhance customer relationships and complement our position as the foremost provider of package distribution services, offering high quality and excellent value in every service.
- People—Be a well-regarded employer that is mindful of the well-being of our people, allowing them to develop their individual capabilities in an impartial, challenging, rewarding, and cooperative environment and offering them the opportunity for career advancement.
- Shareowners—Maintain a financially strong, manager-owned company earning a reasonable profit, providing long-term competitive returns to our shareowners.
- Communities—Build on the legacy of our company's reputation as a responsible corporate citizen whose well-being is in the public interest and whose people are respected for their performance and integrity.

Source: Patricia Jones and Larry Kahaner, *Say It and Live It: The 50 Corporate Mission Statements That Hit The Mark* (New York: Doubleday, 1995).

Blockbuster's focus is on video rentals. But with video rentals losing market share to satellite/pay-per-view movies and videos offered as loss-leaders by discount stores, Blockbuster may have to redefine its mission again.[6]

Mission stability refers to the frequency of modifications in an organization's mission statement. Of all the pieces of the strategic plan, the mission should change least frequently. It is the one element that will likely remain constant through multiple rounds of strategic planning. Goals, objectives, and other plan elements will typically change with each new plan, usually an annual or quarterly event. When the mission changes, the cornerstone has been moved and everything else must change as well. The mission should change only when it is no longer in sync with the firm's capabilities, when competitors drive the firm from certain markets, when new technology changes the way customer benefits are delivered, or when the firm identifies a new opportunity that matches its strengths and expertise. Technological changes, for example, can substantially alter or even destroy a company's reason for being, as was the case with the railroads early in this century. In such cases, a total revision of the mission may be necessary to ensure survival. As the Internet and electronic commerce have gained increasing acceptance, many industries have been affected. For example, the importance and role of travel agencies has decreased because travelers can compare fares faster on the Internet than they can call their travel agent. If a business is moving away from its mission statement, it should refocus by redefining its mission.

Marketing Goals and Objectives

Once the firm has carefully developed a mission statement that clearly delineates what it is, what it stands for, and what it does for others, it can then begin to lay out what it hopes to achieve. These statements of desired accomplishments are goals and objectives. The terms *goals* and *objectives* are sometimes used interchangeably. However, failure to understand the key differences between them can severely limit the effectiveness of the strategic plan. Goals are general accomplishments that are desired, while objectives provide specific, quantitative benchmarks that can be used to gauge progress toward the achievement of the marketing goals. As you saw in Exhibit 5.1, even the best firms have difficulty diluting a means-focused mission statement with a discussion of these desirable ends. Such a move has a negative effect on the strategic planning process in subtle but important ways.

Developing Goals

As statements of desired general accomplishments, goals are expressed in vague terms and do not contain specific information about where the organization stands now or where it hopes to be in the future. Home Depot, for example, has a goal of having lower prices on all its products than the local competition. To achieve this goal, the company asks customers who find a lower price to let Home Depot know and then gives them an even larger discount. Because of their nature, goals are sometimes referred to as *qualitative objectives*. We will use the term goals here for clarity in developing and evaluating marketing plans.

Goals are important because they indicate the direction the firm is attempting to move and the set of priorities it will use in evaluating alternatives and making decisions. For example, a firm might have a goal to improve service quality by providing more training for customer-contact employees. As with all stages of planning, it is important that all functional areas of the organization be considered in the goal-setting process. In developing goals for the marketing plan, it is important to keep in mind several key issues at all times: All marketing goals should be attainable, consistent, comprehensive, and involve some component of uncertainty. Failure to consider these issues will result in goals that are less effective, and perhaps even dysfunctional. Let's look more closely at these issues.

ATTAINABILITY   Setting realistic goals is important because the key parties involved in reaching them must see each goal as reasonable. Determining whether a goal is realistic requires an assessment of both the internal and external environments. For example, it would not be unrealistic for a firm in second place in market share, trailing the leading brand by just 2 percent, to set a goal of becoming the industry leader in terms of sales. Other things equal, such a goal could help motivate employees toward becoming "number one." In contrast, a firm in sixth place, trailing the fifth place firm by 5 percent and the leader by 30 percent, could set the same goal, but it would not be realistic. Unrealistic goals tend to be demotivational because they show employees that management is out of touch with reality. This is a major concern because one of the primary benefits of having goals is to motivate employees toward performance at a higher level.

CONSISTENCY   In addition to being realistic, management must work to set goals that are consistent with one another. Enhancing market share and working to have the highest profit margins in the industry are both reasonable goals by themselves, but together they tend to be inconsistent. Goals to increase sales and market share would be consistent, as would goals to enhance customer service and customer satisfaction. However, reducing inventory levels and increasing the level of customer service are usually incompatible goals. Goals across and within functional areas should also mesh together. Failure to do so causes some concern that "the left hand does not know what the right hand is trying to do." This is a major concern in large organizations, and it highlights the need for a great deal of information sharing during the goal-formulation process. Consider Home Depot's goals for hiring employees as it relates to desired customer service:

> We hire the best people. We are a knowledgeable, career-oriented and motivated group. Many of the Home Depot store associates join us with trade skills or direct experience in their respective store areas. We may appear uniform in our orange aprons, but we value individuality, creativity and fresh thinking. We teach each other. Our "do-it-yourself" concept makes product knowledge mandatory.[7]

COMPREHENSIVENESS   The goal-setting process should also be comprehensive. This means that each area of the firm should be able to develop its own goals that relate to the organization's goals. If goals are set only in terms of advancing the technology associated with a firm's products, members of the marketing department may wonder what role they will play in this accomplishment. The goal should be stated so that both marketing and research and development can work together to help advance the organizational goal of offering the most technologically advanced products. Marketing will need to work on the demand side of this effort (measuring customer needs and staying in tune with trends in customers' lives and businesses), while research and development focuses on the supply side (keeping up with basic research break-throughs and working on applied research related to the development of specific products). Goals should help clarify the roles of all parties in the organization. Functional areas that do not match any of the organization's goals should question their need for future resources and their ability to acquire them.

UNCERTAINTY   Finally, goals should involve some degree of uncertainty. Some planners have been known to confuse strategies, and even tactics, with goals. A goal is not some action the firm can take; it is an outcome the organization hopes to accomplish. "Hiring 100 new salespeople," for example, is not a goal. Any firm with adequate resources can hire 100 new salespeople. An example of a goal in this area might be "to have the largest, best-trained sales force in the industry." Thus, although "doubling the advertising budget" is not a goal, "having the best-recognized and most effective advertising campaign in the industry" could be a goal in the promotions area. Note the uncertainty that stems from using terms such as "largest," "best-trained," and "best-recognized" to indicate comparison with other firms.

Developing Objectives

Objectives provide specific and quantitative benchmarks that can be used to gauge progress toward the achievement of the marketing goals. Goals without objectives are essentially meaningless because progress is impossible to measure. A typical marketing objective might be "for the sales department to decrease unfilled customer orders from 3 percent to 2 percent between January and June of this fiscal year." Note that this objective contains a high degree of specificity. It is this specificity that sets goals and objectives apart. Objectives involve measurable, quantitative outcomes, with specific assigned responsibility for their accomplishment, and a definite time period for their attainment. Texaco, for example, has an objective of increasing its annual oil and gas production more than 50 percent by the end of the century.[8] Again, this objective specifies a measurable outcome and a definite time period for attainment.

Generally, individuals are much more comfortable setting vague goals to spur motivation and direct resource allocation decisions. The tough part is translating those goals into objectives that can be used to evaluate the degree to which units and individuals are helping the organization move forward. Ritz-Carlton Hotels, for example, has a quality goal of making its guests' visit a "memorable experience." To achieve this goal, Ritz-Carlton set an objective of having 92 percent of its customers indicate a memorable experience when surveyed.[9]

In some cases, a particular goal may require several objectives to monitor its progress. The organization's goal will usually require the establishment of objectives in various functional areas of the firm. For example, a goal of "creating a high-quality image for the firm" cannot be accomplished by better inventory control if mistakes are being made in the accounts receivable area and customer complaints about the firm's salespeople are on the rise. If Coca-Cola's U.S. market share is 43 percent and PepsiCo's is 31 percent, then Pepsi will have to have many objectives in fundamental areas of the business to support a goal of increasing market share to 35 percent. Let's now look at the specific characteristics of marketing objectives.

ATTAINABILITY   As with goals, marketing objectives should be realistic given the internal and external environments identified during the environmental and SWOT analyses. This does not mean that a good objective is one that can be accomplished with just average effort. Likewise, the outcome level should not be based on the assumption that everything will go perfectly or that all employees will give 150 percent effort. In some cases, competitors will establish objectives that include taking customers and sales away from the firm. Setting objectives that assume inanimate or inept competitors, when history has shown this not to be the case, creates objectives that quickly lose their value as employees recognize them as unreasonable. Silicon Graphics, for example, found that its objective of 50 percent annual growth became unrealistic in an increasingly competitive computer industry. After the firm lowered its expectations to a more attainable 20 percent objective, performance improved.[10] Likewise, easily achieved objectives will motivate few people to move to higher levels of productivity. All marketing objectives should be attainable at reasonable levels of effort, given what is known about internal strengths and weaknesses and with respect to key external opportunities and threats (competitors, customers, suppliers, the economy, regulators, and technology).

CONTINUITY   The need for realism brings up a second consideration: continuity. Desired marketing outcomes can be of two types: continuous objectives or discontinuous objectives. A firm uses continuous objectives when its current objectives are similar to those set in the previous planning period. For example, an objective to "increase market share from 20 percent to 22 percent (a 10 percent increase) between January 1 and June 30" could be carried forward to the subsequent period (July 1 to December 31). This would be a continuous objective because the factor in question and the magnitude of change are similar, or even identical, from period to period.

Marketing objectives should lead people to perform at higher levels than would otherwise have been the case. However, continuous objectives that are identical, or only slightly modified, from period to period often do not need new strategies, increased effort, or better implementation to be achieved. People naturally tend to be objective-oriented. Once the objective is met, the level of creativity and effort tends to fall off. There are internal and external circumstances where continuous objectives are appropriate, but they should not be set simply as a matter of habit.

Discontinuous objectives significantly elevate the level of performance on a given outcome factor, or bring new factors into the set of objectives. Discontinuous objectives could establish a new objective, such as market share, to measure to obtain an outcome factor such as sales. If sales growth has been averaging 10 percent, and the SWOT analysis suggests that this is an easily obtainable level, an example of a discontinuous objective might be "to increase sales 18 percent during the next period." This would require new strategies to sell additional products to existing customers, to expand the customer base, or at the very least to develop new tactics and/or enhance the implementation of existing strategies. Discontinuous objectives require more analysis and linkage to strategic planning than continuous objectives.

Developing discontinuous objectives is one of the major benefits a company can gain from applying for the Malcolm Baldrige Quality Award. The seven quality categories identified in Exhibit 5.2 list areas for objective setting that have until recently

EXHIBIT 5.2	Categories of the Malcolm Baldrige Quality Award, with Point Values

CATEGORIES	ITEMS	POINTS
1. Leadership		**110**
	1.1 Leadership System	(80)
	1.2 Company Responsibility and Citizenship	(30)
2. Strategic Planning		**80**
	2.1 Strategy Development Process	(40)
	2.2 Company Strategy	(40)
3. Customer and Market Focus		**80**
	3.1 Customer and Market Knowledge	(40)
	3.2 Customer Satisfaction and Relationship Enhancement	(40)
4. Information and Analysis		**80**
	4.1 Selection and Use of Information and Data	(25)
	4.2 Selection and Use of Comparative Information and Data	(15)
	4.3 Analysis and Review of Company Performance	(40)
5. Human Resource Development and Management		**100**
	5.1 Work Systems	(40)
	5.2 Employee Education, Training, and Development	(30)
	5.3 Employee Well-Being and Satisfaction	(30)
6. Process Management		**100**
	6.1 Management of Product and Service Processes	(60)
	6.2 Management of Support Processes	(20)
	6.3 Management of Supplier and Partnering Processes	(20)
7. Business Results		**450**
	7.1 Customer Satisfaction Results	(130)
	7.2 Financial and Market Results	(130)
	7.3 Human Resource Results	(35)
	7.4 Supplier and Partner Results	(25)
	7.5 Company-Specific Results	(130)
Total Points		**1000**

Source: 1997 Award Criteria: Malcolm Baldrige National Quality Award, 2.

been ignored by many organizations. To demonstrate proficiency in these areas, a firm must first establish benchmarks, which typically are the quantitative performance levels of the leaders in the industry. The firm then develops objectives that center on improving performance in each area. Companies that have applied for the award feel that one of its most positive aspects has been the impetus it has had on organizations to set discontinuous objectives. This is true both for organizations who formally enter the competition, as well as those who use the Baldrige guidelines as a planning aid.

TIME FRAME   Another key consideration in the establishment of objectives is the time frame for their achievement. Although marketing plans are often established on an annual basis, marketing objectives may differ from this period in their time frame. Sales volume, market share, customer service, and gross margin objectives may be established for terms less than, equal to, or exceeding one year. Bath & Body Works, for example, has a short-term objective to open 200 new stores nationwide in one year, and a long-term objective to increase sales by nearly $2.5 billion over the next five years.[11] The time frame should be appropriate and allow for accomplishment within the period with reasonable levels of effort. To set a target of doubling sales for a well-established company within six months would likely be unreasonable. On the other hand, objectives having an excessively long time frame may be attained without any increased effort or creativity. Given that Bath & Body Works grew from 95 stores with sales of $20 million to 750 stores with sales of $753 million in five years, its short- and long-term objectives will likely be challenging but not unreasonable.[12] The combination of managerial expertise and experience, along with the information acquired during the environmental and SWOT analyses, should lead to the establishment of an appropriate time frame.

For objectives with longer time frames, it is important to remind employees of the objective on a regular basis and to provide feedback on progress toward its achievement. For example, employees at FedEx's main terminal in Memphis, Tennessee, can see a real-time "accuracy gauge" that displays the company's current performance in terms of getting packages in the right place. Whether a weekly announcement, a monthly newsletter, or an up-to-date "thermometer" on the wall that charts progress toward the objective, feedback should be a large part of the objective-setting process, particularly for longer-term objectives.

ASSIGNMENT OF RESPONSIBILITY   One final aspect of objectives that sets them apart from goals is that the person, people, or business function/unit responsible for their achievement is identified. By explicitly assigning responsibility, the firm can limit the problems of stealing credit and avoiding responsibility. A bank might give the marketing department the responsibility of achieving the objective of "having 40 percent of its customers list the bank as their primary financial institution within one year." If by the end of the year, 42 percent of all customers list the bank as their primary financial institution, the marketing department gets credit for this outcome. If the figure is only 38 percent, the marketing department must provide an explanation.

Moving from Goals to Objectives and Beyond

Marketing goals and objectives identify the desired ends, both general and specific, that an organization hopes to achieve during the planning period. However, properly set goals and objectives are not attained automatically or through wishing and hoping. They set in motion a chain of decisions and serve as a catalyst for the subsequent stages in the strategic-planning process. Organizational goals and objectives must lead to the establishment of consistent goals and objectives for each functional area of the firm. Having recognized the desired ends, each area, including marketing, must next determine the means that will lead to these targeted results.

In the next chapter, we focus our attention on this means issue as we address marketing strategy development. Although the steps of the market planning process are considered sequentially, in reality the firm must move back and forth between steps. If marketing strategies that have the potential to achieve the marketing goals and objectives cannot be developed, the goals and objectives may not be reasonable and may require adjustments before the marketing strategy is developed. Given that the marketing plan must be a working document, it is never *truly* finalized.

Key Insights from Chapter 5

Mission, goals, and objectives:

- are sometimes overlooked as managers move quickly to develop the firm's marketing strategy and marketing plan.
- guide the next stages of the strategic planning process.

The mission statement:

- is a clear and concise statement that explains the organization's reason for being.
- formally identifies what the firm stands for and its basic philosophy for operating.
- should answer five basic questions about the firm:
  - who are we?
  - who are our customers and what do they value?
  - what does our organization stand for?
  - what makes our organization unique?
  - what impression do we want key publics to have of us?
- should not be kept secret but instead communicated to everyone—customers, employees, investors, competitors, regulators, and society in general.
- should be customer-focused.
- should be neither too broad nor too narrow.
- should be the least changed part of the strategic plan.

Marketing goals:

- are desired general accomplishments that are stated in vague terms.
- indicate the direction the firm is attempting to move and the set of priorities it will use in evaluating alternatives and making decisions.
- should be attainable and realistic.
- should be internally consistent.
- should be comprehensive and help to clarify the roles of all parties in the organization.
- should involve some degree of uncertainty.

Marketing objectives:

- provide specific and quantitative benchmarks that can be used to gauge progress toward the achievement of the marketing goals for which they are developed.

- should be attainable with a reasonable degree of effort.

- may be either continuous or discontinuous, depending on the degree to which they depart from present objectives.

- should specify the time frame for their completion.

- should assign responsibility for accomplishment to specific areas, departments, or individuals.

Marketing Strategy Decisions

Introduction

Marketing strategy involves selecting a specific target market and making decisions regarding the crucial elements of product, price, promotion, and distribution in order to satisfy the needs of customers in that market. Choosing the "right" strategy from among many possible alternatives is the ultimate test in developing good marketing strategy. There are literally thousands of possible marketing mix combinations that, when matched with good environmental analysis, can give a firm a chance to satisfy the needs of target customers, differentiate its products from competitors, and achieve its marketing goals and objectives.

This chapter explores several issues that need to be considered in selecting the "right" marketing strategy. We begin our examination with the customer, or more specifically, target market selection decisions such as mass marketing, market segmentation, niche marketing, and even customized (one-on-one) marketing. Until a firm has chosen and analyzed a target market, it cannot make effective decisions regarding other elements of marketing strategy. Next, we briefly review major issues relating to the major marketing mix activities—product, price, promotion, and distribution—that are appropriate for the chosen target market(s). We will conclude by considering decisions related to differentiating and positioning products.

Market Segmentation and Target Marketing Decisions

Because marketing strategy has the primary role of placing the firm in an optimal position with respect to customer needs, we first consider decisions related to target markets and market segmentation. The information used to make these decisions should come from the environmental analysis, particularly the analysis of the customer environment, as described in Chapter 2. Based on this information, the marketing manager must decide whether to target the entire market for a product or one or more segments of it. All firms have two basic alternatives in determining the scope of the markets they will serve or attempt to attract—mass marketing and market segmentation. Some firms opt to target small niches of a market, or even the smallest of market segments, individuals.

Mass Marketing

Mass marketing (or undifferentiated marketing) is aimed at the total market for a particular type of product. Companies that adopt mass marketing assume that all customers in the product market have similar needs, and that these needs can be reasonably satisfied with a single marketing mix. This marketing mix typically consists of a single product (or, in the case of retailers, a homogeneous set of products), one price, one promotional program, and one distribution system. Wal-Mart, for example, offers a set of quality name brands to consumers who tend to be both price and quality conscious. Likewise, Duracell offers a collection of different size batteries (D, C, A, AA, AAA, 9–volt), but they are all disposable batteries marketed to be used by consumers in toys and appliances.

Mass marketing works best when the needs of an entire market are relatively homogeneous. In reality, very few product markets are suited for mass marketing, if for no other reason than companies desiring to reach new customers often modify their product lines. Vaseline is a good example. For most of its existence, the company manufactured and offered a single product to consumers. In recent years, Vaseline modified this strategy by launching its Intensive Care line of products and extending customers' perception of Vaseline's uses to various needs in the home, including the garage/workshop.

Market Segmentation

Most firms use some form of market segmentation by dividing the total market into groups of customers having relatively common or homogeneous needs and attempting to develop a marketing mix that appeals to one or more of these groups. This approach may be necessary when customer needs are similar within a single group, but their needs differ across groups. Through well-designed and carefully conducted research, firms can identify the particular needs of each market segment to create marketing mixes that best match those needs and expectations.

VARIABLES FOR SEGMENTING MARKETS   The purpose of segmenting markets is to divide the entire population into groups with relatively homogeneous needs. There are a variety of factors that can be used to divide markets into these homogeneous groupings. Most fall into one of three general categories—state of being, state of mind, and benefit(s) sought.

State-of-being segmentation divides markets into segments using demographic factors such as gender (e.g., Virginia Slims cigarettes for women), age (e.g., Limited Express retail clothing stores for young women/teenagers), income (e.g., Lexus automobiles for wealthy consumers), and education (e.g., Executive MBA programs for business professionals with an undergraduate degree). *State-of-mind segmentation* deals not with the way consumers actually are, but how they think and feel. Attitudes, interests, and opinions are generally used to categorize consumers into state-of-mind segments. For example, "True Greens" tend to be the most environmentally conscious consumers, and therefore those to whom recycled products are most likely to appeal.

Both state-of-being and state-of-mind segmentation are really surrogates for the true issue in market segmentation, *benefits sought.* Some people buy a new car for transportation; others buy one for sex-appeal and social reasons; while still others buy one to gain a sense of power and speed. Many senior citizens view their cars as a sign of independence. Car companies would be most effective in marketing cars to each of these segments if they knew what specific benefits the people being marketed to are seeking.

State-of-being segmentation tends to be the most widely utilized because demographic variables are relatively easy to measure. In fact, much of this information was already obtained during the environmental analysis through secondary sources. For example, the U.S. Census Bureau offers data about the size of state-of-being segments by state, county, and even zip code. State-of-mind issues are more difficult to measure, and often require primary marketing research (e.g., survey questions) to classify people properly and assess the size of various segments.

MARKET SEGMENTATION APPROACHES   Within the market segmentation option, there are two sub-options: the multisegment approach and the market concentration approach.

Firms using the multisegment option seek to attract buyers in more than one market segment by offering multiple marketing mixes that will appeal to more parts of the total market. In using this option, the firm can increase its share of the market by responding to the heterogeneous wants and desires of different segments or submarkets. If the segments have enough buying potential, and the product is successful, the resulting sales increases can more than offset the increased costs of offering multiple marketing mixes.

The multisegment option is the most widely used alternative in medium- to large-sized firms. Packaged goods firms often make liberal use of multisegmentation. Maxwell House, for example, began by marketing one type of coffee and one brand. Today, that division of General Foods offers at least five brands and six or more varieties under the Maxwell House label in addition to providing private label brands for retailers. A walk down the cereal aisle of your local supermarket offers additional examples; firms such as Kellogg's and Nabisco offer seemingly hundreds of brands of breakfast cereals targeted at specific segments including children (Fruit Loops, Apple Jacks), health-conscious adults (Shredded Wheat, Total), parents looking for healthier foods for their children (Life, Kix), and so on.

Firms using the market concentration approach focus on a single market segment. These firms often find it most efficient to seek a maximum share in one segment of the market. The German-made Porsche and the Italian-made Ferrari are produced by organizations using this strategy. Armor All markets appearance chemicals primarily to young driving-aged males. Small book publishers tend to focus their offerings toward readers with certain tastes. The market concentration approach is almost universal in the fine arts. For instance, musical groups hone their talents and plan their performances to satisfy the tastes of one market segment, such as country, rock, or classical music.

The main advantage of market concentration is specialization, as it allows the firm to focus all its resources toward understanding and serving a single segment. Specialization is also the major disadvantage of this approach. By "putting all of its eggs in one basket," the firm can be vulnerable to changes in its market segment, such as economic downturns and demographic shifts. Gerber experienced this effect in the 1970s and 1980s when birth rates declined just as it was proclaiming, "Babies are our business. Our only business."

Niche Marketing

Some companies narrow the market concentration approach even more and focus their marketing efforts on one small, well-defined market segment that has a unique, specific set of needs; this approach is known as niche marketing. One example of successful niche marketing is sports camps for youth. Such camps offer a specific level of sports training for children of a well-defined category of ages and specific ability levels. Nike, for example, sponsors five-day camps for sports ranging from white-water rafting to golf and in-line skating for $500–$625. Other organizations, including Bolletieri Sports and Kutsher's Sports Academy, offer camps lasting for up to two months of intensive instruction, with prices as high as $4,950.[1] Obviously, these offerings are for a small and very well-defined set of parents who have the money and children with the athletic interest and potential to send to such camps. The key with niche marketing is to understand and meet the needs of target customers so completely that, despite the small size of the niche, the firm's substantial share makes the segment highly profitable.

Customized Marketing

When a company creates an entirely unique marketing mix for each customer in the target segment, it is employing customized marketing. This approach is common in business-to-business marketing where unique programs and/or systems are designed for each customer. Airborne Express, for example, customized an 8:30 early delivery of parts to repair technicians for Xerox.[2] Insurance companies, such as The Royal, and insurance brokers, such as Sedgwick, often design programs to meet a corporation's specific needs. The unique needs of moderate to large-size companies dictate that promotion, price, product and distribution are all modified to meet the specifics of the client's situation.

This type of one-on-one marketing is used less often in consumer marketing, although Burger King took this approach with its "have it your way" promotional campaign. Here the price, distribution, and promotion were the same for all consumers, but the product varied slightly (depending on what the customer wanted on the Whopper). More extensive customization takes place when a consumer buys a large sail or motor boat, jet, or a custom-built home. In such instances, the product is significantly modified to meet unique customer needs and preferences. Many service firms — such as hairstylists, lawyers, doctors, educational institutions — also customize their marketing mixes to match individual customer needs.

Identifying the Characteristics and Needs of the Target Market

Once the marketing manager has selected the target market—whether it be the total mass market or one or more segments of it—he or she must next identify the characteristics and needs of customers within that target market. This step involves selecting the most relevant variables to identify and define the target market. Many of these variables, including customer demographics, lifestyles, and product-usage characteristics, are derived from the environmental analysis section of the marketing plan.

It is at this stage of market planning where the target market variables are revised or carried over from previous planning periods. A new or revised marketing strategy often requires changes in target market definition or identification to correct any problems in the previous marketing strategy that led to reduced performance, or that are likely to do so in the future. Changes here might include reducing price (to enhance value), increasing price (to connote higher quality), updating the advertising message to keep the communication current, adding a new product feature to make the benefits delivered more meaningful, or selling through retail stores instead of direct distribution to add the convenience of immediate availability. Sometimes it takes major changes to deliver fairly minor improvements in mix performance, while at other points a relatively minor modification can deliver significant improvements.

Developing the Marketing Mix

Marketing strategy decisions for the marketing mix involve creating a combination of product, price, promotion, and distribution that, to the greatest extent possible, matches the needs of customers in the chosen target market segment(s). In-depth, current data about the target market is necessary to provide information on customer preferences for product features, attitudes toward competitors' products, price/budget considerations, and the frequency and intensity with which the product is used. With this information, the SBU or marketing manager has the potential to develop a marketing mix that delivers value and customer satisfaction better than competitors' mixes. Exhibit 6.1 provides a partial list of decisions and activities associated with each element of the marketing mix. As we look more closely at the strategic options available within each marketing mix element, keep in mind that an exhaustive discussion of each element is beyond the scope of this book. We assume that the reader is already familiar with many of these concepts from earlier marketing courses and/or previous experiences with the marketing discipline.

Product Decisions

The product is at the core of the marketing strategy. It is important to keep in mind that products refer to more than tangible goods. Products are usually some amalgam of goods, services, ideas, and even people. The best way to view a product is as a set of features and advantages that have the capacity to satisfy customer needs and wants, thus delivering valued benefits. Products can also be exchanged for something else of value. When a consumer buys a Lexus automobile, for example, transportation is only one benefit of the product that he or she obtains. The buyer may also receive luxury, prestige, sex appeal, comfort, a brand name, and countless other attributes in exchange for the price he or she pays.

As we consider products through the reminder of this chapter—and throughout the rest of this book—it is important to remember that products in and of themselves are of little value. The real value a product provides is derived from its ability to deliver benefits that enhance the buyer's situation. Consumers don't buy pest control, they buy a bug-free living environment. Students patronizing a night spot are not really thirsty, they want to fulfill their need for social interaction. Likewise, companies do not really want computers, they want a tool to store, retrieve, distribute, and analyze data and information. Thus, organizations that keep their sights set on developing products, systems, and processes that identify and meet needs of the target market are more likely to be successful, while those that take an internal

EXHIBIT 6.1	Possible Decisions and Activities Associated with Marketing Mix Elements

Marketing Mix Variables	Possible Decisions and Activities
Product	Develop and test-market new products; modify existing products; eliminate products that do not satisfy customers' desires; formulate brand names and branding policies; create product warranties and establish procedures for fulfilling warranties; plan packages, including materials, sizes, shapes, colors, and designs.
Distribution	Analyze various types of distribution channels; design appropriate distribution channels; design an effective program for dealer relations; establish distribution centers; formulate and implement procedures for efficient product handling; set up inventory controls; analyze transportation methods; minimize total distribution costs; analyze possible locations for plants and wholesale or retail outlets.
Promotion	Set promotion objectives; determine major types of promotion to be used; select and schedule advertising media; develop advertising messages; measure the effectiveness of advertisements; recruit and train salespeople; formulate compensation programs for sales personnel; establish sales territories; plan and implement sales promotion efforts; prepare and disseminate publicity releases; integrate all promotional communications.
Pricing	Analyze competitors' prices; formulate pricing policies; determine method(s) to be used to set prices; set prices; determine discounts for various types of buyers; establish conditions and terms of sales.

Source: Adapted from William Pride and O.C. Ferrell, *Marketing: Concepts and Strategies,* 10th ed. (Boston: Houghton Mifflin, 1997), 13-15.

focus of designing the best "widget" possible are following a map to failure once widgets are no longer the best method of meeting a need.

One of the key decision areas related to products deals with the introduction of new products. What is considered to be a new product depends on the point of view of both the firm and its customers. There are at least six marketing strategy options related to the newness of products. These options follow in decreasing degrees of product change:

1. *Innovation,* the most radical option, involves the firm in a pioneering effort, as did FedEx in providing an overnight, small package delivery service. Innovations of this type can even result in new product categories (e.g., Henry Ford with cars and Xerox with copy machines).

2. *New product lines* allow a firm to enter new markets with a new group of closely related product items that are considered as a unit based on technical, or end-use, considerations. For instance, Caterpillar, long known for powerful construction equipment, has in recent years developed engines for boats, trucks, and generators.[3]

3. *Product line extensions* supplement an existing product line with new styles or models. Mazda, for example, introduced the Miata to compete in the market for small, two-seat sports cars, while both Lincoln (Navigator) and Mercedes-Benz (ML320) added sport utility vehicles to their product lines.[4]

4. *Improvements or changes in existing products* offer customers improved performance or greater perceived value, such as the yearly design changes in the

automobile industry. This option also includes changes to make an existing product "new and improved," a common option in packaged goods. Clorox Co., for example, spiced up sales after adding lemon and floral scents to its perennial bleach product, and a lemon fragrance to Pine-Sol.[5]

5. *Repositioning* involves the modification of existing products (either real or through promotion) so that they can be targeted at new markets or segments. The famous "Orange juice is not just for breakfast anymore" campaign is a good example. Carnival Cruise Line's effort to attract senior citizens to supplement its younger crowd is another example.

6. *Cost reductions* involve modified products that offer similar performance at a lower price, such as Plymouth's Neon, a lower-cost version of Plymouth's entry level cars, to compete with Kia and Chevrolet's Metro and Prism.

The first two options are the most effective and profitable when the firm wants to differentiate itself significantly from competitors. The consulting firm of Booz, Allen found that 30 percent of the product introductions they studied were innovations or new product lines, and 60 percent of the profitable product changes were of this type.[6] A firm may have ample reason, nevertheless, to pursue one of the last four product modification options, particularly if resource constraints are a significant issue. We will take a closer look at new product development and strategy issues in Chapter 7.

Pricing Decisions

Price can be the most critical, the most visible, and the most overmanipulated element of the marketing mix. Price is an extremely important consideration as customers decide whether to purchase the firm's products. For this reason, the marketing manager must set the price correctly to achieve the right balance between customers' needs, alternative solutions, and the firm's need to cover its direct and indirect costs, while also making an acceptable profit. Price is also the most flexible element of the marketing mix as it can be adjusted to meet changing market conditions. Changing the price of a product can be very risky, however, because price is ultimately connected to customer perceptions of product quality, prestige, and image. Pricing decisions are best guided by a deliberate strategy to achieve marketing goals and objectives, not by knee-jerk reactions to changing customer needs, competitive activities, or short-term reductions in overall mix performance (e.g., sales or share).

There are two points of view to consider with regard to price. First, to the firm, price is the amount of money that the firm is willing to accept in exchange for a product. This sum should be high enough to cover costs and clear a profit without being so high that the product does not sell well. To customers, price is anything they are willing to give up in exchange for the product. In addition to money, customers pay certain nonmonetary prices to obtain products, such as time, effort, risk, and opportunity costs. Although customers may not explicitly consider these costs to be prices, they are nonetheless vitally important in customers' decisions on what products to buy and where to obtain them.

Marketing strategies can be designed around price to make a relatively low price economically feasible. When companies employ a competitive strategy of operational excellence (discussed in Chapter 4), they focus on efficiency of operations that lowers costs and allows them to deliver goods and services to their customers at lower prices and thus a better value. For example, some lower-priced motel chains (such as Motel 6 and Red Roof Inns) make low prices their main customer benefit and base their entire marketing mix and appeal on the price variable alone. Ongoing discount, or *everyday low pricing (EDLP)*, is another commonly employed strategy, particularly in retailing. In the past decade, this strategy has been immensely successful for Wal-Mart and Kmart, as well as their suppliers, including Procter & Gamble and Coca-Cola. Car makers, such as GM's Saturn, also exploit the price element with their increasingly popular "no-dicker sticker" policies.

Regardless of their appeal, we must reiterate that low price strategies are frequently not sustainable over time. They are successful only when the firm has a significantly lower cost of operation to support the lower prices. Circuit City, for example, can sell electronic products for less than department stores and specialty stores on an ongoing basis only because the firm's volume buying translates to lower unit invoice costs and other related scale economies.

On the other side of the coin, price can also be the focal point of a marketing mix oriented toward a high quality, prestige product image. When Honda launched the Acura line, for example, it dropped the Honda brand name, enlisted new dealers, and increased prices to create a high status, quality image. Toyota did the same thing with its Lexus brand. In order for this strategy to be successful, customers must perceive the firm's product to be of significantly higher quality than competing products. The key word is "perceived" because prestige products can possess an image that is entirely unrelated to the product's actual quality. Compare the quality of a Timex watch and a Rolex watch, for example. Most consumers would say that a Rolex watch possesses a superior quality image, even though the quality of a Timex in terms of its ability to keep accurate time is comparable to that of the Rolex. This is an example of the "set of features and advantages" that define a product. A Rolex is obviously much more than a timepiece to the consumers who own them: It is frequently a reward for, and symbol of, professional or personal success. Thus, price is much more than a financial or economic issue, it also has significant social and psychological connotations.

Promotion Decisions

Promotion activities are necessary to communicate the features and benefits of a product to its intended target market(s). For example, to raise awareness of its newly acquired Altoids peppermints beyond their limited counterculture devotees, Kraft employed the Leo Burnett ad agency to develop a campaign to tout the mints without diluting their already "curiously strong" word-of-mouth advertising. The resulting low-key campaign, which featured quirky posters in bus shelters, subways, and alternative weekly newspapers, helped swell the product's share to nearly 10 percent of the market in just two years.[7] The role of advertising, sales promotion, personal selling, and public relations (the promotion mix) in a particular marketing strategy will vary depending on the nature of the product. Industrial products, such as heavy equipment, tend to rely more heavily on personal selling, while consumer products often require greater use of advertising, sales promotion, and publicity. Simple products, like the Altoids peppermints, are more suited for advertising, while technologically complex products rely more heavily on personal selling.

The role of promotion mix elements also varies by stage in the product purchase process (awareness, interest, desire, and action). Mass elements such as advertising and publicity tend to be used more heavily to stimulate awareness and interest due to their efficiency per target member contact. The enhanced communication effectiveness of personal selling makes it better suited for moving target members through desire and into action. Promotion mix decisions are also affected by product price, as lower-priced products tend to have a lower profitability per unit that would dictate advertising (e.g., chewing gum and soft drinks), while higher-priced products include a level of margin that makes covering the costs of personal selling feasible (e.g., cars, jet skis, dress clothing, and accessories).

The wide variety of promotion methods makes it necessary to assess the promotional mix in terms of its role in the overall promotional strategy. The advantages and disadvantages of each promotion method must be carefully weighed against their costs and the firm's marketing and promotion objectives. The marketing manager must also decide on the relative weight to give to each method in the total promotion mix. This decision typically comes down to how to best divide the promotion budget across different methods. As the SBU or marketing manager selects promotional methods for the new marketing plan, the product's current position should be assessed with respect to customers. Then, promotion objectives can be set for the upcoming planning period. Making these decisions requires the marketing manager to specify what each method is capable of delivering in customers' decision-making processes. Promotion directed toward the trade is growing in importance for manufacturers as they seek to expand shelf space at the retail level. In fact, outside of personal selling expenses, roughly two-thirds of manufacturers' promotional expenses are directed toward the trade in an effort to push products through the channel of distribution.

When selecting promotion methods to include in the promotion mix, it is important to take an integrated marketing communication perspective, that is, to coordinate promotion elements and other marketing efforts that communicate with target customers to maximize the total impact on those customers. This requires a marketer to look at the "big picture" when planning marketing and promotional programs and coordinating the total set of communication functions to deliver the intended message on a consistent basis.[8] For example, if the promotional campaign stresses quality, while the sales force is talking about low price, and the Web site features product innovations, what is the customer to believe? Not readily seeing that a product can deliver all of these, the customer is likely to become confused and go to a competitor with a more consistent set of messages.

All too frequently, managers find themselves in the midst of promotion campaigns or activities that have no *clear* promotion objectives. Marketing managers must understand that most promotion activities do not simply create results in the short term. Thus, the firm must have long-term promotion objectives and the patience to continue the promotion strategy long enough to gauge true success, and, hopefully, to build a solid market position. Promotion activities based on creativity alone and not linked to the rest of the marketing strategy can waste precious marketing resources.

Distribution Decisions

Distribution is the most costly marketing activity for many products. Good distribution, however, is essential because it can make a critical difference in how easily and well customers are served. Thus, it has a major impact on the perceived value of exchanges by customers with a particular firm. Distribution refers to either or both of the following:

1. *Marketing channels:* a system of organizations through which a product, resources, information, and/or product ownership flows from producers to consumers.

2. *Physical distribution:* moving products to the right place in the right quantities at the right time, and in a cost-efficient manner. Logistics strategies address physical distribution issues, such as transportation, storage, materials handling, and the systems and equipment necessary for these functions.

Distribution tends to be the most difficult marketing activity to modify. Distribution channels and physical distribution systems may not change substantially for years, but they still need to be considered as major elements in short-term strategy. Retailers' recent moves from unique buying decisions to managing categories of products have significantly heightened the need to be effective and efficient in the management of the distribution component.

For many firms, distribution provides an avenue for creating a sustainable competitive advantage. Several firms have achieved notable success with this strategy, including Wal-Mart, Home Depot, and Dell Computer. Highly efficient distribution is one of Dell's main competitive advantages: speed and rigorous inventory control permit the computer giant to ship computer orders in 36 hours, while keeping costs ultra low so that it can undercut its rivals' prices by 10 to 15 percent.[9] Distribution is also the key marketing activity that is responsible for making products more convenient for customers to purchase—a topic we will address later in this chapter.

MARKETING CHANNEL ALTERNATIVES   There are many strategic options for distribution, and these strategies are often complex and very costly to implement. However, a good distribution strategy is essential for success because once a channel is selected and commitments are made, distribution often becomes highly inflexible due to long-term contracts, investments, and commitments with channel members. There are three basic strategic options for distribution in terms of the amount of market coverage and level of exclusivity between vendor and retailer:

1. Exclusive distribution gives one merchant or outlet the sole right to sell a product within a defined geographic region. This option is most commonly associated with prestige products, or with firms that are attempting to give their products an exclusive image. Many car makers, such as Saturn and Mercedes-Benz, use exclusive distribution. Companies that pursue this option are usually targeting a single, well-defined segment and need a significant amount of input regarding how their products are positioned to the ultimate consumer.

2. Selective distribution gives several outlets the right to sell a product in a defined geographic region. McDonald's and most other franchisers utilize selective distribution in the allocation of franchises. Such selectivity may be based on population (e.g., one franchise per 250,000 people), or dollar volume (e.g., when sales

reach $5 million in an area, another franchise is awarded), or some other factor. Selective distribution is desirable when customers need the opportunity to comparison shop and after-sale services are important. Pioneer and Panasonic stereo components, for example, are often available through a number of electronics stores and even discount stores where shoppers can compare them with other brands.

3.   Intensive distribution makes a product available in the maximum number of outlets in each region to gain as much exposure and as many sales opportunities as possible. This option is closely associated with consumer convenience goods, such as bread, soft drinks, or cigarettes. Firms that take the mass marketing approach to segmentation often employ an intensive distribution strategy.

IMPLICATIONS OF CHANNEL ALTERNATIVES   The configuration of the marketing channel helps to direct the flow of products and resources from producers to consumers and back. There are many options in designing marketing channels. Unfortunately, the nature of competition and customer behavior may limit the marketing manager's options. The traditional channel of producer to wholesaler to retailer is alive and well today and is used to distribute a wide range of products. However, some changes have occurred in this traditional arrangement as very large retailers, such as Sears, Kmart, Circuit City, Toys "R" Us, Home Depot, and Wal-Mart, are now performing their own wholesaling activities and buying directly from producers.

Distribution activities have also changed as a result of increased distribution from producers directly to consumers. In some cases, producers are selling to consumers through their own retail outlets. Nike, for example, continues to expand its Nike Town locations. The growth and popularity of factory outlet malls also testifies to this trend. However, most of the activity in direct distribution is the result of increasing sales being made through nonstore retailing.[10] Millions of satisfied customers are now purchasing products from catalog marketers, such as Lands' End and J. Crew; door-to-door marketers, such as Avon and Fuller Brush; home shopping programs, like QVC and the Home Shopping Network; and interactive marketers, such as those found through America Online or on the World Wide Web. Dell Computer, for example, sells $1 million worth of computers *a day* on its Web site, leaving rivals IBM and Compaq scrambling to develop their own Web-based marketing strategies.[11]

The growth in direct distribution has been sparked primarily by consumer demands for convenience and safety and the growing desire of producers to cut distribution expenses and capture higher margins. As personal computers and Internet access become more widespread, the World Wide Web is likely to become a more important channel for both manufacturers and retailers to consider. Even when the purchase is not made from the Web, it is increasingly viewed as an important source of information in the decision-making process of both consumers and organizational buyers. For example, a homeowner doing a kitchen remodel can "surf the Web" to find information about product features and specifications from a variety of manufacturers including Jenn-Air, KitchenAid, Maytag, Thermador, Kraftmaid, and many other firms.

Distribution strategies often need multiple channels to reach various markets. The use of multiple channels may arise out of necessity in order to meet customer needs, or by design. Multiple channels enable a producer to offer two or more lines of the same merchandise through two or more means, thus increasing sales coverage. Distribution strategy is also changing as a result of mass retailers like Toys "R" Us, Home Depot, and Wal-Mart that have gained increasing power relative to their suppliers. This change compels manufacturers to accommodate the objectives and methods of these large retailers. Indeed, these retailers have become the distribution strategists for many lines of consumer goods such as cosmetics, electronics, and toys.

SUPPLY CHAIN MANAGEMENT   In an effort to improve distribution channel relationships among manufacturers and other channel intermediaries, several forms of distribution alliances have evolved, with names like seamless pipelines, value-added partnerships, collaborative trade alliances, and supply chain management. Regardless of the name used, in most instances, the motivation behind such alliances is fairly simple—to drive out uncertainty and improve cooperation between channel members. Supply chain management, in particular, refers to long-term partnerships among marketing channel members working together to reduce costs, waste, and unnecessary movement in the entire marketing channel in order to satisfy customers.[12] Moreover, it moves beyond traditional channel members (producers, wholesalers, retailers, customers) to include *all* organizations involved in moving products from the producer to the ultimate customer, including facilitating agencies such as component parts suppliers and shipping companies.

Although relatively simple to describe, the implementation of a relationship driven by supply chain management is quite difficult. It requires a fundamental change in how distribution channel members work together. Among these changes is a move from a "win-lose" attitude to a "win-win" attitude in which all parties in the chain must prosper. It shifts the participants from short-term to long-term assessments in evaluating decisions affecting the relationship. The focus shifts from one of selling to the next level in the channel to one of selling products *through* the channel to a satisfied ultimate customer. Information flows move from a guarded "as needed" basis, to open, honest, and ongoing. Perhaps most importantly, the points of contact in the relationship expand from one-on-one at the salesperson-buyer level to multiple interfaces at all levels and in all functional areas of the various organizations.

The most advanced form of supply chain management in existence today was designed by a group of consumer food product manufacturers and leading supermarket chains that were dissatisfied with the highly competitive relationship that existed among them. To improve their relationship, the group developed the concept of category management through their Joint Industry Project on Efficient Consumer Response (ECR). This group defines category management as "a supplier process of managing categories (of products) as strategic business units, producing enhanced business results by focusing on delivering continuously enhanced consumer value."[13] In addition to being customer-oriented, the group has determined that category management should also be:

1. Customer-driven: Manufacturers and wholesalers should make all decisions with a concern for the challenges facing retailers in the channel.
2. Strategically driven: The relationship between the parties should be driven by a strategic plan to advance the relationship, and through this, advance the outcomes for the parties involved.

3. Mutlifunctional: Contact points should go beyond marketing and buying to include areas such as finance, logistics, quality control, and facilities management, in addition to the senior management teams of all firms.

4. Financially based: Solid financial targets should be set and met in terms of profitability and hard and soft cost management.

5. Systems-dependent: Systems (operational and technical) should be designed and put in place to support the activities of the relationship.

6. Focused on immediate consumer response: Successful channel members implementing category management should be able to give consumers what they want more rapidly than firms operating as traditional marketing channels.[14]

Exhibit 6.2 outlines six components of an ongoing category management process that must be jointly managed by both the category manager (retail buyer and merchandising position) and channel consultant (manufacturers' or wholesalers' account manager or salesperson). Each of the components in the process depends on the quality planning and performance of the other five components. In recent years, firms outside the consumer products industries have begun to adopt components of the ECR category management process to drive their own relationships.

Differentiation and Positioning

After selecting a target market(s) and developing a mix of marketing elements to satisfy the needs of members of that target market, the marketing manager should attempt to differentiate the product from competitive offerings and position it so that it seems to possess the characteristics the target market most desires.

Differentiation Strategies

One of the most important product strategy motives is to find ways to differentiate the firm's products from those of competing firms. Customer perception is of utmost importance in this process because differences between products can be based on real qualities (product characteristics, features, or style) or psychological qualities (the product's image). Generally, the most important element that communicates the differences between one product and another is the brand. However, there are other bases for differentiation. Three of the more important of these bases are product descriptors, customer support services, and image.

PRODUCT DESCRIPTORS   Information about products is generally provided in one of four contexts. The first context is product features, which are factual (hopefully) descriptors of the product. A feature of Diet Coke, for example, is zero calories per serving. A feature of a Xerox DocuPrint laserjet printer is that it produces three color copies per minute. Features, while telling customers something about the nature of the product, are not generally the pieces of information that lead people to buy. Advantages are performance characteristics that communicate how the features make the product behave, hopefully in a fashion that is distinctive and appealing to the target customers. The advantage of a zero-calorie drink is lower contribution to daily calorie intake, while an advantage of the color copier is less

EXHIBIT 6.2	Major Components of Category Management

Component	Description
1. Strategy	This step involves an informed choice by the retailer to move from managing brands or SKUs (stock-keeping units) to managing groups of products that satisfy similar consumer needs. Such groups are known as categories (e.g., deli meats, fresh cut floral, appearance chemicals, home bath cleaning products).
2. The Business Process	This is an eight-step process that includes: (1) defining categories and subcategories; (2) determining the categories' role in meeting retailer goals and objectives; (3) assessing the present performance of the defined category; (4) setting scorecard targets for measuring performance; (5) jointly developing strategies for achieving scorecard targets; (6) selecting specific tactics to implement selected strategies; (7) implementing plans with calendars and assigned responsibilities; and (8) appraising categories and refining plans for return to step 1.
3. Scorecard	An ongoing process of setting targets and setting up the means to monitor and improve performance in targeted areas (e.g., profit per square foot of category space, or average dollars purchased in the category per consumer).
4. Organization Capabilities	Changes in the design and structure of organizations, the required skill bases of the parties to the relationship, and the performance measurement and reward and recognition systems of the people involved.
5. Information Technology	Address the acquisition, analysis, and movement of information within and between the organizations involved. It must involve the supplier's marketing information system (MIS), the retailer's MIS, and external syndicated data suppliers (e.g., Nielsen).
6. Collaborative Trading Partners	The methods used to structure and conduct interactions between members of both the supplier and retailer organizations in a win-win fashion with the open and honest exchange of information for the purpose of identifying and solving problems.

Source: *Category Management Report* © 1995 by the Joint Industry Project on Efficient Consumer Response.

waiting time. But, as we have said before, the real reason people buy products is to gain benefits, the positive outcomes or need satisfactions they acquire from purchased products. The zero-calorie soft drink may facilitate weight loss, a more attractive figure, and longer life. At three copies per minute, the copier will reduce employee waiting time, which increases their satisfaction and productivity and ultimately helps the organization attain its goals.

For the soft drink, marketers can get by with just communicating product features. The price is low, the product simple, and the consumer can make his or her own translation to health and appearance. In the situation of the copier, however, promotional messages must incorporate all product descriptors to help the customer recognize the attractiveness of the product: "At three copies per minute, your employee waiting time will be reduced, freeing employees for more productive activities than watching pages slowly come out of the existing copier." Despite this fact, firms often focus on communicating just features, leaving customers to their own devices to come up with benefits.

Increasingly, one aspect of a product's description that is highly valued by customers is quality, which refers to the overall characteristics of a product that allow it to perform as expected in the satisfaction of customer needs. The words *as expected* are crucial to this definition because quality means different things to different people. Research suggests that U.S. consumers view the following characteristics (in order of importance) as evidence of high quality: reliability, durability, ease of maintenance, ease of use, and a known and trusted brand name.[15] For business-to-business customers, characteristics such as technical suitability, ease of repair, and company reputation are significant indicators of quality. In general, higher product quality—whether real or imagined—means that a company can charge a higher price for the product and simultaneously build customer loyalty. This relationship between quality and price (inherent in the concept of value) forces the marketing manager to consider product quality carefully in his or her marketing mix decisions.

CUSTOMER SUPPORT SERVICES   A firm may have difficulty differentiating its products when all products in a market have essentially the same quality, features, and benefits. In such cases, providing good customer support services—both before and after the sale—may be the only way to differentiate the firm's products and thus move them out of a price-driven commodity status. Services include anything the firm can provide in addition to the main product that adds value to that product for the customer. Examples include assistance in identifying and defining customer needs, delivery and installation, technical support for high-tech systems and software, financing arrangements, training, extended warranties and guarantees, repair, layaway plans, convenient hours of operation, affinity programs (e.g., frequent flier/buyer programs), and adequate parking. If you buy a Sears Kenmore refrigerator, for example, you may count on Sears to provide financing, install the appliance, and, if necessary, repair the appliance through a designated warranty period. Through research, the marketing manager can discover the types of support services that customers value most. The importance of having good support services has increased in recent years, directing many firms to design their customer services as carefully as they design their products.

IMAGE   The image of a product, or organization, is the overall impression, positive or negative, that target customers have of it. This impression includes what the entity has done in the past, what it presently offers, and projections about what it will do in the future. All aspects of the firm's marketing mix as perceived by target customers will affect this overall impression. Consider the Macintosh computer. Despite Apple's financial woes, its Macintosh maintains a fiercely devoted following of consumers who perceive the computer as being easier to use and more versatile than personal computers offered by IBM, Compaq, and other firms. Marketers can manipulate the marketing mix elements to position and enhance a product's image (typically through promotion activities) in consumers' minds.

Positioning Strategies

To create a positive image for a product, a marketing manager can choose from among several positioning strategies, including strengthening the current position, moving to a new position, or attempting to reposition the competition.

STRENGTHEN CURRENT POSITION   The key to strengthening a product's current position is to monitor constantly what target customers want and the extent to which the product or firm is perceived as satisfying those wants. Any complacency in today's dynamic marketplace is likely to result in lost customers and sales. It can be easy for a company known for excellent customer service after the sale to stagnate in this area as it focuses on improving other areas. But if after-sale service is a key ingredient in the company's strategy, this just simply cannot be allowed to happen. The firm must continue to invest time, money, talent, and attention in after-sale service to protect its market share and sales from competitors.

Strengthening a current position is all about continually "raising the bar" of customer expectations, and being perceived by customers as the only firm capable of reaching the new height. For example, when Houghton Mifflin launched the third edition of its *American Heritage Dictionary,* it heavily promoted the fact that the *AHD* offers more definitions than condensed dictionaries yet costs half the price of unabridged dictionaries. By strengthening its middle-of-the-road position through advertising and publicity (including associations with *Jeopardy* and *Wheel of Fortune*), Houghton Mifflin made the *American Heritage Dictionary* useful and hip enough to spend 16 weeks on the *New York Times* Best Seller list, a rarity for a reference work.[16] Companies that fail to strengthen their position often find themselves sliding backward on key dimensions of their market offering.

MOVE TO A NEW POSITION   At times, declining sales or market share may signal that customers have lost faith in a product's ability to satisfy their needs. In such cases, strengthening the present position may well accelerate the downturn in performance; a new position may be the best response. Repositioning may involve a fundamental change in any of the marketing mix elements, and perhaps even all of them. J. Crew, for example, has dropped its "preppy" style of clothing in favor of more "urban and hip" merchandise. The traditional catalog-based retailer is also expanding the number of stores where its clothes are sold. As its traditional baby boom customers age, J. Crew needs to attract younger shoppers who have traditionally favored stores like Banana Republic.[17]

REPOSITION THE COMPETITION   Sometimes, it is advantageous to attempt to reposition the competition rather than change your own position. A direct attack on a competitor's strength may put its products in a less favorable light, or even force the competitor to change its positioning strategy. This was the tactic taken by Barnes & Noble in the book retailing business when it launched a Web site to compete with online bookstore pioneer, Amazon.com. Barnes & Noble's electronic storefront forced Amazon.com to reposition on two fronts: price and in-stock product. Barnes & Noble inaugurated its site with 30–percent discounts on all hard-cover books. To remain competitive, Amazon.com had to respond with similar discounts. As a traditional store-based retailer with 400,000 frequently stocked titles, Barnes & Noble also heavily promoted immediate availability of most ordered books. Amazon.com had to increase the number of titles it stocks, a position it had previously avoided in an effort to keep costs low.[18]

Whether to strengthen or reposition is just one of many complex decisions required in the development of a marketing strategy. Along with thorough environmental analyses, a strong marketing mix can effectively differentiate a firm's products and position them in such as way that customers perceive them as satisfying their desires. However, there are many other decisions and issues to be considered in developing the "right" marketing strategy, as we shall see in the next chapter.

Key Insights from Chapter 6

Marketing strategy involves:

- selecting a specific target market and
- making decisions regarding the crucial elements of product, price, promotion, and distribution in order to satisfy the needs of customers in that market.

Target market alternatives include:

- mass (or undifferentiated) marketing, which is aimed at the total market for a particular type of product.
- market segmentation, which divides the total market into groups of customers having relatively homogeneous needs and attempting to develop a marketing mix that appeals to one or more of these groups. The multisegment approach and the market concentration approach are two options under market segmentation.
- niche marketing, which focuses marketing efforts on one small, well-defined market segment that has a unique, specific set of needs.
- customized marketing, which involves the creation of an entirely unique marketing mix for each individual in the target segment.

Marketing mix alternatives:

- involve the creation of a combination of product, price, promotion, and distribution that, to the greatest extent possible, matches the needs of customers in the chosen target market segment(s).
- must be carefully integrated to create the marketing mix.

Product alternatives:

- must acknowledge the product as a set of features and advantages that have the capacity to satisfy customer needs and wants, thus delivering valued benefits that can be exchanged for something else.
- include at least six marketing strategy options related to the newness of products—innovation, new product lines, product line extensions, improvements or changes in existing products, repositioning, and cost reductions.

Price alternatives:

- must achieve the right balance between customers' needs, other product alternatives, and the firm's need to cover its direct and indirect costs, while also making an acceptable profit.
- include a low-price strategy, which requires operational efficiency and low costs.
- include a higher-price strategy for products perceived as having high quality and prestige.

Promotion alternatives:

- are necessary to communicate the features and benefits of a product to its intended target market(s).
- must integrate elements of the promotion mix (advertising, personal selling, publicity, and sales promotion) cost effectively, consistently, and appropriately for the nature of the product and stage of the product purchase process.

Distribution alternatives:

- include both marketing channels and physical distribution or logistics activities necessary to move products from producer to ultimate consumer.
- are often inflexible due to long-term contracts, investments, and commitments with channel members.
- include three basic strategic options related to the amount of market coverage and level of exclusivity between producers and retail outlets:
  - exclusive distribution
  - selective distribution
  - intensive distribution
- may be enhanced through supply chain management of channel member relationships and category management.

Differentiation strategies:

- are necessary to distinguish a firm's offering from those of competitors.
- may communicate differences in product descriptors (features, advantages, benefits, quality), customer support services, and/or image.

Positioning strategies:

- help create a positive image of the product and/or organization.
- include:
  - strengthening the current position.
  - moving to a new position.
  - repositioning the competition.

CHAPTER 7

Selecting and Developing the Marketing Strategy

Introduction

In the previous chapter, we considered those aspects of marketing strategy selection that drive the direction of an entire organization or SBU, including target market selection and marketing mix options, which help guide the selection of a specific marketing strategy. We begin this chapter by examining the criteria for selecting a marketing strategy for a specific product or line of products, including strategic characteristics and life cycle considerations. Later, we explore how marketers can create a competitive advantage based on customer value. Finally, we consider marketing strategies for specialized products, including service and nonprofit organizations, as well as business-to-business markets.

Criteria for Selecting a Marketing Strategy

There are a variety of factors a firm must keep in mind in selecting and developing a marketing strategy for a product or group of products. Included in this set of factors are the strategic characteristics of the firm and environment and the stage of the item or line in the product life cycle. The weight given to each of these factors will vary depending on the situation, but each should be carefully considered before a final strategy for the product line or item is crafted, finalized, and ultimately implemented.

Strategic Characteristics

Exhibit 7.1 presents an overview of the steps involved in selecting a marketing strategy. The marketing manager evaluates all strategy options in light of the firm's mission, goals and objectives, strengths and weaknesses, and opportunities and threats to craft a marketing strategy that produces the best overall strategic fit. To use an analogy of a jigsaw puzzle, the best marketing strategy is the piece of the puzzle that correctly joins the firm to its environment. If the fit is incorrect, the pieces of the puzzle cannot join together properly. A good fit allows the firm to make the most of the potential capabilities that the internal and external environment combination provides.

EXHIBIT 7.1	Steps in Selecting a Marketing Strategy

Considerations in Selecting a Strategy

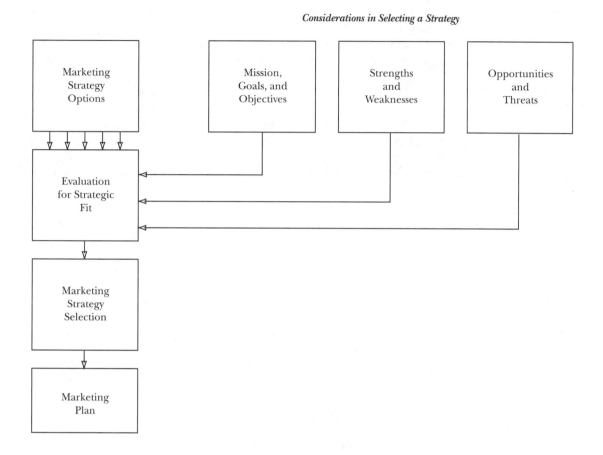

Unfortunately, there are no universal criteria for determining strategic fit. Much of the strategy selection process is based on years of experience with the product in a particular market (or set of markets), careful and comprehensive research, and ultimately, managerial intuition. Although the list here is obviously incomplete, we believe that the best marketing strategies will be differentially advantageous, sustainable, timely, feasible, and affordable.

The marketing strategy should contain a differential advantage—a feature or attraction that competitive offerings lack—that will provide satisfaction or understandable benefits to buyers. Such an advantage makes it possible for the firm to exploit fully the potential of its marketing plan. Differential advantages are usually based on matching an internal strength with an external opportunity to create a capability. Taco Bell, for example, identified two distinct groups of frequent customers: "penny pinchers" (18–24 year-olds looking for low-priced fast-food products), and "speed freaks" (time-poor, two-income-family couples or parents). To satisfy these "frequent buyers," the firm sharply cut back its menu to reduce inventory costs and accelerate food production and delivery. This strategy helped Taco

Bell's sales grow from $1.6 billion to $4.5 billion over a six-year period, with earnings growing from $82 million to $273 million during the same time period.[1]

A good marketing strategy is also one that competitors cannot copy, or can copy only slowly over the long term with significant investments. This gives the firm a sustainable competitive advantage that allows it to exploit its differential advantage over a longer period of time. Many firms create sustainable advantages based on lower costs or higher efficiency. Of all marketing mix elements, low prices are often the least sustainable, unless they are backed up by significantly lower costs. Returning to Taco Bell, the firm's low-price strategy was sustainable only because of the cost reductions realized by the significant decreases in the number of menu items.

There is a right or ideal time for every strategy. Marketers often use the term *strategic window* to refer to the timeliness of an opportunity. Before the "window" is open, the market is not ready. But if the firm is too slow to act on the opportunity, the window may close due to the presence of valued options from competitors or declining demand. Due to varying response times and the fact that strategic windows close more rapidly than ever today because of nimble, intense competition, it is crucial that a firm do all it can to anticipate the opening of a strategic window. If this is not feasible, the firm must be prepared to respond with increasing speed once an opening has been identified. In every instance, the attractiveness of an open (or opening) window must be evaluated relative to the strengths and weaknesses of the firm. Consider a window opening for computer manufacturers and retailers to sell made-to-order computers directly to consumers and small businesses. Dell Computer opened the window with a line that yielded a two-thirds increase in sales and more than doubled its profits. Consumers and small business owners like the idea of computers made specifically to meet their needs with lower prices from direct sales. Retailers CompUSA, Office Max, and Radio Shack, and manufacturers Hewlett-Packard, IBM, Packard Bell, NEC, and Compaq recognized the wide-open window and quickly followed suit with their own direct-sale made-to-order strategies.[2]

Although a marketing strategy may be sound, a firm may lack the venture spirit, willingness to accept risk, patience, experience, technical know-how, or resources necessary to implement the strategy. In short, a good marketing strategy is feasible because the firm possesses the required skills, experience, resources, and strengths to do so. Overly aggressive short-term objectives frequently result in the lack of patience or perspective to capitalize effectively on an otherwise solid opportunity.

Finally, a good marketing strategy is one that is affordable given the level of the firm's financial resources. Affordability also includes the level of financial resources devoted to the marketing plan instead of other functional areas. One of the primary reasons why marketing plans fail is because the firm did not devote the necessary financial resources to implement them, or failed to devote resources for a long enough period of time.

Of these criteria, building a differential advantage is perhaps the most critical for long-term success and survival. What unique benefit does, or can, the firm offer to customers? A differential advantage can be real or based exclusively on image. In either case, creating the *perception* of differentiation is the key. For example, lacking anything exclusive, a firm might find some feature that no competitor has claimed and promote it before the competition can retaliate. This is often a highly creative process. Consider the car rental industry. In the industry's early years, Hertz not only stood first but maintained a vast lead over second-place Avis. The management of Avis, intent on capturing a larger portion of Hertz's customers, asked its

EXHIBIT 7.2   **A Typical Product/Market Life Cycle**

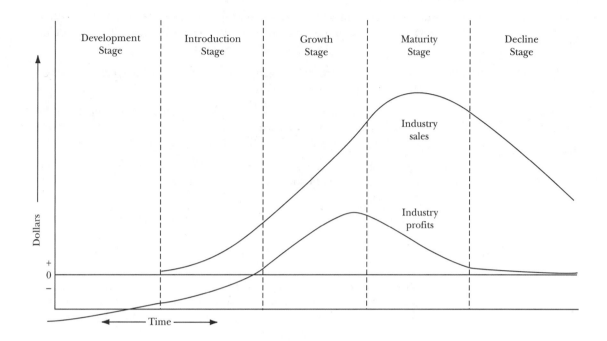

advertising agency to find an effective marketing strategy. After searching for any advantage that Avis held over Hertz, the agency concluded the only difference was that Avis was number two! Avis management decided to claim this fact as an advantage, using the theme, "We're number two. We try harder!" Avis rentals soared, putting the company in a much stronger number-two position.

The criteria for a good marketing strategy will vary across companies, markets, products, and over time. In some cases, what makes a good marketing strategy depends on the person reviewing it. In some firms, the best marketing strategy may be the one that is capable of being approved by top management. Thus, in the process of selecting a marketing strategy, it is important for the SBU or marketing manager to do an occasional "reality check" to understand better what can and cannot be achieved. The manager should also do a reality check of the firm's own strengths and weaknesses. Key weaknesses that cannot be overcome in the short term can make an otherwise attractive marketing strategy impossible to implement.

Life Cycle Considerations

Because many marketing strategy decisions are made at the SBU level, it is beneficial to consider the issue of life cycle stages of the product, brand, or market. Other approaches to planning and managing products are equally valid, but you are probably most familiar with the product life cycle in terms of how sales, resources, investments, and profits vary over time. To the usual four stages, we add a fifth: the product's development period from conception to commercialization. With that addition, Exhibit 7.2 charts the typical life cycle, while Exhibit 7.3 describes each of the life cycle stages.

EXHIBIT 7.3	Description of Life Cycle Stages
Development	Determine target customers' desired benefits. Conceive or select product ideas. Direction and specifications for marketing strategy development. Move rapidly but prudently toward commercialization that begins in the next stage.
Introduction	Determine best strategy for introducing the new product and gaining customer acceptance. Launch of marketing strategy.
Growth	Establish the product in a defensible competitive position and broaden its market. Sales should rise rapidly and profits should peak.
Maturity	Extend the life of the product. Innovate to maintain profits while sales curve peaks and starts to decline. Severe competition with many brands. Curtail, but do not eliminate, resource investments of financial and human capital.
Decline	Find solutions that will slow or postpone the decline of demand, or find ways to terminate the product. Cut marketing expenses to maximize profits.

Exhibit 7.2 shows the growth and decline in sales volume over the life of a product in a curve that is a generalization, but appropriate for our discussion. The relative time length of the stages can vary greatly. For a fad, such as Tamagotchi virtual pets or Beanie Babies, the life cycle might be measured in weeks or months, while the cycle for a staple item may last for years or even decades. Let's briefly consider these stages and how they relate to marketing strategy development.

DEVELOPMENT STAGE   As Exhibit 7.2 shows, a firm has no sales revenue during the product development stage. In fact, the firm experiences a net cash outflow due to the expenses of product invention and development. For most innovations, a substantial investment of financial resources and time, as well as risk assumption, are necessary for invention and development. For example, the development of the Gulfstream V, an ultra-long-distance corporate jet aircraft, required four years and an $800 million investment.[3] Such investments are no guarantee of success and, in fact, many products fail. A study of 11,000 new products manufactured by 77 firms found that only 56 percent were still on the market five years after introduction. In the food and beverage industry alone, 80 percent of all new products fail.[4] The high product failure rate underscores the need to identify target customer needs correctly *before* developing a marketing strategy.

The development stage usually begins with a product concept, which has several components:

- An understanding of the specific uses and benefits that target customers seek in a new product.
- A description of the product, including its potential uses and benefits.
- The potential for creating a complete product line that can produce synergy in sales and income and place the firm in a strong market position.

- An analysis of the feasibility of the product concept, including such issues as anticipated sales, required return on investment, time of market introduction, length of time to repay investment, etc.

Although marketing activities do not typically occur in the development stage, planning efforts at this point can greatly influence marketing activities in later stages of the life cycle. In creating a new product or product line, a group of closely related product items is desired because of the scale economies that are created, along with increased efficiency in operations and marketing. New products that match customers' needs and have strong advantages over competing products are simply easier to market as the new product enters the introduction stage of its life cycle.

INTRODUCTION STAGE   The introduction stage begins when development is complete and ends when sales indicate that target customers are widely accepting the product. The marketing strategy devised during the development stage should be fully implemented during the introduction stage, and should relate to issues that arose during the SWOT analysis. Marketing strategy goals that are common to the introduction stage include:

- Attract customers by raising awareness of and interest in the product through advertising, public relations, and publicity efforts that stress key product features and benefits.
- Induce customers to try and buy the product through the use of various sales tools and pricing activities.
- Strengthen or expand channel relationships to gain sufficient product distribution to make the product accessible to target customers.
- Build on the availability and visibility of the product through trade promotion activities.
- Engage in customer education activities that teach target market members how to use the new product and convince them to repurchase the product.

Although all marketing mix activities are important during the introduction stage, good promotion and distribution are essential to make customers aware that the new product is available, how to use it, and where to purchase it.

After the product is introduced, the marketing manager must employ the firm's marketing information system to determine market share, revenues, store placement/channel support, costs, and rate of product usage to assess whether the new product is paying back the firm's investment. Even when the firm has patent protection or hard-to-copy technology, the manager must carefully track competitors' reactions. Tracking this information is critical if the firm is to continue along the gradually rising sales curve shown in Exhibit 7.2.

Industrial products often have long periods of introduction while buyers are being convinced to adopt them. Pharmaceuticals in particular may experience long delays while being tested and before doctors become convinced of drug safety and efficacy. A packaged consumer good, on the other hand, may see an immediate upsurge in sales as consumers and retailers take advantage of special introductory offers. Unfortunately, many product introductions never enjoy rising demand, leading to significant losses for an organization. The success of product introduction determines whether the product will make the grade and enter the profitable growth stage, where bottom-line enhancement and resources for subsequent revisions and additional new product introductions occur.

GROWTH STAGE   Marketing managers should be ready for growth as sustained sales increases may begin quickly. The product's upward sales curve may be steep, as shown in Exhibit 7.2. The length of the growth stage varies according to the nature of the product and competitive reactions. Disposable diapers had a long growth stage as they experienced over 30 percent yearly growth for a decade. A short growth stage is typical for games and toys—Barbie dolls notwithstanding.

Regardless of the length of the growth stage, the firm has two main priorities: (1) establish a strong market position and defend it from competitors, and (2) achieve financial objectives that repay investment and earn enough to justify a long-term commitment to the product. Within these two priorities, there are a number of pertinent marketing strategy issues:

- Utilize the product's *perceivable* differential advantages in terms of quality, price, value, etc., to secure market leadership.
- Establish a clear product/brand identity through image-oriented advertising and personal selling campaigns.
- Create a unique product position, or niche, through the use of advertising that stresses product features and benefits for target customers relative to other solutions/products available to target market members.
- Maximize availability of the product through extensive trade promotion activities that capitalize on the product's popularity at this stage and thereby enhance the firm's ability to deliver profits to key channel members, especially retailers.
- Find the ideal balance between price and demand and determine a general estimate of price elasticity.
- Maintain control over product quality to assure customer satisfaction.

The overall strategy in the growth stage shifts toward generating repeat purchases and building brand loyalty. Typically, the overall product/market is growing as well, thus the firm should not only focus on sales increase percentages, but also on achieving as high a market share as possible. Consider Ty Inc., the marketer of Beanie Babies. Ty experienced nearly four-digit sales increase rates in the late 1990s by continuously introducing new stuffed animals and retiring mature editions of these cuddly collectibles. This strategy has kept the firm in a growth mode and pleased collectors who now sell retired Babies via classified newspaper ads and Web sites at premium prices.[5]

The growth stage is the most expensive stage for marketing. A deep negative cash flow is likely because strong marketing efforts are needed to sustain growth. One of the most difficult questions that a marketing manager must ask is how long should the firm expend cash and other resources to establish the product? This decision should be influenced by the growth rate of the *total* market. The answer to this question is complicated by the price/quality/earnings tradeoff: Low prices build market share but sacrifice profit and can lower customer perceptions of the product's quality. A good estimate of price elasticity (percentage change in quantity demanded for a particular percentage change in product price) is important. One option at this point is to create a prestige image by fortifying quality perceptions and holding to premium prices.

Increasing competition should be expected as the product moves through the growth stage and into the maturity stage, and the product's sales growth and emerging profitability encourages other firms to develop competitive product entries. These firms may be traditional rivals or nontraditional competitors. Photography giant Kodak, for example, now faces competition from Hewlett Packard, best known for its laser and ink-jet printers, in the emerging market for digital photography products.[6] If a firm is the first to market a new product, it has a better chance of capturing and maintaining market leadership, assuming that the product's competitive advantages can be sustained against competitive inroads. Whatever competitive role the marketing manager selects during the growth stage, it is important to commit to it. Competitors who enter with comparable products later have narrower options.

MATURITY STAGE   In the typical product life cycle, we expect maturity to be the longest stage. When the relatively fast growth has tapered, there will be some "shake-out" of the competition that built during the growth stage. As the strategic window of opportunity has all but closed for the product/market, no more firms will enter the market unless they have found some product innovation significant enough to attract large numbers of target customers. The window of opportunity often remains open, however, for new product features and variations. A good example is the introduction of light, dry, ice, microbrew, and low-alcohol products in the beer industry. These variations can be quite important as firms attempt to gain market share. In the face of limited or no growth within the product market, the only way for a firm to gain market share is to steal it from a competitor. Such theft often comes only with significant promotional investments or cuts in gross margin as prices are lowered.

For the manager who has survived the growth stage, maturity can be a relatively status quo stage. As long as sales volume is maintained, keeping market share constant, a more long-term perspective can be taken due to decreasing market uncertainty. Typically, the marketing manager has three general objectives that can be pursued during the maturity stage:

1. *Generate Cash Flow.* By the time a product reaches maturity, it should be yielding a very positive cash flow. This is essential to recoup the initial investment and to generate the excess cash necessary for the firm to grow and develop new products.

2. *Hold Market Share.* Marketing strategy should still stress holding market share among the dominant brands in the market. Firms having a marginal market share must decide whether they have a reasonable chance of improving their position or they should drop out.

3. *Increase Share of Customer.* Where market share refers to the percentage of total customers held by the firm, *share of customer* refers to the percentage of each customer's needs being met by the firm. Many banks, for example, have added

a variety of services to gain more of each customer's business in financial services (brokerage, auto leasing, retirement planning, etc.). Likewise, many larger grocery stores gain share of customer by adding features ranging from restaurants to video rentals to dry cleaning services in an effort to create one-stop shopping for household needs.

To achieve these objectives, the marketing manager has at least four general options for strategy selection throughout the maturity stage: (1) develop a new product image; (2) find and attract new users to the product; (3) discover new applications and uses for the product; or (4) apply new technology. Kraft General Foods, for example, launched a massive advertising campaign to create a new product image for Jell-O after a nine-year decline in sales. Today, Jell-O has once again achieved gourmet status with American children. After sales of baking soda went flat, Arm & Hammer began touting the product's uses as a deodorizer. Today, baking soda is found in products ranging from toothpaste to kitty litter.

Holding market share or increasing share of customer often requires heavy expenditures in marketing, particularly in promotion. Increasing share of customer may also require additional expenditures in creating new product features or modifications, as was the case in the beer industry. Likewise, when Clorox added lemon and floral scents to its bleach product and a lemon fragrance to Pine-Sol, sales for both products accelerated despite a slow-growing market.[7] A holding strategy also requires a careful coordination of marketing activities as the firm attempts to maintain its image against possible attacks by competitors. Due to the expense, only firms in an already strong market position should attempt a holding strategy.

DECLINE STAGE   A product's sales plateau will not last forever, and eventually it begins a persistent decline in revenue that marks the beginning of the decline stage. Very popular brands can postpone this stage longer than weaker brands. The decline stage, and the product's life, ends when the product is terminated.

The marketing manager has two options during the decline stage: attempt to postpone the decline or accept its inevitability. Should the firm decide to attempt to postpone the decline, the manager must find ways to renew the product's demand, perhaps through repositioning, developing new uses or features for the product, or applying new technology. Whatever the method, postponing the decline stage often takes a great deal of time and a substantial investment of resources. Many firms, however, do not have the resources or opportunity to renew a product's demand and are forced to accept the inevitability of decline. In such instances, the marketing manager can either harvest profits from the product while demand declines or divest the product, taking steps to abandon it or sell it to another firm.

The *harvesting* approach calls for a gradual reduction in marketing expenditures, and uses a less resource-intensive marketing mix. A harvesting strategy allows the firm to funnel its increased cash flow into new products. Chrysler, for example, gradually pulled all resources and development efforts from the Eagle brand of its Jeep/Eagle SBU. Harvesting the Eagle brand enabled the auto maker to consolidate its organizational structure and funnel extra resources into its more prosperous Jeep, Chrysler, and Plymouth brands.[8]

A company using the *divesting* option withdraws all marketing support from the product or SBU. It may continue to sell the product until losses are sustained, or arrange for the product to be acquired by another firm. Home Depot, for example, made the tough decision to divest its Crossroads stores for farm dwellers, and to move human and financial resources to Home Depot Expo (a chain for upscale consumers doing significant renovations or remodeling projects) and a program to attract more professional contractors into its home improvement centers.[9]

There are several factors that the marketing manager should examine before making a decision to harvest or divest:

- the rate of market deterioration—the faster the rate, the sooner the manager should divest.

- market segment potential—loyal customer segments might continue to buy.

- the market position of the product—a leading product with a good image in a declining industry may be profitable and generate excess cash by attracting customers from competitors' abandoned products.

- the firm's price and cost structure—this may remain strong in the face of declining sales if the firm no longer has to invest significantly in maintaining the product.

Although the marketing manager should study all of these factors, he or she should not be sentimental about dropping a failing product. On the other hand, the marketing manager should not quickly dismiss a renewal attempt, particularly if the firm does not have a better alternative use for its resources.

Bear in mind that throughout all of these life cycle stages, the marketing manager should stay focused primarily on changes in the market, not the firm's products. Products have life cycles only because markets and customer needs—and options for meeting those needs—change. By focusing on changing markets, the manager can attempt to create new and better quality products to match customer needs. Only in this way can a firm grow, prosper, remain competitive, and continue to be seen as a viable source of solutions for the target market members' needs.

Creating a Competitive Advantage Based on Customer Value

The motivation behind any change in marketing strategy is to increase the degree to which successful performance can be continued into the next planning period, or to improve the performance of a product that is failing to meet its share of the SBU's objectives. Over the years, marketers have used many approaches to organize marketing strategy decisions to achieve these ends, including the recent interest in product/service quality and total quality management. One of the more prevalent approaches is the concept of value. Value may be an effective way to integrate marketing activities because (1) it includes the concept of quality, although it is a much broader term, (2) it takes into account all four marketing mix elements, and (3) it can be used to consider explicitly customer perceptions of the marketing mix in the strategy development process. Value can also be used, like total quality management, as a means of organizing the internal aspects of marketing strategy development. Let's look at value in more detail.

The Value Formula

Value is a difficult term to define because it means different things to different people.[10] Some people equate good value with high product quality, while others see value as nothing more than a low price. The most common definition of value relates customer benefits to costs, or to use a more colloquial expression, gives "more bang for the buck." Value is also a relative term in that it can be judged only in comparison to the offerings of other firms. For our purposes, we define value as a customer's subjective evaluation of benefits relative to costs to determine the worth of a firm's product relative to the offerings of other firms. A simple formula for value might look like this:

$$\text{Perceived Value} = \frac{\text{Customer Benefits}}{\text{Customer Costs}}$$

Although this formula is simple in design, it is not very useful in developing marketing strategy. To see how each marketing mix element relates to this formula, we need to break down customer benefits and customer costs into their component parts, as shown in Exhibit 7.4.

Customer Benefits

Customer benefits can include anything that a customer receives in his or her dealings with the firm. These benefits are most closely associated with the product element of the marketing mix. Examples include the benefits that customers receive from the quality of the firm's products, including all of the features possessed by its products. For service firms, product quality refers to the inherent quality of the core service, such as a bed or room in a hotel. Customers also receive benefits from the firm's customer (product support) services, such as installation, delivery, training,

---

EXHIBIT 7.4	Components of Customer Benefits and Costs that Create Value

Customer Benefits

Benefits derived from:	Examples:
Product Quality	Product features, styling, brand name, warranties, durability, ease of use, image, prestige
Customer Service Quality	Reliability, responsiveness, employee friendliness and empathy
Experience-Based Quality	Retail atmosphere/decor, in-store promotion, advertising, publicity

Customer Costs

Costs associated with:	Examples:
Monetary Prices	Retail price, sales taxes, delivery charges
Nonmonetary Costs	Time, effort, risk, opportunity costs

or layaway programs. The quality of customer service depends on how reliable and responsive the firm is to customer requests, and on employee characteristics, such as friendliness and empathy.

Customers also receive benefits based on their experiences. For example, many customers derive benefits from the act of shopping itself. These benefits are affected by the atmosphere and decor of the retail store. Many promotional activities are included in experience benefits. These activities range from instore promotion(s) (e.g., point-of-purchase displays, demonstrations, or fashion shows) to out-of-store promotion (e.g., advertising and publicity to provide product information to customers). Promotional activities are also partly responsible for creating the image and prestige characteristics that are a part of product quality.

Customer Costs

Customer costs include anything that the buyer must give up to obtain the benefits provided by the firm. The most obvious cost is the monetary price of the product, including any sales taxes or additional charges. Nonmonetary costs, however, are not so obvious. Two such costs are the time and effort customers expend to find and purchase desired products. These costs are closely related to a firm's distribution activities. To reduce time and effort, the firm must increase product availability, thereby making it more convenient for customers to purchase the firm's products. The growth in nonstore retailing is a direct result of firms taking steps to reduce the time and effort required to purchase their products and thereby reduce these costs to customers.

Another nonmonetary cost, risk, can be reduced by offering good basic warranties, or extended warranties for an additional charge. Retailers reduce risk by maintaining liberal return and exchange policies. The final nonmonetary cost, opportunity costs, is harder for the firm to control. Some firms attempt to reduce opportunity costs by promoting their products as being the best or by promising good service after the sale. To anticipate opportunity costs, the firm must consider all competitors, including total budget competitors, that offer customers alternatives for spending their money.

Competing on Value

After breaking down value into its component parts, we can better understand how a firm's marketing strategy can be designed to optimize customer value. By altering each element of the marketing mix, the firm can enhance value by increasing product, customer service, or experience-based quality and/or reducing monetary or nonmonetary prices. Different retail firms provide good examples of how value can be delivered by altering one or more parts of the value equation. Convenience stores offer value to customers by reducing nonmonetary costs (time and effort) and increasing monetary prices. These high-priced (in dollars) stores stay in business because many customers value their time and effort more than money in some instances. In such instances, a gallon of milk purchased from a convenience store may be perceived as having the same or greater value as an identical gallon purchased at a large supermarket at a lower monetary price. Customers searching for the best quality may consider their nonmonetary costs to be less important. These customers may be willing to spend large sums of money and/or drive long distances to search for top-quality merchandise.

Obviously, different target markets will have different perceptions of good value. The marketing manager must understand the different value requirements of each target market and adapt the marketing mix accordingly. From a strategic perspective, it is important to remember that all four marketing mix elements are important to delivering value. Strategic decisions about one element alone can change perceived value for better or worse. If these decisions lower overall value, the marketing manager should consider modifying other marketing mix elements to offset this decrease.

Marketing Strategy for Specialized Products

Although we have focused largely on strategies for tangible goods thus far, it is important to remember that products can be more intangible services and ideas as well. Recall also that marketing strategies can be applied to nonprofit organizations, government agencies, and individuals, as well as for-profit businesses. In many cases, the products offered by a nonprofit organization such as the American Cancer Society (information, research funding) or the National Wildlife Federation (financial assistance for endangered species and habitats) lie closer to the intangible end of the service continuum. Although most aspects of marketing planning can be applied regardless of type of organization or product, we believe it will be beneficial to explore a few issues regarding marketing strategies for services and business-to-business markets.

Services

Nonprofit and for-profit organizations that market services and ideas face additional considerations in creating an appropriate marketing mix. These factors are the direct result of the unique characteristics of services that distinguish them from goods; these distinctions and their resulting challenges are summarized in Exhibit 7.5. Obviously, the primary difference between a good and a service is that a service is less tangible. Some services, such as business consulting and education, are almost completely intangible, while others have more concrete elements. The services provided by UPS and FedEx, for example, include tangible airplanes, trucks, boxes, and airbills. Still other firms, such as restaurants, market products that are a mixture of both goods and services. As the intangible elements begin to dominate the total product offering, the firm will experience a new set of considerations in designing a marketing mix.

PRODUCT CONSIDERATIONS   Because of the intangibility of services, it is quite difficult for customers to evaluate the product before they actually use it. This forces customers to place some degree of trust in the service provider to perform the service correctly and in the time frame promised or anticipated. One way companies can address this issue is by providing satisfaction guarantees to customers. For example, Hampton Inn, a national chain of mid-priced hotels, offers guests a free night if they are not 100 percent satisfied with their stay.[11]

Moreover, because most services are people-based, they are susceptible to variations in quality and inconsistency. Such variations can occur from one organization to another, from one outlet to another within the same organization, from one service

EXHIBIT 7.5	**Unique Service Characteristics and Resulting Marketing Problems**

Unique Service Characteristics	*Resulting Marketing Problems*
Intangibility	• Difficult for customers to evaluate • Firm is forced to sell a promise • Difficult to advertise and display • Prices are difficult to set and justify
Inseparability of production and consumption	• Service employees are critical to delivery • Customers must participate in production • Other customers affect service outcomes • Customers cannot derive possession utility • Services are difficult to distribute
Customer contact	• Service employees are critical to delivery • Training and motivating service employees • How to change a high-contact service into a low-contact service to lower costs
Perishability	• Services cannot be inventoried • Difficult to balance supply and demand • Unused capacity is lost forever • Demand is very time sensitive
Heterogeneity	• Service quality is difficult to control • Difficult to standardize service delivery
Client-based relationships	• Success depends on satisfying and keeping customers in the long term • How to generate repeat business • Relationship marketing becomes critical

Sources: J. Paul Peter and James H. Donnelly, Jr., *A Preface to Marketing Management,* 6th ed. (Burr Ridge, IL: Richard D. Irwin, 1994), 220-228; and Valarie A. Zeithaml, A. Parasuraman, and Leonard L. Berry, *Delivering Quality Service: Balancing Customer Perceptions and Expectations* (New York: The Free Press, 1990).

to another within the same outlet, and even from one employee to another within the same outlet. Service quality can further vary from week to week, day to day, or even hour to hour. And because quality is a subjective phenomenon, it can also vary from customer to customer, and for the same customer from one visit to the next. As a result, standardization and service quality are very difficult to control. The lack of standardization, however, actually gives service firms one advantage: Services can be customized to match the specific needs of any customer. Such customized services are frequently very expensive for both the firm and its customers. This creates a dilemma: How does a service firm provide efficient, standardized service at an acceptable level of quality while simultaneously treating every customer as a unique person? This dilemma is especially prevalent in the health care industry today.

PRICE CONSIDERATIONS   Price is a key issue in the marketing mix for services because it can be used to connote quality in advance of the purchase experience (e.g., "I want better than an $8 haircut just before the big interview.") However, determining the costs of producing and delivering a service is complicated for service providers. Part of this complexity is that services often do not have well-defined units of measure. For example, what is the unit of measure for hairstyling? Is it time, hair length, type of style, or gender of the customer? Many female customers complain that they are charged more for a haircut than men, even when a man's hair is longer. This illustrates the challenge that service firms often face in justifying their prices to customers.

Customers often balk at the high prices of legal, accounting, or medical services because they have no way to evaluate the product's worth prior to purchase. This issue can be especially critical when customers emphasize price in selecting a service provider. Consider the pricing problems in the airline industry where many customers perceive all airlines as being about the same. Airline companies often resort to fare wars to ensure that they get their desired share of customers' business. Pricing tactics can also help a firm balance peak and off-peak demand times. Most service firms offer lower prices during off-peak demand times to encourage more customers to use the service (such as half-price movie matinees and off-season vacations).

PROMOTION CONSIDERATIONS   Because a service cannot be directly shown or displayed, the marketer faces the difficult task of explaining the service to customers. As a result, service advertising typically focuses on tangible cues that symbolize the service.[12] Insurance firms are good examples: Prudential's rock, Allstate's good hands, and Travelers' umbrella. Although these symbols have nothing to do with the service, they make it easier for customers to understand the intangible features and benefits associated with insurance.

Endorsements from other customers in the target market who have had a positive experience are often a key to successful promotion. In fact, in order to create a group of satisfied clients, the service provider must be able to generate positive word-of-mouth advertising. For example, some doctors provide such good service and generate so much good word-of-mouth that they actually have to turn clients away. Consistently bad service can cause the opposite effect to take place.

DISTRIBUTION CONSIDERATIONS   It is practically impossible to distribute services in the traditional sense because customers cannot take physical possession of a service. Distribution systems must be developed to provide service in a convenient manner (e.g., Enterprise Car Rental's pick-up and drop-off service), and in locations where they are expected to be found (e.g., shoe shine stands in airports and hotels). Service distribution often requires multiple outlets to increase customer convenience.

Another way to distribute a service is to separate production and consumption by creating a tangible representation of the service. A credit card, for example, is not a service, but rather a tangible representation of a line of credit service offered by a bank or other financial institution. Although the production and consumption of this service remain inseparable, the credit card increases convenience by giving the customer something tangible to possess. This also allows the firm to distribute its credit services through the mail.

If any one of these marketing mix elements is inappropriately designed or implemented, it can lead to the failure of the entire mix to reach developed goals and objectives. Many service providers have found that successful marketing mixes create and maintain client-based relationships, with satisfied customers who repeatedly use a service over time.[13] Some service providers, such as doctors, lawyers, accountants, and financial consultants/advisers, actually refer to their customers as clients. These service providers are successful only to the degree that they can develop a marketing mix that builds relationships with a group of clients who use their services on an ongoing basis.

Business-to-Business Markets

As with service marketing, business-to-business marketing does not totally depart from the issues regarding SBU or product marketing strategy discussed to this point, but it does raise some additional considerations that must be addressed for successful strategies to be developed and implemented. The foundation, however, remains the same. The marketing manager must determine target customers' needs, assess the extent to which those needs are being met with existing products from the firm and its competitors, and then determine the ways in which these needs and competitive offerings may be changing in the future.

UNIQUE CHARACTERISTICS OF BUSINESS-TO-BUSINESS MARKETS   Business-to-business marketing differs from consumer product marketing in at least four ways. These key differences relate to the nature of the decision-making unit, the role of hard and soft costs in making and evaluating purchase decisions, reciprocal buying relationships, and the dependence of the two parties on each other. As a general rule, these differences are more acute for firms attempting to build client relationships than for those businesses that practice transactional marketing. Traditional transactional marketing focuses on delivering largely standardized products to a sizable group of customers at the lowest price possible. Client-relationship building is longer term in nature and tends to focus more on overall goal attainment than simply getting the lowest possible price. At the present time, client-relationship building represents a growing, albeit still relatively small, portion of business-to-business marketing.

The first key difference relates to the role of the decision-making unit (DMU)—the individual or group responsible for making purchasing decisions. For consumer products, the DMU is fairly straightforward: The adult household head(s) tend(s) to make most major purchase decisions for the family, with input and assistance from children and other family members if applicable. In an organization, however, the DMU tends to be much more complex and difficult to identify, in part because it may include three distinct groups of people—economic buyers, technical buyers, and users—each of which may have its own agendas and unique needs and desires in the buying decision.

Any effort to build a relationship between the selling and buying organization must include economic buyers (senior managers with the overall responsibility of achieving the buying firm's objectives) in the DMU mix. In recent years, economic buyers have become increasingly important as major product purchase decisions based on value factors beyond price have moved up the organization chart. This has made economic buyers a greater target for promotional activities.

Technical buyers (buying firm personnel with the responsibility for procuring products to meet the needs of the firm on an ongoing basis) include purchasing agents and materials managers. They have the responsibility of delivering product solutions within budget and to narrow the number of product options that are presented to the economic buyer(s). They are critical for transactional marketing, and are important to the day-to-day maintenance for client-relationship building.

Users (managers and employees who have the responsibility of using a product purchased by the firm) comprise the last segment in the DMU. The user is often not the ultimate decision maker, but frequently is included in the decision process, particularly in the case of technologically advanced products. For example, a vice-president of information systems often has a major role in hardware and software purchase decisions.

The second key difference between business-to-business marketing and consumer product marketing relates to the significance of hard and soft costs. Consumers and organizations both consider hard costs, which include monetary price and related costs associated with the purchase, such as shipping and installation. Organizations, particularly those attempting to build client relationships, also consider soft costs, such as downtime, opportunity costs, and human resource costs associated with the compatibility of systems in the buying decision. Activity-based costing is a critical part of the process of building client relationships as hard and soft costs are identified, and total cost targets are set for all major purchase decisions.

The third key difference involves the existence of reciprocal buying relationships. With consumer purchases, the opportunity for buying and selling is usually a one-way street: The marketer sells and the consumer buys. Business-to-business marketing, however, is more often a two-way street, with each firm marketing products that the other firm buys. For example, a company may buy office supplies from another company that in turn buys copy machines from the first firm. In fact, such arrangements can be an upfront condition of purchase in transactional marketing. Reciprocal buying is less likely to occur under client-relationship building *unless* it helps both parties achieve their respective goals.

Finally, in business-to-business marketing, the buyer and seller are more likely to be dependent on one another, particularly in client relationships. For consumer-marketer relationships and transactional marketing, the level of dependence tends to be low. If a store is out of a product, or a marketing organization goes out of business, customers simply switch to another source to meet their needs. Likewise, the loss of a particular customer through competitive inroads, geographic relocation, or death is unfortunate for a company, but not itself particularly damaging.

This is not the case with client-relationship building where sole-source or limited-source buying may leave an organizational customer's operations severely distressed when a product provider shuts down or cannot deliver. The same is true for the loss of a customer. The selling firm has invested significantly in the client relationship, oftentimes modifying products and altering information systems and other systems central to the organization. Each client relationship represents a significant portion of the firm's profit, and the loss of a single customer can take months and even years to replace, if it can be done at all. After Rubbermaid and Wal-Mart experienced a rift in their relationship, the impact for both firms was significant. Rubbermaid was particularly affected as Wal-Mart used the situation, along with its significant resources and buying power, to build Sterilite, a small Massachusetts manufacturer, into a major competitor for Rubbermaid.[14]

MARKETING MIXES FOR BUSINESS-TO-BUSINESS MARKETS   Although our discussion above certainly involves generalizations (e.g., some consumer product marketers are much better at building close relationships than many business-to-business marketers), business-to-business marketing mixes do tend to have some key differences from consumer marketing mixes, particularly as a firm moves toward client-relationship building. Central to this switch for relationship-focused buyers and sellers is a shift from a *win-lose strategy*—the only way for one side to get more is for the other side to get less—to a *win-win strategy*—a focus more on growing the "size of the pie" where both sides win.

Authors Karl-Heinz Sebastian and Ralph Niederdrenk highlight some of the marketing mix changes that must take place to be consistent with a shift to client-relationship building:

- *Change in buyers' and sellers' roles*: Both buyers and sellers will need to move from competitive negotiators trying to drive prices up and down to true communications specialists. This represents a major change in all aspects of the promotion mix for the selling firm.

- *Single sourcing*: Supplying firms will continue to sell directly to large customers or move to selling through "systems suppliers" that put together a set of products from various suppliers to deliver a comprehensive solution to buyers.

- *Decision-making teams*: Although transactional marketers will continue to market their products primarily one-on-one (personal selling to a purchasing agent or user), client-relationship builders employing strategic purchasing will have teams on both sides of the table representing different perspectives and areas of expertise that are central to the success of both firms. Increasingly, senior management of both the buying and selling firm will be represented on these teams as economic buyers for both sides play a major role in assessing objective attainment.

- *Global sourcing*: Increasingly, both buyers and sellers will be scanning the globe in search of suppliers or buyers that represent the best match with their specific needs and requirements. The relationship-building process is costly and complex enough that only the best potential partners should be pursued.

- *Advanced earning power though productivity enhancement*: The focus must be to identify regularly any inefficiencies in the buying and selling relationship so that they can be removed. Only the most efficient channels of sellers and buyers will survive; thus all hard and soft cost inefficiencies must be identified and driven from the relationship.[15]

The fundamental changes in the structure of the buyer-seller relationship outlined above will dictate a close examination of, and likely many changes in, the way marketing and buying organizations work together. Only those firms willing to make strategic, as opposed to cosmetic, changes in the way they are set up to work with their customers/suppliers are likely to prosper as we move into the next century. Effective implementation of marketing strategies will become even more important, as we shall see in the next chapter.

Key Insights From Chapter 7

The criteria for selecting a marketing strategy:

- are focused toward identifying the marketing strategy that has the best strategic fit.
- are based on the notion that a good marketing strategy is one that is differentially advantageous, sustainable, timely, feasible, and affordable.

The product/market life cycle:

- consists of five stages (development, introduction, growth, maturity, decline), each having unique strategy options for achieving marketing and organizational objectives.
- should assist the manager in focusing on changes in the market, not the firm's products. Products have life cycles only because markets and customer needs change.

Value:

- works well as an integrating framework because it is a broad concept that takes into account all four marketing mix elements.
- is defined as a customer's subjective evaluation of benefits relative to costs to derive the worth of a firm's offering relative to the offerings of other firms. Value is subjective as it means different things to different people.
- can be broken down into customer benefits (product quality, customer service quality, and experience-based quality) and customer costs (monetary and non-monetary prices).
- can be increased by changing one or all of the marketing mix elements.

Marketing services:

- is similar to the marketing of goods, but includes additional issues that stem from differences between goods and services, including intangibility, inseparability, perishability, heterogeneity, client-based relationships, and customer contact.
- requires adjustments to the marketing mix to compensate for these differences.

Business-to-business marketing:

- is similar to consumer product marketing, but includes additional issues that stem from differences that relate to the nature of the decision-making unit, the role of hard and soft costs in making and evaluating purchase decisions, reciprocal buying relationships, and the dependence of the two parties on each other.
- requires adjustments to the marketing mix to compensate for these differences and to ensure that all parties benefit from the exchange, particularly in client-relationship building.

CHAPTER 8

Marketing Implementation

Introduction

Historically, most organizations placed a tremendous emphasis on strategic planning. This emphasis occurred because managers believed that strategic planning, by itself, was the key to marketing success. This belief was and is based on the logical premise that before a company can determine where it is going, it must have a plan for getting there. Unfortunately, this emphasis on strategic planning comes at the expense of marketing implementation. Today, many firms are quite effective at devising strategic plans, but totally unprepared to cope with the realities of implementing those plans. Strategic planning without effective implementation can produce unintended and counterproductive consequences that result in high levels of customer dissatisfaction and feelings of frustration within the firm. In addition, ineffective implementation will likely result in the firm's failure to reach its organizational or marketing objectives.

In this chapter, we continue through the strategic market planning process by examining a number of important issues related to marketing implementation. First, we define implementation and discuss a number of issues associated with effectively implementing marketing strategies. Second, we discuss the major components of marketing implementation—all of which must work together effectively in order for implementation to be successful. Then we examine the relative advantages and disadvantages of four major approaches to marketing implementation. We next concentrate on the importance of people in the implementation of marketing activities. This discussion also describes how an internal marketing approach can be used to motivate employees to implement the marketing strategy. Finally, we look at the steps involved in creating a timetable for implementing marketing activities.

As we begin our examination of marketing implementation, keep in mind the "implementation axiom" that we introduced in Chapter 2: *Organizations do not implement strategies, people do!* Because a strategy cannot implement itself, organizations depend on employees to carry out all marketing activities. As a result, the organization must devise a plan for implementation just like it devises a plan for marketing strategy.

Marketing Implementation Defined

In Chapter 2, we defined marketing implementation as the process of executing the marketing strategy by creating specific actions that will ensure that the marketing objectives are achieved. Simply put, implementation refers to the "how" part of the marketing plan. Because marketing implementation is a very broad term, it is often used but frequently misunderstood.

Some of this misunderstanding may stem from the fact that marketing strategies almost always turn out differently than anticipated because of the difference between intended marketing strategy and realized marketing strategy.[1] Intended marketing strategy is what the organization wants to happen; it is the organization's planned strategic choice. The realized marketing strategy, on the other hand, is the strategy that actually takes place. More often than not, the difference between the intended and realized strategy is the result of the way the intended marketing strategy is implemented. This is not to say that an organization's realized marketing strategy is necessarily better or worse than the intended marketing strategy, just that it is different in some way. Such differences are often the result of internal and external environmental factors that change during implementation. As a result, when it comes to marketing implementation, Murphy's Law usually applies: If anything can possibly go wrong, it will. This serves as a warning to all managers that the implementation of the marketing strategy should not be taken lightly.

Issues In Marketing Implementation

Marketing implementation is critical to the overall success of any organization because it is responsible for putting the marketing strategy into action. Unfortunately, many organizations repeatedly experience failures in marketing implementation. We often encounter examples of these failures in our daily lives—out-of-stock items at the local supermarket, overly aggressive salespeople at automobile dealerships, long checkout lines at the local department store, and unfriendly or inattentive employees at a hotel. Such examples illustrate that even the best planned marketing strategies are a waste of time without effective implementation to ensure their success. In short, a good marketing plan combined with bad marketing implementation is a guaranteed recipe for disaster.

One of the most interesting aspects of marketing implementation is its relationship to the strategic planning process. Many managers assume that planning and implementation are interdependent, but separate issues. In reality, planning and implementation are intertwined within the marketing planning process. Many of the problems of marketing implementation occur because of this relationship to strategic planning. Let's look at three of the most common issues.

Planning and Implementation Are Interdependent Processes

Many marketing managers assume that the planning and implementation process is a one-way street. That is, strategic planning comes first, followed by marketing implementation. Although it is true that the content of the marketing plan determines how it will be implemented, it is also true that how a marketing strategy is to be implemented determines the content of the marketing plan. This two-way relationship between marketing strategy and marketing implementation is depicted in Exhibit 8.1.

| EXHIBIT 8.1 | Two-Way Relationship Between Strategy and Implementation |

Marketing Strategy

Organizational
Resources,
Policies,
and
Processes

Marketing Implementation

Source: Adapted from Frank V. Cespedes, *Organizing and Implementing the Marketing Effort* (Reading, MA: Addison-Wesley, 1991), 18.

Certain marketing strategies will dictate some parts of their implementation. For example, a company such as Southwest Airlines with a strategy of improving customer service levels may turn to employee training programs as an important part of that strategy's implementation. Through profit sharing, many Southwest Airlines employees are also stockholders with a vested interest in the firm's success. Employee training and profit-sharing programs are commonly used in many companies to improve customer service. However, employee training, as a tool of implementation, can also dictate the content of the company's strategy. A Southwest Airlines competitor, in the process of implementing its customer service program, may realize that it does not possess adequate resources to carry out extensive employee training. Perhaps the company lacks the financial resources for a profit-sharing program and does not employ, or cannot cost effectively acquire, a staff that is qualified to perform the training. As a result, the company must go back to the planning stage to adjust its customer service strategy. These continual changes in marketing strategy make implementation more difficult. Clearly a SWOT analysis conducted with an eye toward what the company can reasonably implement can reduce, but not completely eliminate, this problem.

Planning and Implementation Are Constantly Evolving

The reality of marketing is that critically important environmental factors are constantly shifting. As customers change their wants and needs, as competitors devise new marketing strategies, and as the organization's own internal environment changes, the firm must constantly adapt. In some cases, these changes occur so fast that once the organization decides on a marketing strategy, it is already out of date. Because of the interrelationship between marketing strategy and marketing implementation, both must constantly change. The process is never static because environmental changes require changes in strategy, which require changes in implementation, which require changes in strategy, and so on.

A related issue is that managers often assume there is one correct way to implement a given strategy. This is simply not true. Just as strategy often results from trial and error, so does marketing implementation. The fact that marketing is customer-driven requires that the organization be flexible enough to alter its implementation to counter changes in its customers' preferences or the competitive environment. The airline industry provides a good example. Regardless of any one company's marketing strategy, all airlines quickly alter their pricing strategy when a competitor announces a fare reduction. Such rapid changes require that the organization be flexible in its marketing strategy and its implementation.

Planning and Implementation Are Separated

The ineffective implementation of marketing strategy is often a self-generated problem stemming from the planning process itself. Although strategic planning is carried out by top managers, the responsibility for implementing marketing plans falls on lower-level managers and frontline employees. This separation of planning and implementation is depicted in Exhibit 8.2. Top managers often fall into a trap of believing that a good marketing strategy will implement itself. Because these top managers are separated from the "front line" of the organization, they often do not understand the unique problems associated with implementing marketing strategies. Conversely, those employees who do understand the problems of marketing implementation usually have no voice in developing the marketing plan.

Another trap that top managers often fall into is believing that lower-level managers and frontline employees will be excited about the marketing strategy and motivated to implement it. However, because they are separated from the planning process, these managers and employees often fail to identify with the organization's goals and objectives or to understand the marketing strategy.[2] It is unrealistic for top managers to expect lower-level managers and employees to be enthused about or committed to a strategy they had no voice in developing, or to a strategy that they do not understand or feel is inappropriate.[3]

The Components of Marketing Implementation

Marketing implementation involves a number of interrelated components and activities. Exhibit 8.3 shows the components that must work together for strategy to be implemented effectively. Because we examined marketing strategy in Chapters 6 and 7, we now look briefly at the remaining components.

| EXHIBIT 8.2 | Separation of Planning and Implementation |

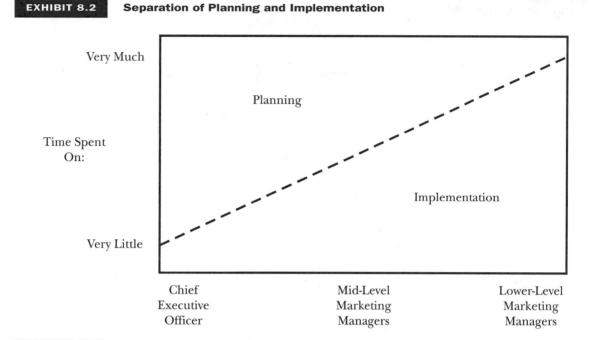

Ferrell, O.C., George H. Lucas, Jr., David Luck, *Strategic Marketing and Management: Text and Cases* (Southwestern, 1994).

Shared Goals and Values

Shared goals and values among all employees within the organization are the "glue" of successful marketing implementation because they bind the entire organization together as a single, functioning unit. When the firm's goals and values are shared by all employees, all actions will be aligned and directed toward the betterment of the organization. Without a common direction to hold the organization together, different areas of the company may work toward different outcomes, thus limiting the success of the entire organization.

Institutionalizing shared goals and values within a firm's culture is a long-term process. The primary means of creating shared goals and values is through employee training and socialization programs.[4] Although creating shared goals and values is a difficult process, the rewards are worth the effort. Some have argued that creating shared goals and values is the most important part of marketing implementation because it stimulates organizational commitment where employees become more motivated to implement the marketing strategy and meet customer needs.[5]

Marketing Structure

Marketing structure refers to how an organization's marketing activities are organized. The organization's marketing structure establishes formal lines of authority (i.e., who reports to whom), as well as the division of labor within the marketing function.

One of the most important decisions that managers must make is how to divide and integrate marketing responsibilities. This question typically comes down to the centralization versus decentralization issue. In a centralized marketing structure,

| EXHIBIT 8.3 | **Components of Marketing Implementation** |

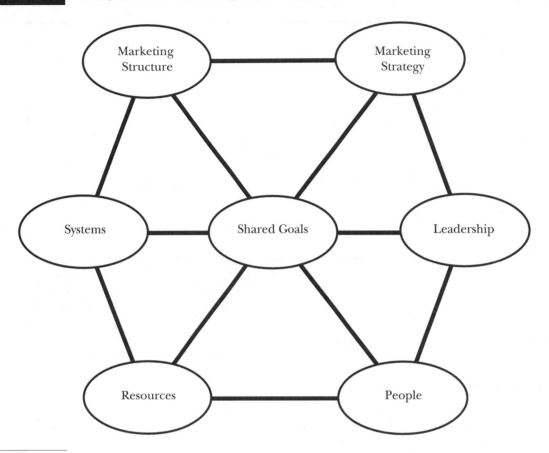

Source: Adapted from Lawrence R. Jaunch and William F. Glueck, *Strategic Management and Business Policy,* 3rd ed. (New York: McGraw-Hill, 1988), 305.

all marketing activities and decisions are coordinated and managed from the top of the marketing hierarchy. Conversely, in a decentralized marketing structure, marketing activities and decisions are coordinated and managed from the front line of the organization. Typically, decentralization means that frontline marketing managers are given the responsibility of making day-to-day marketing decisions.

Both marketing structures have advantages. Centralized structures are very cost-efficient and effective in ensuring standardization within the marketing program. These advantages can be particularly critical to organizations whose competitiveness depends upon maintaining a tight control over costs and programs.[6] For example, companies employing a strategy of operational excellence, such as Wal-Mart and Southwest Airlines, may find a centralized structure beneficial for ensuring operational efficiency and consistency. Decentralized marketing structures have the important advantage of placing marketing decisions close to the front line where customer needs are the priority. By decentralizing marketing decisions, frontline managers can be creative and flexible, allowing them to adapt to changing market conditions.[7] For this reason, companies employing a strategy of customer intimacy, such as Airborne Express and Nordstrom's, may decentralize to ensure that they can respond to customers' needs. In many cases, the decision to centralize or decentralize marketing activities is a trade-off between reduced costs and enhanced flexibility. However, there is no one correct way to organize the marketing function. The right structure will depend on the specific organization, the nature of its internal and external environments, and its chosen marketing strategy.

Systems and Processes

Organizational systems and processes are collections of work activities that take in a variety of inputs to create information and communication outputs that ensure the consistent day-to-day operation of the organization.[8] Examples include information systems, strategic planning, capital budgeting, purchasing, order fulfillment, manufacturing, quality control, and performance measurement. Although all systems are important, the marketing information system (MIS) is a critical part of the planning and implementation process. By providing a continuous flow of information, the MIS can assist in the analysis of the internal and external environments before marketing strategies are developed. The MIS is also used during implementation to assist in the evaluation and control of all marketing activities.

Resources

An organization's resources can include a wide variety of assets that can be brought together during marketing implementation. These assets may be tangible or intangible. Tangible resources include financial resources, manufacturing capacity, facilities, and equipment. Though not quite as obvious, intangible resources such as marketing expertise, customer loyalty, and external relationships/strategic alliances are equally important.

Regardless of the type of resource, the amount of resources available can make or break a marketing plan. However, a critical and honest evaluation of available resources during the environmental and SWOT analyses can help ensure that the marketing strategy and marketing implementation are within the realm of possibility. Once the marketing plan is completed, the planner must seek the approval of needed resources from top management. It is important to remember that resources will be allocated for the marketing plan based on its ability to help the organization reach its goals and objectives.

People

By "people," we obviously mean the human side of marketing implementation. In fact, people are considered by many to be the "5th P" of marketing. The implementation of any marketing strategy is extremely dependent on the quality, diversity, and skill of the firm's work force. The people component also includes employee selection and training, reward policies, employee motivation, commitment, and morale. Because employees are critical to successful marketing implementation, we will discuss the people component in detail later in this chapter.

Leadership

The leadership provided by an organization's management and the behaviors of employees go hand in hand in the implementation process. As the art of managing people, leadership includes how managers communicate with employees, as well as how they motivate their people to implement a marketing strategy. Leaders are responsible for establishing the corporate culture necessary for implementation success.[9] A good deal of research has shown that marketing implementation is more successful when leaders create an organizational culture characterized by open communication between employees and managers. In this way, employees are free to discuss their opinions and ideas about implementation tasks. This type of leadership also creates a climate where managers and employees have full confidence and trust in each other.

One of the most important tasks leaders perform is to motivate their employees to give their best effort. Being a good motivator is not an easy task because employee motivation consists of many factors. The key is to understand each employee's personal characteristics and adapt leadership tasks appropriately. For example, leaders must recognize that some employees are smarter and work harder than others.[10] These differences can stem from innate ability but are more often the result of employee selection and training practices. Leaders must also recognize that different employees are motivated by different factors. Some employees want financial gain, some want important titles and large offices, and others are simply rewarded by doing a good job. The same employee may be motivated by a different factor at different points in time. Thus, treating employees as if they were all the same will often create a situation where employees are not motivated to do their best.

A final trait that all leaders possess is a leadership style, or way of approaching a given task. Because a manager's leadership style is important to implementation success, we will devote the next section to a discussion of several approaches that managers can take in implementing marketing strategies.

Approaches to Marketing Implementation

Managers can use a variety of approaches in implementing marketing strategies and motivating employees to perform implementation tasks. In this section, we'll examine four of these approaches—the command approach, the change approach, the consensus approach, and the cultural approach.[11]

The Command Approach

With the command approach, marketing strategies are evaluated and selected at the top of the organization and forced downward to lower levels where frontline managers and employees are expected to implement them. The approach has two advantages: (1) It makes decision making easier, and (2) it reduces uncertainty as to what is to be done.

Unfortunately, the command approach suffers from several disadvantages. First, it does not consider the feasibility of implementing the marketing strategy. The only consideration in the command approach is that top managers have the power to force the implementation of the strategy. Second, the approach divides the organization into *strategists* and *implementers,* with no consideration for how strategy and implementation affect each other. Those developing the strategy are often far removed from the targeted customers it is intended to attract. Third, the command approach often creates employee motivation problems. Many employees are not motivated to implement strategies in which they have little confidence. This can create problems in the implementation of the chosen strategy.

McDonald's came to appreciate the limitations of the command approach when it tried to force franchisees to implement its "Campaign 55" promotion. The promotion offered discounted prices on select sandwiches when customers purchased fries and a drink. However, the company's franchisees balked at the plan when they lost money because customers bought only small fries and drinks to get the discounts. The original "Campaign 55" strategy also included a 55–second service guarantee, or customers would get their food for free. Franchisees flatly refused to implement the guarantee. In total, "Campaign 55" lasted less than 55 days.[12]

The experience of McDonald's illustrates how a marketing strategy can fail when those responsible for its implementation do not believe in it. However, the command approach can be a viable method of marketing implementation under the proper conditions. The command approach tends to work best when the organization is headed by a powerful leader, the strategy is simple to implement, and the strategy poses few threats to employees. Faced with the difficulty of meeting these criteria in today's business environment, few companies practice the command approach.

The Change Approach

The change approach is similar to the command approach except that it focuses explicitly on implementation. The basic premise of the change approach is to modify the organization in ways that will ensure the successful implementation of the chosen marketing strategy. For example, the organization's structure can be altered; employees can be transferred, hired, or fired; new technology can be adopted; the employee compensation plan can be changed; or the organization can merge with another firm.

Because many top managers are reluctant to give up control over the organization, the change approach is used quite often in business today, sometimes with great success. For example, when Lee Iacocca purchased AMC and Jeep/Eagle as a part of the long, slow process of rebuilding the Chrysler Corporation, he was applying the change approach. Today, Chrysler's products are winning industry awards as well as the loyalty of many car buyers. A more recent example of the change approach is GM's move to a brand management marketing structure. Faced with a continuing loss of market share, GM shifted to brand management to be more responsive to customer tastes and better differentiate between the products in its own divisions. The new structure is designed to focus each division and brand on its own target customers.[13] Time will tell whether GM's use of the change approach leads to success as it did in the case of Chrysler.

As opposed to the command approach, the manager taking the change approach toward implementation is more of an architect and politician, skillfully crafting the organization to fit the requirements of the chosen marketing strategy. However, the change approach still suffers from the separation of planning and implementation. By clinging to this "power-at-the-top" mentality, employee motivation often remains an issue. Likewise, the changes called for in this approach often take a great deal of time to design and implement. This can create a situation where the organization becomes frozen while waiting on the chosen strategy to take hold. As a result, the organization becomes vulnerable to changes in the marketing environment.

The Consensus Approach

In the consensus approach, top managers and lower-level managers work together to evaluate and develop marketing strategies. The underlying premise of this approach is that managers from different areas and levels of the organization come together as a team to "brainstorm" and develop the marketing strategy. Each participant has different opinions as well as different perceptions of the marketing environment. The role of the top manager is that of a coordinator, pulling different opinions together to ensure that the best overall marketing strategy is created. Through this collective decision-making process, a marketing strategy is agreed upon and a consensus is reached as to the overall direction of the organization.

Thermos, for example, was able to achieve an impressive market share in the outdoor grill market through the use of the consensus approach. Thermos is organized into market-based interdisciplinary teams, which bring together people from different functional areas to focus on a specific product or market. The "Lifestyle" team was given the task of developing a new product for the outdoor grill market. The leadership of the team rotated depending on which aspect of the project—design, development, manufacturing, marketing—was most important at any given time. The outdoor electric grill that the team developed won industry awards and a large share of the market. Because they "owned" the project from beginning to end, team members reported an overwhelming sense of pride and accomplishment.[14]

The consensus approach is more advantageous than the first two approaches in that it moves some of the decision-making authority closer to the front lines. Lower-level managers who participate in the strategy-formulation process have a unique perspective on the marketing activities necessary to implement the strategy. These managers are also more sensitive to the needs and wants of the organization's target market customers. In addition, because they are involved with developing the marketing strategy, these lower-level managers are often much more committed to the strategy and more motivated to see that it is implemented properly. This is the approach Japanese managers have historically used to enter international markets successfully.

However, like the first two approaches, the consensus approach often retains the barrier between strategists and implementers. This occurs because top managers are unwilling to give up their centralized decision-making authority. The end result of this barrier is that the full potential of the organization's human resources is not realized. Thus, for the consensus approach to be truly effective, managers at all levels within the organization must communicate openly about strategy on a daily basis, not just during formal strategy development sessions. The consensus approach tends to work best in complex, uncertain, and highly unstable environments. The collective strategy-making approach works well in this environment because it brings multiple viewpoints to the table.

The Cultural Approach

The cultural approach carries the participative style of the consensus approach to the lower levels of the organization. Its basic premise is that marketing strategy is a part of the overall organizational vision. Thus, the goal of top managers using this approach is to shape the organization's culture in such a way that all employees—top managers to janitors—participate in making decisions that help the organization reach its objectives. As a result, the cultural approach breaks down the barrier between strategists and implementers so that all employees work toward a single purpose.

With a strong organizational culture and an overriding corporate vision, the task of implementing marketing strategy is about 90 percent complete.[15] Employees are allowed to design their own work procedures, as long as they are consistent with the organizational mission, goals, and objectives. This extreme form of decentralization is often called *empowerment*. Empowering employees means allowing them to make decisions on how to perform their jobs.[16] The strong organizational culture and a shared corporate vision ensures that empowered employees make the right decisions.

We should add a cautionary note on the use of empowerment. Although the concept is oft touted as the panacea for many marketing problems, empowering employees can have some added costs and negative consequences for marketing activities. First, the firm must spend more money on employee selection and training to ensure that empowered employees are capable of performing their expanded jobs. Until they learn their jobs correctly, empowered employees may actually slow down or disrupt many customer service activities. Second, empowered employees have to work harder due to their added decision-making authority. Simply having this extra responsibility can cause some employees to become dissatisfied. Third, empowered employees sometimes suffer from excessive job ambiguity, especially if they have not been trained properly. This ambiguity can be a real detriment to the successful implementation of marketing activities. Finally, empowered employees will be more prone to make mistakes. As a result, the organization should expect some bad decisions and giveaways that could adversely affect the bottom line.[17]

The prime example of the cultural approach in action is FedEx. At the heart of the FedEx culture is its "People, Service, Profits" philosophy. Because people are the most important business of the company, all FedEx employees know that their opinions and jobs actually matter. The company's supportive culture where employees feel important is responsible for FedEx's remarkable levels of efficiency and effectiveness: 99.9 percent of all packages and letters are delivered on time. CEO Fred Smith has reported that he spends a full 25 percent of his time on personnel issues, ranging from employee recognition programs to responding to employee suggestions and complaints.[18]

Obviously, creating a culture like FedEx's does not happen overnight. However, a strong culture that simultaneously frees and controls employees is absolutely necessary before employees can be empowered to make decisions. Employees must be trained and socialized to accept the organization's mission and to become a part of the organization's culture. The use of the cultural approach in an organization that has never used it before can be especially troublesome. Despite the enormous amount of time involved in developing and using the cultural approach, its rewards of enhanced implementation and increased employee commitment are often well worth the investment.

To summarize, managers can use any one of these four approaches for implementing marketing strategy. They all have advantages and disadvantages as shown in Exhibit 8.4. The choice of any approach will depend heavily on the organization's resources, its current culture, and the manager's personal preference. Many managers today are unwilling to give up total control over marketing decision making. For these managers, the cultural approach may be out of the question.

EXHIBIT 8.4   **Advantages and Disadvantages of the Four Implementation Approaches**

Command Approach

Basic Premise: Marketing strategies are evaluated and selected at the top of the organizational hierarchy and forced downward to lower levels where frontline managers and employees are expected to implement them.

Advantages: Makes decision making easier.
Reduces uncertainty.
Good when the organization is headed by a powerful leader.
Good when the strategy is simple to implement.

Disadvantages: Does not consider the feasibility of implementing the strategy.
Divides the organization into strategists and implementers.
Does not consider how strategy and implementation affect each other.
Can create employee motivation problems.

Change Approach

Basic Premise: The organization is modified (changed) in ways that will ensure the successful implementation of the chosen marketing strategy.

Advantages: Specifically considers how the strategy will be implemented.
Considers how strategy and implementation affect each other.
Used successfully by a large number of U.S. businesses.

Disadvantages: Clings to a "power-at-the-top" mentality.
Requires a skilled leader who can be both an architect and a politician.
Changes often take a great deal of time to design and implement.
Organization can become frozen while waiting on the chosen strategy to take hold.
The time required for changes to occur can make the organization vulnerable to changes in the marketing environment.

Consensus Approach

Basic Premise: Managers from different areas of the organization come together to "brainstorm" and develop the marketing strategy. Through this collective decision-making process, a marketing strategy is agreed upon and a consensus is reached as to the overall direction of the organization.

Advantages: Incorporates multiple opinions and viewpoints into the marketing strategy.
Leader coordinates by pulling different opinions together.
Organizationwide commitment to the strategy makes implementation easier.
Top-level and lower-level managers work together, thus moving some of the decision making closer to the front lines of the organization.
Good in complex, uncertain, and highly unstable environments.

Disadvantages: Top managers are often unwilling to give up their decision-making authority.
Can lead to groupthink.
Process of strategy development and implementation is very slow.
Requires ongoing, open communication between all levels of the organization.

Cultural Approach

Basic Premise: Marketing strategy is a part of the overall organizational vision. The goal of top managers using this approach is to shape the organization's culture in such a way that all employees participate in making decisions that help the organization reach its objectives.

Advantages: Completely breaks down the barrier between strategists and implementers.
Committed employees who work toward a single organizational goal.
Participative style leads to an overriding corporate vision.
If done correctly, makes implementation very easy to accomplish.
Allows for the empowerment of employees.

Disadvantages: Must spend more money on employee selection and training.
Creating the needed culture is a painful, time-consuming process.
Quickly changing to this approach from another approach causes many problems.

Regardless of the approach taken, one of the most important issues that a manager must face is how to deal with the people who are responsible for implementing marketing strategy. Let's now take a closer look at the "people part" of marketing implementation.

People: The Human Side of Marketing Implementation

The quality, diversity, and skill of an organization's work force are all important considerations in implementing marketing strategy. Consequently, human resource issues are becoming more important to the marketing function, especially in the areas of employee selection and training, evaluation and compensation policies, and employee motivation, satisfaction, and commitment. In fact, the marketing departments of many organizations have taken over the human resources function to ensure that employees are correctly matched to required marketing activities.[19]

Employee Selection and Training

One of the most critical aspects of marketing implementation is matching employees' skills and abilities to the marketing tasks to be performed.[20] The first step in this process is employee recruitment and selection. It is no secret that some people are better at some jobs than others. All of us know individuals who are born salespeople. Some individuals are better at working with people while others are better at working with tools or computers. The key is to match these employee skills to marketing tasks. Corporate downsizing and tight job markets in recent years have forced companies to become more demanding in finding the right employee skills to match their required marketing activities.

One of the best ways to ensure a match of skills to activities is to select individuals with raw abilities and train them to perform certain tasks. Through training and socialization programs, employees learn to understand what is expected of them in implementing a marketing strategy.[21] Most marketing training programs emphasize product or customer knowledge, selling skills, and/or customer service. Other employees may be trained on less people-intensive marketing skills such as inventory control, warehousing, or distribution. The important point is that all marketing tasks are important to implementation success. Managers must select and train employees to perform these tasks effectively. Unfortunately, this is not always the case. A recent study of training practices in U.S. companies found that 59 percent of employees do not receive any type of formal training. Of those that do receive training, only 7.3 percent receive training in sales or customer service activities. Further, these employees receive an average of only 3.2 hours in formal sales or customer service training.[22] This lack of customer service training is particularly troubling for organizations that seek to implement a marketing strategy based on customer intimacy.

An increasingly important aspect of selection and training practices is the management of employee diversity, whether it be ethnic or generational. As the U.S. population becomes more ethnically diverse, many companies are taking steps to ensure that the diversity of their employees matches the diversity of their customer groups. Xerox, for example, recruits and manages a very diverse work force: of its 47,000 employees, 32 percent are women and 26 percent are minorities. Plus, about one-fourth of the company's corporate officers are women and minorities.[23] A common form of diversity faced by most organizations is generational diversity. Although most middle and upper managers come from the baby-boomer ranks (born 1946–1964), most entry-level positions are filled by members of Generation X (born 1965–1976) or Generation Y (born after 1976).[24] In many cases, these younger employees are better trained, more technologically sophisticated, and less politically minded than their baby-boomer bosses. These differences, combined with limited economic and career prospects for many Generation X employees, can create a great deal of tension in the workplace.[25] Managers must recognize these issues and adapt selection and training practices accordingly.

Employee Evaluation and Compensation Policies

Employee evaluation and compensation are also important to successful marketing implementation. Although employee compensation is a highly visible part of managing the human side of marketing, it is not always the most important. Many individuals are rewarded simply by doing a job well. Others are interested only in financial gains. The key is to balance these differing perceptions and develop an evaluation and compensation program that ties employee rewards to performance levels on required marketing activities.

One of the most recent debates in employee evaluation and compensation is outcome- versus behavior-based control systems.[26] Outcome-based control evaluates and compensates employees based on measurable, quantitative standards, such as sales volume or gross margin levels. This type of system is fairly easy to use, requires less supervision, works well when market demand is fairly constant, the selling cycle is relatively short, and all efforts directly affect sales or profits. However, outcome-based control is not tied directly to customer satisfaction levels and may penalize employees for factors beyond their control (e.g., a recession). Conversely, behavior-based control evaluates and compensates employees based on subjective, qualitative standards such as effort, motivation, teamwork, and friendliness toward or problem solving with customers. This type of system is tied directly to customer satisfaction and does reward employees for factors they can control. However, behavior-based control is extremely difficult to administer because of its subjective nature. It requires a great deal of supervision and expanded data collection. As a result, it can be more costly to use.

The choice between outcome- and behavior-control depends on the type of company, type of product, type of market, and customer needs. For example, a manager that uses the cultural approach to implementation may have a difficult time using an outcome-based control system. Likewise, many service firms are discovering that behavior-based control systems better match the activities that are required in the employee/customer interface. In the end, the key is to match the employee evaluation and compensation system to the activities that employees must perform in order to implement the marketing strategy.

Employee Motivation, Satisfaction, and Commitment

Other important factors in the implementation of marketing strategy are the extent to which employees are motivated to implement a strategy, their overall feelings of job satisfaction, and the commitment they feel toward the organization and its goals. For example, one of the contributors to the highly successful implementation at FedEx is the motivation and commitment of the company's employees. These employees are so dedicated to FedEx that they are often said to have purple blood—one of the company's official colors.[27] Likewise, Home Depot employees wear orange aprons to indicate stock ownership in the company.

Although factors such as employee motivation, satisfaction, and commitment are critical to successful implementation, they are highly dependent on other components, especially training, the evaluation/compensation system, and leadership. Marketing structure and processes can also have an impact on employee behavior. The key is to recognize the importance of these factors to successful marketing implementation and to manage them accordingly.

The Expanding Role of Internal Marketing

As more companies come to appreciate the importance of people in the implementation process, they are becoming disenchanted with traditional approaches to marketing implementation. These forces for change have been caused by several factors: American businesses losing out to foreign competitors, high rates of employee turnover and its associated costs, and continuing problems in the implementation of marketing strategy. These problems have led many organizations to adopt alternative approaches to marketing implementation. One of these alternatives is internal marketing.

The Internal Marketing Approach

The concept of internal marketing comes primarily from service organizations where it was first practiced as a tactic for making all employees aware of the need for customer satisfaction.[28] Generally speaking, internal marketing refers to the managerial actions necessary to make all members of the organization understand and accept their respective roles in implementing marketing strategy. This means that *all* employees, from the chief executive officer to frontline marketing personnel, must realize how each individual job assists in implementing the marketing strategy.

Under the internal marketing approach, every employee has two sets of customers: external and internal. For department store managers, for example, the people who shop in the store are called external customers, while the employees who work in the store are the manager's internal customers. In order for implementation to be successful, the store manager must serve the needs of both customer groups. If the internal customers are not dealt with properly, then it is unlikely that the external customers will be completely satisfied.

This same pattern of internal and external customers is repeated throughout all levels of the organization. Even the CEO is responsible for serving the needs of his or her internal and external customers. Thus, unlike traditional approaches where the responsibility for implementation rests with lower levels of the organization, the internal marketing approach places this responsibility on all employees, regardless of organizational level. In the end, successful marketing implementation comes from an accumulation of individual actions where all employees are responsible for implementing the marketing strategy.

Wal-Mart founder Sam Walton was keenly aware of the importance of internal marketing. He visited Wal-Mart stores on a regular basis, talking with customers and employees about how he could better serve their needs. He felt so strongly about the importance of his associates (his term for store personnel), that he always allowed them the opportunity to voice their concerns about changes in marketing activities. He felt that if he took care of his associates, they would take care of Wal-Mart's customers.

The Internal Marketing Process

The process of internal marketing is straightforward and rests on many of the same principles used in external marketing. The overall internal marketing framework is presented in Exhibit 8.5. In this framework, internal marketing is seen as an output of and input to both marketing implementation and the external marketing program. That is, neither the marketing strategy nor its implementation can be designed without some consideration for the internal marketing program.

The product, price, distribution, and promotion elements of the internal marketing program are similar, yet different from the elements of the external marketing program. Internal products refer generally to marketing strategies that must be sold internally. More specifically, however, internal products refer to those employee tasks, behaviors, attitudes, and values necessary to ensure implementation of the marketing strategy.[29] The implementation of any marketing strategy requires certain changes on the part of employees. They may have to work harder, change job assignments, or even change their attitudes and expand their abilities. The changes that employees must undergo in implementing the marketing strategy are called internal prices. Employees pay these prices through what they must do, change, or give up when implementing a new marketing strategy.

Internal distribution refers to how the marketing strategy is communicated internally. Planning sessions, workshops, formal reports, and personal conversations are all examples of internal distribution. Internal distribution also refers to employee training and education programs designed to assist in the transition to a new marketing strategy. Finally, all communication aimed at informing and persuading employees about the merits of the marketing strategy comprise internal promotion. Internal promotion can take the form of speeches, video presentations, audio tapes, and/or internal company newsletters. With the vast age disparity of today's employees, it is unlikely that any one medium will successfully communicate with all employees. Managers must realize that telling employees important information once in a single format is not communicating. Until they "get it," communication has not taken place.

Implementing an Internal Marketing Approach

Successfully using an internal marketing approach requires an integration of many factors already discussed in this chapter. First, the recruitment, selection, and training of employees must be considered an important component of marketing implementation, with marketing having input to the personnel function as necessary.[30] This ensures that employees will be matched to the marketing tasks to be performed. Second, top managers must be completely committed to the marketing strategy and overall marketing plan. It is naive to expect employees to be committed when top managers are not. Simply put, the best planned strategy in the world cannot successfully proceed if the employees responsible for its implementation do not believe in it and are not committed to it.[31]

EXHIBIT 8.5	Internal Marketing Framework

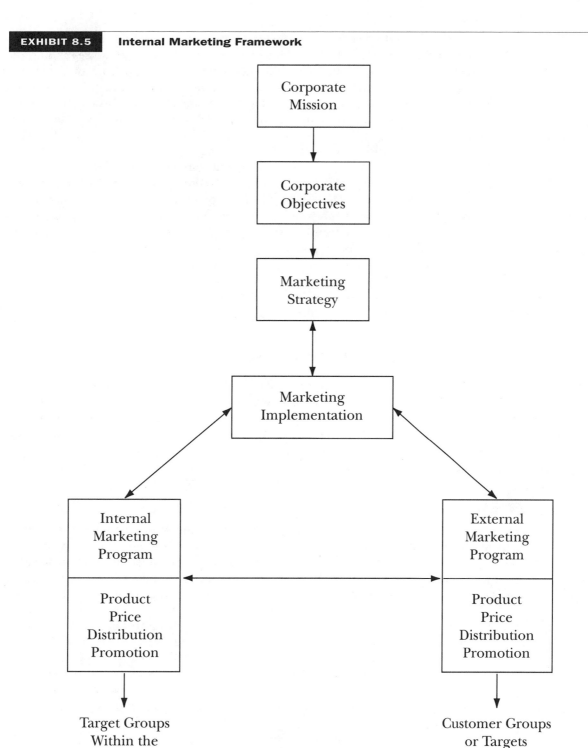

Source: Adapted from Nigel F. Piercy, *Market-Led Strategic Change* (Stoneham, MA: Butterworth-Heinemann, 1992), 371.

Third, employee compensation programs must be linked to the implementation of the marketing strategy. This generally means that employees should be rewarded on the basis of their behaviors rather than on their work outcomes.[32] In an organization guided by a strong culture and a shared marketing plan, outcome-based control systems may not adequately capture the effort put forth by employees. Fourth, the organization should be characterized by open communication among all employees, regardless of organizational level. Through open, interactive communication, employees come to understand the support and commitment of top managers, and how their jobs fit into the overall marketing implementation process.

Finally, organizational structures, policies, and processes should match the marketing strategy to ensure that the strategy is capable of being implemented. On some occasions, the organization's structure and policies constrain employees' ability to implement the marketing strategy effectively. Although eliminating these constraints may mean that employees should be empowered to creatively fine tune the marketing strategy or its implementation, empowerment should be used only if the organization's culture can support it. However, if used correctly as a part of the internal marketing approach, the organization can experience more motivated, satisfied, and committed employees as well as enhanced customer satisfaction and improved business performance.[33]

Implementing Marketing Activities

Through good planning and organizing, marketing managers provide purpose, direction, and structure for marketing activities. However, the manager must understand the problems associated with implementation, understand how the various components of implementation are coordinated, and select an overall approach to implementation before actually executing marketing activities. As we have stated before, people (employees) are ultimately responsible for implementing marketing activities. Therefore, the manager must be good at motivating, coordinating, and communicating with all marketing personnel. In addition, the manager must establish a timetable for the completion of each marketing activity.

Good communication is the key to motivating and coordinating marketing personnel. One of the most important types of communication flows upward from the frontline of the firm to management. Frontline employees interact daily with customers, putting them in a unique position to understand their perceptions, wants, and needs. By taking steps to encourage upward communication, managers gain access to a fertile source of information about customer requirements, how well products are selling, whether marketing activities are working, and the problems that occur during implementation.[34] Upward communication also allows management to understand the problems and needs of employees, an integral part of the internal marketing approach.

Successful implementation also requires that employees know the specific activities for which they are responsible and the timetable for completing each activity. Establishing an implementation timetable involves several steps:

1. Identifying the specific activities to be performed,
2. Determining the time required to complete each activity,
3. Separating the activities that must be performed in sequence from those that can be performed simultaneously,

4. Organizing the activities in the proper sequence, and

5. Assigning the responsibility for completing each activity to one or more employees, teams, or managers.

Although some activities must be performed before others, other activities can be performed simultaneously or later in the implementation process. This requires tight coordination between departments—marketing, production, advertising, sales, etc.—to ensure that all marketing activities are completed on schedule. Pinpointing those activities that can be performed simultaneously can greatly reduce the total amount of time needed to execute a given marketing strategy. Because scheduling is a complicated task, most organizations use sophisticated computer programs to plan the timing of marketing activities.

Key Insights from Chapter 8

Marketing implementation:

- is every bit as important as planning the marketing strategy.
- is the process of executing marketing strategies by creating specific actions that will ensure that marketing objectives are achieved.
- usually causes the difference between intended marketing strategy—what the organization wants to happen—and realized marketing strategy—the strategy that actually takes place.

Three issues in marketing implementation are:

- planning and implementation are interdependent.
- planning and implementation are constantly evolving.
- planning and implementation are separated.

The components of marketing implementation include:

- marketing strategy.
- shared goals and values.
- marketing structure.
- systems and processes.
- resources.
- people.
- leadership.

Four approaches to implementing marketing strategy:

- *Command approach*: evaluating and selecting marketing strategies at the top of the organization and forcing them downward to lower levels where frontline managers and employees are expected to implement them.
- *Change approach*: modifying the organization in ways that will ensure the successful implementation of the chosen marketing strategy.
- *Consensus approach*: top managers and lower-level managers working together to develop and evaluate a marketing strategy.

- *Cultural approach*: carrying the participative style of the consensus method to the lower level of the organization. The organization's culture guides the implementation of the marketing strategy.

The "people" component of marketing implementation includes:

- employee selection and training.
- evaluation and compensation policies.
- employee motivation, satisfaction, and commitment.

Internal marketing:

- refers to the managerial actions necessary to make all members of the organization understand and accept their respective roles in implementing marketing strategy.
- involves two sets of customers: external and internal. Every employee in the organization has these two sets of customers.

Implementing marketing activities:

- requires good communication to motivate and coordinate marketing personnel properly. Upward communication is especially important to implementation.
- requires that employees know the specific activities for which they are responsible and the timetable for completing each activity. The steps in this process are:

  1. Identify the specific activities to be performed,
  2. Determine the time required to complete each activity,
  3. Separate the activities that must be performed in sequence from those that can be performed simultaneously,
  4. Organize the activities in the proper sequence,
  5. Assign the responsibility for completing each activity to one or more employees, teams, or managers.

CHAPTER 9

Financial Assessment and Marketing Control

Introduction

Will the marketing plan or marketing strategy assist the firm in reaching its goals and objectives? This is a complex question for the marketing manager that, despite its difficulty, simply cannot be ignored. As we consider the tools related to assessing the financial impact of and controlling the marketing plan, you will see that we have come full circle. We have moved from analyzing the environment, to establishing goals and objectives, to developing and selecting specific marketing strategies, to marketing implementation. We are now ready to consider the extent to which the marketing strategies are likely to deliver the desired outcomes through the processes of evaluation and control.

In reality, budgetary considerations must play a role in the identification of alternative strategies as well as the evaluation and control of those strategies. Developing a marketing plan that ignores the financial realities of the organization is a waste of time and shows great naiveté on the part of the marketing manager. Even when funds are available for marketing activities, they are not assured. Top managers must be convinced that the marketing plan and strategy are a good value for the firm. Like external customers, these executives will determine value by assessing the relationship between benefits and costs. The ratio of the plan's cost compared to expected returns will be a critical deciding factor in determining which plans receive management approval and funding. This is true regardless of the size of the firm and the cost of the plan. In larger firms, the sophistication and depth of the assessment will be greater, but the same principles apply. Marketing managers must prepare and submit convincing proposals to compete successfully against the plans of other product or SBU managers, as well as managers from other functional areas, who are also seeking their share of a limited set of resources.

Performing a financial assessment of the marketing plan requires a working understanding of both finance and statistical analysis. It also involves basic concepts from microeconomics. Our discussion in this chapter will combine all of these areas using a hypothetical case for illustration. We begin our discussion by looking at the financial assessment process, including several tools that marketing managers can use to estimate the financial results of implementing specific marketing strategies. Later in the chapter, we will turn our attention to the evaluation and control (formal and informal) of marketing activities.

The Financial Assessment Process

Determining the potential financial impact of a marketing plan is a similar process at all levels of the organization. Our discussion and example here are oriented around the activities of a marketing manager for a single product/market combination. This approach allows for simplicity, because only one product and market are involved, and it is this first level of the organization where comprehensive financial analysis is likely to occur. Like other area managers, the marketing manager strives to develop a plan that will achieve goals and objectives set at higher levels of the organization. The question then becomes the same for managers at all levels of the firm: Does the proposed plan (or combination of plans) lead to the outcomes that must be generated within my unit?

To introduce our ongoing example for this chapter, let us assume that it is late 1998. Austin Wood is the marketing manager for a line of convection ovens sold by Zonko Electronic Products, Inc. (ZEP)—a firm that manufacturers and markets electronic appliances for household markets. Although ZEP's convection ovens have been quite successful, our manager, Austin, faces the challenge of determining how much sales volume must increase to provide the $1 million increase in gross margin sought by top management to meet organizational goals and objectives. Achieving this objective will be critical if Austin is to secure more marketing funds to expand promotional efforts to the extent called for in his marketing plan. We will now consider the tools Austin can use in his effort to justify the desired budget increase. These tools or techniques are contribution analysis, response analysis, and the systematic planning model.

Contribution Analysis

Contribution analysis attempts to determine the amount of output (revenues) that can be expected from a given set of inputs (costs). You are probably familiar with break-even analysis, a type of contribution analysis used to determine the amount of revenue necessary to cover both variable and fixed costs. In our example, Austin is seeking to demonstrate the ability of his marketing plan to increase gross margin. Gross margin is calculated by subtracting the cost of goods sold and all marketing costs from sales volume in dollars. Four different factors figure into this form of contribution analysis: expected sales in dollars, fixed costs, variable costs, and the gross margin objective. Fixed costs (such as rent, salaries, utilities) do not fluctuate with changes in volume, while variable costs (such as costs of product inputs, commissions, transportation charges) do. Austin's motive in using contribution analysis is to find the level of sales that would be required, given the costs that are within his control, to generate the desired increase in gross margin. The formula for this type of contribution analysis is:

$$\text{Required sales volume in units} = \frac{\text{Total fixed costs (\$) + Desired gross margin (\$)}}{\substack{\text{Gross margin contributed per unit} \\ \text{or} \\ \text{(Unit selling price} - \text{variable costs per unit)}}}$$

Austin has been able to collect the following information about the costs associated with producing convection ovens:

Selling price per unit	$200
Variable costs per unit	$110
Total fixed costs	$5,000,000
Gross margin target	$4,000,000

Using these numbers, the gross margin contribution per unit is $90 ($200 – $110). Substituting these numbers into the formula yields the following result:

$$\text{Required sales volume in units} = \frac{\$5,000,000 + \$4,000,000}{\$90} = 100,000 \text{ units}$$

At the present 100,000 unit sales level, total revenues are $20 million and total variable costs equal $11 million.

Austin is next interested in determining how changes in any one of these numbers will affect the results. For example, ZEP's top management has asked for a $1 million increase in gross margin. This changes Austin's gross margin target from the current $4 million to $5 million. The required sales volume increase can be estimated by substituting this larger gross margin figure into the equation, as follows:

$$\frac{\$5,000,000 + \$5,000,000}{\$90} = 111,111 \text{ units}$$

The size of the current convection oven market is approximately 500,000 units per year. ZEP holds a 20 percent share of this market, so Austin is presently selling 100,000 units, exactly what is required to meet the $4 million gross margin target. To increase this target by the required $1 million, Austin must find a way to sell 11,111 additional units per year, an 11.1 percent increase. This increase may be quite difficult to achieve because the total market for convection ovens is growing at only 4 percent per year. Thus, to achieve the required increase in sales, Austin must capitalize on overall industry growth and find ways to take market share away from his competitors.

Let's assume that in his search for options, Austin first considers a price cut to generate increased sales. If the price were reduced by $10 to $190 (a 5 percent drop), what would be the impact? Keeping other factors constant, gross margin per unit would fall to $80 ($190 – $110). Substituting the $80 figure into the denominator of our contribution analysis equation yields the following result:

$$\text{Required sales volume in units} = \frac{\$5,000,000 + \$5,000,000}{\$80} = 125,000 \text{ units}$$

Austin must now address the likelihood that a 5 percent price reduction will generate a 25 percent increase in unit sales volume. This issue is assessed by considering demand response through our second tool, response analysis.

Response Analysis

Accurate financial assessment depends on the marketing manager's ability to predict costs and revenues over the course of the planning period. A key aspect of this prediction centers around the question of how large a percentage change in sales can be anticipated when a variable in the marketing mix is altered. Response analysis is the category of tools used to address this question of incremental change. The goal of response analysis is to estimate accurate response coefficients that can be used to predict the change in sales volume based on a change in one or more elements of the marketing mix.

Let us first address the issue of price changes. Price and sales volume should vary inversely, with the exception of certain prestige products (which have upward sloping demand curves) or products with totally inelastic demand (the quantity sold is constant at all price levels). Thus, higher prices should result in a smaller number of units sold, and visa versa. A response coefficient of −2.0 means that if price falls 5 percent, as was the case in our example, sales would be expected to grow by twice that level, or 10 percent.

Most other marketing mix elements would be expected to have positive response coefficients, whereby increased spending would be expected to result in increased sales volume. Let us assume that Austin is considering an increase in advertising expenditures for the 1999 planning period. In 1998, $200,000 was budgeted for advertising, and Austin wants to analyze the impact of a 50 percent increase in this figure (to $300,000). The change in sales volume from such an increase in expenditures would be expected to be positive, but would it contribute to the objective of a $1 million increase in gross margin?

Estimating response coefficients can be a very difficult process. However, several sources of information are usually available. Historical relationships between advertising and sales volume for the convection oven market, or other similar markets, could be calculated. Trade association figures may also be used to estimate response coefficients. These figures are usually provided as averages for the items addressed. ZEP might also conduct primary research to better understand these relationships when no historical data is available. Such research usually involves manipulating advertising, pricing, or another element with the goal of determining the affect of these changes on sales volume. The use of multiple methods should increase the manager's confidence in the coefficients that are estimated.

For the sake of example, we will assume that Austin has evidence leading him to estimate a response coefficient of + 0.3 for the advertising in question. Based on this estimate, the proposed 50 percent increase in advertising expenditures would result in a sales volume increase of 15 percent (0.5 x 0.3), assuming that all other marketing mix elements remain unchanged from the previous period. This means that sales would increase from $20 million to $23 million.

Marketing managers should not attempt to utilize response coefficients without understanding the *implicit assumptions* associated with them. These assumptions are displayed graphically in Exhibit 9.1. The line from S to S_1 shows what Austin expects to happen as advertising expenditures rise from $200,000 to $300,000. The 15 percent increase in sales is associated with the single-year planning period. Although the primary interest in our example is the particular change in question, it is useful for the planner to have an understanding of how the response varies over a range of values. This issue is addressed by the line from S_1 to S_2. Above a certain point, increases in advertising expenditures have a decreasing marginal impact on sales volume. In Exhibit 9.1, expenses above the $300,000 level, while generating marginal increases in sales volume, may not be worth the effort, especially if competitors are well entrenched and spending large sums on their own advertising.

| EXHIBIT 9.1 | Sales Response to Advertising Expenditures |

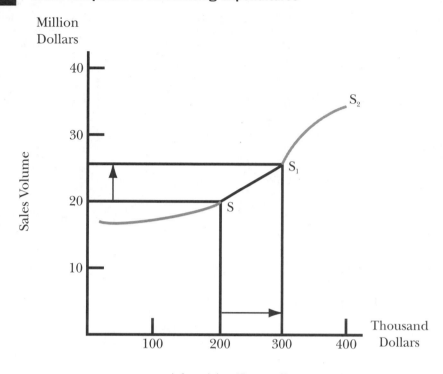

Advertising Expenditure

In practice, it would be rare if a marketing plan called for the modification of only a single marketing mix element. As multiple changes in planning elements are considered, response analysis becomes more sophisticated, using tools such as regression analysis to analyze the impact of multiple independent variables (marketing mix elements) on a single dependent variable (sales volume). The estimated response functions can be used to make predictions and to develop a hypothetical (pro forma) income statement for the marketing plan. For a comprehensive discussion of regression analysis, you should consult a multivariate statistics text.

Systematic Planning Models

Marketing managers often use a model that indicates the financial effects of marketing activities proposed in the marketing plan. The systematic planning model that we will use to map out the impacts of these decisions is outlined in Exhibit 9.2. This model has nine steps that collectively show the projected bottom-line impact of all aspects of the plan. We will examine each of these steps in this section.

Several essential predictions, representing the first three steps, are critical pieces of input for the model. First, *industry sales* for the product are required. This figure should be expressed in units, not dollars, because dollars are closely tied to the price variable. Industry sales in units can then be used to develop a forecast for the planning period. Second, the firm's *market share* is needed. This can be expressed as the number of units sold by the firm divided by the total units sold in the industry. This

EXHIBIT 9.2   **A Systematic Planning Model**

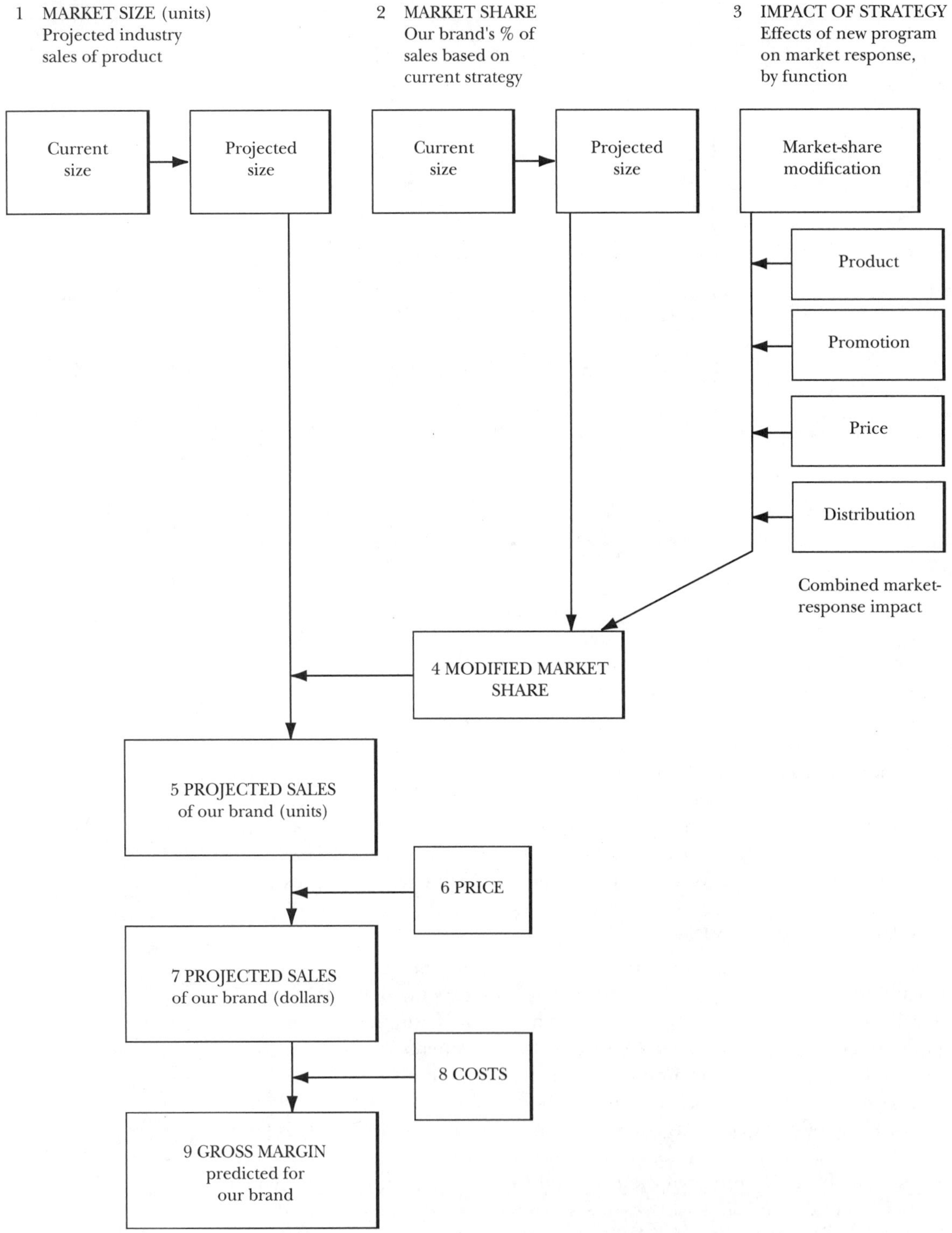

1   MARKET SIZE (units)
Projected industry
sales of product

2   MARKET SHARE
Our brand's % of
sales based on
current strategy

3   IMPACT OF STRATEGY
Effects of new program
on market response,
by function

| Current size | → | Projected size |

| Current size | → | Projected size |

| Market-share modification |

| Product |

| Promotion |

| Price |

| Distribution |

Combined market-
response impact

4 MODIFIED MARKET
SHARE

5 PROJECTED SALES
of our brand (units)

6 PRICE

7 PROJECTED SALES
of our brand (dollars)

8 COSTS

9 GROSS MARGIN
predicted for
our brand

figure is then used to forecast market share for the planning period. Because this forecast is the base level for the planning period, it should be calculated with the assumption that the present marketing strategy will be continued.

In step three, *response coefficients* are estimated for each element of the new marketing strategy. The estimation of these coefficients was discussed in the previous section. Calculating a group of coefficients for a strategy is more complex, as interactions between marketing mix elements may produce a combined effect that is different from each coefficient if estimated independently. Both the positive and negative effects for the various elements are combined into an aggregate rate of sales change for the new marketing mix. This is referred to as the *combined market response impact* at the bottom of step three.

In steps four through nine, the bottom line effects of the three input categories are calculated. In step four, *modified market share* is calculated by multiplying the projected share (step 2) by the combined market-response impact (step 3). The result indicates the relative merits of continuing the old strategy versus adopting the new one. In step five, modified market share is multiplied by the projected total market in units (step 1). The result is a *unit sales prediction* for the brand. Step six adds the unit's *sales price* to the process, as it is multiplied by the unit sales prediction to get *projected brand sales* in dollars (international operations would require the use of multiple currencies here).

In steps eight and nine, we move from sales to gross margin. In step eight, the cost of the new marketing mix is subtracted from projected brand sales volume. All costs, excluding those associated with administration and finance, are subtracted at this time. The result in step nine is the *gross margin* predicted for the brand under the new marketing strategy. Gross margin was chosen as the outcome in this case because it was the targeted improvement area for Austin's new marketing strategy. With slight modifications, the model could produce whatever outcome is being considered by top management.

Now, let's return to Austin's efforts to demonstrate the use of the model. Exhibit 9.3 provides an example of how valuable a tool the model can be for managers in the financial analysis phase. Hypothetical numbers have been inserted for each of the steps in Exhibit 9.2 to show how the model progresses toward the desired outcomes.

In step one, Austin takes the 500,000-unit sales level for convection ovens in 1998, and combines this amount with the current industry growth rate of 4 percent to get the projected industry sales figure of 520,000 units for 1999. Although ZEP's marketing plan for 1998 had yielded a 20 percent market share in convection ovens, Austin projects that a repeat of the same strategy would lead to a 10 percent decline in market share—down to 18 percent (step 2).

In step three, the effects of the proposed marketing plan on ZEP's market share are addressed. Austin is proposing a fresh look for the brand, as well as the addition of a warming feature that keeps food left in the oven at a constant temperature once the timer goes off. Austin has reason to believe that this change will represent the greatest product improvement in the industry. Thus, he expects a 6 percent share increase from changes in the product element (calculated using a 1.06 multiplier). The proposed advertising program has tested well, and with an increase in media expenditures of $50,000 ($200,000 to $250,000), Austin projects a 20 percent increase in share from changes in the promotion element (multiplier of 1.20).

EXHIBIT 9.3 Projected Financial Impact for Convection Oven Marketing Plan

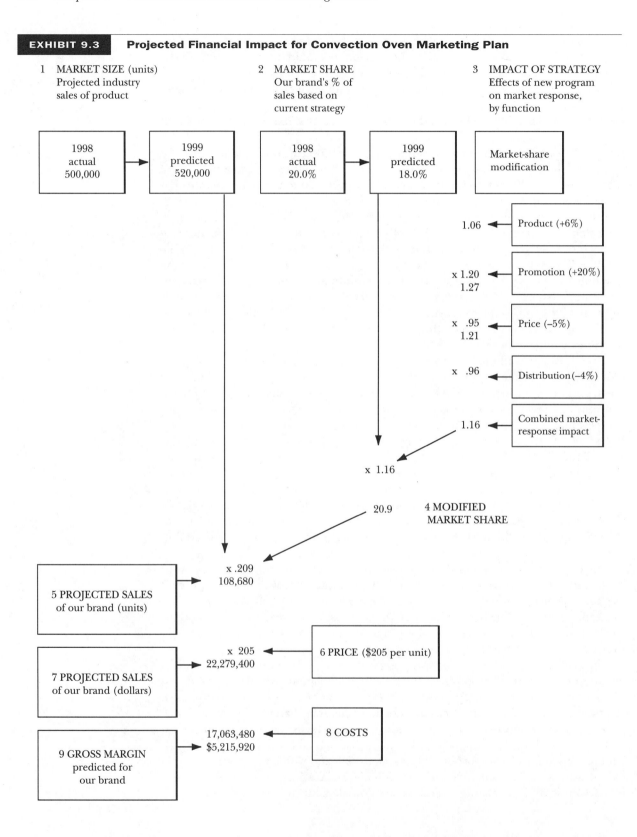

Not all elements of the new plan will have positive effects on the brand's market share. The termination of some discounting to dealers that is seen as excessive, as well as a slight price increase that will likely not be matched by major competitors, will hurt ZEP's share by an estimated 5 percent (multiplier of 0.95). In the distribution area, the elimination of some small, remote dealers, who were found to be unprofitable for ZEP to maintain, will also cut market share. Although these dealers presently represent 6 percent of the unit's volume, it is anticipated that ZEP will only lose 4 percent in market share as a result of dropping these dealers (multiplier of 0.96). Sequentially multiplying for each element (1.06 x 1.20 x 0.95 x 0.96) yields a combined market response impact of 1.16 for the new marketing strategy.

Austin uses the combined market response figure to calculate modified market share in step four. Taking the projected share for 1999 under the existing plan, and correcting it for the anticipated impact of the new marketing plan, yields a modified market share of 20.9 percent—a gain in share of just under 1 percent. In step five, modified market share is multiplied by the projected 520,000-unit industry sales for 1999 to arrive at ZEP's projected sales level of 108,680 units. As Austin proposes a selling price of $205 per unit, the resulting projected revenues for the new plan are $22,279,400 (step seven).

Now that revenues have been estimated, Austin must next consider costs in step eight. Working with the cost accounting department, Austin expects a $1 increase in unit variable costs ($110 to $111), while fixed costs are expected to remain the same. Based on these numbers, Austin arrives at a figure of just over $17 million to produce and market the 108,680 units:

$$(108,680 \times \$111) + \$5,000,000 = \$17,063,480$$

Costs are usually much easier to predict accurately than revenues because the firm has more control over its costs. In the final step, Austin gets to the bottom-line result of his proposed marketing plan: a gross margin of over $5.2 million for ZEP's line of convection ovens. Thus, based on the new marketing strategy, Austin expects to generate $1.2 million more in gross margin—a result that should please ZEP's top management.

The systematic model has allowed Austin to conduct a thorough assessment of the cost and revenue generation associated with his proposed marketing plan. The inclusion of a detailed model (like the one shown in Exhibit 9.3) will assist the marketing planner in convincing top management that all the implications of the proposed plan have been carefully considered. Management can clearly see the route that the planner has taken to arrive at the bottom-line impact of the proposed plan. This does not mean that management will not question the estimates utilized, but that the process will be clear and sound.

Evaluating and Controlling Marketing Activities

To this point in the chapter, we have dealt with assessing the financial impact of the proposed marketing plan. However, before the expected financial results can be realized, the plan must be implemented. The marketing plan can achieve its desired results only if it is implemented properly. *Properly* is the key word here. Remember from our discussion of marketing implementation (Chapter 8) that a firm's intended marketing strategy often differs from the realized strategy (the one that actually takes place). This also means that actual performance is often different from what the manager expected. Typically, there are three possible causes for this difference:

1. The marketing strategy was inappropriate or unrealistic.
2. The implementation was inappropriate for the strategy or was simply mismanaged.
3. The internal and/or external environments changed substantially between the development of the marketing strategy and its implementation.

To reduce the difference between what actually happened and what was expected, and to correct any of these three problems, marketing activities must be evaluated and controlled on an ongoing basis. Obviously, the best way to handle implementation problems is to recognize them in advance. However, no manager can successfully recognize all of the subtle and unpredictable warning signs of implementation failure.

The best way to prevent implementation problems is to have a system of marketing controls in place that allows the manager to spot potential problems before they cause real trouble. Exhibit 9.4 outlines a framework for marketing control. Marketing controls fall under two major types: formal controls and informal controls.[1] While the following discussion examines each type of marketing control separately, most organizations will use a combination of these control types at the same time.

Formal Marketing Controls

Formal marketing controls are mechanisms designed by the marketing manager to help ensure the implementation of the marketing plan. The elements of formal control are designed to influence the behaviors of employees before, during, and after the implementation of the marketing plan. These elements are referred to as input, process, and output control mechanisms.

INPUT CONTROL MECHANISMS   Any actions taken prior to the implementation of the marketing plan are referred to as input control mechanisms. The premise of input control is that the marketing plan cannot be implemented unless the proper tools are in place for it to succeed. Among the most important input control mechanisms are recruiting, selecting, and training employees. Most marketing strategies require that the right employees be matched to the job. These employees must then be trained on the best way to perform their jobs. For example, a marketing plan that focuses on increased customer service must also emphasize the selection and training of people-oriented employees. Other examples of input controls include resource allocation decisions (manpower and financial), capital outlays for needed facilities and equipment, or increased expenditures on research and development.

PROCESS CONTROL MECHANISMS   Process control mechanisms include activities that occur during the implementation of the marketing plan and that are designed to influence the behavior of employees so they will support the marketing plan and

EXHIBIT 9.4	Framework for Marketing Control

Formal Control Mechanisms — initiated by the marketing manager

Input control mechanisms – actions taken prior to implementation

    Employee recruitment and selection procedures

    Employee training programs

    Employee manpower allocations

    Financial resources

    Capital outlays

    Research and development expenditures

Process control mechanisms – actions taken during implementation

    Employee evaluation and compensation systems

    Employee authority and empowerment

    Internal communication programs

    Lines of authority/structure (organizational chart)

    Management commitment to the marketing plan

    Management commitment to employees

Output control mechanisms – evaluated after implementation

    Performance standards (e.g., sales, market share, product availability, recognition and recall of promotion, etc.)

    Marketing audits

Informal Control Mechanisms —unwritten controls initiated by employees

Employee self-control – individualized control

    Job satisfaction

    Organizational commitment

    Commitment to the marketing plan

Employee social control – small group control

    Shared organizational values

    Social and behavioral norms

Employee cultural control – culture of the entire organization

    Organizational culture

    Organizational stories, rituals, and legends

    Cultural change

its objectives. While the potential number of process controls is limitless and will vary from one organization to the next, there are examples of universal process controls that all organizations must use and manage well (see Exhibit 9.4).

One of the most important process control mechanisms is the system used to evaluate and compensate employees. In general, employees must be evaluated and compensated based on criteria that are relevant to the marketing plan.[2] For example, if a marketing plan requires that salespeople increase their efforts at customer service, they should be rewarded on the basis of this effort, not on other criteria such as sales volume or new accounts. Another important control issue is the amount of authority and empowerment that is granted to employees. While some degree of authority or empowerment can lead to increased performance, employees who are given too much authority often become confused and dissatisfied with their jobs.[3] Having good internal communication programs—another type of process control—can help to alleviate these problems.

The process control mechanism that stands out above all others is management commitment. Several research studies have confirmed that management commitment to the marketing plan is the single most important determinant of whether the plan will succeed or fail.[4] Management commitment is critical because employees learn to model the behavior of their managers. If management is committed to the marketing plan, it is more likely that employees will be as well. Commitment to the marketing plan also means that managers must be committed to employees.

OUTPUT CONTROL MECHANISMS   Output control mechanisms are designed to ensure that the outcomes of marketing activities are in line with anticipated results. The primary means of output control is the setting of performance standards against which actual performance can be compared. To ensure an accurate assessment of marketing activities, all performance standards should be based on the marketing objectives. Some performance standards are broad, such as those based on sales, profits, or costs. We say these are broad standards because many different marketing activities can affect them. Other performance standards are quite specific, such as many customer service standards (e.g., number of customer complaints, repair service within 24 hours, overnight delivery by 10:00 a.m.). In many (if not most) cases, how the firm performs relative to these specific standards will determine how well it performs relative to broader standards.

But how specific should performance standards be? Standards should reflect the uniqueness of the firm and its resources, as well as the critical activities needed to implement the marketing plan. In setting performance standards, it is important to remember that employees are always responsible for implementing marketing activities, and ultimately the marketing plan. For example, if an important part of increasing customer service requires that employees answer the telephone by the second ring, then a performance standard should be established in this area. Performance standards for marketing personnel are typically the most difficult to establish and enforce.

One of the best methods of evaluating whether performance standards have been achieved is to use a marketing audit to examine systematically the firm's marketing objectives, strategy, and performance.[5] The primary purpose of the marketing audit is to identify problems in ongoing marketing activities and to plan the necessary steps to correct those problems. A marketing audit can be long and elaborate or short and simple. A sample marketing audit is shown in Exhibit 9.5. This example is just that, only a sample. In practice, the elements of the audit should match the elements of the marketing strategy. The marketing audit should also be used in concert with the actual implementation of marketing activities—not just when problems arise.

Regardless of how the audit is organized, it should aid the marketing manager in evaluating marketing activities by:

1.   Describing current marketing activities and their results,
2.   Gathering information about changes in the external or internal environments that may affect ongoing marketing activities,

EXHIBIT 9.5   **A Sample Marketing Audit**

Identification of Marketing Activities
1. In what specific marketing activities is the company currently engaged?
   Product activities: research, concept testing, test marketing, quality control, etc.
   Customer service activities: repairs, maintenance, technical assistance, complaint handling, training, etc.
   Pricing activities: financing, billing, cost control, discounting, etc.
   Distribution activities: availability, channels used, customer convenience, etc.
   Promotion activities: media, sales promotion, personal selling, public relations, etc.
2. Are these activities conducted or provided solely by our company, or are some conducted or provided by outside contractors? If outside contractors are used, how are they performing? Should any of these outside activities be brought in-house?
3. What additional marketing activities do customers want, need, or expect?

Review of Standard Procedures for Each Marketing Activity
1. Do written procedures (manuals) exist for each marketing activity? If so, are these procedures (manuals) up to date? Are these procedures (manuals) being followed by our employees?
2. What oral or unwritten procedures exist for each marketing activity? Should these procedures be formally included in the written procedures or should they be eliminated?
3. Do marketing personnel regularly interact with other functional areas to establish standard procedures for each activity?

Identification of Performance Standards for Each Marketing Activity
1. What specific, quantitative standards exist for each activity?
2. What qualitative standards exist for each activity?
3. How does each activity contribute to customer satisfaction within each marketing mix element (i.e., product, pricing, distribution, promotion)?
4. How does each activity contribute to our marketing goals and objectives?
5. How does each activity contribute to the goals and objectives of the company?

Identification of Performance Measures for Each Marketing Activity
1. What are the internal, profit-based measures for each marketing activity?
2. What are the internal, time-based measures for each marketing activity?
3. How is performance monitored and evaluated internally by management?
4. How is performance monitored and evaluated externally by customers?

Review and Evaluation of Marketing Personnel
1. Are the company's current recruiting, selection, and retention efforts consistent (matched) with the requirements of our marketing activities?
2. What is the nature and content of our employee training activities? Are these activities consistent with the requirements of our marketing activities?
3. How are customer-contact personnel supervised, evaluated, and rewarded? Are these procedures consistent with customer requirements?
4. What effect do employee evaluation and reward policies have on employee attitudes, satisfaction, and motivation?
5. Are current levels of employee attitudes, satisfaction, and motivation adequate?

Identification and Evaluation of Customer Support Systems
1. Are the quality and accuracy of our customer service materials (e.g., instruction manuals, brochures, form letters, etc.) consistent with the image of our company and our products?
2. Are the quality and appearance of our physical facilities (e.g., offices, furnishings, layout, store decor, etc.) consistent with the image of our company and our products?
3. Are the quality and appearance of our customer service equipment (e.g., repair tools, telephones, computers, delivery vehicles, etc.) consistent with the image of our company and our products?
4. Is our record keeping system accurate? Is the information always readily available when it is needed? What technology could be acquired to enhance our record keeping abilities (e.g., bar code scanners, portable computers, cellular telephones)?

Source: Adapted from Christopher H. Lovelock, *Services Marketing*, 2nd ed. (Englewood Cliffs, NJ: Prentice-Hall, 1991), 270.

3. Exploring different alternatives for improving the ongoing implementation of marketing activities, and

4. Providing a framework to evaluate the attainment of performance standards, as well as marketing goals and objectives.

The information in a marketing audit is often based on a series of questionnaires that are given to employees, managers, customers, and/or suppliers. In some cases, this ongoing evaluation is done by people outside the firm. Using outside auditors has the advantages of being more objective and less time consuming for the firm. However, outside auditors are typically quite expensive. A marketing audit can also be very disruptive, especially if employees are fearful of the scrutiny.

Despite their drawbacks, marketing audits are usually quite beneficial for the firms that use them. They are flexible in that the scope of the audit can be broad (as in to evaluate the entire marketing strategy) or narrow (as in to evaluate only a specific marketing mix element). The results of the audit can be used to reallocate marketing efforts, correct implementation problems, or even to identify new opportunities. The end results of a well-executed marketing audit are usually better performance and increased customer satisfaction.

Informal Marketing Controls

Although formal marketing controls such as the marketing audit are overt in their attempt to influence employee behavior, informal controls are more subtle. Informal marketing controls are unwritten, employee-based mechanisms that subtly affect the behaviors of employees, both as individuals and in groups.[6] Here we are dealing with personal objectives and behaviors, as well as group-based norms and expectations. There are three basic types of informal control: employee self-control, social control, and cultural control. As you read the descriptions of each type below, note that the elements of informal control are affected to a great extent by the formal control mechanisms employed by the marketing manager. However, the premise of informal control is that some aspects of employee behavior cannot be influenced through formal mechanisms and therefore must be controlled informally through individual and group mechanisms.

EMPLOYEE SELF-CONTROL   Through employee self-control, employees manage their own behavior (and thus the implementation of the marketing plan) by establishing personal objectives and monitoring their results. The type of personal objectives that employees set depends on how employees feel about their jobs. If they are satisfied with their jobs and committed to the organization, they are more likely to establish personal objectives that are consistent with the aims of the organization. Further, when employees are committed to the marketing plan, they are more likely to establish personal objectives that are consistent with the marketing goals and objectives. Employee self-control also depends on how employees are rewarded. Some employees prefer the intrinsic rewards of doing a good job rather than the extrinsic rewards of pay and recognition. Employees who are intrinsically rewarded are likely to exhibit more self-control.

EMPLOYEE SOCIAL CONTROL   Social, or small group, control deals with the standards, norms, and ethics that are found within work groups within the organization.[7] The social interaction that occurs within these work groups can be a powerful motivator of employee behavior. The social and behavioral norms of work groups provide the "peer pressure" that causes employees to conform to expected standards of performance. If employees fall short of these standards, the group will pressure them to increase effort and performance.

EMPLOYEE CULTURAL CONTROL   Cultural control is very similar to social control, only at a much broader level. Here we are concerned with the behavioral and social norms of the entire organization. One of the most important outcomes of cultural control is the establishment of shared values among all organizational members. Marketing implementation is most effective and efficient when every employee is committed to the same organizational goal and guided by the same organizational values. Companies such as FedEx and Hewlett-Packard are noted for their strong organizational cultures that guide employee behavior. Unfortunately, cultural control is very difficult to master. It takes a great deal of time to create the appropriate organizational culture to ensure implementation success.

Key Insights from Chapter 9

Assessment of the financial impact of a proposed marketing plan:

- is important if the marketing manager is to convince top management that the marketing plan and strategy are a "good value" for the firm.
- answers two important questions:
    1. Will the marketing plan help the firm reach its goals and objectives?
    2. Will the marketing plan lead to the specified outcomes?
- uses contribution analysis to determine the amount of revenues that can be expected from implementing the marketing plan.
- uses response analysis to estimate response coefficients that can be used to predict the change in sales volume based on a change in one or more elements of the marketing mix.
- uses a systematic planning model to map the financial impact of specific marketing mix decisions.

Evaluating and controlling marketing activities:

- is an important step in the planning process because the marketing plan must be implemented before the expected financial results can be realized.
- is necessary if the manager is to reduce the difference between expected performance (the intended marketing strategy) and actual performance (the realized marketing strategy).

Differences between the intended marketing strategy and the realized marketing strategy may be due to:

- an inappropriate or unrealistic marketing strategy.
- mismanaged or inappropriate implementation for the strategy.
- substantial changes in the internal and/or external environments between the development of the marketing strategy and its implementation.

Formal marketing controls:

- involve mechanisms that are initiated by managers in an attempt to influence employee behavior toward implementing the marketing plan.

- include input controls (actions taken prior to implementation), process controls (actions taken during implementation), and output controls (setting performance standards and monitoring the results).

Informal marketing controls:

- are unwritten, employee-based mechanisms that center around individual objectives and behavior, as well as group-based norms and expectations.

- include employee self-control (individual objectives and behavior), social control (norms and expectations of small groups), and cultural control (norms and expectations of the entire organization).

Social, Electronic Commerce, and Global Considerations In Strategic Market Planning

Introduction

Now that we have examined the basic framework for strategic market planning, we turn our attention to several important issues that should be considered during the planning process. The first of these issues is the role of ethics and social responsibility in the strategic market planning process. Being ethical and socially responsible is a necessity in light of public demands and changes in federal law. We also believe that being ethical and socially responsible improves marketing performance and profits. Another issue is exploring how marketers can use electronic commerce through the Internet and the World Wide Web to achieve strategic marketing plan goals and objectives. This interactive medium represents a unique opportunity to communicate, foster exchanges, and build long-term relationships with customers, suppliers, and others. Another issue of importance is strategic planning in an increasingly global economy. Environmental analysis is particularly critical for firms with target markets outside their own countries. Finally, we examine the issue of market planning as it is actually practiced today.

The Role of Ethics and Social Responsibility In Strategic Market Planning

Motivated by news reports of scandals and misconduct, customers are increasingly demanding that marketers behave ethically and socially responsible. Such demands are often expressed by "voting with dollars": A recent survey found that nearly 90 percent of customers say they would be more likely to buy from the company that has the best reputation for social responsibility when quality, service, and price are otherwise equal among competitors.[1] In response to these demands, along with the threat of increased regulation, more and more firms are incorporating ethics and social responsibility into the strategic market planning process. Orange and Rockland Utilities (O&R), for example, developed an ethics program that includes a code of conduct, an ethics office, and a 12–member ethics council comprised of representatives from all levels and departments of the firm, even union employees.[2] Because of the prominence of marketing ethics and social responsibility today, in this section we explore the dimensions of these concepts, examine research that relates ethics and social responsibility to marketing performance, and discuss their role in the strategic market planning process.

Dimensions of Social Responsibility

Social responsibility is a broad concept that relates to an organization's obligation to maximize its positive impacts on society while minimizing its negative impacts. As shown in Exhibit 10.1, social responsibility consists of four dimensions, or responsibilities: economic, legal, ethical, and philanthropic.[3]

From an economic perspective, all companies must be responsible to their stockholders, who are primarily interested in proper accounting procedures, relevant

---

EXHIBIT 10.1   The Pyramid of Social Responsibility

RESPONSIBILITIES

Philanthropic
*Be a good
corporate citizen*
▶ Contribute resources to the
community; improve quality of life

Ethical
Be ethical
▶ Obligations to do what is right, just, and fair
▶ Avoid harm

Legal
Obey the law
▶ Law is society's codification of right and wrong
▶ Play by the rules of the game

Economic
Be profitable
▶ The foundation upon which all others rest

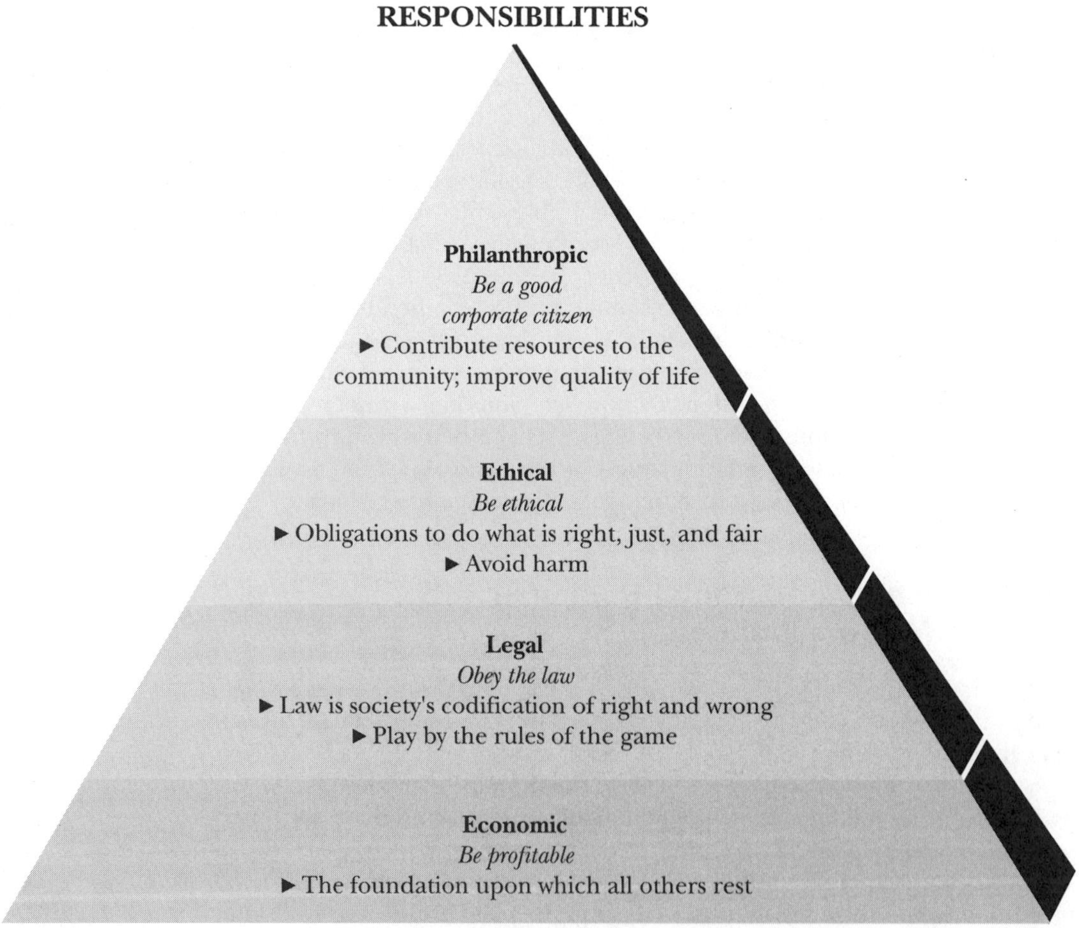

Source: Archie Carroll, "The Pyramid of Corporate Social Responsibility: Toward the Moral Management of Organizational Stakeholders," *Business Horizons* 34 (July/August 1991): 42.

information about the current and projected performance of the firm, and, of course, earning a return on their investment. The economic responsibility of making a profit also serves employees and the community at large due to its impact on employment and income levels in the area where the firm is located. Marketers are also expected, at a minimum, to obey laws and regulations. Economic and legal concerns are the most basic levels of social responsibility for a good reason: without them, the firm may not be around long enough to engage in ethical or philanthropic activities.

At the next level of the pyramid, marketing ethics refers to principles and standards that define acceptable conduct as determined by the public, government regulators, private interest groups, competitors, and the organization itself. The most basic of these principles have been codified as laws and regulations to induce marketers to conform to society's expectations of conduct. However, it is important to understand that marketing ethics goes beyond legal issues: Ethical marketing decisions foster trust, which helps build long-term marketing relationships.

There is ample evidence that ignoring these issues can destroy trust with customers and prompt government intervention. At Columbia/HCA, for example, allegations of health care fraud made the company a target of federal and state investigations of its Medicare and home-health care billing practices. The scandal has claimed at least four casualties: Three executives were indicted for overcharging Medicare, and founder Rick Scott stepped down as CEO. The hospital chain also faces ethics issues such as conflict of interest stemming from its doctors' investments in the company, profit goals that may have sacrificed the quality of patient care, and charges of unfair competition related to its buyout of nonprofit hospitals.[4] When companies engage in activities that deviate from accepted principles to further their own interests, continued marketing exchanges become difficult, if not impossible. The best way to deal with such problems is during the strategic planning process, not after major problems materialize.

It is imperative that marketers become familiar with many of the ethical and social issues that may occur in marketing so that these issues can be identified and resolved when they occur. Some of these issues are shown in Exhibit 10.2. Essentially, any time an activity causes marketing managers, or customers in their target market, to feel manipulated or cheated, an ethical issue exists, regardless of the legality of the activity. Many ethical issues can develop into legal problems if they are not addressed in the planning process. Once an issue has been identified, marketers must decide how to deal with it.

Being ethical and responsible requires commitment. For this reason, many firms simply ignore these issues and focus instead on satisfying their economic and legal responsibilities, with the overall bottom line being profit maximization. While the firm may do nothing wrong, it misses out on the long-term benefits that can be derived from satisfying ethical and philanthropic responsibilities. Firms that choose to take these extra steps are concerned with increasing their overall positive impact on society, their local communities, and the environment, with the bottom line being increased goodwill toward the firm as well as increased profits. Recognizing this community responsibility, Ralph Wilson, Jr., owner of the Buffalo Bills football team, decided not to move the Bills from Buffalo at a time when football teams and cities were playing a game of high-dollar musical chairs. Said Wilson, "I never even spoke to another city, though the team could make more money in

---

EXHIBIT 10.2   **Possible Ethical Issues in Marketing**

Product Issues
   Reducing package sizes while holding prices constant
   Product quality dishonesty (shortcuts in design/manufacture)
   Unsafe products (particularly for children)
   Poor service or no service after the sale
   Adding useless features to command higher prices

Promotion Issues
   Bait-and-switch advertising
   Puffery
   Push money (spiffs) paid to salespeople
   Advertising to children
   Sex or fear as an advertising appeal
   Exaggerated product benefits
   High-pressure or misleading salespeople
   Bribery of salespeople or purchasing agents

Pricing Issues
   Price fixing between competitors
   Predatory pricing
   Excessive pricing
   Misleading credit/financing practices
   Fraudulent warranty or refund policies

Distribution Issues
   Opportunistic behavior among channel members
   Slotting allowances paid to retailers to gain shelf space
   Extortion
   Tying contracts
   Distribution of counterfeit products

Sources: Adapted from J. Paul Peter and James H. Donnelly, Jr., A *Preface to Marketing Management*, 6th ed. (Burr Ridge, IL: Richard D. Irwin, 1994), 274; and William M. Pride and O. C. Ferrell, Marketing: Concepts and Strategies, 10th ed. (Boston: Houghton Mifflin Company, 1997), 59.

Los Angeles. I just did not feel it would be right to leave."[5] In short, being socially responsible is not only good for customers, employees, and the community, it makes good business sense.

   Philanthropic activities make very good marketing tools. Thinking of corporate philanthropy as a marketing tool may seem cynical, but it points out the reality that philanthropy is good for the firm. By the mid 1990s, charitable donations by corporations amounted to $6.1 billion, although these donations have declined significantly since 1987 when tax reform and downsizing affected business dramatically.[6] Nike, for example, sponsors sporting events at local boys' and girls' clubs and then features these events in its national advertising. This approach has been called "strategic philanthropy," or financially sound goodwill.[7] Companies that engage in philanthropic activities win the trust and respect of their employees, customers, and society, thus allowing them to earn higher profits in the long run.

Many firms focus their philanthropic efforts on education. Acknowledging that today's students are tomorrow's customers and employees, firms such as Kroger, Campbell's Soup, Kodak, American Express, Apple Computers, and the Coca-Cola Company have donated money, equipment, and employee time to help improve local schools around the nation. McDonald's, for example, provides scholarship money for high school students who work part time in its restaurants. Although some members of the public fear "strategic philanthropy" initiatives in education and other social areas, business participation is necessary in helping to educate future employees and customers.

Marketers are also beginning to take more responsibility for the hard-core unemployed, spurred in recent years by welfare reform efforts. Marriott International, for example, puts welfare recipients through its welfare-to-work program, called Pathways to Independence, which includes training in self-confidence, budgeting and checking-account management, as well as specific job skills. The hotel chain then hires graduates of the program.[8] In addition to fostering self-support, such opportunities enhance self-esteem and help people become productive members of society.

Ethics and Social Responsibility Improve Marketing Performance

One of the more powerful arguments for including ethics and social responsibility in the strategic market planning process is increasing evidence of a link between social responsibility, ethics, and marketing performance.[9] One study found that an ethical climate is associated with employee commitment to quality and intrafirm trust.[10] Employee commitment, customer loyalty, market orientation, and profitability have also been associated with companies identified as socially responsible.[11]

Research also suggests a relationship between a market orientation and ethics and social responsibility. Market-oriented businesses support the generation of thorough market intelligence and the use of this information at every level of the organization. This implies that in market-oriented organizations, employees are not only concerned about changes in market forces, but are also sensitive and responsive to the demands of customers and other stakeholders. Thus, by encouraging their employees to understand their markets, companies can help them respond to their stakeholders' demands.

In contrast, a competitive orientation in the workplace can be a negative force creating conflict and damaging the opportunity to improve ethics and social responsibility. A competitive orientation encourages personal success, which may come at the expense of openness and teamwork. Internal competition between employees may encourage the achievement of financial performance levels without regard for their potential effects on other parties both inside and outside the organization. Consequently, employees of such organizations are unlikely to incorporate the demands and concerns of society, business, and its customers in their decisions.

It should come as no surprise that satisfied employees are more likely to satisfy customers.[12] In fact, research has shown that in companies where there is a significant relationship between employee satisfaction and customer satisfaction—including companies such as MCI Communications, Chick Fil-A, and Xerox—there are more repeat purchases and more familiarity with customer needs and ways to meet those needs.[13] And, yet another study on service contact employees discovered a correlation between employee satisfaction and customer perceived service quality.[14] Allegheny Industrial Sales, Inc., believes that "advancement of quality as a leading management theory will be heavily influenced by the degree to which it can focus upon and improve ethical behavior in organizations."[15] Because there is a correlation between service quality and the ethical climate of the organization,[16] we conclude that employee satisfaction, customer loyalty, and service quality are all positively interrelated with ethics and social responsibility.

Companies that do not develop strategies and programs to incorporate ethics and social responsibility into their organizational culture will pay the price with potentially poor marketing performance and will face the potential costs of legal violations, civil litigation, and damaging negative publicity when questionable activities are discovered by the public. Consider, for example, the issue of silicon breast implants, which may have contributed to health problems in thousands of women. Faced with a protracted class-action lawsuit and negative publicity, several marketers of silicone-gel implants tentatively agreed to a $4.2 billion global settlement to compensate women who claim they have been harmed by the implants. On the other hand, organizations that do incorporate ethics and social responsibility into their strategic plans are likely to experience improved marketing performance.

Unfortunately, because marketing ethics and social responsibility are not always viewed as organizational performance issues, many managers do not believe they need to be considered in the strategic planning process. Individuals also have different ideas as to what is ethical or unethical, leading them to confuse the need for workplace ethics and the right to maintain their own personal values and ethics. Although it is true that the concept of ethics is controversial, it is possible—and desirable—to incorporate ethics and social responsibility into the planning process.

Incorporating Ethics and Social Responsibility into Strategic Market Planning

Many firms are integrating ethics and social responsibility into their strategic planning through ethics compliance programs or integrity initiatives that make legal compliance, ethics, and social responsibility an organizationwide effort.[17] Such programs establish, communicate, and monitor a firm's ethical values and legal requirements through codes of conduct, ethics offices, training programs, and audits. Most organizations have established codes of conduct, which are formalized rules and standards that describe what the company expects of its employees. One of the most widely adopted professional codes is that of the American Marketing Association, whose code of conduct is shown in Exhibit 10.3.

The *Federal Sentencing Guidelines for Organizations (FSGO)*, approved by Congress in 1991, codified into law incentives for organizations to develop ethics and legal compliance programs to detect and deter misconduct.[18] The FSGO hold both employees *and* the firms that employ them accountable for violations of federal law. (Before 1991, laws punished mainly those employees directly responsible for an offense.) Companies that fail to develop effective compliance programs can incur severe penalties if their employees violate the law. Under the new law, several firms, including Daiwa Bank of Japan and Archer-Daniels-Midland, have been disciplined with fines exceeding $100 million for the illegal activities of their employees. However, those

| EXHIBIT 10.3 | American Marketing Association Code of Ethics |

Members of the American Marketing Association (AMA) are committed to ethical professional conduct. They have joined together in subscribing to this Code of Ethics embracing the following topics:

Responsibilities of the Marketer

Marketers must accept responsibility for the consequences of their activities and make every effort to ensure that their decisions, recommendations, and actions function to identify, serve, and satisfy all relevant publics: consumers, organizations, and society. Marketers' professional conduct must be guided by:

1. The basic rule of professional ethics: not knowingly to do harm;
2. The adherence to all applicable laws and regulations;
3. The accurate representation of their education, training, and experience; and
4. The active support, practice, and promotion of this Code of Ethics.

Honesty and Fairness

Marketers shall uphold and advance the integrity, honor, and dignity of the marketing profession by:

1. Being honest in serving consumers, clients, employees, suppliers, distributors, and the public;
2. Not knowingly participating in conflict of interest without prior notice to all parties involved; and
3. Establishing equitable fee schedules including the payment or receipt of usual, customary and/or legal compensation for marketing exchanges.

Rights and Duties of Parties

Participants in the marketing exchange process should be able to expect that:

1. Products and services offered are safe and fit for their intended uses;
2. Communications about offered products and services are not deceptive;
3. All parties intend to discharge their obligations, financial and otherwise, in good faith; and
4. Appropriate internal methods exist for equitable adjustment and/or redress of grievances concerning purchases.

It is understood that the above would include, but is not limited to, the following responsibilities of the marketer:

In the area of product development management:

Disclosure of all substantial risks associated with product or service usage

Identification of any product component substitution that might materially change the product or impact on the buyer's purchase decision

Identification of extra-cost added features

In the area of promotions:

Avoidance of false and misleading advertising

Rejection of high pressure manipulations, or misleading sales tactics

Avoidance of sales promotions that use deception or manipulation

In the area of distribution:

Not manipulating the availability of a product for purpose of exploitation

Not using coercion in the marketing channel

Not exerting undue influence over the resellers' choice to handle a product

In the area of pricing:

Not engaging in price fixing

Not practicing predatory pricing

Disclosing the full price associated with any purchase

continued

EXHIBIT 10.3	American Marketing Association Code of Ethics *(continued)*

In the area of marketing research:

Prohibiting selling or fund raising under the guise of conducting research

Maintaining research integrity by avoiding misrepresentation and omission of pertinent research data

Treating outside clients and suppliers fairly

Organizational Relationships

Marketers should be aware of how their behavior may influence or impact on the behavior of others in organizational relationships. They should not encourage or apply coercion to obtain unethical behavior in their relationships with others, such as employees, suppliers or customers.

1. Apply confidentiality and anonymity in professional relationships with regard to privileged information.
2. Meet their obligations and responsibilities in contracts and mutual agreements in a timely manner.
3. Avoid taking the work of others, in whole, or in part, and represent this work as their own or directly benefit from it without compensation or consent of the originator or owner.
4. Avoid manipulation to take advantage of situations to maximize personal welfare in a way that unfairly deprives or damages the organization or others.

Any AMA members found to be in violation of any provision of this Code of Ethics may have his or her Association membership suspended or revoked.

Source: Reprinted by permission of the American Marketing Association.

organizations that take steps to establish high ethical and legal standards and thereby prevent misconduct in the first place may receive mitigated penalties should one of their employees break the law.[19] To avoid such penalties, a company must develop corporate values, enforce its own code of ethics, strive to prevent misconduct, and, in short, be a "good citizen" corporation.[20]

The marketing plan should include distinct elements of ethics and social responsibility as determined by top-level marketing managers. Marketing strategy and implementation plans should be developed that reflect an understanding of (1) the ethical and social consequences of strategic choices, and (2) the values of organizational members and stakeholders.[21] To help ensure success, top managers must demonstrate their commitment to ethical and socially responsible behavior through their actions—words are simply not enough. In the end, a marketing plan that ignores social responsibility—or is silent about ethical requirements—leaves the guidance of ethical and socially responsible behavior to the work group, risking ethical breakdowns and damage to the firm.

Electronic Commerce: Strategic Market Planning and The Internet[22]

The *Internet* has emerged as one of the hottest buzzwords of the 1990s. The Internet has been around since the early 1960s, but it wasn't until the development of the World Wide Web—which organizes the vast amount of information on the Internet into interconnected "pages" of text, graphics, audio, and video—that use of the Internet for research and entertainment exploded in the early 1990s. Online use is increasing by 50 percent a year."[23]

Astute marketers recognize that they can exploit the opportunities created by the interactive nature and growth of the World Wide Web to communicate and foster commerce and relationships with customers, suppliers, and others. Through FedEx's Web site, for example, customers can track their shipments, find the nearest drop-off site or request a pickup, download software for printing packing labels, and request invoice adjustments. The FedEx site experiences about 5 million "hits," or visits, per month, which save the company money by not going through its Call Center.[24] Such effective use of the interactive nature of the Internet enables companies to build long-term relationships with customers and to stand tall among competitors. As a result, more and more firms are incorporating the Internet, and more specifically the World Wide Web (WWW), into their strategic market planning efforts to gather marketing intelligence, create effective marketing strategies, and build relationships with customers. For more information about strategic marketing and the Internet, view our Web site at http://www.dryden.com/mktg/ferrell/.

Using the Web to Improve Environmental Analysis

The Internet offers a growing opportunity to gather data for analyzing an organization's external environments. Using the World Wide Web, marketers can obtain vast amounts of demographic and usage-related marketing data to better understand their target customers. Secondary data, for example, is available through numerous government sources such as U.S. Census data, or private databases such as those from A.C. Nielsen or American Demographics' Marketing Tools Web site. Useful information may also be found in the many newspapers and trade magazines available online, including *Business Week, USA Today,* and *The Wall Street Journal.* The Web also gives marketers a rare opportunity to gather information about competitors' product offerings, services, prices, and more through their Web sites.

A more direct means of gathering marketing information is by requiring Web users to register in order to gain access to a particular Web site or to premium areas of the site. Registration forms often ask for basic information such as name, e-mail address, age, and so on, from which marketers can develop user profiles for their own use or to sell to other companies. Firefly, for example, asks users to supply information about their musical and movie tastes so that the online CD and video marketer can recommend new music. Marketers can also conduct surveys through their Web pages to learn more about the people who access their pages.

Using the Internet to Create Effective Marketing Strategies

The exponential growth of the Internet and the World Wide Web presents exciting opportunities for marketers to reach customers with marketing mixes that take advantage of the technology.

NEW PRODUCTS FOR THE INTERNET   Obviously, the computer industry—both hardware and software—is best positioned to take advantage of the Internet. Many computer programs, including Netscape's Communicator, Microsoft's Internet Explorer, and Sun's Java programming language have been developed to help consumers exploit the World Wide Web. Internet access service is another growing market. Commercial online services, such as America Online (AOL), provide subscribers with ready access to the Internet as well as unique content and services. AOL and other commercial services also compete fiercely with local and national

Internet service providers (ISPs), such as Netcom, Flashnet, and TexasNet, which offer full Internet access at very competitive rates. Many telecommunications firms—including AT&T, Southwestern Bell, and MCI—have launched Internet service providers as well. It's not even necessary to own a computer to access the Web. Through Web TV, consumers can surf the Web using their television and a special remote control device.

Several enterprising organizations have developed indexes and search engines that keep track of and catalog the information available on the World Wide Web. Users of these services can type in a key word to locate, usually in seconds, a Uniform Resource Locator (URL)—a Web site "address"—or piece of data that otherwise might take hours to find. Consequently, services such as Yahoo!, Infoseek, and Lycos are among the most heavily accessed sites on the Internet.

Marketers are also using the Web to create unique products to satisfy the needs of specific target market segments. GolfWeb, for instance, offers links to 35,000 golf-related Web pages, a virtual ProShop, and the opportunity to subscribe to special services such as handicapping and online games. GolfWeb users also see golf-related advertising, which accounts for 35 percent of GolfWeb's revenues.[25] City guides, like those offered by CitySearch, Sidewalk, and Digital City, are another hot Internet offering. At CitySearch Austin, for example, Net surfers in Austin, Texas, can find out about sporting events and recreation opportunities, live music, movies, restaurants and businesses, museums, and local news, and exchange opinions on topics ranging from favorite local swimming holes to politics and the weather.

The most successful Web sites evolve as "virtual communities" where "like-minded cybernauts congregate, swap information, buy something, and come back week after week."[26] One such community is Women's Wire, a sort-of hybrid news magazine/talk show/beauty salon targeted primarily at working women. In addition to editorial content and columns on current events, work, finance, fashion, entertainment, health, and shopping, users can chat and exchange messages on virtual bulletin boards about a variety of topics. They also see advertising from GTE, Bank of America, Ford, and many other firms. Women's Wire, like many online communities, is free, but users are encouraged to register to access the site. Online communities like Women's Wire succeed by taking advantage of the interactive nature of the Internet, and they encourage Web browsers to hang out and contribute to the community instead of clicking elsewhere. Because these communities have well-defined demographics and common interests, they represent a valuable audience for advertisers.[27]

PROMOTION   In fact, advertising is one of the more lucrative ways marketers can capitalize on the World Wide Web. Thousands of well-known firms, from Levi Strauss to Boeing, from Wal-Mart to Blue Cross/Blue Shield, have set up Web sites to tout their products, display their mission and code of ethics, list job opportunities, entertain and inform users, and interact with customers. More and more companies are recognizing the value of the Web to provide "infotainment" that can foster brand identity and loyalty and develop long-term relationships with customers.[28]

Most online directory and search engine services now sell advertising on their directory pages. As you search Yahoo! for a topic, for instance, you see advertising banners for products from Microsoft, IBM, Nike, and many more firms. Increasingly, these banners are targeted to the user accessing the Web page. A student using Yahoo! to search for "beer," for example, is likely to see a banner for Miller

Brewing.[29] Clicking on these banners takes the searcher to the advertiser's Web site for more information. Many Web services and communities, including GolfWeb, Women's Wire, Parent Soup, ESPNet SportsZone, and the Internet Movie Database fund their Web sites by accepting such advertising.

Promotion is increasingly occurring through corporate sponsorship of Web sites. For instance, Parent Soup, an online community of more than 200,000 parents, not only relies on corporate "partners," it even creates companion Web sites closely linked to Parent Soup for some of its sponsors. One such "bridge site," ParentsClub.com for Triaminic children's cough syrup, offers child safety tips and other parenting information in addition to promotional content for the product. These sponsorships have been so beneficial for Parent Soup and its sponsors that 80 percent of its advertisers come back.[30]

The actual dollar amount of advertising on the World Wide Web is the subject of some debate, but no one doubts that Web advertising generates millions of dollars in revenues for companies that choose to carry such advertising. Jupiter Communications projects that advertising on the World Wide Web and commercial online services will generate $8 billion in revenues by the year 2002, about 4.1 percent of total advertising dollars. Until recently, the bulk of Web ads have been for high-tech products such as computers, office equipment, and telecommunications. However, consumer goods companies, recognizing the opportunity to reach specific target markets, are increasing their budgets for online advertising as well. Yahoo! has seen its mix of advertising shift from 80 percent technology to nearly 80 percent consumer brands in two years.[31]

A NEW CHANNEL OF DISTRIBUTION   Beyond advertising, the Internet is increasingly becoming a retail venue. From airline reservations to automobiles, and CDs to wine, the World Wide Web presents an opportunity for marketers to encourage electronic commerce. With online security improving through new technology, online retail sales are expected to reach $7 billion in 2000.[32] Dell Computer already sells more than $1.5 million worth of computers online every day.[33] Chrysler Corp. projects that 25 percent of its sales will be online by 2000.[34]

Astute marketers have expanded the concept of electronic commerce further by creating virtual shopping malls where online shoppers can "walk" from store to store and place goods in a "shopping cart." At Shop.com, a list of virtual malls, storefronts, and other information for the online shopper is organized by short descriptions and rated with a system of one to five stars. netMarket is an online shopping club/electronic superstore that offers members discounts of 10 to 50 percent off manufacturers' list prices on some 250,000 brand name products. Members pay $69.95 a year to access deals on new and used cars, travel services, games, books, videos, flowers, an auction, a flea market, and more.[35] Another retailing adventure is supplied by online auctioneers, such as First Auction, Haggle Online, and Onsale Inc., which auction everything from fine wines and golf clubs to computer goods and electronics online.[36]

PRICE   For most marketers, the Internet's effect on pricing strategies relates to its capability to give consumers quick access to prices. For instance, users can access many auto makers' Web pages, configure an ideal vehicle, and get instant feedback on its cost from the manufacturer. This facilitates comparison shopping and gives manufacturers that want to make price a key element in their marketing mix another opportunity to get pricing information to customers.

Some firms are using the Internet to implement low-price policies. One of these is Auto-By-Tel, a service that aids customers in finding the best deal on new cars and trucks. Auto-By-Tel helps customers negotiate a final price, then contracts with member dealers, who pay a fee to participate, to deliver the vehicle to a dealership near the customer. Most major airlines are now publicizing their fares over the Internet and, in some cases, offering lower prices to customers who are willing to wait to book their flights until the last moment. American Airlines, for example, makes seats available over the Internet and gives customers a chance to save money by making travel arrangements online.

Incorporating the Internet into a Marketing Plan

Media hype notwithstanding, the Internet is not a license to mint money. In fact, several vaunted Web sites have been major black holes for corporate funds. Time Warner's Pathfinder Web site, for example, has lost about $5 million a year, and American Cybercase, which produces the "cybersoap operas," *The Pyramid* and *The Spot,* filed for bankruptcy.[37] Nevertheless, many companies *are* finding success through the Internet, but they have done so through careful analysis and planning. Exploiting the opportunities offered by the Internet requires marketing research to understand the Internet community, technological resources, creativity, and, most importantly, a well-thought-out marketing strategy that integrates Internet marketing with other aspects of the marketing plan.

Strategic Market Planning In A Global Economy

Technological advances like the Internet, along with falling political and economic barriers, are creating opportunities for more and more companies to sell their products overseas as well as in their own countries. As these changes narrow cultural and other differences among nations, the trend toward the globalization of marketing is becoming increasingly important. Global marketing occurs when companies treat the entire world as the focus for marketing planning and implementation. It involves decisions about marketing activities for the whole world, including the United States. It is a broader concept than international marketing, which occurs anytime a company crosses national boundaries to buy or sell products.

There are many reasons to engage in international and global marketing activities. One of the most attractive is market potential. The consulting firm Deloitte and Touche estimates that about 95 percent of the world's population and two-thirds of its total purchasing power are outside the United States. Global marketing also affords an opportunity to extend the life cycle of maturing products by introducing them into new markets. Global marketing can help minimize seasonal sales fluctuations. For example, a firm that markets sunscreen might sell its product in Australia when summer ends in the United States. Finally, foreign products often command higher prices because consumers in many countries expect foreign products to cost more.[38]

Already, consumers around the world drink Coca-Cola and eat at McDonald's and Pizza Hut; shop at Wal-Mart and Home Depot; see movies from Mexico, France,

Australia, Japan, and China; and watch CNN and MTV on Toshiba and Sony televisions. The products you consume today are just as likely to have been made in Korea or Germany as in the United States. Likewise, consumers in other countries buy Western electrical equipment, clothing, music, cosmetics, and toiletries, as well as computers, robots, and earth-moving equipment. Brands such as Coca-Cola, Sony, British Petroleum, and Levi Strauss seem to make year-to-year gains in the global market.

Competing in this global economy offers both challenges and opportunities for today's marketing managers. For example, we cannot overemphasize the importance of solid environmental analysis before entering foreign markets. In this section, we will look at several specific global marketing issues, including strategic involvement in international marketing and marketing strategy adaptations.

Strategic Involvement in Global Marketing

Companies engage in global marketing at many levels—from a small Nigerian firm that occasionally exports African crafts, to a huge multinational corporation such as Unilever that sells products around the globe. The degree of commitment of resources and effort required increases according to the strategic level the firm chooses to involve itself in global marketing. In this section, we examine several levels of global marketing involvement from importing and exporting, trading companies, licensing and franchising, and contract manufacturing, to direct investment and joint ventures.

IMPORTING AND EXPORTING   Importing and exporting require the least amount of effort and commitment of resources. Importing is the purchase of products from a foreign source. Exporting—the sale of products to foreign markets—enables businesses of all sizes to participate in global business. In fact, according to the U.S. Department of Commerce, 60 percent of U.S. firms engaging in exporting have fewer than 100 employees.[39]

A company may choose to export its wares overseas directly or import goods directly from their manufacturer, or it may deal with an export agent. Export agents either purchase products outright or take them on consignment. When they purchase them outright, they generally mark up the price they paid and attempt to sell the product in the international marketplace. These intermediaries are also responsible for storage and transportation. An advantage of exporting through an agent is that the company does not have to deal with foreign currencies or the red tape (paying tariffs and handling paperwork) of international business. A major disadvantage is that because the export agent must make a profit, the price of the product must be increased or the domestic company must provide a larger discount than it would in a domestic transaction.

TRADING COMPANIES   A marketer seeking international sales may also do business with a trading company, a firm that buys products in one country and sells them to buyers in another country. Trading companies handle all activities required to move products from one country to another, including purchasing the products outright, consulting, marketing research, advertising, insurance, product research and design, warehousing, and foreign exchange services. Trading companies are similar to export agencies, but their role in international trade is larger. By linking sellers and buyers of goods in different countries, trading companies promote international trade.

LICENSING AND FRANCHISING   Licensing is a trade arrangement in which one company—the licensor—allows another firm—the licensee—to use its name, products, patents, brands, trademarks, raw materials, and/or production processes in exchange for a royalty fee. Coca-Cola and PepsiCo frequently use licensing as a means to market their soft drinks in other countries. Licensing allows companies to enter the global marketplace without spending large sums of money abroad and hiring or transferring personnel to handle overseas affairs. It minimizes problems associated with shipping costs, tariffs, and trade restrictions. Licensing also allows a firm to establish goodwill for its products in a foreign market. However, if the licensee does not maintain high standards of quality, the product's image may be damaged; therefore, it is important for the licensor to monitor its products overseas and to enforce its standards of quality.

Franchising is a form of licensing in which a company—the franchiser—agrees to provide a franchisee a name, logo, methods of operation, advertising, products, and other elements associated with the franchiser's business, in return for a financial commitment and the agreement to conduct business in accordance with the franchiser's standard of operations. KFC, Wendy's, McDonald's, and Holiday Inn are well-known franchisers with international visibility.

CONTRACT MANUFACTURING   Contract manufacturing occurs when a company hires a foreign firm to produce a designated volume of the firm's product to specification, and the final product carries the domestic firm's name. Spalding, for example, relies on contract manufacturing for its sports equipment; Reebok uses Korean contract manufacturers to manufacture many of its athletic shoes. Marketing may be handled by the contract manufacturer or by the original company.

DIRECT INVESTMENT   Companies that want more control and are willing to invest considerable resources in global business may consider direct investment, the ownership of overseas production and marketing facilities. With direct investment, a company may control the facilities outright, or it may be the majority stockholder in the company that controls the facilities. Many firms have direct investments in production plants and companies around the globe. Ford Motor Company and 3M, for example, own subsidiaries and manufacturing facilities all over the world. Japanese-owned Nissan owns a plant in Smyrna, Tennessee, as well as other facilities around the world.

JOINT VENTURES   Many nations, particularly less developed countries, do not permit direct investment by foreign companies or individuals. Or, a company may lack sufficient resources or expertise to operate in a country. In such cases, a company that wants to do business in another country may set up a joint venture by finding a local partner (occasionally, the host nation itself) to share the costs and operation of the business. General Electric and Hungary's Tungsram have formed such a venture to manufacture light bulbs in Budapest.

A relatively new form of international joint venture is the strategic alliance, a partnership formed to create competitive advantage on a worldwide basis. In some industries, such as automobiles and airlines, strategic alliances are becoming the predominate means of competing. Competition is so fierce and the costs of competing on a global basis so high that few firms have the resources to go it alone.

Thus, individual firms that lack the resources essential for international success may seek to collaborate with other companies. An example of such an alliance is the agreement between Delta and Virgin Atlantic, which improves Delta's ability to offer more nonstop flights to Europe.

Developing a Global Marketing Strategy

Developing a global marketing strategy employs the same strategic market planning process as developing a marketing strategy for domestic markets. However, in global marketing efforts, environmental analysis takes on even greater significance. Success in global marketing requires an analysis of the target country's social and cultural differences, political stability, and legal background as well as tariffs, quotas, and currency. Failure to research these areas adequately can result in huge financial and goodwill losses.

Because we have already devoted the previous chapters of this book to the strategic market planning process and marketing strategy, we will concentrate here on those elements of the marketing mix that may require adaptation for foreign markets.

PRODUCT AND PROMOTION   There are five possible approaches to adapting product and promotion for international markets: (1) keep product and promotion the same worldwide, (2) adapt promotion only, (3) adapt product only, (4) adapt both product and promotion, and (5) invent new products.[40]

Using the same product and promotion worldwide is desirable wherever possible because it eliminates the expense of marketing research and product development. PepsiCo and Coca-Cola use this approach in marketing soft drinks. Although both firms translate promotional messages into the language of the target country, the product and promotional message do not vary around the world. Despite certain inherent risks that stem from cultural differences in interpretation, exporting advertising copy does provide the efficiency of international standardization.

The approach of marketing the same product but adapting its promotion may be necessary because of language, legal, or cultural differences associated with the advertising copy. Promotional adaptation is a low-cost modification compared with the costs of redeveloping engineering and production and even physically changing products. Generally, the strategy of adapting only promotion infuses advertising with the culture of people who will be exposed to it. This approach often combines "thinking globally and acting locally." At company headquarters, a basic global marketing strategy is developed, but promotion is modified to fit each market's needs.

The basic assumption in modifying a product without changing its promotion is that the product will serve the same function under different conditions of use. Honda, for example, is attempting to revamp its top-selling Accord automobile into the first truly "world car" despite strong differences among its target markets in the United States, Europe, and Japan. By creating a unique modifiable platform, Honda can market a family-sized Accord that competes head on with the Ford Taurus in the United States, a stylish, sportier compact Accord for the Japanese, and a smaller Accord for Europe's narrower roads.[41] Household appliances have also been altered to use different types of electricity.

When a product serves a new function or is used differently in a foreign market, then both the product and its promotion require alteration. Cranberries, for example, are unfamiliar outside the United States. Ocean Spray Cranberries, Inc., therefore had to make adjustments in order to tempt foreign consumers into trying cranberry products in hopes of reaching $500 million in foreign sales by the year 2000. In Great Britain, Ocean Spray sales faltered until the firm mixed cranberry juice with black currant juice, a favorite of British children, and began using juice boxes, which the British prefer over the bottles Ocean Spray uses in the United States.[42] Adaptation of both product and promotion is the most expensive strategy discussed thus far, but it should be considered if the foreign market potential appears large enough.

When existing products cannot meet the needs of a foreign market, a firm may choose to invent new ones. General Motors, for example, developed an all-purpose jeeplike motor vehicle that can be assembled in underdeveloped nations by mechanics with no special training. The vehicle was designed to operate under varied conditions; it has standardized parts and is inexpensive. Colgate-Palmolive Co. created an inexpensive, all-plastic, hand-powered washing machine that has the tumbling action of a modern automatic machine. The product, marketed in underdeveloped countries, was invented for households that have no electricity. Strategies that involve the invention of products are often the most costly, but the payoff can be great.

DISTRIBUTION   Distribution system decisions are also important in developing the international marketing mix. A firm can sell its own product to an intermediary that is willing to buy through existing market channels in the United States, or it can develop new international marketing channels. Obviously, a service company needs to develop its own distribution system to market its products. However, many goods, such as toothpaste, can be distributed through intermediaries and brokers. The firm must consider distribution both between countries and within the foreign country. If a foreign country has a segmented retail structure consisting primarily of one-person shops or street vendors, it may be difficult to develop new marketing channels for such products as packaged goods and prepared foods.

If a product being sold across national boundaries requires service and information, then control of the distribution process is desirable. Caterpillar, for example, sells more than half its construction and earth-moving equipment in foreign countries. Because it must provide services and replacement parts, Caterpillar has established its own dealers in foreign markets. Regional sales offices and technical experts are also available to support local dealers. A manufacturer of paint brushes, on the other hand, would be more concerned about agents, wholesalers, or other manufacturers that would facilitate the product's exposure in a foreign market. Control over the distribution process would not be so important for that product because services and replacement parts are not needed. Distribution problems can arise, however, when an exporting firm sells, knowingly or unknowingly, to an unauthorized agent that competes with the exporter's official agent.[43]

Political instability can jeopardize the distribution of products. When the United States invaded Panama in 1989, the Panama Canal was closed for several days, delaying shipments of goods through the canal. Similarly, during the political unrest in China, military activity and fighting made it difficult to move goods into and out of certain areas. Thus we want to stress again the importance of monitoring the environment when engaging in international marketing. Companies that market products in unstable nations may need to develop contingency plans to allow for sudden unrest or hostility and ensure that the distribution of their products and employee safety are not jeopardized.

PRICING   Foreign prices of products are often higher due to increased costs of transportation, supplies, taxes, tariffs, and other expenses necessary to adjust a firm's operations to international marketing. A cost-plus approach to international pricing is commonly used because of the compounding number of costs necessary to move products from the United States to a foreign country.

The price charged in other countries is also a function of foreign currency exchange rates. Fluctuations in the international monetary market can change the prices charged across national boundaries on a daily basis. Because of a trend toward greater fluctuation (or float) in world money markets, a sudden variation in exchange rate, which occurs when a nation devalues its currency, can have wide-ranging effects on consumer prices. The sudden devaluation of the Mexican peso in 1994, for example, had drastic effects on Mexico-U.S. trade.

A key marketing strategy decision is whether the firm will change its basic pricing policy when moving beyond the United States. If it is a firm's policy not to allocate fixed costs to foreign sales, then lower foreign prices could result. Of course, understanding consumer demand and the competitive environment is a necessary step in selecting a price, as well as other elements of the marketing mix.

Strategic Market Planning in Practice

True adherence to strategic market plans was rare among U.S. business firms until the 1970s. Then economic shocks occurred that awakened many to its value—or necessity. Consider American Airlines. Until 1978, the U.S. airline industry was comfortable because competition was regulated by the government. In that year, American Airlines enjoyed the largest revenues among all U.S. airlines. The federal government deregulated the industry in 1978, and the "friendly skies" turned decidedly turbulent. Among the shocks: entry of many new competitors, growth of new routes, large expansions of equipment, and a multiplicity of fare schedules. More would come: two oil crises that escalated fuel prices to ruinous levels, fare wars, and sharply falling customer demand during the Persian Gulf War. By the mid 1990s, more startup competitors, mergers, and fierce fare wars were destroying profit margins. Where did American Airlines rank after all that? Still number one in the United States. That remarkable achievement was explained by American's chief executive, Robert Crandall, in this way:

> "I would like to report that we at American anticipated all this . . . (but) . . . any such claim would be an exaggeration . . . . We did foresee the probability of major change and we did put in place a strategic plan."[44]

Strategic market planning has many important benefits. In fact, merely going through the process improves decision making. This improvement occurs because of the vertical and horizontal flow of information and communication the process generates within an organization. However, the full potential of strategic market planning is realized only when plans are implemented. In this final section of this chapter, we examine several issues that can affect the practice of strategic market planning.

Balancing relationships with customers, employees, and other key stakeholders is necessary for long-term success. The most successful foreign companies, particularly

Japanese firms, plan strategies for the long term. These firms then adhere to their plans regardless of short-term effects, unless key internal or external environmental factors materially change. Unfortunately, ignoring long-range strategy to plan only for the next quarter has been far too typical of North American firms. Diversification, takeovers, leveraged buyouts, and downsizings, especially in the 1980s, resulted in economic failures, recession, and American weaknesses in world markets. Rather than develop long-term marketing strategies for growth, many firms focus on financial strategies aimed at quickly increasing earnings per share to improve short-term performance. When these strategies do not seem to work immediately, the firms shift strategies "in midstream" so to speak. Apple Computer, for example, has shifted its strategic focus numerous times, leading to consumer confusion about its products. Such situations are not necessarily the result of bad planning. In many cases, the reward structure of the organization leads management to focus on short-term financial results, especially those that improve the performance of the firm's stock. The end result: Foreign firms that plan for the long term pose serious threats to most U.S. businesses.

Many firms are forced to downsize, reorganize, merge, or be sold because of the inherent short-term focus of their strategic planning processes. This is certainly a compelling argument. A long-term strategic planning effort could uncover future trends, and the firm's strengths and weaknesses, to determine whether the firm was prepared for its future. In practice, however, all strategic planning takes place in a dynamic environment. Managers must be aware of these dynamics and remain flexible in the face of ever-changing market conditions.

Key Insights from Chapter 10

Social responsibility:

- refers to a business's obligation to maximize its positive impacts on society while minimizing its negative impacts.
- consists of four dimensions or responsibilities: economic, legal, ethical, and philanthropic.
- can include activities that are effective marketing tools in creating a positive image and goodwill for the firm.

Marketing ethics:

- refers to principles and standards that define acceptable marketing behavior.

Ethics and social responsibility as inputs to marketing planning:

- have caused some firms to incorporate these issues formally in their planning structure through codes of ethics, ethics offices, and organizationwide ethics compliance programs.

Electronic commerce via the Internet:

- represents an opportunity to communicate and foster commerce and relationships with customers, suppliers, and others through interactive technology.
- can be used to gather data for environmental analysis.
- can be a major ingredient in a marketing plan through effective use of specific marketing mixes that take advantage of the graphical, audio, and interactive technologies available.

- requires marketing research to understand the Internet community, techno-logical resources, creativity, and a well-thought-out marketing strategy that integrates Internet marketing with other aspects of the marketing plan.

Global marketing:

- occurs when companies treat the entire world as the focus for marketing plan-ning and implementation. It is a broader concept than international market-ing, which occurs anytime a company crosses national boundaries to buy or sell products.
- is becoming increasingly important because of technological advances, falling political and economic barriers, and increasingly strong foreign markets.

Strategic involvement in global marketing may take the form of:

- importing and exporting.
- trading companies.
- licensing and franchising.
- contract manufacturing.
- direct investment.
- joint ventures.

Developing a global marketing strategy:

- is the same as developing any marketing strategy except that environmental analysis is even more critical and some adaptations to the marketing mix may be necessary.
- includes product and promotion decisions such as whether to:
  - keep product and promotion the same worldwide.
  - adapt promotion only.
  - adapt product only.
  - adapt both product and promotion.
  - invent new products.
- includes distribution decisions such as:
  - whether to sell products to an intermediary willing to buy from existing market channels or to develop new international marketing channels.
  - how much control of the distribution process is desirable and possible.
- includes pricing decisions:
  - that are affected by increased costs of transportation, supplies, taxes, tariffs, and other expenses necessary to adjust a firm's operations to international marketing, as well as fluctuating currency exchange rates.
  - that include whether to change the basic pricing policy when moving beyond the United States.

The practice of strategic market planning:

- often comes about out of necessity rather than design.
- is impeded by taking a short-term perspective—the typical response of most North American firms.

- will be affected by the reward structure of the organization, especially if it leads management to focus on short-term financial results.
- can lead to growth and expansion if a long-term approach is taken that correctly identifies important environmental trends.
- takes place in a dynamic environment. Managers must be aware of these dynamics and remain flexible in the face of ever-changing market conditions to ensure that the firm is prepared for its future.

CASES

Cross Listing of Cases Matched to Specific Chapters

All of the cases were designed to complement any of the ten chapters in the text. However, the thrust and teaching emphasis of each case can be aligned with the content of specific chapters. The grid cross lists each case with the specific chapters that most closely match each case in terms of content and strategic emphasis.

Case #	Case Title	1	2	3	4	5	6	7	8	9	10
1	Saturn	X	X	X	X						
2	The Cola War	X	X			X					X
3	Sigma Press		X	X			X	X			
4	Nissan	X				X		X	X		X
5	Eagle Hardware and Garden, Inc.	X				X	X	X	X		
6	Apple Computer, Inc.	X	X	X	X	X					
7	IBM					X	X	X			X
8	Bass Pro Shops	X		X	X				X		
9	H-E-B					X	X	X			X
10	U.S. Learning, Inc.					X	X	X			
11	Dr. Pepper/Seven-Up, Inc.	X		X	X	X					
12	Wm. Wrigley Jr. Company		X	X	X	X					X
13	Benckiser				X		X	X			X
14	Maybelline	X	X	X	X						X
15	Texas Instruments						X	X	X		
16	AutoZone	X				X	X				
17	USA Today	X			X		X	X		X	
18	The Gillette Company					X	X	X			X
19	Columbia/HCA										X
20	Federal Express	X			X				X		X
21	Sears Logistics Group			X			X	X	X		
Integrating	Kentucky Fried Chicken and the Global Fast-Food Industry	X	X	X	X	X	X	X	X	X	X

Saturn[1]

In 1990 after seven years of incubation, Saturn, a division of General Motors Corp., debuted in the crowded market of compact cars. Since 1985, GM's share of the U.S. passenger car market had fallen 11 points to 33 percent. Moreover, a J.D. Powers & Associates study revealed that 42 percent of all new car shoppers didn't even consider a GM car. Saturn's mission, then, was to sell 80 percent of its cars to drivers who would not otherwise have bought a GM car.

GM established Saturn as a separate and independent subsidiary in 1985 with an investment of $5 billion. Former GM Chairman Robert B. Smith envisioned Saturn as a "laboratory" to find better ways to manufacture and market cars. GM believed that Saturn was the key to its long-term competitiveness and survival. Saturn managers spent years developing the new company from scratch. They viewed partnerships as a key element of Saturn's future-relationships between management and labor, between company and supplier—with everyone sharing the risks and rewards. To truly separate Saturn from the traditional Detroit auto-building mentality, GM decided to build Saturn in Spring Hill, Tennessee. GM lent its financial support to Saturn by providing the latest in technology, manufacturing methods, pace-setting labor relations, and participatory management ideas. Saturn represents the largest single-construction project in the history of GM. While other GM plants merely assemble parts, Saturn manufactures almost everything, including power trains, moldings, and instrument panels, at its facility.

Production Quality and Employee Participation

At first, management expected to totally automate the Saturn assembly line. However, in recent years, GM has learned many costly lessons about robotics, including the fact that robots do not always perform as expected. A joint venture with Toyota in California taught GM and Saturn that good labor-management relations could do more for productivity and quality. Consequently, Saturn adopted the outlook that technology takes a back seat to people.

---

[1] This case was prepared by O. C. Ferrell, Colorado State University, for classroom discussion rather than to illustrate either effective or ineffective handling of an administrative situation. Research assistance was provided by Donald P. Roy, University of Memphis.

The United Auto Workers Union (UAW) and General Motors management both wanted Saturn to succeed from the start and, in a partnership unprecedented in the auto industry, the two entities joined hands and decided to work side by side. Now, all decisions at Saturn are reached by consensus. UAW members, for example, help select supplies, Saturn's advertising agency, and dealers. All employees—blue- and white-collar—have to be approved by both union members and management. New employees at Saturn's Tennessee plant also face extensive training to teach them how to work in teams and how to keep track of costs. Saturn provides an on-site MBA program for employees in a cooperative effort with Middle Tennessee State University. Classes are available after each shift is over.

Even the plant's design reflects thought for cost efficiency and people. For example, there are many entrances to the plant instead of one main entrance, and each is designed to be no more than a five-minute walk to an employee's station. Parking was designed so that no one has to dodge delivery trucks. Street names around the plant—Handshake Road and Greater Glory Road—also reflect a people-oriented philosophy. Inside, cars on the assembly line can be raised or lowered to make the workers' jobs easier. Another first in North America is that the final assembly line is made of wood, which is easier on employees' feet.

The Marketing Strategy

Promotion

The story of Saturn is inseparable from its advertising history because Saturn involved all marketing entities from the advertising agency to the dealers in all decisions from the very beginning. In 1987, Saturn began looking for an advertising agency to handle what would become a $100 million account, searching for an agency that could understand the importance of partnership. After reviewing applications from more than 50 agencies, Saturn decided to widen its search. San Francisco's Hal Riney & Partners had already attracted attention in the car industry with its work for Austin Rover Cars of North America, with an ad for the Sterling that showed only brief glimpses of the car itself. In May 1988, after a review by a panel of company executives, two dealers, and a UAW representative, Saturn named Riney its advertising agency, 29 months before the first car went on sale.

Riney immediately became involved with many aspects of the company's innovative start-up. Unlike other ad agencies handling automotive accounts, Riney did not open a satellite office in Detroit because it wanted to remain free of Detroit's limited world view, where 80 percent of the cars are domestic. Riney understood that Saturn had to cater to baby boomers who preferred Japanese automobiles for their perceived higher quality and value.

Riney, along with a panel of 16 Saturn dealers, contributed to many Saturn decisions. Keeping in mind the target market of college-educated men and women aged 25 to 49, they decided to adopt a "straight talk" philosophy, which was applied to many aspects of the Saturn brand. For example, all Saturn retail stores would be called "Saturn of [Location] "to stress the Saturn name rather than the dealer's. Car color descriptions are also simple, using names like "red" rather than "raspberry red."

Riney's first real promotion task was internal communication. When members of his agency interviewed Saturn employees for this task, they found the Saturn employees enthusiastic and emotionally involved with their new company, a fact that Riney would use to advantage in both internal and external promotions. In April 1989, Riney produced a 26-minute documentary film called, "Spring in Spring Hill," which chronicled the startup of a new company dedicated to building cars "in a brand new way." The film is used to help explain Saturn to new employees and suppliers and for training; dealers use it to make presentations; and the film has aired on some cable television networks. The film features employees explaining, often quite emotionally, just what Saturn is all about and what it means to them.

Riney applied the straight-talk, people-oriented philosophy in consumer advertising, stressing Saturn, the company, rather than the car. "A different kind of company. A different kind of car," was the theme line. The first commercials told stories about the Spring Hill heartland and about Saturn employees. All Saturn ads have a down-home feeling and feature ordinary people talking about the cars and the Saturn concept. They tell the story of how employees took a risk and left Detroit for something new and exciting—to start from the drawing board and "build cars again . . . but in a brand new way. "The ads stress that, by recapturing the USA's can-do spirit, Saturn knows how to make cars.

Later ads featured the stories of Saturn customers, focusing on Saturn buyers' lifestyles and playing up product themes that baby boomers hold dear, such as safety, utility, and value. One commercial, for example, highlighted a recall order Saturn issued to fix a seat problem and showed a Saturn representative traveling to Alaska to fix the Saturn owned by Robin Millage, an actual customer who had ordered her car sight unseen from a dealer in the continental United States. The result of Riney's folksy, straight-talk campaign is a sharply focused brand image for Saturn.

Most Saturn dealers have salespersons working in teams and avoid high pressure sales techniques. Usually salespersons split commissions and cooperate in providing a relaxed, inviting showroom environment, allowing customers to browse and offering service and advice only as customers seek it.

Product

Initially, Saturn offered only four products: the Saturn SC1 and SC2 coupes and the Saturn SL1 and SL2 sedans. A SW1 and SW2 station wagon and entry-level coupe (SL) were introduced in 1993. The EV1 (a limited production electric car) was introduced in late 1996 and the LS (mid-size car) is to be introduced in spring 1999. The ad agency/dealer advisory panel felt the cars should not be given descriptive names (such as Chevrolet Camaro) because they didn't want anything to dilute the Saturn name. Saturn's entire philosophy means that the cars have a higher level of quality than other General Motors-made vehicles.

Distribution

With marketing and distribution of new cars accounting for 30 to 35 percent of a car's cost, Saturn planned its distribution very carefully. Dealers are given large territories so that each competes with rival brands rather than each other. Saturn generally has only one dealership in a metropolitan area. The first dealerships were set up in areas where import car sales are high, and most were located on the East and West coasts to avoid cannibalizing sales of other GM cars. In addition, Saturn chose dealers that know how to appeal to import car buyers.

Pricing

The revolutionary ideas employed at Saturn continue with its pricing strategy. Base prices range from $11,035 (SL) to $15,295 (SC2), competitive with import car prices, but options can increase prices up to $20,000. Other base prices are SL1 ($11,735), SL2 ($13,195), SC1 ($13,035), SW1 ($12,735), and SW2 ($14,695). For most dealers, there are no rebates or promotions, and no haggling or dealing. A price tag of $11,035 means that the customer pays $11,035, period. Saturn cannot set prices or control the one-price policy because of legal considerations. However, dealers have found the one-price policy very desirable because of tight profit margins and the high integrity sales approach that is a part of this marketing strategy. Potential buyers can access the Interactive Pricing Center (http://www.saturn.com/cgi-bin/welcome.cgi) where they can "build" their own Saturn, starting with a base car and adding options. Monthly payments can be estimated and financing options chosen.

Implementation Of The Saturn Strategy

First-day sales of Saturn cars were tremendous. One Memphis dealership sold all nine of its Saturns on the first day, with a backlog of orders. Similar success stories occurred all over the country. However, the company experienced great difficulty meeting demand, with many customers waiting more than six weeks to receive their automobiles. For example, in late 1992, the Plymouth, Michigan, dealer had only four Saturn cars on hand, instead of the usual 200, and she had sold the nine demonstration models her sales staff had been driving. Saturn officials say part of the problem with shortages was due to the fact that they were unwilling to compromise on quality. Saturn expected to hit peak production of 300,000 cars per year at Spring Hill in 1993.

With serious troubles of its own, General Motors wanted Saturn to stand on its own and was reluctant to invest more money in the project. Specifically, GM wanted the Spring Hill plant to be more productive, saying there was room for improvement. However, Saturn employees said quality suffered when personnel and equipment were pushed too hard. Because their pay is tied to quality targets, they were especially concerned about the quality of Saturn cars. In October 1991, they held a slowdown during a visit by then GM Chairman Robert C. Stempel to protest a production increase that resulted in higher defect rates. Saturn president Richard G. "Skip" LeFauve tried to increase production without harming quality, partly by adding a third shift to the Spring Hill plant. Saturn's future was further threatened by the fact that GM had yet to commit money to fund new Saturn models beyond 1995. This could have been a real problem because it takes a minimum of three years to develop a new car. However, GM pinned hopes on today's baby boom Saturn buyers graduating to larger, more expensive GM models such as Buick and Cadillac in future years.

Despite production restraints and other problems, Saturn sold 170,495 cars in the 1992 model year, a 236 percent increase over its first-year sales in 1991. That gave Saturn a 2.1 percent share of the U.S. auto market, helping it leapfrog over Hyundai, Subaru, Volkswagen, and Mitsubishi. More significantly, Saturn ranked third in J.D. Power & Associate's measurement of new car buyer satisfaction, behind only Lexus and Infinity.

May 1993 was the first profitable month for the Saturn Corporation since its first car was produced. Saturn expected to sell 300,000 cars in the 1993 calendar year but failed to reach this objective. A third production shift was added to cut overtime costs. With 20 hours of production, six days a week, quality was still the company's main concern. If a car is not up to standards, Saturn employees stop the assembly line.

Until 1996, Saturn was able to maintain its sales momentum by developing a cult-like following with its down-home advertisements and successful picnics where all Saturn owners were invited to Spring Hill, Tennessee, to celebrate the joy of Saturn ownership. Since then, even creative advertising and high profile customer events have not overcome the decreasing sales in the sub-compact market. Fewer people want to buy small, fuel-efficient cars. Another factor was the Asian currency crisis in 1997 that helped foreign small car makers drop prices.

There is a question concerning Saturn's decision to focus on small cars. The company may have missed an opportunity to build on Saturn's success as a respected, high quality small car manufacturer. Should GM have developed Saturn into a company selling many different types and sizes of cars and trucks? Even Saturn workers suggested in 1996 that the company should be selling a small sport utility vehicle. Then they watched as Honda (CR-V) and Toyota (RAV4) sold all they could make.

The Need for New Products and Sales Growth

Despite the early success of Saturn, the company faces challenges in order to sustain its early momentum. Unit sales peaked during calendar year 1994 at approximately 286,000 units. Since then, unit sales declined to approximately 250,000 in 1997, a 10 percent decrease from the previous year. Saturn's rather narrow product line is cited as one reason for the sales decline. The Company's focus on small cars leaves it vulnerable to the shift in demand toward bigger vehicles, including minivans and sport utility vehicles.

Saturn is considering the development of a small sport utility vehicle, but this product cannot hit the market before 2002. Instead of letting Saturn sell the Catera, a small, near luxury sedan that was given to Cadillac, there appeared to be a corporate (GM) strategy to keep Saturn from having new product lines.

The good news is that in the spring of 1999 Saturn dealers will begin selling the LS, the first new product for Saturn in almost a decade. This mid-size vehicle should provide a significant opportunity to get current owners who have outgrown their small cars to buy another Saturn. With a trend toward the purchase of larger cars and low gas prices, a mid-size vehicle is long overdue. The Saturn LS was developed in Europe as an Opal Astra and will be built at a spare factory GM owns in Wilmington, Delaware. An important consideration is how this new manufacturing facility will fit into the Saturn image of Spring Hill, Tennessee and a "different kind of car company and a different kind of car." Finally, instead of increasing Saturn's autonomy, GM is integrating it into the corporate organization. The reason given is that GM has a strategy to capitalize on worldwide efficiencies by using common parts and processes for many of its cars.

Keeping with GM's vision of Saturn as a laboratory for new product development, GM selected the Saturn unit to market the company's first electric vehicle, named EV1. This two-seat coupe, which goes from 0 to 60 miles per hour in 8.5 seconds, was introduced at select Saturn dealers in Arizona and California in late 1996 and was supported by a $25 million marketing campaign. The development of the EV1 is in response to mandates passed in California, Massachusetts, and New York that require that a certain percentage of vehicles sold in any given year be "zero-emissions vehicles." GM was the first company to have an electric vehicle on the market, but other manufacturers including Chrysler, Honda, and Nissan have similar products available, too.

Electric vehicles may hold promise for the future, but their impact on Saturn today is minimal. Many consumers are not ready to change from gasoline-powered automobiles to ones powered by electricity. A survey by J.D. Power found that only 23 percent of consumers would consider buying or leasing an electric vehicle. Forty percent said the technology of electric vehicles was too new. Saturn is carefully offering the EV1 to consumers in test markets. The EV1 is available only by lease (monthly rate ranges from $399 to $549 depending on location), and prospective customers are screened to determine if the EV1 would be a fit with the customer. Saturn's plans for the EV1 are modest; it plans to lease only about 300 per year for the next few years.

Declining sales also have created inventory problems for Saturn with the company having an 84-day supply at the end of 1997 that was well above a desired level of 65 days. This situation resulted in Saturn's announced plans to reduce production for the first six months of 1998 from 160,000 cars to 130,000 cars. The planned cuts will not affect the status of Saturn's employees because the United Auto Workers' contract with Saturn does not allow employees to be laid off. Any downtime resulting from decreased production is filled with training activities or performing such projects as painting miles of white wooden fence around the Saturn facility.

Another challenge for Saturn lies in its attempt to establish itself in the Japanese market. Saturn began selling right-side-drive cars in Japan in 1997 via a small number of retailers. The entry into Japan was complicated by a strong dollar versus all Asian currencies, thus hurting Japanese consumers' purchasing power. Also, Saturn's small-car products face intense competition in Japan from domestic producers Toyota, Honda, and Nissan. These challenges posed by the Japanese market as well as demand shifts in the American automobile market are sure to test the strength of the young Saturn company in the 21st century.

Questions for Discussion

1. Analyze strategic market planning at Saturn.
2. What should Saturn do as competitors attempt to copy its pricing and dealer service policies?
3. Can General Motors change its corporate culture and implement some of Saturn's successes within its organizational structure?

Sources

These facts are from http://www.gm.com/ (Apr. 22, 1998); http://www.saturn.com (Apr. 16, 1998); Robyn Meredith, "As Sales Fall, Saturn Workers to Vote on Ditching Contract," *The Commercial Appeal*, Mar. 8, 1998, C1, C3; Michelle Maynard, "Sales Slump Forces Saturn to Cut Production," *USA Today*, Jan. 21, 1998, B1; Ian P. Murphy, "Charged Up: Electric Cars Get Jolt of Marketing," *Marketing News*, Aug. 18, 1997, 1, 7; Kristine Breese, "First Saturn Day: Diary of a Dealer," *Advertising Age*, Oct. 29, 1990, 68; Rich Ceppos, "Saturn-Finally, It's Here. But Is It Good Enough?," *Car and Driver*, Nov. 1990, 132–138; Stuart Elliott, "Campaign Takes Aim at Heartstrings," *USA Today*, Nov. 1, 1990, 1B, 2B; Bob Garfield, "Down-to-Earth Ads Give Saturn an Underrated Liftoff," *Advertising Age*, Oct. 29, 1990, 68; James R. Healey, "Saturn Demand Delivers Excitement to Dealers," *USA Today*, Nov. 5,1990, B1; James R. Healey, "Saturn, Day One: Business Is Brisk," *USA Today*, Oct. 26, 1990, 1B, 2B; Barbara Lippert, "It's a Saturn Morning in America," *Adweek*, Oct. 15, 1990, 67; Micheline Maynard, "Fulfilling Buyers' Wishes, Saturn's Well Runs Dry," *USA Today*, Aug. 18, 1992, B1; Raymond Serafin, "Saturn's Goal: To Be Worthy," *Advertising Age*, Nov. 5, 1990,

21; Raymond Serafin, "The Saturn Story," *Advertising Age*, Nov. 16, 1992, 1, 13, 16; Raymond Serafin and Patricia Strand, "Saturn People Star in First Campaign," *Advertising Age*, Aug. 27, 1990, 1, 38; Neal Templin and Joseph B. White, "GM's Saturn, In Early Orbit, Intrigues Buyers," *The Wall Street Journal*, Oct. 25, 1990, B1, B6; James B. Treece, "Here Comes GM's Saturn," *Business Week*, April 9, 1990, 56–62; "23 More Dealers Open Doors to Saturn Buyers," *USA Today*, Nov. 15, 1990, 6B; Joseph B. White and Melinda Grenier Guiles, "Rough Launch," *The Wall Street Journal*, July 9, 1990, A1, A12; David Woodruff, with James B. Treece, Sunita Wadekar Bhargava, and Karen Lowry Miller, "Saturn: GM Finally Has a Real Winner. But Success Is Bringing a Fresh Batch of Problems," *Business Week*, Aug. 17, 1992, 86–91; Cindy Wolff, "First Saturn Here Runs Jag Off Road," *The Commercial Appeal*, Oct. 26, 1990, A1, A12; Phil West, "Saturn Corp. Rings up First Profitable Month," *The Commercial Appeal*, June 11, 1993, B2.

The Cola War[1]

Perhaps one of the most fascinating competitive rivalries (the "Cola War") has been between the Coca-Cola Company and PepsiCo, Inc. This long "war" (nearly 75 years old) will be summarized by comparing the histories of the two opponents and providing descriptions of their recent strategic positions.

The Coca-Cola Company

It began in 1878 as an Atlanta druggist's creation. He concocted a soft drink syrup containing ground kola nuts (from an African tree) for his soda fountain. These nuts contain cocaine, a substance with much more of a side effect than understood at the time, which provided a "stimulus" to the drinker. For many reasons, this drink was immediately popular, so the inventor began to bottle it with carbonated water. A catchy brand name denoting the kola ingredient ("Coca-Cola") was developed, and the company was incorporated with the inventor keeping majority control.

Sales began briskly in Atlanta but were confined to the region. Market potential beyond Atlanta was evident from the local success. The founder, however, was adamantly opposed to advertising at first, but later, Coca-Cola became a leading advertiser. The next issue to address was channels of distribution. The bottled product was too heavy for shipment, so the company found several independent bottlers and franchised them. Then, the company needed to ship only the syrup, leaving the bottlers to add the carbonated water. When expansion was limited by cash flow, another solution was taken. The plants were sold back to regional bottlers and the company maintained control with a 49 percent interest. In other words, the company maintained a large minority interest in locally owned bottling plants.

The Coca-Cola Company became a very effective marketer with its full-page magazine advertisements and billboards. Its theme, "The Pause that Refreshes," was seen everywhere, especially on soda fountains and grocery stores. The drink was the national thirst quencher, and its makers aimed to put it "within arm's reach of every American." The company became dedicated to creating a distribution network in the United States, then Canada and beyond.

---

[1] This case was prepared by David J. Luck, emeritus, Southern Illinois University, and O.C. Ferrell, Colorado State University, for classroom discussion rather than to illustrate either effective or ineffective handling of an administrative situation.

Although the company was financially strong, capable of financing expansion in other directions, it did not choose to expand its product line in beverages, sticking with Coca-Cola, its sole beverage. The company was free to plot its strategy, protected by a copyrighted brand name, a secret formula, and its widespread infrastructure of bottlers and distributors.

The Pepsi-Cola Company Begins the Cola War

The Pepsi-Cola Company's business was founded at the turn of the century by a New Bern, North Carolina druggist who formulated the product. When a firm in New York launched Pepsi Cola, the Coca-Cola Company sued for infringement. When the final decision came down, the winner was Pepsi. The copyright of "cola" was held invalid, for that is only a generic term for a product containing kola. Thus began the war of the colas.

Pepsi-Cola scarcely seemed a match for the Coca-Cola Company, but it attacked its giant rival with even more effective marketing. A low price strategy was used for years with emphasis on lower price and slightly larger quantity. The initial theme was "Pepsi-Cola hits the spot." Pepsi-Cola struggled into the 1930s, but it became the number two cola in the United States.

Both companies experienced strong demand into the World War II era. Pepsi-Cola broadened its product line with new products such as Mountain Dew. However, a minor brand—RC Cola—was the first to respond to consumers' diet-consciousness with Diet Rite. Pepsi-Cola introduced Diet Pepsi and quickly led in this new diet category. The Coca-Cola Company introduced Tab, then Diet Coke. When Sprite (a lemon-lime drink) was introduced by the Coca-Cola Company, Pepsi-Cola followed with its Slice (a fruit drink). The battle continued with added varieties, containers, and advertising campaigns.

Pepsi-Cola was a leader in promotion and dedicated to maximizing sales growth. It recognized the key importance of the youth segment and launched the "Join the Pepsi Generation" campaign with great success. The Coca-Cola Company responded with huge, but less flamboyant, campaigns. The next smashing success was the "Taste the Pepsi Challenge," in which consumers made blind sampling of the two top brands, Pepsi and Coke. Of course, Pepsi was always the winner in the commercials aired.

The impact of that success alarmed Coca-Cola management, which decided to counter by introducing a new "flavor" of Coke. However, the "New Coke" was not accepted well and was soon pulled from the market. The company had not properly assessed the emotional feeling consumers had for the original formula that the company returned to and called "Classic Coke." It had made a serious marketing mistake in implying that the time-honored "secret" formula was inferior. The rivalry between Pepsi-Cola and the Coca-Cola Company was intensified when Pepsi-Cola gloated about the fiasco in a derisive book.

The Coca-Cola Company and Pepsi-Cola Diversify

While the competition continued, changes were being made in the two companies through diversification. The Coca-Cola Company pursued many ventures outside the soft drink business, including the purchase of the number two film producer, Columbia Pictures, which was later sold for $1.5 billion, making it an overall success. Another venture included citrus orchards and juice production. The orchards were eventually sold, but juice packing thrived. Its brand, Minute Maid, became the leader in citrus juices. With the addition of Hi-C and other juice products, the Coca-Cola Company became the world leader in fruit drinks. The main emphasis continued to be strengthening the distribution system and penetration of world markets. A major achievement was winning the Chinese government's permission to be the first foreign bottler there.

Pepsi-Cola was active in diversification as well, driven by top executives who saw sales growth as their main ambition. Their first foray was to buy Frito-Lay, the leader in snack foods. Frito-Lay was an excellent firm whose success rested on its many new snack varieties and its delivery system. Buoyed by this successful endeavor, Pepsi-Cola made a bold move into restaurants with the purchase of Pizza Hut in 1974, followed by two other major fast food chains, Kentucky Fried Chicken and Taco Bell. Pepsi-Cola management now had many facets, including continuing efforts in battling Coke in foreign markets.

The Coca-Cola Company Maintains Leadership in Soft Drinks

The Coca-Cola Company maintains global soft drink industry leadership with 1997 revenues of $18.9 billion, net income of $4.1 billion, and nearly 30,000 employees. Every day, consumers enjoy an average of almost a billion servings of Coca-Cola (known as Coca-Cola Classic in the United States and Canada), Diet Coke (known as Coca-Cola Light in some countries), Sprite, Fanta, and other products of the Coca-Cola Company, such as Surge. Syrups, concentrates, and beverage bases for Coca-Cola, the company's flagship brand, and other company soft drinks are manufactured and sold by the Coca-Cola Company and is subsidiaries in more than 195 countries around the world. By contract with the company or its local subsidiaries, local businesses are authorized to bottle and sell company soft drinks within certain territorial boundaries and under conditions that ensure the highest standards of quality and uniformity providing 50 percent world market share.

Coca-Cola Enterprises, Inc. sells 65 percent of the canned and bottled Coke in the United States and is 44 percent owned by the Coca-Cola Company. Coca-Cola Enterprises continues to acquire large regional bottlers that control local operations and serves as a "master bottler" with the financial resources to continue expansion.

The company takes pride in being a worldwide business that is local. Bottling plants are, with some exceptions, locally owned and operated by independent business people who are native to the nations in which they are located. Bottlers provide the required capital for investments in land, buildings, machinery, equipment, trucks, bottles, and cases. Most supplies are purchased from local sources, often creating new supply industries and areas of employment within local economies.

The company continues to supply concentrates and beverage bases used to make its products and provides management assistance to help its bottlers ensure the profitable growth of their businesses. Product manufacturing, quality control, plant and equipment design, marketing, and personnel training are just a few of the areas in which the company shares its expertise.

The company's operating management structure consists of five geographic groups plus the Minute Maid Company. The North America Group comprises the United States and Canada. The Latin America Group includes the company's operations across Central and South America from Mexico to the tip of Argentina. The company's most populated operating group, the Middle and Far East Group, ranges from the Middle East to India, China, Japan, and Australia. The Greater Europe Group stretches from Greenland to Russia's Far East, including some of the most established markets in western Europe and the rapidly growing nations of eastern and central Europe. The Africa Group includes the company's business in 47 countries in sub-Saharan Africa.

PepsiCo Reorganizes for Soft Drink and Snack Food Growth

PepsiCo, Inc., founded in 1965 through the merger of Pepsi-Cola Company and Frito-Lay, Inc., is among the most successful consumer products companies in the world with 1997 annual revenues of over $21 billion, net income of $1.5 billion, and about 140,000 employees.

PepsiCo has achieved a leadership position in each of its two major packaged goods businesses: beverages and snack foods. The company is a world leader in soft drink bottling and the world's largest producer of snack chips. PepsiCo's brand names are some of the best known and most respected in the world. Pepsi, Diet Pepsi, Mountain Dew, Slice, and other brands account for nearly one-third of total soft drink sales in the United States, a consumer market totaling about $54 billion. Today, PepsiCo products account for about 23 percent of all soft drinks sold internationally. In addition to brands marketed in the United States, major products include Mirinda and Pepsi Max. Pepsi-Cola North America includes the United States and Canada. Key Pepsi-Cola international markets include Argentina, Brazil, China, Mexico, Saudi Arabia, Spain, Thailand, and the United Kingdom. The company has also established operations in the emerging markets of the Czech Republic, Hungary, India, Poland, Slovakia, and Russia, where Pepsi-Cola was the first United States consumer product to be marketed.

Today, Frito-Lay brands account for more than 60 percent of the $12.2 billion United States snack chip industry. PepsiCo's international snack food operations are the leading multinational snack chips company, accounting for about one-fifth of international retail snack chip sales. Frito-Lay Company operations in 39 markets supply products to more than 80 countries. Frito-Lay North America includes Canada and the United States. Major Frito-Lay international markets include Australia, Brazil, France, Mexico, the Netherlands, Poland, Spain, and the United Kingdom.

PepsiCo has achieved a continuing record of growth. This record is based on high standards of performance, distinctive competitive strategies, and superbly executed marketing strategies. PepsiCo's objective is to increase the value of its shareholders' investment through concentration of resources on internal growth and carefully selected acquisitions. These strategies are continually fine-tuned to address the opportunities and risks of the global marketplace. The corporation's success reflects a continuing commitment to growth.

In early 1997 PepsiCo management announced plans to spin off its restaurant divisions to focus on the company's packaged goods businesses. This decision was implemented on October 6, 1997, the day PepsiCo spun off its three principal restaurant businesses—Pizza Hut, KFC, and Taco Bell—into a new, independent publicly held company called TRICON Global Restaurants, Inc.

Questions for Discussion

1. Briefly describe the strategies of the Coca-Cola Company and PepsiCo. In your opinion, which company's management team is following the better strategy? What key factors impact your opinion?

2. What are the most important differences between the Coca-Cola Company and PepsiCo?

3. What major strategy should each company adopt for the next ten years? What changes would you make in their current strategies and why?

Sources

These facts are from PepsiCo, Inc. 1997 Annual Report; http://www.pepsico.com; The Coca-Cola Company 1997 Annual Report; and http://www.cocacola.com/co/chairman97.html.

CASE 3

Sigma Press[1]

In the fall of 1970, Donald Sapit was faced with a dilemma. His company, Weston Laboratories, of which he was president, had been sold to a larger corporation. At the age of 41, he was faced with the prospect of unemployment for the first time in his life. Employment prospects in his town, Ottawa, Illinois, were not good for someone with a degree in mechanical engineering and an MBA from the University of Chicago. He was not looking forward to having to move his family of four school-age children, given the anticipated disruptions in their lives and resulting stress and unhappiness. He had received offers in Chicago, 80 miles away, but it would have required a full-fledged move to the city or suburbs. The alternative was to stick it out in Ottawa and rectify his company's badly damaged financial situation.

As president of Weston Laboratories, a small research facility, Sapit had gained an excellent background in the administration and operation of a small business. During the two years prior to the sale of Weston Laboratories, he had returned to school on a part-time basis to earn his MBA at the University of Chicago. As in most small businesses, Sapit wore many hats, one of which was supervising most of the purchasing functions. Over the previous two or three years, he had dealt, on a continuing basis, with a small printer, Dayne Printing Company, of Streator, Illinois, a town 15 miles away. In 1967, Dayne, on the verge of bankruptcy, was offered to Weston Laboratories at an attractive price. Sapit saw it as an opportunity for a good personal investment that would not conflict with the Weston Labs operation. He felt the present Dayne managers, who indicated their desire to stay on after the sale, could manage the day-to-day operations with little outside help. Sapit personally made the purchase and felt that, with the increased volume that Weston would provide, the operation could become profitable within a 12-month period.

One problem Dayne had experienced over the years had been establishing a sound, effective sales program. To help mend some of Dayne's image problems with its customers, the name was changed to Sigma Press, Inc., and the business was

---

[1] This case was provided by Donald and Mike Sapit, Sigma Press, 1543 Kingsley Ave., Bldg. 16, Orange Park, Florida 32073 for classroom discussion rather than to illustrate either effective or ineffective handling of an administrative situation. O. C. Ferrell, Colorado State University, developed the final draft of this case.

incorporated in the state of Illinois. A new salesman/manager was hired and given the authority to establish new sales policies. Sapit had decided to be involved only on a limited basis and, in effect, took the position of an absentee owner. Over the next few years, several salespeople came and went, and the sales effort provided only minimal increases in volume. The business held its own, but made little progress. The results were typical of those experienced by most absentee-owned businesses.

In spite of the fact that Sigma was making little progress, Sapit continued to see the potential for making it into a quality-oriented printing business that could make substantial gains against its local competition. The area served by the shop covered a radius of approximately 30 miles around the city of Streator. The area had a number of major manufacturing plants that were potential users of substantial quantities of printing. Unfortunately most of these plants were headquartered in other cities and did not have authority for local purchasing of anything beyond the basic necessities required for daily plant operations.

The Desk Calendar: A Strategic Opportunity

In seeking other alternatives to improve sales, Sapit and Sigma staff had developed an advertising desk pad calendar for distribution as a gift to its customers. Its purpose was to keep the Sigma name, phone number, and list of services in front of the customer as a constant reminder of its existence. It was freely offered to any customer thought to have sufficient volume potential to justify the expense of the calendar and its distribution costs.

One of the customers that had received the calendar, Oak State Products, an Archway Cookie Bakery, asked the salesman if Sigma could produce similar calendars for them with the Archway advertisement printed at the top. Sigma filled this initial order and it proved popular with Archway's customers. The next year Archway asked if the calendars could be produced with a color photo of its plant in the ad space. This version was so well received that Oak State recommended the use of the calendar as a marketing tool to all the other Archway Bakeries around the country. Sigma recognized that the opportunity for a new marketing strategy was developing.

The sales volume realized from the calendar sales was not substantial, but Sapit saw in it a good possibility for a totally new market, divorced from the limitations imposed by Sigma's present sales territory. Furthermore, he perceived a market that could be developed by a direct marketing effort. This direct marketing effort would permit sales penetration into a much larger geographical area than was practical to serve with Sigma's limited sales staff.

It was at this time that the sale of Weston Laboratories took place, and because of philosophical differences with the new management, Sapit was forced to make the decision to leave the company. Although Sigma was starting to show potential for very modest profitability and good growth, it was still just barely able to support itself. After a family council meeting where the decision was made to "tough it out," Sapit made the decision to enter the Sigma operation on a full-time basis and to prove that it really could become a first-class operation. The change was made in 1971.

A New Marketing Strategy

The first major strategic organizational decision for Sapit was to dismiss the one salesman and assume all sales and management responsibilities himself. He then developed a general marketing strategy. A definite sales territory was established and prime prospects targeted for personal calls on a regular basis. (Previous salespeople had been making calls on a hit or miss basis, with no real continuity.) Customer and prospect lists were developed so that a mailing program could be instituted on a scheduled basis. Each four to six weeks, a specially created mailing piece or a sample of the "job of the month" was sent to each firm. Additionally, a direct marketing calendar program was developed with a crude effort to target specific market segments. At the time, direct mail promotion of printing, and especially direct marketing efforts, were relatively unheard of in the printing industry.

The advertising desk calendar was marketed on the theme of "constant exposure advertising." It was given the name "Salesbuilder." Each customer was offered a standard calendar format with an individual ad imprint customized to fit the needs of the company's business. The imprint could contain line drawings, photos, product lists, or any special information necessary to convey the company's message to customers. Sigma's willingness to encourage attractive and creative designs received immediate attention and acceptance by customers. It set the company apart from the competition, which would allow "four lines of block type, not to exceed 32 letters." In effect, a whole new advertising medium was being created, and Sigma was at the front of the wave.

A Financial and Production Strategy to Promote Expansion

Within a year after Sapit's entry into the business, total volume was up 50 percent; even more important, the response to the calendar marketing effort was starting to show real promise. As a result, Sigma was experiencing the need for additional capital to finance the growth. Sapit offered one third of the stock to Don Vonachen, a long-time friend, who was a practicing attorney from Peoria, Illinois. The transaction was completed, and the cash was used for capital to help fund the day-to-day operations and expanding accounts receivable resulting from the increased volume. Vonachen was not active in the day-to-day operations but functioned as corporate secretary, legal counsel, board member, and advisor.

In the summer of 1972, the sales of commercial printing were gaining at a modest rate of increase, but calendar sales were increasing at a rate of 40 percent per year. It was becoming apparent that larger manufacturing facilities would be required in the immediate future or the sales efforts would have to be scaled back. A search was started for a larger building in a better location. When no suitable building could be found, the board decided to construct its own building on a five-acre site at the intersection of Route 23 and Interstate 80 in Ottawa. It was a site with high visibility and a good measure of prestige. This was a rather ambitious move for a company that, only 18 months prior, was just barely holding its own. The move to the new building, attractively designed and fronting on the Interstate, created a then-unwarranted image success for Sigma. It seemed to Sapit that Sigma should try to capitalize on its new image and high visibility. He decided to change the emphasis of the business and hoped to improve its record of growth and profitability.

A Three-Year Corporate Plan

Over the next few years, Sigma's marketing strategy was oriented toward building a reputation for producing the most creative and highest quality printing in its service area, which had a 35- to 40-mile radius around Ottawa. The firm took a calculated risk. Sapit anticipated that this new direction would give his firm a solid reputation as a quality printer, one that fully justified the higher prices it charged. Several of the larger local companies obtained permission from their corporate offices to procure their printing locally. The downstate division of Carson Pririe Scott & Company, a substantial department store chain, chose Sigma for the production of its catalogs. The new marketing strategy paid off, and total sales volume had increased 220 percent by 1976.

Sales of the calendar increased slowly but steadily. Management wanted growth, but it wanted it in an orderly and controlled manner. Management also wanted its growth to be more profitable than the industry average of approximately 5 percent on sales. It was becoming obvious that to be successful in the printing business, it was necessary to specialize. After long and deliberate discussion and investigation during 1976, the company management wrote a three-year corporate plan.

The corporate plan emphasized marketing, which at this time was considered unique for a small commercial printer. The marketing plan focused a major share of the sales and marketing effort on building a market for the "Salesbuilder" desk calendar. The target market consisted primarily of smaller corporate accounts, while the marketing mix emphasized product and promotion. Space advertising in sales and marketing-oriented publications created substantial numbers of inquiries, but sales levels did not follow. Direct mail, primarily to manufacturers, produced a much higher response and return on investment. Sigma had created a unique product that was very flexible in terms of unusual designs, advertising messages, photographic techniques, and other special requirements-a highly effective marketing tool.

Within the next few calendar seasons, solid accounts such as Serta Mattress, Domino Sugar, and Borden, Inc., were added to the list of satisfied customers. Reorder rates were very high, usually in the 88–90 percent range. Quantities ordered by individual companies tended to increase annually for three or four years and then level off. Total calendar sales had increased at a rate of approximately 40 percent per year during the 1976–1980 period, during which time commercial printing sales increased at a rate of about 15 percent annually.

The Calendar Becomes Sigma's Corporate Strategy

Because of the success of the marketing plan, production capacity was being taxed. In 1979–1980, major capital commitments were made to add a new high-speed two-color press and to purchase, redesign, and rebuild a specialized collating machine to further automate calendar assembly. This opened the way to mass marketing of the "Salesbuilder" calendar line. Direct mail techniques were improved to allow selection of prospects by SIC number and sales volume. A toll-free 1-800 number encouraged direct response by interested parties. Whenever possible, Sigma responded to inquiries by sending a sample calendar that contained advertising ideas related to the respondent's line of business. The sample would be followed up with a personal phone call within two to three weeks. Calendar sales continued to improve until, by 1983, they represented 40 percent of total sales and approximately 75 percent of net profit.

In spite of the success of the calendar marketing programs and attractive profit levels, Sapit was disturbed by trends in the printing industry that pointed toward a diminishing market and increased competition for the commercial segment, particularly in Sigma's local Rust Belt area. Rapid development of new technology and high-speed equipment had caused industry-wide investments in new equipment well beyond immediate need, creating excess capacity. The result was cost cutting and reduced margins.

Sigma's management had for some time been considering selling the commercial portion of its business in favor of becoming an exclusive marketer of calendar products. Through its membership in the Printing Industry of Illinois, a buyer was found for the plant, equipment, and the goodwill of the commercial portion of the business. The buyer agreed to enter into a long-term contract to handle all calendar production for Sigma, using the same plant and staff that had been handling the production for the previous 10 years. The sale was completed in June 1983.

Sigma's management now found itself free of the daily problems of production and plant management and able to commit all its efforts to creating and marketing new calendar products. Sapit had a long-standing personal desire to move the business to the Sun Belt for the better weather and, more important, for the better business climate. In May 1985, corporate offices were moved to Jacksonville, Florida. Concurrently, Sapit was joined in the business by his son, Mike, a graduate of Illinois State University in graphic arts.

Actions were taken to expand Sigma's product line to include several additional products, all designed to be highly personalized. The new products included a year-at-a-glance wall planning calendar, desk diary, pocket diary, and a smaller version of the original desk calendar.

Sigma had built its calendar business on items that were basically "off-the-shelf" products that could be imprinted with the customer's advertising message. It was now seeing a growing market and benefiting from the demand for products that were totally customized not only in graphic design, but in product specifications as well. Sigma's management perceived the market for their new line of "supercustomized" calendars to be the medium to large corporation with a substantial customer base. The audience was companies with large advertising budgets that were service-oriented, thus providing the potential for orders of larger magnitudes. The market being studied was relatively small in terms of number of companies, but very large with respect to total sales potential. It would require a totally different marketing approach from those used in the past.

Test advertisements for custom-designed calendars were run in *Advertising Age* and in several marketing journals. These advertisements appealed to larger corporate accounts. In addition, the sales staff became much more aggressive in searching out individual accounts that appeared to have a high potential as customized calendar customers. Prospects were contacted by phone and mail, to determine the individual with the responsibility to specify and authorize this type of purchase. Unsolicited samples of several different customized products were sent by Federal Express in order to attract attention. Each prospect was followed up by a phone call within a few days to confirm interest and provide additional information.

The goal was to establish Sigma as a publisher of high quality, creatively designed custom calendars. Initial response to the new marketing strategy was good, with indications that the blue chip companies could, in fact, be reached through this approach. To reach its growth goals, Sigma felt it had to be successful in this marketing strategy. This type of highly customized product design is very demanding on the creative staff. Because only 10 to 15 new accounts of this type could be handled each year, it was important that creative time be spent on high-potential accounts. The new strategy was successful in landing substantial orders from Nabisco, Fidelity Investments, and FedEx. Realizing that these blue chip companies were consumers, Sigma focused the entire organization on meeting five customer needs:

1. Flexibility
2. The ability to produce a quality product consistent with the client's image and marketing goals
3. Personal service and attention from beginning to end
4. Fair pricing
5. Timely, efficient fulfillment.

With the blue chip accounts, Sigma realized that it had to be able to offer its products on a turnkey, or concept through fulfillment, basis. Many of these corporations wanted to use a calendar program, but were not able to devote staff, time, or expertise to such a project. Sigma offered the solution—handling the entire calendar promotion so that customers could devote their time to more productive efforts, confident that their calendar program was running smoothly and efficiently. It installed new computer equipment and programs that would allow order fulfillment in small or single shipments, even for large quantity orders. Special UPS manifest programs were developed to simplify the handling of large quantities of drop shipments.

The Total Service Package

The business grew rapidly from 1985 to 1990, and by 1991, Don and Mike Sapit saw a new opportunity to expand the business again. After carefully analyzing the characteristics of its buyers and their buying decisions, Sigma found new market opportunities. During its first 15 years in the promotional calendar business, Sigma focused on large companies, which usually distributed their promotional calendars through their sales forces to customers. These companies usually supplied Sigma with the basic idea for their calendar promotion, including an imprint or art design for the firm's individualized calendar. For years, Sigma heard the same story from several top prospects: An effective calendar program required too much of their staff's valuable time. Sigma seized this opportunity by marketing its "Total Service Package," a program in which it handled the entire calendar promotion, including conception, design, production, and delivery.

With its own computer order tracking and manifest system in place, Sigma was able to offer its customers and prospects an efficient and cost-saving order and distribution system. From established customer lists or those generated through Sigma's direct order programs, calendars could be shipped to as many as 20,000 locations for a single account. This was particularly helpful to accounts that had dealers scattered across the country.

This achievement led Sigma to take its experience one step further. Using a customer-supplied list, it began marketing the calendars directly to the customer's distributors.

Flyers and samples were produced and mailed by Sigma. Orders were then returned directly to Sigma. This process allowed individual distributors or a single branch to include its own imprint on the calendar. Currently, a customer list may have over 10,000 names, and a single order may consist of over 1,000 different imprints. Because each customer has its own requirements, a staff member dedicated to personalized service is assigned to each customer. Sigma learned how its customers make decisions about specialty advertising purchases such as promotional calendars and then developed a program to satisfy the needs of purchasing agents and buyers in large organizations.

The strategy appears to be very successful. The company has added to its list of satisfied customers such prime accounts as Milwaukee Electric Tool Corp, Hoffman LaRoche, Inc., International Paper Company, and Nabisco Brands, Inc.

Recent Developments

Since focusing on the "Total Service Package" approach as its marketing strategy, Sigma has experienced a large increase in corporate clientele with very specialized product and service requirements. Because of the high demand for the "Total Service Package," the workload soon placed a serious strain on the limits of Sigma's existing staff and physical space. When one additional full-time employee was added in 1993, Sigma began looking for a new facility. The company moved into its new building in 1995 knowing that the new office would allow for personnel growth for at least five to seven years. Adjacent land was secured in the same purchase, which made possible the early 1996 addition of a complete wing for graphics production. State-of-the-art equipment was purchased to keep Sigma in line with new technology, and two additional full-time employees were added between 1995 and 1997, along with one permanent part-time employee—a total of 11 full-time personnel.

Marketing

In 1994, Sigma's sales had leveled at $2.5 million and its new test product, the School Year Planner, was into its second year, with sales growing at about 3 percent per year. Developed to find an ideal "off season" product that would not interfere with seasonal calendar production, Sigma found coordination of sales and production was cumbersome and was spilling over into the seasonal calendar production. The effort was not worth the increase in sales in terms of demand on staff time and energy, so Sigma ultimately decided to discontinue the project in 1998.

Sigma's reputation for its main product continued to grow. Companies were drawn to the custom calendar vendor known for high quality products and a staff with tremendous flexibility and creativity. In an effort to distance itself from competitors, Sigma improved on the "Total Service Package," which had become an important part of its marketing strategy. Customers are now surveyed before and after they receive the product, and large corporate account contacts receive a visit from their account representative early in the year to review the previous year's program and begin groundwork on the upcoming promotion. In addition, international promotions and shipping have become important aspects of several large accounts. Account representatives are developing large corporate accounts by promoting multiple products, while some promotional items beyond calendars are produced in an effort to maintain exclusivity with a client.

Customer demand led to changes in both the sales and administrative area, as well as the graphics department. A stronger focus on the service aspect of the business was a strategic move for the sales and administrative areas. However, the company has also seen tremendous growth in its graphics capabilities—a response to the printing industry itself, as well as the needs of its customers.

However, Sigma's focus on securing corporate accounts that rely heavily on service, rather than the traditional "salesbuilder, once-a-year accounts" is clearly the right formula. The company has added to its list of satisfied customers such prime accounts as Unisource, Volvo, DitchWitch, BetzDearborn, and Sears. But despite the additional staff and resources, the demand for the "Total Service Package" is so great that the company is in danger of overselling its production capabilities to its vendors. Recognizing that possibility, Sigma has become more selective in its marketing efforts.

Annual marketing meetings, held in a different city each year, have become a tradition. Since 1991, staff members have met to review the past year and solve internal and external problems. The meetings encourage teamwork, foster company loyalty, and increase employees' knowledge about Sigma's status in the marketplace. The firm is forecasting 30 percent annual sales growth over the next five years.

Technology

In the late 1980s and early 1990s, Sigma offered limited in-house design/layout services and film was shot manually on a camera—but utilized service bureaus for scans, separations, digital files, and special film needs. Sigma's capabilities were limited, but very few of its customers had complex needs or technologically capable marketing departments.

The advent of the "digital age" in the 1990s served as the catalyst to transform Sigma's prepress capabilities. Graphics workstations were given the speed and storage capacity to handle larger and more complex files that became an integral part of the business. In 1996, an imagesetter was installed—a tremendous commitment to switch to digital film output and to bring a portion of the production work in-house that had been going to outside vendors. The additional equipment also created an environment of more sophisticated hardware, software use, and training needs. The graphics applications used to create the page layouts and images are very complex and call for continual upgrades.

As more companies utilize desktop publishing, Sigma has taken on some of the functions of a service bureau. Converting disks into usable formats and correcting customer artwork has become routine and time-consuming for the graphics department. The growth of the desktop publishing market has created a large number of self-proclaimed graphic artists, who serve as a reminder that the need for such functions will only continue to increase.

The graphics department continues to face more sophisticated product design, printing processes, and compatibility challenges with data and equipment. A commitment was made toward continued evaluation of resources and education on the part of management and the graphics staff.

Though the majority of the prepress work is now handled in-house, there are still some items that must be sent. Certain capabilities are cost-prohibitive to accommodate when the demand isn't great enough to justify the purchase of the resources. Sigma has developed strong relationships with service providers who complement its ability to respond to customer needs.

The mid-1990s also ushered in the company's Internet presence and on-line capabilities. With a corporate identity on the Web, Sigma is better prepared to compete in the increasingly high-tech world of business.

Upgrading technology on the administrative side has allowed the company to better serve its customers. Sigma is now online with several transportation companies, making package tracking an easy task. Networking the administrative computers has resulted in increased flexibility among the staff. In addition, the company is able to do direct invoicing; credit card sales are now offered as a service.

Management Change/Ownership Issues

During the expansion period, Don began to turn over the daily operations of the business to his son Mike. In early 1996, the transition was complete, with Mike in full charge of the business. Don has retired but remains chairman of the board, acting in an advisory capacity.

One of the major concerns is developing personnel strategies over the next few years. Sigma must plan for the transfer of duties as one key employee prepares for retirement in the next five years. This also raises the question of who would succeed the Sapits. Purchasing, production and scheduling are fully understood only by Mike and Don. In the absence of both Mike and Don's leadership, the business would most likely flounder as it is structured today. Even if a successor were waiting in the wings, the internal knowledge of both men would be lost without documentation. The need for procedure manuals clearly needs to be part of a strategy to educate a successor and keep the business going in the event of the loss of one or both of the leaders.

Questions for Discussion

1. Compare and contrast the need for long-range versus short-range marketing planning at Sigma Press.

2. Compare the changes in Sigma's marketing strategy before and after 1983— the date of the sale of the plant and production activities. What were the primary considerations for marketing strategy changes?

3. If you were Sigma's marketing consultant, what recommendation(s) would you make for future strategic market planning?

4. How has Sigma managed growth, and what do you see as its major environmental threats and opportunities for future growth?

Nissan Motor Company[1]

In 1911 in Tokyo, the Kaishinsha Automobile Company was begun. Three years later, the first car rolled off its production lines. That model was an open-touring automobile typical of its day and was called the "Dat."

Post-World War II Period

Forty years later, when the postwar Japanese industrial revival began, the Kaishinsha firm was among the survivors. Soon it was given a simpler name—Nissan Motor Company. Nissan began to produce compact cars that were popular in its home market. Like other successful Japanese manufacturers, Nissan also built an export business around the Orient. Nissan prospered, as did its major rival, Toyota.

The 1950s' economy facilitated strong markets for automobiles in all major nations. The United States continued to be the world's largest market and its major automakers basked in the success of their ever-larger cars. Henry Ford's strategy of tapping popular demand with his low-priced cars seemed all but forgotten. However, the lesson had not been wasted on the West Germans. With their "people's car" (developed before World War II), they staged a peacetime invasion of other European countries, and by the early 1950s, Volkswagen was enjoying success in the United States. American car manufacturers underestimated the threat from the German (and English and French) compacts and responded weakly by importing compacts of their European subsidiaries, like the Opel.

Crossing The Pacific, 1958

In Japan, Nissan and Toyota controlled most of the automobile market. They watched Volkswagen gain solid success in the United States, where other European compacts were established as well. In 1958, Toyota first entered the U.S. market with

---

[1] This case was prepared by David J. Luck, emeritus, Southern Illinois University, for classroom discussion rather than to illustrate either effective or ineffective handling of an administrative situation.

its inexpensive Crown model. Americans found the car inadequate, and Toyota withdrew it.

Nissan was just a few months behind when it took a compact Japanese model to the United States where it met a reception almost as chilly as Toyota's. Nissan persevered, and in 1960, sent over a top salesman, Yatuka Katayama, to cover the West Coast. With him came another car that the company named the Datsun 210 (reminiscent of their first model's name). It was so underpowered and boxy that Katayama struggled to enlist used car dealers to sell it.

However, Katayama put together a network of dealers who were eager to succeed in new car sales. He taught them Japanese-class service and rewarded them well. Much of the credit for Nissan's new U.S. subsidiary (named Datsun Motors) forging ahead into the United States belonged to Katayama. Datsun's first solid success came with a well-designed 1.6 liter Datsun 510 (designed for the United States) in 1968. Sales zoomed in 1969 when the Datsun 240Z, a two-seater sports car fitting U.S. tastes, hit the United States and created a performance image for Datsun.

The Joys of Success

As the 1970s dawned, Toyota and Nissan were successful competitors in the Orient, the United States, and European markets. This was expanded by a 1973 windfall: the world oil crisis. As Middle Eastern sources withheld supply and prices at the pump soared, sales of gas-saving compacts surged in the United States. Nissan became the front-runner, and in 1975, moved ahead of Volkswagen as the number one import in the United States. Its market share, over 3 percent, was greater than Toyota's. A third Japanese firm, Honda, then seized the opportunity to be an important player in the U.S. market.

At this time, Katayama was head of the Datsun subsidiary, but he did not hold this position long. His personality did not suit Nissan's president, nor was Katayama's boasting of his U.S. role deemed proper in Tokyo. He was recalled to Japan and soon retired. In 1977, a former accountant, Takashi Ishihara, became president of Nissan. He was conservative and domineering, and clashed with Nissan's labor unions, ultimately depressing factory morale. Also, his people discouraged original car designs by haggling over new designs emerging from the studio.

The 1980s

Datsun won acclaim in 1980 by announcing it would be the first Japanese auto company to build a plant in the United States. The plant, built in Tennessee, had a 245,000-unit capacity. Shortly after, Honda announced that its U.S. plant would be built in Ohio. At that time, Datsun's U.S. market share had reached over 5.5 percent, its highest ever. The achievement was dimmed, though, when Toyota's share exceeded 6 percent (continuing the lead it had held for five years). Honda was doing well too, having tripled its U.S. share during the previous five years.

In 1981, Datsun was a very popular automobile manufacturer among Americans. Its slogan, "Datsun—We are Driven!" was engraved in Americans' minds and stood for high performance. That image changed abruptly when the corporate headquarters decided that its cars throughout the world must carry the head company's nameplate, Nissan. Whatever the logic was in Tokyo, the name change confused U.S. consumers. Many Americans continued to refer to the company's cars and trucks as Datsuns because the name Nissan meant very little to them. Further, some even believed Nissan was a division of Toyota. The confusion over the name may explain why Nissan experienced a decline in sales and market share and trouble with its dealer network.

Datsun dealers in the United States reacted very negatively. Dealer resistance included refusal to pay for new Nissan signs or make further investments, a standoff that some maintained for five years. In 1981, an artificial shortage of Japanese cars developed in the United States as the respective governments agreed to limit Japan's exports to 1.68 million cars. This inflated the Japanese firms' U.S. profits, which they used to improve their position in the United States. Toyota employed them to strengthen its U.S. sales force and to ration cars to dealers willing to invest in better facilities and locations. Nissan, however, nervous about declining market share back home, used these excess funds to improve its Japanese dealerships. Given its strained relationship with the U.S. automobile market, Nissan missed the opportunity to develop successful partnerships with large, professionally managed dealerships. Instead, the firm struggled with the image problem presented by dealing with former used car lots.

As gasoline prices decreased in the United States, motorists returned to larger cars. None of the Japanese car manufacturers had such models in their lines. Toyota, however, acted by introducing its family-size Camry line, while Honda brought out its comparable Accord. Nissan continued with its smaller Sentra and thus missed an opportunity to penetrate the higher-profit segment.

In 1985, Nissan's U.S. plant began producing Sentras, but Honda completed its Ohio plant earlier and had already produced 117,000 cars. The Nissan plant cost around 50 percent more than Honda's, yet had only two-thirds the capacity. Nissan achieved higher U.S. sales that year, a peak of 831,000 cars, but from there its market share drifted downward against gradual growth in Toyota's share and even better growth in Honda's. In Japan, these rivals' market shares followed a comparable pattern.

In 1986, Yutaka Kume, a career engineer, became Nissan's president. Then, the yen's value rose steeply against the dollar, hurting Nissan's U.S. profits and causing total earnings to fall into the negative category. However, the company recovered, and its operating profit soared to over $1 billion by 1989. This was fueled in part by success in Europe, following the opening of Nissan's plant in England where the new "Bluebird" was produced. With it, Nissan expanded its lead in European market share over Japanese rivals. Meanwhile, Kume shook the Tokyo bureaucracy: He put one engineer in charge of each car and supported more original styling.

A new president, Hagiwara, was named to head the U.S. subsidiary. Lacking new car models, he concentrated on reforming the dealership system. He hired an American marketing executive from Ford, Thomas Mignanelli, to head Nissan's U.S. marketing activities. The new marketer started on Nissan's confused U.S. image. In 1987, the widely criticized theme "Built for the Human Race" was chosen to replace its weaker theme, "The Name is Nissan." This advertising campaign failed to bring prospective buyers into the showroom as sales fell by 40 percent. The company kept the slogan, but dropped the corresponding advertisements. Soon after, Nissan initiated a sales promotion offering rebates of up to $1,000 on selected cars.

Many industry experts predicted that such sales promotions would bring only short-run sales results, not build the long-term image Nissan wanted. Mazda now had a tight grip on performance positioning, and Honda and Toyota were holding popularity with quality themes. A new image or positioning for Nissan was badly needed.

Meanwhile, under Hagiwara, important steps were taken toward U.S.-oriented car design. A design studio was opened near San Diego, with a GM designer, Gerald Hirshberg, as chief. The company brought out a luxury car—the Infiniti—designed in Japan for world markets in 1989. The introduction was preceded with novel "tease" commercials, showing images of waves, fields, or clouds, but no automobiles. A market research firm named these Zen-inspired spots third in the top 10 most-remembered television advertisements, the best showing ever for a new car campaign. However, Toyota won the race to market with its Lexus luxury line and led Nissan's Infiniti in American sales. Although Infiniti dealers were overwhelmed with prospective buyers, sales lagged about 30 percent behind Nissan's goals. Largely in response to dealer insistence, later Infiniti ads were more typical of automotive advertising (i.e., the ads emphasized steering and comfort instead of rocks and trees). Two-page ads in newspapers across the country not only displayed the car at last, but did it from 15 different angles. For Infiniti, however, the goal remained to establish an identity that would make it stand out from its toughest competitor, the Toyota Lexus.

As the 1980s ended, Nissan's market share in Japan had declined to 23 percent, but was steady. In the United States, its share revived slightly (after 1988) to around 4.5 percent. However, over 60 percent of Nissan's sales were for smaller, less expensive models. Overall corporate profits slipped moderately from their 1989 peak.

The 1990s

The 1990s began adversely for the automotive industry worldwide. The Japanese companies avoided the deep losses sustained in most countries, but profits shrank drastically. Nissan's profits fell to around $200 million in 1991 and kept declining. This occurred despite the success of Nissan's Maxima line. The Maxima SE represented a successful venture in image-building efforts. Selected by *Road & Track Magazine* as the best coupe/sedan of 1991, the Maxima SE represented a mid-price "family" car offering responsiveness, durability, and attractive styling. The Maxima helped Nissan's repositioning efforts as a leader in Japanese design. Described as a quiet, elegant sedan, the Maxima SE maintained a midlevel image and represented a major force behind the revival of Nissan's presence in the United States market. The luxury-market Maxima GXE met with similar success.

Continued profit pressures in 1992 put Nissan in a tough spot because it was a relatively high-cost producer in Japan and was still trying to recover in the United States. Nissan took steps to meet the needs of the immediate future. Capacity was doubled at the Tennessee plant (with a $425 million investment) and at the English plant. New cars, including three from its California design center, were introduced: the Altima, a larger sedan intended to surpass the Accord and Camry (and the reason for the U.S. plant expansion), the Infiniti J30, to expand the line with touches appealing to the U.S. luxury car market, and the Quest, a minivan that was Nissan's third effort to crack the U.S. minivan market.

By the mid-1990s, efforts were well underway to reorganize Nissan's U.S. operations. These steps included (1) moving decision-making authority to a dealer-operations manager who would live in the dealers' communities and be sole advisor to a group of them, (2) consolidating each model's marketing decisions at headquarters under a brand manager rather than having decisions diffused among functions, and (3) reducing regional offices from 11 to 7 and moving much of headquarters staff to them. The same reorganization was taking place in Tokyo, where Yoshifumi Tsuji—the former head of production—had become the new Nissan CEO. His mission was to increase Nissan's productivity by 10 percent during his first three years, a task to which he was well-suited. By rationalizing production methods and reducing line workers by 2 percent per year, total cost savings reached $770 million. With the savings, Nissan tried to hold its place in the auto race.

In the United States, a new ad campaign was developed that featured "Mr. K" and the "Enjoy the Ride" slogan. The ads were seen as creative masterpieces, with consumers shown as being rejuvenated as they drove around in Nissan products. However, the ads did very little to sell cars. Despite early optimism, sales in the late 1990s have been disappointing. In 1997 alone, total sales dropped over 45 percent from 1996 sales figures. In addition, sales for the Altima, one of Nissan's most successful car introductions, fell to disappointing levels.

To combat these problems, Nissan began to take some bold and creative steps. First, Nissan announced an aggressive pricing strategy for the 1998 Altima—about $1,500 less than the 1997 model. However, a lower price does not always mean lower quality. Instead, Nissan's goal was to provide a higher quality car at a lower price. This goal was achieved in part by using more U.S.-based plants to produce parts for the Altima. Hundreds of small improvements (both in manufacturing processes and operations) were made in order to introduce car buyers to an affordably priced luxury car. Nissan's "Value Strategy" was later universally adopted for all Nissan products, with hopes that consumers will think "extraordinary value" when they think of Nissan. Nissan was so confident in its new strategy that it forecasted sales to increase 13 percent—a very bold forecast given the fiercely competitive market for midsize sedans.

Second, Nissan shifted its strategic focus to creating cohesion between manufacturing, finance, and marketing. In addition, Nissan moved aggressively into enhanced customer service. Nissan implemented a "no-pressure" customer-oriented buying situation, where consumers are treated fairly. In the future, Nissan will likely expand customer services to include such amenities as roadside assistance and post-purchase service. The new strategy will uphold the notion that the initial sale is merely the beginning of an overall long-term buyer–seller relationship.

Third, Nissan introduced a new advertising campaign in early 1998. The new ads kept the "Enjoy the Ride" slogan, but no longer featured "Mr. K." Instead, the new ads focused on product features and Nissan's new worldwide positioning statement: "dependability, quality, and reliability." The overriding goal of the new campaign was to focus on each product by touting the fun-to-drive benefits of each Nissan model.

A part of this new promotional effort was Nissan's launch of its restored vintage "Z-car" promotion. Z-cars refer to Nissan classic cars (e.g., 1969 Datsun 240Z). Nissan began efforts to market fully restored versions of their famed classics at 10 select "Z-stores" across the United States. In doing so, Nissan became the first major car manufacturer to undertake this type of restoration and marketing effort. The restoration process lasts two months, and involves locating original parts (when available) and rebuilding parts that are no longer manufactured. The cars are all being restored by Pierre Perrot (a former race car driver), along with Nissan's quality department. The goal is to make restored Z-cars virtually equal to the original. Nissan's revitalization strategy may prove beneficial, as rare commodities—waterfront property, stamp collections, and now Z-cars—continue to be lucrative investments.

Looking Ahead

Nissan North America, Inc. (NNA) announced its intentions to pioneer the U.S. electric vehicle (EV) market with the new "Altra EV." The compact van is equipped with cutting-edge lithium-ion (Li-ion) battery technology. Li-ion batteries allow drivers to travel approximately 120 miles at one time and provide acceleration levels comparable to gasoline-powered vans. The "EV" represents a high-tech van for practical use. Nissan began testing the "EV" in several driving conditions (e.g., summer weather and urban driving). The carmaker also began testing the concept with California and Arizona consumers. The purpose of this testing is to help Nissan deliver a reliable electric vehicle that meets the needs of American drivers. The Altra EV will be manufactured on an all-new platform at Nissan's Tochigi (Japan) plant. Nissan provided approximately 30 Altra EVs to some fleet users in 1998. Further, 90 demonstration units will be tested by fleet users in 1999 and 2000. Given positive results, retail sales will begin soon after. NNA also plans to participate in a National Low Emission Vehicle (NLEV) Program. In 1999, NLEV will begin striving to provide consumers with environmentally cleaner cars (up to 70 percent cleaner).

In early 1998, Nissan introduced two "new" vehicles to the U.S. market: the seven-passenger 1999 Quest minivan and the Frontier four-door pickup. The new Quest offers Nissan's minivan customers increased passenger roominess, more cargo space, many performance enhancements, and a refreshing new style. The hallmark of the new Quest is its ability to provide a car-like ride without compromising comfort or cargo space. The new Frontier represents uncharted territory for Nissan, as it boasts a family-sized cab and much larger body. Nissan basically created the U.S. compact pickup market in 1959, and has continuously stayed at the forefront of small-truck innovation ever since.

In sum, the late 1990s have brought some innovative strategies to Nissan. Nissan is striving to build a "value" image among auto customers. To do so, it has made significant improvements in both Nissan cars and trucks. Moreover, Nissan has made innovative efforts to protect the environment (e.g., electric vehicles and NLEV). Nissan also plans to put customer needs at the forefront of its corporate mission. Given these changes, Nissan may experience exciting and prosperous times in the next decade.

Questions for Discussion

1. How would you characterize the strategy-making performance of Nissan in general and in the United States since World War II?
2. What were the major forces behind this performance?
3. Appraise Nissan's actions and programs as it prepares for the next millennium. What would you have changed or added?

4. Evaluate Nissan's plans to be a pioneer in the electric car market. Do you agree with their decision? How would you market such vehicles?

5. Nissan spends a great deal of resources on environmentally friendly strategies. Given the expense of these strategies in both time and cost, do you feel that these strategies are a wise decision? Will such strategies help the long-term profitability of Nissan? If so, how?

Sources

These facts are from Larry Armstrong, "In reverse at Nissan," *Business Week,* Mar. 9, 1998; 42; James R. Crate, "Nissan unveils Altra in effort to zoom ahead in EV race," *Automotive News,* Oct. 27, 1997, 50; Paul J. Deveney, "Nissan Motor Co. expects domestic sales to fall," *Wall Street Journal,* Dec. 18, 1997, A16; Jean Halliday and Alice Z. Cuneo, "Nissan reverses course to focus on the product," *Advertising Age,* Feb. 16, 1998, 1; Michiyo Nakamoto, "Nissan warning as domestic sales slip," *The Financial Times,* Mar. 3, 1998, 29; Nissan's homepage, www.nissan.co.jp; "Nissan says all is well with TBWA Chiat/Day," *ADWEEK Eastern Edition,* Mar. 2, 1998, 6; "Nissan says profits will be disappointing," *The New York Times,* Mar. 13, 1998, C2; Mark Rechtin, "Nissan cleans house in U.S.," *Automotive News,* Feb. 23, 1998, 1; Daniel Taub, "Nissan continues to flail, despite management change," *Los Angeles Business Journal,* Mar. 9, 1998, 8; "3 Nissan executives in U.S. are removed as sales slump," *The New York Times,* Feb. 24, 1998, C9; James B. Treece, "Hanawa tries to stir the stew at Nissan," *Automotive News,* Mar. 16, 1998, 39; and "Upping the EV ante: Nissan hopes to charge up image of electric vehicles," *Ward's Auto World,* Dec. 1997, 124.

C A S E **5**

Eagle Hardware and Garden, Inc.[1]

Eagle Hardware & Garden is a leading operator of retail home improvement centers in the Pacific Northwest. In its first full fiscal year of operation, Eagle generated over $50 million in revenues, averaging approximately $500,000 in sales per week per store; new stores turned profitable an average of 120 days after opening. Eagle's first six stores were opened in the greater Seattle, Washington area. Since its founding in 1989, the company has opened 32 home centers throughout Washington, Utah, Colorado, Hawaii, Alaska, California, Idaho, Oregon, and Montana. Sales and net income for the fiscal year ended January 30, 1998 totaled $971.5 million and $29.9 million, respectively. Eagle opened four stores in fiscal 1997 and seven stores in fiscal 1998. Of the eight to 10 stores currently planned for opening in fiscal 1999, four are located in southern California.

Eagle has succeeded in its markets against its more established competitors by offering customer-friendly store environments, a large product selection, exceptional service, convenient locations and competitive prices. The company's home centers average 128,000 square feet and depart from warehouse-style chains with clean, well-lighted aisles, attractive displays and clearly marked signs. Eagle locations are stocked with more than 65,000 products per store under its "More of Everything" merchandising philosophy—over 30 percent more items than most of its competitors. The company's product categories provide a selection that is broad enough to allow a customer to purchase virtually every item needed to build a house.

Eagle's Retailing Strategy

Eagle attempts to be a "one-stop-shop" for customers' home improvement needs at competitive prices. By hiring highly competent salespeople and designing the stores to be both inviting and user-friendly, Eagle has effectively eliminated the customer confusion often associated with larger warehouse stores. Each store has 16 to 23 cashier stations, a large convenient return and exchange counter, and a separate checkout and loading area for bulky purchases such as lumber.

---

[1] This case was prepared by O. C. Ferrell, Colorado State University, for classroom discussion rather than to illustrate either effective or ineffective handling of an administrative situation.

Eagle has quickly established itself as the home improvement store leader in the Pacific Northwest. With 65,000 stock-keeping units in each store, Eagle's "more of everything" philosophy has become a reality. Eagle strives for competitive advantage; it delivers both selection and high level customer service. Eagle has, by a very wide margin, the broadest selection of high-quality products in its industry. The expansion philosophy serves large urban markets as well as smaller markets. Eagle ranked first in percentage increase in same store sales and net income of all publicly traded home improvement retailers and second in percentage increase in total sales in 1997.

Eagle has established extreme loyalty among its customers, particularly women, who account for about 50 percent of its sales. Typically, warehouse stores attract only 25–50 percent females. Eagle stores feature innovative "design idea centers," where customers can work with design coordinators to conceptualize and plan virtually any home improvement project. The design idea center is surrounded by a "race track" aisle, which provides convenient access to well-defined departments around the central core of the store. Wide, brightly lit aisles and attractive displays are designed to appeal to a broad range of customers, many of whom the company believes are less attracted to traditional, warehouse-format home centers.

Eagle Hardware strives to attract more experienced and qualified personnel by paying what it believes are the most competitive wages in each of its markets. The company also makes a substantial investment in its employee training program, which emphasizes and rewards superior customer service. "Eagle Experts," many with extensive experience in their respective fields, are available to provide specialized service in each department.

Eagle's commitment to quality customer service goes beyond the basics of having adequate sales personnel on the floor. Eagle believes that sales and product training are essential to satisfying customers' service needs. Eagle invests millions of dollars in employee training annually. Each store has its own training director, and employees receive an average of 60 hours of formal training every year. The "Eagle Expert" program honors employees who successfully complete the "Expert" study course and test. "Experts" receive a salary increase and other recognition. Through the "Expert" program and formal training sessions, sales associates gain the confidence they need to approach customers and offer practical solutions to do-it-yourself questions. Incentives also play an important role in providing outstanding customer service. Store employees are paid bonuses based on customer service reports, and after two years of service, all employees are eligible for the Employee Stock Ownership Plan. Eagle consistently promotes from within. Their strategy is to develop employees who excel at their service-oriented approach—people who can deliver the "Eagle Experience."

Eagle maintains competitive, everyday low prices on products carried by other home centers and does not engage in promotional, "sale" pricing. At the same time, the company benefits from higher margins on hard-to-find merchandise and on products not carried by its competitors.

The result of Eagle's strategy is a hybrid "retail/warehouse home center" concept, which the company believes effectively integrates the selection and value associated with traditional, warehouse-format home centers with the customer-friendly attributes and expertise of service-oriented specialty retailers.

Competition

Eagle operates in a highly competitive environment that includes traditional hardware, plumbing, electrical and home supply retailers; wholesale clubs; discount retail stores; and catalog companies. Despite the growth of warehouse format home centers, the domestic "do-it-yourself" home improvement industry remains fragmented. The Eagle concept was developed after carefully studying successful home improvement stores, such as Home Depot, headquartered in Atlanta, and Orchard Hardware Supply of California. Eagle Hardware's competitors include HomeBase, Home Depot, Builder's Square, Ernst Home Center, and Payless Cashways. Most analysts view Home Depot as Eagle's major competition.

A favorable influence on the growth of Eagle's market share was the closing of a primary competitor that operated in most markets. Ernst Home Center had operated 86 mid-sized home improvement stores in the western United States Over half of these stores competed directly with Eagle stores. In July 1996, Ernst filed for Chapter 11 bankruptcy protection and closed 25 stores. Additional store closures were announced, shrinking the size of the Ernst chain to 53 stores. Of the remaining stores, over 60 percent competed directly with Eagle stores. In November 1996, Ernst announced the liquidation of the company and all remaining stores were closed by February 1997. Eagle experienced an increase in customer transactions as a result of the initial Ernst store closings and is continuing to realize the benefits of the Ernst liquidation.

Fisher Broadcasting, Inc., which operates a Seattle area television network affiliate, assessed the impact of Ernst's withdrawal from the Puget Sound market. As part of an independent survey, 403 people (79 percent of them former Ernst customers) were asked where they planned to shop for home improvement products after the Ernst stores were closed. Over 36 percent of Ernst's shoppers surveyed named Eagle, twice as many as the 18 percent who named Home Depot, the nation's largest home improvement retailer. HomeBase, the eighth largest retailer in the industry, was selected by 11 percent of those surveyed. Eagle was encouraged by the results of this survey considering that over 75 percent of their stores competed with at least one Ernst store during 1996. It is estimated that Ernst's sales in the Puget Sound market were approximately $150 million in 1996. The impact on Eagle sales will be very favorable should they gain the 36 percent of this business that the survey suggested. The survey results were important to Eagle given the strong competition it continues to face in the Puget Sound market. At the time the survey was taken, Eagle operated 10 stores, Home Depot had nine, and HomeBase had seven in this market.

As Eagle began to see substantial increases in customer transactions in many stores from the initial Ernst store closures, they were faced with the decision either to maintain or increase the number of sales associates in stores. They chose to forgo the immediate benefit of "leveraging" payroll dollars and added additional sales staff to provide existing and new customers with a high level of customer service. The decision has been validated by independent customer service surveys that are taken in each store every month. The stores scored higher than ever before on these surveys.

Eagle formed a Canadian subsidiary, Eagle Hardware and Garden (Canada) Ltd. and opened an Edmonton, Alberta store. With advances in the U.S. and Canada Free Trade Agreement and NAFTA, Eagle tried to take advantage of opportunities for expansion into Canada. After Home Depot moved into Canada, Eagle withdrew from this market.

Home Depot

Founded in 1978 in Atlanta, Georgia, Home Depot is North America's largest home improvement retailer, currently operating 584 warehouse-style home centers in 41 states and 32 stores in four Canadian provinces with net sales of over $20 billion. Home Depot has a joint venture with S.A.C.I. Falabella in Chile for its first store outside of North America, which opened in Santiago in 1998.

Home Depot is credited with being the leading innovator in the home improvement retail industry by combining the economies of scale inherent in a warehouse format with a level of customer service unprecedented among warehouse-style retailers. Home Depot stores cater to do-it-yourselfers, as well as home improvement, construction, and building maintenance professionals.

Each Home Depot store stocks approximately 40,000–50,000 different kinds of building materials, home improvement supplies, and lawn and garden products. New stores in the United States and Canada include a 20,000–28,000 square foot garden center. The stores have a design center staffed by professional designers who offer free in-store consultation for home improvement projects ranging from lighting to computer-assisted design for kitchens and bathrooms. Most Home Depot stores offer installation services ranging from single-item installations, such as carpet, to more extensive projects such as kitchen cabinet installation.

Home Depot also operates EXPO Design Centers in Atlanta, Dallas, Miami, San Diego, and Westbury, New York. Unlike traditional Home Depot stores, EXPO does not sell building materials, such as lumber, but focuses on interior design and renovation products, including kitchen and bath, lighting, and floor and wall coverings.

Although most DIY warehouse stores offer deep discounts with minimal service, Home Depot offers low prices and unusually helpful customer service. The company aims to demystify the mechanics of home repairs and improvements for DIYers. The company is successful because of hands-on management that carefully implements its market plan and controls operations. Home Depot's organization is based on expert buying, innovative merchandising, efficient inventory control, and motivated, knowledgeable salespeople.

To determine what products consumers want, Home Depot conducts extensive market research. It adds and deletes products to match demand on the basis of this research and computerized sales tracking records. The company has introduced an advanced inventory control system, which allows inventory to turn over faster than most competitors such as Eagle. It has a smaller inventory than Eagle and needs less working capital to finance it.

Home Depot's salespeople give the firm an edge over its competitors. Of its employees, 90 percent are full-time and earn higher-than-average salaries with full benefits; most of its competitors are staffed by part-time minimum-wage earners. Salespeople are given detailed product information and hands-on training to assist DIYers in purchasing and using all the items needed for a project. Home Depot's hands-on management of its outlets includes regular store visits and training classes for all new and potential store managers, emphasizing the company philosophy of low prices and quality service. In addition, the company regularly hires former construction workers as employees.

Home Depot emphasizes community relations, social responsibility, and the correctness of ethical work relationships. Many Home Depot employees are also stockholders. The company's progressive corporate culture includes a philanthropic budget ($12.5 million in 1998) that is directed back to the communities Home Depot serves and the interests of its employees through a Matching Gift program. The major focuses are affordable housing, at-risk youth, and the environment. Team Depot, an organized volunteer force, was developed in 1992 to promote volunteer activities within the local communities the stores serve. For four consecutive years, the company was ranked by *Fortune* magazine as America's Most Admired Retailer.

EAGLE CHALLENGES HOME DEPOT   Approximately two-thirds of Eagle stores compete in markets with Home Depot. Eagle has the broadest product assortment of any warehouse competitor. The company's per-unit store sales are second only to that of Home Depot in the entire industry. Eagle's extensive inventory heightens the necessity for sophisticated inventory systems to deal with a lower number of inventory turns. On the other hand, Eagle's broad assortment results in consumer loyalty built upon carrying hard-to-find items. There is an increased margin associated with that merchandise.

Eagle's objective in large markets, such as Denver, is to open multiple stores to achieve long-term market share. Eagle opened its first small-market prototype store in Wenatchee, Washington and added two stores in Colorado. Denying prime retail locations to Eagle competitors and realizing certain operating efficiencies are additional benefits of employing this strategy. More importantly, by opening multiple stores in certain markets, they make goods and services more convenient to a broader base of customers. Surveys have indicated that convenience is the most important criteria customers use when selecting a home improvement store. By opening stores in smaller single-store markets, Eagle typically encounters less competition and lower operating costs and is able to achieve higher gross margins. There are numerous expansion opportunities in markets of this size.

Home Depot continues to increase same store sales at an impressive rate and deliberately opens new stores to cannibalize existing stores. This strategy may keep Home Depot from moving as rapidly into new markets. As Home Depot has moved into the Washington area, severe competition with Eagle has resulted because of its cannibalization strategy. Home Depot can be called a "category killer" store in the home improvement industry. Eagle can be called a "newcomer" with a differentiated retail strategy designed not to dominate but to cash in on the warehouse-store home improvement market.

CURRENT ECONOMIC CLIMATE IN EAGLE MARKETS   General economic conditions improved in most Eagle markets recently. Lower interest rates in 1995–98 resulted in increased sales of existing homes. Because consumers typically purchase home improvement products prior to selling and after buying a home, demand for Eagle products improved with the increase in housing turnover.

The economy in the Puget Sound area, Eagle's home market, improved dramatically. Growth in this region, where Eagle now has 12 stores, shifted into high gear at the start of 1996. Regional employment growth was expected to peak halfway through 1997 at 3.7 percent, well above the predicted national average of 1.7 percent. Within three years, according to recent economic forecasts, the Puget Sound area will add 220,000 jobs and 290,000 residents. These newcomers will need approximately 20,000 new units of housing stock per year. Old housing will need to be replaced, and the turnover of existing homes will accelerate. The economic forecast for the Eagle core market has never been better.

The overall economic climate of the Denver and Salt Lake City markets is also expected to be robust. The six-county region that includes Denver is projecting a 3.1 percent increase in employment and more than 140,000 new residents over the next three years. Utah, according to a survey by regional Financial Associates, will enjoy a job growth rate of 4.7 percent, the highest in the nation. More than 78,000 new residents are expected to settle in the Salt Lake City area by 2001. Eagle is very encouraged by the economic forecasts for major markets and is well prepared to benefit from the opportunities that this dynamic growth presents.

The Future

Most investment analysts remain positive on Eagle Hardware and Garden, Inc. To expand rapidly and increase profits, a successful strategy seems to be in place, with individual store sales increasing beyond expectations. On the other hand, there are threats to Eagle's continued success.

Home Depot, the industry's leader, is one of the most successful specialty retailers in the United States. Home Depot has 584 stores in the United States and 32 in Canada compared to Eagle's 32 stores. Eagle planned to open seven new stores in fiscal 1998 and eight to 10 in fiscal 1999 compared to Home Depot's plan to operate over 1,100 stores by the end of 2000.

Eagle's primary emphasis will continue to be offering customers a unique shopping experience, one that cannot be found at any competitor. Eagle is committed to leading the industry in merchandise assortment, innovative display techniques, and store design. Eagle wants to sharpen its focus on customer service and continue to reward the efforts of Eagle associates for achieving results that maximize customer service.

Questions for Discussion

1. Compare Eagle's strategy to the successful Home Depot strategy.
2. The Seattle, Washington market is the 15th largest market in the nation for building material sales. Will the Home Depot or Eagle strategy win in this market?
3. If Home Depot is to defeat Eagle in Seattle, what strategy will it have to use?
4. How can Eagle, with sales that are only a fraction of Home Depot's sales, succeed and reach its objectives?

Sources

These facts are from http://www.eaglehardware.com/annual.htm (3/31/98); http://biz.yahoo.com/bw/980306/profile_ea_1.html (3/31/98); http://www.HomeDepot.com/dykfacts/dukful.htm (4/1/98); Eagle Hardware and Garden, Inc. Prospectus, Montgomery Securities, Alexander Brown & Sons Inc., July 15, 1992; Montgomery Securities Basic Report Vol. 23, Specialty Retailing, Aug. 10, 1992; Alexander Brown & Sons Inc. Research Growth Retailers' Group, Oct. 2, 1992; Northern Exposure, Eagle Hardware and Garden, Sept., 1992; and Bill Saporito, "The Fix Is In at Home Depot," *Fortune,* Feb. 29, 1988, 73–74, 79.

Apple Computer, Inc.[1]

Apple Computer, Inc. designs, manufactures, and markets microprocessor-based personal computers and related personal computing and communicating solutions for sale primarily to education, home, business, and government customers. Substantially all of the company's net sales to date have been derived from the sale of personal computers from its Apple Macintosh line of computers and related software and peripherals. Apple is considered the true American entrepreneurial legend. Founded in a garage in 1976 by two college dropouts, Steven Jobs and Stephen Wozniak, the company grew to reach its high point in 1995 with worldwide revenues of $11.1 billion. However, the company earned just $424 million on those phenomenal sales, and it lost $69 million in the last quarter of the year. Although Apple customers tend to be vehement in their support of the company's products, Apple's share of the world computer market fell to 7.1 percent in 1995, down from 8.2 percent in 1994. In 1996, Apple announced it would take a $125 million restructuring charge and lay off 1,300 employees. By 1997, Apple continued to decline, with sales decreasing 28 percent from 1996 to $7.1 billion, and the company posted a $1 billion loss. Apple's market share dipped to 3 percent. To many outsiders, it appears that Apple has lost its technological edge, and its future as an independent entity looks doubtful. To understand how the company found itself in this bleak predicament in 1998, we will consider the firm's history, culture, and marketing strategy changes. Exhibit 1 provides an overview of Apple's financial performance over the last five years.

Birth of an Icon

Stephen Wozniak developed Apple's first product, the Apple I computer, which he and Steven Jobs built in Jobs's garage and sold without a monitor, keyboard, or casing. The Apple I's success helped Jobs recognize a demand for small, "user-friendly"

---

[1] This case was prepared by O. C. Ferrell, Colorado State University, and Gwyneth Vaughn for classroom discussion rather than to illustrate either effective or ineffective handling of an administrative situation. Research assistance was provided by Donald P. Roy, University of Memphis.

EXHIBIT 6.1

Apple Computer, Inc. Financial Performance—Five Fiscal Years Ended Sept. 26, 1997
(in millions except per share amounts)

	1997	1996	1995	1994	1993
Net sales	$7,081	$9,833	$11,062	$9,189	$7,977
Net income (loss)	$(1,045)	$(816)	$424	$310	$87
Earnings (loss) per common and common equivalent share	$(8.29)	$(6.59)	$3.45	$2.61	$0.73
Total assets	$ 4,233	$5,364	$6,231	$5,303	$5,171
Long-term debt	$951	$949	$303	$305	$7

Source: United States Securities and Exchange Commission Form 10-K for Apple Computer, Inc., Dec. 4, 1997, p. 8.

computers. Wozniak added a keyboard, color monitor, and eight slots for peripheral devices, giving the firm's next product, the Apple II, greater versatility and encouraging other firms to develop add-on devices and software. It worked: Jobs and Wozniak sold more than 13,000 Apple IIs by 1980, and revenues climbed from $7.8 million in 1978 to $117 million in 1980. The next ventures, the Apple III and Lisa computers, flopped, but Apple scored a huge success with the Macintosh, introduced in 1984. The Mac, which incorporated an easy-to-use graphical interface, was billed as the computer "For the Rest of Us." The Mac's rapid popularity soon established Apple as a leader in the expanding computer industry. Apple moved into the office market in 1986 with the Mac Plus and the LaserWriter printer. Wozniak left in 1983, and Jobs brought in John Sculley, a former PepsiCo executive, to manage the growing firm.

From Apple's garage-bound birth, Jobs and Wozniak, iconoclasts themselves, so engraved their personalities on Apple Computer's culture that it survived long after their departures. Their do-your-own-thing, ignore-the Establishment philosophy gave Apple a unique culture of rebels, right down to the pirate flag flying over headquarters. Scorning dress codes, formal meetings, and other traditional business trappings, Apple's creative, defiant culture nurtured the development of the groundbreaking Macintosh computer and operating system, as well as numerous other successful products, and propelled Apple to the top of the computer industry.

Cultural Conflict

The do-it-your-way culture also created strife within the company, pitting the inventive "gearheads" and "wizards"—the engineers and programmers who developed products—against the managers Jobs imported to bring order and good business practices to the firm. Jobs, in fact, left the firm in 1985 in a power struggle with Sculley, largely over the future of the Macintosh platform. When Sculley took over the reins, he realized that Apple's employees would resent the big-business systems he wanted to implement. He also recognized that he had to retain Apple's technical wizards if the firm was to succeed. He decided not to tinker with Apple's unique culture. However, glorifying Apple's technical personnel made them very tough to supervise. Combined with Sculley's feel-good approach to management, the result was a company run largely by consensus, and decisions were rarely final. One joke on the Apple grapevine was that "a vote can be 15,000 to 1 and still be a tie."

The Revolving Door

Apple's culture contributed to frequent power struggles and a seemingly revolving door on management offices. In 1995 alone, 14 of 45 vice presidents left or were dismissed. Major management upheavals occurred in 1981, 1985, 1990, 1993, 1996, and 1997 with numerous minor ones in between. Several of these disturbances led to the removal of chief executives. Sculley, for example, was dethroned in 1993 after an 84 percent drop in earnings. His replacement, Michael "Diesel" Spindler, brought a focus on business basics to the firm and quickly worked to address Apple's problems: overpriced products, inflated costs, and sluggish product development. He laid off 2,500 workers, cut R&D costs by more than $100 million a year, and launched a new product line based on the PowerPC microprocessor (which Apple developed with IBM and Motorola). Spindler's back-to-the-basics approach helped Apple rebound, but Spindler soon stumbled under Apple's consensus culture. An insider close to Spindler says, "It was fine for awhile. But the system converts people." Spindler was ousted in 1996 and replaced by Gilbert Amelio as president and CEO. By July 1997, Amelio departed and was replaced on an interim basis by Steven Jobs, who stepped in to reverse the company's declining performance. Each of these management upheavals brought restructuring and changes in strategy.

Frequent Strategy Changes

These frequent strategy changes may be the biggest source of Apple's disappointing performance in recent years. Over the years, Jobs, Sculley, Spindler, then Jobs again reversed, delayed, or evaded outright key decisions while trying to push their own agendas. For example, in April 1995, Spindler implemented a major reorganization of Apple but was forced to recant that decision six months later under fiscal pressures. A late 1995 decision to launch an all-out bid for market share failed after executives misread the market. The result was a storehouse of low-end computers, at a time when consumers wanted expensive powerhouse machines, and an $80 million inventory write-off. Meanwhile, savvy rivals IBM, Hewlett-Packard, and Compaq raked in the bucks and made further inroads into Apple's market share.

In fact, Apple has been consistent only in its inconsistency over the years. For example, Apple has traditionally relied on high-priced products to fund development and marketing of new technology. However, in a desperate bid to boost market share and improve efficiency, the firm has occasionally deviated from this strategy by introducing lower-priced Apple machines. But management has never given the latter strategy time to work, and it failed to implement other tactics that might have generated the same results.

One of the most significant examples of this inconsistency and wavering was the issue of whether to license the Mac operating system to other computer makers in order to create a "clone" industry that would increase market share for the Mac platform, much as IBM had done with its personal computer. The clone decision was debated as early as 1985, but until 1994, every time top management came close to making the licensing decision, it was stymied by lack of consensus. As one former Apple executive says, "I've never understood why somebody didn't just say: 'I'm the leader. This is the way it's going to be. Thanks for the discussion, but if you don't want to do it, leave.'"

When Spindler finally made the decision to license the technology in 1994, the rising popularity of Microsoft's Windows operating environment for the IBM-PC platform made the clone decision too late. Apple executives asserted that they could raise the Mac's share of the global market to 20 percent in five years, adding 1 percent each year, with the clones bringing in the rest. However, even though Apple executives said they would "aggressively" pursue licensees, thus far, Apple has licensed the Mac design only to Pioneer, Power Computing, Unmax, and Daystar. Together, these firms sold about 200,000 Mac clones in 1995, a drop in the bucket compared with the 4.5 million shipped by Apple. In a last-ditch attempt to revive Mac software's faltering market share, Apple gave Motorola the rights to use its current and future operating systems, as well as the right to sublicense the operating system to other computer makers likely to produce Apple clones. However, Motorola grew tired of Apple's tough anti-licensing stance and announced in late 1997 that it would halt development of Mac clones. In another move that signaled an about-face on licensing, Apple acquired Power Computing Corp., the largest cloner of Macs, in 1997.

Other strategy changes were implemented by Jobs after he returned as CEO. The thrust of his strategy changes was to reduce many new product ideas and concentrate on a small number of key new products. Among the most notable products scrapped by Jobs was the Newton hand-held computer. The company spent over a decade attempting to develop the hand-held technology. Performance problems with the Newton Message Pad and competition from the 3Com Palm Pilot led to Newton's dismal performance. In early 1998, Apple announced it would cease all further development of Newton technology.

Another delayed decision may be more risky for Apple—whether to merge with or sell the company to another firm. During his tenure, Michael Spindler held serious talks with IBM starting in 1994. IBM seemed like a perfect match. The two firms had collaborated with Motorola on the PowerPC chip, which both were committed to using in their products, and they shared two software joint ventures—Kaleida Labs and Taligent (both now defunct). Negotiations between Spindler and IBM's Louis Gerstner even generated a proposed marketing strategy for the merged firm, with IBM bringing out a new line of PCs based on the PowerPC chip already used in Power Macs, and the two firms using Apple's software, beefed up with IBM's OS/2 for the merged PowerPC line. However, with Spindler making many demands, negotiations deteriorated, and the merger talks broke down. A second attempt at negotiating a merger with IBM in 1995 also failed. Attempts to find another partner or suitor have failed thus far, though Apple is reportedly holding talks with Sun Micro Systems.

Another major issue for Apple has been the thorn of Microsoft's Windows. Windows, with its graphical interface, makes PCs work much like the Macintosh. When the first successful version of Windows appeared in 1990, Apple executives dismissed the threat, although they filed a lawsuit against Microsoft and Hewlett-Packard, claiming copyright protection for the "look and feel" of the Macintosh user interface. Apple lost the suit in 1992. Macintosh users continue to be passionate in their insistence that the Macintosh is a better machine than a Windows-based PC, but Apple has failed to capitalize on their fervor. At the same time, Microsoft has been very aggressive in upgrading Windows to the point where buyers just entering the market fail to see significant differences between a PC and a Mac beyond the fact that the Apple machine costs more. A new Mac operating system tentatively called Copland, the one project that could have countered the Windows 95 and Windows 98 onslaughts, is several years behind schedule.

In August 1997, Apple and Microsoft entered into patent cross licensing and technology agreements. Under these agreements, the companies provided patent cross licenses to each other. In addition, for a period of five years beginning in August 1997, Microsoft will make future versions of its Microsoft Office and Internet Explorer products for the Mac OS. Apple will bundle the Internet Explorer product with Mac OS system software releases and make that product the default Internet browser for such releases. In addition, Microsoft purchased 150,000 shares of Apple Series 'A' non-voting convertible preferred stock for $150 million. While the company believes that its relationship with Microsoft will be beneficial to Apple and its efforts to increase the installed base for the Mac OS, the Microsoft relationship is for a limited term and does not cover many of the areas in which the company competes with Microsoft, including the Windows platform. In addition, the Microsoft relationship may have an adverse effect on, among other things, the company's relationship with other partners. There can be no assurance that the benefits to Apple of the Microsoft relationship will not be offset by the disadvantages.

Current Marketing Strategies

Due to the highly volatile nature of the personal computer industry, which is characterized by dynamic customer demand patterns and rapid technological advances, Apple must continuously introduce new products and technologies and enhance existing products in order to remain competitive. Recent introductions include new PowerBook and Power Macintosh products and the introduction of Mac OS 8 in July 1997.

In the meantime, Apple is narrowing its focus to market segments in which it already has a solid presence, a strategy that may mean forever abandoning the possibility of regaining the position of industry leader. And, like apparently everyone else inside and outside the computer industry, Apple is turning to the Internet. In February 1997, Apple acquired NeXT which developed, marketed and supported software that enables customers to implement business applications on the Internet, intranets, and enterprise-wide client/server networks. "Any project that doesn't have the word Internet in it doesn't get approved anymore," says one Apple manager. Apple plans to support its Internet emphasis by introducing the MacNC, a network computer designed primarily for Internet and intranet applications. The firm's expertise in media and entertainment, where many content providers are moving to the Web, may enhance its edge. Says one industry executive, "This whole Internet explosion is a real opportunity for Apple. It's not so much an advantage for them, but it takes away some of their disadvantages." The company is introducing a low-end personal computer, iMac, to compete with firms such as Compaq and Packard Bell in the $1,200-$1,600 market.

Apple has announced plans for two operating systems. The company plans to continue to introduce major upgrades to the current Mac OS and later introduce a new operating system (code named "Rhapsody") that is expected to offer advanced functionality based on Apple and NeXT software technologies. However, the NeXT software technologies that Apple plans to use in the development of Rhapsody were not originally designed to be compatible with the Mac OS. As a result, there can be no assurance that the development of Rhapsody can be completed at reasonable cost or at all. In addition, Rhapsody may not be fully backward-compatible with all existing applications, which could result in a loss of existing customers.

As a supplemental means of addressing the competition from Windows and other platforms, Apple had previously devoted substantial resources toward developing personal computer products capable of running application software designed for the Windows operating systems. These products include an add-on card containing a Pentium or 586-class microprocessor that enables users to run applications concurrently that require the Mac OS, Windows 3.1, or Windows 95 operating systems. Apple plans to transition the cross-platform business to third parties during 1998. There can be no assurance that this transition will be successful.

To capitalize on these opportunities, Apple must develop new products and market them astutely and consistently. Shareholders and staunch Apple customers hope that Steven Jobs, as interim chief executive officer, will bring to Apple much-needed focus, consistency, and competitive products and marketing strategies. Whether Apple remains a viable firm depends on the strength of its interim chief executive to overcome problems and guide Apple through the process of a possible merger with a stronger firm so that it may continue to satisfy devout Macintosh customers. The future of Steven Jobs as CEO is unclear. When he took over for the ousted Amelio in 1997, Jobs insisted he was an interim CEO and had no intention of taking the position on a permanent basis. However, in early 1998, Apple's board said that Jobs could stay on as CEO for as long as he wanted, and he gave no outward indications that he was eager to step down.

Questions for Discussion

1. Describe how Apple's unique culture has contributed to its present situation. If you were the chief executive, how would you deal with this culture?

2. How have Apple's frequent strategy changes brought it to where it is today? What do you see as the single most costly error made by executives?

3. Describe Apple's current strategy.

4. Propose a strategy to take Apple Computer into the 21st century. Keep in mind such factors as Microsoft Windows and the Internet. Describe how you would implement your strategy.

Sources

These facts are from Jim Carlton, "Apple Drops Newton, An Idea Ahead of Its Time," *The Wall Street Journal*, Mar. 2, 1998, B1, B8; "Claris to Reorganize as FileMaker, Inc.," Apple Press Release, Jan. 27, 1998; United States Securities and Exchange Commission Form 10-K for Apple Computer, Inc.; Peter Burrows, "A Peek at Steve Jobs' Plan," *Business Week*, Nov. 17, 1997, 144; "Apple Buys Assets of Clone Maker Power Computing," Reuters, Sept. 3, 1997; "Apple Drives Away Motorola from Cloning, IBM Next," Reuters, Sept. 12, 1997; Peter Burrows, "An Insanely Great Paycheck," *Business Week*, Feb. 26, 1996, 42; Kathy Rebellow and Peter Burrows, "The Fall of an American Icon," *Business Week*, Feb. 5, 1996, 34–42; and *Hoover's Company Profile* database (Austin, Texas: Reference Press, 1996) via America Online.

IBM[1]

International Business Machines (IBM), or "Big Blue," consistently maintained a position of leadership in the computer industry for most of the last three decades. For much of that time, experts and novices alike held the IBM name to be synonymous with the United States computer industry. A number of IBM products—including the System/360 mainframe computer, the AS/400 minicomputer, and its line of personal computers—have set industry standards. Despite a reputation for providing high quality computers and strong customer service, increasing levels of consumer dissatisfaction and declining sales, profits, and market share in recent years forced IBM's upper echelon into turmoil early in 1993.

During the 1980s, the company's share of the world computer market fell from 36 percent to 23 percent; its share of the $50 billion personal computer market dropped from 42 percent to a mere 14 percent. By late 1992, IBM posted its first operating loss, and share prices dropped by half. During that year, the firm lost more than $5 billion. Many of IBM's major customers voiced complaints about the company's inability to keep up with computer technology, citing the firm's lack of applications software, poor integration of its different computer product lines, and unwieldy systems. The early 1990s represent a dark page in IBM's corporate story. Recognizing that Big Blue's performance had deteriorated to an alarmingly critical low, its board of directors called, in January 1993, for the replacement of Chairman John Akers and two top members of his executive team. This move was coupled with an unprecedented 55 percent reduction in the company's dividend. These moves were met with confusion and skepticism from Wall Street and the computer industry as to whether IBM's drastic attempts to regain its top position in the computing industry were too little, too late.

The future hopes of IBM were pinned on an outsider with no background in technology, Louis V. Gerstner. On April Fool's Day, 1993, he became the first outsider to hold the CEO position at IBM. Gerstner's background included positions as an executive vice president at American Express and CEO of RJR Nabisco. His mission was to restore prominence to an ailing Big Blue; the company famous for

---

[1] This case was prepared by O. C. Ferrell, Colorado State University, for classroom discussion rather than to illustrate either effective or ineffective handling of an administrative situation. Research assistance was provided by Donald P. Roy, University of Memphis.

lifetime employment was in the process of slashing its workforce from 406,000 in 1986 to 219,000 in 1994. It had taken $20 billion-plus in write-offs, and its debt rating was deteriorating.

Reorganizing Big Blue

Early in 1988, then-Chairman John Akers announced a reorganization to make the computer giant more responsive to customers' needs, allowing it to respond more competitively in the stagnating computer market. At that time, the company combined its personal computer and typewriter divisions based on the rationale that customers of those products have similar needs. It also merged its mainframe computer operation with the less profitable midsize computer division. Akers decentralized IBM somewhat, pushing decision-making responsibilities down to six major product and marketing divisions to help reduce the bureaucracy that had been slowing down new product development—one of the most frequent and loudly voiced complaints from dissatisfied customers. Still attempting to maintain its long-standing policy of no layoffs, IBM asked 15,000 employees—mostly managers—to retire early, and left another 25,000 positions vacant. It retrained and moved thousands of employees to new positions within the company. Although these efforts helped improve the company's performance, IBM continued to struggle with slow, at times negligible, growth, in part because of increasingly intense competition in its mainframe and personal computer markets.

In January 1990, IBM announced another restructuring in an attempt to reduce its costs. Company executives said they would make the company more competitive by slashing costs by $1 billion and by eliminating 10,000 jobs, again through early retirements and attrition rather than layoffs. The company took a $2.3 billion pretax charge against fourth quarter 1989 earnings to cover severance pay, consolidations, and other expenses associated with reorganizing. Akers vowed that IBM would generate "modest growth" in revenues for the first time since 1985.

Despite Akers' declaration, industry analysts continued to predict gloom for Big Blue, pointing out that IBM had repeatedly forecast turnarounds that did not materialize. Critics blamed John Akers for IBM's dismal performance, particularly for the manufacturing problems, product delays, and managerial decisions that blemished IBM's reputation and its earnings. Some argued that IBM had maintained its policy of no layoffs at the expense of shareholder value and that IBM's board of directors was reluctant to criticize executives or enact tough cost-cutting measures. They also accused IBM of clinging to its old line of mainframe computers at the expense of developing technologically sophisticated new products that could help boost the company's revenue and image. IBM's continued slow performance in an increasingly competitive and fast-paced industry seemed to lend merit to these criticisms.

IBM announced yet another restructuring late in 1991, in which it further decentralized decision-making authority and created dozens of nearly independent operations. Some divisions were given almost complete autonomy: Facilities Management, which operates customer data centers; Maintenance, which repairs and upgrades systems; Software, the world's largest software company with projected 1991 revenues of $10.6 billion; Systems Integration, which provides custom programming and networking; Personal Computers and Workstations; Printers; Storage Products, which includes the company's high quality Rochester, Minnesota, operation; and Semiconductors.

The new IBM functioned essentially like a holding company, with control over many mostly autonomous divisions. Managers of each operation effectively became CEOs with freedom to make decisions, particularly regarding the development and marketing of products for their divisions. Their new decision-making authority should allow the company to speed up development of innovative products and allow it to be more effective against stiff global competition. With freedom, however, comes accountability and responsibility for a division's performance; if managers fail to perform adequately, they may be fired. In fact, with the 1991 restructuring, IBM abandoned its no-layoff policy, eliminating 20,000 jobs.

Additionally, in 1991, IBM announced that it had formed a joint venture with rival Apple Computer and Motorola Inc. to develop future personal computing technology. The same year, the company formed another joint venture with Siemens AG to develop and produce more advanced memory chips. More such alliances were likely as IBM executives believed that no single company can provide all the technologies, goods, and services that customers want. By the end of 1992, two former executives, Paul Rizzo and Kaspar Cassini, had been called from retirement to bolster IBM Chairman John Akers' fading position although he vehemently denied pressure to resign. In just over a month, following the report of IBM's first quarterly operating loss of $45 million, Akers' departure became a reality.

When Lou Gerstner became CEO in 1993, he faced decisions that would decide IBM's fate and had to move quickly to address the company's mounting financial losses. Gerstner's predecessor, John Akers, was attempting to split Big Blue 13 ways and possibly divest some of the parts. That strategy was immediately dropped, and Gerstner made mainframes his priority for the company. The logic behind the emphasis on mainframes was not to sell hardware, but rather to offer customers expertise in the implementation of computer systems. Another major decision involved changing the company's organization structure. Gerstner mandated that IBM dismantle its geographic organization structure in favor of an organization structure in which every function, from development to sales, was organized along industry lines.

Changes in product offerings were made after Gerstner's arrival through divestitures and acquisitions. IBM sold its online service, Prodigy. Gerstner added brands such as Lotus, which gave IBM a major player in desktop software and groupware, and Tivoli, which aided in the ability to build corporate networks. In addition to adding new products to the IBM line, Gerstner demanded that the company accelerate product development.

IBM's Products

Analysts have argued for years that IBM suffered stagnation in responding to the changes taking place constantly within the computer industry. Particularly in high-technology industries, innovation and rapid responsiveness are essential components of the success, and oftentimes, the very survival, of competing firms. Industry watchers place much of the blame for IBM's resistance to innovation on the sheer size of the organization. Particular criticisms include having too many employees, staggeringly high overhead, near-sighted reliance on its cash cow (mainframe computers), and dangerous inbreeding of management teams, resulting from the strong corporate culture, which was the company's greatest asset. Mainframe computer sales made up the largest percentage of the company's $78 billion annual sales in

EXHIBIT 7.1	Percent of Revenue by Business Segment

Segment	1997 Percent of Total Revenue	1996 Percent of Total Revenue	1995 Percent of Total Revenue
Hardware	46.1	47.8	49.5
Services	24.6	20.9	17.7
Software	16.4	17.2	17.6
Maintenance	8.1	9.2	10.3
Rentals/Financing	4.8	4.9	4.9
Total	100	100	100

Source: IBM 1997 Annual Report

1997. The multimillion-dollar mainframes link the company to its largest, most profitable customers, and they also heavily influence computer and software purchases. But as the IBM-dominated mainframe market matures, growth is slow, and competition has become fierce.

The product mix of IBM is now composed of five business segments: hardware, services, software, maintenance, and rentals and financing. Exhibit 1 indicates progress in these business units from 1995 to 1997. The company's reliance on hardware sales has decreased in recent years as IBM positions itself as a "solutions company" rather than a marketer of computer hardware. This strategy of being a more comprehensive technology company is evident in the increase of the services segment as IBM has taken a more active role in managing customers' computer networks.

Hardware

Trends in the hardware segment continued to be disappointing for IBM into the late 1990s. The company has experienced flat sales (sales increased 4 percent in 1997). Mainframe revenue has experienced modest growth, but server revenue declined in both 1996 and 1997, thus adversely impacting the hardware segment. Furthermore, IBM has experienced decreased revenue from storage products, particularly high-end products. One bright spot in the hardware area has been a marked increase in original equipment manufacturer (OEM) revenue. This increase has been sparked by strong growth in HDD storage products.

To overcome some of the problems in the hardware area, IBM is completely upgrading and adding new products to the entire server product line. The new system/390 G4 enterprise servers represent the complete conversion of mainframes to microprocessor technology. The system/390 product line delivered 30 percent growth in shipments of processing capacity. The company recently introduced Web-enabled RS/6000s and AS/400 servers. In addition, after lagging behind the industry, IBM is introducing a number of new products from the disk storage area. The company announced the world's highest capacity desktop PC disk drive. It is claimed to be new, breakthrough technology and has given the company the world's most sensitive sensor for reading and writing computer data on magnetic disk.

The market for personal computers remains a battleground for IBM. Over the years, intense competition from makers of clones of IBM's XT and AT personal computer lines cut sharply into the company's market share. Savvy competitors such as Gateway 2000, Dell Computers, and others have won market share at IBM's expense by offering good value and strong customer support; other clone makers won customers through ultra low prices. Although IBM is fighting back with new high-quality computers, consumers have been reluctant to pay higher prices just for the IBM name.

IBM is using its rediscovered prowess in the PC market to win back major customers. It has won contracts to supply PC products for such corporations as Signa, Barnes & Noble, United Parcel Service, and Home Depot. Despite the resurgence of the PC unit and an impressive list of new customers, IBM still finds itself behind Compaq and Dell in PC market share. However, the company believes its faster, simpler distribution system will enable it to bolster profit margins and increase market share.

It appears that IBM has made progress in reversing its missteps in the personal computer market. The PC unit reached a low point in 1994, when it reported a $1 billion operating loss. Inefficient operations that included a 3,400 model assortment of machines, an excessive number of available options, and excessive parts inventory contributed to IBM's poor performance. Today, the company's PC unit is much more efficient, offering fewer models and reducing available options. Streamlined product offerings have enabled IBM to reduce the number of different parts it keeps in inventory to less than one-third of 1994 levels. Also, the company has reduced inventory levels by having suppliers replenish parts on a daily basis, with 62 percent of all parts replenished daily in 1997, up from 5 percent in 1994. Finally, the PC unit has become more efficient due to distributors assembling PCs rather than IBM assembling them in-house. Today, almost one-third of the company's PCs are assembled by distributors compared to no outside assembly in 1994. The results of this increased efficiency are evident for IBM. Sales grew 18 percent in 1997, and the company has been able to maintain the low profit margins PCs offer.

Services

Another bright spot for IBM has been the growth of its services segment. Services revenue increased 28 percent in 1997, growing from revenues of about $4 billion in 1990 to $19.3 billion in 1997. Today, IBM is the market leader in global services and has the highest customer satisfaction rating in the industry. The growth in the services segment is consistent with the company's desire to become a complete information technology company and not just a hardware manufacturer. Revenues from services accounted for about 25 percent of total company revenues in 1997. Growth in this segment has come from managed operation of systems and networks. Emphasis on the services segment has come from the top levels of management, as Lou Gerstner himself occasionally speaks at conferences attended by current and prospective IBM services clients. Despite the company downsizing activities following Gerstner's arrival in 1993, the services segment has added employees, hiring over 15,000 employees in both 1996 and 1997 to keep pace with the segment's growth.

Software

IBM is growing its software business unit at a faster rate than the industry. This is the result of IBM focusing on distributed software. In 1992, distributed software represented only 10 percent of software revenue, and by 1997, it represented 40 percent. Lotus Notes sales doubled for the third straight year in 1997 and Tivoli's systems management products are growing twice as fast as those in the industry. The company is also making other software products that are growing rapidly such as a new product, DB2, a universal database.

Lotus' new eSuite (Applets) is redefining personal productivity applications like word processors and spreadsheets. With Enterprise Java Beans, IBM and Lotus are taking Java into high volume transaction processing. More than 200 software developers are working with IBM to create Java for general ledger, order entry, and other business functions as a part of IBM's San Francisco project.

IBM Responds to Competition

IBM's newest organizational structure has somewhat improved the company's decision-making time, allowing it to respond more quickly to changes in the marketplace. To increase sales, IBM discounted prices on many products by up to 40 percent. After the debut of its new mainframe, the company reduced the price of older 3090 models by 50 percent. When rival Compaq cut prices on its 386 personal computers by as much as 32 percent, IBM followed suit within hours (rather than the months it would have taken the company before reorganization). For example, IBM's Value Point PCs, which do not come with a monitor or hard drive, cost less than Compaq's. IBM's new discounting policy marks the beginning of a price-competition strategy, which it hopes will eliminate many "clone" marketers from the PC market.

Although many industry experts warn that IBM may confuse its customers by broadening its product line, the company has implemented this strategy. Knowing that in the computer industry, equipment can become obsolete in a matter of years, IBM continues to develop products and technology critical to its survival. With the mainframe ES/9000 as its flagship, IBM is introducing the System/390. This 400 product package possesses a broad array of technology and the ability to network between IBM and non-IBM systems.

IBM is also cultivating a long-term approach by entering the education sector more aggressively, an arena it once left to Apple. Discounting means the education sales will not generate high profits, but company executives recognize that schools represent a reliable and growing market, and that the children getting familiar with IBMs in the classroom today will be the adults who buy computers tomorrow.

With the worst of times hopefully behind it, IBM is optimistic about its future. The company has renewed its commitment in two key areas. First, it has reaffirmed its desire to be the company for mainframe computers. Second, it has reaffirmed its commitment to its customers. For years, IBM's customer service was legendary. However, as the company fell on hard times in the early 1990s, customer confidence in Big Blue fell, too. With its increased emphasis in providing complete network management services to its customers, organizing the company along industry lines, and restructuring its distribution system to be more responsive to market needs, IBM appears to be in position to be competitive in the coming years.

Questions for Discussion

1. Characterize IBM's current situation. What are the firm's unique strengths? Weaknesses?

2. Evaluate the most recent series of changes taking place at IBM. Does the firm seem to be on the "right track" again? Why or why not?

3. Evaluate the record of Louis V. Gerstner, IBM CEO since 1993.

Sources

These facts are from IBM 1997 Annual Report; Betsy Morris and Joe McGowan, "He's Smart, He's Not Nice. He's Saving Big Blue," *Fortune*, April 14, 1997, 68; Raju Narisetti, "How IBM Turned Around Its Ailing PC Division," *The Wall Street Journal*, March 12, 1998, B1, B4. "Big Blue Sees Red," *USA Today*, Oct. 20, 1992, 2B; Paul B. Carroll, "Big Blues: Hurt by a Pricing War, IBM Plans a Writeoff and Cut of 10,000 Jobs," *The Wall Street Journal*, Dec. 6, 1989, A1, A8; Harris Collingwood, "IBM May Be Crowding Its Own Turf," *Business Week*, Feb. 19, 1990, 42; "Computer Makers Find Schools a Reliable Market," *The Kansas City (MO) Business Journal*, Aug. 13, 1990; John Hillkirk, "As IBM Falters, Shareholders and Critics Take Aim at Akers," *USA Today*, Dec. 6, 1989, 10B; "IBM slashes dividend to stem red ink," *USA Today*, Jan. 27, 1993; IBM 1991 Annual Report; Louise Kehoe, "The New Big Blue," *Electronics*, July 1990, 27–28; Carol J. Loomis, "Can John Akers Save IBM?" *Fortune*, July 15, 1991, 40–56; Sharon Machlis, "'Big Blue' Makes Push for Engineering Market," *Design News*, March 26, 1990, 186; Jim McNair, "IBM Rolls Out Next Generation," *The Miami Herald*, Sept. 6, 1990; Jeff Moad and Susan Kerr, "How Customers Help the New IBM," *Business Month*, Jan. 1990, 13; Therese Poletti, "IBM unveils system, enters 'super' market," *The Commercial Appeal*, Feb. 3, 1993, B-4; Larry Reibstein, "IBM's Plan to Decentralize May Set a Trend-But Imitation Has a Price," *The Wall Street Journal*, Feb. 19, 1988, 17; Frank Ruiz, "IBM Blazes Trail with New 16-Megabit Computer Chip," *The Tampa (FL) Tribune*, Feb. 14, 1990; Robert L. Scheier, "IBM Redraws its Big Blueprint," *PC Week*, Dec. 2, 1991, 1, 6; John Schneidawind, "Apple Computer Seizes IBM's PC Crown," *USA Today*, Oct. 23, 1992, 1B; John Schneidawind, "IBM faces dilemma in CEO quest," *USA Today*, Jan. 27, 1993; John W. Verity "Guess What: IBM Is Losing Out in Mainframes Too," *Business Week*, Feb. 8, 1993, 106–107;John W. Verity, "A Slimmer IBM May Still Be Overweight," *Business Week*, Dec. 18, 1989, 107–108; John W. Verity, "What's Ailing IBM? More Than This Year's Earnings," *Business Week*, Oct. 16, 1989, 75–86; and John W. Verity, Thane Peterson, Deidre Depke, and Evan I. Schwartz, "The New IBM," *Business Week*, Dec. 16,1991, 112–118.

Bass Pro Shops[1]

Bass Pro Shops is the privately owned parent of Outdoor World, a large retail store and catalog operation headquartered in Springfield, Missouri, and Tracker marine, a manufacturer of fishing boats. Bass Pro Shops has 1,806 employees and a $200 million economic impact on Springfield. Outdoor World is a 280,000 square foot retail operation organized by departments that, in some ways, resembles a mall because it includes a variety of entertainment and service offerings. Over four million people visit Outdoor World in Springfield each year. The Bass Pro Shops organization primarily serves the outdoor enthusiast, with a strong emphasis on hunting and fishing.

President Johnny Morris of Bass Pro Shops calls Outdoor World the "world's greatest sporting goods store." Opened in 1981, Outdoor World was designed to be a showcase for the thousands of items offered in the Bass Pro catalog. It has become a mecca for those who enjoy outdoor activities such as hunting, fishing, boating, canoeing, bicycling, and camping. Merchandise of a particular type, such as fishing equipment, is grouped together in one area, using a unified promotional theme that varies with the seasons. Services and entertainment are provided in hopes that customers will stay in the store for longer periods of time and spend more money.

Outdoor World was originally intended to be a special store that would provide "red carpet" treatment for catalog customers who could see and buy products unavailable from other retailers. Because half of Outdoor World's customers come from outside Missouri, rifle, pistol, and archery ranges were included in order to allow customers to try out merchandise, such as a new rifle, before taking it home. Although the retail store operation has taken on a life of its own, the telemarketing operation continues to sell a high volume of merchandise from the Outdoor World catalog and thus, indirectly, encourages store visits.

Catalog and Telemarketing

About 500 operators are busy around the clock, seven days a week, answering about 170 incoming WATS lines at the catalog operation. Bass Pro managers won't reveal

---

[1] This case was prepared by Neil Herndon, City University of Hong Kong, for classroom discussion rather than to illustrate either effective or ineffective handling of an administrative situation.

sales or profit figures for the privately owned company, but they say they distribute about 36 million catalogs a year, keeping United Parcel Service (UPS) and the U.S. Postal Service busy with 400,000 packages shipped to catalog customers monthly. The Bass Pro Shops Outdoor World Master Catalog, with 388 full-color pages, lists more than 17,000 items. There are also specialty catalogs for sportsmen's clothing, hunting, fishing, and marine enthusiasts. The customer pays $2 for the master catalog but receives with the catalog a coupon good for $3 off merchandise purchases. About 90 percent of the catalog orders are filled on initial request and do not have to be backordered.

Catalogs are printed a season in advance, and there is always the danger that customers may wait too long to order. The biggest reason for backorders is manufacturers' underestimating the popularity of an item. Manufacturers keep track of items that are most popular and try to prepare for the buying season but, unfortunately, are not always accurate. A missed projection of anticipated sales for a certain fishing lure quickly resulted in 3,000 backorders for the product and, presumably, as many unhappy fishermen. The catalog is one of the most convenient ways of getting needed items with minimum effort. In addition, many of the items that Bass Pro offers are not available in many rural and smaller towns.

The Outdoor World Store

The departments within the store contain a wide variety of merchandise with many choices within each line. There are about 200 types of bows available, and seven display cases, each about six feet long, hold about 15 handguns each. While signs help customers find departments, merchandise lines, and clothing sizes, promotion elements attract special attention to the merchandise. Flyers call attention to special in-store sales. There are the usual shelf-talker cards attached to display shelves. There are also mounted Northern geese, suspended in mid-air, that appear to be preparing to land over the Tracker Marine boat showroom area. Nearby, a mounted raccoon raids a Cracker Jack box on a display of men's caps. People often point out the raccoon and, hopefully, the caps are noticed in the process.

Outdoor World offers two restaurant options to shoppers. Near the entrance to Hemingway's Blue Water Cafe, a four-story waterfall cascades in a 64,000-gallon reflecting pool stocked with fish native to Missouri. Stairs and two glass-enclosed elevators provide access to the fourth-floor cafe, which contains a 29,000-gallon saltwater aquarium. The cafe is decorated with antique fishing and hunting equipment, as well as mounted animal trophies and African ritual masks, providing an exotic decor. Local businesspeople frequently dine in the cafe. Former president George Bush had biscuits and gravy at Hemingway's in 1991. Cafeteria-style family dining is available at the Gravel Bar located across from Hemingway's on the same floor.

Outdoor World customers can also visit the Tall Tales Barbershop on the fourth floor, just across the waterfall from Hemingway's. The decor features four barber chairs for patrons, which are real "fighting chairs" that a fisherman might use on a deep sea fishing boat. The barbershop's location provides an excellent view of the Tracker Marine boat showroom below, and customers can have strands of their freshly cut hair made into a fishing lure.

Visitors can see both a trout stream and scuba divers hand-feeding freshwater fish at Uncle Buck's 250-seat auditorium on the lower level. There are six aquariums at

Outdoor World, as well as a live alligator pit (in the hunting department), and an aquarium with a 96-pound alligator snapping turtle (in the boat showroom). There is also a large display of antique fishing lures, mounted trophy fish, and mounted trophy animals, including a lion posed to leap with claws aimed at the visitor's chest. Many visitors pose by the gaping mouth of a 3,247-pound great white shark and have a friend take their picture using a loaner camera from Outdoor World.

Outdoor World contains indoor shooting ranges for rifles, handguns, and bows that provide a variety of stationary and moving targets. Rods and reels are repaired and knives sharpened. Trophy animals can be mounted at Wildlife Creations, the award-winning taxidermy shop. Golfers can test putters on an indoor putting green and test other clubs on an indoor driving range.

Outdoor World provides both entertainment and a variety of services for the four million visitors who come to the store each year. More people visit Outdoor World than the Gateway Arch in St. Louis, making Outdoor World the most visited tourist attraction in Missouri. Bass Pro provides useful product information to help customers select equipment suited to their interests. Camping equipment, such as tents, is displayed as it would be used. Salespeople are trained not only to sell the product but to show its proper use and maintenance. Videotapes are shown near the equipment they feature. Free pamphlets explain how to select items such as baseball bats, bows, camp foods, canoes, golf clubs, rifle scopes, slalom water skies, sleeping bags, and water fowl decoys. All Outdoor World products receive a 100 percent satisfaction guarantee.

Sales Promotion

Special events are an important part of marketing at Outdoor World. The Bass Pro Shops World's Fishing Fair, held in the spring, draws about 50,000 people each of its five days. It features about 150 fishing seminars (such as fly tying demonstrations) and about 200 displays. The Fall Hunting Classic draws a total of about 80,000 visitors over its four-day run. Rock star Ted Nugent, an avid bowhunter, presented a bowhunting seminar at the 1990 Fall Hunting Classic, which also promoted a bow he designed that is sold at Outdoor World. Former president Jimmy Carter, an avid fisherman and hunter, attended the 1988 Fall Hunting Classic to autograph copies of his book about the outdoors.

The Bass Pro organization pays careful attention to the local Ozark region. Coins tossed into Outdoor World aquariums and fountains are collected by Outdoor World employees, cleaned and sorted by community volunteers, and then donated to the Ronald McDonald House, which benefits critically ill children and their families. The 400,000 packages mailed each month by the Bass Pro catalog division feature biodegradable packing material made from recycled ground paper rather than the less environmentally safe foam "peanuts" formerly used.

When Berkley Inc., a fishing equipment manufacturer, asked anglers purchasing Berkley Trilene or Trimax fishing line to send in a postcard attached to the fishing line package in order to have a fish stocked in their name, Bass Pro Shops President Johnny Morris promised to match the number of fish stocked by Berkley. The result was that Fellows Lake near Springfield received 5,000 channel catfish from Berkley and 5,000 walleye from Bass Pro.

Bass Pro also uses drawings as a sales promotion tool. More than half a million people nationwide submitted entries in the Skoal Sportsman's Sweepstakes sponsored by the U.S. Tobacco Sales and Marketing Company, Inc. and Bass Pro. The winner received a $100,000 line of credit at Outdoor World.

Bass Pro executives say their key operating philosophy has not been to add more and more to their organization. Rather, they have added items that seem important to the outdoor enthusiast in terms of providing them with a new experience or element of pleasure. The key idea for the executives seems to be the value-added notion of meeting the needs of the outdoor enthusiast, an idea at the very heart of the marketing concept.

Tracker Marine

Originally, Outdoor World wanted to provide the angler with everything necessary to go fishing, such as rod, reel, tackle box, seating, electronic fish finders, motor, and boat. At first, boats were purchased by Bass Pro from other companies. Then in 1978, the Tracker Marine subsidiary was developed to build boats. Today, Tracker Marine produces 41 different models, ranging from a line of pontoon boats to a line of aluminum boats to a line of fiberglass bass boats, including boat trailers. All of these boats and trailers used to be manufactured within 50 miles of Springfield. Now, they are manufactured at five plants in Missouri and Florida.

Tracker Marine has been successful in part because it was the first company to provide the customer with a complete fishing package—boat, motor, lure, electronics, steering, seating—everything needed to go fishing without having to assemble the individual items.

Tracker Marine now sells its own boats and trailers through a network of about 250 dealers across the United States There are about 25 dealers in Canada and one in Australia. Tracker plans to expand the number of its dealerships in Canada and to enter the market in Europe and other unspecified parts of the world. Tracker Marine executives attribute expansion to the fact that volume helps Tracker keep its prices competitive.

Outdoor World is Tracker Marine's largest boat customer, and Tracker Marine is Outdoor World's largest advertiser in the Outdoor World master catalog. Together the two subsidiaries of Bass Pro Shops employ about 4,000 people in the peak season (a minimum of about 1,800 in Outdoor World and about 1,500 in Tracker Marine year round) and have an annual payroll of about $40 million. Even though Bass Pro has acquired the Spectrum and Fisher boat lines from Brunswick Corporation, there are no plans to sell them through Outdoor World.

Environmental and Competitive Threats

Outdoor World's emphasis on hunting and large displays of mounted animals are a potential target of protest by animal rights activists. Despite the argument advanced by hunters that hunting preserves the balance of nature by reducing wild animal populations that cannot be supported by existing vegetation, some people feel any killing of animals is unethical. Others would hold that wildlife should be observed in the wild, not in retail stores, especially those who believe that wildlife should not even be displayed in zoos. Using mounted animals for commercial purposes would appear to be a further source of displeasure for animal rights activists. Also, some parents may find the narrated exhibitions of scuba divers hand-feeding live goldfish to gamefish in Uncle Buck's auditorium objectionable.

Bass Pro does not seem to have direct competitors. Small tackle shops, marine dealers, and sources of other outdoor products generally cannot match prices or selection. L.L. Bean operates a retail store specializing in outdoor products in Freeport, Maine and also offers products through several catalogs supported by a telemarketing operation in Lewiston, Maine. However, Bean appears to be targeting a more upscale market with its offerings. Bean displays only a few mounted animals in its store, has fewer and smaller aquariums, and is located among upscale outlets like Ralph Lauren and London Fog. Although neither Bass Pro nor L.L. Bean offers firearms through their catalogs because of federal regulations, Outdoor World offers a very large selection of rifles, shotguns, and handguns in store, while L.L. Bean offers a smaller selection of only rifles and shotguns in store. Bass Pro executives, however, do keep an eye on L.L. Bean.

New Retailing Directions

Bass Pro Shops' retail activities have been centered in one store location in Springfield. However, in March 1995, Bass Pro opened a second store in Atlanta, Georgia, called "Sportsman's Warehouse." This store has an outdoor feel similar to the Outdoor World operation and could be a concept test for a warehouse style retailing operation. Worldwide Sportsman, another Bass Pro owned store in Islamorada, Florida, stocks goods mainly for saltwater fishermen.

Although the Sportsman's Warehouse may change its name and atmospherics to match that of its parent store, four new stores are opening under the Outdoor World name. One will be in a mall location in Gurnee, Illinois, another near a megamall in Grapevine, Texas, one in Nashville, Tennessee, and the fourth in Fort Lauderdale, Florida. The 133,000 square foot Grapevine store—which could add another 90,000 square feet for a boating center or other attraction—is expected to produce $100 million in gross sales annually. A wilderness-themed hotel and convention center is being built nearby. The Nashville location will be close to a "shoppertainment" music-themed megamall on the site of the former Opryland Theme Park. The Fort Lauderdale store will be next to the International Game Fish Association Hall of Fame to be built on land donated by Bass Pro Shops President Morris.

The stores operated under the Outdoor World name will be extremely similar to the parent Springfield store. They will have similar decorations, entertainment qualities, and merchandise. However, a new facade pioneered at the Gurnee store location is being added to the Springfield store. This new entrance will likely be a signature of all Outdoor World stores.

Bass Pro Shops is locating its stores next to family attractions. To accomplish this in Springfield, Morris is donating $10 million in cash, land, and exhibits and seeking the balance from state and local taxes to build a $40 million world-class American National Fish and Wildlife Living Museum and Aquarium on land next to the Springfield Outdoor World store. Although the Missouri Conservation Commission views this as a positive effort to promote conservation and is donating $2.5 million to the museum, critics envision a big room full of stuffed dead animals created to boost business for Outdoor World.

Questions for Discussion

1.   What is the corporate and marketing strategy at Bass Pro Shops?

2.   What are the external opportunities and threats and the internal strengths and weaknesses facing Outdoor World?

3.   What promotion components are emphasized at Bass Pro Shops? Why?

4.   Does your SWOT analysis suggest the need for changes in Outdoor World's promotion strategy? Support your position with facts from the case.

Sources

These facts are from Bass Pro Shops, "Outdoor World," promotional pamphlet, undated, CL-670; Bass Pro Shops, "The Outdoor World Showroom," *Springfield News-Leader*, Special Advertising Supplement, Aug. 20, 1989, 1; Kate Marymount, "Hemingway's Makes Debut with Flavor," *Springfield News-Leader*, Apr. 24, 1987, 1-C; Matt Hiebert, "Restaurant Offers More Than Delicious Food," *Springfield News-Leader*, Special Advertising Supplement, Aug. 20, 1989, 6; Kathleen O'Dell, "Old Sea Tales: Bass Pro Barbershop Cuts Hairs with Nautical Flair," *Springfield News-Leader*, Oct. 1, 1987, 8-B, 6-B; Bass Pro Shops, "Welcome to Outdoor World," promotional pamphlet, undated, CL-902; Kathleen O'Dell, "Bass Pro Plans Big Renovation," *Springfield News-Leader*, Jan. 6, 1988, 1-A, 10-A; Robert E. Carr, "Bass Pro Challenges Vendor Price Policies," *Sporting Goods Business*, Feb. 1994, 8; "Bass Pro Shops: An RV/Fishing Venue," *RV Business*, July 1996, 34, 41–42; Jeff Kurowski, "Bass Pro Shops Goes to Illinois, Texas," *Boating Industry*, Sept. 1996, 16; Steve Koehler, "A New Zenith for Bass Pro," *Springfield News-Leader*, Jan. 16, 1997, 1-A; Dan Sewell, "After the Strike: UPS Tries to Recoup Losses," *The Commercial Appeal*, Aug. 21, 1997, B-8; "Wildlife Museum Backers Seek Millions from Public," *St. Louis Post-Dispatch*, May 3, 1997, 18; Andrew Backover, "Bass Pro Shops Signs Grapevine Superstore Deal," *Fort Worth Star-Telegram*, Oct. 7, 1997, 1; Eddie Bass, "Renovations Add More Retail Space," *Springfield Business Journal*, Dec. 1, 1997, 11; Michael Grunwald, "Megamall Sells Stimulation," *Boston Globe*, Dec. 9, 1997, 1-A; John Rogers, "State Conservation Department Pledges $2.5 Million Toward Wildlife Museum," *St. Louis Post-Dispatch*, Dec. 19, 1997, 6-C; Paul Flemming, "Civic Park Tops List of Tax Beneficiaries," *Springfield Business Journal*, Jan. 26, 1998, 1.

CASE 9

H-E-B[1]

Established in 1905 as a small family business, H. E. Butt Food Stores (H-E-B) has grown into one of the most successful food retail businesses in the United States with sales of $6 billion. What began as a small mom-and-pop store in Kerrville, Texas, has become a complex operation with 245 grocery stores in Texas, Louisiana, and Mexico, yet H-E-B retains its ability to blend the ever-changing concept of grocery marketing with the needs and tastes of the local communities that it serves. The company's growth over the past 93 years reflects both the history of Texas and the evolution of the supermarket concept.

Company History

Mrs. Florence Butt opened the door of the Mrs. C. C. Butt Staple and Fancy Groceries store in Kerrville, Texas in 1905 with a $60 investment. Mrs. Butt's store was probably like most grocery stores of the time, with merchandise stored in open barrels or cans on shelves cooled by ceiling fans. Customers carried merchandise in wicker baskets or wooden wagons, and most probably purchased goods on credit with the store. The small store thrived enough to sustain the family.

In 1919, Mrs. Butt's son, Howard, fresh from World War I, took over the family business. Howard E. Butt began his tenure with the idea of expanding the business beyond Kerrville. After four unsuccessful attempts, a second store was opened in Del Rio, Texas, in 1927. The following year, Howard Butt decided to move the base of operations to Rio Grande City in south Texas. He borrowed $38,000 (think what this kind of money would represent in 1928!) to acquire three similar stores, thus initiating the first expansion of the business.

During the tough years of the Great Depression and through the late 1930s, the company continued its expansion with new stores in the central and coastal regions of Texas. During those early years, the company adopted many practices that continue to be part of its strategy today. For example, with the acquisition in 1936 of its own bakery in Corpus Christi, Texas, the company began a process of vertical integration that eventually included milk, ice cream, and meat processing plants, as well as a

[1] This case was prepared by Salvador Trevino-Martinez, ITESM/University of Memphis, for classroom discussion rather than to illustrate either effective or ineffective handling of an administrative situation.

photo processing lab. This process of integration led to the concept of one-stop shopping, turning the simple grocery store into a comprehensive supermarket with drugstore, fish and flower markets, and butcher and delicatessen shops, all under the same roof. Along with this successful expansion, the firm moved to San Antonio, Texas, renovating a historic U.S. Army Arsenal complex for its current headquarters.

Company Philosophy

H-E-B's business philosophy is based on three principles. First, the entire organization is committed to offering superior customer service. Second, the company pledges to offer the best quality and freshness in its products. Finally, the firm aims to offer the best overall buying experience along with great value.

H-E-B's mission statement reflects the elements by which these principles become a day-to-day reality. The mission statement opens with a "Bold Commitment" in which the organization pledges to build what it calls, "The Greatest Retailing Company," a phrase that provides a sense of direction, yet leaves room to adapt the concept to the configuration of the retailing industry itself. The mission statement also provides guidance regarding members of the organization whom the firm refers to as partners. Partner promises are also incorporated into the mission's pledge with specific commitments in the areas of customer service, product quality, and value for every dollar spent in the stores. The mission statement concludes with a phrase that could only be the product of the partners' view on the statement itself: "We promise ... to keep our promises."

H-E-B: A Regional Business?

There are several characteristic traits innate to the H-E-B concept of business. The first is the fast adaptation to the markets it serves. This adaptation extends beyond the mere allocation of shelf space to local products and food staples. For example, the company's 73 Pantry Foods stores are smaller in size, offer a wide variety of name-brand merchandise and fresh meat and produce, and are known for their convenience and low prices, which appeal to citizens of east Texas, where the stores are primarily located. In 1991, the company launched a new supermarket concept in San Antonio under the name Marketplace. The larger size of this store and its product variety and availability made it a benchmark for other food retailers. The concept turned out to be so successful that the firm soon opened more Marketplace stores throughout Texas. In 1995, the company introduced another version of a modern store, the Central Market, in Austin, Texas. This upscale concept brings a wide assortment of fresh products and ready-to-cook prepared items under the same roof and features an eclectic arrangement of shopping and entertainment alternatives to appeal to local tastes. The store has been generating positive comments since its opening, and plans are under way for two more Central Markets.

A second distinct feature is technological innovation. The company has instituted state-of-the-art computer-based Point-of-Sale systems, satellite communications, and video surveillance, and is an industry leader in testing electronic shelf labels. According to Fully Clingman, H-E-B's president and COO, "If [technology] can improve the quality of life for our partners [employees], improve the quality of our products for consumers, help deliver products in a more cost-effective manner, then whether it's smoke signals, satellites or infrared, we don't care." This attitude has generated praise from both industry analysts and competitors who see H-E-B's approach to technology as a benchmark for the entire industry.

Another interesting characteristic of the H-E-B operation has to do with its distribution system. Since its inception, the company has held to a strict regional expansion trend. This focus has allowed the company to build a comprehensive 1,000-truck transportation network operated from a large distribution center in San Antonio. The delivery system is further supported by warehouses in San Marcos, Corpus Christi, and Houston.

Despite its regional scale, H-E-B has capitalized on its 93 years of experience to rack up some impressive industry records, such as double the average weekly sales of other national grocery chains, three times the average of industry leaders in same store sales growth, and a sales volume that has tripled in 10 years, all of which have propelled the firm to the rank of 12th-largest food retailing chain in the United States But not everything is on the bright side: The company is presently undergoing a period of expansion amidst increasing competition, some technological overturns in the retailing business, and changing customer demands for better value and more services. Given these circumstances, the company must carefully decide on the strategies that will not only assure its current standing but also guide future development.

Options for Expansion

H-E-B faces three options for growth. The first is to expand north within the state of Texas. The company already has a dominant position in the Rio Grande Valley, central Texas, and in the coastal area that stretches from the Mexican border to Houston. However, the company has no presence in the north and northeastern regions of the state.

A second option for expansion is into neighboring U.S. states. Demographic trends indicate that strong population growth in the Sun Belt states will continue, so a natural route for expansion would be into the promising markets of states such as New Mexico, Arizona, Louisiana, and Mississippi. These states have similar sociodemographic consumer profiles as the firm's current markets and have the additional advantage of geographical proximity. In 1996, the company tested this strategy when it opened its first store outside of Texas with the inauguration of a pantry-type store in Lake Charles, Louisiana, a growing city of 70,000.

H-E-B's third option for expansion is south of the Texas border, where the marketing environment is quite different. However, factors such as geographical proximity, ethnic composition of the indigenous market, and the shopping habits of the Mexican middle class make the prospects of expansion into Mexico not only feasible but also appealing. If the company can thrive in a market where the economy, culture, language, and laws are different, then it can build a position to capitalize on its experience and adopt an even more aggressive expansion stance into international markets.

H-E-B's First International Market

Perhaps the boldest expansion move taken thus far is the opening of a store in San Pedro Garza García, an upscale suburb of Monterrey, in the northeastern state of Nuevo Léon, Mexico. Open to the public in 1997, the 70,000 square-foot store has elicited favorable comments from customers, many of whom were already familiar with H-E-B from shopping trips to neighboring cities on the Texas border such as Laredo, McAllen, and Brownsville. The company has already announced plans to open a second store in the southern part of Monterrey.

Monterrey is a logical choice for expansion, given its status as an industry and services capital and its location just 150 miles south of Laredo, Texas. The city's large population (3.5 million), income per capita above the national average, and increasing economic activity make it an appealing market for H-E-B. Monterrey represents a primary market for both national and international firms willing to consolidate operations in the country.

Of course, H-E-B will face challenges in the Monterrey market. Among its most significant local competitors are Gigante, a national chain with many outlets throughout Mexico and within Monterrey, and Soriana, a supermarket chain with 90 outlets in the northern region of Mexico and 30 outlets in Monterrey. Wal-Mart already has two stores in the area, as well as two Sam's Club stores. The French chain Carrefour opened a hypermarket in 1997, and Price Costco, another shopping club chain, has also started operations in the market. Moreover, Monterrey, like most Mexican cities, is still feeling the lingering effects of a severe economic crisis that nearly collapsed the Mexican economy in 1994. As current CEO Charles Butt commented, "We have found it very challenging to do business in another country. It is even more complex then we expected: Different laws, a different culture. It has been really stretching for our company."

Supermercados H-E-B S.A. *de C.V.* (the name the company adopted for its operations in Mexico) is a long-term project based on the strong belief that the company is moving into Mexico as part of a natural evolution process that can be traced back to the early days when Howard E. Butt moved the business to the Rio Grande Valley, a region with a distinct Mexican influence. H-E-B's commitment to the Monterrey market is best explained by CEO Butt, "We have had a relationship with the people of Northern Mexico for decades in our company, going back to the 1930s when my father established stores in the Rio Grande Valley. . . . It is our real desire here to be a part of this nation in a strong way. Many people have talked to us about out timing in Mexico. My father used to say to me, 'Son, the border will always go up and down, but it will always come back.' I have never been terribly concerned about whether we hit things here on the downturn or in the upswing. We are in this game for the long haul. . . . Yes, I think Mexico is coming out of the crisis, as they refer to it here. So maybe our timing is fine, but that's not the major part of our concern. We want to serve people here in a way that will build customer relationships for the longer term."

Questions for Discussion

1. What factors are behind the success of H-E-B?
2. Evaluate the three potential strategies H-E-B is considering for future expansion.
3. What are some of the foreseeable challenges that the company is likely to face in the future if it continues with expansion in Mexico?

Sources

"HEB: The Tech Leader?" *Progressive Grocer,* May, 1996 and *http://www.hebgrocery.com,* April 2, 1998.

U.S.Learning, Inc.[1]

Upon graduation, many students wrestle with the following pressing question; "Will I ever be in a position to have my own company, or will I always work for someone else?" Don Hutson, the present chairman of the board and CEO of U.S.Learning, Inc., faced that question in 1967. Today, he is one of the limited, but growing, number of people who successfully start a company that achieves prominence in an industry. This case should give significant hope to all budding entrepreneurs who wish to follow. It also provides examples of the potholes encountered on the road to this type of success.

Background

Don Hutson started in the training business in August 1967 when he went to work for the National Association of Sales Education (NASE) promoting and selling seats in sales seminars. Fresh out of the sales program at what was then Memphis State University (now the University of Memphis), Don was looking for a challenge that would allow him to demonstrate and refine his sales skills. He found it in NASE. Don worked in this capacity for a year and a half. His responsibilities included giving short speeches to small groups with the goal of successfully creating interest in upcoming seminars and the ultimate objective of selling tickets to the programs. His first 1,500 speeches in this job were 30-minute talks to groups of anywhere from five to 20 people.

After a year and a half of successes that included a significant amount of tutoring from NASE president Dick Gardner, Don Hutson started his first true entrepreneurial venture, Sales Corporation of America (SCA). The challenge was basically the same, selling tickets to public seminars, but now the responsibility for developing and directing this new organization was Don's alone. At the age of 24 he hired several sales associates and SCA was off and running. Sales Corporation of America stayed in business for three and one-half years. During this period the small but growing firm promoted anywhere from four to 20 training seminars per year.

---

[1] This case was prepared by Robert Peterson, University of Portland, for classroom discussion rather than to illustrate either effective or ineffective handling of an administrative situation.

At its peak, SCA had approximately a dozen salespeople working for it, most of them doing what Don had done for NASE. The company had a national flair, with sales-people in numerous different cities.

It was in 1973 that Don Hutson made a major decision that would forever alter his companies and the career he would pursue. He was a good speaker and began giving fee-paid speeches at various company meetings and conferences. "We kind of bowed out of the public seminar promotion business gradually and I started Sales Education Institute (SEI). We basically just shut down Sales Corporation of America," he said. The formulation of SEI represented a much different initiative than anything Don had been involved with before. "I was pretty much on my own— just me and a secretary at that point. I was looking for a simplified life process and I wanted to write and speak, so that's what I started doing." Don had realized sev-eral important entrepreneurial lessons. First, it is not how many people you have working for you, or how much money you take in, that determines success. Suc-cess in the training and speaking business was and is driven by two issues: (1) cash flow, and (2) net profit. Second, the entrepreneur who runs a large organization may have very little time to do what he/she loves, and spend a lot of time on activi-ties he/she dislikes. For Don, the love was working with clients in a speaking and training capacity. SEI gave him the chance to focus more of his energies on suc-cess and satisfaction.

With SEI off and running, Don began delivering as many as 180 fee-paid speak-ing dates across the country each year. These dates (the speaking industry's term for speeches that may last anywhere from 45 minutes to a full day) were largely sold by Don himself. Over time his relationships with some of America's most prominent speakers bureaus have contributed to the momentum he has enjoyed in the mar-ketplace. In addition to this source of income, Don consulted for clients primarily in the Memphis area about 30 to 40 days a year. Over time he began to phase out most of the consulting and began to focus on speaking and training. He also began to increase his fee per date and reduce the number of his paid speeches. "Most of those speeches were (and still are) out of town, with a lot of travel and that was really tough, so I finally realized that I would burn out in a hurry doing that and cut the number back." He realized the difference between activity and profitability, partic-ularly for a speaker who has only himself to sell.

In 1986 Don made a significant move into the tangible training product arena. This year marked the incorporation of the Ultimate Success Library, Inc. (The Library), which was both a company name and also a product. This singular product was comprised of 40 audio cassette audio tape albums, 10 videotapes and 50 books. All the items in the collection were selected or developed to be effective in skill building for the areas of sales, employee motivation, personal development, and interpersonal communications and leadership. A skills assessment checklist came with The Library, which was designed for companies to ascertain specific training needs of all individual employees. This completed assessment directed employees and their managers to certain components in The Library. In his appraisal of his suc-cess with this organization and product, Don states, "It was a great product and we sold it initially for $3,688, which I realize in retrospect was an underpriced product with insufficient margin. Of course, hindsight is 20-20. We should have sold it for $4,988. We would have sold just as many and made enough money from the venture that we could have sustained the process and really gotten it going."

The Birth of U.S.Learning, Inc.

In 1988 the Ultimate Success Library changed its organizational name to U.S.Learning, Inc.. U.S.Learning at that time had revenues of just under $1.5 million and was making a profit. In the 1990s, The Library remained a viable product, but more momentum was created in his new company, The Don Hutson Organization, with his speeches and seminars for corporate organizations and a growing number of trade association clients. "Frankly I started to get a little less enamored with some of the training products like the Ultimate Success Library and another video series that we had simply because there was greater profitability and more career promise on the speaking and training side for me personally. We phased out some of those products over time and I started gaining some additional excellent momentum, and it made a speaking focus more viable as it enabled me to enjoy significant fee increases over time."

Exposure and Skill Development Activities

One of the key sources of this momentum was Don's involvement with Speakers Roundtable. Early in his career (1974) he had served on the founding board of the National Speakers Association (NSA). Hutson was elected the third president of NSA, the principal association of professional trainers and speakers. At that time the group had just over 200 members. This activity enabled him to gain some tremendous personal visibility nationally, and to a degree, internationally.

Another key personal development activity was Hutson's active participation on the speakers staff of the Positive Thinking Rallies. Other nationally recognized personalities involved were Paul Harvey, Norman Vincent Peale, Earl Nightingale, Dr. Robert Shuler, Ira Hayes, Cavett Robert, Art Linkletter, and Zig Ziglar. At any given rally six or seven of the speakers would address as many as 15,000 attendees. The first year and a half Don was the emcee, and the next two or three years he was one of the featured speakers.

Demand and Revenues Increase

The result of this exposure and skill development was higher fees and more invitations for speaking engagements. Don's first fee in 1971 was $150. "While that sounds very low, it was questionable whether they got their money's worth." The speech was for a trade association in Atlanta.

From this starting level, his fees went to $250 for a short time, then $350, with subsequent increases up to $500, $600, $750, and $1,000, over a period of several years. By 1980 Don's fee was $1,500–$2,000. Over the years his fee per speech, the primary source of revenue for U.S.Learning, has gone up in increments of about $500 approximately every 18 months. At about the $5,000 level, speakers and trainers generally start increasing their fees in $1,000 increments. As of 1998 the investment required to hire Don Hutson for a speech of up to 90 minutes averaged $10,000, a figure that includes travel. His reputation and impact have shown that in recent years fee increases have actually resulted in a higher demand for his quickly filled calendar dates.

Speakers bureaus, organizations that center their business around booking speakers for program slots ranging from keynote speeches to break-out group facilitation and seminars, have always played an important role in sales for Don Hutson.

These bureaus require about 25 percent of the fee for matching the speaker and the booking. Historically about half of Don's speeches have been through his organization's direct sales efforts, with the other half coming from bureaus. Either way, a key component in obtaining a booking/sale is the video demonstration tape produced and distributed by the speaker. Many organizations will review five to 10 tapes sent by speakers or bureaus before selecting a speaker for a slot on a program. Don has regularly updated his video every 12 to 18 months, at an investment cost of $5,000 to $10,000. On the average about five to 10 tapes must be sent out for each sold date.

Product Sales as a Profit Builder

Although the Ultimate Success Library ceased being the major source of revenue for Don's organization in the late 1980s, tangible learning product sales have always played a major role in enhancing his firm's profitability. Hutson produced his first six–tape audio cassette album in 1971 entitled "The Techniques and Tactics of Professional Selling." Over the years, several revisions of this product have been completed. Today the current album is entitled "High Performance Selling—50 Skills That Will Make You Rich." Hutson has also produced several other audio tape albums. Some are multi-tape albums that have as a model six different tapes of different speakers in each set. Don's largest writing project to date has been "The Sale," a comprehensive handbook on the profession of selling, with the focus on successfully building customer relationships. He has also written and co-authored four other books—"The Winning Spirit," and "Inspiring Others to Win" (two collaborative projects to benefit the U.S. Olympic Committee), "Insights Into Excellence" and "Speaking Secrets of the Masters," co-authored by Don and his colleagues in Speakers Roundtable.

These products are promoted through web sites, catalogs and direct mail pieces, but most of them generally have been sold following one of Don's speeches or training presentations. With the client's permission, Don informs participants of a package of products they can receive simply by providing him with a business card. The package is structured so as to support the learning of concepts related to the speech material. Those participants who supply a card are shipped and billed directly for the price of the package, plus shipping. Some clients will purchase product packages in advance to provide to their attendees. This product business has traditionally represented about 25 to 30 percent of firm revenues, a figure that has demonstrated consistent gains over the past decade.

The Environment for Training and Speaking Firms

The environment for firms and individuals that develop and deliver products in U.S.Learning's industry provides both positives and negatives at this point in time. Three of the key factors and forces in the external environment are outlined in the sections below.

COMPETITION   As evidenced by the rapid growth in the membership of the National Speakers' Association (as of May, 1998 just over 3,800 members), the business of training has seen a tremendous increase in competition in recent years. Much of this increase has been caused by downsizing in organizations that has led many former managers to seek careers in speaking. The barriers to entry are very low in this industry, and just about anyone with a telephone, and preferably a computer and fax machine, can become a speaker or trainer. The vast majority of these new entrants find the business extremely difficult for achieving financial success. Experience, references and a high quality demonstration tape are essential to book enough dates to cover expenses and generate some profit. All of these require delivered speeches, so many new speakers spend a great deal of time speaking for free early in their career. At the other end of the spectrum are large regional and national training and consulting firms such as Dun and Bradstreet, the Boston Consulting Group and McKinsey. These firms generally offer speaking and training as part of an overall consulting and management support initiative.

TECHNOLOGY   Technological advances have primarily impacted the ways in which firms in this industry communicate to and with their clients. Laptop computer-driven video projection is increasingly becoming a staple in training presentations. These units, from firms such as In Focus and Proxima, cost anywhere from $3,000 to over $9,000. Portability (some models are now under seven pounds excluding carrying case), simplicity, and enhanced image brightness have greatly expanded their use.

Web sites have become increasingly popular for communicating information about presentation topics and training materials (U.S.Learning's web address is www.USLearning.com). In addition, e-mail and voice-mail systems have made staying in touch with clients much easier and faster. Customer information file management software, and more powerful hardware, have also made this process more efficient and effective.

Technology has also greatly impacted the cost, speed, and quality of audio and videotape products. What used to take weeks can now be done in a less than a day through computerized digital editing. The production of the edited tapes has also become faster and less costly.

ECONOMIC/BUSINESS TRENDS   During the latter part of the 1980s and early 1990s, many large organizations attempted to achieve profitability by a comprehensive program centered around reducing expenses, especially in the area of training. Success is based on building profitable relationships with suppliers and customers, but development of employees capable of forming and advancing these types of relationships had failed without training initiatives. Leadership, sales and customer service skills had deteriorated at a time when customers and clients were demanding more as they had more options from which to choose. This has led many firms to reinvest in the human resource as we move into the next century. Such reinvestment has been accelerated by low unemployment rates (making it harder to attract and retain employees), low interest rates, and generally steady economic growth.

In addition to a renewed training focus in organizations, trade associations have also refocused their efforts in this area. This is because training is regularly shown to be one of the top three reasons an organization joins and pays dues to a trade association (the other two being trade information and networking opportunities). Associations are generally looking to produce better training components to their meeting programs, with more "actionable" ideas from the speakers on the agenda.

USL Toward the New Millennium

The Corporate/Association University Concept

The middle of 1997 marked a major expansion in U.S.Learning's structure and focus. It was at this point that under Don Hutson's direction the firm decided to focus increasingly on long-term client relationships in addition to one-time or once a year speaking engagements. These relationships are structured with contracts for the delivery of customized training products to meet the unique needs of an organization's employees, distributors, and increasingly, its customers. Training a firm's customers has been found to be one of the best ways to strengthen a business relationship and also grow demand by moving more product through the distribution channel. The first such contract in the new era was put in place with World's Finest Chocolate (WFC), the fundraising product manufacturer and marketer headquartered in Chicago, Illinois. These contracts frequently involve the development of "corporate universities" for the client. This is done for the purpose of focusing attention on learning and providing greater human resource asset development coordination for the organization. Due to downsizing, these are often organizations that no longer have the personnel or expertise in-house to devote to these initiatives. Since WFC, several other contracts have been undertaken, with an objective of completing four to six projects/project phases per year. Included in this mix is Green Tree Commercial Finance, the dominant firm in the financing of manufactured housing inventories, and Cavalier, the third-largest producer of manufactured homes.

The university concept has proven to be a successful approach in a variety of settings and is designed to accomplish the following objectives:

- Assess the client's present training and development practices to identify matches and gaps with respect to the organization's current plan.
- Design a learning environment and curriculum under a university logo that will be housed within the client organization and will lend credibility to all client training and development activities.
- Provide a process for monitoring the future training and development needs of the client organization and a vehicle for efficiently delivering such training.

In an effort to support this strategic move to expand existing speaking business and develop and implement corporate university concepts and customized training products under a relationship approach, the management team at USL was expanded. Don Hutson hired George Lucas, Ph.D. to serve as the new president and COO of U.S.Learning. Lucas had gained extensive training and consulting experience while on the business faculties at Texas A&M and the University of Memphis. He played a central role in the development and implementation of Sedgwick University for the third-largest insurance broker in the world and a similar initiative for the largest wallcovering producer and marketer (Imperial). His client base also included small local and regional firms, as well as other global giants, such as FedEx. Lucas' responsibilities beyond contract work include speaking and training sessions for the clients he brings to U.S.Learning, as well as providing additional expertise to U.S.Learning's extensive existing customer base of organizations and associations. In addition he is responsible for the identification and development of new product areas for the firm's continued growth.

Other key changes in 1997–98 included the promotion of Linda Hightower to the position of vice-president of operations. Linda has extensive experience in the training and speaking industry, having worked for Hutson since 1987, and other speakers and trainers for over 20 years. Her responsibilities include personnel management, finance, and working with USL's vendors and supplier partners. At that same time, Scott Hutson became vice-president of sales for USL. Scott has a proven track record in telephone sales and data-base management and marketing. An average day for him is comprised of 60 outgoing calls, 15 incoming calls, and 40 faxes and e-mails. Scott books dates for Don and George both directly and through the many bureaus that seek their talent. He also directs the distribution of an average of 50 video demo tapes and press kits to prospective clients each week. January 1998 also marked the firm's move into its own building in a prime commercial location in the eastern part of Memphis.

The USL Corporate and Marketing Strategy

In building relationships with its clients, U.S.Learning works via a process-driven approach. This approach is based on the perspective that training works only when people learn and organizations become more successful. The firm consistently applies some degree of a consultative approach to every opportunity it identifies and pursues. That approach begins with the thorough discovery of the clients' or prospects' business needs as they apply to their own employees, customers, vendors and alliance partners. After researching the dynamics that drive training in the organization, U.S.Learning can then work with the organization's management team to establish a creative set of solutions and then implement those solutions in a seamless fashion. Commenting on this process, Lucas states, "Our objective is to work with the client so that all training and development needs are clearly identified. At that point we operate as an extension of the firm or association to deliver the highest quality programs and products consistent with the achievement of the group's goals and objectives. Generally, the more we work together, the more needs we identify that either USL can address or bring in our alliance partners to help the client identify a more comprehensive set of options." This approach is reflected in the U.S.Learning mission statement presented below.

U.S.Learning Mission Statement

U.S.Learning is dedicated to assisting our clients in keeping their people skills at an advanced level in order to grow their enterprises. We do this through teaching skills that will result in the formation of strong business relationships and trade alliances. We believe that human resource development should not be an event, but an ongoing process with clear objectives and applications crafted to help our clients turn vision into reality.

U.S.Learning is committed to the enrichment of our clients, our alliance partners and our colleagues through assurance of the highest quality learning experiences possible. Our efforts reflect a combination of advanced technologies, social responsibility and superior ethical conduct.

Concluding Thoughts

In many ways, U.S.Learning represents a virtual organization. Don Hutson has made the strategic decision not to build diverse capabilities in-house. The firm instead uses strong relationships with its alliance partners in the areas of software development, videotaping, video and audio duplication and order fulfillment, and publishing. Don describes what he envisions as his ideal firm going forward: "We will have available and bring to bear the types of resources that are dictated by our client's needs. That does not mean that we will carry the overhead for those resources in-house. Instead, we will continue to develop the best possible alliance partners who are committed to working with us seamlessly in a fashion that meets the ever-evolving needs of the organizations and associations that are our clients."

Questions for Discussion

1. What have been some of the key factors that you see in this case that impact the success of an entrepreneurial marketing venture?
2. What are USL's strengths and weaknesses at the conclusion of the case?
3. What opportunities and threats do you see given USL's present industry positioning and strategy?
4. What other types of products might add to the success of U.S.Learning?

Dr Pepper / Seven Up, Inc.[1]

In 1988, The Holding Company, a Delaware corporation, acquired the Dr Pepper Company and the Seven Up Company in a leveraged buyout transaction. The two companies were merged as part of a recapitalization effort in 1992, the result being the formation of Dr Pepper/Seven Up, Inc. In 1995, Cadbury Schweppes PLC, Great Britain's oldest bottler, bought Dr Pepper/Seven Up. Today, the company is the third largest soft drink concentrate manufacturer in the United States, behind the Coca-Cola Company and PepsiCo. Dr Pepper/Seven Up's products, which include a broad range of brands and flavors, account for more than one-third of total non-cola soft drink sales. This case will provide a closer look at the situation facing Dr Pepper/Seven Up by examining its operations and competitive position.

The Soft Drink Industry

Soft drinks constitute one of the largest consumer food and beverage categories in the United States. Although the soft drink industry is highly competitive, it is generally considered to be relatively stable and non-cyclical, with steady sales growth in each of the past 10 years.

The soft drink industry can be divided into two broad segments, colas and non-colas. The cola segment includes products such as Pepsi, Coca-Cola, RC, and so on. This segment represents approximately 70 percent of all soft drink sales. The non-cola segment includes products such as Dr Pepper, 7 UP, Sprite, Barq's Root Beer, and so on. Over the last five years, the non-cola segment has experienced growth rates well above those in other industry segments. Also included in the non-cola segment are the new lines of seltzers, flavored waters, juice drinks, and natural sodas. This segment has emerged in response to consumer demand for healthier, less traditional refreshments.

Most soft drink companies sell concentrates and extracts to authorized bottlers under license agreements. These licensed bottlers produce finished soft drink products by adding carbonated water and sweeteners and then packaging and selling the

---

[1] This case was prepared by Brent Wren, University of Alabama-Huntsville, and Thomas S. Corcoran, Louisiana State University, for classroom discussion rather than to illustrate either effective or ineffective handling of an administrative situation.

carbonated beverages to various distributors for resale to consumers. The licensed bottlers also produce and sell syrups for fountain outlets. Most soft drink companies maintain some degree of control over the marketing mix of their products by setting uniform prices for concentrate, by controlling the mixing of its soft drink formulas, and by engaging in cooperative advertising and promotion plans.

Once the licensed bottlers have produced the various soft drink products, there are four major channels of distribution: take-home, convenience, fountain/foodservice, and vending. The take-home channel primarily consists of grocery stores, drug stores, mass merchandisers, warehouses, and discount stores. This channel has seen many changes recently as mass merchandisers such as Wal-Mart now offer their own private label soft drinks. Explanations for this move include the increased demand for less expensive products and the growing popularity of discount mass merchandisers. The convenience channel includes convenience stores and gas minimarkets. The fountain/foodservice channel primarily includes fountain syrup sales in retail store outlets and restaurant single drink sales. Finally, the vending channel is comprised of bottle and can sales through vending machines.

How Does Dr Pepper/Seven Up Compete?

The overall product positioning strategy of Dr Pepper/Seven Up is to market leading brands in the non-cola segment, where the company believes there is less intense direct competition. This is a viable segment of the domestic soft drink market, representing roughly 30 percent of all soft drink sales. In 1997, Dr Pepper/Seven Up held approximately 14.2 percent of the total soft drink market.

The company's operations can be divided into four business units: Dr Pepper, Seven Up, Foodservice/Fountain Operations, and Other Beverages. Dr Pepper's international distribution has been handled by PepsiCo since the mid-1980s. Dr Pepper and Seven Up sell concentrate formula to licensed bottlers for processing into bottle and can products, which are sold through the take-home, convenience, and vending channels of distribution. The foodservice unit is fully devoted to the marketing and sale of the company's brands through the fountain/foodservice channel. Dr Pepper/Seven Up also markets many other beverage brands, including Schweppes, A&W, Welch's, Canada Dry, Sundrop, Sunkist, and Squirt. The business operations and strategic directions of each of these business units are discussed more fully in the following sections.

Dr Pepper

Formulated in 1885, Dr Pepper is the oldest nationally distributed soft drink brand in the United States. In 1997, all Dr Pepper brands accounted for an estimated 5.9 percent of the total domestic soft drink market. The company expects Dr Pepper's sales volume to grow at a rate of 7 percent per year.

In the late 1960s, Diet Dr Pepper was introduced as one of the soft drink industry's first diet soft drinks (the first diet soft drink was from Royal Crown and was known as Diet Rite Cola). After the introduction of the artificial sweetener NutraSweet—which led to better tasting, competitive diet soft drinks—Diet Dr Pepper lost market share in the early to mid 1980s. To combat lagging sales, the Diet Dr Pepper brand was reformulated and repackaged in early 1991. The brand registered an increase in sales volume of 127.8 percent compared to 1990, making it the 14th-largest selling soft drink brand. The brand is currently being given close attention by its marketing department. New promotional campaigns and strategies are being adopted to help continue its growth. In addition to regular and diet Dr Pepper, the company markets a caffeine-free version of each product.

Dr Pepper is bottled by the same companies that bottle Coca-Cola and PepsiCo products, as well as by a network of independent bottlers. Nationally, 36 percent of Dr Pepper's volume is bottled by Coca-Cola Enterprises, Inc., which will bottle Dr Pepper products at least until the end of 2005. Dr Pepper has long believed that selling products through Coca-Cola and PepsiCo bottlers provides greater efficiencies and economies of scale in the areas of manufacturing, purchasing, and distribution, and offers greater financial resources relative to independent bottlers. This is especially true in geographic areas with a sparse population. However, the use of such bottlers forces Dr Pepper to compete with Coke and Pepsi for marketing focus.

To help combat this problem, Dr Pepper introduced the "Priority Brand" strategy to its bottlers. This strategy is designed to provide incremental sales to bottlers when Dr Pepper is treated as a priority brand. It is placed on display alongside cola brands, featured at an attractive price, made available in the desired packages, and given adequate grocery shelf space. Another radical change occurred in 1997 with a change in the shape of Dr Pepper's bottle. The 20-ounce bottles were given an angular shape to help differentiate them from Coca-Cola and PepsiCo products. The strategy worked as Dr Pepper sales grew at nearly double the market rate.

Market research has consistently shown that Dr Pepper has a loyal core group of consumers who drink only Dr Pepper. The remaining Dr Pepper consumers tend to be above-average consumers of soft drinks who occasionally drink Dr Pepper. Realizing the potential to appeal to a wider variety of consumers, Dr Pepper targeted its "Just What the Dr Ordered" campaign to a very broad audience. The campaign targeted consumers aged 12–34, a market segment that consumes approximately 52 percent of all soft drinks.

Although the company is the third-largest domestic soft drink advertiser, it spends its money cautiously. The company has set very strict guidelines concerning the promotion of its products, including criteria that: (1) the promotion be long enough to drive consistent volume growth, (2) the promotion be supported with value-added packaging, and (3) the promotion be simple enough for the consumer to understand immediately. The result of these guidelines has been an increase in unaided brand and advertising awareness among its target consumers. Dr Pepper also engages in cooperative advertising through national media with its bottlers.

Seven Up

During the early to mid 1990s, both 7 UP and Diet 7 UP experienced significant losses in market share. These declines were attributed to operating and financial difficulties that were experienced by certain bottlers (especially in the New York area), the popularity of diet soft drinks sweetened with NutraSweet, and 7 UP's focus on grocery sales to the exclusion of other avenues of distribution. In addition, the lemon-lime market segment became more competitive due to Coca-Cola's increased promotion of its Sprite brand (6.2 percent of the total market) and the promotion of similar soft drinks, including PepsiCo's Mountain Dew brand (6.3 percent of the total market). Both Coca-Cola and PepsiCo employed vigorous advertising campaigns aimed at 7 UP's narrow 18–25 year old market segment.

Like the marketing efforts of Dr Pepper, the advertising and promotion of 7 UP brands tends to be very focused. In fact, the target market for 7 UP was so narrowly defined in the early 1990s that approximately 76 percent of 7 UP volume was consumed by only 29 percent of U.S. households. The company also relied on an ad campaign that was originally designed in 1967. This tried-and-true campaign had been modernized with the use of the animated 7 UP Spot character. While it increased the unaided recall of the product, it did very little to sell to its target market. Seven Up had plans to continue to penetrate into the remaining 71 percent of U.S. households with the use of promotional tie-ins, sampling programs, and increased availability in vending machines.

Seven Up's past problems seem to have subsided. Market research shows that 7 UP has gained a considerable increase in sales since just a few years ago. It now holds 2.2 percent of the total soft drink market and has shown an increase of 30 percent in 20-ounce bottle sales. This result is exceptional when one considers that 7 UP had its advertising cut by 50 percent when Coca-Cola increased Sprite's expenditures by over 35 percent.

Foodservice/Fountain Operations

Dr Pepper/Seven Up's foodservice/fountain operation focuses on foodservice and fountain beverage sales and distribution. It has grown from one brand, Dr Pepper, to a full line of premium non-colas, including Dr Pepper, Diet Dr Pepper, 7 UP, Diet 7 UP, Cherry 7 UP, Diet Cherry 7 UP, Sunkist, Canada Dry, and Tahitian Treat brands. A senior management official at Dr Pepper/Seven Up commented that the company plans to make its brands constitute roughly 50 percent of all fountain sales by the year 2000. The executive also stated that the expected increase would result from a better promotional strategy, with tie-ins to national brand promotion. The strategy has been working. Despite Coca-Cola's drive to increase its number of exclusive contracts with major accounts (such as McDonald's), Dr Pepper's fountain volume is growing twice as fast as the total market.

Other Beverages

Though Dr Pepper and 7 UP receive most of the attention, the company also markets other soft drink brands and flavors: Welch's, A&W Root Beer and Cream Soda, Canada Dry, Schweppes, Sunkist, Sundrop, and Squirt. These additional products permit the company to offer a full line of high-quality, non-cola options. The recognition and awareness of the Welch's brand have made its grape soda the number one selling grape-flavored, carbonated beverage in the United States. The growth of the market in these areas can be partly attributed to the increase in popularity of fruit-based and all-natural drinks.

The company's strategy for these brands has been to build sales by building demand for 7 UP, as many of these brands are bottled by the same companies that bottle 7 UP. Schweppes, A&W, Canada Dry, and Sundrop have experienced the largest sales increases among Dr Pepper/Seven Up's other brands. Recently, however, Dr Pepper/Seven Up pulled the Sunkist and Welch's bottling contracts from Coca-Cola and PepsiCo bottlers and signed new contracts with independent bottlers. This move came as Coca-Cola and PepsiCo began dropping non-owned brands from their distribution networks.

Recent Marketing Activities

Dr Pepper/Seven Up started to experience lagging sales and loss of market share. Particularly hard hit in the mid-to-late 90s was the 7 UP brand. The "red dots" that were supposed to be the advertising campaign to reign in consumers did not fare well. One of the suspected reasons was that it did not effectively target the "ideal" consumer. One bottler commented on the dots, "7 UP is dead: Sprite just crushes our market. It needs a new angle, and I hope those cutesy 'dots' are dead and gone, because that was just an awful campaign." Sure enough, those dots are gone. The new campaign for 7 UP includes promotions on ESPN and MTV in an attempt to capture the attention of the 18–24 year old consumer. Seven Up sponsored the 1998 NCAA Basketball Championship Week Festivities and the MTV program "Drive Thru America." The new "Refreshing Moments" campaign began in the summer of 1998. These new promotional activities are accompanied by a 25 percent increase in advertising expenditures. The most drastic change is the launch of 7 UP's "Crisp, New Taste" reformulation of the product. The new taste is designed to appeal to consumers who want a soft drink that is refreshing and not sticky sweet. The "Crisp, New Taste" and "Refreshing Moments" campaigns are expected to complement each other.

Dr Pepper was given a record media budget for 1998—over $40 million dollars. The company planned to begin an international marketing campaign and to sponsor several sporting events. The "Dr Pepper . . . This is the taste" campaign also began during 1998. However, the new campaign does not focus solely on the familiar Dr Pepper delivery truck workers used in past ads. The new campaign focuses on the "taste" of Diet Dr Pepper using a "fantasy becoming reality" theme. Dr Pepper is trying to avoid the mistake of 7 UP's dots and prevent wearout of its delivery truck theme.

What's Ahead for Dr Pepper/Seven Up?

The company's executives look ahead to the future with mixed feelings. The company has many strengths, not the least of which is the growth rate for Dr Pepper, which continues to be well above the industry average. Likewise, the managerial experience of Cadbury Schweppes is a tremendous advantage. The size of Cadbury also gives Dr Pepper/Seven Up more leverage in purchasing raw materials, particularly the bulk buying of sugar and sugar substitutes. However, the company has several concerns that must be addressed. The poor performance of 7 UP's previous promotional campaigns has dragged down sales for 7 UP. The company is now very careful not to repeat any of its past mistakes.

Dr Pepper/Seven Up also faces threats from three major forces in its external environment—competition, suppliers, and bottlers. Competition in the soft drink industry refers not only to competition for consumer acceptance, but also for shelf space in supermarkets and for marketing focus by the company's licensed bottlers. Although it is often considered a two-horse race (between Pepsi and Coca-Cola), competition within the domestic soft drink industry is actually much broader. Dr Pepper/Seven Up competes not only with the two industry giants, but also with all other liquid refreshments such as bottled water, fruit juices, and regional and private label producers of soft drinks. These special market segments are especially volatile as consumer tastes change rapidly. By offering low-priced private brands, highly diversified and capital-rich mass merchandisers, such as Wal-Mart and Sam's, make the market even more difficult to manage.

A second external force affecting Dr Pepper/Seven Up is the battle for fair prices from sweetener suppliers. Other than aspartame sweeteners used by the company to manufacture diet soft drink products, other raw materials are essentially commodities and are available from several alternative suppliers. However, aspartame is currently available from only one supplier, the NutraSweet Company, which owns the exclusive patent to aspartame. NutraSweet's patent protection allows the company to manipulate prices at will. Another sugar substitute, Sucralose, was recently introduced to the market, and more sugar substitutes are on the way. However, changing from NutraSweet to Sucralose or another sweetener could possibly change the taste of Diet Dr Pepper. Given the taste claims used in the advertising for Diet Dr Pepper, the company is reluctant to make any changes to the product's formulation until there are several sweetener options on the market. Until the patent for NutraSweet expires, Dr Pepper/Seven Up, like all soft drink manufacturers, will face concerns over the price of aspartame sweetener.

The third major issue facing Dr Pepper/Seven Up is the ongoing relationship with its bottlers. Though the company has long-term contracts with Coca-Cola and PepsiCo bottlers for Dr Pepper and 7 UP, its other brands are feeling the squeeze. Both Coca-Cola and PepsiCo are trying to eliminate non-owned brands from their bottling and distribution systems. Dr Pepper/Seven Up has responded by moving the bottling contracts for these brands to independent bottling companies. In order to ensure that brands like Welch's, A&W, Schweppes, and Canada Dry receive adequate marketing support, Dr Pepper/Seven Up may have to invest in building the infrastructure required to consolidate these brands into the independent bottling network.

The relationship between Dr Pepper/Seven Up and its Coca-Cola and PepsiCo bottlers is so important to the company that it has been reluctant to expand into the cola segment of the soft drink market. A long-standing industry rumor is that Dr Pepper/Seven Up will buy out RC Cola, and thus round out its product line with both cola and non-cola brands. Dr Pepper/Seven Up executives agree that a combination with RC makes perfect sense from a strategic perspective. However, the company's relationship with Coca-Cola and PepsiCo currently prevents such a move.

Questions For Discussion

1. Having just read Dr Pepper/Seven Up's situation, perform a thorough examination of its competitive position, including company strengths, weaknesses, opportunities, and threats.

2. What marketing mix variables are most relevant to Dr Pepper/Seven Up's past success?

3. What marketing mix variables could be altered to help ensure the company's future success?

4. Generate a list of strategic alternatives for Dr Pepper/Seven-Up. Define each alternative and tell which strengths, weaknesses, opportunities, and/or

threats the alternative is designed to exploit and/or combat.

5. What benefits does Dr Pepper/Seven Up gain by being associated with Cadbury Schweppes? How can these benefits be leveraged to increase sales and market share for the company's brands?

6. In your opinion, should Dr Pepper/Seven Up look into acquiring RC Cola? What would be the advantages and disadvantages of such a move?

Sources

These facts are from Karen Benezra, "DP/7 UP beats marketing drums, but Pepsi alliance in offing?" *Brandweek*, Sept. 22, 1997, 9; Karen Benezra, "Fizz or Fizzle?" *Brandweek*, Oct. 13, 1997, 29; Karen Benezra, "Three's charm," *Brandweek*, Oct. 13, 1997, 32; Beverage World Homepage: www.beverageworld.com/liquidstats.html; "Cadbury Schweppes offers 1.6 billion pounds sterling for Dr Pepper," *Eurofood*, Feb. 1995, 12; Cadbury Schweppes Homepage, Global Beverages Review: www.cadburyschweppes.com/finance_investor/global_bevs.html; "The Cadbury shuffle," *Beverage World*, July 1996, 16; Jacqueline Doherty, "A sparkling strategy; Cadbury Schweppes to fiddle with formula for 7-Up to try for market effervescence," *Barron's*, Sept. 15, 1997, 12; "Dr Pepper/Cadbury," *Beverage World*, Mar. 1996, 71; "FDA Approves Johnson & Johnson's Artificial Sweetener Sucralose," *Knight-Ridder/Tribune Business News*, April 4, 1998, 404B; "FTC finale," *Beverage World*, June 1995, 8; Joan Holleran, "Dr Pepper/Seven Up ups the ad ante," *Beverage Industry*, Nov. 1997, 33; Joan Holleran, "Fountain of gold: beverage marketers pump up fountain sales with promotions, tie-ins," Beverage Industry, Oct. 1996, 10; Larry Jabbonsky, "Bring the family," *Beverage World*, Oct. 1995, 6; Susan Jackson and Nicole Harris, "Can Cadbury dodge big cola's bullets?" *Business Week*, Aug. 12, 1996, 70; Sharon Marshall, "Cadbury and Coke end CCSB deal," *Marketing*, June 6, 1996, 1; Dan McGraw, "7 UP: Remaking the Uncola," *U. S. News & World Report*, Sept. 22, 1997, 54; "Move over colas: Peppers and lemon-limes have arrived," *Beverage Industry*, March 1995, SD10; Hilary Rosenberg, "How Tom Hicks survived the cola wars," *Institutional Investor*, April 1995, 11; Sarah Theodore, "Breaking new ground: Dr Pepper/Seven Up recreates itself for its new role in the soft drink industry," *Beverage Industry*, Jan. 1997, 36; Louise West, "Cadbury Schweppes gulps down Dr Pepper," *Mergers & Acquisitions International*, Jan. 30, 1995, 1; and "Y&R unveils new Dr Pepper/7 UP campaigns," *ADWEEK Eastern Edition*, Sept. 22, 1997, 6.

Wm. Wrigley Jr. Company[1]

William Wrigley Sr. was a soap manufacturer in Philadelphia. His rebellious son sold Wrigley's Scouring Soap from a basket in that city's streets. After being expelled from school, William Wrigley Jr. sharpened his skills as a full-time salesman for his father by selling to stores in country towns. However, William Junior had ambitions of his own.

William Wrigley Jr. went west to Chicago in spring 1891. His newly founded firm sold his father's scouring soap to retailers. Wrigley Jr. offered baking powder as a premium to induce soap sales. When he discovered the baking powder was more popular than the soap, Wrigley discontinued sale of the soap. Later Wrigley offered two sticks of chewing gum as a premium with the purchase of a can of baking powder. Again, he found that the premium was more popular than the product it was to promote. In 1892, his firm began a long and flourishing career in the chewing gum industry.

The Company

The chewing gum industry was difficult to enter because a dozen or more companies were already selling gum. But at age 29, Wrigley had the energy and marketing insight to succeed. He understood his consumers and readily adapted to their tastes. He inspired his sales force, continued to offer enticing premiums, used pioneering advertising, and understood the importance of national brands.

In the early 1900s, Wrigley decided to concentrate on a spearmint-flavored gum, as he began his expansion into eastern U.S. cities. He eventually won over consumers through innovative advertising. He used the same means to enter the New York City market and, by 1910, had succeeded in making Wrigley's Spearmint gum America's favorite. He also succeeded in establishing Juicy Fruit and Doublemint as very popular brands.

Domestic Business

The company forged ahead, achieving a leading position in American markets with its three primary brands. However, World War II brought disruptions in the supply

---

[1] This case was prepared by David J. Luck, emeritus, Southern Illinois University, for classroom discussion rather than to illustrate either effective or ineffective handling of an administrative situation. Research assistance was provided by Salvador Trevino-Martinez, ITESM/The University of Memphis.

of top grade ingredients. Rather than risk its quality reputation, the company took Spearmint, Juicy Fruit, and Doublemint off the civilian market. Until 1945, these brands were supplied only to the armed forces. To maintain a presence in the public eye, Wrigley introduced Orbit chewing gum to the civilian market during World War II. The company launched a successful advertising campaign to keep the former brands alive with a picture of the old wrappers and the slogan, "Remember This Wrapper." After the war, the three brands were reintroduced and surpassed their prewar volume.

During the 1970s, several new brands were introduced to combat the competition from sugarfree gums. Wrigley introduced Freedent (1974) for denture wearers; cinnamon-flavored Big Red (1975); a sugarfree Orbit (1977) which later failed; and Hubba Bubba bubblegum in 1978. Wrigley introduced Extra sugarfree gum in 1984 and supported it with unprecedented advertising spending. It, too, became a profit leader and the best-selling sugarfree gum in the United States.

Amurol, the subsidiary that introduced Hubba Bubba, launched an outstanding success in 1991. Shredded bubble gum, labeled "Michael Jordan Hang Time," was a hit with the younger markets and improved Amurol's earnings. Along with its sustained growth trend, Amurol has also maintained a sound marketing strategy evolution. By 1996, the brand was working out a licensing deal with the cable channel Nickelodeon in order to launch a Nickelodeon branded extension of its candy and chewing gum product lines. The deal included the right to carry the TV network's name in those lines of products. Similar to the case of Amurol, industry reportings indicated that the ratings of the Nickelodeon channel were experiencing sustained growth.

Since World War II, Wm. Wrigley Jr. Company has been expanding the scope and reach of its operations in the U.S. market. Its four plants manufacture and distribute Wrigley's core product lines and brands: established (Spearmint, Doublemint, Juicy Fruit, Big Red, and Winterfresh), Extra Sugar-Free (Spearmint/Peppermint, Cinnamon, Original, and Classic Bubble Gum and Winterfresh), and Freedent (Spearmint, Peppermint, and Winterfresh), assuring a dominant position in the U.S. market. Notwithstanding its dominant position, the company has also experienced the effects of a more aggressive competitive environment in which sales of sugarfree products and levels of distribution are major issues.

International Business

Early in its history, the company exported to other countries. Foreign production began in Canada in 1910, and by 1939, plants were operating in Australia, Great Britain, and New Zealand. New types of products and flavors were produced to meet varying consumer preferences in international markets. Wrigley's most popular product abroad was "P.K.," sugar-coated gum pellets.

After World War II, Wrigley intensified international expansion by opening sales offices throughout Asia, Africa, and Europe. The company manufactures its products on a worldwide basis with 14 manufacturing factories—four in North America, four in Europe, one in Africa, and five in the Asia/Pacific region. Company sources also report a new factory currently under construction in Russia. According to the president's letter accompanying the 1997 annual report, the size of the "overseas business has nearly doubled in the five-year period ending in 1997." Wrigley's products now enjoy a market coverage that reaches over 100 nations.

Marketing Activities

Wrigley defends all its markets fiercely with special attention to the United States, a market that as of the end of 1997 represented almost $2 billion in retail sales for the company. Part of Wrigley's strength is a constant quest for efficiency in production and physical distribution. Yet, marketing in general, and advertising specifically, are the keys to its defense.

The firm's basic approach is to "pull" products through the distribution channels with strong advertising. That is followed by in-store shelf and point-of-purchase displays to present the gums attractively. Wrigley's sales representatives visit stores often to aid retailers with placement, filling, and straightening of display fixtures.

Wrigley's principal advertising medium is television. Chewing gum is bought by a broad spectrum of consumers, and TV can reach the widest audience at the lowest cost per capita. Commercials are placed between programs that have the widest cross sections of viewers. The ads are correspondingly broad in their appeal. Two lesser used media are transit advertising (on buses, in rapid transit cars and stations) and outdoor posters that have a strong visual impact.

Advertising consistently aims to create a wholesome image for gum chewing and for Wrigley brands. Its most memorable feature was created for 1930s radio programs. Ads for Doublemint featured double pianists, double comedians, and so forth. Outdoor posters for the brand repeated the theme with twins in matching hats. The idea of twins proved to have universal appeal and is still featured in Doublemint advertising today.

Wrigley's advertising outlays are representative of an aggressive marketer. Controlling nearly half of the U.S. market, Wrigley's advertising outlays have been among the highest in relation to dollar sales in the food industry. A striking example of this aggressiveness occurred in 1989. The American economy was starting to decline and leveling sales were expected for the gum industry. Wrigley's response was to raise advertising expenditures from $134 million to $158 million in 1990. As of December 1997, advertising expenditures were over $280 million. Wrigley has been ranked in the *Advertising Age* "100 Leading National Advertisers" list for several years.

Three of Wrigley's most outstanding campaigns in recent years were developed by the BBDO agency: (1) creative and strategic positioning for cinnamon-flavored Big Red; (2) positioning for Extra sugar-free gum; and (3) the "no-smoking" campaign for Spearmint. The no-smoking campaign received much critical attention as a substantial change from Wrigley's traditional whimsical campaigns. The multi-media campaign introduced a simple, straightforward message-"If you can't smoke, chew gum"—in print, television, outdoor, and in-store formats. The ads feature smokers confronted with a number of non-smoking situations (restaurants, airplanes, and the workplace) and offer Wrigley's Spearmint gum's "pure chewing satisfaction" as an attractive alternative. The competitive situation has caused the relationship between BBDO and Wrigley to evolve accordingly. In April 1997, *Advertising Age* reported that Wrigley decided to change the compensation scheme for the agency (business with Wrigley was $130 million) from the traditional system to one based on market performance of the brands.

The View From the Top

A Wrigley executive scanning the view from the corporate offices in Chicago would see the gently rising Illinois terrain. The near-future prospects of the gum industry for the last two years of the millennium would offer a similar view. Observers of the industry believed that foreseeable sales volume would rise only at the U.S. demographic rate and Wrigley profits were expected to show continued, but slower, growth. See Exhibits 1 and 2 for financial results through 1997.

EXHIBIT 1	Wm. Wrigley Jr. Company Financial Results 1987–1997 ($ in millions)	

Year	*Sales*	*Net Profit*
1987	781.1	70.2
1988	891.4	87.2
1989	992.9	106.2
1990	1110.6	117.4
1991	1148.9	128.7
1992	1286.9	148.6
1993	1428.5	174.9
1994	1596.6	230.5
1995	1754.9	223.7
1996	1836.0	230.2
1997	1954.2	271.6

Sources: Standard & Poor's/Foods and Nonalcoholic Beverages, May 29, 1997, 27 and Wm. Wrigley Jr. Company 1997 Annual Report.

EXHIBIT 2	Wm. Wrigley Jr. Company Current Position, 1996–97 ($ in millions)	

	1996	*1997*
Current Assets		
Cash Assets	181.2	206.6
Receivables	165.1	176.0
Inventories	233.2	247.4
Other Assets	19.7	30.5
Deferred Income		
Taxes	11.0	16.4
Total	729.4	797.7
Current Liabilities		
Accounts Payable	75.4	71.0
Accrued Expenses	66.4	78.4
Dividends Payable	19.7	22.0
Other Liabilities	56.7	54.4
Total	218.2	225.8
Current Ratio	3.34	3.53

Source: Wm. Wrigley Jr. Company 1997 Annual Report

There are no signs of Wrigley's long-range strategy changing notably. When asked about new ventures, one director was quoted as saying: "The only thing Wrigley would consider as a new venture is something else in the gum business." That is likely to remain the main principle guiding strategic marketing planning in the near future. However, competitors' moves, efficiency rationalization moves and other internal pressures like reduction of tax credits are changing the typical composition of the company's domestic business environment.

As the millennium approaches, the company faces the prospects of increasing competition in the sugar and sugarfree segments of the North American market, the need to rationalize product lines and promotional activities in both domestic and foreign markets, and the rising trend of business opportunities in the overseas markets. With these and other circumstances affecting the business situation, the marketing strategy for chewing gum products would need to be altered to accommodate this change—an action that Wrigley executives should be considering now.

Questions for Discussion

1. Describe Wrigley's strategic planning. How do you think Wrigley's image would vary among different stakeholders?

2. What are the strengths and weaknesses in Wrigley's marketing strategies?

3. Imagine yourself as Wrigley's top vice president for marketing. What are the alternative strategies that you would consider seriously? What do you recommend?

SOURCES

These facts are from http://www.wrigley.com; Sloan, Pat and Judann Pollack, "Wrigley to Compensate BBDO on Performance," *Advertising Age*, Apr. 14, 1997, 4; Kate Fitzgerald, "Wrigley's Amurol Unit Joins Nickelodeon Brand Wagon," *Advertising Age*, Jan. 20, 1997, 10; *Wall Street Journal*, May 29, 1991, 1; information from the Consumer Affairs unit of the Wrigley Company; *Hoover's Handbook* 1991, 591; "100 Leading National Advertisers," *Advertising Age*, Sept. 25, 1991, 69–71; Jay Palmer, "Shipshape Financials," *Barron's*, Oct. 22, 1990, 20, 22; Judith Crown, "Chew on this: Longer-lasting gum," *Advertising Age*, May 11, 1992; 32–34; Bob Garfield, "Forging Strong Partnerships," *Advertising Age*, Sept. 30, 1991, S30–S31; Bob Garfield, "Wrigley Ads Tied to Smoking Are Tasteful Winners, by Gum," *Advertising Age*, Feb. 11, 1991, 46; and Julie Liesse, "Wrigley Sticks It Out," *Advertising Age*, June 10, 1991, 14.

Benckiser[1]

Marketers around the world were beginning to take notice of the success of a German company in the early 1990s. It came into the global market with a two-pronged strategy: acquisition of strong brands, followed by a back-to-basics marketing strategy for those brands. In just a few short years, Benckiser (pronounced Ben-Keezer) has become a global powerhouse in the detergent and cosmetics markets. The majority of Benckiser N.V.'s revenues are earned in niche growth markets where the company holds one or more brands. The company's initial success in the United States occurred because Benckiser provided high quality products at lower prices due to less packaging, advertising, and other expenses.

German-based Benckiser was founded as a chemical business during the reign of Prussian King Frederick William III. It began divesting its industrial chemicals operations and moving into consumer goods in the late 1980s. Then the company went on a spending spree, buying eight companies in 10 countries over a period of five years, acquiring ownership of leading household products in Italy, Spain, and the United States. Benckiser's acquisitions placed it in competition with such marketing giants as Procter & Gamble, Unilever, and Japan's Kao Co.

One of the most important of Benckiser's acquisitions was Ecolab, Inc. of St. Paul, Minnesota, which gave it entry into the competitive world of U.S. consumer products and ownership of five well-known brands: Electrasol dishwashing detergent, Jet-Dry dishwasher additive, Scrub Free and Lime-A-Way cleaners, and Clean & Smooth liquid hand soap. Its purchase of Smith Kline Beecham's Cling Free line gave it four more powerful brands: Cling Free fabric softener sheets, Delicare detergent, Calgonite dishwashing detergent, and Calgon bath products. Other major acquisitions included Quintessence, Inc., with its Jovan fragrance line, Revlon's Germaine Monteil lines, and the Coty division of Pfizer, Inc. Benckiser also owns the U.S. rights to market Astor and Lancaster cosmetics lines, as well as many leading household products in Italy, including S.A. Camp.

Benckiser's current principal product lines are Calgonite, Finish, Electrasol, Jet Dry (automatic dishwashing products), Calgon (bath additives and water softener),

---

[1] This case was prepared by O. C. Ferrell, Colorado State University, and Thomas S. Corcoran, Louisiana State University, for classroom discussion rather than to illustrate either effective or ineffective handling of an administrative situation.

Vanish (in-wash or out-wash stain removers), Cillit, and Lime-A-Way (limescale cleaners). Its subsidiary company Coty oversees all of the brands in the cosmetics and personal fragrance operations of Benckiser.

Benckiser's Structure And Reach

Benckiser N.V., the private parent corporation, is controlled by a five-person board from its headquarters in Germany's Rhine Valley. The board makes all corporate decisions, but leaves all other decisions and planning to its strong regional offices and their presidents. Benckiser offices or subsidiaries can be found around the world in Turkey, France, Denmark, Canada, Puerto Rico, Greece, Great Britain, Portugal, Czechoslovakia, Belgium, Japan, Australia, New Zealand, Switzerland, Austria, Italy, Hungary, Spain, Monaco, and India. The company also has plans to establish branches in major Russian cities and in Ukraine. Each subsidiary functions as a local operating unit and is directly responsible for its own sales and earnings. Benckiser N.V. Chairman and CEO Peter Harf believes that consumer goods marketing requires a local, decentralized touch. This view has been growing in importance as Benckiser has started to follow a strategy of exploiting niche categories with high growth potential.

Until 1997, Benckiser N.V. was divided into two corporate divisions: Benckiser Consumer Products and the Lancaster Group AG. However, the Lancaster Group—which markets selective cosmetics worldwide under the brand names Bogner, Chopard, Davidoff, Jil Sander, Joop!, Lancaster, and Monteil—ceased to function as a separate entity when it was "folded into" Coty, Inc. in 1997. Coty also absorbed many of Benckiser's other assets, including Quintessence, a Chicago-based fragrance company. All of Coty's operations are now overseen by Benckiser Group USA, a subsidiary of the parent corporation. The second corporate division, Benckiser Consumer Products of Ludwigshafen, Germany, is further divided into detergents (household laundry, dishwashing, and cleaning products) and cosmetics (medium-priced fragrances and color and skin care cosmetics). In 1997, the detergent group alone had sales of $1.57 billion.

Benckiser's Marketing Strategy

Benckiser's strategy isn't just buying out strong brand names: It follows through with canny marketing for those brands and the consolidation of vital resources. Benckiser believes that consumers want high-quality products with minimum advertising and related marketing expenses. A senior manager at Benckiser stated, "Marketers have taught their consumers that they lie about their products. . . . We learn from birth that every product is a lie. . . . The result has been a loss of brand loyalty and the rise of commercialism based on packaging and advertising. Either the product really does work better or it doesn't. If shoppers could talk to me, I think they'd say, 'Give me a break, save the buck on advertising and give me something I can afford'." This common sense philosophy allows Benckiser to offer consumers high quality products at lower prices with less packaging and hype. Consider Benckiser's handling of Electrasol, for example. The company decided not to launch an advertising campaign to make dishwashing detergents fit any typical consumer psychological profile. Instead, the company cut the product's advertising, lowered its price to less than $2, and insisted on printing the price on the box so shoppers would know the price wouldn't change.

Benckiser has also followed the popular business trends of consolidation and downsizing, where many divisions or SBUs are consolidated and run under a parent corporation. For example, the Coty subsidiary absorbed Lancaster Group and Quintessence. Then shortly afterward, both companies were run from Coty's home office. Although Lancaster and Quintessence maintained their individual product lines, everyone had to report ultimately to the CEO of Coty, Inc. Additionally, Coty cut 75 positions at Lancaster and 70 positions at Quintessence during the merger. To put this in perspective, Lancaster had 169 positions prior to the consolidation, while Coty had approximately 1,400. As a percentage, Lancaster's staff was cut almost in half.

Cutting the staff is not the only thing that Coty CEO Jerry Abernathy did. Because of its size and capacity, Coty was able to take over the distribution functions of both newly acquired companies. The distribution is now handled by Coty's manufacturing complex in Sandford, North Carolina. Abernathy also made plans to eliminate products that performed below expectations. Joop!, Femme, and Zino Davidoff were placed on hold due to some concerns about their performance.

Benckiser's detergent and cosmetics strategies seem to be working. Benckiser's margins and sales figures continue to grow, and its low prices have cut into the market shares of higher-priced competitors. Before Benckiser bought Electrasol from Ecolab, the detergent had a 3 percent market share. Under Benckiser's strategy, Electrasol quickly gained more than 10 percent of a market previously dominated by Procter & Gamble's Cascade. Now, Electrasol holds one of the top positions in the dishwashing detergent market. Benckiser used the same high quality/low price strategy when it acquired Cling Free and doubled its sales every month. Other well-known American brands purchased by Benckiser—Jet-Dry, Scrub Free, Lime-A-Way, and Clean & Smooth—have done equally well in competition with other U.S. products.

Searching for a Better Way

While Benckiser's strategy has been to buy out companies and brands and then revamp their marketing mixes, the company is also seeking growth through innovation. The company's research and development emphasizes the creation of environmentally safe product formulas, reduction of bulk, and the design of recyclable packaging, all of which save raw materials. Among Benckiser's innovations are new formulas and applications for concentrated dishwashing detergents in powder form, which contain citrates and polymers rather than environmentally unfriendly phosphates. Many Benckiser detergents contain an environmentally safe oxygen bleach rather than chlorine bleach.

Benckiser's support of research doesn't always support the bottom line. A major effort by the company is its financial and managerial support of DKMS, the German Bone Marrow Donor Base. This Tubingen-based nonprofit entity is working to establish a German bone marrow donor database and link it to a worldwide network. It has grown to 70,000 potential bone marrow donors, quickly making it the world's third largest such database. In its first year, DKMS made numerous bone marrow transplants possible for leukemia patients, and it hopes to make many more possible in years to come. Benckiser believes it is more efficient to focus its philan-thropic support on this one organization rather than giving small contributions to many social causes and programs.

Benckiser's strategy of acquisitions, cost-cutting strategies through elimination of shared competencies, minimal marketing and its research and development activities have positioned it for a strong future in the global economy. In following consumer desires and the environmentalists' credo "think globally, act locally," the company has enabled its brands to survive and thrive in competitive global markets.

Questions For Discussion

1.   What are the major SWOT considerations for Benckiser N.V.'s Consumer Products Group?

2.   From the facts in this case, try to describe Benckiser's strategic market plan for Coty, Inc. and its relationship with Lancaster and Quintessence.

3.   Compare Benckiser's detergent marketing strategy to the marketing strategies used by Procter & Gamble.

4.   What do you think about Benckiser's strategy to focus all of its philanthropic support on a single organization rather than giving small contributions to many different causes?

Sources

These facts are from "Benckiser Breaks All Records," *European Cosmetic Markets*, May 1991, 129; "Benckiser Establishes a NYSE-listed New York Share Program with J.P. Morgan," Company Press Release, Yahoo! Finance, http://www.yahoo.com; "Benckiser: From Calgon to Cosmetics in 18 Months," *European Cosmetic Markets*, Oct. 1991, 285; Benckiser Group 1997 Annual Report; Pete Born, "Lancaster folded into Coty," *WWD*, Feb. 2, 1996, 6; Peter Harf, "Dramatic Departure from the Status Quo," *Director & Boards*, Fall 1991, 35–37; "Lancaster Acquisitions Boost Benckiser Sales, *Cosmetics Communications*, Nov. 10, 1991, 11–12; Soren Larson, "Monteil returning to the launch game," *WWD*, Sept. 8, 1995, S9; Fara Warner, "Benckiser Who?," *Adweek's Marketing Week*, July 22, 1991, 16–17; and "What's in a name?: Benckiser cosmetic opera-tions revamped," *Drug & Cosmetic Industry*, March 1996, 6.

CASE *14*

Maybelline[1]

Maybelline is a leading brand name in the mass-market color cosmetics business. It manufactures and markets eye, face, lip, and nail cosmetics and other personal care products for sale in the United States and in selected international markets. The company's Maybelline brand, established in 1915, held the second-largest domestic share in the mass-market color cosmetics business through the mid-1990s. Maybelline is the leading brand in domestic sales of eye cosmetics products, which include mascara, eye shadow and eyeliner; it maintains the second- and third-place positions in the domestic market in face and lip cosmetics, respectively. The company markets its products under such well-established brand names as "Great Lash," "Expert Eyes," "Revitalizing," "Moisture Whip," "Shine Free," "Shades of You," and "Yardley of London." Maybelline products are carried by virtually every major domestic mass-market retailer.

Description Of Maybelline's Businesses

The Maybelline business was founded in 1915 with the introduction of the first modern eye cosmetics products for daily use. This business remained in the control of the founding family until 1967 when it was sold to the Schering-Plough Corporation. Under this ownership, the company introduced face and lip products in 1974 and its first nail color products in 1977.

In 1990, the Maybelline business was acquired from Schering-Plough by three limited partnerships related to Wasserstein Perella Management Partners Inc. Maybelline's new management team began to pursue a three-part, growth-oriented strategy designed to: (1) revitalize the company's core color cosmetics business, (2) develop or acquire select new personal care product lines and brands to complement the firm's core business, and (3) expand the company's market presence internationally.

Revitalizing Maybelline's Cosmetics Business

Maybelline's principal product groups are eye, face, lip, and nail products. The company also manufactures and markets cosmetics-related products under the

[1] This case was prepared by Debbie Thorne LeClair, The University of Tampa, for classroom discussion rather than to illustrate either effective or ineffective handling of an administrative situation. Research assistance was provided by Sergio Balsera, The University of Tampa.

Maybelline brand name, including make-up removers, eyelash curlers, and cosmetic applicators.

EYE PRODUCTS   Mascara, eyeliner, eyebrow products, and eye shadow are the main components of Maybelline's eye product line. The company believes Maybelline has held the number one U.S. market share continuously since 1915. Maybelline has a 31 percent market share in mascara products. The company produces and markets eyeliner products under seven brand names including "Blooming Colors" and "Expert Eyes." Maybelline has held the leading position in eyeliner and eyebrow products for the last 20 years. The company ranks second in domestic sales of eye shadow.

FACE PRODUCTS   Maybelline's face products include foundation, blush, concealer, and powder. The company sells several basic types of foundation under seven brand names, including "Shades of You" for women of color and "Shine Free" for teenagers and younger women. Maybelline ranks second in unit sales of foundation and blush products. The company offers several basic blush products under three brand names. In concealer products, Maybelline sells under four brand names and has a 21 percent market share. The firm markets pressed and loose powder under four brand names. Maybelline is ranked second in powder by unit sales, with an approximate 12 percent market share. All of the company's face products are non-comedogenic (won't close pores), non-achegenic (won't cause acne), and dermatologist-tested.

LIP PRODUCTS   The company sells numerous lip products under eight brand names, including "Moisture Whip," "Revitalizing," "Long Wearing," "Kissing Koolers," and "Lip Liner." Maybelline is ranked third in lip product unit sales with an approximate 11 percent market share based on units sold.

NAIL PRODUCTS   Maybelline markets nail products under two brand names, "Revitalizing" and "Long Wearing." The company's nail products have held the number five position in the market for the last two years.

COSMETIC IMPLEMENTS AND OTHER PRODUCTS   The company also markets cosmetic implements and related accessories, including sharpeners, tweezers, make-up sponges, powder puffs, false eyelashes, eye make-up remover, eyelash curlers, and mascara remover under various brand names.

In 1991, Maybelline redesigned and updated the packaging of most of its cosmetics products, upgraded and improved many product formulations, and launched a $60 million, 16-month multimedia advertising campaign featuring the slogan "Maybe she's born with it. Maybe it's Maybelline." The new management team substantially lowered operating costs by eliminating about 145 of approximately 700 stock keeping units ("SKUs," the individual products manufactured and marketed within various product categories), and redirected the company's marketing focus from promotional programs to its core product lines. Maybelline also adopted a comprehensive value-analysis program designed to enhance product quality and consumer appeal while reducing unit costs. Finally, the firm developed and introduced the "Shades of You" product line.

Acquiring New Product Lines and Brands

In September 1991, Maybelline acquired the "Yardley of London" trade name and related intellectual property rights in North America. The Yardley acquisition provided a strategic platform for the company to enter the soap and bath luxuries product category, which Maybelline believed was one of the fastest growing segments of the personal care products market. The company has revitalized the Yardley bar and liquid soap lines by, among other things, updating and improving the quality of existing Yardley products and reformulating high-quality liquid and bar soaps. In addition, Maybelline has developed its upscale Yardley Bath Shoppe line of luxury bath products. This consists of a wide variety of high-quality, attractively packaged soaps, gels, powders, and related luxury bath products, which were introduced to consumers in the mass market in early 1993. Maybelline positioned its Yardley Bath Shoppe products to be similar in quality and appearance to luxury bath products traditionally sold only through department stores and specialty boutiques. In 1993, the company introduced a line of face cosmetics for mature women under its "Revitalizing" brand.

International Market Presence

While international sales accounted for approximately 10 percent of Maybelline's net sales in 1991, management has adopted various strategies designed to expand the company's core color cosmetics business in existing international markets, including Canada, Mexico, Latin America, and southeast Asia. Maybelline's products are currently sold, either directly by the company or through licensees or distributors, in approximately 25 countries. Management believes that the Maybelline brand is broadly recognized around the world and that the international cosmetics and personal care markets represent a significant growth opportunity. The company developed a four-part strategy to expand its international core color cosmetics business. First, it sought to increase its sales in Canada, Guatemala, Hong Kong, and Puerto Rico, the markets in which the firm directly sells its products, by establishing a more uniform image for its products and utilizing the updated packaging, product formulations, and advertising currently used domestically.

Second, it is strengthening its relationships with existing licensees and distributors and seeking to establish similar new relationships, in each case to ensure the consistent delivery of Maybelline products, customer service, and quality in markets served by licensees and distributors. In that regard, the company is also seeking to identify strategic markets with both sufficient sales volume and adequate growth potential where it would be beneficial to discontinue ineffective licensee and distributor relationships and begin direct sales. Third, the company is establishing licensee and distributor relationships in new markets by developing channels of distribution in order to protect the brand image and preserve future growth opportunities. Finally, Maybelline is evaluating additional markets for possible expansion where it is believed that the firm's products could be successfully marketed to consumers.

In 1991, the company sold its intellectual property rights to manufacture and market Maybelline cosmetics and personal care products in Japan to a third party. Other companies, such as Revlon's Max Factor and Betrix cosmetic brands, were already established in Europe and Japan. Procter & Gamble owns these Revlon divisions and used its well-established distribution and marketing network in Europe and Japan to facilitate its global expansion in the cosmetics industry. Previously, Procter & Gamble's Japanese sales of fragrances and cosmetics were zero, but immediately reached $237 million after the firm acquired two of Revlon's cosmetic brands.

Many companies recognize the strong profit potential of selling cosmetics in the global marketplace, but there is much competition and some cultural barriers. Japan's Kao Corporation and the Anglo-Dutch Unilever Group are powerful and well-entrenched competitors for any new entrants. Further, marketing cosmetics around the world presents cultural obstacles and considerations. Maybelline is interested in the international marketplace, but these sales accounted for only 10 percent of the firm's net sales in 1991.

Marketing At Maybelline

Customers

Maybelline distributes its products directly to over 23,000 mass-market retail stores in the United States and Canada and believes its products are sold in approximately 80,000 retail outlets. The company's products are sold to nearly every major food, drug and mass-merchandise retailer in the United States, as well as to various wholesalers. Maybelline's largest customers include Wal-Mart, Kmart, Target, and Walgreens. Net sales of the company's products to Wal-Mart exceeded 10 percent of 1991 net sales. With the exception of Wal-Mart, no single customer or affiliated group of customers represents 10 percent or more of the firm's sales.

Consumers and Advertising

Based upon various independent attitude and usage studies prepared on behalf of the company, approximately 78 percent of all women 13 and older purchase cosmetics in mass-market outlets. Of these women, approximately 73 percent have used one or more Maybelline products in the past six months. Women of all ages purchase Maybelline products, with slight over-representation of those women 13–24 and slight under-representation of those women 50 and older. The Maybelline consumer represents all income levels and ethnic backgrounds.

Maybelline expends a significant portion of its revenue for the advertising and promotion of its products. In the late 1980s and early 1990s, over $350 million was spent on advertising and promotional activities for Maybelline products. These expenditures were necessary to maintain and increase market share in an industry highly dependent upon product image and consumer trends. The company spent $59.3 million in 1991, or 23.3 percent of its 1991 net sales, for these purposes. These expenditures are an integral component of Maybelline's overall marketing effort.

As part of the Maybelline Restage in September 1991, the company initiated a comprehensive marketing program designed to enhance the image of its products with its ultimate consumers and to increase their usage. Elements of this program included: (1) a $60 million, 16-month advertising campaign created by the company's new advertising agency, Lintas Group: New York, featuring the company's new theme, "Maybe she's born with it. Maybe it's Maybelline"; (2) improved product formulations reflecting recent technological advances and changing consumer preferences, including products with sheerer textures; (3) new primary packaging and product packaging cards for both regular Maybelline and "Shine Free" products; and (4) new products supported by extensive consumer advertising.

The program is part of Maybelline's effort to focus on its core cosmetics products and business lines. One of the principal objectives for the marketing program is to revitalize the company's packaging, advertising, retail displays, and product formulas. The result desired is that consumers perceive the firm's cosmetics as equivalent in quality and appearance to department and specialty store brands. The campaign has included extensive television advertising; print ads will appear in many leading beauty magazines, including *Vogue, Glamour, Seventeen,* and *Teen.* The company expects to continue to maintain substantial levels of advertising.

Distribution and EDI Systems

Maybelline's sales to mass merchandisers and chain and other drug stores are generated principally by its own salesforce (approximately 300 people in North America) and, to a lesser extent, by a network of food brokers in selected domestic markets. International sales are generated through a combination of the company's own salesforce and exclusive distributors. The salesforce makes frequent sales presentations at the headquarters or home office of its major customers and to various individual retail outlets. The sales representatives focus their efforts both on sales of products to direct customers and on designing and executing programs to ensure sales to ultimate-product consumers. Programs directed at ultimate-product consumers provide innovative on-shelf and stand-alone displays, offer price reductions and discounts, and include cooperative advertising efforts.

Maybelline emphasizes and believes it is well positioned to provide responsive service to its customers. It has developed advanced capabilities in electronic data interchange ("EDI") telecommunications technology. As a result, the company is electronically able to receive and confirm customer purchase orders and transmit sales invoices. Additionally, through EDI, the company has access to up-to-date data regarding product movement through retail stores. EDI technology is utilized by many of Maybelline's customers who have similar technology, including Wal-Mart, Kmart, and Target.

Changes in Maybelline's Ownership

Despite management's efforts at revitalizing Maybelline's business, the results did not come soon enough. By the mid-1990s, with more than $150 million in debt, the company was targeted for a takeover. French cosmetics giant L'Oreal and German manufacturer Benckiser battled it out for the Maybelline acquisition in 1996. L'Oreal emerged the winner. L'Oreal is one of the world's largest cosmetics companies and markets a broad line of makeup, perfumes, hair care products, and skin care products. This change in ownership was barely noticeable to the average consumer, and Maybelline continues its reign as a leading mass-market cosmetics brand.

L'Oreal kept the Maybelline brand name, even though it has its own brand of mass-marketed products. Mass market products account for more than half of L'Oreal's total sales, which reached over $11 billion in 1997. The company also markets upscale cosmetics through the Lancome brand name and provides products for professional hairdressers with its Redken line. The company's sales in the United States exceeded $2 billion in 1997. In the United States, all L'Oreal products are distributed and marketed through a subsidiary, Cosmair. Cosmair is also the exclusive distributor of Ralph Lauren fragrances. Thus, the L'Oreal organization has a substantial and concerted effort in many lines of the personal care business.

L'Oreal considers itself to be a world leader in cosmetics and is very committed to products that complement a wide range of beauty cultures and aesthetic traditions around the world. Behind western Europe, North America is L'Oreal's second largest market. Other growing markets include Latin America, eastern Europe, and parts of Asia. The international expansion efforts for Maybelline have also continued under L'Oreal's ownership. The brand is available in many countries, including a recent introduction in China. In a surprise move, L'Oreal decided to keep Maybelline's U.S.-based advertising agency, Gotham New York, after the 1996 acquisition. One major consideration was how effectively the tagline, "Maybe she's born with it. Maybe it's Maybelline," would translate into other languages.

Questions For Discussion

1. Evaluate Maybelline's current position in the cosmetics industry. What are the brand's strengths and weaknesses?

2. What kinds of opportunities and threats are in Maybelline's marketing/business environment? What competitive, social, and economic forces influence this environment?

3. What other types of products could be marketed effectively under the Maybelline brand name? Consider the company's current brand equity and how new products would integrate with the brand's current marketing mix.

4. Conduct a secondary research effort or a brief primary research study to understand the similarities and differences between the mass marketed brands, Maybelline and L'Oreal. What do your results indicate about brand and corporate strategy?

SOURCES

These facts are from http://www.loreal.com/us/group/world/loreal-usa.asp; http://www.loreal.com/us/group/group.asp; wysiwyg://main.82/http://www.hoovers.com/capsules/41772.html; http://www.adage.com; Gretchen Morgenson, "Where Can I Buy Some?," *Forbes*, June 24, 1991, 82; "Maybelline Expands its Cosmetic Offerings for Women," *Drug* Topics, July 9, 1990, 46; "For Years Maybelline Played 'Me-Too' with Cover Girl," *Adweek's Marketing Week*, April 3, 1989, 22;"A New Face in Cosmetics Research: Maybelline Sets Up A Research Group to Improve its Ingredients," *Chemical Week*, Nov. 23,1988,15; Cara Applebaum, "A New World of Beauty for P&G," *Adweek's Marketing Week*, April 15, 1991,4–5; Randall Smith, Kathleen Deveny and Alecia Swasy, "Perelman Launches Sales of Revlon Units to Procter & Gamble for $1.4 Billion," *The Wall Street Journal*, April 11, 1991, A4; and Prospectus, Maybelline, Inc., 1992.

CASE *15*

Texas Instruments[1]

Founded in the 1930s, Texas Instruments (TI) employs 75,000 people worldwide, with major manufacturing sites in North America, South America, Europe, Asia, and Australia. TI serves a wide range of electronics markets and is divided into six major groups of specific applications.

Semiconductors are TI's principal business, and the company is striving to become one of the world's leaders in semiconductor innovations and applications. TI is successful in defense electronics, as well, and serves both U.S. and international defense markets. The materials and controls portion of TI's business is a world leader in electromechanical controls technology. Through its research and development division, TI strives to convert research and development activities into useful products and services. TI earns adequate returns on investments through intellectual property, as recognized through patents and inventions. Finally, information technology combines TI's capabilities in both computing hardware and software. The Information Technology Group is comprised of Computer Systems, Industrial Automation, and Peripheral Products. The Peripheral Products Division (PPD), located in Temple, Texas, produces printers and portable computers and terminals. Because all phases of a new product introduction—including engineering, manufacturing, and marketing—are located together, the communication and coordination needed for a successful product launch exists.

The Laser Printer Market

The popularity of personal computers has prompted the growth of printers as a complementary product. Throughout the 1990s, laser printers were the fastest growing segment of the entire printer industry. Laser technology has become popular because it offers excellent print quality, fast printing, quiet operation, and flexibility with graphics and styles of letters. Laser printers are designed for environments where data/word processing, specialty publishing, and business communications

---

[1] This case was prepared by Debbie Thorne LeClair, The University of Tampa, for classroom discussion rather than to illustrate either effective or ineffective handling of an administrative situation. Research assistance was provided by Sergio Balsera, The University of Tampa.

are integral to daily operations. Laser printers require minimal user training and are considered a commodity in some markets. For this reason, the price of laser printers has decreased dramatically over the past several years.

The Introduction Of The Microlaser Printer

In late 1989, TI introduced the microLaser printer. TI hoped that the microLaser would become the laser printer of choice in the world. When compared to leading competitors, the microLaser offered greater functionality in a smaller package. It was designed to fit easily on a desktop and perform numerous applications.

By virtue of its size, ease of use, and affordability, the microLaser had been positioned as a personal laser printer. It was small and relatively inexpensive. TI marketers hoped these attributes would encourage companies to purchase one microLaser for every personal computer they owned.

TI Explores New Distribution Channels

As with any new product introduction, careful attention was given to a distribution strategy. In the past, TI had relied on distributors, original equipment manufacturers (OEMs), and value-added resellers (VARs) to market its laser printers. OEMs would specify a high level of customization and remarket the printer under their brand name, usually as a part of a system. The OEM might even request functional modifications to meet its customers' needs. The printer was usually integrated with a computer and software to form a system that the OEM would sell as its own. A VAR was more likely to purchase the printer with the TI name on it and then integrate it with other brands of computers and software to form a system. Texas Instruments' authorized distributors, VARs, and OEMs usually sold to large volume accounts, such as governmental agencies, financial institutions, and Fortune 1000 companies.

At first, little attention was given to retailers and less sophisticated end-users. Although the Texas Instruments name was recognized by many consumers, market research showed that little was known about TI laser printers. Most people either associated TI with its educational products, semiconductors, or for being forced out of the personal computer market. Perhaps these associations explain in part why retail distribution was not pursued by the Peripheral Products Division. Additionally, from 1986 to 1989, Peripheral Products had no products suitable for the retail market.

The development of the microLaser prompted PPD Marketing to explore new channels of distribution. Research revealed that 48 percent of laser printer purchases were made through retailers. Distributors and wholesalers accounted for an additional 20 percent of laser printer sales. Texas Instruments had mainly sold through the reseller market. However, data such as these proved that the market demanded new distribution channels. Retailers did sell to individual users and small business owners, but now larger corporations with decentralized buying were going to retail outlets for their purchases.

After much thought and analysis, TI executives decided to re-enter the retail market. The nature of the printer market and the increased popularity of laser printers demanded new distribution channels. However, the move into retail would be gradual. Support for retailers, including promotional campaigns, had to be designed, tested, and implemented. This channel demanded more support than the others and required that TI "pull" customers into the stores. PPD Marketing had to build name recognition, establish TI as a producer of high-quality printers, and reach end-users and purchasers.

TI Enters The Retail Market

Although nearly half of all laser printer purchases are made through retailers, the microLaser printer presented several challenges to TI. There are many laser printers from which to choose, and there is little difference among products, so buyers will often use price as a means of choosing between competing products. This elastic price situation means that new entrants into the laser printer market should have a very low price to encourage sales. The TI microLaser had a price lower than two-thirds of its competitors in the laser printer industry.

Although the printer had a reasonable price, TI did not provide the promotional support necessary to "pull" end-users into retail stores. TI advertised in trade journals but did little else to establish itself as a viable competitor in the laser printer market. Co-op advertising and sales force incentives might have been successful strategies for building recognition among retailers.

The microLaser was similar to other products and there were few end-users specifically requesting the printer. Further, entrenched competitors, such as Hewlett Packard and IBM, made it difficult for TI to persuade retailers to add another laser printer to their product mix. Finally, TI had much more experience in dealing with large accounts and industrial merchandising, which may have put them at a disadvantage in dealing with the competitive retail market.

Although TI enjoyed only moderate success with its microLaser printer, the company expanded on the microLaser product line. In the 1990s, the microLaser PS17 and PS35, the microLaser XL, microLaser Turbo printers, microLaser Plus printers, and others were introduced by TI. Each of the new printers offered either improved print-engine speed or greater font capability at an affordable price. Despite these improvements, TI's presence and movement in retail markets remained relatively slow. However, the company has signed agreements to distribute the microLaser product line through an original equipment manufacturer (OEM) and a national computer distributor.

TI Printer Business Sold

On July 23, 1996, TI announced the sale of its worldwide printer and supplies business to GENICOM Corporation, a Washington, D.C.-based company. By this time, the microLaser printer line was part of TI's Personal Productivity Products business. The company indicated that the agreement with GENICOM would allow it to invest additional resources in mobile computing and educational calculators. For GENICOM, the acquisition increased its market share in several printer categories and doubled the size of its core business. Under the ownership of GENICOM, the microLaser line has expanded with special emphasis on commercial and heavy users, not the personal laser printer market.

Questions for Discussion

1. The microLaser was introduced in a highly competitive and price-sensitive market. Explain how these factors affected the marketing strategy for the microLaser.

2. Evaluate TI's decision to enter retail markets. What could the company have done differently?

3. Now that TI has a product line of laser printers, explain how the company might position itself to end users, to retailers, and to distributors.

4. Why would TI decide to sell its printer business to GENICOM? Conduct some research on both companies to better understand their current core businesses.

Sources

These facts are from http://www.genicom.com/drivers/; http://www.genicom.com/about/7900.htm; http://www.ti.com/corp/docs/pressrel/1996/96037.htm; http://www.ti.com/corp/docs/investor/ar95/ary-outi.htm; Daniel M. Kehoe, "Fonts Unlimited: Seven Smart Lasers for Under $3,000," *PC World*, Sept. 1990; Alfred Poor, "Small-Footprint 6-ppm TI microLaser," *PC Magazine*, April 24, 1990; a marketing study on Texas Instruments prepared by John Barnes, Jamie Holmes, Danny Lester, Truman Murray, and Mike Shelton, Memphis State University, 1991; Peter H. Lewis, "Texas Instruments Gets Personal," *New York Times*, Nov. 5, 1989, A2; Whitney Lynn, "Selling Computer Products in Changing Channels," *Computer Reseller News*, Aug. 28, 1989, 83–84; Personal interview with Bruce Foster (Channel Marketing Manager for Texas Instruments' Peripheral Products Division), Aug. 16, 1989; Rowland T. Moriarty and Thomas J. Kosnick, "High Tech Marketing: Concepts, Continuity, and Change," *Sloan Management Review*, Summer 1989, 7–17; Texas Instruments, (promotional booklet), 1988; Marketrends/1988: The State of the Printer Industry, 3–4; and "Desktop Publishing Drives a High-Tech Company," *Modern Office Technology*, May 1988, 80, 85, 88.

C A S E *16*

AutoZone[1]

AutoZone is a chain of 1,728 retail auto parts stores operating in 32 states. Originally named AutoShack, the company was created as a division of Malone and Hyde in 1979. Following a lawsuit by the Tandy Corporation, which contended that the name "AutoShack" was too similar to that of its Radio Shack electronics chain, the company name was changed to AutoZone in 1987. Today, AutoZone is one of the fastest growing companies in the highly competitive auto parts industry.

After 20 years of constant growth, AutoZone has emerged as number one in market share in the auto parts retail industry. AutoZone sells a broad line of vehicle replacement parts, accessories, chemicals, and motor oil. The company projects opening 350 new stores per year and rapid geographic expansion. Both the do-it-yourself (DIY) market and the professional mechanic sector (commercial market) continue to expand. AutoZone continues to improve comparable store sales by approximately 7–10 percent per year and is attempting to leverage expenses through a culture of thrift and tight expense control.

How Does AutoZone Compete?

AutoZone targets the DIY auto repair market with an extensive selection of automotive replacement parts and accessories. The DIY market is attractive for several reasons. First, due to rising prices for new cars, the average age of cars is about eight years. This means that approximately two out of every three—or 113 million—cars are over five years old, beyond the coverage of most warranty periods, and well into the repair cycle. Secondly, with the increasing costs of professional mechanics and auto repair labor, many people are opting to do their own auto repair work. Finally, many people prefer to do their own repair and maintenance because of the difficulty in finding trustworthy mechanics. Due to these factors, the number of "shade tree" mechanics has grown rapidly in recent years. AutoZone provides do-it-yourselfers with quality, brand name products at affordable prices.

---

[1] This case was prepared by Brent Wren, University of Alabama-Huntsville, for classroom discussion rather than to illustrate either effective or ineffective handling of an administrative situation.

Two years ago, AutoZone kicked off the commercial program to expand its market into the professional mechanic sector. AutoZone is especially well suited to cater to small repair shops because it provides services—like free testing of starters, alternators, batteries, and engine management components. In addition, service to the commercial market includes delivery to professional repair shops. After two years of service to commercial markets, this business accounts for more than 10 percent of total sales.

The AutoZone product line includes both new and remanufactured auto parts and accessories, which can be broadly classified into three categories. The majority of the retailers' sales come from "hard" parts, such as alternators, starters, and water pumps, which are often much more costly when obtained through a professional garage. The second category of products is a fairly complete "soft" line of regular maintenance items, such as oil, windshield wiper fluid, waxes/polishes, and antifreeze. Finally, the chain also offers accessory items such as floor mats, special auto repair tools, and car stereos.

Currently, the majority of AutoZone outlets are located in the Sun Belt region. Tennessee and Texas represent the greatest areas of market penetration for the chain. In the last fiscal year, AutoZone entered five new states—California, Iowa, Maryland, Nevada, and New York. The company is well on its way to being a strong national auto parts chain. The AutoZone strategy is to try to expand the store count faster than any competitor in the industry. In addition, there is a desire to always look for new opportunities to create more value for customers, especially in the areas of technology, store design, and product quality.

What Makes AutoZone Different?

AutoZone offers quality, brand name parts at low prices. However, pricing and product offerings alone do not set AutoZone apart. AutoZone stores differentiate themselves from the typical auto parts store in two primary ways: their appearance and their customer service. First, they strive to erase the perception of auto parts stores as dirty, unfriendly environments where only advanced mechanics dare tread. AutoZone stores are designed to effect a positive visual impact on the customer. The high-tech appearance of the stores is achieved through the use of exposed beams and ductwork and vivid orange, black, and red coloring. Also, a strategic emphasis is placed on cleanliness, as stores are kept both orderly and very clean.

In addition to dispelling myths about the appearance of the typical auto parts store, AutoZone has worked very hard to establish a reputation for customer service unequaled in the parts industry. They have developed employee hiring and training procedures to counter the stereotypical image of a surly mechanic as clerk in the parts store. All potential employees go through an extensive screening and testing process before a hiring decision is reached. Newly hired employees are then given a thorough training program that allows them to specialize in one particular aspect of the store's operation. Most AutoZone employees have had some experience or exposure to automotive repair, and this background is supplemented through the company's training program. This is evident in the level of technical assistance that AutoZone employees are willing and able to give customers.

In addition to the technical aspects of the training, AutoZone provides employees with extensive training in customer satisfaction. The chain's unique "Drop/Stop/30/30" policy illustrates the firm's emphasis on maintaining high standards of customer service. This policy states "a customer should be approached by a salesperson within 30 seconds of entering the store or within 30 feet of the front door. If the salesperson is working on something, that is put aside when a customer enters the store."

Customer service is further enhanced by two technological innovations. The first innovation is the registering of all customer parts warranties on computer. Knowing that customers sometimes misplace their receipts, this innovation enhances customer service by reducing the hassles often involved in returned or defective parts. A second innovation is the electronic parts catalog. AutoZone installed electronic catalog terminals in their stores to help customers select appropriate parts and locate the needed items. In addition, the Store Management System (SMS) allows a central computer system to measure the operations of any store at any given time. As an automatic replenishing system, SMS allows for reduced administrative requirements, improved personnel scheduling, enhanced merchandising information, and improved inventory control.

AutoZone is constantly fine tuning the way stores are designed and operated. This includes the development of new products for the DIY market and the development of automotive diagnostic and repair software. In Memphis, AutoZone is experimenting with a test store that is open 24 hours every day to be available to unlucky drivers who have a night-time car emergency. If this concept proves workable, AutoZone may consider keeping other stores open 24 hours, but, of course, customer demand must justify the extra cost of 24-hour service. It is possible in urban areas where there are large second and third shift flows that the 24-hour service could differentiate AutoZone from the competition.

Beyond image management, one of the major factors in AutoZone's success is its state-of-the-art distribution network, which is similar to that utilized by Wal-Mart. AutoZone is able to buy in large quantities directly from manufacturers. In fact, purchasing for all stores is done centrally at the Memphis headquarters, while distribution is accomplished through seven distribution centers, in Danville, Illinois; Phoenix, Arizona; San Antonio, Texas; Lafayette, Louisiana; Lavonia, Georgia; Lexington, Tennessee; and Zanesville, Ohio. Memphis is also the location of an Express Parts center, which handles special orders and slower moving stock.

With this elaborate distribution system, the chain is able to have the right product at the right place at the right time. For example, in a Memphis AutoZone store, 28 brands of car wax and 11 brands of oil filters were stocked on the shelves. Substantial savings realized from economies of scale may be passed along to the firm's customers. In fact, AutoZone strives to maintain everyday low prices and positions itself as the price leader of "hard" parts.

AutoZone also expends considerable effort in site selection. In the past, expansion has meant obtaining high-visibility sites in high-traffic locations. Before entering new markets, the company undertakes substantial market research. Several factors are involved in market and site selection, including population demographics, vehicle profile, and the number and strength of competitive stores. The company attempts to cluster development in new urban markets in a relatively short period of time in order to achieve economies of scale in advertising and distribution costs.

Finally, AutoZone succeeds because of the dedication of its highly motivated work force. AutoZone has tried to develop a family atmosphere at all levels of the company, which has led to a fiercely loyal group of employees. In fact, all AutoZoners know the company pledge by heart:

1. AutoZoners always put customers first;
2. We know our parts and products;
3. Our stores look great;
4. And we've got the best merchandise at the right price!

The execution of this pledge has led to the current success of AutoZone.

Financial Performance

AutoZone's financial performance has been nothing less than impressive. Exhibit 1 provides sales, profits, and store growth over the last 10 years. The chain has shown steady increases in sales, profits, and geographic expansion to 32 states. In 1992, AutoZone reached a milestone by topping $1 billion in sales. Even more amazing is the fact that this feat was accomplished in just 13 years.

Although AutoZone's performance has been remarkable, substantial investments in the future are still being made. AutoZone continually opens, replaces, or remodels its retail locations. It also continues to invest in new technology, such as an electronic catalog, and development of software.

The Industry Outlook

According to many predictions, U.S. auto parts firms can expect slow growth. Forecasters say that the industry is mature and the aftermarket is likely to be weak. New car sales will also significantly affect the health of the aftermarket. The greater number of new cars means better designed parts and increasingly complicated diagnostic technologies, which makes it tougher for do-it-yourselfers to repair their cars.

Foreign expansion is expected to provide a possible growth opportunity for U.S. auto parts suppliers. The major destinations were Canada, Mexico and the European

EXHIBIT 1	AutoZone Sales, Profit, and Total Stores, 1987–1997 (in $hundred thousands, except # of stores)		
	Sales	*Profits*	*# of Stores*
1997	2,691	321	1,728
1996	2,242	269	1,423
1995	1,808	228	1,143
1994	1,508	191	933
1993	1,217	141	783
1992	1,002	104	678
1991	818	79	598
1990	672	49	538
1989	536	25	504
1988	437	17	440
1987	354	16	396

community. Canada and Mexico combined to represent 80 percent of this figure. The current trend toward incorporating complex computer-based components in vehicles could provide the U.S. auto parts industry with a significant international competitive advantage. Increased sales opportunities may also unfold with the unification of the European market and as Eastern Europe opens to Western trade and investment. Standardized specifications and simplified commercial producers in Europe will provide more market opportunities. However, in this increasingly competitive environment, auto parts dealers will have to manage marketing efforts successfully to excel.

What Is Next for AutoZone?

AutoZone executives expect that increases in overall industry volume will be only moderate, but they see considerable room for growth. Estimates of the size of the DIY market range up to $30 billion in sales. Using this estimate, AutoZone's 1997 sales of $2.7 billion represent just 9 percent of the overall market. The continued growth and successful financial performance of the company may be dependent upon management's ability to open new stores on a profitable basis in existing and new markets. The company feels new stores must be opened and operated on a timely and profitable basis in order to compete. AutoZone executives feel confident that they can continue to grow by satisfying their customers. In fact, they are so sure customer service will prove successful as a long-run strategy that they have increased staffing to ensure typical AutoZone service.

In 1998, AutoZone executives are looking for new, innovative alternatives that will allow them to control a larger share of the market. Continuing with their current marketing strategy may not be enough to ensure the kind of growth they think is possible. AutoZone is looking for new ways to market itself and achieve even greater differentiation from its competition. For example, some store managers have heard customers complain that they have no facilities or knowledge to repair or install parts in their cars. Some executives have suggested that AutoZone install "DIY repair bays," giving customers a place to install the parts they purchase at AutoZone. This would also allow customers to be close to the technical support of AutoZone employees. However, AutoZone would be moving away from its area of expertise. Also, this service could be competition with AutoZone's new emerging commercial market of repair shops that represents 10 percent of its business.

The problem faced by AutoZone is "Where to go now?" The company must decide if continued expansion would be a proper step or if another alternative would be better. Executives are considering several strategies but are still uncertain what the future will hold for AutoZone.

Questions for Discussion

1. Having just read AutoZone's situation, perform a thorough examination of its competitive position, including company strengths and weaknesses and opportunities and threats.

2. What variables within the marketing mix are most relevant to AutoZone's past success? Which are going to be most relevant in their future success?

3. Generate a list of strategic alternatives for AutoZone. Define each alternative and tell which strengths, weaknesses, opportunities, and/or threats the strategy is designed to capitalize on and/or combat.

4. What actions do you recommend for AutoZone? Are these actions a long-term plan or a short-term fix?

Sources

These facts are from AutoZone's 1997 Annual Report; Laurel Campbell, "AutoZone to open 24 hours in test at store on Summer," *The Commercial Appeal*, Apr. 9, 1998, B4; http://www.autozone.com/sitemap.html; AutoZone 1992 Annual Report; AutoZone Common Stock Prospectus, Lehman Brothers, Goldman, Sachs and Co., Oct. 3, 1991; Neumeierm, Shelley, "Companies to Watch," *Fortune*, Dec. 2, 1991, 110; and Shearson Lehman Brothers, AutoZone Stock Report, April 29, 1991.

USA Today: The Nation's Newspaper[1]

USA Today, billed as "the nation's newspaper," debuted in 1982 as America's first national general-interest daily newspaper. The paper was the brainchild of Allen H. Neuharth, Chairman of Gannett Co., Inc., a diversified news and information company that publishes newspapers, operates broadcast television stations and outdoor advertising businesses, and is involved in research, marketing, commercial printing, a newswire service, and news programming. Gannett is currently the largest U.S. newspaper group, with 92 daily newspapers, including *USA Today*, *USA Weekend*, and a number of nondaily publications.

Pre-Launch Strategy

In February 1980, Allen Neuharth met with "Project NN" task force members for the first time to discuss his vision for producing and marketing a unique wide-focus daily newspaper that would ultimately be distributed nationwide. Previously, national newspaper circulation had not been technologically feasible, but satellite technology had since solved the problem of limited geographical distribution. Neuharth was ready to take advantage of two seemingly disparate trends in the reading public—an increasingly short attention span among a generation nurtured on television rather than print, coupled with a growing hunger for more information. Neuharth believed that readers face a time crunch in a world where so much information is available, but there is so little time to absorb it. *USA Today*'s primary mission would be to provide more news about more subjects in less time. Task force members were enthusiastic about the concept. Research suggested that *USA Today* should target primarily achievement-oriented men in professional and managerial positions who are heavy newspaper readers and frequent travelers.

By early 1982, a team of news, advertising, and production personnel from the staffs of Gannett's daily newspapers developed, edited, published, and tested several different prototypes. Gannett sent three different 40-page prototype versions of *USA Today* to almost 5,000 professional people. Along with each prototype, they sent

---

[1] This case was prepared by Geoffrey Lantos, Stonehill College, for classroom discussion rather than to illustrate either effective or ineffective handling of an administrative situation. Research assistance was provided by James G. Maxham, Louisiana State University.

readers a response card that asked what they liked best and least about the proposed paper, whether or not they would buy it, as well as whether they would give it approval. The content of each prototype was basically the same. What differed were the layout and graphics presentations. For example, one prototype included a section called "Agenda" that included comics and a calendar of meetings to be held by various professional organizations. According to marketplace feedback, readers liked the prototypes. The Gannett Board of Directors unanimously approved the paper's launch, and so, on April 20, 1982, Gannett announced that the first copies of *USA Today* would soon be available in the Washington/Baltimore area.

Product Launch

On September 15, 1982, 155,000 copies of the newspaper's first edition hit the newsstands. On page one, founder Neuharth wrote a short summary of *USA Today*'s mission statement. He wanted to make *USA Today* enlightening and enjoyable to the public, informative to national leaders, and attractive to advertisers. The first issue featured a cover story on *Batman,* the movie, an abridged report on the assassination of the Lebanese president-elect, and an article on celebrities discussing their weight problems. The issue sold out. A little over a month following its debut, *USA Today*'s circulation hit 362,879, double the original year-end projection. In April 1983, just seven months after its introduction, the newspaper's circulation topped the one million mark.

Gannett did not plan a grand nationwide debut. In order to monitor results carefully and modify the paper and its marketing as needed, the paper implemented a regional rollout distribution strategy. Produced at facilities in Arlington, VA, *USA Today* was transmitted via satellite to printing plants across the country. The newspaper's marketers divided the country into 15 geographical market segments. *USA Today* was available within a 200-mile radius of these 15 major markets, making the paper accessible to 42 percent of U.S. households. Significantly, these markets contained 23 million of the 35 million adults who read two or more newspapers daily. Gannett's focus group research indicated that many readers were bringing the paper into their homes rather than reading it on their commute or at work. Consequently, Gannett launched a home delivery subscription service in 1984. Home delivery caused problems at first, because the in-house computer technology could not handle subscription mailing lists efficiently, and the postal service did not always deliver the paper on its publication day. Nevertheless, subscriptions grew, and by 1991, nearly half of *USA Today*'s distribution was via home and office delivery.

Clearly, the paper filled a gap in the market, satisfying several unmet needs and wants. *USA Today*'s success came from listening to its readers and giving them what they wanted. *USA Today* communicated with readers on a personal level very quickly (many of the short, fact-filled stories are under 250 words), clearly, and directly, in an upbeat and positive way. The color is riveting, and so are the space-defying number of stories, factoids, larger-than-usual pictures, bar graphs, and charts, all squeezed onto each page without seeming too crowded. Instead of confusion, readers get neatness and order. Very few stories are continued on another page. The paper's dependably consistent organization enables readers to go directly to any one of *USA Today*'s major sections. It takes an average of only 25 minutes for a reader to peruse the paper.

USA Today strives to be a balanced newspaper, reporting positive stories along with negative ones and reflecting America's diversity. The editorial page always presents opposing views. *USA Today*'s own editorial position on most major social, economic, and political issues can be described as middle-of-the-road, a position its staff believes is in tune with the general public. The newspaper's intent is to allow readers to have the information and opinions they need to form their own views.

Marketing Mix Changes

During the mid-1980s, the media dubbed *USA Today* "McPaper"—the fast food of the newspaper business. Critics denounced what they called its junk-food journalism. In spite of the criticism, circulation surpassed 1.4 million by late 1985 as the paper expanded to 56 pages in length. The cover price of the paper had also increased to 50 cents, double its original price of 25 cents per issue. By this time, *USA Today* had become the second largest paper in the country, with a circulation topped only by *The Wall Street Journal*. Although *USA Today* competes more directly with news weeklies and business newspapers than with local papers, many papers began to adopt some of *USA Today*'s style. Publishers began adding color and beefing up circulation campaigns to compete with "The Nation's Newspaper."

Product Innovation

To stay ahead of the competition, which was increasingly borrowing its format, *USA Today* had to continue to innovate. Gannett began incorporating less traditional value-added features to keep readers interested. The paper added 1-800 and 1-900 "hot-line" numbers that readers could call for expert information on financial planning, college admissions, minority business development, taxes, and other subjects. Shortly after their introduction, over three million readers called the hot-line numbers, with over half of these readers calling for up-to-the-minute information on sports, weather, stocks, and lottery numbers. Thousands of readers responded to reader-opinion polls and write-in surveys on political and current event issues. The editorial pages were also redesigned to provide more room for guest columnists and to encourage debate. The change was popular: The volume of letters to the editor increased by over 500 percent. Gannett also initiated a high school "Academic All Star" program that it later expanded to include colleges and universities. In hard news, *USA Today* was able to offer more up-to-date coverage by rolling the presses over four hours earlier than *The Wall Street Journal* and almost three hours later than the *New York Times*.

Promotional Innovation

USA Today also began to innovate in its promotional activities. Historically, the paper limited its promotions mostly to outdoor advertising and television. However, in the late 1980s, Neuharth undertook a "BusCapade" promotion tour, traveling to all 50 states and talking with all kinds of people, including the governors of each state. Neuharth succeeded in raising public awareness of his paper, allowing *USA Today* to make money for the first time. Encouraged by his success, Neuharth forged ahead with a "JetCapade" promotion where Neuharth and a small news team traveled to 30 countries in seven months, stimulating global demand for the paper. During a visit to the troops of Operation Desert Storm in the Persian Gulf, General Norman Schwarzkopf expressed a need for news from home. *USA Today* arranged for delivery of 18,000 copies per day. The overseas success of *USA Today* led to the publication of *USA Today International*, which is available in more than 90 countries in Western Europe, the Middle East, North Africa, and Asia.

The paper continued to drum up demand among advertisers by adding marketing enhancements. Selling space to Madison Avenue advertisers presented a challenge to *USA Today*, because those agencies weren't convinced that it would pay to advertise in the paper. Gannett's first strategy for enlisting advertisers was called the Partnership Plan, which provided six months of free space to those who purchased six months of paid advertising. *USA Today* also began to accept regional advertising across a wide variety of categories such as regional travel, retail, tourism, and economic development. Color advertisements could arrive as late as 6 p.m. the day before publication, giving local advertisers increased flexibility. The paper also moved aggressively into "blue-chip circulation," where bulk quantities of *USA Today* are sold at discounted prices to hotels, airlines, and restaurants, and provided free-of-charge to customers. Today, roughly 500,000 copies of *USA Today* are distributed through blue chip circulation every day.

Spinoff Activities

A decade after *USA Today*'s launch, Gannett found itself in the enviable position of owning one of America's most successful newspapers. *USA Today* was the most widely read newspaper in the country, with daily readership of over 6.5 million. In an era when nearly all major national media were suffering declines in readership or viewing audience, *USA Today* continued to grow. Rising distribution and promotion costs, however, were beginning to make the newspaper slightly unprofitable. To reverse this trend, *USA Today* created several spinoffs, including its first special interest publication, *Baseball Weekly*. During its first month of operation, *Baseball Weekly*'s circulation reached 250,000 copies. Today, the weekly's circulation is roughly 425,000. Venturing into news media, *USA Today* joined with Cable News Network to produce a football TV program, and launched SkyRadio to provide live radio on commercial airline flights.

Another major spinoff was *USA Today Online*, which the company introduced in 1993. The online version allows readers to receive up-to-the-moment news that incorporates colorful visuals and crisp audio. Given the surge in Internet subscribers, *USA Today* made a strategic decision to link their online news with popular Internet providers' web sites. These Internet providers agreed to incorporate *USA Today Online* as their default news source. This strategy allowed *USA Today* to increase its readership substantially, while also increasing its name recognition. Ad revenues also increased as new advertisers were attracted to the online format and the potentially huge worldwide reach. The online version was seen as a natural companion to the print version of *USA Today*, given the paper's worldwide distribution.

Looking Ahead

In looking at the total national newspaper market, *USA Today* is quite successful. Today, over 6.5 million consumers read *USA Today* on a daily basis and approximately

2.2 million people subscribe to the paper. This success has occurred during a time when newspaper readership overall is declining. Of all the national, daily papers in the United States, only *USA Today*, the *Los Angeles Times*, and the *Denver Post* are experiencing large gains in circulation. Given the success of *USA Today*, advertisers are obviously quite attracted to the paper's large volume of readers. To help cope with advertiser demand, the paper recently implemented the necessary technology to allow advertisers to transmit advertising copy electronically 24 hours per day. However, despite *USA Today*'s positive performance and national appeal, the firm is concerned about its future.

Some analysts have argued that no matter what *USA Today* does, its huge distribution costs will keep the paper's profits marginal for the foreseeable future. This problem is due in large part to the volatility of newsprint prices, which have increased 40 percent in the last few years. Given the unstable paper market, firms often pay extraordinarily high fixed costs to deliver their paper. This problem is compounded for *USA Today*, as it pays comparatively high distribution fixed costs. As such, *USA Today* often yields profit margins as much as 50 percent below other newspaper firms.

Because newspapers are often subjected to high newsprint costs, many newspaper firms are looking at online news as a means to increase readership and cut distribution expenses. However, online news poses a major threat to *USA Today* and other newspaper firms. Some experts suggest that approximately 14 percent of readers will switch from newspaper to online news, effectively cannibalizing the readership of printed news. And, despite the enormous potential of online news, many companies have yet to turn a profit on their online ventures. *USA Today Online* will break even for the first time in 1998 despite earning over $4 million from online ad revenues.

To help combat this problem, *USA Today* has moved to increase the value-added components of both its print and online versions. In the print version, *USA Today* recently split its Friday Life section into two separate sections: Weekend Life and Destinations & Diversions. This format change, the first major change in the history of *USA Today*, allows the paper to devote more space to weekend entertainment and travel news. This entertainment and travel focus has been mirrored in the online version of *USA Today* in its Travel Marketplace. *USA Today* recently signed six travel partners that will offer online travel services via the *USA Today* web site. Adopting a value-added strategy can help *USA Today* differentiate itself from other national news providers. In the future, the key will be to ensure that both the print and online versions of *USA Today* provide readers with content they cannot find anywhere else.

Questions for Discussion

1. What opportunities in the marketing environment did Gannett seize in launching *USA Today*? How did it learn about these opportunities? How did it respond to the opportunities identified?

2. What is *USA Today*'s competition? What are the implications for its marketing strategy?

3. What competitive growth strategies did Gannett use in introducing *USA Today* and in developing the paper over time? Were these strategies appropriate?

4. What performance standards did Gannett measure in assessing *USA Today*'s success? According to these measures, is the paper a success?

5. Evaluate *USA Today*'s decision to enter the online news market. What strategy should *USA Today Online* employ? Should the marketing strategy for the print version of *USA Today* be changed?

Sources

These facts are from "Baseball Weekly hits record circulation," *PR Newswire*, April 13, 1998, 413; "Circulation slide for newspapers," *Editor & Publisher*, May 10, 1997, 3; R. Cook, "Gannett hits heights in print but fall short of TV stardom," *Campaign*, Jan. 17, 1997, 24; Gannett Company, Inc., 1997 Annual Report; Gannett Company, Inc., 1996 Form 10-K (on file with the Securities and Exchange Commission); A. M. Kerwin, "Daily paper's circulation woes persist into '97," *Advertising Age*, May 12, 1997, 26; J. McCartney, "*USA Today* grows up," *American Journalism Review*, Sept. 1997, 19; T. Noah, "At least it's free, right?" *U.S. News & World Report*, Dec. 2, 1996, 60; J. Sullivan, "Where are newspapers headed?" *Editor and Publisher*, June 28, 1997; R. Tedesco, "Internet profit sites elusive," *Broadcasting & Cable*, Nov. 17, 1997, 74; "*USA Today*: A Case Study," prepared by M. Condry, R. Dailey, F. Gasquet, M. Holladay, A. Johnson, S. Menzer, and J. Miller, University of Memphis, 1997; "*USA Today* launches new Life section Friday format," *PR Newswire*, Mar. 16, 1998, 316; *USA Today* Press Kit, 1997, Gannett Company, Inc.; and I. Wada, "*USA Today* Marketplace signs up six for on-line services," *Travel Weekly*, April 28, 1997, 44.

The Gillette Company[1]

The Gillette Company has established itself as the leading producer and seller of grooming products. The corporate history of Gillette will be described briefly in order to provide an overview of the strategy behind Gillette's phenomenal success. Closer attention will then be paid to the situation as it existed at the end of 1997, and the prospects, outlook, options, and opportunities that were present then. The major focus of the case will be on the corporate strategy, business segments, and product mix.

A Sharp Beginning

Founded in 1901 by King C. Gillette, the Gillette Company was one of the first great multinational organizations and a marvel of marketing effectiveness. Only four years after founding the firm in Boston, King Gillette opened a branch office in London and rapidly obtained sales and profits throughout western Europe. About 20 years later, he said this of his safety razor:

> There is no other article for individual use so universally known or widely distributed. In my travels, I have found it in the most northern town in Norway and in the heart of the Sahara Desert.

Gillette set this goal for himself: to offer consumers high-quality shaving products that would satisfy basic grooming needs at a fair price. Having gained more than half of the entire razor and blades market, Gillette's manufacturing efficiency allowed it to implement marketing programs on a large scale, which propelled Gillette forward in profits and in market leadership. Riding this tide of good fortune, the company was able to weather the storm brought on by World War II and emerged in a very healthy condition. In 1948, Gillette set its all-time performance record with profits per share of $6.80. Gillette has not approached this level of success since that time.

---

[1] This case was prepared by Donald P. Roy, University of Memphis, and Brent Wren, University of Alabama-Huntsville, for classroom discussion rather than to illustrate either effective or ineffective handling of an administrative situation.

In 1955, Gillette decided to tread new waters and undertook two unrelated acquisitions. The first acquisition was the Toni Company, maker of do-it-yourself home permanent wave kits. Although this was a profitable venture initially, sales and profits soon faded. The second major acquisition was the Paper Mate pen company, which at that time made only retractable, refillable ballpoint pens. It, too, was profitable, but soon Bic's low-priced, disposable (nonrefillable) pens came over from France. Partly due to these two acquisitions, Gillette slowly began to lose its edge, and net profit slumped to $1.33 per share in 1964.

A Tough Lesson Learned

In 1962, Gillette's U.S. market share hovered around 70 percent while its success abroad was even better. Around this time, the English firm Wilkinson Sword introduced a stainless steel blade in the United States and began taking a substantial portion of Gillette's market share. Partly due to the time devoted to experimenting with the home permanent wave and pen businesses and partly due to the small size of the Wilkinson Sword company, Gillette underestimated the potential impact on its core business. Also, Gillette executives were unsure how to react. Should they introduce their own stainless steel blade or ignore the rival and hope that its market niche would remain small?

Gillette was lucky. Although it eventually introduced its own stainless steel blade, the real break came when Wilkinson was unable to exploit the niche it had created. Due to its lack of resources, Wilkinson Sword was unable to compete with the powerful Gillette machine and eventually sold much of its blade business to Gillette. However, the impact of this dilemma had already been felt. In 1965, Gillette's market share hit an all-time low of 49 percent. The lessons learned from this debacle are still with Gillette today and guide many of its decisions and actions.

The Move Toward Diversification

Attempting to resolve the crises of the early 1960s was Gillette's new CEO, Vincent Ziegler. Ziegler was aggressive, marketing-oriented, and ambitious for the company, believing in diversification through the acquisition of companies in other business segments. Within the next few years, Ziegler spearheaded the acquisition of the following companies:

Braun AG (German manufacturer of small appliances)

S.T. Dupont (French maker of luxury lighters)

Eve of Roma (high-fashion perfume)

Buxton Leather goods

Welcome Wagon, Inc.

Sterilon hospital razors

Jafra Cosmetics (home sales)

Four of these acquisitions proved to be unprofitable or unsuitable and were divested, and the other three yielded low profits by Gillette's standards. Other troubles came from the French manufacturer Bic, which excelled in disposable products. Its 19-cent disposable stick pens particularly affected the Paper Mate line of refillable pens and drove Paper Mate's share of the retail ballpoint pen market from over 50 percent down to 13 percent, approximately a 75 percent drop. Gillette had retaliated quickly with its new Write Brothers line of disposable pens, which failed on the first introduction in 1972, but succeeded in building market share when reintroduced to the market in 1975 with heavy price promotions. Bic was also threatening Gillette's strengths with two other products-its disposable razors and lighters-which were being marketed very successfully in Europe and elsewhere.

The Ziegler era had its successes. Cricket disposable lighters were brought on through the Dupont firm and did well. Soft & Dri antiperspirant joined Right Guard, expanding Gillette's position in the deodorant market. However, the belief that aerosols destroy the ozone layer caused sales of spray versions of these products (along with all other brands of spray) to plummet suddenly, creating a crisis in these segments. Meanwhile, Gillette's Trac II razor was a great success, and the razor segment continued its dominance. Earnings per share rose to $2.83 in 1974, but slipped again the next year.

At this juncture, Ziegler retired from active direction of the company and sought to hire a successor. The first choice candidate did not remain in the position very long, and Colman Mockler was then asked to step into this position, which he accepted in 1976. Under Mockler, Gillette's strategy was to cut costs dramatically and pour the money saved into ad and product development budgets. The Mockler era was one of the most successful in Gillette history, producing such memorable innovations as the Atra razor, the Good News! disposable razor, and the Daisy razor for women. With such product additions, Gillette not only held a majority of the U.S. shaving market (including the leading shaving cream), but up to 75 percent of market shares in countries around the world.

During this period, Gillette's major marketing war was in disposable lighters. When Cricket was launched in 1972, it was an instant success. Then Bic entered the U.S. market and enticed smokers to "Flick your Bic." A long-term price war ensued in which Bic succeeded in outselling the Cricket by a small margin, but Gillette was persistent.

A principal aim of the Mockler management team in the 1980s was the recovery of the company's earnings to previously established levels. Through a series of aggressive economizing measures and acquisitions, the company was able to show strong growth in earnings per share throughout the decade. Two outside acquisitions played key roles in Gillette's resurgence in the early 1980s. First, Gillette acquired the Liquid Paper Company, the leading maker of typewriter correction fluids. This gave a much needed boost to its writing instruments segment. Second, in what appeared to be a minor acquisition at the time, Gillette purchased a small maker of skin care products, Aapri.

Along with these acquisitions, the introduction of new products that were developed in the Gillette laboratories helped boost sales in the razor and blades, personal care, and writing instruments segments. First, in the razor and blades segment, Gillette introduced the Atra-Plus shaving system, which featured a refillable Atra cartridge with a lubricating strip. This overtook the Trac-II as the number one selling razor. Also, Gillette updated the Good News! line to include a disposable razor with a lubricating strip.

In the personal care segment, Gillette made several introductions, including Aapri facial care products, Dry Idea deodorant, Bare Elegance body lotion, Mink

Difference hair spray, White Rain hair care products, and Silkience shampoo and moisturizers. These additions had mixed results and left Gillette still searching for the keys to success in this business segment.

In the writing instruments segment, Gillette achieved moderate success with the development of Eraser Mate erasable, disposable pens. Also, the steady sales of Paper Mate pens and Liquid Paper correction fluids helped to maintain company performance.

Despite its ability to post above-average performance during the 1980s, many analysts saw Gillette as a stagnant, lazy, sleeping giant, with earnings potential far above current realizations. The analysts based this evaluation on Gillette's considerable name recognition and market power, and its well-established marketing and production channels worldwide. In fact, Gillette's attractiveness led to an unsuccessful takeover attempt in 1986.

Current Business Segments and Products

Having provided the background information on Gillette's activities, we will now review the situation in the various business segments in the latter part of the 1990s. This section is designed to give you an idea of the scope of operations and current product offerings, as well as strategies being pursued in each segment. Exhibits 1 through 3 depict the financial situation as it existed toward the end of 1997. Sales and profits for most segments were well ahead of 1996 numbers and were projected to continue the upward trend of recent years. As Exhibit 1 shows, Gillette is involved in business activities worldwide.

Blades And Razors

Gillette is still the world leader in blades and razors, and this business is growing at a brisk pace. The company holds dominant market share in the United States (68

| EXHIBIT 1 | Financial Information by Geographic Area |

(Millions of Dollars)	Western Europe	Latin America	Other	Total Foreign	United States	Corporate	Total
1996							
Net Sales	$3,067.70	$1,105.20	$1,944.10	$6,117.00	$3,580.70	$–	$9,697.70
Profit from Operations	534.80	210.20	306.10	1,051.10	719.70	-134.50–	1,636.30
Identifiable Assets	3,838.00	1,109.90	$1,549.60	$6,477.50	$3,517.50	440.30–	10,435.30
1995							
Net Sales	$3,031.00	$1,043.10	$1,663.40	$5,737.50	$3,097.00	$–	$8,834.50
Profit from Operations	639.80	235.70	302.80	1,178.30	681.30	– 60.40–	1,799.20
Identifiable Assets	3,754.80	874.10	1,018.40	5,647.30	2,952.00	340.80–	8,940.10
1994							
Net Sales	$2,650.70	$1,031.10	$1,375.00	$5,056.80	$2,878.30	$–	$7,935.10
Profit from Operations	533.90	259.90	234.60	1028.40	636.90	– 50.60–	1,614.70
Identifiable Assets	3,237.20	825.90	887.40	4,950.50	2,496.00	320.80–	7,767.30

percent), Europe (73 percent), and Latin America (91 percent). As Exhibits 2 and 3 illustrate, sales and profits have shown a strong upward trend over the past several years, during which annual gains in sales and profits averaged approximately 10 percent. The blades and razors segment accounts for about 30 percent of its sales and over 50 percent of the company's profits. Sales in this segment have more than doubled to $2.8 billion since 1989, and the outlook for this segment is promising as the shaving population increases, particularly in such locations as Asia, Eastern Europe, and Latin America, and with the increased popularity of shaving among women. The company's progress in its principal line of business reflects the outstanding market success of its technologically superior products, including the Sensor family of shaving systems.

The original Sensor was introduced in early 1990 and is now sold in over 80 markets worldwide. It remains the best seller in the United States and most other major markets. The current top-of-the-line product, the SensorExcel, registered gains in sales and market share in 1996. Gillette leveraged both the Sensor and SensorExcel brand names by developing versions of these products targeted at women. The Sensor for Women system, launched in 1992, holds about one-fourth of the market share for female razor products in the United States. The SensorExcel for women, launched in 1996, was very successful in the key markets where it was introduced. The continued success of the Sensor family of shaving systems has led to the gradual decline of the Atra and Trac II twin blade shaving systems. These systems, key brands since the 1970s, have yielded their standing as market leaders. Despite this gradual decline, both systems continue to hold sizable share positions worldwide. The company's disposable twin blade razors' moderate increases in sales have enabled it to maintain its position as the number one seller in this product category worldwide. Gillette's Good News! brand was the number one disposable razor in the United States for the twenty-first consecutive year in 1996.

In 1998, Gillette introduced a new razor with three thin blades called the Mach3 designed to provide a closer shave in fewer strokes with less irritation than any other razor on the market. To develop this new product, Gillette made major investments in research and development and a strong commitment to gain market share. It is the first major product launch since Gillette introduced Sensor's independently floating double blades in 1977. The Mach3 blades are mounted on tiny springs like Gillette's Sensor Excel. Many analysts believe the razor will help the company continue to exceed its annual earnings increases of 17 percent over the past five years. The introduction of this new razor helps to carry out Gillette's strategy to get customers to switch to more expensive razors with better features. The primary market for the new razor will be current Sensor users. Gillette currently makes six of the top 10 selling razors in the $1.1 billion U.S. market and generates half its earnings from sales of blades. The company planned to make 600 million of the new Mach3 razors the first year and increase that number to 1.2 billion the second year. Gillette plans to have the razor available around the world in two and one-half years.

Gillette is actively pursuing two main growth strategies to strengthen its global blade and razor position. The first is to upgrade the value of the blade market worldwide. In the more developed countries this means further developing its Sensor system franchise and introducing the Mach3. In developing countries, increasing blade value involves accelerating the conversion from double-edge blades to more profitable twin blade products. The second strategy is continued geographic expansion, with the company taking such steps as creating selling organizations in Romania and the former Yugoslavia and the acquisition of blade firms in the former Soviet Union and the Czech Republic.

Toiletries And Cosmetics

The toiletries and cosmetics line includes deodorants, antiperspirants, shave preparations, hair care products, and Jafra skin care and cosmetic products. The strategy for toiletries is to focus resources on core grooming product categories such as deodorants/antiperspirants and shave preparations, while providing supporting products in key markets.

The current product lineup includes Gillette Gel, Satin Care for Women gel, and Foamy shaving creams; Right Guard, Gillette Series, Soft & Dri, and Dry Idea deodorants/antiperspirants; White Rain hair care products; and Jafra skin creams. Sales in this category have increased each year since 1993, and by the end of 1996, the toiletries and cosmetics segment sales were almost 42 percent higher than five years ago. Recent growth in this segment has been fueled by strong demand for clear gel versions of all brands of deodorants/antiperspirants. Other brands contributing to the improved performance of this segment are Gillette Series and Satin Care for Women shaving gels, Gillette Series after shave, and Satin Care skin replenishing system for women. The White Rain brand experienced a decline in sales in 1996 despite strong showings by the White Rain Solutions hair care line and White Rain body wash. Gillette expects this segment to continue its growth through accelerated new product development, technologically superior products, and an expanding world presence.

Stationery Products

Despite intense competition, Gillette has strengthened its position as the worldwide leader in the writing products and correction products businesses. This segment includes Parker, Paper Mate, and Waterman pens and Liquid Paper correction products. With its current writing instrument franchises, Gillette holds a strong position within all writing systems, price levels, distribution channels, and geographic areas. This segment has experienced solid growth in sales and profits in each of the last three years (see Exhibits 2 and 3).

Gillette has been able to grow the Stationery Products segment with a combination of new products and geographic expansion. The company introduced the

EXHIBIT 2   Net Sales and Net Profit Contribution by Business Segment

Year	Blades & Razors Net Sales	Segment Profit	Toiletries & Cosmetics Net Sales	Segment Profit	Stationery Products Net Sales	Segment Profit	Braun Products Net Sales	Segment Profit	Oral-B Products Net Sales	Segment Profit	Duracell Products Net Sales	Segment Profit
1996	29%	52%	14%	4%	10%	6%	18%	14%	6%	3%	23%	21%
1995	30%	51%	14%	4%	10%	6%	18%	14%	5%	2%	23%	23%
1994	30%	53%	15%	5%	10%	6%	17%	12%	5%	1%	23%	23%
1993	30%	53%	15%	5%	10%	6%	17%	12%	5%	1%	23%	23%
1992	29%	51%	14%	7%	8%	4%	20%	12%	5%	3%	24%	23%

EXHIBIT 3	Financial Information by Business Segment

	Blades & Razors	Toiletries & Cosmetics	Stationery Products	Braun Products	Oral-B Products	Duracell Products	Other	Corporate	Total
1996									
Net sales	$2,835.70	$1,375.2	$914.6	$1,773.4	$547.5	$2,250.8	$0.5	–	$9,697.7
Profit from Operations	1,061.80	86.9	122.2	300.3	57.6	142.3	−0.3	−134.5	1,636.3
Identifiable Assets	2,591.2	874.0	1,244.4	1,533.8	595.3	3,153.60	2.7	440.3	10,435.3
Capital Expenditures	353.4	64.7	43.1	119.8	38.1	200.7	0.1	9.8	829.7
Depreciation	95.7	26.4	20.2	77.9	14.8	50.9	0.6	6.1	292.6
1995									
Net sales	$2,634.7	$1,236.2	$862.2	$1,621.1	$440.0	$2,039.8	$0.5	–	$8,834.5
Profit from Operations	960.7	74.9	108.7	254.9	32.9	427.9	−0.4	−60.4	1,799.2
Identifiable Assets	2,123.0	695.3	1,171.2	1,483.1	523.6	2,599.8	3.3	340.8	8,940.1
Capital Expenditures	219.5	54.4	43.5	110.5	39.6	122.0	0.1	3.5	593.1
Depreciation	84.6	28.4	19.1	69.8	11.6	48.0	0.4	3.6	265.5
1994									
Net sales	$2,350.7	$1,162.2	$806.7	$1,348.2	$401.9	$1,864.9	$0.7	–	$7,935.1
Profit from Operations	878.2	79.3	94.9	200.4	25.0	388.0	−0.5	−50.6	1,614.7
Identifiable Assets	1,833.6	615.2	1,103.4	1,089.9	347.5	2,453.9	3.0	320.8	7,767.3
Capital Expenditures	181.1	33.0	30.4	110.0	38.2	98.2	0.4	6.7	498.0
Depreciation	72.5	20.2	23.8	57.3	8.0	42.8	0.4	1.9	226.9

Parker Frontier line of mid-priced writing instruments, Paper Mate Gel-Writer pen, and the Expert II and Phileas lines of Waterman pens. A major geographic expansion occurred in this segment when Gillette began a joint venture with Luxor, the largest writing instrument manufacturer in India. The company instantly assumed leadership in this important market as a result of this joint venture.

Braun

The Braun segment turned in a record performance in 1996, continuing a trend of increased sales and profits (see Exhibits 2 and 3). Growth in this segment was fueled by strong demand for oral care appliances and ThermoScan infrared ear thermometers. The launch of the Oral-B Interclean marked the introduction of the first interdental plaque remover, providing an alternative to manual flossing. The ThermoScan infrared ear thermometer recorded major sales gains and secured market leadership in its first year under Braun management. Geographic expansion of this product was extended to selected markets in Europe and Asia, where customer response was very favorable.

Two other major products in the Braun segment are hair removal products and household appliances. Braun continues to maintain worldwide leadership of the men's electric shaver market, although sales were hurt by unfavorable foreign exchange rates. This leadership position was supported by the Flex Integral family of pivoting head shavers. Women's hair removal products experienced a considerable increase in sales, strengthened by the Braun-epil brand of electric hair eliptors. In the household products area, Braun hand blenders maintained its number one position in the world hand blender market, and the MultiGourmet food steamer and a new range of steam irons were introduced in Europe. However, the household appliance category experienced a decline in sales.

The foundation of Braun's growth strategy is its product philosophy of high-quality, innovative features and outstanding design and efficiently producing a steady stream of technologically superior new products through Braun's vertically integrated and highly automated manufacturing facilities. These strengths, combined with Braun's name recognition and marketing expertise, provide the company with the vital components for success. Braun is expanding the number of its geographic markets, most recently establishing sales operations in Indonesia, Vietnam, and Peru.

Oral-B

In a strong and well-established partnership with dental professionals, Oral-B develops and markets a broad range of superior oral care products worldwide. Led by toothbrushes, the Oral-B line also includes interdental dental products, specialty toothpastes, mouth rinses, and professional dental products. Sales and profits continue to increase for this segment (see Exhibits 2 and 3), and developments in product technology are largely responsible for this increase. For example, the Advantage and Advantage Control Grip models of Oral-B toothbrushes feature micro-textured bristles that are specifically designed to fight plaque with the whole bristle, not just the tip.

Oral-B's strategy for growth relies on a combination of new product development and geographical expansion. The toothbrush category has experienced growth due to the introductions of the Oral-B Pro Plus, Squish Grip and Gripper children's toothbrushes, and a new dental floss that is easy to insert between teeth and resists shredding. Geographic expansion continues with the establishment of sales organizations in Portugal and India, and opening a joint venture toothbrush manufacturing plant in Vietnam. These two strategies for growth will be supported by advertising and promotion in an effort to sustain Oral-B's worldwide growth.

Duracell—Powering Up the Future

With a merger between Gillette and Duracell International at the end of 1996, Gillette instantly achieved worldwide leadership in the alkaline battery business. This segment is key to Gillette's portfolio, with Duracell products generating over one-fifth of the company's sales and profits (see Exhibits 2 and 3). Sales of Duracell products have increased in recent years, and the prospects for growth continue to be promising. The Duracell product line includes alkaline batteries, specialty batteries such as lithium batteries used in cameras and zinc air batteries used to power hearing aids, and high-power rechargeable batteries for use in such consumer products as cellular phones and camcorders.

Gillette's strategies for sustaining growth in the Duracell segment are similar to strategies developed for its existing segments. First, the company emphasizes research and development for new product introductions. For example, Duracell introduced PowerCheck AA batteries, which feature an on-battery, heat-sensitive strip that gauges remaining battery power when activated. This innovative technology was made available on AAA, C, and D batteries in 1997. Second, geographic expansion opportunities exist in this segment. In 1996, Duracell purchased Eveready South Africa, whose zinc carbon battery is the best seller in that country, and Sunpower, a leading alkaline battery brand in South Korea.

Although Gillette has enjoyed solid performances in sales and profits from each of its existing business segments, the company sees the Duracell merger as adding a long-sought "new leg" to its portfolio. Duracell is considered to be an excellent fit with Gillette's focus on technologically driven consumer products. Also, Duracell and Gillette share numerous characteristics, including global brand franchises, common distribution channels, and geographic expansion potential. The company sees opportunities for Duracell to enjoy significant economies of scale and greater market penetration through Gillette's worldwide distribution network.

Perhaps the most attractive aspect of Duracell for Gillette is the market potential of the alkaline batteries category. Duracell has market leadership in alkaline batteries, and the global battery market is expected to nearly double in size, to an estimated $7 billion annually, by the year 2000. Among the reasons for this growth are the booming popularity of portable electronic products, aggressive merchandising by battery manufacturers, and constant performance improvements, especially in battery lifetime (for instance, the "run time" of a portable personal stereo powered by a pair of AA batteries had been stretched from 11-12 hours in 1984 to nearly 20 hours in 1997).

Duracell can benefit from the growing market in three ways. First, geographic expansion opportunities exist for Duracell given the fact that only one-fifth of Duracell's business is now in markets outside Europe and North America. In international markets where Duracell has not been strongly represented, there are quick, clear benefits to be gained from the linkage with Gillette's well-established marketing and distribution networks. Second, opportunities exist in both new and established markets to upgrade customers from lower-value zinc carbon batteries to better-performing, longer-lasting Duracell alkaline technology. Alkaline batteries deliver five to six times the life for two to three times the price. This upgrade opportunity is strikingly clear in the emerging countries of China, India, and Russia. These three countries account for some 30 percent of the world's consumer battery market but less than 5 percent of batteries currently sold in these countries is alkaline. Third, Duracell's focus on improving its alkaline technology could significantly expand the capabilities of alkaline batteries, thus dramatically expanding their worldwide market. In February 1998, Duracell set a new standard in quality with Duracell Ultra, a new line of AA and AAA batteries specially designed to be used in powerful digital cameras, cellular phones, and remote-controlled toys. It is estimated that the Ultra has a 50 percent longer life than current alkaline batteries. The company believes that the 20 percent price above regular alkaline batteries will be accepted because of the extended battery life.

Ultra was the result of four years of development in which Duracell improved the performance of the alkaline design by reducing electrical resistance and reformulating the battery's chemistry. However, Duracell was not the only company tweaking batteries for high-tech products. Eastman Kodak, the fourth-place player in the battery battle, launched the Photolife AA which claims to outlast competitors' batteries in digital cameras. Also, number two Energizer promoted AA and AAA batteries as superior for high drain devices such as mini-disc players and cell phones.

Alkaline batteries face competition from rechargeable batteries, as well. However, alkaline offers more convenience to consumers because the internal construction allows for storage of more than twice as much energy as a comparably sized rechargeable. To exploit Ultra's potential, Duracell must convince rechargeable users to switch to alkaline.

Toward The Future

Gillette has plans to continue its impressive performance into the 21st century. CEO Zeien leads the emphasis on development of new products; he predicts that 50 percent of Gillette's sales will soon come from products introduced within the past five years. Two segments seem to demand special attention from top management in the coming years. First, the stationery products segment lacks "home-run" products similar to the SensorExcel and Mach3 in the Blades and Razors segment, and competition is intense. Second, the Duracell merger gives the company an established brand in the battery product category, but it must integrate Duracell into Gillette's intensive product development efforts.

Questions for Discussion

1. What are the current conditions in each of Gillette's business segments? Is each business segment moving in the right direction? Do you see new products that should be added or old products that should be eliminated? Which products and why?

2. Identify the environmental variables (market, competition, government, technology) that have affected Gillette over its life. Which have had the greatest positive and negative impacts? At the present time, what do you perceive to be the chief environmental forces with which Gillette must cope?

3. What actions would you recommend over the next five years? What specific marketing mix decisions would you recommend for each business segment? What is the time frame for your actions?

SOURCES

These facts are from Wes Conard, "3-blade razor a cut above, Gillette says," *The Commercial Appeal,* Apr. 15, 1998; Gillette 1997 Annual Report; "Gillette's Edge," Business Week, January 19, 1998, 70-77; "How Gillette is Honing Its Edge," *Business Week,* Sept. 28, 1992, 60; Gillette Company, 1991 Annual Report; Gillette Series Marketing Support Report, Gillette Company 1992; Lawrence Ingrassia, "Gillette Ties New Toiletries to Hot Razor," *Wall Street Journal,* Sept. 18, 1992, B1, B6; Lawrence Ingrassia, "Keeping Sharp," *Wall Street Journal,* Dec. 10, 1992, Al; A6; and Seema Nayyar, "Gillette Jumps Into Men's Toiletries," *Brandweek,* July 20, 1992, 6.

Columbia/HCA[1]

Columbia/HCA Healthcare Corporation is one of the largest health care services companies in the United States. As of December 31, 1996, the company operated 343 hospitals, 136 outpatient surgery centers, and approximately 550 home health locations and provided extensive outpatient and ancillary services in 37 states, the United Kingdom, and Switzerland. With revenues of nearly $20 billion, Columbia was the seventh-largest U.S. employer. The stated mission of Columbia was "to work with our employees, affiliated physicians and volunteers to provide a continuum of quality healthcare, cost-effectively for the people in the communities we serve." The vision for Columbia was "to work with employees and physicians to build a company that is focused on the well-being of people, that is patient-oriented, that offers the most advanced technology and information systems, that is financially sound, and that is synonymous with quality, cost-effective healthcare."

Columbia/HCA built the nation's largest chain of hospitals based on cost effectiveness and financial performance. New hospitals were acquired and health services provided throughout the nation by developing competitive advantages with internal control of costs and sales activities. The focus was bottom line performance and new business acquisition. Although Columbia had a stated mission and value statement, quality care of patients was only a small part of that statement. Quality efforts were run by nonphysicians from sales and marketing departments. For example, the frequency of home health care visits often increased dramatically after a new unit was acquired.

A number of critics have charged that health care services and staffing often took a back seat to the focus on profits. For example, short training periods were used as opposed to training time provided by competitive hospitals. One former administrator indicated that training that typically takes six months was sometimes done in as little as two weeks in a Columbia/HCA hospital. In 1995, a Columbia women's hospital in Indianapolis decreased nursing staff to save money. The hospital was fined $25,000 for failing to keep appropriate staffing. The company reorganized and re-engineered job titles and redefined duties of many staff at

---

[1] This case was prepared by O. C. Ferrell, Colorado State University, for classroom discussion rather than to illustrate either effective or ineffective handling of an administrative situation. Research assistance was provided by Rachel Smith, The University of Memphis.

Columbia/HCA hospitals. For example, in one hospital, the concept of a "patient's support associate" included unlicensed personnel—housekeepers, patient-care assistants, physical therapy aides, orderlies, EKG technicians, and others—who are trained to perform some, but not all, of each other's duties. Some housekeepers, for example, received a few weeks of training in drawing blood and other skills (there is no license required to draw blood). In addition, the company was accused of patient dumping. Patient dumping involves discharging emergency room patients or transferring them to other hospitals without the patient being in a stable condition. In 1997, officials at the Department of Health and Human Services Inspector General's office indicated that they were considering imposing fines on Columbia/HCA for an unspecified number of patient dumping cases.

Columbia/HCA aggressively recruited doctors to be co-owners in the growing business of outpatient surgical centers. Local doctors were often asked to buy stock through a limited partnership agreement. The company's hard-driving sales tactics came under scrutiny as the outpatient surgical units were considered a conflict of interest by many critics.

The Problems Begin

In late July 1997, a hospital in Florida was named as the focal point of the biggest case of health care fraud in the health care industry. The focus of a government probe was Fawcett Memorial Hospital in Port Charlotte, Florida. An investigation resulted in the indictment of three mid-level Columbia/HCA Healthcare Corporation executives that charged them with filing false cost reports for Fawcett resulting in losses of more than $4.4 million from government programs. Federal investigators seized hospital documents relating to its home health care services and its close relationships with doctors, as well as charges of defrauding the Federal Medicare and military healthcare programs by inflating reimbursement requests. The government declared a criminal investigation, meaning that there was evidence to indict not only individual Columbia executives but also alleging that the company was involved in systematic organizational efforts to defraud the government. The government alleged that at least part of the profit obtained by Columbia was gained by overcharging for Medicare and other federal health programs by unscrupulous executives who billed the government for non-reimbursable interest expenses. Other concerns were illegal incentives to physicians and possible overuse of home health services.

Top Columbia Officials Are Seen As Key to Problems

Federal investigators claimed that Columbia/HCA Healthcare Corporation engaged in a "systematic effort to defraud government health care programs." In a 74-page document made public, federal investigators quote confidential witnesses saying that former Columbia Chief Executive Officer Richard Scott and former President David Vandewater were routinely briefed on issues relating to Medicare reimbursement claims that the government charged were fraudulent. It was also claimed that Samuel Greco, Columbia's former chief of operations, also knew of alleged fraud that resulted in the indictment of three Columbia officials affiliated with Fawcett Memorial Hospital in Port Charlotte.

In addition, confidential witnesses said that Columbia made an effort to hide internal documents from federal regulators that could have disclosed the alleged fraud and that Columbia's top executive in charge of internal audits instructed employees to soften the language used in internal financial audits critical of Columbia practices. According to the affidavit signed by FBI agent Joseph Ford, "investigation by the [Federal Bureau of Investigation] and the [Defense Criminal Investigative Service] has uncovered a systematic corporate scheme perpetrated by corporate officers and managers of Columbia's hospitals, home health agencies, and other facilities in the states of Tennessee, Florida, Georgia, Texas, and elsewhere to defraud Medicare, Medicaid, and the [Civilian Health and Medical Program of the Uniformed Services]."

Columbia officials indicted pleaded "not guilty" and defense lawyers for Columbia tried to diminish the importance of the allegations contained in the government's affidavits. Although a Columbia spokesperson said the company is cooperating with the government, other allegations included:

- Columbia officials at the Nashville headquarters transferred $800,000 in fictitious expenses to a Columbia hospital in Florida so that it could show higher costs and get higher Medicare reimbursements.
- Columbia stamped "attorney/client privilege" on audit reports to hide results.
- Officials under indictment told a co-worker to steer a Medicare auditor away from sensitive cost figures or offer the auditor a job.
- Columbia had a "corporate policy" to shift hospitals' overhead costs to its home health care units so it could bill Medicare for more money.
- A former administrator alleged in a lawsuit that the hospital fired her for whistle-blowing that other executives had destroyed documents.

Developing a New Corporate Culture at Columbia/HCA

Soon after the investigation was launched, Dr. Thomas Frist, Jr. was hired as chairman and chief executive. Frist had been president of Hospital Corporation of America, which had been merged with Columbia. Frist vowed to cooperate fully with the government and develop a 100-day plan to change the corporate culture. Under the Federal Sentencing Guidelines for Organizations, companies with effective due diligence compliance programs may receive reduced organizational fines if convicted of fraud. Although the requirements are that a senior executive be in charge of compliance, Columbia's general counsel had been overseeing the company's existing compliance program. In order for penalties to be reduced, an effective compliance program must be in place before misconduct occurs, and any crimes that occur after indictment for criminal activities will be even more severely punished.

After 100 days as chairman and chief executive of Columbia/HCA, Dr. Frist outlined changes that would reshape Columbia. His reforms included a new mission statement and support for the new senior executive to oversee legal compliance and quality issues. The new mission statement emphasizes a commitment to quality medical care and honesty in business practices. It makes no mention of financial performance.

"We have to take the company in a new direction," Dr. Frist said. "The days when Columbia/HCA was seen as an adversarial or in your face, a behind-closed-doors kind of place, is a thing of the past." The corporate culture was viewed as so unethical by some managers that they had resigned before the fraud investigation.

Columbia/HCA hired corporate ethics specialist, Alan Yuspeh, as senior vice president of ethics, compliance, and corporate responsibility. Yuspeh was given a staff of 12 at the corporate headquarters and was assigned to work with group, division, and facility presidents to create a "corporate culture where Columbia workers feel compelled to do what is right." Yuspeh indicated that his first initiatives would be to refine monitoring techniques, boost workers' ethics and compliance training, develop a code of conduct for employees, and create an internal mechanism for workers to report any wrongdoing. The Inspector General's office of the Department of Health and Human Services has developed a model compliance programs for hospitals. Yuspeh said he wanted to build the model ethics and compliance program for the health care industry. Because only about 5 percent of the 5,400 hospitals and medical schools in the United States have comprehensive compliance programs, the Department of Health and Human Services plans to release its suggestions for a model program.

Columbia/HCA Changes Rapidly

Immediately after announcing a new mission and vision for the company, organizational restructuring started. The company announced that it would be changing its name to create a new image as it continues to battle the federal fraud investigation. The company removed large, lighted Columbia signs with the company icon from the sites of its headquarters building and canopies over its entrances in Nashville, Tennessee. This act indicated the Columbia name had been damaged by negative publicity. Within a few weeks, 25 percent of the hospitals had dropped "Columbia" from their name. Consumers, doctors, and the general public had lost confidence in Columbia as an institution. Columbia's stock price dropped over 50 percent from its 1997 high and new management was much more concerned about developing a compliance program than growth and profits. At a conference in Phoenix, 20 Columbia managers were asked by a show of hands how many of them had escaped taunts from friends about being a crook. No hands went up, and the discussion was not on surgery profit margins but on resolving the investigation and the importance of the intangible corporate image and values.

As of mid-1998, Columbia had not held serious settlement talks with the government concerning allegations of overbilling Medicare. A number of health care fraud experts have predicted that Columbia could pay fines as high as $1 billion to settle the allegations.

In addition, a restructuring may include the possible sale of one-third of its 340 hospitals and the spinoff or sale of 33 of its 148 freestanding surgery centers. Currently, the company is consolidating into 18 divisions from 36 and reorganizing its core hospital business into five groups, of which three are slated for spinoff or sale. The goal is to return the company's attention to local hospitals and health care networks. It is estimated that the restructuring may take 12 to 18 months and is unlikely to be completed until after Columbia resolves its conflict with the federal government.

The efforts to quickly change the corporate culture and become the model corporate citizen in health care is a real challenge for what was Columbia/HCA.

This health care provider learned the hard way that maintaining an organizational ethical climate is the responsibility of top management.

Developing an Ethical Compliance Program

Compliance, including both ethical and legal issues, will continue to be at the forefront of organizational concerns as managers and employees face increasingly complex decisions in the 21st century. An organizational compliance effort establishes formal accountability and responsibility for appropriate organizational conduct. An effective program has the potential to encourage all employees to understand organizational values and ethical climate and to comply with policies and codes of conduct that create a good citizen organization. It takes into account values, ethics, and legal requirements, helping an organization develop trust and prevent misconduct.

The federal government created the United States Sentencing Commission to institutionalize ethical compliance programs and help prevent illegal activity. Its Federal Sentencing Guidelines for Organizations (FSGO), approved by Congress in 1991, broke new ground by codifying into law incentives for organizations to develop effective internal compliance programs to prevent misconduct. Of critical importance is the fact that these guidelines hold businesses accountable for the misconduct of their employees. The sentencing guidelines take a carrot-and-stick approach. Companies that lack effective ethical compliance programs can incur severe penalties if their employees violate the law. The seven recommended steps to develop an effective program include: (1) establishing codes of conduct, (2) appointing or hiring a high-level compliance manager, (3) taking care in delegation of authority, (4) instituting a training program and communication system, (5) monitoring and auditing for misconduct, (6) enforcing and providing for discipline, and (7) revising the program as needed. Many organizations are implementing integrity programs based on these seven recommendations. Alan Yuspeh, the new Columbia/HCA senior vice president of ethics, compliance and corporate responsibility, was a leader in developing this seven-step compliance program for firms in the defense industry.

Creating an ethical workplace requires an understanding of the challenges and pressures that most employees face on a daily basis. Developing a strategic approach to compliance will provide an organization with a way to manage legal and ethical issues and to improve its relationships with employees, customers, and other constituencies. An ethics program will only be effective if it becomes a part of the core values and corporate culture that influence decisions on a daily basis. Just as quality management principles have become commonplace, the future will require that organizations also have an effective program for workplace integrity.

Health Care Provider Compliance Programs

The Office of Inspector General (OIG) and the Department of Health and Human Services (HHS) have supplied health care providers with industry-specific compliance program guidelines. Fashioned upon the framework of the Federal Sentencing Guidelines for Organizations' seven-step program previously discussed, these two agencies have embarked upon a mission to provide for various health care provider segments a more specific and targeted set of guidelines. The specific guidelines strive to assist health care providers in developing effective internal controls that promote adherence to applicable federal and state law and the program requirements of federal, state, and private health plans by expanding upon each guideline. In February 1998, a "Compliance Program Guidance for Hospitals" was released. It represents the OIG's suggestions on how a hospital can best establish internal controls and monitoring procedures to correct and prevent fraudulent activities. Based on the seven steps, these guidelines specify requirements for a minimum comprehensive compliance program.

The guidelines are only a framework for organizing a specific program that addresses risks. The seven steps are necessary but not sufficient for an effective compliance program. One of the prevailing tenets of the guidelines is that there is no one special compliance program for all providers. No prototype exists that fits all organizations. It is not a procedure but a guide for planning compliance activities. The seven basic elements of the hospital guidelines can be used by all hospitals, regardless of size, location, and structure. The OIG recognizes that all entities must internalize the guidelines, and it implores organizations to structure them to fit their unique organization. The Sentencing Guidelines acknowledge that different organizations require different kinds of compliance programs. It follows then that larger organizations will have more formal compliance programs.

According to the OIG, the adoption and implementation of voluntary compliance programs significantly advance the prevention of fraud, abuse and waste in health care plans while furthering the fundamental mission of all hospitals—providing quality care to patients. Compliance programs guide a provider's governing body, chief executive officer, managers, employees, physicians, and other health care professionals in the management and operation of the organization. The program is especially germane in the reimbursement and payment areas where claims and billing operations can be the source of fraud and abuse. Compliant efforts help to establish a culture within a health care provider that promotes prevention, detection, and resolution of conduct that does not conform to federal and state regulations. In the past, health care compliance endeavors have included statistical audits, medical reviews, and fraud detection. Typically the reviews were funded by the Health Care Financing Administration (HCFA) in its contracts with intermediaries such as Blue Cross/Blue Shield.

Soon after the investigation into Columbia, regional FBI officers urged hospital executives to reform their own industry because law enforcement's interest in health care fraud was not waning. The FBI defined physician referral fees as "kickbacks" and urged executives to be upfront in any gray areas related to Medicare reimbursements. Not only has the FBI brought on former hospital administrators as agents, but it has also encouraged competing hospitals and insurance companies to blow the whistle on improper billing practices and referrals. The statement has been made that hospital administrators are the ones responsible for making sure that the health care industry operates ethically. On the other hand, if the FBI and the U.S. Attorney's office can prove "a pattern of corruption and conspiracy" in a hospital, federal law allows the government to seize the hospital's property and ban it from participating in federal health care programs. It is estimated that three out of four hospitals face scrutiny from the Department of Justice's probe of Medicare billing. To help hospitals set up compliance programs, the American Hospital Association is working with Coopers & Lybrand to offer a video, workbook, help line, and web site. The case of Columbia/HCA is ongoing but provides an incentive for other hospitals to install an ethical compliance program as suggested by the Federal Sentencing Guidelines for Organizations.

Columbia/HCA Launches Ethics and Compliance Training Program

By February 1998, Columbia released a press statement indicating it was taking a critical step in developing a company-wide ethics, compliance, and corporate responsibility program. The company designated more than 500 employees as facility Ethics and Compliance Officers (ECOs). The new ECOs started with a two-day training session in Nashville. The facility ECOs will be the key links in making sure the company continues to develop a culture of ethical conduct and corporate responsibility. Local leadership for each facility will bring the overall ethics program for Columbia/HCA to its full implementation. As the compliance officer, Alan Yuspeh was focused on developing a world-class ethics and compliance program for the company. Yuspeh made a 15-minute videotape that was sent to managers throughout the Columbia/HCA system announcing the launch of the compliance training program and the unveiling of a code of ethics that was designed to communicate effectively Columbia's new emphasis on compliance, integrity, and social responsibility. Columbia's chairman and chief executive officer, Thomas F. Frist, Jr., M.D., said, "we are making a substantial investment in our ethics and compliance program in order to ensure its success" and "instituting a values-based culture throughout this company is something our employees have told us is critical to forming our future. The ethics and compliance initiative is a key part of that effort."

Actions taken to date at Columbia/HCA include: (1) development of a Code of Conduct intended to guide employees through ethical and compliance issues in their daily work, (2) production of a videotaped training program on the code, (3) creation of numerous policies to support the code of conduct, (4) establishment of a compliance committee of the board of directors and an internal compliance committee, (5) appointment of ECOs at each facility, and (6) development of an enhanced ethics hotline for employees to report ethics and compliance issues.

The training seminars include introductions to the training program that each ECO will be expected to implement locally, as well as the code of conduct and the overall ethics and compliance program. The program also includes presentations from senior management and small group discussions in which participants will discuss application of the new code of conduct in ethics related scenarios.

Yuspeh has said he does not believe that the program will have to change personal values. Although the company wants individuals to bring their highest sense of personal values to work each day, the purpose of the program is to help employees understand how strictly a company defines ethical behavior. Columbia/HCA's ethical guidelines tackle basic issues like whether nurses can accept tips—they can't—and complicated topics, such as what constitutes Medicare fraud. In addition to random audits and continuing education on ethics topics, the hotline deals with employees' billing questions. The company has developed certification tests for employees who determine billing codes. A 40-minute training video was shown in April 1998 to all 285,000 employees and featured three ethical scenarios for employees to examine.

Questions for Discussion

1. Columbia developed competitive advantages with internal control of cost and sales activities. What was the fundamental marketing strategy mistake in developing long-term profitability?

2. Evaluate the progress made in changing corporate and marketing strategy in the "new" Columbia.

3. Evaluate the ethical compliance program that Alan Yuspeh has established at Columbia.

Sources

The OIG's Compliance Program Guidelines for Hospitals, 1998; Columbia/HCA Healthcare Corporation 1996 Annual Report to Stockholders; Kurt Eichenwald and N.R. Kleinfield, "At Columbia/HCA, scandal hurts," *The Commercial Appeal*, Dec. 21, 1997, C1, C3; "Columbia/HCA Launches Ethics and Compliance Training Program," AOL News, Feb. 12, 1998; Charles Ornstein, "Columbia/HCA prescribes employee ethics program," *The Tampa Tribune*, Feb. 20, 1998, 4; Tom Lowry, "Loss warning hits Columbia/HCA stock," *USA Today*, Feb. 9, 1998, 2B; "Columbia/HCA changing name and revising signs," *The Commercial Appeal*, Nov. 19, 1997, B7; Kevin Drawbaugh, "Columbia to refocus business," *The Commercial Appeal*, Nov. 18, 1997, B5, B10; Michael Connor, "Whistle-blowing got woman fired, suit says," *The Commercial Appeal*, Nov. 6, 1997, B4, B8; Kurt Eichenwald, "Reshaping the Culture at Columbia/HCA," *The New York Times*, Nov. 4, 1997, C2; Tom Lowry, "Columbia/HCA hires ethics expert," *USA Today*, Oct. 14, 1997, 4B; Lucette Lagnado, "Columbia Taps Lawyer for Ethics Post: Yuspeh Led Defense Initiative of 1980s," *The Wall Street Journal*, Oct. 14, 1997, B6; Eva M. Rodriguez and Lucette Lagnado, "Top Columbia Officials Seen Key to Fraud," *The Wall Street Journal*, Oct. 7, 1997, A3; Chris Woodyard, "FBI alleges systemic fraud at Columbia," *USA Today*, Oct. 7, 1997, 1B; Tom Lowry, "Columbia still woos doctors as business partners," *USA Today*, Oct. 3, 1997, 1B; Vickie Chachere, "Fraud warning issued," *The Tampa Tribune*, Sept. 26, 1997, 5; Kris Hundley, "In the Eye of a Storm," *Times*, Sept. 15, 1997, 8– 10; "Executive departs besieged Columbia," *Times*, Sept. 12, 1997, 1; Eva M. Rodriguez, "Columbia/HCA Probe Turns to Marketing Billing," *The Wall Street Journal*, Aug. 21, 1997, A2; Joseph B. White, "Suits by Two Big Public Pension Funds Broaden the Attack on Columbia/HCA," *The Wall Street Journal*, Aug. 19, 1997, A20; Anita Sharpe, "Columbia/HCA Confirms Departures of Another 2 Executives, More Expected," *The Wall Street Journal*, Aug. 15, 1997, B5; Lucette Lagnado and Steven Lipin, "Columbia/HCA Is Object of HealthSouth Interest," *The Wall Street Journal*, Aug. 15, 1997, A3; Eva M. Rodriguez, "Columbia May Have Destroyed Data," *The Wall Street Journal*, Aug. 14, 1997, A3; Eva M. Rodriguez, "Health Giant Is Targeted in U.S. Probe," *The Wall Street Journal*, Aug. 13, 1997, A3; Greg Jaffe, Anita Sharpe, and Eva M. Rodriguez, "Columbia/HCA Turns Over Key Cost Records," *The Wall Street Journal*, Aug. 8, 1997, B3; Eva M. Rodriguez, "Florida Becomes Third State to Probe Medicaid Billings of Columbia/HCA," *The Wall Street Journal*, Aug. 6, 1997, B6; and Anita Sharpe, "Bovender Joins Frist Team at Columbia/HCA," *The Wall Street Journal*, Aug. 5, 1997, A3.

Federal Express[1]

Frederick W. Smith founded the Federal Express Corporation in 1973 with part of an $8 million inheritance. At the time, the U.S. Postal Service and United Parcel Service (UPS) provided the only means of delivering letters and packages, and they often took several days or more to get packages to their destinations. While a student at Yale in 1965, Smith wrote a paper proposing an independent, overnight delivery service. Although he received a C on the paper, Smith never lost sight of his vision. He recognized that time is money in today's high-tech world, and he believed that many businesses would be willing to pay more to get letters, documents, and packages delivered overnight. He was right.

Federal Express began shipping packages overnight from Memphis, Tennessee on April 17, 1973. On that first night of operations, the company handled six packages, one of which was a birthday present sent by Smith himself. Today, FedEx, as the company is now called, handles about 3 million packages and documents per day—a figure that gives the company more than 50 percent of the total overnight delivery market and 43 percent of the total express delivery market. FedEx's total revenue in 1997 was an astounding $11.5 billion. According to the company, FedEx is not in the package and document transport business; it moves information around the globe for both private consumers and industrial customers.

FedEx offers a valuable service to anyone who needs letters, documents, and packages delivered overnight. When a customer needs a package shipped, a FedEx courier picks up the package and takes it to a local FedEx office, where it is trucked to the nearest airport. FedEx serves roughly 325 airports worldwide. The package is usually flown to one of the company's distribution hubs for sorting, and then flown to the airport nearest its destination. The package is then trucked to another FedEx office where a courier picks it up and hand delivers it to the correct recipient. All of this takes place overnight, with many packages being delivered before 10:30 a.m. the next day. Couriers use handheld computers to keep track of packages. FedEx confirms that more than 98 percent of its deliveries are made on time.

To accomplish this amazingly high delivery rate, FedEx maintains an impressive infrastructure of equipment and processes. The company owns approximately

---

[1] This case was prepared by O. C. Ferrell, Colorado State University, and Michael D. Hartline, Louisiana State University, for classroom discussion rather than to illustrate either effective or ineffective handling of an administrative situation.

34,000 drop boxes and 14,000 service centers and airport facilities around the world. FedEx owns a fleet of 610 airplanes and 40,500 trucks and vans that travel 2.5 million miles every day to ensure accurate delivery. The company even has its own weather forecasting service, ensuring that most of its flights arrive within 15 minutes of schedule. Most packages shipped within the United States are sorted at the Memphis superhub, where FedEx takes over control of the Memphis International Airport at roughly 11 p.m. each night. FedEx planes land side-by-side on parallel runways every minute or so for well over one hour each night. After the sorting of packages, all FedEx planes take off in time to reach their destinations. Not all packages are shipped via air. When possible, FedEx uses ground transportation to save on expenses. For international deliveries, FedEx uses a combination of direct services and independent contractors.

FedEx's pricing structure is based on the distance a package must travel to reach its final destination. FedEx charges $12.50 to $19 for its Priority Overnight Service, which offers next-day delivery of letter packages by 10:30 a.m. The company's Standard Overnight Delivery Service, which offers next-day afternoon delivery by 3 p.m., costs from $10.75 to $17.50. For an extra $3, customers can have a courier pick up the package rather than having to drop it off at a FedEx office or drop box. Prices vary for larger packages and international shipments. Although the U.S. Postal Service charges less for its Express Mail delivery service and UPS charges less for its overnight letter delivery, FedEx believes it offers customers more service and efficiency for its price.

Growing Pains

Despite its tremendous success, FedEx has had to face some difficult times in its efforts to grow and compete against strong rival firms. The overnight delivery market matured very rapidly as intense competition from the U.S. Postal Service, UPS, Emery, DHL, RPS, and electronic document delivery (i.e., fax machines and e-mail) forced FedEx to search for viable means of expansion. In 1984, facing a growing threat from electronic document delivery, FedEx introduced its ZapMail service for customers who could not afford expensive fax machines. For $35, FedEx would fax up to 10 pages of text to any FedEx site around the world. The document was then hand delivered to its recipient. Soon after the service was introduced, the price of fax machines plummeted, ultimately forcing FedEx to drop ZapMail after losing over $190 million. Many analysts still argue that the overnight delivery market could eventually lose as much as 30 percent of its letter business to electronic document delivery, especially to e-mail.

After its experience with ZapMail, FedEx began to focus its resources on expanding its overseas operations, the most rapidly growing area of the overnight market. In an increasingly global economy, businesses must be able to communicate quickly with employees around the world, with partners in other nations, with other businesses, and with customers. Though FedEx had been shipping packages from the United States to Canada since 1975, its acquisition of Gelco International in 1984 enabled FedEx to expand its operations to Europe and the Far East. Political changes in foreign markets—such as the establishment of the European Economic Community and the dismantling of once-closed Eastern European markets—allowed FedEx to gain entry into large, untapped markets.

FedEx's most important strategic move into international markets was its 1988 purchase of Tiger International Inc., owner of the Flying Tiger Line air freight service. The $880 million purchase gave FedEx valuable routes, airport facilities, and expertise in European and Asian markets that it had been struggling to enter. Such valuable assets would have taken the company years to develop on its own. The purchase also gave the company valuable landing slots in Sydney, Singapore, Bangkok, Hong Kong, Seoul, Paris, Brussels, and Tokyo. However, the purchase of Flying Tiger created some problems for FedEx. The purchase left the company with a debt of $2.1 billion. It also thrust FedEx into the heavy-freight distribution market, which was more cyclical and capital intensive than small-package distribution. In addition, many of Tiger's key customers, including UPS, were competitors of FedEx. Finally, FedEx had trouble integrating Tiger's 6,500 union employees into its own nonunion work force. Despite the difficulties in merging the two companies, the merger was a key ingredient in making FedEx a powerful global delivery service.

By 1991, the company had taken advantage of its opportunities and was offering international service to more than 100 countries. By 1992, next-morning service was available to and from major markets including Paris, London, Frankfurt, Milan, Brussels, Geneva, Zurich, Antwerp, Amsterdam, Hong Kong, Tokyo, Singapore, and Seoul. FedEx's Canadian operations remained strong, and the company's operations in Latin America were growing. Despite this success, however, FedEx's international operations were troublesome. This was particularly true in Europe, where the total volume of express shipments between European countries was only 150,000 packages per night. Deciding that the intra-European market lacked potential, FedEx abandoned it and closed some domestic businesses in Italy, Germany, France, and the United Kingdom. The company took a $254 million restructuring charge in the third quarter of its 1992 fiscal year to cover the closures. FedEx then restricted its European focus to shipments to and from Europe, rather than within Europe. By the end of 1992, FedEx experienced a total loss of $113 million and a negative earnings per share of $2.11. Company officials pointed to several reasons for the losses. First, the company was still recovering from its purchase of Flying Tiger, which increased its fixed costs in international operations. Second, FedEx had difficulty building a global infrastructure to support its operations. Negotiating for landing rights, dealing with foreign customs regulations, and establishing information networks all proved to be very costly.

Despite the problems in Europe, FedEx was doing very well in Asia. The Asian economy was growing rapidly—seven of the top 10 growth economies at the time were in Asia. Additionally, Asia's manufactured product exports were increasing at a rate of 28 percent per year. To capitalize on this growth, FedEx introduced its "AsiaOne" network in 1995. AsiaOne is an express network that offers effective "late-day" pick ups and "next-day" deliveries not only across Asia, but also between Asia and North America. This quick service is due in part to FedEx's unparalleled capability to gain Asian air-route authority. For instance, FedEx is the only U.S.-based cargo firm allowed to fly its own planes throughout China, or to fly between Asia and Tokyo. The AsiaOne network attempts to provide quick, reliable package delivery to and from Asia, backed up by a money-back guarantee. Customers could now purchase next-day delivery from Asia to the United States, Canada, or Latin America, and vice-versa. The overall growth of the Asian market is forecasted to continue for some time. FedEx's 1996 Asian revenue was approximately $100 million. By 2016, Asian revenue is expected to reach over $325 million.

Recent Developments

In 1997, FedEx became the only cargo carrier allowed to fly its own aircraft and utilize its own warehousing facilities in Moscow. This was a breakthrough for FedEx because the Moscow market is forecasted to grow at least 30 percent by 2000. This exclusive capability allows FedEx customers to receive reliable next-business-day service (by 10:30 a.m.) from Moscow to North America and Western Europe. Likewise, FedEx offers two- to three-day service between Moscow and many Asian cities. FedEx has instituted a similar plan from the United States to Argentina, as projections indicate that the South American market will grow substantially.

FedEx has recently introduced several new services. The "International First" service, which refers to next-day or two-day international service by 8:00 a.m., is now available to the United States from 18 international countries (United Kingdom, France, Germany, Belgium, Italy, Switzerland, The Netherlands, Luxembourg, Spain, Ireland, South Africa, Israel, Japan, Hong Kong, Macao, Taiwan, Puerto Rico, and Canada). FedEx also improved its International Priority service from noon delivery to 10:30 a.m. delivery. This enhanced delivery schedule is available from the United States to over 12 European cities. Given that firms are increasingly working seven day weeks, FedEx added Sunday delivery in early 1998. Customers can now ship letters and packages on a Priority Overnight basis that guarantees delivery by 3 p.m. Sunday to the 50 largest U.S. markets. All of FedEx's traditional service features are available for the new Sunday service (e.g., 24 hour package tracking and money-back guarantees).

By far the most important recent development for FedEx is its acquisition of Caliber System, a trucking company whose RPS subsidiary is second only to UPS in ground shipments. The $2.7 billion merger created a new holding company, called FDX, which owns both FedEx and Caliber System. FedEx and RPS will be run as separate companies; however, they will share a common information interface that will allow FedEx customers to track packages with all FDX subsidiaries. RPS's fleet of 13,500 trucks will help FedEx grow and compete more effectively with UPS in the non-express, ground-delivery business. The purchase of Caliber System, along with the 1997 strike by UPS employees, allowed FedEx to steal business from UPS and increase its market share by two points to 43 percent—far and away the dominant share in the industry. The purchase of RPS not only makes FedEx more profitable, it also makes FedEx more attractive to current and potential customers. Now, FedEx has the ability to fulfill any customer's needs by providing one-stop shopping for express and non-express shipping and delivery.

Looking Toward the Future

FedEx is now concentrating on a new corporate strategy, termed "V3" (i.e., Vision, Value, and Virtual), to lead it into the next decade. The first component of the new strategy, Vision, focuses on satisfying customers' dynamic shipping and delivery needs. To do so, FedEx continuously strives to improve its express delivery services by enhancing its distribution networks, transportation infrastructure, information technology, and employee performance. Currently, no other package carrier can match FedEx's global capabilities. However, FedEx is not ready to rest on its laurels. Instead, FedEx aggressively pursues new routing authorities, information technology advancements, and more efficient and effective routing plans.

FedEx's employees and corporate culture are also important parts of the Vision of V3. Because FedEx depends heavily on its employees to deliver its services, the company strives to hire the best people and offers them the best training and compensation in the industry. As a result, FedEx employees are loyal, highly efficient, and extremely effective in delivering good service. In fact, FedEx employees claim to have "purple blood" to match the company's official color.

The second component of the V3 strategy is Value. FedEx strives to provide more value to its customers. A recent example of this effort is the company's move to distance-based pricing, where the price of FedEx services depends on how far the package must travel to reach its destination. For example, New York customers now pay less to ship a package to Michigan than to ship the same package to California. Distance-based pricing helps customers save money on short-distance shipments. The change has also increased FedEx's yield—or average revenue per package—to $15.11. Another way FedEx attempts to increase customer value is by improving its own transportation efficiencies to the point where customers can turn over some or all of their own distribution to FedEx. FedEx provides consultants to its customers to help them redesign their distribution networks to include FedEx services. Due to FedEx's massive distribution network and economies of scale, the end result is a major cost savings for the customer. For example, IBM employed FedEx to warehouse parts for its workstations, which enabled IBM to cut its delivery costs and close 120 parts depots.

The third component of the V3 strategy is Virtual. In the past several years, FedEx has invested heavily in information technology by installing computer terminals at 100,000 customers' offices and giving away its proprietary tracking software to another 650,000 customers. Now, customers electronically generate over 60 percent of all FedEx delivery requests. FedEx electronically receives its notification to pick up a package without having to deal with telephone calls or paperwork. The company can also pick up and deliver packages using fewer employees. To remain competitive, FedEx will continue to seek improvements in packaging and information technologies so customers can send and track packages in a more convenient manner.

In sum, FedEx hopes that its V3 strategy will improve customer service and increase the company's global dominance. The company has been highly successful because it recognized a need and filled it well. There is no doubt that Fred Smith's C paper has become an indispensable part of the business world.

Questions for Discussion

1. Evaluate the methods used by FedEx to expand into global markets. Why do you think the company had so many problems in its global operations?

2. How did FedEx recover from these global problems to become a global leader? What did FedEx do differently on the global front that spurred this recovery?

3. What are the major SWOT considerations in FedEx's attempt to continue its dominance in the domestic and global overnight delivery markets?

4. Comment on the acquisition of Caliber System and RPS. If you were a senior manager for UPS, how would you react?

Sources

These facts are from "FedEx announces domestic rate hike," *The Daily Advocate* (Baton Rouge, LA), Jan. 7, 1998; FedEx Corp. 1997 Annual Report; FedEx homepage, www.fedex.com; Linda Grant, "Why FedEx is flying high," *Fortune,* Nov. 10, 1997, 155; Nicole Harris, "Flying into a rage?" *Business Week,* April 27, 1998, 119; Michele Kayal, "FedEx launches Sunday service amid skepticism," *Journal of Commerce and Commercial,* Mar. 11, 1998, 1A; Richard Tomkins, "The bear and the alligator enter into a race to deliver," *The Financial Times,* March 13, 1998, 30; and Michael Weingarten and Bart Stuck, "No substitutions?" *Telephony,* Feb. 2, 1998, 26.

Sears Logistics Group[1]

The throb of the helicopter blades intensified as the helicopter lifted off the helipad outside of Sears Roebuck and Co. (Sears) Corporate headquarters in Hoffman Estates, IL. Retired Lieutenant General Gus Pagonis was starting out on another trip to visit the Sears Logistics Services, Inc. (SLS) Distribution Centers (DC) in Columbus, Ohio. Gus Pagonis, unaware of the ghostbusters (special problem solving team within the Sears Logistics Group)[2] traveling with him, was concentrating on the meeting scheduled for later that evening with his Distribution Center managers. Even though Gus has been able to make many financially beneficial changes in the Sears Logistics Group, there is still another challenge ahead, making the Columbus DCs operate more financially efficient. The charge which he must deliver to his managers is to develop a plan which will provide a more efficient and stronger strategic alliance among the distribution centers in Columbus. The directive to reduce costs was given to him by Arthur Martinez, CEO of Sears, in the wake of unexpected escalating costs and stiffer competition.

History of SLG

Logistics was an area which had not always had a high priority in Sears. Prior to Gus coming on board at Sears, the logistics functions had literally bounced all around the company. At one time, logistical functions were divided among four different executives. Upon the development of SLS in 1990, which controlled transportation and a portion of logistics, the Director reported to the Chief Financial Officer (CFO).

Prior to Gus taking on the role of Senior Executive Vice President of Logistics, logistics had more of a functional perspective than a process perspective. Upon

---

[1]This case was prepared by Keith C. Jones and Stewart Husted, both of Lynchburg College, for classroom discussion rather than to illustrate either effective or ineffective handling of an administrative situation. The case is based on an extensive interview trip to Hoffman Estates and the Columbus, Ohio Distribution Centers. This case was developed with the permission and approval of Gus Pagonis and SLG.

[2]Sears Logistics Group is comprised of the logistics functions within Sears Roebuck and Co. and Sears Logistics Services, Inc., a wholly owned subsidiary of Sears. These two entities work in conjunction to support Sears logistical requirements.

Gus entering the logistics area, he insisted that all areas of logistics report directly to him, and he would report directly to Arthur Martinez. This required upper management in Sears to make changes within the current executive board since logistics had not been previously represented in this group. This change was very important and crucial to the success of logistics. When Gus arrived in 1993 he created the Sears Logistics Group (SLG).

The Sears Logistics Group is structured around 14 functions which report directly to Gus. SLG is composed of vendor relations, full lines store logistics, direct delivery channel, off-mall stores logistics, finance, human resources, logistics systems, legal, logistics cell operations and administration, strategy, transportation, outlet stores, and SLS. Four of these individuals are responsible for overseeing the Channel operations within SLG. These four positions are the VP of Full-Line Stores, VP of Off Mall Stores, the VP of Direct Delivery and the Director of Specialized Channel. All other areas are support functions for these channels.

The main strategic control of merchandise movement is handled within the three Channel management groups. These three groups are the Full-Line Channel, the Direct Delivery Channel, and the Off-Mall Channel. The Full-Line Channel controls the Fashion Merchandise Distribution Center (FMDC) (with five Fashion Centers, five consolidation centers, four Import Centers, two Shoe Warehouses, and International Logistics), the Takewith Channel (with seven Retail Replenishment Centers (RRC), five Flow Thru Centers (FTC), and four Specialty Centers). The Direct Delivery Channel focuses on the functions of delivering products from Brand Central (appliance) store orders, Home Improvement stores, and Homelife stores. The function is divided into two channels. The Brand Central and Home Improvement products are channeled through Market Delivery Operations (MDO) which are under the coordination of 21 Direct Delivery Support Offices (DDSO) and the Homelife furniture orders which are delivered out of 5 Home Delivery Centers (HLDC). The Off-Mall Channel controls the logistics functions associated with the Tire Warehouse group, Western Auto, and the Orchard Supply and Hardware in addition to Home Solutions, and the Retail Special Order System.

Under the current operating system, each of the main distribution centers are responsible for the distribution of the specific products which flow through their centers. Each center is then responsible for loading trucks for delivery to each of the stores. Thus, based on the routing, each truck would carry merchandise for multiple stores. Each store would receive trucks from each of the distribution centers.

Structure of SLG

The SLG Mission statement is the driving force behind the maintenance and control of the system. The Mission Statement says:

> SLG's mission is to develop logistics capabilities in conjunction with the Full Line Stores and Off Mall businesses to create a competitive advantage for Sears. The priorities of SLG focus on the reduction of costs, improvement of services, management of cycle time and improved asset productivity.

By achieving these goals, SLG will continue to improve profit for Sears. All decisions which are made within SLG must be measured against the mission statement and goals. If the concept will not advance this perspective, then the concept is not developed.

Formation of SLG

SLG was formed in 1993. Prior to the formation of SLG the transportation component of Sears was a subsidiary of the company. In 1939 the Terminal Freight Cooperative Association was created with 168 members. This cooperative serviced more than just Sears. With the deregulation of the Transportation Industry in 1980, 165 members of the cooperative pulled out and in 1985 the Terminal Freight Cooperative was dissolved.

Following the dissolution of the cooperative, Sears started moving from an asset management transportation group to a lane management transportation group. As the transportation fleet became more expensive to maintain, Sears started developing third party transportation partners to carry the freight. Sears Logistics Services, Inc., a wholly owned subsidiary of Sears was formed in 1990 to manage the distribution and transportation function of Sears.

Under SLG, SLS continues as a subsidiary coordinating the transportation and logistics functions for SLG. SLS provides all potential transportation vendors with projected freight usage for all of the lanes (routes). The transportation vendors are then allowed to submit a bid for the routes of interest. Once that carrier has been awarded a lane, the carrier can subcontract up to 5% of its total volume, but not more than 20% of volume on any one lane if the company is awarded more than one lane.

Multiple "Customer" Perspective

The success of Sears is dependent on its ability to meet the needs of its customers. Gus also saw this as being the situation within the SLG. The difference is how the SLG defines its customers. The SLG has three different customers. The first is the retail consumer. As with any retailer, the logistics system must be able to provide the retail consumer with the merchandise which he or she wants to purchase when he or she wants to purchase it. This includes not only delivery of the merchandise but also the condition upon arrival. It also means that the product is priced at the desired level from the customer's perspective. That is why it is important to control the costs associated with the logistics function in Sears. Logistics can account for as much as 5 percent of the cost of an item if not properly managed.

The retail store is the second customer which SLG must satisfy. There have been many changes made within SLG to make the experience of the retail store better. A short list would include: shorter lead time for orders, undamaged merchandise, garment-on-hanger, inspection free off-loading of orders, and improved communications. Through these various changes within SLG, stores have realized cost savings through reduction in labor costs and inventory carrying costs as well as freeing up store backroom space. Because of these enhancements, many of the stores have remodeled and expanded their sales floors recapturing valuable floor space which is no longer needed for merchandise preparation and storage.

The third customer is the Vertical Merchandising Business. These are functional areas within Sears which support the success of the store (the buying organization and store operations). These areas are not under the control of SLG, but have direct impact upon its ability to meet its mission and priorities.

Ghostbusters/SPOC

To achieve the desired level of customer satisfaction, Gus installed two concepts into SLG structure: Ghostbusters and SPOC. Ghostbusters are a specialized team designed to solve problems which arise within the organization and impact any of the three customer types. Ghostbusters are an empowered management team designed to fix the problems and assist in keeping the group profitable. The Ghostbusters evaluate the situation, develop a solution, and implement that solution. They are not required to receive permission from Gus or any of the report directs prior to their actions. This team consists of six people who function as a team but must also be able to act independently. Ghostbusters may work on projects ranging from a dissatisfied consumer (e.g. product delivered damaged, not all parts arrived, or incorrect product delivery) to working on problems associated with delivery errors to stores or poor product quality from a vendor. The ghostbuster must be cross-trained and be able to handle and control multiple tasks at one time. Gus rarely travels without at least one ghostbuster accompanying him.

The other concept which Gus implemented was the SPOC (Single Point Of Contact). Prior to the implementation of this concept into the logistics group, there was no clear path of responsibility or problem resolution. A lot of passing the buck occurred. Under the SPOC program, the SPOC acts as a liaison between the SLG customer and logistics. If any problems arise, the customer knows who to call. The SPOC is responsible for investigating and resolving the situation. If the problem cannot be solved by the SPOC, then the problem is passed on to a ghostbuster. Depending on the urgency of the problem, the problem will be tagged as a HOT item. These items receive special attention. The ghostbuster must drop whatever he or she is working on and immediately work on the HOT item.

Current Logistics Situation in Columbus, Ohio

Columbus, Ohio is the home of major distribution centers for Sears. A Hardware Distribution Center (HDC), a Market Delivery Operations (MDO), a Fashion Merchandise Distribution Center (FMDC), a Direct Delivery Center (DDC), and a Retail Replenishment Center (RRC) are all located in the Columbus area in four separate facilities. Because of this situation, Columbus has become one of the areas which Gus is reviewing for potential cost reductions. In addition to the above, a Western Auto distribution center is also located in the area. Gus is in the process of incorporating this into the SLG as Western Auto is now a part of Sears.

HARDWARE DISTRIBUTION CENTER   The Hardware Distribution Center (HDC) is responsible for items carried in the Orchard Hardware Stores and in some cases are the same as those carried in the RRC, but need to be separated due to ordering systems constraints.

FASHION MERCHANDISE DISTRIBUTION CENTER   Flow through is the name of the game in the FMDC. The philosophy of the management in the FMDC is "We are in the business of moving merchandise, not warehousing." If the merchandise ever stops moving, something is wrong. Several changes have occurred within the FMDC to achieve this flow. One of the biggest challenges was the implementation of garment-on-hanger (GOH) concept. This required the third party transportation provider to specially equip trucks to haul merchandise which comes pre-hung on hangers into the distribution center. This was accomplished through installing a hanging rope system inside the trailer on which garments are hung. The garments are taken off of the truck and placed on a conveyor system which carries them to a sorting area. In this area the garments are then sorted based on store need. Getting the right garment to the right store is important. Under the old box system, stores had to receive the merchandise as it was boxed. This normally consisted of a specific number of each size, regardless of the store's actual needs. Currently about 50 percent of the clothing items arrive GOH, while 20 percent arrive in flat pack to be displayed on tables and 30 percent is prepacked from the vendor.

Once the items have been sorted by store, the merchandise is scanned and a shipping invoice is printed and the merchandise is loaded onto the GOH-equipped trucks. The boxed and crated (non-hanger) items are stacked on the floor of the truck, beneath the GOH merchandise. The trucks then deliver to the various stores which are on the route of the truck.

By employing a "flow through" system, Sears has been able to reduce the lead time of fashion merchandise from 31 days to 6.7 days. Sears is not planning on lowering this time since it will require air freighting merchandise to the store. The FMDC is currently remodeling. It has now recaptured over 25 percent of its space because of flow through. This area was used to inventory merchandise to accommodate high demand periods under the old stack and store philosophy.

DIRECT DELIVERY CENTER/MARKET DELIVERY OPERATIONS   The Direct Delivery Center (DDC) and the Market Delivery Operations (MDO) are housed within the same facility. The DDC is responsible for those items which are delivered to the customer's home. These items include household appliances, lawn equipment, and snowblowers. The DDC is 1 million square feet with 127 doors for DDC and 14 doors for MDO. Their products are very seasonal in nature which requires the DDC to properly manage the flow and location of merchandise in the facility. While the DDC would like to accomplish a flow through operation policy, unlike the other facilities, it must maintain a certain level of stock to meet the demands of the consumer. The DDC delivers products to the Dealer Stores, the Mall Stores and the MDO. By having the MDO located in the same facility, this promotes more efficient use of resources.

The MDO is responsible for the delivery of merchandise directly to the customer's home. Under the current system, the customer will go to a store and see the merchandise on the floor. The customer will then place an order for the merchandise. This order is normally delivered the next day in major markets. For the other markets it may take two days for a delivery. Sears currently operates under a "four hour window" program. They can tell the customer within a four hour time period when a product will be delivered. SLG is currently reviewing the process and trying to determine how it can narrow that window to two hours without raising the costs. The MDO group for Sears, not just Columbus, will handle 10 million pieces of merchandise and will deliver that to 4 million homes in a given year. There are 130 delivery markets.

RETAIL REPLENISHMENT CENTER   The Retail Replenishment Center (RRC) in Columbus is 1.5 million square feet. It carries the "takewith" merchandise. Takewith is the non-fashion, non-deliverable merchandise in Sears stores. This merchandise is either in break pac, full case or non-conveyable. Merchandise is picked and placed onto a conveyor belt or in a box which is placed onto a conveyor belt. The box has a scan tag attached to it based on the store which has ordered the merchandise. The conveyor belt routes the box or item to the appropriate truck for shipment. Upon leaving the RRC, 97 percent of the merchandise is scanable and ready to be displayed once it arrives at the store.

To assist the retail store and reduce its costs, the current system in the RRC does not require the merchandise be counted at the receiving dock of the store. SLG has implemented a validation system. After the trucks have been loaded and dispatched, the RRC is notified which trucks will be checked for accuracy. Upon arrival at the store, a team is there ready to count the merchandise. If the count is inaccurate, the RRC is notified as to the truck and the picking group responsible for the error. There can be no variances in the printed invoice and the merchandise which is on the truck.

WESTERN AUTO DISTRIBUTION CENTER   The final facility in Columbus is the Western Auto Distribution Center (WADC). It is the farthest away from the other facilities (over a 45 minute drive in light traffic). The WADC carries the merchandise necessary to stock a Western Auto Store. There is a much wider product mix in the WADC. The products it carries include motor oils, tires, engines, mufflers and tail pipes, weed eaters, screwdrivers, screws, and small appliances, just to name a few items. The WADC also acts as a warehouse for some Sears merchandise. Since Sears is the parent company for National Tire and Battery and it already has its own Tire and Automotive Center in many of its own stores, Western Auto will no longer carry tires.

Merchandise Control

Each distribution center is operated with a separate profit statement. When a piece of merchandise arrives into the center, it is inventoried and charged to that center. When the item leaves the distribution center it is billed to the customer (retail or consumer). It is billed out at a rate which will cover the costs and value added contributions the distribution center made to the product. Under this system, no product is shipped between the distribution centers since this would increase the cost of the product. While this is being reviewed by management, there is no quick or easy solution in sight. Also, because of the locations of the facilities, it is not practical to partially load trucks at one center and then complete the load at another center. There are two reasons. First, you have the loss of time for transportation across town. Second, to do this, the truck would have to be partially unloaded so merchandise could be separated by store on the truck.

Future Complications

While the SLG faces these current situations, the future will become more complicated. With the introduction of the Orchard Store Concept (Lawn and Garden type centers), The Great Indoor Stores, and the reduction of the return outlet stores, logistical issues will continue to plague Gus and his team.

The Orchard Store is a chain of stores located mainly in California. The store is designed around an outdoor and home improvement merchandise mix. While part of the store is hardware oriented, other portions of the store focus on lawn care, small home repairs, small household merchandise, and lawn decorations. The acquisition of this store will allow Sears and Craftsman to expand their product offerings and customer contact. It will also broaden the overall product offerings of Sears.

The Great Indoors store debuted in Denver, Colorado. This new retail format concept allows the consumer to experience remodeling and interior design of a home from a new perspective. The 150,000 square feet stores target women who are interested in home remodeling. Unlike the warehouse atmospheres of its competitors, the Great Indoors stores use wide aisles and bright lights designed to replicate rooms in a home to see the actual use of the merchandise. The merchandise includes linens and towels, consumer electronics, housewares and decorative accessories, wall and floor coverings and a complete line of specialty paints.

The store will not use the Sears name anywhere in its advertising or signage. The strategic plan is to create an entirely different feel for the store.

The meeting which is about to happen is crucial to the continued success of SLG. It is critical that this group of individuals address and attack the current situation prior to the introduction of other logistic issues.

Dinner with Unit Managers at DaVanci's Italian Restaurant

As the helicopter landed, one of the center managers was waiting to chauffeur the group to the meeting. Upon arrival at the restaurant, Gus individually greeted all of those attending the meeting. Those in attendance were the managers and assistants of the distribution centers located in Columbus, OH. At that point there was some casual conversation until the wait staff arrived to take the orders. Immediately following the placement of orders, Gus began the meeting. Similar to his Stand-ups[3] (with the exception that everyone is seated), Gus had everyone report current situations.

After the meal was over, Gus presented his ideas to the group: "As you know, in the past year we have made some great accomplishments in SLG and we have been able to save the company a considerable amount of money. All of the Executive VP's have been asked to trim their budgets for the remainder of the year. Our budget is very lean and the only way I can see us trimming the budget is by developing more efficient ways to continue to deliver our services to our customers. Here is my challenge to you as a group, how can we run a tighter ship in Columbus, Ohio? As you know, many of you service the same customers which means we still have multiple trucks leaving Columbus headed for the same stores. In some cases, the size of the order warrants such moves. In other situations, and probably the majority of such situations, this is not warranted. How can we fix this problem?"

---

[3]Stand-ups are a style of meeting which Gus or one of his report directs facilitates every morning at Hoffman Estates for the SLG division. The Stand-up lasts approximately 30 minutes. All report directs are responsible for being there or must be represented. Each person in attendance is required to either update Gus and the others to any issues of importance or "pass" if there is nothing which must be mentioned. These meetings are called stand-ups because no one in the room is allowed to sit down. To say the least, the meetings are very efficient.

Questions for Discussion

1. What has been the main success of SLG since the arrival of Gus Pagonis at Sears?

2. What internal factors must be considered when determining the potential actions that the group can take to develop a more efficient system in Columbus?

3. What external factors must be considered when determining the potential actions that the group can take to develop a more efficient system in Columbus?

4. What impact will the expansion of Sears to include Western Auto, Orchard Stores, and The Great Indoors have on the management and control of the logistics function of SLG?

Sources

Other facts of this case are from Tom Andel, "Could you work for a three-star general?" *Transportation & Distribution*, Nov. 1996, 113; Adam Blair, "Sears' logistics chief pushes for open dialogue: William 'Gus' Pagonis wants to know the good and the bad," *Daily News Record*, Nov. 19, 1997, 12; James Aaron Cooke, "A view of logistics from the front lines," *Logistics Management*, Mar. 1996, 46; Laura Heller, "Sears' Great Indoors draws crowds in Denver market," *Discount Store News*, March 9, 1998, 7-8; William G. Pagonis, "The work of a leader," *Harvard Business Review*, Nov.-Dec. 1992, 118; Sears Logistics Group Bulletin, No. 1, May 5, 1997; and Valerie Seckler, "Winning the battle at Sears logistics," *WWD*, July 2, 1997, 10.

Kentucky Fried Chicken and the Global Fast-Food Industry[1]

Kentucky Fried Chicken Corporation (KFC) was the world's largest chicken restaurant chain and third largest fast-food chain. KFC held over 55 percent of the U.S. market in terms of sales and operated over 10,200 restaurants worldwide in 1998. It opened 376 new restaurants in 1997 (more than one restaurant a day) and operated in 79 countries. One of the first fast-food chains to go international during the late 1960s, KFC has developed one of the world's most recognizable brands.

Japan, Australia, and the United Kingdom accounted for the greatest share of KFC's international expansion during the 1970s and 1980s. During the 1990s, KFC turned its attention to other international markets that offered significant opportunities for growth. China, with a population of over one billion, and Europe, with a population roughly equal to the United States, offered such opportunities. Latin America also offered a unique opportunity because of the size of its markets, its common language and culture, and its geographical proximity to the United States. Mexico was of particular interest because of the North American Free Trade Agreement (NAFTA), a free trade zone between Canada, the United States, and Mexico that went into effect in 1994.

Prior to 1990, KFC expanded into Latin America primarily through company-owned restaurants in Mexico and Puerto Rico. Company-owned restaurants gave KFC greater control over its operations than franchised or licensed restaurants. By 1995, KFC had also established company-owned restaurants in Venezuela and Brazil. In addition, it had established franchised units in several Caribbean countries. During the early 1990s, KFC shifted to a two-tier strategy in Latin America. First, it established 29 franchised restaurants in Mexico following enactment of Mexico's new franchise law in 1990. This allowed KFC to expand outside of its company restaurant base in Mexico City, Guadalajara, and Monterrey. KFC was only one of many U.S. fast-food, retail, and hotel chains to begin franchising in Mexico following the new franchise law. Second, KFC began an aggressive franchise building program in South America. By 1998, it was operating franchised restaurants in 32

---

[1] This case was prepared by Jeffrey A. Krug, University of Illinois at Urbana-Champaign, for classroom discussion rather than to illustrate either effective or ineffective handling of an administrative situation.

Latin American countries. Much of this growth was in Brazil, Chile, Colombia, Ecuador, and Peru.

Company History

Fast-food franchising was still in its infancy in 1952 when Harland Sanders began his travels across the United States to speak with prospective franchisees about his "Colonel Sanders Recipe Kentucky Fried Chicken." By 1960, "Colonel" Sanders had granted KFC franchises to over 200 take-home retail outlets and restaurants across the United States. He had also succeeded in establishing a number of franchises in Canada. By 1963, the number of KFC franchises had risen to over 300 and revenues had reached $500 million.

By 1964, at the age of 74, the Colonel had tired of running the day-to-day operations of his business and was eager to concentrate on public relations issues. Therefore, he sought out potential buyers, eventually deciding to sell the business to two Louisville businessmen—Jack Massey and John Young Brown Jr.—for $2 million. The Colonel stayed on as a public relations man and goodwill ambassador for the company.

During the next five years, Massey and Brown concentrated on growing KFC's franchise system across the United States. In 1966, they took KFC public and the company was listed on the New York Stock Exchange. By the late 1960s, a strong foothold had been established in the United States, and Massey and Brown turned their attention to international markets. In 1969, a joint venture was signed with Mitsuoishi Shoji Kaisha, Ltd. in Japan, and the rights to operate 14 existing KFC franchises in England were acquired. Subsidiaries were also established in Hong Kong, South Africa, Australia, New Zealand, and Mexico. By 1971, KFC had 2,450 franchises and 600 company-owned restaurants worldwide, and was operating in 48 countries.

Heublein, Inc.

In 1971, KFC entered negotiations with Heublein, Inc. to discuss a possible merger. The decision to seek a merger candidate was partially driven by Brown's desire to pursue other interests, including a political career. (Brown was elected governor of Kentucky in 1977.) Several months later, Heublein acquired KFC. Heublein was in the business of producing vodka, mixed cocktails, dry gin, cordials, beer, and other alcoholic beverages. However, Heublein had little experience in the restaurant business. Conflicts quickly erupted between Colonel Sanders, who continued to act in a public relations capacity, and Heublein management. Colonel Sanders became increasingly distraught over quality control issues and restaurant cleanliness. By 1977, new restaurant openings had slowed to about 20 per year. Few restaurants were being remodeled and service quality had declined.

In 1977, Heublein sent in a new management team to redirect KFC's strategy. A "back-to-the-basics" strategy was immediately implemented. New unit construction was discontinued until existing restaurants could be upgraded and operating problems eliminated. Restaurants were refurbished, an emphasis was placed on cleanliness and service, marginal products were eliminated, and product consistency was reestablished. By 1982, KFC had succeeded in establishing a successful strategic focus and was again aggressively building new units.

R.J. Reynolds Industries, Inc.

In 1982, R.J. Reynolds Industries, Inc. (RJR) merged Heublein into a wholly owned subsidiary. The merger with Heublein represented part of RJR's overall corporate strategy of diversifying into unrelated businesses, including energy, transportation, food, and restaurants. RJR's objective was to reduce its dependence on the tobacco industry, which had driven RJR sales since its founding in North Carolina in 1875. Sales of cigarettes and tobacco products, while profitable, were declining because of reduced consumption in the United States. This was mainly the result of an increased awareness among Americans about the negative health consequences of smoking.

RJR had no more experience in the restaurant business than did Heublein. However, it decided to take a hands-off approach to managing KFC. Whereas Heublein had installed its own top management at KFC headquarters, RJR left KFC management largely intact, believing that existing KFC managers were better qualified to operate KFC's businesses than its own managers were. In doing so, RJR avoided many of the operating problems that plagued Heublein. This strategy paid off for RJR as KFC continued to expand aggressively and profitably under RJR ownership. In 1985, RJR acquired Nabisco Corporation for $4.9 billion. Nabisco sold a variety of well-known cookies, crackers, cereals, confectioneries, snacks, and other grocery products. The merger with Nabisco represented a decision by RJR to concentrate its diversification efforts on the consumer foods industry. It subsequently divested many of its non-consumer food businesses. RJR sold KFC to PepsiCo, Inc. one year later.

PepsiCo, Inc.

Corporate Strategy

PepsiCo, Inc. was formed in 1965 with the merger of the Pepsi-Cola Co. and Frito-Lay Inc. The merger of these companies created one of the largest consumer products companies in the United States. Pepsi-Cola's traditional business was the sale of soft drink concentrates to licensed independent and company-owned bottlers that manufactured, sold, and distributed Pepsi-Cola soft drinks. Pepsi-Cola's best known trademarks were Pepsi-Cola, Diet Pepsi, Mountain Dew, and Slice. Frito-Lay manufactured and sold a variety of snack foods, including Fritos Corn Chips, Lay's Potato Chips, Ruffles Potato Chips, Doritos, Tostitos Tortilla Chips, and Cheetos Cheese Flavored Snacks. PepsiCo quickly embarked on an aggressive acquisition program similar to that pursued by RJR during the 1980s, buying a number of companies in areas unrelated to its major businesses. Acquisitions included North American Van Lines, Wilson Sporting Goods, and Lee Way Motor Freight. However, success in operating these businesses failed to live up to expectations, mainly because the management skills required to operate these businesses lay outside of PepsiCo's area of expertise.

Poor performance in these businesses led then-chairman and chief executive officer Don Kendall to restructure PepsiCo's operations in 1984. First, businesses that did not support PepsiCo's consumer product orientation, such as North American Van Lines, Wilson Sporting Goods, and Lee Way Motor Freight were divested. Second, PepsiCo's foreign bottling operations were sold to local businesspeople who better understood the culture and business environment in their respective countries. Third, Kendall reorganized PepsiCo along three lines: soft drinks, snack foods, and restaurants.

Restaurant Business And Acquisition Of Kentucky Fried Chicken

PepsiCo first entered the restaurant business in 1977 when it acquired Pizza Hut's 3,200-unit restaurant system. Taco Bell was merged into a division of PepsiCo in 1978. The restaurant business complemented PepsiCo's consumer product orientation. The marketing of fast-food followed many of the same patterns as the marketing of soft drinks and snack foods. Therefore, PepsiCo believed that its management skills could be transferred easily among its three business segments. This was compatible with PepsiCo's practice of frequently moving managers among its business units as a way of developing future top executives. PepsiCo's restaurant chains also provided an additional outlet for the sale of Pepsi soft drinks. Pepsi-Cola soft drinks and fast-food products could also be marketed together in the same television and radio segments, thereby providing higher returns for each advertising dollar. To complete its diversification into the restaurant segment, PepsiCo acquired Kentucky Fried Chicken Corporation from RJR-Nabisco for $841 million in 1986. The acquisition of KFC gave PepsiCo the leading market share in chicken (KFC), pizza (Pizza Hut), and Mexican food (Taco Bell), three of the four largest and fastest-growing segments within the U.S. fast-food industry.

Management

Following the acquisition by PepsiCo, KFC's relationship with its parent company underwent dramatic changes. RJR had operated KFC as a semi-autonomous unit, satisfied that KFC management understood the fast-food business better than it. In contrast, PepsiCo acquired KFC in order to complement its already strong presence in the fast-food market. Rather than allowing KFC to operate autonomously, PepsiCo undertook sweeping changes. These changes included negotiating a new franchise contract to give PepsiCo more control over its franchisees, reducing staff in order to cut costs, and replacing KFC managers with its own. In 1987, a rumor spread through KFC's headquarters in Louisville that the new personnel manager, who had just relocated from PepsiCo's headquarters in New York, was overheard saying, "There will be no more home grown tomatoes in this organization."

Such statements by PepsiCo personnel, uncertainties created by several restructurings that led to layoffs throughout the KFC organization, the replacement of KFC personnel with PepsiCo managers, and conflicts between KFC and PepsiCo's corporate cultures created a morale problem within KFC. KFC's culture was built largely on Colonel Sander's laid-back approach to management. Employees enjoyed relatively good employment stability and security. Over the years, a strong loyalty had been created among KFC employees and franchisees, mainly because of the efforts of Colonel Sanders to provide for his employees' benefits, pension, and other non-income needs. In addition, the Southern environment of Louisville resulted in a friendly, relaxed atmosphere at KFC's corporate offices. This corporate culture was left essentially unchanged during the Heublein and RJR years.

In stark contrast to KFC, PepsiCo's culture was characterized by a strong emphasis on performance. Top performers expected to move up through the ranks quickly. PepsiCo used its KFC, Pizza Hut, Taco Bell, Frito Lay, and Pepsi-Cola divisions as training grounds for its top managers, rotating its best managers through its five divisions on average every two years. This practice created immense pressure on managers to continuously demonstrate their managerial prowess within short periods, in order to maximize their potential for promotion. This practice also left many

KFC managers with the feeling that they had few career opportunities with the new company. One PepsiCo manager commented that "You may have performed well last year, but if you don't perform well this year, you're gone, and there are 100 ambitious guys with Ivy League MBAs at PepsiCo who would love to take your position." An unwanted effect of this performance-driven culture was that employee loyalty was often lost and turnover tended to be higher than in other companies.

Kyle Craig, president of KFC's U.S. operations, was asked about KFC's relationship with its corporate parent. He commented:

> The KFC culture is an interesting one because I think it was dominated by a lot of KFC folks, many of whom have been around since the days of the Colonel. Many of those people were very intimidated by the PepsiCo culture, which is a very high performance, high accountability, highly driven culture. People were concerned about whether they would succeed in the new culture. Like many companies, we have had a couple of downsizings that further made people nervous. Today, there are fewer old KFC people around and I think to some degree people have seen that the PepsiCo culture can drive some pretty positive results. I also think the PepsiCo people who have worked with KFC have modified their cultural values somewhat and they can see that there were a lot of benefits in the old KFC culture.
>
> PepsiCo pushes their companies to perform strongly, but whenever there is a slip in performance, it increases the culture gap between PepsiCo and KFC. I have been involved in two downsizings over which I have been the chief architect. They have been probably the two most gut-wrenching experiences of my career. Because you know you're dealing with peoples' lives and their families, these changes can be emotional if you care about the people in your organization. However, I do fundamentally believe that your first obligation is to the entire organization.

A second problem for PepsiCo was its poor relationship with KFC franchisees. A month after becoming president and chief executive officer in 1989, John Cranor addressed KFC's franchisees in Louisville, in order to explain the details of the new franchise contract. This was the first contract change in 13 years. It gave PepsiCo greater power to take over weak franchises, relocate restaurants, and make changes in existing restaurants. In addition, restaurants would no longer be protected from competition from new KFC units and it gave PepsiCo the right to raise royalty fees on existing restaurants as contracts came up for renewal. After Cranor finished his address, there was an uproar among the attending franchisees, who jumped to their feet to protest the changes. The franchisees had long been accustomed to relatively little interference from management in their day-to-day operations (a tradition begun by Colonel Sanders). This type of interference, of course, was a strong part of PepsiCo's philosophy of demanding change. KFC's franchise association later sued PepsiCo over the new contract. The contract remained unresolved until 1996, when the most objectionable parts of the contract were removed by KFC's new president and CEO, David Novak. A new contract was ratified by KFC's franchisees in 1997.

Pepsico's Divestiture of KFC, Pizza Hut, and Taco Bell

PepsiCo's strategy of diversifying into three distinct but related markets—soft drinks, snack foods, and fast-food restaurants—created one of the world's largest consumer products companies and a portfolio of some of the world's most recognizable brands. Between 1990 and 1996, PepsiCo grew at an annual rate of over 10 percent, surpassing $31 billion in sales in 1996. However, PepsiCo's sales growth masked troubles in its fast-food businesses. Operating margins (profit as a percent of sales) at Pepsi-Cola and Frito Lay averaged 12 and 17 percent between 1990 and 1996, respectively. During the same period, margins at KFC, Pizza Hut, and Taco Bell fell from an average of over 8 percent in 1990 to a little more than 4 percent in 1996. Declining margins in the fast-food chains reflected increasing maturity in the U.S. fast-food industry, more intense competition among U.S. fast-food competitors, and the aging of KFC and Pizza Hut's restaurant base. As a result, PepsiCo's restaurant chains absorbed nearly one-half of PepsiCo's annual capital spending during the 1990s. However, they generated less than one-third of PepsiCo's cash flows. Therefore, cash was diverted from PepsiCo's soft drink and snack food businesses to its restaurant businesses. This reduced PepsiCo's return on assets, made it more difficult to compete effectively with Coca-Cola, and hurt its stock price. In 1997, PepsiCo spun off its restaurant businesses into a new company called Tricon Global Restaurants, Inc. (see Exhibit 1). The new company was based in KFC's headquarters in Louisville, Kentucky. PepsiCo's objective was to reposition itself as a packaged goods company, to strengthen its balance sheet, and to create more consistent earnings growth. PepsiCo received a one-time distribution from Tricon of $4.7 billion, $3.7 billion of which was used to pay off short-term debt. The balance was earmarked for stock repurchases.

Fast-Food Industry

According to the National Restaurant Association (NRA), food-service sales topped $320 billion in 1997 for the approximately 500,000 restaurants and other food outlets making up the U.S. restaurant industry. The NRA estimated that sales in the fast-food segment of the food service industry grew 5.2 percent to $104 billion in 1997, up from $98 billion in 1996. This marked the fourth consecutive year that fast-food

---

EXHIBIT 1   **Tricon Global Restaurants, Inc. Organizational Chart (1998)**

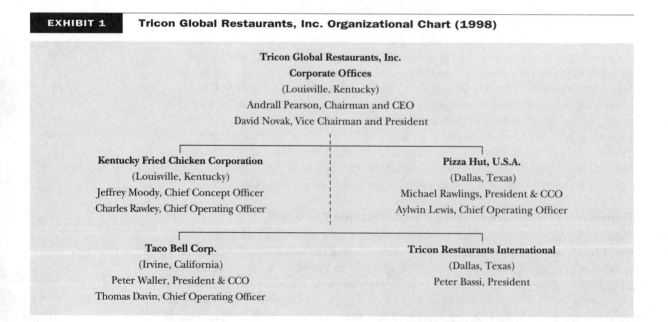

Tricon Global Restaurants, Inc.
Corporate Offices
(Louisville, Kentucky)
Andrall Pearson, Chairman and CEO
David Novak, Vice Chairman and President

Kentucky Fried Chicken Corporation
(Louisville, Kentucky)
Jeffrey Moody, Chief Concept Officer
Charles Rawley, Chief Operating Officer

Pizza Hut, U.S.A.
(Dallas, Texas)
Michael Rawlings, President & CCO
Aylwin Lewis, Chief Operating Officer

Taco Bell Corp.
(Irvine, California)
Peter Waller, President & CCO
Thomas Davin, Chief Operating Officer

Tricon Restaurants International
(Dallas, Texas)
Peter Bassi, President

sales had either matched or exceeded sales in full-service restaurants. The growth in fast-food sales reflected the long, gradual change in the restaurant industry from one once dominated by independently operated sit-down restaurants to one quickly becoming dominated by fast-food restaurant chains.

Major Fast-Food Segments

Six major business segments made up the fast-food segment of the food service industry. Sales data for the leading restaurant chains in each segment are shown in Exhibit 2. Most striking is the dominance of McDonald's, which had sales of over $16 billion in 1996. This represented 16.6 percent of U.S. fast-food sales, or nearly 22 percent of sales among the nation's top 30 fast-food chains. Sales at McDonald's restaurants averaged $1.3 million per year, compared to about $820,000 for the average U.S. fast-food restaurant. Tricon Global Restaurants (KFC, Pizza Hut, and Taco Bell) had U.S. sales of $13.4 billion in 1996. This represented 13.6 percent of U.S. fast-food sales and 17.9 percent of the top 30 fast-food chains.

Sandwich chains made up the largest segment of the fast-food market. McDonald's controlled 35 percent of the sandwich segment, while Burger King ran a distant second with a 15.6 percent market share. Competition had become particularly intense within the sandwich segment as the U.S. fast-food market became more saturated. In order to increase sales, chains turned to new products to win customers away from other sandwich chains, introduced products traditionally offered by non-sandwich chains (such as pizzas, fried chicken, and tacos), streamlined their menus, and upgraded product quality. Burger King recently introduced its "Big King," a direct clone of the Big Mac. McDonald's quickly retaliated by introducing its "Big 'n Tasty," a direct clone of the Whopper. Wendy's introduced chicken pita sandwiches and Taco Bell introduced sandwiches called "wraps," breads stuffed with various fillings. Hardee's successfully introduced fried chicken in most of its restaurants. In addition to new products, chains lowered pricing, improved customer service, co-branded with other fast-food chains, and established restaurants in non-traditional locations (for example, McDonald's has installed restaurants in Wal-Mart stores across the country) to beef up sales.

The second largest fast-food segment was dinner houses, dominated by Red Lobster, Applebee's, Olive Garden, and Chili's. Between 1988 and 1996, dinner houses increased their share of the fast-food market from 8 to over 13 percent. This increase came mainly at the expense of grilled buffet chains, such as Ponderosa, Sizzler, and Western Sizzlin'. The market share of steak houses fell from 6 percent in 1988 to under 4 percent in 1996. The rise of dinner houses during the 1990s was partially the result of an aging and wealthier population that increasingly demanded higher quality food in more upscale settings. However, rapid construction of new restaurants, especially among relative newcomers, such as Romano's Macaroni Grill, Lone Star Steakhouse, and Outback Steakhouse, resulted in overcapacity within the dinner house segment. This reduced per restaurant sales and further intensified competition. Eight of the 16 largest dinner houses posted growth rates in excess of 10 percent in 1996. Romano's Macaroni Grill, Lone Star Steakhouse, Chili's, Outback Steakhouse, Applebee's, Red Robin, Fuddruckers, and Ruby Tuesday grew at rates of 82, 41, 32, 27, 23, 14, 11, and 10 percent, respectively.

The third largest fast-food segment was pizza, long dominated by Pizza Hut. Although Pizza Hut controlled over 46 percent of the pizza segment in 1996, its market share has slowly eroded because of intense competition and its aging restaurant

EXHIBIT 2	Leading U.S. Fast-Food Chains (Ranked by 1996 Sales, $000s)	

Sandwich Chains	*Sales*	*Share*
McDonald's	16,370	35.0 percent
Burger King	7,300	15.6 percent
Taco Bell	4,575	9.8 percent
Wendy's	4,360	9.3 percent
Hardee's	3,055	6.5 percent
Subway	2,700	5.8 percent
Arby's	1,867	4.0 percent
Dairy Queen	1,225	2.6 percent
Jack in the Box	1,207	2.6 percent
Sonic Drive-In	985	2.1 percent
Carl's Jr.	648	1.4 percent
Other Chains	2,454	5.2 percent
Total	46,745	100.0 percent
Dinner Houses	*Sales*	*Share*
Red Lobster	1,810	15.7 percent
Applebee's	1,523	13.2 percent
Olive Garden	1,280	11.1 percent
Chili's	1,242	10.7 percent
Outback Steakhouse	1,017	8.8 percent
T.G.I. Friday's	935	8.1 percent
Ruby Tuesday	545	4.7 percent
Lone Star Steakhouse	460	4.0 percent
Bennigan's	458	4.0 percent
Romano's Macaroni Grill	344	3.0 percent
Other Dinner Houses	1,942	16.8 percent
Total	11,557	100.0 percent
Grilled Buffet Chains	*Sales*	*Share*
Golden Corral	711	22.8 percent
Ponderosa	680	21.8 percent
Ryan's	604	19.4 percent
Sizzler	540	17.3 percent
Western Sizzlin'	332	10.3 percent
Quincy's	259	8.3 percent
Total	3,116	100.0 percent

base. Domino's Pizza and Papa John's Pizza have been particularly successful. Little Caesars is the only pizza chain to remain predominately take-out, though it recently began home delivery. However, its policy of charging customers $1 per delivery damaged its perception among consumers as a high-value pizza chain. Home delivery, successfully introduced by Domino's and Pizza Hut, was a driving force for success among the market leaders during the 1970s and 1980s. However, the success of home delivery drove competitors to look for new methods of increasing their customer bases. Pizza chains diversified into non-pizza items (e.g., chicken wings at Domino's, Italian cheese bread at Little Caesars, and stuffed crust pizza at Pizza Hut), developed non-traditional units (e.g., airport kiosks and college campuses), offered special promotions, and offered new pizza variations with an emphasis on high quality ingredients (e.g., "Roma Herb" and "Garlic Crunch" pizza at Domino's and "Buffalo Chicken Pizza" at Round Table Pizza).

EXHIBIT 2	**Leading U.S. Fast-Food Chains** **(Ranked by 1996 Sales, $000s)** *(continued)*	

Family Restaurants	*Sales*	*Share*
Denny's	1,850	21.2 percent
Shoney's	1,220	14.0 percent
Big Boy	945	10.8 percent
Int'l House of Pancakes	797	9.1 percent
Cracker Barrel	734	8.4 percent
Perkins	678	7.8 percent
Friendly's	597	6.8 percent
Bob Evans	575	6.6 percent
Waffle House	525	6.0 percent
Coco's	278	3.2 percent
Steak 'n Shake	275	3.2 percent
Village Inn	246	2.8 percent
Total	8,719	100.0 percent
Pizza Chains	*Sales*	*Share*
Pizza Hut	4,927	46.4 percent
Domino's Pizza	2,300	21.7 percent
Little Caesars	1,425	13.4 percent
Papa John's	619	5.8 percent
Sbarros	400	3.8 percent
Round Table Pizza	385	3.6 percent
Chuck E. Cheese's	293	2.8 percent
Godfather's Pizza	266	2.5 percent
Total	10,614	100.0 percent
Chicken Chains	*Sales*	*Share*
KFC	3,900	57.1 percent
Boston Market	1,167	17.1 percent
Popeyes Chicken	666	9.7 percent
Chick-fil-A	570	8.3 percent
Church's Chicken	529	7.7 percent
Total	6,832	100.0 percent

Source: *Nation's Restaurant News.*

Chicken Segment

KFC continued to dominate the chicken segment, with 1997 sales of $4 billion (see Exhibit 3). Its nearest competitor, Boston Market, was second with sales of $1.2 billion. In 1998, KFC operated 5,120 restaurants in the United States, eight fewer restaurants than in 1993. Rather than building new restaurants in the already saturated U.S. market, KFC focused on building restaurants abroad. In the United States, KFC focused on closing unprofitable restaurants, upgrading existing restaurants with new exterior signage, and improving product quality. The strategy has paid off. Although overall U.S. sales during the last 10 years remained flat, annual sales per unit increased steadily in eight of the last nine years.

Despite KFC's continued dominance within the chicken segment, it has lost market share to Boston Market, a new restaurant chain emphasizing roasted rather than fried chicken. Boston Market has successfully created the image of an upscale deli offering healthy, "home-style" alternatives to fried chicken and other "fast-foods." It has broadened its menu beyond rotisserie chicken to include ham, turkey, meat loaf, chicken pot pie, and deli sandwiches. In order to minimize its image as a "fast-food" restaurant, it has refused to put drive-thrus in its restaurants and has established most of its units in outside shopping malls rather than in freestanding units at intersections so characteristic of other fast-food restaurants.

In 1993, KFC introduced its own rotisserie chicken, called "Rotisserie Gold," to combat Boston Market. However, it quickly learned that its customer base was considerably different than that of Boston Market's. KFC's customers liked KFC chicken despite the fact that it was fried. In addition, customers did not respond well to the concept of buying whole chickens for take-out. They preferred instead to buy chicken by the piece. KFC withdrew its rotisserie chicken in 1996 and introduced a new line of roasted chicken called "Tender Roast," which could be sold by the piece and mixed with its Original Recipe and Extra Crispy Chicken.

Other major competitors within the chicken segment included Popeye's Famous Fried Chicken and Church's Chicken (both subsidiaries of AFC Enterprises in Atlanta), Chick-fil-A, Bojangle's, El Pollo Loco, Grandy's, Kenny Rogers Roasters, Mrs. Winner's, and Pudgie's. Both Church's and Popeye's had similar strategies—to compete head-on with other "fried chicken" chains. Unlike KFC, neither chain offered rotisserie chicken and non-fried chicken products were limited. Chick-fil-A focused exclusively on pressure-cooked and char-grilled skinless chicken

EXHIBIT 3	Top U.S. Chicken Chains						
Sales ($ M)	1992	1993	1994	1995	1996	1997	Growth Rate (%)
KFC	3,400	3,400	3,500	3,700	3,900	4,000	3.3
Boston Market	43	147	371	754	1,100	1,197	94.5
Popeye's	545	569	614	660	677	727	5.9
Chick-fil-A	356	396	451	502	570	671	11.9
Church's	414	440	465	501	526	574	6.8
Total	4,758	4,952	5,401	6,118	6,772	7,170	8.5
Number of U.S. Restaurants							
KFC	5,089	5,128	5,149	5,142	5,108	5,120	0.1
Boston Market	83	217	534	829	1,087	1,166	69.6
Popeye's	769	769	853	889	894	949	4.3
Chick-fil-A	487	545	534	825	717	762	9.0
Church's	944	932	937	953	989	1,070	2.5
Total	7,372	7,591	8,007	8,638	8,795	9,067	4.2
Sales per unit ($ 000s)							
KFC	668	663	680	720	764	781	3.2
Boston Market	518	677	695	910	1,012	1,027	14.7
Popeye's	709	740	720	743	757	767	1.6
Chick-fil-A	731	727	845	608	795	881	3.8
Church's	439	472	496	526	531	537	4.1
Total	645	782	782	782	782	782	3.9

Source: Tricon Global Restaurants, Inc., *1997 Annual Report;* Boston Chicken, Inc., *1997 Annual Report;* Chick-fil-A, corporate headquarters, Atlanta; AFC Enterprises, Inc., *1997 Annual Report.*

breast sandwiches, which it served to customers in sit-down restaurants located predominately in shopping malls. As many malls added food courts, often consisting of up to 15 fast-food units competing side-by-side, shopping malls became less enthusiastic about allocating separate store space to food chains. Therefore, in order to complement its existing restaurant base in shopping malls, Chick-fil-A began to open smaller units in shopping mall food courts, hospitals, and colleges. It also opened freestanding units in selected locations.

Demographic Trends

A number of demographic and societal trends contributed to increased demand for food prepared away from home. Because of the high divorce rate in the United States and the fact that people married later in life, single-person households represented about 25 percent of all U.S. households, up from 17 percent in 1970. This increased the number of individuals choosing to eat out rather than eat at home. The number of married women working outside of the home has also increased dramatically during the last 25 years. About 59 percent of all married women have careers. According to the Conference Board, 64 percent of all married households will be double-income families by 2000. About 80 percent of households headed by individuals between the ages of 25 and 44 (both married and unmarried) will be double-income. Greater numbers of working women increased family incomes. According to *Restaurants & Institutions*, more than one-third of all households had incomes of at least $50,000 in 1996. About 8 percent of all households had annual incomes over $100,000. The combination of higher numbers of dual-career families and rising incomes mean that fewer families have time to prepare food at home. According to Standard & Poor's Industry Surveys, Americans spent 55 percent of their food dollars at restaurants in 1995, up from 34 percent in 1970.

Fast-food restaurant chains met these demographic and societal changes by expanding their restaurant bases. However, by the early 1990s, the growth of traditional freestanding restaurants slowed as the U.S. market became saturated. The major exception was dinner houses, which continued to proliferate in response to Americans' increased passion for beef. Since 1990, the U.S. population has grown at an average annual rate of about 1 percent and reached 270 million people in 1997. Rising immigration since 1990 dramatically altered the ethnic makeup of the U.S. population. According to the Bureau of the Census, Americans born outside of the United States made up 10 percent of the population in 1997. About 40 percent were Hispanic, while 24 percent were Asian. Nearly 30 percent of Americans born outside of the United States arrived since 1990. As a result of these trends, restaurant chains expanded their menus to appeal to the different ethnic tastes of consumers, expanded into non-traditional locations such as department stores and airports, and made food more available through home delivery and take-out service.

Industry Consolidation and Mergers & Acquisitions

Lower growth in the U.S. fast-food market intensified competition for market share among restaurant chains and led to consolidation, primarily through mergers and acquisitions, during the mid-1990s. Many restaurant chains found that market share could be increased more quickly and cheaply by acquiring an existing company rather than building new units. In addition, fixed costs could be spread across a larger number of restaurants. This raised operating margins and gave companies an opportunity to build market share by lowering prices. An expanded restaurant base also gave companies greater purchasing power over suppliers. In 1990, Grand Metropolitan, a British company, purchased Pillsbury Co. for $5.7 billion. Included in the purchase was Pillsbury's Burger King chain. Grand Met strengthened the franchise by upgrading existing restaurants and eliminating several levels of management in order to cut costs. This gave Burger King a long-needed boost in improving its position against McDonald's, its largest competitor. In 1988, Grand Met had purchased Wienerwald, a West German chicken chain, and the Spaghetti Factory, a Swiss chain.

Perhaps most important to KFC was Hardee's acquisition of 600 Roy Rogers restaurants from Marriott Corporation in 1990. Hardee's converted a large number of these restaurants to Hardee's units and introduced "Roy Rogers" fried chicken to its menu. By 1993, Hardee's had introduced fried chicken into most of its U.S. restaurants. Hardee's was unlikely to destroy the customer loyalty that KFC long enjoyed. However, it did cut into KFC's sales, because it was able to offer consumers a widened menu selection that appealed to a variety of family eating preferences. In 1997, Hardee's parent company, Imasco Ltd., sold Hardee's to CKE Restaurants, Inc. CKE owned Carl's Jr., Rally's Hamburgers, and Checker's Drive-In. Boston Chicken, Inc. acquired Harry's Farmers Market, an Atlanta grocer that sold fresh quality prepared meals, in 1997. The acquisition was designed to help Boston Chicken develop distribution beyond its Boston Market restaurants. Also in 1997, AFC Enterprises, which operated Popeyes and Church's, acquired Chesapeake Bagel Bakery of McLean, Virginia, in order to diversify away from fried chicken and to strengthen its balance sheet.

The effect of these and other recent mergers and acquisitions on the industry was powerful. The top 10 restaurant companies controlled almost 60 percent of fast-food sales in the United States. The consolidation of a number of fast-food chains within larger, financially more powerful parent companies gave restaurant chains strong financial and managerial resources that could be used to compete against smaller chains in the industry.

International Quick-Service Market

Because of the aggressive pace of new restaurant construction in the United States during the 1970s and 1980s, opportunities to expand domestically through new restaurant construction in the 1990s were limited. Restaurant chains that did build new restaurants found that the higher cost of purchasing prime locations resulted in immense pressure to increase annual per restaurant sales, in order to cover higher initial investment costs. Many restaurants began to expand into international markets as an alternative to the United States. In contrast to the U.S. market, international markets offered large customer bases with comparatively little competition. However, only a few U.S. restaurant chains had defined aggressive strategies for penetrating international markets by 1998.

Three restaurant chains that had established aggressive international strategies were McDonald's, KFC, and Pizza Hut. McDonald's operated the largest number of restaurants. In 1998, it operated 23,132 restaurants in 109 countries (10,409 restaurants were located outside of the United States). In comparison, KFC, Pizza Hut, and Taco Bell together operated 29,712 restaurants in 79, 88, and 17 countries, respectively (9,126 restaurants were located outside of the United States). Of these four chains, KFC operated the greatest percentage of its restaurants (50 percent) outside of the United States. McDonald's, Pizza Hut, and Taco Bell operated 45, 31, and 2 percent of their units outside of the United States. KFC opened its first restaurant outside of the United States in the late 1950s. By the time PepsiCo acquired KFC in 1986, KFC was already operating restaurants in 55 countries. KFC's early expansion abroad, its strong brand name, and managerial experience in international markets gave it a strong competitive advantage over other fast-food chains that were investing abroad for the first time.

Exhibit 4 shows *Hotels'* 1994 list of the world's 30 largest fast-food restaurant chains (*Hotels* discontinued reporting these data after 1994). Seventeen of the 30 largest restaurant chains (ranked by number of units) were headquartered in the United States. There were a number of possible explanations for the relative scarcity of fast-food restaurant chains outside of the United States. First, the United States represented the largest consumer market in the world, accounting for over one-fifth of the world's gross domestic product (GDP). Therefore, the United States was the strategic focus of the largest restaurant chains. Second, Americans were quick to accept the fast-food concept. Many other cultures had strong culinary traditions that were difficult to break down. Europeans, for example, had histories of frequenting more mid-scale restaurants, where they spent several hours in a formal setting enjoying native dishes and beverages. Although KFC was again building restaurants in Germany by the late 1980s, it previously failed to penetrate the German market, because Germans were not accustomed to take-out food or to ordering food over the counter. McDonald's had greater success penetrating the German market, because it made a number of changes in its menu and operating procedures, in order to better appeal to German culture. For example, German beer was served in all of McDonald's German restaurants. KFC had more success in Asia and Latin America, where chicken was a traditional dish.

Aside from cultural factors, international business carried risks not present in the U.S. market. Long distances between headquarters and foreign franchises often made it difficult to control the quality of individual restaurants. Large distances also caused servicing and support problems. Transportation and other resource costs were higher than in the domestic market. In addition, time, cultural, and language differences increased communication and operational problems. Therefore, it was reasonable to expect U.S. restaurant chains to expand domestically as long as they achieved corporate profit and growth objectives. As the U.S. market became saturated, and companies gained expertise in international markets, more companies turned to profitable international markets as a means of expanding restaurant bases and increasing sales, profits, and market share.

Kentucky Fried Chicken Corporation

KFC's worldwide sales, which included sales of both company-owned and franchised restaurants, grew to $8 billion in 1997. U.S. sales grew 2.6 percent over 1996 and accounted for about one-half of KFC's sales worldwide. KFC's U.S. share of the chicken segment fell 1.8 points to 55.8 percent in 1997 (see Exhibit 5). This marked the sixth consecutive year that KFC sustained a decline in market share. Market share fell from 72.1 percent of the market in 1988 to 55.8 percent in 1997, a total market share loss of 16.3 points. Boston Market, which established its first restaurant in 1992, increased its market share from 0 to 16.7 percent over the same period. On the surface, it appeared as though Boston Market's market share gain was achieved by taking customers away from KFC. However, KFC's sales growth has remained fairly stable and constant over the last 10 years. Boston Market's success was largely a function of its appeal to consumers who did not regularly patronize KFC or other chicken chains that sold fried chicken. By appealing to a market niche that was previously unsatisfied, Boston Market was able to expand the existing consumer base within the chicken segment of the fast-food industry.

Refranchising Strategy

The relatively low growth rate in sales in KFC's domestic restaurants during the 1992–1997 period was largely the result of KFC's decision in 1993 to begin selling company-owned restaurants to franchisees. When Colonel Sanders began to expand

	EXHIBIT 4	The World's 30 Largest Fast-Food Chains (Year-end 1993, ranked by number of countries)		
	Franchise	*Location*	*Units*	*Countries*
1	Pizza Hut	Dallas, Texas	10,433	80
2	McDonald's	Oakbrook, Illinois	23,132	70
3	KFC	Louisville, Kentucky	9,033	68
4	Burger King	Miami, Florida	7,121	50
5	Baskin Robbins	Glendale, California	3,557	49
6	Wendy's	Dublin, Ohio	4,168	38
7	Domino's Pizza	Ann Arbor, Michigan	5,238	36
8	TCBY	Little Rock, Arkansas	7,474	22
9	Dairy Queen	Minneapolis, Minnesota	5,471	21
10	Dunkin' Donuts	Randolph, Massachusetts	3,691	21
11	Taco Bell	Irvine, California	4,921	20
12	Arby's	Fort Lauderdale, Florida	2,670	18
13	Subway Sandwiches	Milford, Connecticut	8,477	15
14	Sizzler International	Los Angeles, California	681	14
15	Hardee's	Rocky Mount, North Carolina	4,060	12
16	Little Caesar's	Detroit, Michigan	4,600	12
17	Popeye's Chicken	Atlanta, Georgia	813	12
18	Denny's	Spartanburg, South Carolina	1,515	10
19	A&W Restaurants	Livonia, Michigan	707	9
20	T.G.I. Friday's	Minneapolis, Minnesota	273	8
21	Orange Julius	Minneapolis, Minnesota	480	7
22	Church's Fried Chicken	Atlanta, Georgia	1,079	6
23	Long John Silver's	Lexington, Kentucky	1,464	5
24	Carl's Jr.	Anaheim, California	649	4
25	Loterria	Tokyo, Japan	795	4
26	Mos Burger	Tokyo, Japan	1,263	4
27	Skylark	Tokyo, Japan	1,000	4
28	Jack in the Box	San Diego, California	1,172	3
29	Quick Restaurants	Berchem, Belgium	876	3
30	Taco Time	Eugene, Oregon	300	3

Source: *Hotels,* May 1994; 1994 PepsiCo, Inc. Annual Report.

| EXHIBIT 5 | Top U.S. Chicken Chains - Market Share (percent) |

	KFC	Boston Market	Popeye's	Chick-fil-A	Church's	Total
1988	72.1	0.0	12.0	5.8	10.1	100.0
1989	70.8	0.0	12.0	6.2	11.0	100.0
1990	71.3	0.0	12.3	6.6	9.8	100.0
1991	72.7	0.0	11.4	7.0	8.9	100.0
1992	71.5	0.9	11.4	7.5	8.7	100.0
1993	68.7	3.0	11.4	8.0	8.9	100.0
1994	64.8	6.9	11.3	8.4	8.6	100.0
1995	60.5	12.3	10.8	8.2	8.2	100.0
1996	57.6	16.2	10.0	8.4	7.8	100.0
1997	55.8	16.7	10.1	9.4	8.0	100.0
Change	-16.3	16.7	-1.9	3.6	-2.1	0.0

Source: *Nation's Restaurant News.*

the Kentucky Fried Chicken system in the late 1950s, he established KFC as a system of independent franchisees. This was done in order to minimize his involvement in the operations of individual restaurants and to concentrate on the things he enjoyed the most—cooking, product development, and public relations. This resulted in a fiercely loyal and independent group of franchisees. PepsiCo's strategy when it acquired KFC in 1986 was to integrate KFC's operations into the PepsiCo system, in order to take advantage of operational, financial, and marketing synergies. However, such a strategy demanded that PepsiCo become more involved in decisions over franchise operations, menu offerings, restaurant management, finance, and marketing. This was met by resistance by KFC franchisees, who fiercely opposed increased control by the corporate parent. One method for PepsiCo to deal with the conflict with KFC franchises was to expand through company-owned restaurants rather than through franchising and to use strong PepsiCo cash flows to buy back unprofitable franchised restaurants, which could then be converted into company-owned restaurants. In 1986, company-owned restaurants made up 26 percent of KFC's U.S. restaurant base. By 1993, they made up about 40 percent of the total (see Exhibit 6).

While company-owned restaurants were relatively easier to control compared to franchises, they also required higher levels of investment. This meant that high levels of cash were diverted from PepsiCo's soft drink and snack food businesses into its restaurant businesses. However, the fast-food industry delivered lower returns than the soft drink and snack foods industries. Consequently, increased investment in KFC, Pizza Hut, and Taco Bell had a negative effect on PepsiCo's consolidated return on assets. By 1993, investors became concerned that PepsiCo's return on assets failed to match returns delivered by Coca-Cola. In order to shore up its return on assets, PepsiCo decided to reduce the number of company-owned restaurants by selling them back to franchisees. This strategy lowered overall company sales, but it also lowered the amount of cash tied up in fixed assets, provided PepsiCo with one-time cash flow benefits from initial fees charged to franchisees, and generated an annual stream of franchise royalties. Tricon Global continued this strategy after the spinoff in 1997.

EXHIBIT 6	KFC Restaurant Count (U.S.A.)				
	Company-Owned	% Total	Franchised/Licensed	% Total	Total
1986	1,246	26.4	3,474	73.6	4,720
1987	1,250	26.0	3,564	74.0	4,814
1988	1,262	25.8	3,637	74.2	4,899
1989	1,364	27.5	3,597	72.5	4,961
1990	1,389	27.7	3,617	72.3	5,006
1991	1,836	36.6	3,186	63.4	5,022
1992	1,960	38.8	3,095	61.2	5,055
1993	2,014	39.5	3,080	60.5	5,094
1994	2,005	39.2	3,110	60.8	5,115
1995	2,026	39.4	3,111	60.6	5,137
1996	1,932	37.8	3,176	62.2	5,108
1997	1,850	36.1	3,270	63.9	5,120
1986–1993 Compounded Annual Growth Rate					
	7.1 percent		-1.7 percent		1.1 percent
1993–1997 Compounded Annual Growth Rate					
	-2.1 percent		1.5 percent		0.1 percent

Source: Tricon Global Restaurants, Inc., *1997 Annual Report;* PepsiCo, Inc., *Annual Report,* 1994, 1995, 1996, 1997.

Marketing Strategy

During the 1980s, consumers began to demand healthier foods, greater variety, and improved service in a variety of non-traditional locations such as grocery stores, restaurants, airports, and outdoor events. This forced fast-food chains to expand menu offerings and to investigate non-traditional distribution channels and restaurant designs. Families also demanded greater value in the food they bought away from home. This increased pressure on fast-food chains to reduce prices and to lower operating costs in order to maintain profit margins.

Many of KFC's problems during the late 1980s surrounded its limited menu and its inability to bring new products to market quickly. The popularity of its Original Recipe Chicken allowed KFC to expand through the 1980s without significant competition from other chicken competitors. As a result, new product introductions were never an important element of KFC's overall strategy. One of the most serious setbacks suffered by KFC came in 1989 as KFC prepared to add a chicken sandwich to its menu. While KFC was still experimenting with its chicken sandwich, McDonald's test-marketed its McChicken sandwich in the Louisville market. Shortly thereafter, it rolled out the McChicken sandwich nationally. By beating KFC to the market, McDonald's was able to develop strong consumer awareness for its sandwich. This significantly increased KFC's cost of developing awareness for its own sandwich, which KFC introduced several months later. KFC eventually withdrew its sandwich because of low sales.

In 1991, KFC changed its logo in the United States from Kentucky Fried Chicken to KFC, in order to reduce its image as a fried chicken chain. It continued to use the Kentucky Fried Chicken name internationally. It then responded to consumer demands for greater variety by introducing several products that would serve as alternatives to its Original Recipe Chicken. These included Oriental Wings, Popcorn Chicken, and Honey BBQ Chicken. It also introduced a dessert menu that included a variety of pies and cookies. In 1993, it rolled out Rotisserie Chicken and began to promote its lunch and dinner buffet. The buffet, which included 30 items, was introduced into almost 1,600 KFC restaurants in 27 states by year-end. In 1998, KFC sold three types of chicken—Original Recipe and Extra Crispy (fried chicken) and Tender Roast (roasted chicken).

One of KFC's most aggressive strategies was the introduction of its "Neighborhood Program." By mid-1993, almost 500 company-owned restaurants in New York, Chicago, Philadelphia, Washington, D.C., St. Louis, Los Angeles, Houston, and Dallas had been outfitted with special menu offerings to appeal exclusively to the African-American community. Menus were beefed up with side dishes such as greens, macaroni and cheese, peach cobbler, sweet-potato pie, and red beans and rice. In addition, restaurant employees wore African-inspired uniforms. The introduction of the Neighborhood Program increased sales by 5 to 30 percent in restaurants appealing directly to the African-American community. KFC followed by testing Hispanic-oriented restaurants in the Miami area, offering side dishes as fried plantains, flan, and tres leches cake.

One of KFC's most significant problems in the U.S. market was that overcapacity made expansion of freestanding restaurants difficult. Fewer sites were available for new construction and those sites, because of their increased cost, were driving profit margins down. Therefore, KFC initiated a new, three-pronged distribution strategy. First, it focused on building smaller restaurants in non-traditional outlets such as airports, shopping malls, universities, and hospitals. Second, it experimented with home delivery. Home delivery was introduced in the Nashville and Albuquerque markets in 1994. By 1998, home delivery was offered in 365 U.S. restaurants. Other non-traditional distribution outlets being tested included units offering drive-thru and carry-out service only, snack shops in cafeterias, scaled-down outlets for supermarkets, and mobile units that could be transported to outdoor concerts and fairs.

A third focus of KFC's distribution strategy was restaurant co-branding, primarily with its sister chain, Taco Bell. By 1997, 349 KFC restaurants had added Taco Bell to their menus and displayed both the KFC and Taco Bell logos outside their restaurants. Co-branding gave KFC the opportunity to expand its daytime business. While about two-thirds of KFC's business was dinner, Taco Bell's primary business occurred at lunch. By combining the two concepts in the same unit, sales at individual restaurants could be increased significantly. KFC believed that there were opportunities to sell the Taco Bell concept in over 3,900 of its U.S. restaurants.

Operating Efficiencies

As pressure continued to build on fast-food chains to limit price increases, restaurant chains searched for ways to reduce overhead and other operating costs, in order to improve profit margins. In 1989, KFC reorganized its U.S. operations in order to eliminate overhead costs and to increase efficiency. Included in this reorganization was a revision of KFC's crew training programs and operating standards. A renewed emphasis was placed on cleaner restaurants, faster and friendlier customer service, and continued high-quality products. In 1992, KFC reorganized its middle-management ranks, eliminating 250 of the 1,500 management positions at

KFC's corporate headquarters. More responsibility was assigned to restaurant franchisees and marketing managers and pay was more closely aligned with customer service and restaurant performance. In 1997, Tricon Global signed a five-year agreement with PepsiCo Food Systems (which was later sold by PepsiCo to AmeriServe Food Distributors) to distribute food and supplies to Tricon's 29,712 KFC, Pizza Hut, and Taco Bell units. This provided KFC with significant opportunities to benefit from economies of scale in distribution.

International Operations

Much of the early success of the top 10 fast-food chains was the result of aggressive building strategies. Chains were able to discourage competition by building in low population areas that could only support a single fast-food chain. McDonald's was particularly successful as it was able to expand quickly into small towns across the United States, thereby preempting other fast-food chains. It was equally important to beat a competitor into more largely populated areas where location was of prime importance. KFC's early entry into international markets placed it in a strong position to benefit from international expansion as the U.S. market became saturated. In 1997, 50 percent of KFC's restaurants were located outside of the United States. Although 364 new restaurants were opened outside of the United States, only 12 new restaurants were added to the U.S. system in 1997. Most of KFC's international expansion was through franchises, though some restaurants were licensed to operators or jointly operated with a local partner. Expansion through franchising was an important strategy for penetrating international markets, because franchises were owned and operated by local entrepreneurs with a deeper understanding of local language, culture, and customs, as well as local law, financial markets, and marketing characteristics. Franchising was particularly important for expansion into smaller countries such as the Dominican Republic, Grenada, Bermuda, and Suriname, which could only support a single restaurant. Costs were prohibitively high for KFC to operate company-owned restaurants in these smaller markets. Of the 5,117 KFC restaurants located outside of the United States in 1997, 68 percent were franchised, while 22 percent were company-owned, and 10 percent were licensed restaurants or joint ventures.

In larger markets such as Japan, China, and Mexico, there was a stronger emphasis on building company-owned restaurants. By coordinating purchasing, recruiting and training, financing, and advertising, fixed costs could be spread over a large number of restaurants and lower prices on products and services could be negotiated. KFC was also better able to control product and service quality. In order to take advantage of economies of scale, Tricon Global Restaurants managed all of the international units of its KFC, Pizza Hut, and Taco Bell chains through its Tricon International division located in Dallas, Texas. This enabled Tricon Global Restaurants to leverage its strong advertising expertise, international experience, and restaurant management experience across all its KFC, Pizza Hut, and Taco Bell chains.

LATIN AMERICAN STRATEGY   KFC's primary market presence in Latin America during the 1980s was in Mexico, Puerto Rico, and the Caribbean. KFC established subsidiaries in Mexico and Puerto Rico, from which it coordinated the construction and operation of company-owned restaurants. A third subsidiary in Venezuela was closed because of the high fixed costs associated with running the small subsidiary. Franchises were used to penetrate other countries in the Caribbean whose market size prevented KFC from profitably operating company restaurants. KFC relied exclusively on the operation of company-owned restaurants in Mexico through 1989. Although franchising was popular in the United States, it was virtually unknown in Mexico until 1990, mainly because of the absence of a law protecting patents, information, and technology transferred to the Mexican franchise. In addition, royalties were limited. As a result, most fast-food chains opted to invest in Mexico using company-owned units.

In 1990, Mexico enacted a new law that provided for the protection of technology transferred into Mexico. Under the new legislation, the franchisor and franchisee were free to set their own terms. Royalties were also allowed under the new law. Royalties were taxed at a 15 percent rate on technology assistance and know-how and 35 percent for other royalty categories. The advent of the new franchise law resulted in an explosion of franchises in fast-food, services, hotels, and retail outlets. In 1992, franchises had an estimated $750 million in sales in over 1,200 outlets throughout Mexico. Prior to passage of Mexico's franchise law, KFC limited its Mexican operations primarily to Mexico City, Guadalajara, and Monterrey. This enabled KFC to better coordinate operations and minimize costs of distribution to individual restaurants. The new franchise law gave KFC and other fast-food chains the opportunity to expand their restaurant bases more quickly to more rural regions of Mexico, where responsibility for management could be handled by local franchisees.

After 1990, KFC altered its Latin American strategy in a number of ways. First, it opened 29 franchises in Mexico to complement its company-owned restaurant base. It then expanded its company-owned restaurants into the Virgin Islands and re-established a subsidiary in Venezuela. Third, it expanded its franchise operations into South America. In 1990, a franchise was opened in Chile and in 1993, a franchise was opened in Brazil. Franchises were subsequently established in Colombia, Ecuador, Panama, and Peru, among other South American countries. A fourth subsidiary was established in Brazil, in order to develop company-owned restaurants. Brazil was Latin America's largest economy and McDonald's primary Latin American investment location. By June 1998, KFC operated 438 restaurants in 32 Latin American countries. By comparison, McDonald's operated 1,091 restaurants in 28 countries.

Exhibit 7 shows the Latin American operations of KFC and McDonald's. KFC's early entry into Latin America during the 1970s gave it a leadership position in Mexico and the Caribbean. It had also gained an edge in Ecuador and Peru, countries where McDonald's had not yet developed a strong presence. McDonald's focused its Latin American investment in Brazil, Argentina, and Uruguay, countries where KFC had little or no presence. McDonald's was also strong in Venezuela. Both KFC and McDonald's were strong in Chile, Colombia, Panama, and Puerto Rico.

ECONOMIC ENVIRONMENT AND THE MEXICAN MARKET   Mexico was KFC's strongest market in Latin America. Although McDonald's had aggressively established restaurants in Mexico since 1990, KFC retained the leading market share. Because of its close proximity to the United States, Mexico was an attractive location for U.S. trade and investment. Mexico's population of 98 million people was

EXHIBIT 7	Latin America Restaurant Count—KFC and McDonald's (as of December 31, 1997)			
	KFC Company Restaurants	*KFC Franchised Restaurants*	*KFC Total Restaurants*	*McDonald's*
Argentina	–	–	–	131
Bahamas	–	10	10	3
Barbados	–	7	7	–
Brazil	6	2	8	480
Chile	–	29	29	27
Colombia	–	19	19	18
Costa Rica	–	5	5	19
Ecuador	–	18	18	2
Jamaica	–	17	17	7
Mexico	128	29	157	131
Panama	–	21	21	20
Peru	–	17	17	5
Puerto Rico & Virgin Islands	67	–	67	115
Trinidad & Tobago	–	27	27	3
Uruguay	–	–	–	18
Venezuela	6	–	6	53
Other	–	30	30	59
Total	207	231	438	1,091

Source: Tricon Global Restaurants, Inc.; McDonald's, *1997 Annual Report.*

approximately one-third as large as the United States and represented a large market for U.S. companies. In comparison, Canada's population of 30.3 million people was only one-third as large as Mexico's. Mexico's close proximity to the United States meant that transportation costs between the United States and Mexico were significantly lower than to Europe or Asia. This increased the competitiveness of U.S. goods in comparison with European and Asian goods, which had to be transported to Mexico across the Atlantic or Pacific Ocean at substantial cost. The United States was, in fact, Mexico's largest trading partner. Over 75 percent of Mexico's imports came from the United States, while 84 percent of its exports were to the United States (see Exhibit 8). Many U.S. firms invested in Mexico in order to take advantage of lower wage rates. By producing goods in Mexico, U.S. goods could be shipped back into the United States for sale or shipped to third markets at lower cost.

While the U.S. market was critically important to Mexico, Mexico still represented a small percentage of overall U.S. trade and investment. Since the early 1900s, the portion of U.S. exports to Latin America has declined. Instead, U.S. exports to Canada and Asia, where economic growth outpaced growth in Mexico, increased quickly. Canada was the largest importer of U.S. goods. Japan was the largest exporter of goods to the United States, with Canada a close second. U.S. investment in Mexico was also small, mainly because of government restrictions on foreign investment. Most U.S. foreign investment was in Europe, Canada, and Asia.

The lack of U.S. investment in and trade with Mexico during this century was mainly the result of Mexico's long history of restricting trade and foreign direct investment. The Institutional Revolutionary Party (PRI), which came to power in Mexico during the 1930s, had historically pursued protectionist economic policies, in order to shield Mexico's economy from foreign competition. Many industries were government-owned or controlled and many Mexican companies focused on producing goods for the domestic market without much attention to building export markets. High tariffs and other trade barriers restricted imports into Mexico and foreign ownership of assets in Mexico was largely prohibited or heavily restricted.

Additionally, a dictatorial and entrenched government bureaucracy, corrupt labor unions, and a long tradition of anti-Americanism among many government officials and intellectuals reduced the motivation of U.S. firms for investing in Mexico. The nationalization of Mexico's banks in 1982 led to higher real interest rates and lower investor confidence. Afterward, the Mexican government battled high inflation, high interest rates, and labor unrest, and lost consumer purchasing power. Investor confidence in Mexico, however, improved after 1988, when Carlos Salinas de Gortari was elected president. Following his election, Salinas embarked on an ambitious restructuring of the Mexican economy. He initiated policies to strengthen the free market components of the economy, lowered top marginal tax rates to 36 percent (down from 60 percent in 1986), and eliminated many restrictions on foreign investment. Foreign firms can now buy up to 100 percent of the equity in many Mexico firms. Foreign ownership of Mexican firms was previously limited to 49 percent.

PRIVATIZATION   The privatization of government-owned companies came to symbolize the restructuring of Mexico's economy. In 1990, legislation was passed to privatize all government-run banks. By the end of 1992, over 800 of some 1,200 government-owned companies had been sold, including Mexicana and AeroMexico, the two largest airline companies in Mexico, and Mexico's 18 major banks. However, more than 350 companies remained under government ownership. These represented a significant portion of the assets owned by the state at the start of 1988. Therefore, the sale of government-owned companies, in terms of asset value, was moderate. A large percentage of the remaining government-owned assets was controlled by government-run companies in certain strategic industries such as steel, electricity, and petroleum. These industries had long been protected by government ownership. As a result, additional privatization of government-owned enterprises until 1993 was limited. However, in 1993, President Salinas opened up the electricity sector to independent power producers and Petroleos Mexicanos (Pemex), the state-run petrochemical monopoly, initiated a program to sell off many of its nonstrategic assets to private and foreign buyers.

NORTH AMERICAN FREE TRADE AGREEMENT (NAFTA)   Prior to 1989, Mexico levied high tariffs on most imported goods. In addition, many other goods were subjected to quotas, licensing requirements, and other non-tariff trade barriers. In 1986, Mexico joined the General Agreement on Tariffs and Trade (GATT), a world trade organization designed to eliminate barriers to trade among member nations. As a member of GATT, Mexico was obligated to apply its system of tariffs to all member nations equally. As a result of its membership in GATT, Mexico dropped tariff rates on a variety of imported goods. In addition, import license requirements were

EXHIBIT 8	Mexico's Major Trading Partners % Total Exports and Imports					
	1992		1994		1996	
	Exports	*Imports*	*Exports*	*Imports*	*Exports*	*Imports*
U.S.A	81.1	71.3	85.3	71.8	84.0	75.6
Japan	1.7	4.9	1.6	4.8	1.4	4.4
Germany	1.1	4.0	0.6	3.9	0.7	3.5
Canada	2.2	1.7	2.4	2.0	1.2	1.9
Italy	0.3	1.6	0.1	1.3	1.2	1.1
Brazil	0.9	1.8	0.6	1.5	0.9	0.8
Spain	2.7	1.4	1.4	1.7	1.0	0.7
Other	10.0	13.3	8.0	13.0	9.6	12.0
Total	100.0	100.0	100.0	100.0	100.0	100.0
Value ($M)	46,196	62,129	60,882	79,346	95,991	89,464

Source: International Monetary Fund, *Direction of Trade Statistics Yearbook*, 1997.

dropped for all but 300 imported items. During President Salinas' administration, tariffs were reduced from an average of 100 percent on most items to an average of 11 percent.

On January 1, 1994, the North American Free Trade Agreement (NAFTA) went into effect. The passage of NAFTA, which included Canada, the United States, and Mexico, created a trading bloc with a larger population and gross domestic product than the European Union. All tariffs on goods traded among the three countries were scheduled to be phased out. NAFTA was expected to be particularly beneficial for Mexican exporters, because reduced tariffs made their goods more competitive in the United States compared to goods exported to the United States from other countries. In 1995, one year after NAFTA went into effect, Mexico posted its first balance of trade surplus in six years. Part of this surplus was attributed to reduced tariffs resulting from the NAFTA agreement. However, the peso crisis of 1995, which lowered the value of the peso against the dollar, increased the price of goods imported into Mexico and lowered the price of Mexican products exported to the United States. Therefore, it was still too early to assess the full effects of the NAFTA agreement.

FOREIGN EXCHANGE AND THE MEXICAN PESO CRISIS OF 1995   Between 1982 and 1991, a two-tiered exchange rate system was in force in Mexico. The system consisted of a controlled rate and a free market rate. A controlled rate was used for imports, foreign debt payments, and conversion of export proceeds. An estimated 70 percent of all foreign transactions were covered by the controlled rate. A free market rate was used for other transactions. In 1989, President Salinas instituted a policy of allowing the peso to depreciate against the dollar by one peso per day. The result was a grossly overvalued peso. This lowered the price of imports and led to an increase in imports of over 23 percent in 1989. At the same time, Mexican exports became less competitive on world markets.

In 1991, the controlled rate was abolished and replaced with an official free rate. In order to limit the range of fluctuations in the value of the peso, the government fixed the rate at which it would buy or sell pesos. A floor (the maximum price at which pesos could be purchased) was established at Ps 3,056.20 and remained fixed. A ceiling (the maximum price at which the peso could be sold) was established at Ps 3,056.40 and allowed to move upward by Ps 0.20 per day. This was later revised to Ps 0.40 per day. In 1993, a new currency, called the new peso, was issued with three fewer zeros. The new currency was designed to simplify transactions and to reduce the cost of printing currency.

When Ernesto Zedillo became Mexico's president in December 1994, one of his objectives was to continue the stability of prices, wages, and exchange rates achieved by ex-president Carlos Salinas de Gortari during his five-year tenure as president. However, Salinas had achieved stability largely on the basis of price, wage, and foreign exchange controls. Although giving the appearance of stability, an over-valued peso continued to encourage imports, which exacerbated Mexico's balance of trade deficit. Mexico's government continued to use foreign reserves to finance its balance of trade deficits. According to the Banco de Mexico, foreign currency reserves fell from $24 billion in January 1994 to $5.5 billion in January 1995. Anticipating a devaluation of the peso, investors began to move capital into U.S. dollar investments. In order to relieve pressure on the peso, Zedillo announced on December 19, 1994 that the peso would be allowed to depreciate by an additional 15 percent per year against the dollar compared to the maximum allowable depreciation of 4 percent per year established during the Salinas administration. Within two days, continued pressure on the peso forced Zedillo to allow the peso to float freely against the dollar. By mid-January 1995, the peso had lost 35 percent of its value against the dollar and the Mexican stock market plunged 20 percent. By November 1995, the peso had depreciated from 3.1 pesos per dollar to 7.3 pesos per dollar.

The continued devaluation of the peso resulted in higher import prices, higher inflation, destabilization within the stock market, and higher interest rates. Mexico struggled to pay its dollar-based debts. In order to thwart a possible default by Mexico, the U.S. government, International Monetary Fund, and World Bank pledged $24.9 billion in emergency loans. Zedillo then announced an emergency economic package called the "pacto" that included reduced government spending, increased sales of government-run businesses, and a freeze on wage increases. Exhibit 9 includes selected economic data for Canada, the U.S. and Mexico.

LABOR PROBLEMS   One of KFC's primary concerns in Mexico was the stability of labor markets. Labor was relatively plentiful and wages were low. However, much of the work force was relatively unskilled. KFC benefited from lower labor costs, but labor unrest, low job retention, high absenteeism, and poor punctuality were significant problems. Absenteeism and punctuality were partially cultural. However, problems with worker retention and labor unrest were primarily the result of workers' frustration over the loss of their purchasing power due to inflation and government controls on wage increases. Absenteeism remained high at approximately 8 to 14 percent of the labor force, though it was declining because of decreasing job security fears. Turnover continued to be a problem and ran at between 5 and 12 percent per month. Therefore, employee screening and internal training were important issues for firms investing in Mexico.

Higher inflation and the government's freeze on wage increases led to a dramatic decline in disposable income after 1994. Further, a slowdown in business activity,

EXHIBIT 9	Selected Economic Data for Canada, the United States, and Mexico				
Annual Change (percent)	*1993*	*1994*	*1995*	*1996*	*1997*
GDP Growth					
Canada	3.3	4.8	5.5	4.1	–
United States	4.9	5.8	4.8	5.1	5.9
Mexico	21.4	13.3	29.4	38.2	–
Real GDP Growth					
Canada	2.2	4.1	2.3	1.2	–
United States	2.2	3.5	2.0	2.8	3.8
Mexico	2.0	4.5	-6.2	5.1	–
Inflation					
Canada	1.9	0.2	2.2	1.5	1.6
United States	3.0	2.5	2.8	2.9	2.4
Mexico	9.7	6.9	35.0	34.4	20.6
Depreciation Against $U.S.					
Canada (C$)	4.2	6.0	-2.7	0.3	4.3
Mexico (NP)	-0.3	71.4	43.5	2.7	3.6

Source: International Monetary Fund, *International Financial Statistics,* 1998.

brought about by higher interest rates and lower government spending, led many businesses to lay off workers. By the end of 1995, an estimated one million jobs had been lost as a result of the economic crisis sparked by the peso devaluation. As a result, industry groups within Mexico called for new labor laws giving them more freedom to hire and fire employees and increased flexibility to hire part-time rather than full-time workers.

Risks And Opportunities

The peso crisis of 1995 and resulting recession in Mexico left KFC managers with a great deal of uncertainty regarding Mexico's economic and political future. KFC had benefited from economic stability between 1988 and 1994. Inflation was brought down, the peso was relatively stable, labor unrest was relatively calm, and Mexico's new franchise law had enabled KFC to expand into rural areas using franchises rather than company-owned restaurants. By the end of 1995, KFC had built 29 franchises in Mexico. The foreign exchange crisis of 1995 had severe implications for U.S. firms operating in Mexico. The devaluation of the peso resulted in higher inflation and capital flight out of Mexico. Capital flight reduced the supply of capital and led to higher interest rates. In order to reduce inflation, Mexico's government instituted an austerity program that resulted in lower disposable income, higher unemployment, and lower demand for products and services.

Another problem was Mexico's failure to reduce restrictions on U.S. and Canadian investment in a timely fashion. Many U.S. firms experienced problems getting required approvals for new ventures from the Mexican government. A good example was United Parcel Service (UPS), which sought government approval to use large trucks for deliveries in Mexico. Approvals were delayed, forcing UPS to use smaller trucks. This put UPS at a competitive disadvantage vis-a-vis Mexican companies. In many cases, UPS was forced to subcontract delivery work to Mexican companies that were allowed to use larger, more cost-efficient trucks. Other U.S. companies such as Bell Atlantic and TRW faced similar problems. TRW, which signed a joint venture agreement with a Mexican partner, had to wait 15 months longer than anticipated before the Mexican government released rules on how it could receive credit data from banks. TRW claimed that the Mexican government slowed the approval process in order to placate several large Mexican banks.

A final area of concern for KFC was increased political turmoil in Mexico during the last several years. On January 1, 1994, the day NAFTA went into effect, rebels (descendants of the Mayans) rioted in the southern Mexican province of Chiapas on the Guatemalan border. After four days of fighting, Mexican troops had driven the rebels out of several towns earlier seized by the rebels. Around 150—mostly rebels—were killed. The uprising symbolized many of the fears of the poor in Mexico. Although ex-president Salinas' economic programs had increased economic growth and wealth in Mexico, many of Mexico's poorest felt that they had not benefited. Many of Mexico's farmers, faced with lower tariffs on imported agricultural goods from the United States, felt that they might be driven out of business because of lower priced imports. Therefore, social unrest among Mexico's Indians, farmers, and the poor could potentially unravel much of the economic success achieved in Mexico during the last five years.

Further, ex-president Salinas' hand-picked successor for president was assassinated in early 1994 while campaigning in Tijuana. The assassin was a 23-year-old mechanic and migrant worker believed to be affiliated with a dissident group upset with the PRI's economic reforms. The possible existence of a dissident group raised fears of political violence in the future. The PRI quickly named Ernesto Zedillo, a 42-year-old economist with little political experience as their new presidential candidate. Zedillo was elected president in December 1994. Political unrest was not limited to Mexican officials and companies. In October 1994, between 30 and 40 masked men attacked a McDonald's restaurant in the tourist section of Mexico City to show their opposition to California's Proposition 187, which would have curtailed benefits to illegal aliens (primarily from Mexico). The men threw cash registers to the floor, cracked them open, smashed windows, overturned tables, and spray-painted slogans on the walls such as "No to Fascism" and "Yankee Go Home."

KFC faced a variety of issues in Mexico and Latin America in 1998. Prior to 1995, few restaurants had been opened in South America. However, KFC was now aggressively building new restaurants in the region. KFC halted openings of franchised restaurants in Mexico, and all restaurants opened since 1995 were company-owned. KFC was aggressively building restaurants in South America, which remained largely unpenetrated by KFC through 1995. Of greatest importance was Brazil, where McDonald's had already established a strong market share position. Brazil was Latin America's largest economy and a largely untapped market for KFC. The danger in ignoring Mexico was that a conservative investment strategy could jeopardize its market share lead over McDonald's in a large market where KFC long enjoyed enormous popularity.

Marketing Plan Worksheets

The worksheets in this appendix are designed to assist you in writing a formal marketing plan. Worksheets are a useful planning tool because they help ensure that you do not omit important information from the marketing plan. Answering the questions on these worksheets will enable you to:

1. Organize and structure the data and information you collect during the environmental analysis.
2. Use this information to better understand the strengths and weaknesses of your organization and to recognize the opportunities and threats that exist in the marketing environment.
3. Develop goals and objectives that capitalize on the strengths of your organization.
4. Develop marketing strategies that create competitive advantages.
5. Outline a plan for implementing the marketing strategies.

These worksheets match the marketing plan outline in Exhibit 2.1 and the exhibits in Chapter 3 on environmental analysis. If you need additional help in putting together your marketing plan, refer to Appendix B, where you will find a sample marketing plan. The headings in the sample plan also match the headings in these worksheets.

As you complete the worksheets, it might be useful to refer back to Chapters 3–10. In completing the environmental analysis section, be sure to be as comprehensive as possible. The viability of your SWOT analysis depends on how well you have identified all of the relevant environmental issues. Likewise, as you complete the SWOT analysis, you should be honest about your organization's characteristics. Do not depend on strengths that your organization really does not possess. Being honest also goes for your listing of weaknesses.

You should begin by downloading a copy of these worksheets from our web site. Having an electronic version of these worksheets will allow you to change the outline or add additional information that is relevant to your situation. Remember that there is no one best way to organize a marketing plan. Our outline was designed to serve as a starting point and to be flexible enough to accommodate the unique characteristics of your organization. Now, let's get started.

I. **Executive Summary**

The executive summary is a synopsis of the overall marketing plan. The executive summary is easier to write if you do it last, after you have written the entire marketing plan.

II. **Environmental Analysis**

A. **The External Environment**

Competitive forces

Who are our major competitors? What are their characteristics (size, growth, profitability, strategies, target markets)?

Brand competitors:

Product competitors:

Generic competitors:

Key total budget competitors:

What are our competitors' key strengths and weaknesses?

What are our competitors' key marketing capabilities in terms of products, distribution, promotion, and pricing?

What response can we expect from our competitors if environmental conditions change or if we change our marketing strategy?

Is this competitive set likely to change in the future? If so, how? Who are our new competitors likely to be?

Economic growth and stability

What are the general economic conditions of the country, region, state, and local area in which our firm operates?

Overall, are our customers optimistic or pessimistic about the economy?

What is the buying power of customers in our target market(s)?

What are the current spending patterns of customers in our target market(s)? Are they buying less or more of our product and why?

Political trends

Have recent elections changed the political landscape within our domestic or foreign markets? What type of industry regulations do newly elected officials favor?

What are we currently doing to maintain good relations with elected officials? Have these activities been effective? Why or why not?

Legal and regulatory factors

What changes in international, federal, state, or local laws and regulations are being proposed that would affect our marketing activities?

Do recent court decisions suggest that we should modify our marketing activities?

Do the recent rulings of federal, state, local, and self-regulatory agencies suggest that we should modify our marketing activities?

What effect will changes in global trade agreements have on our international marketing opportunities?

Changes in technology

What impact has changing technology had on our customers?

What technological changes will affect the way we operate or manufacture our products?

What technological changes will affect the way we conduct marketing activities, such as distribution or promotion?

Do current technologies exist that we are not using to their fullest potential in making our marketing activities more effective and efficient?

Do any technological advances threaten to make our product(s) obsolete?

Cultural trends

How are society's demographics and values changing?

What effect will these changes have on our:

product(s)?

pricing?

distribution?

promotion?

people?

What problems or opportunities are being created by changes in the cultural diversity of our customers and employees?

What is the general attitude of society about our industry, company, and product(s)? Could we take actions to improve this attitude?

What consumer or environmental groups could intervene in the operations of our industry or company?

What ethical issues should we address?

B. The Customer Environment

Who are our current and potential customers?

Demographic characteristics: gender, age, income, occupation, education, ethnic background, family life cycle, etc.

Current customers:

Potential customers:

Geographic characteristics: location, density, etc.

Current customers:

Potential customers:

Psychographic characteristics: attitudes, opinion, interests, motives, lifestyles

Current customers:

Potential customers:

Do the purchasers of our products differ from the users of our products? Who are the major influencers of the purchase decision?

Who is financially responsible for making the purchase?

What do our customers do with our products?

In what quantities and in what combinations are our products purchased?

How do heavy users of our products differ from light users?

How do customers use complementary products with our products?

What do our customers do with our products after consumption? Do they recycle our products or our packaging?

Where do our customers purchase our products?

From what types of intermediaries are our products purchased?

Retail stores:

Wholesale outlets:

Catalog outlets:

Electronic outlets:

How does electronic commerce affect the purchase of our products? Will this change in the future?

Are our customers increasing their purchasing from nonstore outlets such as catalogs, home shopping networks, or the Internet?

When do our customers purchase our products?

Are the purchase and consumption of our products seasonal?

To what extent do promotional events affect the purchase and consumption of our products?

Do the purchase and consumption of our products vary based on changes in physical/social surroundings, time perceptions, or the purchase task?

Why (and how) do our customers select our products?

What are the basic benefits provided by our products and our competitors' products?

What are the customer needs that are fulfilled by the benefits delivered by our products and our competitors' products?

How well do our products and our competitors' products meet the needs of our customers?

How are the needs of our customers expected to change in the future?

What methods of payment do our customers use when making a purchase?

Are our customers prone to developing close long-term relationships with us and our competitors, or do they buy in a transactional fashion (primarily on price)?

Why do potential customers not purchase our products?

What are the basic needs of noncustomers that are not being met by our products?

What are the features, benefits, or advantages of competing products that cause noncustomers to choose them over our products?

Are there issues related to distribution, promotion, and pricing that cause customers not to purchase our products?

What is the potential for converting these noncustomers to our products?

C. Internal (Organizational) Environment

Review of marketing goals, objectives, and performance

What are our current marketing goals and objectives?

Are our marketing goals and objectives consistent with the mission, goals, and objectives of the firm? Why or why not?

Are our marketing goals and objectives consistent with recent changes in the marketing or customer environments? Why or why not?

How are our current marketing strategies performing in terms of sales volume, market share, profitability and communication (e.g., awareness and preference) objectives?

How does our current performance compare to other firms in the industry? Is the performance of the industry as a whole improving or declining? Why?

If our performance is declining, what is the most likely cause? Are our marketing objectives inconsistent with changes in the marketing or customer environments? Is the strategy flawed? Was the strategy poorly implemented?

If our performance is improving, what actions can we take to ensure that our performance continues to improve? Is the improvement in performance due to a better than anticipated environment or superior planning and implementation?

Review of current and anticipated organizational resources

What is the state of our current organizational resources (e.g., financial, capital, human, experience, relationships with key suppliers or customers)?

Are these resources likely to change for the better or worse in the near future?

If the changes are for the better, how can we utilize these added resources to our advantage in meeting customer needs better than competitors?

If the changes are for the worse, what can be done to compensate for these new constraints on our resources?

Review of current and anticipated cultural and structural issues

What are the positive and negative aspects of the current and anticipated culture of the firm?

What issues related to internal politics and power struggles might affect our marketing activities?

What is the overall position and importance of the marketing function as seen by other functional areas? Are key executive positions expected to change in the future?

How will the overall customer orientation of the firm (or lack thereof) affect our marketing activities?

Does the firm emphasize a long-term or short-term planning horizon? How will this emphasis affect our marketing activities?

Currently, are there positive or negative issues with respect to motivating our employees, especially those in customer contact positions (e.g., sales, customer service)?

III. SWOT Analysis

A. Strengths

Strength 1:

How does this strength assist us in meeting customer needs?

How does this strength compare to our competitors' strengths? Does this strength make us different from (better than) our competitors in the minds of our customers?

Strength 2:

How does this strength assist us in meeting customer needs?

How does this strength compare to our competitors' strengths? Does this strength make us different from (better than) our competitors in the minds of our customers?

Strength 3:

How does this strength assist us in meeting customer needs?

How does this strength compare to our competitors' strengths? Does this strength make us different from (better than) our competitors in the minds of our customers?

B. Weaknesses

Weakness 1:

How does this weakness hinder us in meeting customer needs?

How does this weakness compare to our competitors' weaknesses? Does this weakness make us different from (worse than) our competitors in the minds of our customers?

Weakness 2:

How does this weakness hinder us in meeting customer needs?

How does this weakness compare to our competitors' weaknesses? Does this weakness make us different from (worse than) our competitors in the minds of our customers?

Weakness 3:

How does this weakness hinder us in meeting customer needs?

How does this weakness compare to our competitors' weaknesses? Does this weakness make us different from (worse than) our competitors in the minds of our customers?

C. Opportunities

Opportunity 1:

How is this opportunity related to serving the needs of our customers?

What actions can we take to capitalize on this opportunity in the short term and in the long term?

Opportunity 2:

How is this opportunity related to serving the needs of our customers?

What actions can we take to capitalize on this opportunity in the short term and in the long term?

Opportunity 3:

How is this opportunity related to serving the needs of our customers?

What actions can we take to capitalize on this opportunity in the short term and in the long term?

D. Threats

Threat 1:

How is this threat related to serving the needs of our customers?

What actions can we take to prevent this threat from limiting our capabilities in the short term and in the long term?

Threat 2:

How is this threat related to serving the needs of our customers?

What actions can we take to prevent this threat from limiting our capabilities in the short term and in the long term?

Threat 3:

How is this threat related to serving the needs of our customers?

What actions can we take to prevent this threat from limiting our capabilities in the short term and in the long term?

E. The SWOT Matrix

Strengths:	*Opportunities:*
•	•
•	•
•	•
•	•
•	•
•	•
•	•
Weaknesses:	*Threats:*
•	•
•	•
•	•
•	•
•	•
•	•
•	•

F. Matching, Converting, Minimizing, and Avoiding Strategies

How can we match our strengths to our opportunities to create capabilities in serving the needs of our customers?

How can we convert our weaknesses into strengths?

How can we convert our threats into opportunities?

How can we minimize or avoid those weaknesses and threats that cannot be successfully converted?

Do we possess any major liabilities (unconverted weaknesses that match unconverted threats) or limitations (unconverted weaknesses or threats that match opportunities)? Are these liabilities and limitations obvious to our customers?

Are there ways that these liabilities and limitations can be minimized or avoided?

IV. Marketing Goals and Objectives

A. Marketing Goal A:

Objective A1:

Specific and measurable outcome:

Time frame:

Responsible unit/person:

Relationship to SWOT:

Objective A2:

Specific and measurable outcome:

Time frame:

Responsible unit/person:
Relationship to SWOT:
Objective A3:
Specific and measurable outcome:
Time frame:
Responsible unit/person:
Relationship to SWOT:
B. Marketing Goal B:
Objective B1:
Specific and measurable outcome:
Time frame:
Responsible unit/person:
Relationship to SWOT:
Objective B2:
Specific and measurable outcome:
Time frame:
Responsible unit/person:
Relationship to SWOT:
Objective B3:
Specific and measurable outcome:
Time frame:
Responsible unit/person:
Relationship to SWOT:
C. Marketing Goal C:
Objective C1:
Specific and measurable outcome:
Time frame:
Responsible unit/person:
Relationship to SWOT:
Objective C2:
Specific and measurable outcome:
Time frame:
Responsible unit/person:
Relationship to SWOT:
Objective C3:
Specific and measurable outcome:
Time frame:
Responsible unit/person:
Relationship to SWOT:
V. Marketing Strategies
A. Target Market(s)
Target market A:
Demographic characteristics:
Geographic characteristics:
Psychographic characteristics:
Basic needs and benefits sought:
Purchasing/shopping characteristics:
Consumption/disposition characteristics:
Justification for selection:
Target market B:
Demographic characteristics:
Geographic characteristics:
Psychographic characteristics:

Basic needs and benefits sought:
Purchasing/shopping characteristics:
Consumption/disposition characteristics:
Justification for selection:

B. Marketing Mix

Marketing mix A (to meet the needs of target market A):

Product
   Description of major features and benefits:
   Differentiation relative to competing products:
   Elements of customer service strategy:
   Brand name and packaging:
   Relationship to delivering value:
   Complementary products:

Pricing
   Description of per unit costs:
   Pricing objectives:
   Discount/markdown policy:
   Relationship to delivering value:

Distribution
   General distribution strategy:
   Intermediaries and channels to be used:
   Relationship to delivering value and convenience:

Promotion
   Summary of overall promotion strategy:
   Basis for product/company positioning:
   Advertising/publicity objectives and budget:
   Elements of the advertising/publicity campaign:
   Personal selling objectives and budget:
   Elements of the personal selling effort:
   Sales promotion objectives and budget:
   Elements of trade sales promotion (push):
   Elements of consumer sales promotion (pull):

Marketing mix B (to meet the needs of target market B):

Product
   Description of major features and benefits:
   Differentiation relative to competing products:
   Elements of customer service strategy:
   Brand name and packaging:
   Relationship to delivering value:
   Complementary products:

Pricing
   Description of per unit costs:
   Pricing objectives:
   Discount/markdown policy:
   Relationship to delivering value:

Distribution
   General distribution strategy:
   Intermediaries and channels to be used:
   Relationship to delivering value and convenience:

Promotion
   Summary of overall promotion strategy:
   Basis for product/company positioning:
   Advertising/publicity objectives and budget:

Elements of the advertising/publicity campaign:
Personal selling objectives and budget:
Elements of the personal selling effort:
Sales promotion objectives and budget:
Elements of trade sales promotion (push):
Elements of consumer sales promotion (pull):

C. Key Customer and Competitor Reactions

What are the likely customer and competitor reactions to marketing mix A?
How does marketing mix A give us a competitive advantage in serving the needs of target market A?
Is this competitive advantage sustainable? Why or why not?
What are the likely customer and competitor reactions to marketing mix B?
How does marketing mix B give us a competitive advantage in serving the needs of target market B?
Is this competitive advantage sustainable? Why or why not?

VI. Marketing Implementation

A. Structural Issues

Description of overall approach to implementation:
Description of internal marketing activities:
  Internal products:
  Internal pricing:
  Internal distribution:
  Internal promotion:
What communication avenues are in place to ensure that all employees understand their role in implementing the marketing strategy?
Will customer-contact employees and managers be empowered to make decisions? If yes, how will the organization ensure that empowered employees make the right decisions?
How can the organization ensure that employees are motivated to implement the required marketing activities?
How can the organization ensure that all marketing activities are coordinated with other functional areas within the firm?

B. Activities, Responsibilities, Budgets, and Timetables

Product activities
  Activity 1:
    Person responsible:
    Budget:
    Other resources needed:
    Target completion date:
  Activity 2:
    Person responsible:
    Budget:
    Other resources needed:
    Target completion date:
  Activity 3:
    Person responsible:
    Budget:
    Other resources needed:
    Target completion date:
Pricing activities
  Activity 1:
    Person responsible:
    Budget:
    Other resources needed:
    Target completion date:
  Activity 2:
    Person responsible:
    Budget:

  Other resources needed:
  Target completion date:
 Activity 3:
  Person responsible:
  Budget:
  Other resources needed:
  Target completion date:
Distribution activities
 Activity 1:
  Person responsible:
  Budget:
  Other resources needed:
  Target completion date:
 Activity 2:
  Person responsible:
  Budget:
  Other resources needed:
  Target completion date:
 Activity 3:
  Person responsible:
  Budget:
  Other resources needed:
  Target completion date:
Promotion activities
 Activity 1:
  Person responsible:
  Budget:
  Other resources needed:
  Target completion date:
 Activity 2:
  Person responsible:
  Budget:
  Other resources needed:
  Target completion date:
 Activity 3:
  Person responsible:
  Budget:
  Other resources needed:
  Target completion date:

VII. Evaluation and Control

A. Financial Assessment

Contribution Analysis

 a. Total fixed costs:
 b. Variable costs per unit:
 c. Per unit selling price:
 d. Current gross margin target:
 e. Future gross margin target:

What is the required sales volume in units needed to meet the *current* gross margin target? $(a + d) \div (c - b)$

What is the required sales volume in units needed to meet the *future* gross margin target? $(a + e) \div (c - b)$

Response Analysis

 a. Estimated product response coefficient:
 b. Estimated price response coefficient:

 c. Estimated distribution response coefficient:

 d. Estimated promotion response coefficient:

 Combined response impact (a × b × c × d):

Systematic Planning Model

 a. Current industry sales (in units):

 b. Projected sales growth (decline) percentage:

 c. Projected industry sales (a × b):

 d. Projected firm market share if current marketing strategy is continued:

 e. Modified market share (multiply d by the combined response impact from above):

 f. Predicted sales in units (c × e):

 g. Projected sales in dollars (multiply f by the per unit selling price):

 h. Projected costs:

 i. Projected gross margin (g - h):

B. Marketing Control

What types and levels of formal control mechanisms are in place to ensure the implementation of the marketing plan?

 Input control mechanisms

 Employee recruitment and selection procedures:

 Employee training programs:

 Employee manpower allocations:

 Financial resources:

 Capital outlays:

 Research and development expenditures:

 Other:

 Process control mechanisms

 Employee evaluation and compensation systems:

 Employee authority and empowerment:

 Internal communication programs:

 Lines of authority/structure (organizational chart):

 Management commitment to the marketing plan:

 Management commitment to employees:

 Output control mechanisms (performance standards)

 Product performance standards:

 Potential corrective actions that can be taken if actual product performance does not match these standards:

 Price performance standards:

 Potential corrective actions that can be taken if actual pricing performance does not match these standards:

 Distribution performance standards:

 Potential corrective actions that can be taken if actual distribution performance does not match these standards:

 Promotion performance standards:

 Potential corrective actions that can be taken if actual promotion performance does not match these standards:

 Output control mechanisms (marketing audits)

 How will marketing activities be monitored?

 What are the specific profit- and time-based measures that will be used to monitor marketing activities?

 Describe the marketing audit to be performed:

 Who will be responsible for conducting this audit?

What types and levels of informal control mechanisms are in place to ensure the implementation of the marketing plan?

 Employee self-control

 Are employees satisfied with their jobs at a level that is sufficient for implementing the marketing plan? If not, how can employee job satisfaction be increased?

 Are employees committed to the organization at a level that is sufficient for implementing the marketing plan? If not, how can employee commitment be increased?

Are employees committed to the marketing plan at a level that is sufficient for its implementation? If not, how can employee commitment to the plan be increased?

Employee social control

Do employees share the organization's values in a manner that enhances the implementation of the marketing plan?

Describe the social and behavioral norms that exist within the organization, and in work groups, that are either beneficial or detrimental to implementation:

Employee cultural control

Is the organizational culture appropriate for the marketing plan? If not, what type of culture would be more appropriate?

Though cultural change is a slow process, what steps can be taken to change the organization's culture to become more conducive to implementing the marketing strategy?

Marketing Plan Example

This marketing plan was developed for a single retail unit of Johnston & Murphy shoes, located in The Regalia Center in Memphis, Tennessee. The overall goal of this marketing plan was to increase customer trial and purchase of Johnston & Murphy (J&M) shoes at this single location. This plan therefore focuses on a narrowly defined product/market: a single retail store in a limited market area. Our example plan is not intended to provide additional content about marketing strategy or the marketing plan, but simply to give you an opportunity to look at a real marketing plan. As you read this example, remember that the analysts adapted the marketing plan outline to fit the needs of a particular situation. As a result, this plan differs somewhat from the general outline presented in Chapter 2.

Before we begin, you might want to know a little about the history of Johnston & Murphy:

The clothing and shoe market has proved to be a challenge to those companies that have ventured into the industry. The task of appealing to consumers' varied tastes, while maintaining quality and value, is one of great importance. One company that has met this challenge is GENESCO, based in Nashville, Tennessee. GENESCO is a diverse company with a wide variety of both footwear and clothing manufacturing facilities and retail locations. GENESCO originated as the General Shoe Corporation, then became involved in the apparel industry in 1956. After changing its name to GENESCO in 1959, the company expanded to overseas operations. Today, GENESCO consists of several companies representing a variety of products sold to a wide array of customers.

GENESCO's footwear division remains a major part of the company. Within this division are brand names such as Code West, Jarman, Dockers, Johnston & Murphy, Mitre, Laredo, and Nautica. These brands represent an assortment of men's casual and dress shoes, sports shoes, and women's boots. These products are sold through GENESCO's own retail facilities, as well as through secondary merchandisers. GENESCO's finest footwear line is Johnston & Murphy.

Founded in 1850 by an English shoemaker, William Dudley, Johnston & Murphy continues to carry on the traditions of excellent craftsmanship in each of its products, now nearly 150 years later. Johnston & Murphy can truly claim to be the "oldest manufacturer of men's dress footwear in America." This title is one of honor and demands that each shoe be meticulously manufactured. Because of this attitude toward quality and value, Johnston & Murphy has become a familiar name among discerning consumers who desire not only an excellent shoe, but an excellent investment.

Marketing Plan for Johnston & Murphy

Executive Summary

Synopsis

This marketing plan is designed for the Johnston & Murphy store in The Regalia Center at 6150 Poplar Avenue, Memphis, Tennessee. Substantial opportunities exist to tap into the market of individuals who currently do not purchase quality footwear and accessories from this location. To take advantage of this opportunity, a specific target market was identified by examining the individual values, attitudes, and lifestyles of consumers. This information will enable the Regalia store to influence the behavior of the target market in ways that will increase Johnston & Murphy's customer traffic and subsequent sales.

The market profile was refined using a survey developed to test attitudes and behaviors related to purchasing dress shoes (See Exhibit B.1). The results were combined with demographic information from zip code regions adjacent to The

EXHIBIT B.1	Men's Dress Shoe Survey

You are being asked to respond to a few questions about men's dress shoes. "Men's dress shoes" include shoes you wear with a suit, dress slacks, etc. Your response is very important to us. The survey will take about 5 minutes, and your responses are anonymous.

The information we receive from this survey will be used to help us understand more about the dress shoe customer. In turn, knowing this will help us develop a marketing plan for a national shoe manufacturer. Thank you for your help.

1. How often do you purchase new dress shoes?
   - _____ 0-1 year
   - _____ 1-2 years
   - _____ 2-3 years
   - _____ 3-4 years
   - _____ 4-5 years
   - _____ More than 5 years

2. Please rank the locations listed below in order of preference. Jot the number 1 next to the location you most prefer to purchase shoes, number 2 by your second choice, and so forth.
   - _____ Specialty Store
   - _____ Department Store
   - _____ Outlet Store
   - _____ Other (please specify)

3. The grid shown below lists four types of "Men's Dress Shoe" brands along the top, and several characteristics of dress shoes along the left side. Please take one brand at a time, and working down the column, pick a number from the scale indicating your evaluation of each characteristic, and jot it in the space in that column to the right of the characteristic. If you are unable to answer, please put "DK" in the appropriate blank. We would like your rating for each brand and characteristic.
   Scale
   Very poor   1   2   3   4   5   6   Excellent

	Allen Edmonds	Bally	Johnston & Murphy	Cole Hahn
Value	_____	_____	_____	_____
Quality	_____	_____	_____	_____
Price	_____	_____	_____	_____
Comfort	_____	_____	_____	_____
Style	_____	_____	_____	_____
Reputation	_____	_____	_____	_____
Convenience	_____	_____	_____	_____

   (Convenient locations to purchase the brand)

4. Do you own more than one pair of dress shoes that you wear at least once every 2 weeks?
   - _____ Yes   If yes, are they different styles?   _____ Yes   _____ No
   - _____ No

5. Do you know where the following brands of shoes are sold?

Yes	No	
_____	_____	Allen Edmonds
_____	_____	Bally
_____	_____	Johnston & Murphy
_____	_____	Cole Hahn

   If you answered yes next to Johnston & Murphy, please specify the location(s) you are aware of.

6. Is there one brand of dress shoe you purchase regularly?
   - _____ Yes   If yes, please specify which brand _____
   - _____ No

7. Do you normally shop for dress shoes
   - _____ Alone
   - _____ With spouse or friend
   If you answered "With spouse or friend," does that person ever help you decide which shoes to buy?
   - _____ Yes
   - _____ No

(continued)

EXHIBIT B.1   **Men's Dress Shoe Survey** *(continued)*

8. Which brands of dress shoes have you purchased at some time in the past?
    _____ Allen Edmonds
    _____ Bally
    _____ Johnston & Murphy
    _____ Cole Hahn
    _____ Other   Please specify _____

9. Which one of the previous brands listed in #8 are you most inclined to purchase now?
    _____ Why? _____

10. Please rank the choices listed below in their order of preference. Jot the number 1 next to the choice indicating what is most important to you when purchasing dress shoes, number 2 by your second choice, and so forth.
    _____ Starting a new job   _____ When your old ones wear out
    _____ For the holidays   _____ When you buy a new suit
    _____ For a special event   _____ When you get a promotion

11. Do you ever get your dress shoes resoled?
    _____ Yes
    _____ No

12. Please rank the choices listed below in their order of preference. Jot the number 1 next to the choice indicating what is most important to you when purchasing dress shoes, number 2 by your second choice, and so forth.
    _____ Value   _____ Style
    _____ Quality   _____ Reputation
    _____ Price   _____ Convenient locations to purchase
    _____ Comfort

13. Please check one the following. How much did you pay for your last pair of dress shoes?
    _____ $25-$75   _____ $176-$225
    _____ $76-$125   _____ $226-$275
    _____ $126-$175   _____ More than $275

14. How much do you spend on accessories (ties, socks, shoe polish, shoe trees, shoe horns, brushes, etc.) when you buy shoes? Please check on the following.
    _____ None, I don't buy accessories when I buy shoes   _____ $46-$60
    _____ $0-$15   _____ $61-$75
    _____ $16-$30   _____ More than $75
    _____ $31-$45

15. What type of non-work activities do you enjoy?
    _____
    _____
    _____
    _____
    _____
    _____

16. What type of business magazines/journals do you read?
    _____
    _____
    _____
    _____
    _____
    _____

17. What is your zip code?
    _____

Regalia Center. This area has the highest concentration of affluent households in the metropolitan Memphis area. The target population is growing very quickly in the surrounding area, and living in this area seems to represent success.

The market is divided into two customer profiles. The first, the achiever, is an affluent, self-assured man who has achieved considerable success. This person is influential and can be an asset as a product advocate. The second customer profile, the striver, is a competitive man with an active lifestyle who aspires to a higher level of success. As this man's tastes are still being refined, he represents a great potential for future market growth. This translates into potential long-term customer relationships with Johnston & Murphy (J&M).

Although nearly half of the survey respondents indicated that they know where Johnston & Murphy shoes might be purchased, only one in twenty were aware of the store in The Regalia. This finding had a significant impact on all decisions related to developing this marketing plan.

Major Aspects of the Marketing Plan

GOALS AND OBJECTIVES   The decision to purchase Johnston & Murphy shoes is a series of dichotomous, yes or no questions, ranging from awareness of the J&M brand, to understanding the value and benefits of J&M products, to an awareness of J&M's Regalia location. For an individual to purchase a pair of Johnston & Murphy shoes at the Regalia store, he or she must pass through all decision levels by answering "yes" to each one. Therefore, the overall goal of this marketing plan is to remove the obstacles to obtaining a "yes" answer during each step in the decision process. To achieve this goal, the marketing plan focuses on the three major capabilities of the J&M line and the Regalia store—outstanding product quality, superior customer service, and convenient location—in an effort to educate current and potential customers about the benefits and value of owning J&M shoes and the existence of the Regalia store location. To address this goal, the following major objective was established:

The objective of the marketing plan for J&M's Regalia store is to increase target consumer awareness of the location from 12 percent to 50 percent within the next three months. The manager of the Regalia store has the primary responsibility for achieving this objective.

Two other objectives that are subsumed within the major objective are to increase customer awareness of the Johnston & Murphy brand and to increase awareness of the value and benefits of Johnston & Murphy products.

MARKETING STRATEGY   To achieve these objectives, demographic and psychographic information was used to develop two target customer profiles. A promotional campaign was developed that incorporates the theme, "Success: the tools that facilitate it, and the rewards that accompany it." The strategy centers on this theme, as well as image differentiation. This includes relating the benefits of Johnston & Murphy shoes to the target market. The strategy will be implemented through three main channels:

1. Two creative radio advertisements designed to appeal to the achiever and the striver.
2. A location awareness sign positioned in front of The Regalia Center.
3. A redesigned window display devised to reflect the characteristics of the target market and to incorporate elements of the promotional theme.

The promotional campaign, as developed, will build upon previous knowledge of Johnston & Murphy products, and will increase brand, location, and value/benefits awareness. The final result should be increased awareness at all levels, increased store traffic, product trial, and increased sales.

Environmental Analysis

Competition

Johnston & Murphy's high end competitors—Allen Edmonds, Bally, and Cole-Haan—were evaluated on several key factors, such as types of stores where the shoes are available, promotional efforts, product offering, and overall presence in the competitive arena. As a basis for comparison, an evaluation of Johnston & Murphy is presented as well.

Johnston & Murphy

Product:

- Variety of styles, predominantly business and dress
- Traditional tones (black, brown, cordovan)
- Accessories available at Regalia store

Availability:

- Discount Chains: Designer Shoe Wearhouse, Steinmart
- Specialty Shops: William Berry, James Davis, Oak Hall
- Department Stores: Dillard's, Goldsmith's

Promotion:

- Media exposure through national fashion magazines
- Limited exposure from local sales promotions
- Word-of-mouth advertising is slowly building

Summary: Johnston & Murphy is the only high-end shoe marketer with its own store in the Memphis area. If used properly, this could represent a tremendous competitive advantage. It is likely that sales at nearby mall stores and discount chains cut into retail sales. Local department stores carry only a limited selection of the J&M line and do not sell any styles over $165. In addition, customers who purchase J&M shoes at department stores do not benefit from the superior sales expertise and service that is offered at the Regalia store.

Allen Edmonds

Product:

- Styles are varied, but the tones are basic (black, brown, cordovan)
- No accessories to support or accompany sales of shoes

Availability:

- Discount Chains: Designer Shoe Wearhouse, Steinmart

- Specialty Shops: William Berry, Oak Hall

Promotion:

- Little or no media advertising in magazines locally or nationally

Summary: Allen Edmonds provides little threat to the local sales of Johnston & Murphy retailers. As indicated in the customer survey, only 16 percent of potential customers shop with previous knowledge of the line's existence. Sales appear to be created by the casual shopper. Some success has been achieved by pricing within a competitive but low-end range.

Bally

Product:

- Multiple styles, including casual, dress, and formal
- Line includes hard-to-find shoe tones
- Name is extended to full line of accessories

Availability:

- Discount Chains: Designer Shoe Wearhouse, Steinmart
- Specialty Shops: Jerry Coletta, Georgio's, William Berry, Oxford Street, Alan Abis
- Department Stores: Dillard's, Goldsmith's
- Formalwear Shops

Promotion:

- Exposure through international advertising in major fashion magazines
- Sales promotions run by local carriers
- Significant word-of-mouth support

Summary: Bally represents a significant threat to Johnston & Murphy. The Regalia Center has a men's clothing store within walking distance of J&M that carries Bally, and this retailer has an advantage in terms of real estate positioning. Some shoppers are surely attracted by the line's international appeal; however its high-end pricing may dissuade less adventuresome shoppers. Approximately 35 percent of those surveyed knew of the line's existence. Sales are supported by shoppers seeking a high profile shoe and accessories. Bally succeeds by positioning itself at the high-end of the price scale and claiming exclusivity.

Cole-Haan

Product:

- Multiplicity of styles
- Clear advantage in tones, ranging from earth to high gloss
- Full line of accessories

Availability:

- Discount Chains: Designer Shoe Wearhouse, Steinmart
- Specialty Shops: William Berry's, James Davis, Bachrach's, Oak Hall
- Department Stores: Dillard's, Goldsmith's

Promotion:

- Major advertising exposure in fashion magazines
- Local media advertising from department stores
- Large word-of-mouth support

Summary: Cole-Haan is easily a direct competitor to the Johnston & Murphy store, as it is sold by competing retailers in very near proximity to the Regalia store. It is sold side-by-side with the Johnston & Murphy line at the James Davis specialty store. Sales of Cole-Haan will especially affect J&M's casual line. The high level of name recognition is a great advantage for Cole-Haan. Sales are supported by intentional and casual shoppers seeking shoes with a conservative and/or traditional appeal, but with a slight European flair in design. The brand succeeds by positioning itself near the high end of the pricing scale and goes after the successful and affluent businessman, as well as the man-about-town. Cole-Haan also capitalizes on the "Made in America" appeal and New York's Fifth Avenue aura.

Economic Conditions

Although national economic conditions are deemed important to J&M's efforts, the local economy is of much greater importance to the success of the Regalia store. On a national level,

retail sales growth for the foreseeable future is expected to be in the 2 to 3 percent range. Likewise, overall consumer spending for clothing and accessories is expected to grow slowly over the next several years. Locally, economic projections match those for the national economy. Local consumers remain a bit more price-sensitive than was the case in the past. Moreover, consumers are demanding greater value for their money, which translates into a desire for high-quality footwear that will last a long time. Upscale consumers are most likely to bridge this gap between price sensitivity and demand for quality. The Regalia store stands to benefit from this trend as it is located in an upscale part of East Memphis.

Political, Legal, and Technological Conditions

The political, legal/regulatory, and technological environments are expected to have very little impact on the operations of the Regalia store. The increased popularity of the Internet might serve as a springboard for future efforts in electronic retailing.

Sociocultural Factors

Several major societal trends stand to affect the marketing of the J&M line and the Regalia store. First, the population of Memphis, particularly East Memphis, is growing rapidly. Most of this influx is comprised of upscale consumers with high discretionary incomes. Second, there is a growing segment of high income, but time-poor consumers who appreciate superior customer service and are willing to pay for it. Research indicates that at least one-third of shoppers would be willing to pay a higher price for better service most of the time. As a result of being short on time, many consumers have turned to other shopping methods. Nonstore retail activities, such as direct mail catalogs and the Internet, have grown in popularity as more and more consumers search for ways to increase the convenience of shopping. A final trend is the growing consumer sentiment toward products that are "Made in America." Today, consumers are beginning to think of American-made products as being just as good as products from overseas.

Customer Environment

The local target market for the Johnston & Murphy store has traditionally been defined in three stages. First, geographic markets are identified that show the greatest potential. Second, the male residents within these geographic markets are profiled in terms of average income, age, interests, and purchasing behavior. Finally, these consumers are identified in psychographic terms using information about their values, attitudes, and lifestyles. The information for this analysis was generated through the following methods:

- Census tracks within the primary and secondary trade zones within the East Memphis area.

- An annual survey to examine demographic information and the media-usage habits of the target market.

- An annual focus group survey of professionals in the target market to further explore their interests and dress shoe purchasing behavior.

- Personal observation and experience are used, along with the other methods, to derive a psychographic profile of consumers in the target market.

Based on the most recent analysis, these combined methods indicate that the primary J&M purchaser resides within the three zip code areas (38119, 38138, and 38139) that are immediately adjacent to The Regalia Center. The average household income of consumers in these zip code areas ranges from $69,000 to $81,000. Other information about the purchasing attitudes and behaviors of the men in the target market includes:

- Forty-seven percent responded that they knew where Johnston & Murphy shoes are sold. However, of that group, only 12 percent knew about the Regalia store location.

- Eighty-five percent own at least two pairs of dress shoes they wear on a regular basis.

- Forty-eight percent indicated some type of brand loyalty by responding that they purchase one brand of shoe on a regular basis.

- Seventy-five percent have their shoes resoled.

- Specialty stores were found to be the preferred location to purchase dress shoes, rather than department and outlet stores.

- Johnston & Murphy shoes were purchased by 36 percent of the target market at some time in the past. This figure is the highest of any brand listed in the survey, and is 10 percent higher than the second place competitor, Cole-Haan.

- Sixty percent shop with someone when buying shoes. Of this group, more than half are influenced in their purchasing decision by the person with them. This shopping companion is generally a woman.

- Business journals/magazines of interest are *The Wall Street Journal, The Memphis Business Journal, Forbes,* and *Money.*

- Favorite activities include golf, fishing, and reading.

Internal Environment

All previous marketing goals and objectives have been aimed at increasing sales at the Regalia location. To achieve this result, J&M has a strong commitment to providing exceptional customer service and high quality footwear. This overall goal is consistent with the J&M philosophy. No other formal marketing goals have been established. However, a simple goal to increase sales may no longer be consistent with certain realities in the market, particularly increased consumer price sensitivity and a general lack of awareness of the Regalia store.

The overall performance of the Regalia store has been consistent, with flat sales over the past year. Although the overall goals and strategy of J&M are good, the marketing activities at the Regalia store need some fine tuning to boost performance.

The current resources of both J&M and the Regalia store are sound. Both businesses maintain strong supplier and customer relationships, and neither is in distress with respect to available financial, capital, or human resources. Likewise, there are no major structural problems within either business. J&M maintains a strong customer orientation that is present in the Regalia store and its employees.

SWOT Analysis

Based on the environmental analysis, a number of important strengths, weaknesses, opportunities, and threats were identified. Although some of these issues pertain to J&M as a whole, most are unique to the Regalia store.

Strengths

- Johnston & Murphy's reputation for superior quality and craftsmanship.
- J&M, and the employees of the Regalia store, have a very high level of experience and product knowledge, and offer excellent personal service.
- The Regalia store experiences good repeat business, indicating a high level of customer satisfaction.
- The Infinity collection of comfort dress shoes, introduced in 1991, indicates J&M's ability to capitalize on consumer trends, in this case the growing market segment of comfort-conscious consumers.
- J&M produces an excellent catalog—it received a Silver Award from the American Catalog Awards.
- J&M's exclusive Refurbishment Service, which allows shoes that have been worn for years to be rebuilt to their original appearance.
- J&M serves a broad customer base with shoes that complement both business and casual wardrobes, as well as unusual sizes for the hard-to-fit customer.
- Through its retail stores and catalog, J&M offers a diverse selection of complementary accessories to suit the needs of its target market.
- The Regalia store is situated near a very high traffic intersection and is convenient to many office buildings, enabling the store to capture lunchtime and after-work traffic.
- The neighborhood immediately surrounding the Regalia store has the highest concentration of affluent households in the Memphis metropolitan area.

Weaknesses

- The J&M store in The Regalia suffers from a severe lack of consumer awareness. The following factors contribute to this weakness:
  - The store is not visible to automobile traffic near The Regalia Center.
  - There is no sign with the Johnston & Murphy name positioned at the shopping center entrance or along the road to increase location awareness.
  - The Regalia currently lacks a complementary men's clothing retailer to attract Johnston & Murphy's target market.
  - There is a very low level of foot traffic past the store.
  - There is no promotional activity directed toward generation of consumer awareness.
  - The current window display does not serve to enhance the store's image.
- The definition of the target audience for J&M's promotional campaign does not adequately define the local target market, nor does it provide for effective product positioning.
- There may be a perception that J&M shoes are too expensive, indicating that the product's value and benefits have not been adequately communicated to the target market.
- The company's product literature would be more effective if the benefits of owning J&M shoes were more clearly emphasized. Currently, the literature focuses only on product features.
- The J&M logo imprinted on the shoe insole becomes illegible over time, thus inhibiting brand recognition at the point of repurchase. Sewing a label into the side of the shoe, or machine-embroidering the logo into the leather lining would be possible solutions to this problem.

Opportunities

- The growing segment of high income but time-poor consumers could be targeted with increased convenience and superior customer service.

- The growing "Made in America" sentiment felt by many consumers is a plus for all American-made products.

- The increasing public awareness of environmental issues leads to an appreciation for consumer goods that are long-lasting and made from natural materials.

- Extravagant consumer spending has been replaced with an appreciation for value. A durable, high quality product may appeal to the value-conscious consumer to the extent that he may not mind paying a little more.

- Many men in the target market are influenced by women in their shoe-purchasing decisions. Thus, promotional efforts directed toward women may be a viable alternative to traditional male-only campaigns.

- Many people do not like to shop in malls, and find that the service and convenience provided by specialty stores makes shopping an easier and more pleasant experience.

- The aging Baby Boom generation (35–54 age group) presents tremendous potential to the men's shoe industry. Likewise, as Generation Xers (23–34 age group) move into management positions, they represent a growing opportunity for dress shoe marketers.

- Over the next five years, men's footwear, currently a $12 billion business, is expected to be the largest growing segment of the footwear industry.

- There are no high-end competitors with dedicated stores in the Memphis area. This limits competition as only parts of the competing product lines are displayed.

- The recent population growth in East Memphis is expected to continue, providing a larger market of affluent consumers in the vicinity of The Regalia Center.

Threats

- Retail sales growth is expected to be only 2 to 3 percent.

- Consumer price sensitivity has resulted in slow growth in consumer spending on clothing and accessories.

- The domestic shoe industry is facing increasing competition from international shoe manufacturers.

- An increase in the popularity of shoe resoling could have a negative impact on overall shoe sales.

- Increasing consumer awareness and acceptance of local discount shoe outlets could negatively affect specialty shoe retailers.

- Jerry Coletta, a specialty retailer in The Regalia Center, currently offers a small but high quality selection of men's shoes. A move by Coletta to enlarge its shoe line would increase the competitive threat.

Assessment

Each element of the SWOT analysis was quantitatively assessed for its magnitude and importance. The final rankings for the most important elements are shown in Exhibit B.2. The final assessment of these issues resulted in the following conclusions:

1. The Regalia store possesses three major capabilities:
   - the demand for high quality and high value products is matched by J&M's reputation for superior quality and workmanship.
   - the demand for good customer service is matched by the Regalia store's reputation for excellent personal service and unmatched product knowledge.
   - consumers' lack of shopping time is matched by The Regalia Center's convenient, high street-traffic location.

2. The Regalia store possesses two major weaknesses:
   - very poor consumer awareness that the store exists.

EXHIBIT B.2	Quantitative Assessment of Elements within the SWOT Matrix

Strengths	M	• I	= R	Opportunities	M	• I	= R
Reputation for quality	3	3	9	Demand for good service	3	3	9
Excellent service	3	3	9	Demand for high quality and value	3	3	9
High car traffic location	3	2	6	Time-poor consumers	2	3	6
Affluent location	2	2	4	No high-end competitors in the area	2	3	6
Excellent J&M catalog	3	1	3	Women are major purchasers	2	2	4
Good repeat business	2	1	2	Growing population in area	2	2	4

Weaknesses	M	• I	= R	Threats	M	• I	= R
Poor awareness of location	-3	3	-9	Consumers are price sensitive	-3	3	-9
Poor foot traffic location	-3	3	-9	No complementary retailers in the shopping center	-3	3	-9
J&M shoes are expensive	-3	2	-6	Slow growth in spending on clothing and accessories	-2	2	-4
J&M's promotion stresses features rather than benefits of ownership	-2	2	-4	Popularity of resoling shoes	-2	1	-2

M = magnitude of element
I = importance of element
R = final rating of the element

Magnitude scale: ranges from +3 for most favorable to -3 for most unfavorable
Importance Scale: ranges from 3 (highest importance) to 1 (lowest importance)

- the inability to capitalize on impulse sales due to the limited foot traffic that passes the store.

3. The Regalia store possesses two long-term limitations:
   - the perceived expense of J&M shoes does not coincide with increasing consumer price sensitivity.
   - the inability to capitalize on consumer convenience and one-stop shopping because there are no complementary retailers in The Regalia Center.

The best way to deal with the weaknesses is to increase the promotional efforts of the Regalia store. This would increase both awareness of the location and the foot traffic passing the store.

These promotional efforts should also emphasize the quality, durability, value, and made-in-America aspects of the J&M product line. These appeals could also offset the problem of J&M's perceived expense by stressing that J&M shoes are an exceptional value. Finally, short of getting a complementary retailer in The Regalia Center, the J&M store must create strong customer loyalty and repeat purchase through its exceptional customer service.

Goals and Objectives

The decision to purchase Johnston & Murphy shoes can be illustrated as a series of dichotomous, yes or no decisions. As shown in Exhibit B.3, the steps in the series are as follows:

EXHIBIT B.3	Purchase Decision Tree

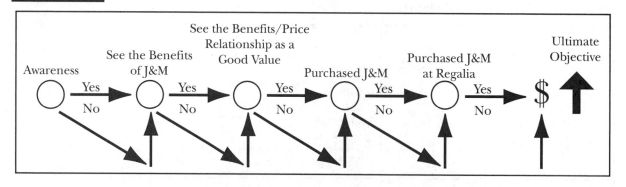

Step 1: Is the customer aware of Johnston & Murphy shoes?

Yes: Proceed to step 2

No: Customer must be educated about Johnston & Murphy

Step 2: Does the customer understand the benefits of Johnston & Murphy shoes?

Yes: Proceed to step 3

No: Customer must be educated about the benefits of J&M products

Step 3: Does the customer see the price/benefit ratio as a good value?

Yes: Proceed to step 4

No: Customer must be educated on the value of Johnston & Murphy shoes

Step 4: Has the customer purchased Johnston & Murphy shoes?

Yes: Proceed to step 5

No: Any remaining obstacles must be removed

Step 5: Will the customer purchase Johnston & Murphy shoes from the Regalia store?

Yes: Objective has been achieved

No: Customer must be educated about the existence of the Regalia store

For a customer to purchase a pair of Johnston & Murphy shoes at the Regalia store, he or she must pass through the five separate decision levels by answering "yes" to each one. Based on this understanding of the purchase decision process, the overall marketing goal of the Regalia store is to remove the obstacles to obtaining a "yes" answer during each step in the decision process. To achieve this goal, the marketing plan must focus on the three major capabilities of the J&M line and the Regalia location: outstanding product quality, superior customer service, and convenient location. To capitalize on these capabilities, however, the marketing plan must also eliminate the store's major weakness of limited customer awareness. Thus, the overall goal of the marketing plan can be formally stated as follows:

Overall Goal: To educate current and potential customers about the benefits of owning J&M shoes (product quality and service), the good value that J&M represents, and the existence of the convenient Regalia store location.

Because the most significant weakness was determined to be an overall lack of awareness of the J&M store in The Regalia Center, this was seen as the largest obstacle to achieving a "yes" answer throughout the purchase decision process. Therefore, the primary objective of the marketing plan is to eliminate this weakness. Formally, this objective can be stated as follows:

Primary Objective: To increase consumer awareness of the Regalia location from 12 percent to 50 percent within the next three months. The manager of the Regalia store has the primary responsibility for achieving this objective.

As a part of its overall goal of customer education, the marketing plan will also have a secondary objective of increasing market share among the target market group. Research indicated that J&M shoes have been purchased by 36 percent of the target market at some time in the past—a full 10 percent higher than the second-place competitor, Cole-Haan. To increase this figure, the Regalia location must increase repeat customer purchases by focusing on its capability in superior customer service. Thus, the secondary objective can be formally stated as follows:

Secondary Objective: To increase J&M's purchase rate among the target market from 36 percent to 40 percent within the next three months. The manager of the Regalia store has the primary responsibility for achieving this objective by maintaining the superior customer service of the store.

Successfully achieving these objectives should lead to increased awareness of the value and benefits of J&M products, as well as increased awareness of the Regalia store. Increasing store awareness will ultimately lead to an increase in foot traffic, thus minimizing this serious weakness. The limitation posed by the perceived expense of J&M shoes can be minimized to some degree by educating consumers on the quality and value of J&M shoes. The limitation posed by the lack of complementary retailers in The Regalia Center is difficult to overcome. Unfortunately, there is little that this J&M store can do to minimize or avoid this limitation.

Once customers are better educated about J&M and the Regalia location, the existing expertise of the sales personnel will be a significant factor in leading to an increase in customers' purchase rates. The level of knowledge and service provided by the sales personnel at the Regalia location is exceptional. Therefore, it is not recommended that their techniques or performance be modified.

Marketing Strategy

Target Customer Profile

The local Johnston & Murphy target market was defined using intrinsic factors such as values, attitudes, and lifestyles rather than demographic information alone. Although the customer descriptions generally fall within the demographics that have been identified, this approach will provide an increased understanding of what motivates the customer and can be used to focus target marketing and positioning efforts more precisely. Two customer profiles have been created: the "Achiever" and the "Striver."[1]

The achiever is affluent and has attained considerable career success; he has "arrived." He is mature, confident, and self assured. He represents mainstream values and his tastes are, for the most part, already formed. This individual is a style and opinion leader, one who sets the standard of the successful and well-dressed man. He knows what he likes and tends to buy the same styles. He is an individual of discerning taste who appreciates status and quality. He operates in a predominantly corporate work environment requiring business dress, but has a need for casual attire at times.

The striver is a man with an active lifestyle and little free time. As he wants to get the most out of life, he is competitive and motivated to succeed in his career and personal life. He aspires to a higher income, social status, and career success. His tastes are still being formed, and he is interested in changing styles and trends. He feels that appearance is important, and has a need for both business and casual attire.

Achievement is the most important desire of both customer profiles. Both categories of men value quality goods as indications of their success and lifestyle. Personal, material, and professional achievement are their paramount life goals. Both the striver and the achiever have more money than time, and thus respond well to high-price/high-service positioning.

Marketing Mix Elements

The main focus of the marketing strategy is a promotional campaign aimed at image differentiation. What benefits do Johnston & Murphy shoes provide that others do not? The basis for this image differentiation is "J&M Quality." This is a phrase that stresses the focus on quality in all aspects of the Johnston & Murphy product offering. No changes are planned for the product, pricing, or distribution elements of the marketing mix.

The strategy will be carried out through a three-pronged coordinated approach that includes the following elements: radio advertisements, a location-awareness sign in front of The Regalia Center, and a window display in the store. All three of these elements are designed to address obstacles that prevent a "yes" response at each of the previously identified decision points. Together, they increase the probability of achieving a "yes" response at each decision phase, leading to the ultimate goal of increased sales.

The three elements of the promotional campaign are coordinated with the overall objective of the marketing plan. The radio campaign is designed to increase customers' awareness of the J&M product line and its benefits, as well as the store's location. The sign in front of The Regalia Center will effectively overcome the anonymity suffered by the store. It is aimed at target customers who have heard the radio ad, as well as traffic passing by on Poplar Avenue. It is important to position the sign for visibility on Poplar Avenue, as the main Regalia sign and entrance to the center is on Ridgeway, and Poplar is the more heavily traveled street. The window display will further attract the radio and drive-by audience, as well as any foot traffic that passes by. Overall, this strategy will incorporate the theme of "Success: the tools that facilitate it, and the rewards that accompany it" as represented through the slogan: "Johnston & Murphy: Don't You Wish You Were In Our Shoes?"

RADIO ADVERTISING   Key to the radio campaign is the target of the advertisement itself. The spots are aimed at the "achiever" and the "striver" and will appeal to specific characteristics of these two types. Both groups are targeted through the use of a father-and-son format in an ad called "The Graduate," and a business-mentor format in an ad called "The Firm." The advertisements target the key characteristics of the achiever (affluent, influential, successful, appreciates value and quality, works in a corporate environment) and the striver (aspires to a higher level of income and status, concerned with appearance, doesn't have much free time). The use of two separate advertisements allows for different features to be emphasized and broadens the message delivered. It allows the audience to think of Johnston & Murphy shoes in more ways, thus increasing the opportunity to make Johnston & Murphy shoes relevant to the consumer's life. (See Exhibits B.4 and B.5 for the scripts of both advertisements.)

"The Graduate" involves a father helping his son get started in the job market, and is designed to evoke an empathic response from the achiever. By calling forth a nostalgic memory, the ad aims to bind Johnston & Murphy to feelings of pride and accomplishment for a father and his son. Essentially, the purchase of one's first pair of Johnston & Murphy's becomes a rite of passage, along with graduating from college and embarking on a career.

"The Firm" involves a mentor situation in a business setting, with one man giving advice to a younger colleague. It emphasizes the investment value of J&M shoes, by making use of the fact that they last much longer than lower-priced competitors. The importance of smart choices, as well as appearance for one's career success, is designed to evoke a response from the striver.

LOCATION AWARENESS SIGN   Location awareness for the J&M store in The Regalia Center was found to be low. The use of a sign in front of The Regalia Center will help anchor the store location in the minds of the radio audience and the general traffic on Poplar Avenue. The sign will carry the Johnston & Murphy logo and the slogan "Don't You Wish You Were In Our Shoes?". Due to the heavy traffic through the nearby intersection and the proximity to office buildings and affluent neighborhoods, the sign will be seen by a significant portion of the target market.

WINDOW DISPLAY   The statement, "first impressions are lasting impressions," cannot be overstated in trying to attract potential customers to a retailer. Window shopping is a favorite pastime of many customers, and display windows offer a glimpse into the psyche of the store and its management. Many shoppers attach a personality to the store by examining what has been provided to them by the store's "face." By redesigning the window displays, the intentional shopper, as well

EXHIBIT B.4   **Script for the "The Graduate" Radio Advertisement**

The son has just graduated from college and has returned home to search for a job. The father helps to put him on the right track with the right shoes.

F: How's the new college graduate?

S: Fine, Dad.

F: So tell me, how soon can we rent out your room?

S: Gee, Thanks. Could you wait until I get a job?

F: We'll see. Speaking of that topic, I hear you have a job interview Monday.

S: You've been talking to Mom, haven't you?

F: I just wanted to see if you needed anything.

S: I appreciate that, but I already have an interview suit.

F: I was thinking more along the line of interview shoes.

S: I have a pair of those, too.

F: Yeah, I've seen them. . . . C'mon-I think it's time you bought a pair of Johnston & Murphy's.

S: Johnston & Murphy? Gee I don't know. Maybe we'd better wait. After all, I don't have the job yet.

F: That's true, but you can't afford to dress like a student anymore. Now I admit that you could spend less on a pair of shoes, but you wouldn't be getting that "J&M quality."

S: Yeah, but, Dad, it's only an interview.

F: That's what I said when your grandfather took me to get my first pair of interview shoes. And you know what he told me? He said, "Son, you can't put a price tag on craftsmanship."

S: That sounds like Granddad all right.

F: And you know what? He was right. Johnston & Murphy shoes are still carrying me through today.

S: I don't know, Dad, I don't think I have time to go to the mall.

F: J&M has a shop in The Regalia Center. They're close by and convenient. You know me, I don't go to the mall unless I have to.

S: OK, so you've convinced me, let's go.

F: Great, while we're there we can see about getting you a tie, too. There will be a lot of guys Monday who will wish they were in your shoes.

S: By the way Dad, what happened at that interview? Did you get that job?

F: What do you think?

Announcer: Johnston & Murphy in The Regalia Center. At Poplar and Ridgeway. Don't you wish you were in our shoes?

as the casual passerby, will be intrigued and drawn into the store. Sales personnel will then be in a position to encourage trial and purchase.

To establish continuity between the various aspects of the promotion campaign, the theme of success will be carried over into the window display. The display will have a feel similar to that found in the Johnston & Murphy catalog. Props and personal items will be included to portray the theme of successful living that the target market can relate to on a personal basis. This technique has proven to be very effective in the catalog, because it allows the customer to view the shoes as fitting in with his lifestyle. The new display will also exhibit a diverse collection of classic footwear with a mix of contemporary styles, as well as stylish accessories. The overall appeal of the display will be enhanced by using gold tones in the window. This works on a psychological level, as gold is a standard by which affluence is judged. The overall appearance of the store front should attract J&M's base customer: the successful male who has made a conscious decision to invest in high-quality, stylish footwear.

EXHIBIT B.5　Script for the "The Firm" Radio Advertisement

A lawyer is advising a younger colleague in a mentor role. This ad places emphasis on the idea of J&M shoes as an investment in long-lasting quality to capitalize on the trend of value over flash.

J:　Bob, come on in, have a seat. I wanted to discuss the Jones case with you.

B:　Sure thing, Jim.

J:　Now, when you meet with the client tomorrow, the first thing to remember is to keep your feet firmly on the floor.

B:　He's pretty tough, huh?

J:　No, I just don't want him to see the soles of your shoes.

B:　Yes, they are getting pretty bad . . . .

J:　How long have you had those things anyway?

B:　Well, just since I joined the firm, actually.

J:　Humph. I thought you were smarter than that. You've still got a lot to learn, don't you? Take it from me, spend your paycheck on something that's really going to last.

B:　Maybe if I had your paycheck.

J:　Bob, if you don't buy quality, you're just throwing your money away. At the rate you're going, you'll outspend me in a couple of years. I bought this pair of Johnston & Murphy shoes when you were still carrying a book bag.

B:　Wow.

J:　Instead of hoping no one notices, why don't you get yourself to The Regalia Center and get a pair of Johnston & Murphy's? Trust me, I don't give much free advice. A pair of Johnston & Murphy's will be an investment in your future. Well, you'd better get cracking on that case.

B:　Thanks.

J:　Oh, and Bob . . . .

B:　Yes?

J:　Get a decent haircut, too.

Announcer:　Johnston & Murphy in The Regalia Center. At Poplar and Ridgeway. Don't you wish you were in our shoes?

Consumer and Competitor Reactions

If the promotional campaign is implemented correctly, consumer awareness should increase dramatically. Foot traffic and sales will also increase as a result of this increased store awareness. The major competitive advantage of the Regalia store is the fact that it sells nothing but J&M products. As a result, the customer will receive only the best in product knowledge and customer service. The promotional campaign will enable the store to capitalize on this advantage. As more customers become aware of, and shop at, the Regalia store, they are likely to become loyal customers.

Major competitors are not likely to react to the new promotional campaign. The most likely competitor to react is Jerry Coletta, who is also located in The Regalia Center. Should the J&M store begin to take sales away from Jerry Coletta, Coletta can be expected to increase promotional efforts in response. Price discounting is not considered to be a major threat because of Jerry Coletta's upscale, quality image.

Marketing Implementation

Prior to implementing the specific campaign elements, all sales personnel will be informed of the strategy. This will be done simply to remind them that exceptional customer service is required to keep a customer coming back to J&M. As all sales personnel are talented and motivated, no extra effort is required on the part of the store's management.

The implementation of all promotional elements is designed to be completed within four weeks. The radio campaign and location awareness sign will run for all four weeks. The window display will be ready in time for the beginning of the radio campaign. The Regalia store manager is responsible for executing all elements of the strategy.

Radio Advertising

Using information gathered from a previous survey on radio listeners, Arbitron information, and personal judgment concerning the preferences of the target market, it was determined that the most effective radio station would be WRVR-104FM. Known as "The River," WRVR plays a variety of popular, easy-listening music, and reaches a wide range of age groups—appealing strongly to the professional and business audience. The time slots chosen for the advertisements were evening drive times and Saturdays. According to earlier survey information, WRVR dominates other Memphis radio stations for the percentage of desired listening audience between the hours of 3 p.m. and 8 p.m. Because of a limited budget (under $1,500 for radio), the radio schedule was narrowed to Thursday and Friday drive times and Saturday midday, between 10 a.m. and 3 p.m. This decision is based on the reasoning that the typical J&M customer would be most attuned to shopping on the weekend or toward the latter part of the week. Sunday advertising was avoided as The Regalia Center is not open on Sunday.

The final copy of the advertisement will be produced at the WRVR facility at no additional cost. Talent for these radio spots will be acquired through Playhouse on the Square, a local professional theater. The actors are currently interns who are willing to provide their talent services at no cost as an opportunity to gain exposure.

Location Awareness Sign

This sign is a form of temporary roadside promotion that can be leased for a one-month period to any one of The Regalia Center's stores. The cost of this lease is $400 per month. The sign is redesigned each month with one business's name and/or logo. Reservations for the sign are made on a first-come, first-served basis. The sign has been leased for one month, with the J&M logo going up on the same day that the radio campaign begins.

Window Display

The items to be located in the store window include a diverse array of Johnston & Murphy products and miscellaneous decor placed in a setting that denotes success in business, personal, and family life. Store products used to represent the success-in-business theme will include Johnston & Murphy's finer dress shoes, belts, braces and suspenders, hosiery, and ties. Additional aesthetic items will include a briefcase/attaché, leather appointment book and pen, a copy of *The Wall Street Journal*, tortoise shell reading glasses, a cellular phone, and a "ladder of success."

Johnston & Murphy store products that will be displayed in a separate window to portray the theme of a successful personal and family life will involve the more casual styles of loafers, boots, socks, belts, and suspenders. For the family success theme, aesthetic items will include a framed photo of a man with his wife and children, attractive books and reading glasses, a brass-handled cane, and a Johnston & Murphy catalog. To denote the theme of a successful personal life, ancillary materials such as a golf club, old baseball and glove, fishing net, wooden oar, driving gloves, and a photo of the "big catch" will be included. The total budget for the window display is not to exceed $120.

Evaluation and Control

Financial Assessment

The total financial impact of the proposed marketing strategy is difficult to estimate given the lead time required for promotional efforts to produce results. Likewise, the intent of this marketing plan is to educate customers and increase location awareness, with an increase in sales volume being an important but secondary concern. However, given the very poor consumer awareness of J&M's store location, the anticipated benefits of this plan are likely to be well worth the minor investment. The following costs are estimated based on rate quotes from WRVR and Boyle Investors of The Regalia Center:

Radio Campaign $1,480
Location Awareness Sign $400
Window Display $120
Total $2,000

Marketing Control

There are no major input controls that are required to implement the marketing plan as all store personnel are highly trained and motivated. It is possible that as store traffic and sales increase, additional employees may be needed. Adequate process control mechanisms are already in place to implement the plan. Employees are empowered to make decisions related to customers. Employees are also well compensated for their efforts. The store manager is highly committed to his employees and the implementation of the marketing plan. Internal lines of communication within the store are excellent.

The major output control mechanism or performance standard to be achieved by this marketing plan is an increase in customer awareness from 12 percent to 50 percent within the next three months. The promotional campaign will take place during the first month of this time frame. To determine the marketing plan's success in achieving the objective of increased awareness, the following steps will be taken:

1. Supplement the annual marketing survey with a follow-up survey to assess customer awareness of the Regalia location. Awareness of the radio advertisements, the location sign, and the window display will also be assessed. This survey will be conducted one month after the completion of the promotional campaign.

2. Test for changes in store traffic by measuring pre- and post-campaign customer traffic within the store. This data will be collected through the use of charts.

3. Test for changes in foot traffic by measuring pre- and post-campaign customer traffic outside the store. This data will be collected through the use of charts.

4. Monitor changes in sales before, during, and after the campaign to test for increases that may be attributable to increased promotion efforts.

5. Changes in customer purchase rate (market share) will be assessed during the annual marketing survey.

If increased promotional efforts do not achieve the desired increase in store awareness, foot traffic, or sales, a direct mail campaign will be used to target J&M's customer profiles more specifically. This campaign will involve the mailing of the J&M catalog to a pre-qualified list of current and potential customers within the census tracts and zip codes immediately surrounding the Regalia store.

END NOTES

Chapter 1

1. Robert F. Hartley, *Marketing Mistakes and Successes* (New York: John Wiley & Sons, 1998), 250–267.
2. Fred Vogelstein, "The Right Connections," *U.S. News & World Report,* September 8, 1997, 44–46.
3. Vogelstein, "The Right Connections."
4. From Intel's Web site at http://www.intel.com/intel/OPPTY/INDEX.HTM.
5. Brian O'Reilly, "Transforming the Power Business," *Fortune,* September 29, 1997, 143–145.
6. Randall E. Stross, "Why Barnes & Noble May Crush Amazon," *Fortune,* September 29, 1997, 248.
7. John Protos, "Profit Makes Perfect," *Smart Money,* October 1997, 61.
8. Protos, "Profit Makes Perfect."
9. Howard Sutton, *The Marketing Plan in the 1990s* (New York: The Conference Board, Inc., 1990).
10 Sutton, *The Marketing Plan in the 1990s,* 9.
11. Sutton, 16.
12. Sutton, 17.
13. Ajay K. Kohli and Bernard J. Jaworski, "Marketing Orientation: The Construct, Research Propositions, and Managerial Implications," *Journal of Marketing* 54 (April 1990): 1-18.
14. "Chili's Grill & Bar Suggestion Selling Training Guide," Brinker International, Inc.; and "Creating the Sizzle Experience," Brinker International Sizzle Service Training Guide, Brinker International, Inc.
15. Jagdish N. Sheth and Rajendras Sisodia, "More than Ever Before, Marketing Is Under Fire to Account for What It Spends," *Marketing Management* 4 (Fall 1995): 13–14.
16. Kohli and Jaworski, "Marketing Orientation: The Construct, Research Propositions, and Managerial Implications."
17. Dale Kurschner, "5 Ways Ethical Busine$$ Creates Fatter Profit$," *Business Ethics* 10 (March/April 1996): 21.
18. Keki R. Bhote, Next Operation as Customer (NOAC): *How to Improve Quality, Cost and Cycle Time in Service Operations* (New York: American Management Association, 1991), 102–104.
19. Bhote, *Next Operation as Customer* (NOAC), 103.
20. Michael Treacy and Fred Wiersema, *The Discipline of Market Leaders* (Reading, MA: Addison-Wesley Publishing Company, 1995).
21. Treacy and Wiersema, *The Discipline of Market Leaders.*

Chapter 2

1. Amy Barrett, with Paul Eng and Kathy Rebello, "For $19.95 a Month, Unlimited Headaches for AOL," *Business Week,* January 27, 1997, 35.
2. James H. Fouss, "Faster and Smarter: Technology and Globalization are Defining the Researcher of Tomorrow," *Marketing Research,* Winter 1996, 16-17.
3. Brian S. Akre, "VW's Bug Staging a Comeback; 1999 Model Beetle to Resemble Original, But It's No Longer Cheap," *Austin American Statesman,* August 14, 1997, D1, D8; and "Bug Caught on Slowly in U.S. But Still World's Most Popular," *Austin American Statesman,* August 14, 1997, D8.
4. Ian P. Murphy, "All-American Icon Gets a New Look," *Marketing News,* August 18, 1997, 6.
5. "Orders Up," *Marketing News,* July 7, 1997, 2.
6. Cyndee Miller, "Marketers Not Worried by Hong Kong Takeover," *Marketing News,* July 7, 1997, 1.
7. Cyndee Miller, "Surreal But So Real: Viacom Is Latest to Make Retailing Entertaining," *Marketing News,* June 23, 1997, 1, 20–21.
8. Ian P. Murphy, "Charged Up: Electric Cars Get Jolt of Marketing," *Marketing News,* August 18, 1997, 1, 7, 13.
9. Miller, "Surreal But So Real."

10. Michael Levy and Barton A. Weitz, *Retailing Management,* 3rd ed. (Boston: Irwin/McGraw-Hill, 1998), 230.
11. Ben M. Enis and Stephen J. Garfein, "The Computer-Driven Marketing Audit," *Journal of Management Inquiry,* December 1992, 306-318; and Philip Kotler, William Gregor, and William Rodgers, "The Marketing Audit Comes of Age," *Sloan Management Review* 30 (Winter 1989): 49-62.
12. This section is based on Howard Sutton, *The Marketing Plan in the 1990s* (New York: The Conference Board, 1990), 21–27, 61–62.

Chapter 3

1. "Whopper Stopper," *Marketing News,* August 4, 1997, 1.
2. Susan Reda, "Beyond Discounting," *Stores,* May 1996, 24–28.
3. Michael Levy and Barton A. Weitz, *Retailing Management,* 3rd ed. (Boston: Irwin/McGraw-Hill, 1998), 108-109.
4. Joseph Coleman, "Big Tobacco Still Calls the Shots in Japan," *Marketing News,* August 4, 1997, 12; and Kirk Davidson, "Proposed Tobacco Settlement Highlights Four Critical Issues," *Marketing News,* August 4, 1997, 17, 19.
5. Maxine Lans Retsky, "Who's Liable and Where On the Internet," *Marketing News,* June 23, 1997, 14.
6. Cyndee Miller, "Gaze Into the Crystal Ball for ë95 and Beyond," *Marketing News,* January 30, 1995, 1, 10.
7. Diane Crispell and William H. Frey, "American Maturity," *American Demographics,* March 1993, 31-42.
8. Levy and Weitz, *Retailing Management,* 67.
9. Patty Ames, "$1,000 PC vs. $2,500 PC," *ComputerLife,* August 1997, 88–89; "New Breed of Computer," *Marketing News,* July 7, 1997, 1.
10. John Rossant, with Gail DeGeorge, "After Versace," *Business Week,* July 28, 1997, 76–81.
11. Amy Cortese, "Here Comes the Intranet," *Business Week,* February 26, 1996, 76–84.
12. Martin Oppermann, "E-mail Surveys Potentials and Pitfalls," *Marketing Research,* Summer 1995, 29.

Chapter 4

1. Nigel Piercy, *Market-Led Strategic Change* (Oxford, United Kingdom: Butterworth-Heineman Ltd., 1992), 257.
2. Piercy, *Market-Led Strategic Change,* 256–266.
3. Larry Rosinski, "Boomers Won't Let Truck Boom Last Forever," *Marketing News,* July 21, 1997, 5.
4. Leonard M. Fuld and Frann Bilus, "Why Bad Intelligence Happens to Good People," *Marketing News,* July 21, 1997, 6, 9.
5. Geoffrey Smith, "A Dark Kodak Moment," *Business Week,* August 4, 1997, 30.
6. Deborah Dougherty and Sarah M. Corse, "What Does It Take to Take Advantage of Product Innovation," *Marketing Science Institute Working Paper Series,* Report No. 96–109, (Cambridge, MA: Marketing Science Institute, 1996).
7. Mary C. Gilly and Mary Wolfinbarger, "Advertising's Second Audience: Employee Reactions to Organizational Communications," *Marketing Science Institute Working Paper Series,* Report No. 96-116. (Cambridge, MA: Marketing Science Institute, 1996).
8. Piercy, 263.
9. George Stalk, Philip Evans, and Lawrence E. Shulman, "Competing on Capabilities: The New Rules of Corporate Strategy," *Harvard Business Review* 70 (March April 1992): 57–69.
10. Stalk, Evans, and Shulman, "Competing on Capabilities," 58–60.
11. *Consumer Reports Annual Auto Issue,* April 1997, and "Four People-Movers," *Consumer Reports,* July 1997, 54–60.
12. Ed Schafer, "Hardware Dealers Battle Each Other and 'Big Boxes'," *Marketing News,* July 21, 1997, 2.
13. "Pace Sets the Tempo; Selling Salsa in the North," *Brandweek,* March 10, 1997, S10.
14. "Salsa Style Ketchup Taps Red Hot Mexican Food Trend," *USA Today,* February 10, 1993, 5D.

15. Ted Anthony, "Where's Farrah Shampoo? Next to the Salsa Ketchup," *Marketing News,* May 6, 1996, 13.
16. Mike France, "So Much for Smoking Out Big Tobacco's Secrets," *Business Week,* July 14, 1997, 28.
17. Cliff Edwards, "Campaign 55' Flop Shows Growing Power of Franchises," *Marketing News,* July 7, 1997, 9.
18. Piercy, 263.
19. Stalk, Evans, and Shulman, 62.
20. Michael Treacy and Fred Wiersema, *The Discipline of Market Leaders* (Reading, MA: Addison-Wesley Publishing, 1995).
21. Treacy and Wiersema, *The Discipline of Market Leaders.*
22. Stephanie Anderson Forest, with Gail DeGeorge and Kathleen Morris, "The Script Doctor Is in at Blockbuster Again," *Business Week,* July 28, 1997, 101.
23. Cyndee Miller, "Exploring Africa: Untapped Market Scares Most Companies," *Marketing News,* July 21, 1997, 1, 38.
24. Jeff Borden, "Outboard Marine Eyes Expansion as Ballast During Industry Cycles," *Crains Chicago Business,* January 29, 1996, 10; Gary Samuels, "After the Storm," *Forbes,* July 3, 1995, 65–66; and "Outboard Marine Corp.," video, (April 4, 1996).
25. Kelly Shermach, "Niche Malls: Innovation for an Industry in Decline," *Marketing News,* February 26, 1996, 1–2.

Chapter 5

1. Sallie Hook, "Remember Location, Location, Location? Forget It, Now It's Image, Image, Image," *Marketing News,* December 4, 1989, 2.
2. "Johnson & Johnson Reincarnates a Brand," *Sales and Marketing Management,* January 16, 1984, 63; and Elyse Tanouye, "Johnson & Johnson Stays Fit by Shuffling Its Mix of Businesses," *The Wall Street Journal,* December 22, 1992, A1, A4.
3. Susan Caminiti, "What Ails Retailing?" *Fortune,* January 30, 1989, 61, 64; and Michael J. McCarthy, "Home Depot's Do-It-Yourself Powerhouse," *The Wall Street Journal,* July 17, 1990.
4. JC Penney, *Managing in the Tradition of Partnership,* 19.
5. Robert D. Hof, with Ira Sager and Linda Himelstein, "The Sad Saga of Silicon Graphics," *Business Week,* August 4, 1997, 66–72.
6. Stephanie Anderson Forest, Gail DeGeorge, and Kathleen Morris, "The Script Doctor Is in at Blockbuster Again," *Business Week,* July 28, 1997, 101–103.
7. The Home Depot 1996 Annual Report, 12.
8. Tim Smart, "Texaco Fills Er Up," *Business Week,* September 1, 1997, 32.
9. Kevin T. Higgins, "Never Ending Journey," *Marketing Management* 6 (Spring 1997): 6.
10. Hof, Sager, and Himelstein, "The Sad Saga of Silicon Graphics," and Robert D. Hof, "Silicon Graphics: Is the Turnaround Here?" *Business Week,* August 11, 1997, 34.
11. Lori Bongiorno, "The McDonald's of Toiletries'," *Business Week,* August 4, 1997, 79–80.
12. Bongiorno, "The McDonald's of Toiletries'."

Chapter 6

1. Brad Wolverton, "Today's Training Ground for Tomorrow's Jocks," *Business Week,* May 12, 1997, 152.
2. Michael Treacy and Fred Wiersema, *The Discipline of Market Leaders* (Reading, Mass.: Addison-Wesley Publishing Company, 1995).
3. Peter Elstrom, "This Cat Keeps on Purring," *Business Week,* January 20, 1997, 82, 84.
4. Sue Zesiger, "It's a Car. It's a 4X4. It's a Benz." *Fortune,* September 29, 1997, 310–311.
5. Joan O'C. Hamilton, "Brighter Days at Clorox," *Business Week,* June 16, 1997, 62, 65.
6. New Products Management for the 1980s (New York: Booz, Allen & Hamilton, 1982), 14.
7. Pat Wechsler, "A Curiously Strong Campaign," *Business Week,* April 21, 1997, 134.
8. George E. Belch and Michael A. Belch, *Introduction to Advertising and Promotion* (Homewood, Ill.: Irwin, 1995), 9.
9. Gary McWilliams, "Whirlwind on the Web," *Business Week,* April 7, 1997, 132–136.
10. Michael Levy and Barton A. Weitz, *Retailing Management,* 2nd ed. (Chicago: Richard D. Irwin, 1995), 48.

11. McWilliams, "Whirlwind on the Web."
12. Lisa Harrington, "How to Join the Supply Chain Revolution," *Inbound Logistics,* November 1995, 21.
13. Category Management Report © 1995 by the Joint Industry Project on Efficient Consumer Response.
14. Category Management Report.
15. Faye Rice, "How to Deal with Tougher Customers," *Fortune,* December 3, 1990, 39-48.
16. William M. Pride and O.C. Ferrell, *Marketing: Concepts and Strategies,* 10th ed. (Boston: Houghton Mifflin Co., 1997), 222–223.
17. Lori Bongiorno, "J. Crew Plays Dress-Up," *Business Week,* May 5, 1997, 127–128.
18. Randall E. Stross, "Why Barnes & Noble May Crush Amazon," *Fortune,* September 29, 1997, 248–250.

Chapter 7

1. Alan W.H. Grant and Leonard A Schlesinger, "Realize Your Customers' Full Profit Potential," *Harvard Business Review* 73 (September-October 1995): 59-72.
2. Stephanie Anderson Forest and Peter Burrows, "And Give Me an Extra-Fast Modem with That, Please," *Business Week,* September 29, 1997, 38.
3. Anthony Bianco, with William C. Symonds, "Gulfstream's Pilot," *Business Week,* April 14, 1997, 64–76.
4. Christopher P. Power, Kathleen Kerwin, Ronald Grover, Keith Alexander, and Robert D. Hof, "Flops: Too Many New Products Fail. Here's Why and How to Do Better," *Business Week,* August 16, 1993, 76-77; "Why Products Fail," *Adweek's Marketing Week,* November 5, 1990, 20, 24.
5. Hoover's Company Capsules, via http://www.hoovers.com/,© 1997, Hoover's Inc., Austin, TX.
6. Peter Burrows, with Geoffrey Smith and Steven V. Brull, "HP Pictures the Future," *Business Week,* July 7, 1997, 100–109.
7. Joan O'C. Hamilton, "Brighter Days at Clorox," *Business Week,* June 16, 1997, 62, 65.
8. "Chrysler's Eagle Faces Extinction," *Marketing News,* July 21, 1997, 12.
9. Nicole Harris, "Home Depot: Beyond Do-It Yourselfers," *Business Week,* June 30, 1997, 86-88.
10. The discussion in this section is based on Michael H. Shenkman, *Value and Strategy: Competing Successfully in the Nineties* (New York: Quorum Books, 1992); and Valarie A. Zeithaml, "Consumer Perceptions of Price, Quality, and Value: A Means-End Model and Synthesis of Evidence," Journal of Marketing 52 (July 1988): 2–22.
11. Louise I. Driben, "The Service Edge," *Sales and Marketing Management,* June 1993, 80–84.
12. Christopher H. Lovelock, *Services Marketing,* 2nd ed. (Englewood Cliffs, NJ: Prentice-Hall, 1991), 248-249.
13. J. Paul Peter and James H. Donnelly, Jr., *A Preface to Marketing Management,* 6th ed. (Burr Ridge, Ill: Richard D. Irwin, 1994), 225.
14. Lee Smith, "Rubbermaid Goes Thump," *Fortune,* October 2, 1995, 90–104.
15. Karl-Heinz Sebastian and Ralph Niederdrenk, "Strategic Purchasing Will Turn Buyer-Seller Confrontation into Cooperation," *Marketing News,* September 15, 1997, 4.

Chapter 8

1. Orville C. Walker, Jr. and Robert W. Ruekert, "Marketing's Role in the Implementation of Business Strategies: A Critical Review and Conceptual Framework," *Journal of Marketing* 51 (July 1987): 15–33.
2. Frank V. Cespedes, *Organizing and Implementing the Marketing Effort* (Reading, MA: Addison-Wesley, 1991), 19.
3. Robert Howard, "Values Make the Company: An Interview with Robert Haas," *Harvard Business Review* 68 (September-October 1990): 132-144.
4. Michael D. Hartline and O. C. Ferrell, "Service Quality Implementation: The Effects of Organizational Socialization and Managerial Actions on Customer-Contact

Employee Behaviors," *Marketing Science Institute Working Paper Series,* Report No. 93–122. (Cambridge, MA: Marketing Science Institute, 1993).

5. Howard, "Values Make the Company."

6. Cespedes, *Organizing and Implementing the Marketing Effort,* 622–623.

7. Robert W. Ruekert, Orville C. Walker, Jr., and Kenneth J. Roering, "The Organization of Marketing Activities: A Contingency Theory of Structure and Performance," *Journal of Marketing* 49 (Winter 1985): 13-25.

8. Michael Hammer and James Champy, *Reengineering the Corporation: A Manifesto for Business Revolution* (New York: Harper Business, 1993), 35.

9. Jeanne M. Plas, *Person-Centered Leadership: An American Approach to Participatory Management* (Thousand Oaks, CA: Sage Publications, 1996).

10. Harish Sujan, "Smarter Versus Harder: An Exploratory Attributional Analysis of Salespeople's Motivation," *Journal of Marketing Research* 23 (February 1986): 41-49.

11. The material in this section has been adapted from L. J. Bourgeois III and David R. Brodwin, "Strategic Implementation: Five Approaches to an Elusive Phenomenon," *Strategic Management Journal* 5 (1984): 241–264; and Steven W. Floyd and Bill Wooldridge, "Managing Strategic Consensus: The Foundation of Effective Implementation," *Academy of Management Executive* 6 (November 1992): 27–39.

12. Cliff Edwards, "'Campaign 55' Flop Shows Growing Power of Franchises," *Marketing News,* July 7, 1997, 9.

13. Mark Stevens, "Brand Management at GM: Panacea or Placebo?" *Marketing News,* July 7, 1997, 6.

14. Plas, Person-Centered Leadership, 55; and Brian Dumaine, "Payoff From the New Management," *Fortune,* December 13, 1993, 103–109.

15. Bourgeois and Brodwin, "Strategic Implementation: Five Approaches to an Elusive Phenomenon."

16. Kenneth W. Thomas and Betty A. Velthouse, "Cognitive Elements of Empowerment: An 'Interpretive' Model of Intrinsic Task Motivation," *Academy of Management Review* 15 (October 1990): 666-681.

17. Michael D. Hartline and O. C. Ferrell, "The Management of Customer-Contact Service Employees: An Empirical Investigation," *Journal of Marketing* 60 (October 1996): 52–70.

18. D. K. Denton, "Keeping Employees: The Federal Express Approach," *SAM Advanced Management Journal,* Summer 1992, 10–13; and Plas, 175–176.

19. Myron Glassman and Bruce McAfee, "Integrating the Personnel and Marketing Functions: The Challenge of the 1990s," *Business Horizons* 35 (May-June 1992): 52-59.

20. Hartline and Ferrell, "Service Quality Implementation."

21. Hartline and Ferrell, "Service Quality Implementation."

22. Lisa Arbetter, "Training Trends," *Security Management,* August 1994, 15; and the *1995 Survey of Employer-Provided Training,* Bureau of Labor Statistics, U.S. Department of Labor.

23. Ron Trujillo, "Good Ethics Pay Off," *USA Today,* October 23, 1995, 2B.

24. Michael Levy and Barton W. Weitz, *Retailing Management,* 3rd ed. (Boston: Irwin-McGraw Hill, 1998), 98.

25. Suneel Ratan, "Why Busters Hate Boomers," *Fortune,* October 4, 1993, 56–70.

26. This discussion is adapted from Erin Anderson and Richard L. Oliver, "Perspectives on Behavior-Based Versus Outcome-Based Salesforce Control Systems," *Journal of Marketing* 51 (October 1987): 76–88; David W. Cravens, Thomas N. Ingram, Raymond W. LaForge, and Clifford E. Young, "Behavior-Based and Outcome-Based Salesforce Control Systems," *Journal of Marketing* 57 (October 1993): 47–59; and Richard L. Oliver and Erin Anderson, "An Empirical Test of the Consequences of Behavior- and Outcome-Based Sales Control Systems," *Journal of Marketing* 58 (October 1994): 53-67.

27. Federal Express Corporation, *Information Book* (Memphis, TN: Federal Express Corporation, 1991).

28. Nigel F. Piercy, *Market-Led Strategic Change* (Stoneham, MA: Butterworth-Heinemann, 1992); Nigel F. Piercy and Neil A. Morgan, "Strategic Internal Marketing: Managerial Frameworks and Empirical Evidence," in *Summer Educators' Conference Proceedings,* A. Parasuraman, et al., eds. (Chicago: American Marketing Association, 1990), 308-313.

29. Piercy, *Market-Led Strategic Change.*
30. William R. George, "Internal Marketing and Organizational Behavior: A Partnership in Developing Customer-Conscious Employees at Every Level," *Journal of Business Research* 20 (January 1990): 63–70; and Glassman and McAfee, "Integrating the Personnel and Marketing Functions."
31. Howard, "Values Make the Company."
32. Kathleen K. Reardon and Ben Enis, "Establishing a Companywide Customer Orientation Through Persuasive Internal Marketing," *Management Communication Quarterly* 3 (February 1990): 376-387.
33. Reardon and Enis, "Establishing a Companywide Customer Orientation Through Persuasive Internal Marketing."
34. Hartline and Ferrell, "Service Quality Implementation."

Chapter 9

1. This section is based on material from Bernard J. Jaworski, "Toward a Theory of Marketing Control: Environmental Context, Control Types, and Consequences," *Journal of Marketing* 52 (July 1988): 23-39.
2. Michael D. Hartline and O. C. Ferrell, "The Management of Customer-Contact Service Employees: An Empirical Investigation," *Journal of Marketing* 60 (October 1996): 52-70.
3. Hartline and Ferrell, "The Management of Customer-Contact Service Employees."
4. Hartline and Ferrell; and Brian P. Niehoff, Cathy A. Enz, and Richard A. Grover, "The Impact of Top-Management Actions on Employee Attitudes and Perceptions," *Group & Organization Studies* 15 (September 1990): 337-352.
5. Ben M. Enis and Stephen J. Garfein, "The Computer-Driven Marketing Audit," *Journal of Management Inquiry,* December 1992, 306-318; and Philip Kotler, William Gregor, and William Rodgers, "The Marketing Audit Comes of Age," *Sloan Management Review* 30 (Winter 1989): 49-62.
6. Jaworski, "Toward a Theory of Marketing Control."

Chapter 10

1. Dale Kurschner, "5 Ways Ethical Busine$$ Creates Fatter Profit$," *Business Ethics* 10 (March/April 1996): 20–23.
2. Andrew W. Singer, "O&R's Ethics Council Includes All Levels of the Company," *ethikos* 10 (November/December 1996): 1-4, 15-16.
3. Archie Carroll, "The Pyramid of Corporate Social Responsibility: Toward the Moral Management of Organizational Stakeholders," *Business Horizons* 34 (July/August 1991): 42.
4. Susan Headen, with Stephen J. Hedges and Gary Cohen, "Code Blue at Columbia/HCA," *U.S. News & World Report,* August 11, 1997, 20–22.
5. Gregg Easterbrook, "Buffalo's Local Hero," *U.S. News & World Report,* September 1, 1997, 16.
6. Stan Crock, "When Charity Doesn't Begin at Home," *Business Week,* November 27, 1995, 34.
7. Nelson Schwartz and Tim Smart, "Giving. and Getting Something Back," *Business Week,* August 28, 1995, 81.
8. Dana Milbank, "Real Work: Hiring Welfare People, Hotel Chain Finds, Is Tough But Rewarding," *The Wall Street Journal,* October 31, 1996, A1, A10.
9. O. C. Ferrell, Isabelle Maignan, and Terry Loe, "Corporate Ethics + Citizenship = Profits," *The Bottom Line: Good Ethics Is Good Business,* University of Tampa, Center for Ethics, 1997.
10. Terry Loe, "The Role of Ethical Climate in Developing Trust, Market Orientation, and Commitment to Quality," unpublished dissertation, University of Memphis, 1996.
11. Isabelle Maignan, "Antecedents and Benefits of Corporate Citizenship: A Comparison of U.S. and French Businesses," unpublished dissertation, University of Memphis, 1997.
12. Maignan, "Antecedents and Benefits of Corporate Citizenship."
13. James L. Heskett, W. Earl Sasser, Jr., and Leonard A. Schlesinger, *The Service Profit Chain* (New York: The Free Press, 1997), 100–102.
14. Michael D. Hartline and O. C. Ferrell, "The Management of Customer-Contact Service Employees: An Empirical Investigation," *Journal of Marketing* 60 (October 1996): 52–70.

15. Dean L. Bottorff, "How Ethics Can Improve Business Success," *Quality Progress* 30 (February 1997): 57–60.
16. Loe, "The Role of Ethical Climate in Developing Trust, Market Orientation and Commitment to Quality."
17. The material on ethics compliance programs and the Federal Sentencing Guidelines for Organizations was adapted from Debbie Thorne LeClair, O. C. Ferrell, and John Fraedrich, *Integrity Management: A Guide to Managing Legal and Ethical Issues in the Workplace* (Tampa, FL: University of Tampa Press, 1998).
18. Richard P. Conaboy, "Corporate Crime in America: Strengthening the Good Citizen Corporation," in *Corporate Crime in America: Strengthening the "Good Citizen" Corporation* (Washington, D.C.: U.S. Sentencing Commission, 1995), 1–2.
19. *United States Code Service* (Lawyers Edition), 18 U.S.C.S. Appendix Sentencing Guidelines for the United States Courts (Rochester, NY: Lawyers Cooperative Publishing, 1995) 8A.1.
20. Conaboy, "Corporate Crime in America," 1.
21. R. Edward Freeman and David R. Gilbert, Jr., *Corporate Strategy and the Search for Ethics* (Englewood Cliffs, NJ: Prentice-Hall, 1988), 7.
22. This section on marketing on the Internet was contributed by Gwyneth M. Vaughn.
23. Don Tapscott, *Growing Up Digital* (McGraw-Hill, 1998).
24. Mark Walsh, "The Air Bill Joins the 8–Track," *Internet World* 8 (August 1997): 43–44.
25. Kathy Rebello, with Larry Armstrong and Amy Cortese, "Making Money on the Net," *Business Week*, September 23, 1996, 104-118.
26. Rebello, Armstrong and Cortese, "Making Money on the Net."
27. Robert D. Hof, with Seanna Browder and Peter Elstrom, "Internet Communities," *Business Week*, May 5, 1997, 64–80.
28. Gary Welz, "The Ad Game," *Internet World* 7 (July 1996): 50–57.
29. Linda Himelstein, with Ellen Neuborne and Paul M. Eng, "Web Ads Start to Click," *Business Week*, October 6, 1997, 128–138.
30. Hof, Browder and Elstrom, "Internet Communities."
31. Himelstein, "Web Ads Start to Click."
32. David Zgodzinski, "Click Here to Pay," *Internet World* 8 (September 1997): 62.
33. Dan McGraw, "Shootout at PC Corral," *U.S. News & World Report*, June 23, 1997, 37–38.
34. Tapscott, Growing Up Digital.
35. Susan Jackson, "Point, Click and Spend," *Business Week*, September 15, 1997, 74–76.
36. Edward C. Baig, "Going Once, Going Twice, Cybersold!" *Business Week*, August 11, 1997, 98–99.
37. Hof, Browder and Elstrom, "Internet Communities."
38. Dom Del Prete, "Winning Strategies Lead to Global Marketing Success," *Marketing News*, August 18, 1997, 1, 2.
39. Del Prete, "Winning Strategies Lead to Global Marketing Success."
40. Warren J. Keegan, *Global Marketing Management*, 4th ed. (Englewood Cliffs, N.J.: Prentice-Hall, 1989), 378–382.
41. Keith Naughton and Emily Thornton, with Kathleen Kerwin and Heidi Dawley, "Can Honda Build a World Car?" *Business Week*, September 8, 1997, 100–108.
42. Joseph Pereia, "Unknown Fruit Takes on Unfamiliar Markets," *The Wall Street Journal*, November 9, 1995, B1.
43. Aspy P. Palia and Charles F. Keown, "Combating Parallel Importing: Views of U.S. Exporters to the Asia-Pacific Region," *International Marketing Review* 8 (no. 1, 1991): 47–56.
44. Robert Crandall, "Challenges to Growth in International Aviation," *Wharton Alumni Magazine*, Spring 1991, 10.

Appendix B

1. These descriptions are based on Michael Levy and Barton A. Weitz, *Retailing Management*, 3rd ed. (Boston: Irwin/McGraw-Hill, 1998), 145; and Martha Farnsworth Rice, "Psychographics for the 1990s," *American Demographics*, July 1989, 24-26ff.

COMPANY INDEX